THE CRISIS BEHIND THE EUROCRISIS

The Crisis behind the Eurocrisis encourages dialogue among scholars across the social sciences in an attempt to challenge the narrative that regarded the Eurocrisis as an exceptional event. It is suggested instead that the Eurocrisis, along with the subsequent crises the EU has come to face, was merely symptomatic of deeper systemic cracks. This book's aim is to uncover that hidden systemic crisis: the 'crisis behind the Eurocrisis'. Through this reading it emerges that what needs to be questioned is not only the allegedly purely economic character of the Eurocrisis, but, more fundamentally, its very classification as an 'emergency'. Instead, the Eurocrisis needs to be regarded as expressive of a chronic, dysfunctional, but 'normal' condition of the EU. By following this line of analysis, this book illuminates not only the causes of contemporary turbulences in the European project, but perhaps the 'true' nature of the EU itself.

Eva Nanopoulos is a Lecturer in Law and academic coordinator for the BA/LLB in Law and Politics at Queen Mary University of London. Her research and teaching interests are in EU law, international law, human rights, constitutional law and critical legal theory. She is co-director of the Centre for Law and Society in a Global Context (QMUL) and currently completing a monograph entitled *Juridification of Sanctions and the Politics of EU Law* (Hart, forthcoming).

Fotis Vergis is Lecturer in Law at the University of Manchester School of Law, where he teaches EU law and labour law. His research interests include EU law and constitutional theory, labour law theory and collective labour law. During his PhD studies at the University of Cambridge he was awarded a Modern Law Review Scholarship for 2013–14 and 2014–15. He is a member of the Labour Law Research Network (LLRN), the Society of Legal Scholars (SLS) and the Industrial Law Society (ILS). He sits on the Editorial Board of the *Greek Labour Law Review* and the Scientific Committee of the 'Moving Labour Collective', a network of progressive labour law scholars. He is also a member of the Thessaloniki Bar, now as a non-practising barrister.

The Crisis behind the Eurocrisis

THE EUROCRISIS AS A MULTIDIMENSIONAL SYSTEMIC CRISIS OF THE EU

Edited by

EVA NANOPOULOS AND FOTIS VERGIS

CAMBRIDGE
UNIVERSITY PRESS

CAMBRIDGE
UNIVERSITY PRESS

University Printing House, Cambridge CB2 8BS, United Kingdom

One Liberty Plaza, 20th Floor, New York, NY 10006, USA

477 Williamstown Road, Port Melbourne, VIC 3207, Australia

314–321, 3rd Floor, Plot 3, Splendor Forum, Jasola District Centre, New Delhi – 110025, India

79 Anson Road, #06–04/06, Singapore 079906

Cambridge University Press is part of the University of Cambridge.

It furthers the University's mission by disseminating knowledge in the pursuit of education, learning, and research at the highest international levels of excellence.

www.cambridge.org
Information on this title: www.cambridge.org/9781108470346
DOI: 10.1017/9781108598859

First published 2019

Printed and bound in Great Britain by Clays Ltd, Elcograf S.p.A.

A catalogue record for this publication is available from the British Library.

ISBN 978-1-108-47034-6 Hardback

You can't be neutral on a moving train
Howard Zinn

Contents

Notes on Contributors   *page* x

Preface   xv

Acknowledgements   xvii

Introduction: The Elephant in the Room: a Tale of Crisis   1
Eva Nanopoulos and Fotis Vergis

1   There Is No (Legal) Alternative: Codifying Economic Ideology
into Law   23
Benjamin Farrand and Marco Rizzi

PART I   THE CRISIS AS A CRISIS OF THE EU'S IDENTITY   49

2   The Roots of the European Crisis: a Historical Perspective   51
Charalampos Kouroundis

3   The End of Self-fulfilling Europe   67
Hent Kalmo

4   The Authoritarian Neoliberalism of the EU: Legal Form
and International Politico-Economic Sources   89
Magnus Ryner

PART II   THE CRISIS AS A CRISIS OF THE EU'S POLITICAL AND
DEMOCRATIC LEGITIMACY   99

5   Authoritarian Liberalism: the Conjuncture behind the Crisis   101
Michael Wilkinson

6   The Inherently Undemocratic EU Democracy: Moving beyond the
    'Democratic Deficit' Debate   122
    Eva Nanopoulos and Fotis Vergis

7   Europe and Constituent Powers: Ruptures with the
    Neoliberal Consensus?   156
    Maria Tzanakopoulou

8   'Who's Afraid of the European Demos?': the Uneasy
    Relationship between the European Union and Referendums   173
    Elia Alexiou

9   Can Public and Voluntary Acts of Consent Confer Legitimacy
    on the EU?   219
    Ozlem Ulgen

    PART III   THE CRISIS AS A CRISIS OF THE EU'S ECONOMIC MODEL   241

10 The Fiscal Compact: a Paradoxical Fiscal Governance Machine   243
    Vanessa Bilancetti

11 The Rise of Unaccountable Governance in the Eurozone   264
    Gunnar Beck

12 Unification from Above, Its Contradictions and the Conjuncture
    Initiated by the Eurozone Crisis   295
    Christakis Georgiou

    PART IV   THE CRISIS AS A CRISIS OF THE EU'S SOCIAL CHARACTER   315

13 A Tale of Two Documents: the Eclipse of the Social Democratic
    Constitution   317
    Alan Bogg and KD Ewing

14 How to Analyse a Supranational Regime That Nationalises
    Social Conflict? The European Crisis, Labour Politics
    and Methodological Nationalism   346
    Roland Erne

15 Which Refugee Crisis? On the Proxy of the Systemic Eurocrisis
    and Its Spatialities   369
    Dimitris Dalakoglou

PART V   JOINING THE DOTS AND THE WAY FORWARD   379

16   The European Crisis of Economic Liberalism: Can the Law Help?   381
      Michelle Everson

17   With Time to Prepare: Planning an Exit from the EMU   403
      Costas Lapavitsas

18   Brexit and the Imperial Constitution of Europe   419
      Alex Callinicos

      Conclusion   430
      Eva Nanopoulos and Fotis Vergis

Index   442

Contributors

Elia Alexiou is a PhD candidate in international law (Université Panthéon-Assas Paris II) and a lecturer in EU law (Université Catholique de Lille). Her PhD thesis focuses on global constitutionalism and her teaching activities on constitutional, European and international law and human rights (Université Paris-Nanterre, Université Panthéon-Sorbonne Paris I). Elia has been a visiting scholar at Columbia Law School and has worked for the United Nations: first in the UN Secretariat at the New York Headquarters (Office of the Secretary General's Envoy on Youth) and recently in the UNHCR Field mission in Greece.

Vanessa Bilancetti holds a PhD in politics from the University of Rome La Sapienza, and has been a visiting PhD and a teaching assistant at the University of Sheffield. Her research focuses on the New Economic Governance, intersecting critical international relations theory, critical European Studies and feminist political economy.

Alan Bogg is Professor of Labour Law at the University of Bristol Law School. Previously he was Professor of Labour Law in the University of Oxford and a fellow of Hertford College, Oxford. He has a broad teaching and research interests in the fields of labour, employment and work laws, which he explores from philosophical, doctrinal and comparative perspectives.

Alex Callinicos is Professor of European Studies (social theory and international political economy) at the Department of European & International Studies at King's College London. He has published extensively on Marxism, social and political theory, political philosophy, political economy, and race and racism.

Gunnar Beck is Reader in EU law and Legal Theory at SOAS. He also practises as a barrister and a Rechtsanwalt, focusing on various aspects of EU law. He has published widely on EU law, as well as legal and political philosophy, including two books, *Fichte and Kant on Freedom, Rights and Law* and more recently, *The Legal Reasoning of the Court of Justice of the EU*.

Dimitris Dalakoglou is Professor and Chair of Social Anthropology at VU University Amsterdam. His research interests lie in the field of anthropology of infrastructures, mobility and urban public spaces and he has carried out an anthropological research of the Greek crisis since 2010. In 2012 he was awarded an ESRC-Future Research Leaders grant for the project 'The City at a Time of Crisis: Transformations of Public Spaces in Athens' (crisis-scape .net).

Roland Erne is Professor and Jean Monnet Chair of European Integration & Employment Relations at University College Dublin, where he teaches international and comparative industrial relations. His work centres on EU governance and the social and political implications of transnational movements of goods, capital, services and people. He has been recently awarded an ERC Consolidator grant for the project 'Labour Politics & the EU's New Economic Governance Regime' at University College Dublin.

Michelle Everson is Professor of European Law in the School of Law, Birkbeck and Assistant Dean for Programme Development. Currently, she sits on the editorial boards of the *European Law Journal*, *Law and Critique* and the *Journal for Socio-Legal Studies*. Professor Everson has researched widely in the field of European law and has particular interests in the areas of European regulatory law, European administrative and constitutional law and European citizenship.

Keith Ewing is Professor of Public Law at the Dickson Pool School of Law, King's College London and the President of the Institute of Employment Rights. He is one of the leading scholars in labour law and public law. His research focuses on labour law and constitutional reform, with special reference to the relationship between social rights and constitutional law.

Benjamin Farrand is Reader in Law and Emerging Technologies at Newcastle University, and coordinates the UACES Research Network 'Communicating Europe'. His research focuses on the interaction between law and politics in European policy-making and technology regulation.

Christakis Georgiou earned his PhD in political science from the University of Montpellier and specialises in the political economy of European integration. He is currently a post-doctoral fellow of the Centre de compétences Dusan Sidjanski en études européennes hosted by the Global Studies Institute at the University of Geneva. His work focuses on the activism and influence of French and European corporate elites in the development of the integration process and are at the intersection of various disciplines: international and comparative political economy, economic sociology and economic history.

Hent Kalmo is a Marie Skłodowska-Curie Global Fellow at the University of Tartu and Harvard Law School. His research has focused mainly on constitutional argumentation. He has written extensively on the doctrine of proportionality, on the primacy of EU law and on the notion of sovereignty.

Charalampos Kouroundis is a postdoctoral researcher at the Aristotle University of Thessaloniki School of Law, Department of Public Law and Political Sciences. His doctoral thesis, 'Constitutional modernisation and the left: the "deep incision" of 1963 and its impact on the constitution of 1975', has recently been published as a monograph. He has published on Marxism, left strategy and the Eurocrisis. He is also a Member of the Thessaloniki Bar.

Costas Lapavitsas is Professor of Economics at the School of Oriental and African Studies, University of London. His research interests include the relationship of finance and development, the structure of financial systems, and the interaction between market and non-market relations in the financial system. He has written widely on economics and published two books addressing directly the Eurocrisis with Verso: *Against the Troika: A Radical Anti-Capitalist Alternative to Eurozone Austerity* and *Crisis in the Eurozone*. In January 2015, he was elected as a member of the Hellenic Parliament for SYRIZA and subsequently stood in the elections with Popular Unity.

Eva Nanopoulos is a Lecturer in Law at Queen Mary University London, having previously taught at King's College, Cambridge. She has teaching and research interests in EU law, international law, human rights and critical legal theory. She is currently completing a monograph entitled *Juridification of Sanctions and the Politics of EU Law*, to be published by Hart/Bloomsbury.

Marco Rizzi is Senior Lecturer at the University of Western Australia, UWA Law School. He was awarded his PhD by the European University Institute in Florence and was previously Senior Lecturer and Head of Department of Law at the University of Seychelles. His research focuses on transnational law, risk regulation, and the interaction between tort law and the public interest.

Magnus Ryner is Professor of International Political Economy and Head of Department at King's College London. His research interests lie in international, European and EU political economy. Magnus is also interested in philosophy of science and sociology of knowledge questions that relate to his empirical concerns. He has a long-standing interest in social democracy and trade unions as sociopolitical phenomena. He has published widely on European political economy and the Eurocrisis; his most recent relevant work is *The European Union and Global Capitalism: Origins, Development, Crisis* (Palgrave, 2017) (with Alan Cafruny).

Maria Tzanakopoulou is a Lecturer at Birkbeck, School of Law. Her doctoral thesis was recently published as a monograph entitled *Reclaiming Constitutionalism: Democracy, Power and the State* (Hart, 2008).

Fotis Vergis is Lecturer in Law at the University of Manchester School of Law, where he teaches EU law and Labour law. His research interests include labour law theory and collective labour law, EU law and constitutional theory, while previously he also worked on various subjects of Greek civil and civil procedure law. He has practised in Greece, working predominantly on labour law and is a member of the Thessaloniki Bar, now as a non-practising barrister.

Ozlem Ulgen is Reader in International Law and Ethics at the School of Law, Birmingham City University, teaching EU law, public law, and corporate regulation. She is also a barrister awarded the Gray's Inn Bedingfield Scholarship and Ann Ebsworth Award. Ozlem is an expert in EU law, public international law, international criminal law and international security and armed conflict law. Her current interests focus on two major research projects: the taxonomy of harm and culpability for robot weapons used in modern warfare; and the legitimacy and accountability of the EU's supranational decision-making.

Michael Wilkinson is Associate Professor of Law at LSE, where he teaches EU law and jurisprudence. His research interests span European integration, constitutional theory and legal, political and social theory. His work has been published in leading journals, including the *Modern Law Review*, the *Oxford Journal of Legal Studies* and the *European Law Journal*. He has published two co-edited collections on constitutional theory, *Constitutionalism beyond Liberalism* (Cambridge University Press, 2017) and *Questioning the Foundations of Public Law* (Hart, 2018).

Preface

The origin of this volume can be traced to a quick exchange on a dark cloudy morning in 2013 between a young lecturer and an old PhD researcher at the Law Faculty of the University of Cambridge. The Eurocrisis was at its apex. In the entrance hall of the (now) David Williams Building, we were coming out of a workshop where the recent *Pringle* judgment had been discussed and criticised. We were not all that surprised that the 'survival of the eurozone' had apparently emerged as the primary objective of the EU that would cast aside any other consideration. But there was a feeling that the established discourses, the optimistic complacency of perpetual 'further integration', and the traditional tools by which EU law was always approached, had suddenly become obsolete. Dozens of similar, yet longer, conversations between us were born out of that brief exchange as the crisis kept unfolding. Being Greek meant we were attuned to developments back home over the months that followed; from the government shutting down the public broadcaster mid-air, to political upheaval and the adoption of successive emergency 'multi Acts' of Parliament that transformed the legal landscape towards a clear neoliberal trajectory, deepening precariousness, uncertainty and inequality, to the emergence of reactionary nationalistic forces that began to shape the public discourse. Our conversations continued, more concerned each time and more frustrated that the emergency narrative seemed to have won the day and academic scepticism was quick to be dismissed.

By autumn 2014 an idea had formed: since there was relatively little critical discussion about the causes of the crisis, the deeper and systemic nature of which was perhaps clearer to those associated with any of the countries that were in the eye of the storm than to those that had the luxury of distance, we would set up a forum to invite such discussion. Supported by some of our colleagues and friends who had recent relevant experience, and to whom we owe our thanks (Dr Alysia Blackham and Dr Amy Ludlow), we pitched the idea to the Centre of European Legal Studies (CELS) of the Cambridge Faculty of Law. With the generous help of the Centre, we were grateful that Prof. David Dyzenhaus and Prof. Emilios

Christodoulidis agreed to participate in a small seminar to discuss the concept of crisis and its contemporary systemic manifestations by placing it within the context of modern constitutionalism and the legacies of the Enlightenment. That event would be the precursor to the conference on the Eurocrisis that led to the present volume.

As the conference was set up during 2015, a wave of dramatic developments unfolded: the election of the SYRIZA government, the risk of Grexit, the Greek referendum and capitulation of July 2015, and, eventually, right as we were about to welcome our speakers, the call for a UK vote on EU membership. Sponsored and supported by CELS as well as King's College, Cambridge, the Eurocrisis conference was held in March 2016 in Cambridge Law Faculty; it was clear that the time was ripe for critical voices.

This volume is the result of the discussions triggered in that conference and to the friendships and collegial relationships that were forged during those days. Some of this volume's contributors based their chapters on their conference presentations or built and expanded on the same themes. Others joined the project later, agreeing it was imperative to engage in more critical debate and situate the narrative of 'crisis' within a discourse as to the nature and condition of its systemic context.

We hope that this volume will be just one of numerous contributions to signify this shift in established discourse. A sincere discussion about the weaknesses of the current variation of the 'European project' can only help expose the true causes of its apparent 'crises', and perhaps facilitate the realisation that another Europe is indeed possible.

Eva Nanopoulos and Fotis Vergis

Acknowledgements

Work on this collection, from its initial conception until its eventual production, has been lengthy, strenuous and not without setbacks at times. During the long process to bring this volume to print both of us moved on from Cambridge to new endeavours. However, we remain grateful to Prof. Kenneth Armstrong and Prof. Catherine Barnard (former Directors of CELS, both professors of EU law at the University of Cambridge), for the unyielding support, guidance, advise and constructive criticism, and to Mrs Felicity Eves-Rey of CELS, without the help and hard work of whom the conference that led to this volume would have been impossible to organise. We are also grateful to those that presented papers or chaired sessions in the March 2016 conference on the Eurocrisis that are not featured in this collection (Prof. John Ryan, Prof. Brendan Simms, Dr Ewan McGaughey, Dr Javor Jancic, Jorge Correcher Mira, Dr Pieter van Cleynenbreugel, Elena Paris) and to all participants that contributed to the discussion. In addition, we wish to thank our colleagues with whom we shared insights and concerns all through the Eurocrisis: Prof. Simon Deakin, Dr Alicia Hinarejos, Dr Albertina Albors-Llorens, Dr Markus Gehring, Dr Niamh Dunne, Dr Samuel Dahan and Dr Rumiana Yotova.

We also wish to express our gratitude to all those who were directly involved with the development of the present collection, which would not have seen the day without their hard work, devotion, academic rigour and patience. This of course includes all the contributing authors of this volume, whether they were committed to the project since its inception or jumped on board at a later stage. Their commitment and the quality of their work is what defines the collection. Equally, however we owe thanks to the hard work of our editors at Cambridge University Press and every member of the its team that was engaged with the project at various points in time: Finola O'Sullivan, Elizabeth Spicer, Rebecca Roberts, Gemma Smith, Tahnee Wager, Marianne Nield, Becky Jackaman, Karthik Orukaimani, Martin Barr and Birgitte Necessary. We also want to thank Jack William Head who helped with the editorial work on some of the chapters in preparation of the full manuscript.

Special thanks are due to Dimitris Naiplis (N_Grams). Dimitris is an Athens-based visual artist working on a wide variety of media and artistic techniques, including sketches, public interventions/installations and street art. His art has been presented in numerous group shows in Greece and cultural festivals around the world. We were delighted he agreed to provide his work, drawn on the eve of the July 2015 referendum, at the apex of the Greek crisis, for our cover.

Lastly, there is a special place in our hearts for those that tolerated our days of stress and sleep deprivation and endured missing holidays and weekends, while we were living, dreaming and breathing Eurocrisis. Eliza and Owen not only had to go through the Eurocrisis itself, but they also had to experience the equally severe effects of partners writing about it. They survived both. And for their patience, they don't just have our utmost gratitude; they have our love.

Eva Nanopoulos and Fotis Vergis
(London – Manchester, 9 May 2018: Europe Day and Victory Day)

Introduction

The Elephant in the Room

A *Tale of Crisis*

Eva Nanopoulos and Fotis Vergis

I BACKGROUND: FIVE 'WISE MEN', A DARK ROOM AND A BEAST

In a version of an old eastern fable, an elephant stands in a great dark room. Five 'wise men', who have never come across such an animal, are granted entrance by the king and asked to describe it. The first goes in, touches the elephant's leg and, as he comes out, firmly declares: 'the elephant is like a pillar'. The second goes in after him, but feels the elephant's tail, thus stating that he disagrees with his colleague; the elephant is like a rope. 'You are both wrong', the third one says, having touched the elephant's ear; 'the elephant is clearly like a fan'. The fourth touches the elephant's belly and describes the beast as a wall, while the fifth is awestruck by touching the tusk, which leads him to conclude without a doubt that the elephant is like a tree's branch. On hearing their conclusion and heated argument, the king scolds them for not having discussed their findings with each other, or not doing as simple a thing as taking the initiative to light a candle before entering the dark room. If they had, they would know the elephant's actual form and nature.

Over the past years, the financial crisis, rooted in part in the 2008 global crisis, shook the EU to its core and tested its institutional structure, if not its very cohesion. In the immediate aftermath of the crisis, numerous analyses across the social sciences emerged to discuss the nature, causes and repercussions of what came to be dubbed the 'Eurocrisis', as well as the steps taken to address it. However, much like the examination of the 'wise men' of the old fable, analyses have tended to contain themselves within narrowly circumscribed limits, dictated by the confines of the analysts' respective fields, with their relevant theoretical preconceptions, assumptions and prejudices.[1]

---

[1] Indicatively, examples include: (a) constitutional and EU constitutional law approaches: K Tuori and K Tuori, *The Eurozone Crisis: A Constitutional Analysis* (CUP 2014); A Hinarejos, *The Euro Area Crisis in Constitutional Perspective* (OUP 2015); M Dawson and F de Witte, 'Constitutional Balance in the EU after the Euro-Crisis' (2013) 76 CMLR 817; M Ruffert, 'European Debt Crisis and European Union Law' (2011) 48 CMLR 1777; (b) legal approaches to the EMU and EU economic governance:

Such analyses, moreover, tended to focus on particular features or symptoms of the crisis,[2] as well as adopted solutions. There seemed to be little appetite to engage with its broader political, social, economic and, indeed, legal context, or to examine it in the light of the normative assumptions and structural parameters underpinning and defining the European project. Partly as a result, the Eurozone crisis was diagnosed as primarily financial in nature and its causes traced to either deficiencies in the institutional structure of the Economic and Monetary Union (EMU) or, especially near the beginning of the crisis, to the Member States' lack of fiscal discipline, or to a combination of the two. Consequently, the relevant patches were applied and the Union called it a day.

Once more, 'wise men' were caught not talking to each other to compare and consolidate their findings. Preoccupied by what seemed to be the obvious form of the subject of their examination, they also failed to pause and simply light a candle to illuminate its nature. The elephant in the room was not a simple financial crisis. It was, and still is, we argue, a deeper, far more complex, systemic crisis of the EU, which, in this instance, manifested itself as a crisis of the mechanics, organisation and function of the EMU.

More recent scholarship has engaged in more comprehensive and in-depth analyses. Some commentators have begun to think more seriously and systemically about the nature and causes of the Eurocrisis itself, even questioning the designation of the events as an alarming 'crisis'.[3] Others,[4] while not necessarily focused on the Eurocrisis itself, have tapped into its events and institutional features to develop broader arguments as to the effects the complex transnational nature and machinery of the EU has had, most notably on the nature of fundamental institutional structures (e.g. statehood itself) and their underlying premises.[5] Others still have looked at the Eurocrisis as one of many different crises, now cutting 'to the very core of the EU

M Dawson, 'The Legal and Political Accountability Structure of 'Post-Crisis' EU Economic Governance' (2015) 53 Journal of Common Market Studies 976; MW Bauer and S Becker, 'The Unexpected Winner of the Crisis: The European Commission's Strengthened Role in Economic Governance' (2014) 36 Journal of European Integration 213; (c) political economy and political sciences analyses: J Caporaso and M Rhodes (eds), *Political and Economic Dynamics of the Eurozone Crisis* (OUP 2016); P Arestis and G Fontana and M Sawyer 'The Dysfunctional Nature of the Economic and Monetary Union' in D Schiek (ed) *The EU Economic and Social Model in the Global Crisis: Interdisciplinary Perspectives* (Routledge 2016); M Matthijs and M Blyth (eds), *The Future of the Euro* (OUP 2015); M Sandbu, *Europe's Orphan: The Future of the Euro and the Politics of Debt* (Princeton UP 2015); C Lapavitsas and others, *Crisis in the Eurozone* (Verso 2012); 23; A Moravcsik 'Europe After the Crisis: How to Sustain a Common Currency' (2012) 91 Foreign Affairs 54.

2   D Chalmers, M Jachtenfuchs and C Joerges (eds), *The End of the Eurocrats' Dream: Adjusting to European Diversity* (CUP 2016); M Dawson, H Enderlein and C Joerges (eds), *Beyond the Crisis: The Governance of Europe's Economic, Political and Legal Transformation* (OUP 2015); S Fabbrini, *Which European Union?* (CUP 2015); G Majone, *Rethinking the Union of Europe Postcrisis: Has Integration Gone Too Far?* (CUP 2014).

3   JE Fossum and AJ Menendez (eds), The European Union in Crisis or the European Union as Crises ARENA Report No 2/14.

4   C Bickerton, *European Integration: From Nation-States to Member States* (OUP 2012).

5   ibid 140–50.

itself.[6] Early such attempts already placed it in the context of a broader set of dynamics that threatened the cohesion of the EU, such as the growing disillusionment of European citizens with the European project,[7] mistrust towards the political process[8] or an insufficient level of economic and social convergence between Member States. More recent work has provided more elaborate topologies of the different dimensions of the crisis (political, economic, social, etc.) as well as examined the Eurocrisis in tandem with the multiple different events that have constituted smaller or larger 'crises' over recent years, including Brexit and the so-called refugee crisis.[9]

These strands of the scholarship move the debate in productive directions and make a number of important contributions. As regards the Eurocrisis, they go beyond the original narrative, which purported that it was an isolated instance, whether it was attributed to structural inefficiencies[10] or to supposedly unforeseeable emergency circumstances (such as the global financial crisis or the 'Greek statistics' trigger of its European variant). They attempt to dig deeper than some of the rather superficial initial reactions to the Eurocrisis, which, perhaps, were affected by established preconceptions about the value of absolute price stability and financial discipline or the 'irresponsibility' of Member States that failed to fully comply with what ought to be the unquestionable core of EMU rules. As such, they begin to reveal a much more complex picture of not only structural, but also substantive and even existential multifaceted issues, that throw a shadow over the triumphalist and teleological narrative of integration that has been constructed over the last decades. In doing so, moreover, they also open up an important, and much awaited, space for more critical engagement with the EU,[11] which has tended to be rather minimal, particularly within EU legal studies. In that sense, the original reactions to the Eurocrisis are also symptomatic of a much deeper reluctance of the academy – itself perhaps the product of the powerful commitment to, and pool of, Europeanisation – to question the more fundamental normative and ideological assumptions of the European project.

Nevertheless, even these more poised critical analyses tend to embrace the symptomatic character of the 'crises' they bring to the fore, without really questioning what the malady that gave rise to the symptoms really is.[12] As a result, they also

---

[6]   D Dinan, N Nugent and W Paterson (eds), *The European Union in Crisis* (Palgrave 2017).

[7]   JC Piris, *The Future of Europe: Towards a Two-Speed EU?* (CUP 2011) 2.

[8]   JC Piris, 'The Five Crises in Europe and the Future of the EU' (King's College London Lecture, London, 28 October 2013) 3 www.kcl.ac.uk/law/research/centres/european/Jean-Claude-Piris-lecture-text.pdf accessed April 2018.

[9]   M Castells and others (eds), *Europe's Crises* (Polity 2018); Dinan and others (n 6).

[10]   eg Arestis and others (n 1).

[11]   I Manners and R Whitman, 'Another Theory Is Possible: Dissident Voices in Theorising Europe' (2016) 54 Journal of Common Market Studies 3.

[12]   It should be noted that this is not the case of works that approach the case of the EU's recent turmoil as but one of the pieces that reveal an overall crisis of modern capitalism, based upon an economic model that has been stretched almost to its limits. See for example, M Ryner and A Cafruny, *The*

tend to approach different symptoms as separate 'crises',[13] linked and mutually reinforcing, but somewhat disassociated as regards their fundamental causes. Tellingly, even in cases where the Eurocrisis specifically is argued to be linked to the other emerging 'crises' as part of an overall systemic problem, analyses once more tend to return to the micro level of the EMU, questioning its institutional and substantive deficiencies, with the question of a deeper connecting thread essentially remaining under-explored.[14] Some contributions, particularly from the field of social sciences, have come closer to, although stayed just clear of, touching upon the essence of this common thread, by suggesting that the Eurocrisis was part of a complex multidimensional socio-economic and sociopolitical crisis, a cumulative process unfolding in the continent.[15] Even those that attempt to predict what the future holds for the Union after the events of the 2010s shy away from enhancing their analysis with a deeper examination of the core characteristics, origins and basic foundations of the Union.[16] In other words, a much richer debate around the Eurocrisis has emerged, important light has been shed, but the nature of the beast, the underlying hidden crisis of the EU, remains to be fully uncovered.

In this volume, we attempt instead to go beyond the comfort of established preconceptions and narratives and try to, once more, comprehend how these fragments fit together and what they can reveal about the true causes of the Eurocrisis and, ultimately, the nature of the EU itself. Therefore, our substantive aim, with the slight temporal distance this collection enjoys from the events that have unfolded over the last ten years, is to begin the work of uncovering the hidden systemic crisis of which the Eurocrisis is merely a component – the 'crisis behind the Eurocrisis' – as the true nature of the beast with which we are confronted. Methodologically, we aim to encourage dialogue about the systemic causes of the Eurocrisis between scholars from different fields and backgrounds, pooling their different perspectives and prompting them to challenge their own established analytical tools, and reach out to ideas, theories and arguments that transcend their respective fields. In other words, we invite social scientists to avoid the mistake of the protagonists of the old eastern fable, constrained by the false security of their individual approaches and theories. This exploration of the hidden systemic nature of the crisis, moreover, is undertaken across different 'dimensions' of the Eurocrisis, which are used as the main themes around which the collection is structured and the material organised.

European Union and Global Capitalism: Origins, Development, Crisis (Palgrave 2017); M Blyth, *Austerity: The History of a Dangerous Idea* (OUP 2013).

[13] Piris (n 8); Piris (n 7) 1–3. See also JC Piris, 'It Is Time for the Euro Area to Develop Further Closer Cooperation among Its Members' (2011) Jean Monnet Working Paper 05/11, 3–4 www .jeanmonnetprogram.org/wp-content/uploads/2014/12/110501.pdf accessed April 2018.

[14] D Dinan, N Nugent and W Peterson 'Conclusions: Crisis without End?' in D Dinan, N Nugent and W Paterson (eds), *The European Union in Crisis* (Palgrave 2017), 360.

[15] 'Conclusion' in Castells and others (n 9) 428.

[16] H Volaard, *European Disintegration: A Search for Explanations* (Palgrave Macmillan 2018); D Webber, 'How Likely Is It That the European Union Will Disintegrate? A Critical Analysis of Competing Theoretical Perspectives' (2014) 20 European Journal of International Relations 341.

As the title of the collection suggests, it is these interdisciplinary, multidimensional and systemic inquiries that we hope will begin to illuminate the 'true' nature of a crisis that is arguably broader than its Eurozone-related financial manifestation.

II SUBSTANTIVE AIM: THE 'EUROCRISIS' AS THE SUBJECT OF BROADER EXAMINATION AND INDICATIVE OF A HIDDEN SYSTEMIC CRISIS

This approach to the Eurocrisis inevitably begs the question: what do we mean by 'crisis' and what exactly is 'in crisis'? Once the Eurocrisis is regarded as symptomatic of deeper inherent issues that are connected to the very nature of the European project, it immediately emerges that what needs to be questioned is not only its allegedly purely economic character, but, more fundamentally, the conceptual framework that underpins its classification and treatment as a 'crisis'. As we explain in this section, our examination of the Eurocrisis as indicative of a hidden systemic crisis moves away from traditional narratives of the Eurocrisis as an emergency triggered by external factors or minor institutional deficiencies and is premised instead on a conception of the Eurocrisis as expressive of a chronic, dysfunctional, but inherent condition of the EU.

A *The Crisis as Emergency Narrative*

A 'crisis', by definition, denotes a critical condition, an intense emergency, that either arises due to inherent failures of the subject plagued by its consequences or because of the influence of factors and circumstances external to that subject. The word can also be used to describe a critical juncture in an endeavour, the moment when a crucial event triggers a fateful decision that might alter the chosen course.

It was primarily in the light of crisis construed as an emergency that the financial and institutional turmoil that hit the EMU since the early 2010s was quickly dubbed a 'crisis', thereby insulating the surrounding events and policy responses from deeper examination of their systemic context. The 'crisis', this narrative went, consisted of an unanticipated set of exceptional events of such magnitude that they created a potentially existential threat for the EU, putting the 'future of Europe' in danger, and therefore called for an unprecedented emergency response. Simultaneously, however, according to this dominant narrative, this 'exceptional set of events' had merely revealed deficiencies and structural flaws in the institutional mechanisms of the EU's economic governance[17] that could be patched; nothing broader or deeper than that.

---

[17] D Schwarzer, 'The Euro Area Crises, Shifting Power Relations and Institutional Change in the European Union' (2012) 3 Global Policy 28.

For the proponents of the current status quo, it might have been logical, if not useful, to regard the events of the first half of the 2010s as a 'crisis'. Doing so, would allow, as it did, the promotion of swift course correction changes, without much political debate, often in blatant disregard of even the commonly agreed fundamental legal framework that governs the EU as we know it. The supposedly urgent existential character of these events facilitated the swift adoption of a particular 'solution' that reflected very specific ideological and political choices but was presented as an absolutely necessary remedy to which there was no practical (legal and political) alternative. The present danger, moreover, meant there was allegedly no time for discussion, no time for reflection, no time to consider other courses of action, much less for criticism or popular input, as they would potentially precipitate disaster. This 'existential crisis' narrative, in other words, allowed for that preordained solution to masquerade as 'imperative' and non-negotiable: there was only one way out of the plight posed by this imminent danger that threatened the Union and its already heavily strained citizens. The result was the creation of new mechanisms of dubious legitimacy and minimal accountability at the fringe of normal EU law, cementing what has led some commentators to characterise as 'embedded neoliberalism'.[18]

That these new mechanisms and embedded dogmas were called for by external factors outside of the EU's own economic objectives and logic is doubtful. On the contrary, the measures adopted by the Eurocrisis could be seen as necessary to ensure the stability and further advancement of the particular variety of market liberalism the EU was set to promote, and of the particular capital/trade flow and wealth distribution structures the combined framework of the EU internal market and the EMU envisage. As with many events characterised as 'emergencies', especially when this occurs so that a convenient pretext for potentially unpopular policies can be created, it is equally doubtful that the crisis of the EMU really threatened the existence of the Union as such. After all, Jean Monnet famously proposed that 'Europe will be forged in crises', expressing the pragmatic view that the overall project would be capable of adapting and changing. Arguably what the real threat was, as regards the events of the Eurocrisis, was that the EMU would be revealed as a conceptual and institutional mistake. The narrative of a 'critical emergency', though, succeeded in brushing aside any real debate on even this particular question, namely the viability of the current construction of the EMU.

What is clear, however, is that, absent the 'existential urgency' the Eurocrisis was perceived to signal, those reforms would not have passed as swiftly and with as

---

[18]   eg B van Apeldoorn, 'Transnationalization and the Restructuring of Europe's Socioeconomic Order: Social Forces in the Construction of "Embedded Neoliberalism"' (1998) 28 International Journal of Political Economy 12, who traces its origins back to Maastricht. See more generally on the use of this concept to offer 'multilevel' legitimacy crisis of the EU, B van Apeldoorn, 'The Contradictions of 'Embedded Neoliberalism' and Europe's Multi-level Legitimacy Crisis: The European Project and Its Limits' in B van Apeldoorn, J Drahokoupil and L Horn (eds), *Contradictions and Limits of Neoliberal European Governance* (Palgrave Macmillan 2009).

minimal scrutiny and debate as they did. As such, the framing of the 'Eurocrisis' was more of an adopted narrative designed to garner social and political 'support' for changes to the European institutional, financial and, ultimately, political architecture and to foster a very specific direction of integration and governance, than it was an actual exogenous emergency. That narrative also facilitated the 'promotion' of specific policies at the level of the Member States where opposition to neoliberal reforms pre-dated the Eurocrisis. There is little doubt that some national governments would have had a hard time – or harder than they eventually did – 'selling' any such further measures to their electorate, absent the language of urgency.

The strategy unsurprisingly backfired. Opposition to austerity and the 'shock therapy' that was imposed on countries of the periphery, particularly Greece, grew and started to be more explicitly directed at the EU, as common solutions were sought at the European level. At the same time, in other quarters of the population, the EU stirred sentiments already brewing in those that had long experienced the consequences of an economic system approaching a critical conjuncture: nationalism, protectionism, mistrust towards established institutions and, eventually, a turn towards extremely conservative political solutions.

In that, the Eurocrisis was neither unique to the EU case nor exceptional. The pattern has been repeating itself in recent political developments on both sides of the Atlantic, with the ascension of President Donald Trump in the US, the reactionary sentiments that coloured the Brexit vote in the June 2016 referendum, and the debate points and results of recent elections, such as those in Italy, where 'anti-establishment' narratives were utilised by essentially every major political player. Nonetheless, in the EU, the Eurocrisis remains a milestone in the European version of a process of political disillusionment. Its mismanagement, its exploitation as a pretext to promote particular agendas and, ultimately, the failure to engage with its underlining ideological roots or address the social needs of those affected by it, fuelled the nationalistic sentiments that lead to endoscopic, reactionary responses to the next crises – the refugee influx and the UK–EU relationship. Ultimately, the return to an entrenched, isolationist perception of the nation state as a response to all contemporary economic and social malaises, was perhaps inevitable. Largely enhanced, if not triggered, by the Eurocrisis, these sentiments and perceptions may have provided the field for the seeds of discontent and populism to flourish, and bear the fruit of utter rejection of the EU.

Ten years on, as Greece is on course to meet its last bailout target, a 'reform map'[19] for the Euro may be about to be released, a full fiscal union seems on the cards, and the EU is 'turning the page on the eurozone crisis',[20] there are signs that a slightly

---

[19] JB Vey, 'Merkel, Macron Plan Roadmap by June on Euro Zone Reform' *Reuters* (16 March 2018) https://uk.reuters.com/article/uk-france-germany/merkel-macron-plan-roadmap-by-june-on -euro-zone-reform-idUKKCN1GS1JY accessed April 2018.

[20] J Valero, 'Turning the Page on the Eurozone Crisis: Economy and Finance in 2018' (*EURACTIV*, 12 January 2018) www.euractiv.com/section/economy-jobs/news/turning-the-page-on-the-eurozone -crisis-economy-and-finance-in-2018 accessed April 2018.

different reading of the crisis is beginning to emerge from within the core of the EU's political establishment. This reading does not diverge from the narrative that the events surrounding the Eurocrisis constituted an existential emergency. Nor does it suggest that a more fundamental critical tipping point had been reached in 2010, either with regard to the EU itself or its broader socio-economic and financial context, of which the Eurocrisis would have been merely a consequence. Nonetheless, this narrative now presents the Eurocrisis not just as an opportunity to 'fix' the flaws of the Eurozone, but as a moment that has cleared the path for a new stage in the development of the EU. Under this new version of the original narrative, the Eurocrisis could retrospectively come to be regarded as one of these 'transformative' moments of opportunity that set the EU onto a different trajectory. Monnet was right after all: the EU is and will continue to be forged in crises.

As with the case of the original language of urgency, deployed to publicly justify the implementation of predetermined solutions that might have been met otherwise with much more intense opposition, however, this retroactive rebranding of the Eurocrisis allows supporters of the fundamental tenets of the European project to pour the old wine of previously criticised ideas into new bottles stamped with aspirational labels that market their content as the supposedly novel vision for the future of the EU. Emmanuel Macron's proposals for a multi-speed Europe,[21] for example, which would have been approached with scepticism, as similar suggestions had been before the crisis,[22] are in line with this new reading of the Eurocrisis. At any rate, regardless of the more positive tone this new approach adopts, the fact remains that the framing, unfolding and responses to the Eurocrisis itself were, and continue to be, infused by the paradigm of the 'emergency' through and through, which remains the dominant narrative about its causes and constitutive features.

B The Crisis as 'Systemic'

Our approach to the Eurocrisis is, necessarily, quite different.[23] If the Eurocrisis itself is but a component of a deeper systemic crisis, the word 'crisis' cannot be understood as an 'intense emergency'. The idea that the crisis is systemic first suggests that the causes of the Eurocrisis must be located in characteristics that are internal to the European project, rather than external factors. It also suggests that the

---

[21] E Maurice, 'Macron Revives Multi-speed Europe Idea' (*EU Observer*, 30 August 2017) https://euobserver.com/institutional/138832 accessed April 2018.

[22] Indicatively, on the multitude of versions of the idea expressed (and criticised) long before the contemporary reinvigoration of the concept, see ACG Stubb, 'A Categorization of Differentiated Integration' (1996) 34 Journal of Common Market Studies 283; Piris (n 7); Piris (n 13).

[23] For examples of critical engagement with the notion of 'crisis', including in the context of the EU see eg N Genova and M Tazzioli (eds), *Europe/Crisis: New Keywords of 'the Crisis' in and of 'Europe'* (Near Futures Online 2016) particularly the 'introduction' and the section entitled 'crisis' http://nearfuturesonline.org/europecrisis-new-keywords-of-crisis-in-and-of-europe; D Baker and P Schnapper, *Britain and the Crisis of the European Union* (Palgrave 2015) 2–6. See also Chapter 1 in this volume.

crisis cannot be reduced to a mere economic and financial crisis and its internal components traced solely to deficiencies in the architecture of the EMU. In addition, if the conditions of what came to be perceived as the 'Eurocrisis' are deeper and inherent in the project of European integration, it would appear somewhat paradoxical to argue that they could come to pose an existential threat to the European project. Finally, this would also suggest that, to the extent that the Eurocrisis is connected to the global financial crisis of 2008, their interrelationship is not solely one of cause (the global financial crisis) and effect (the Eurocrisis) but far more symbiotic and linked to characteristics that are inherent in the European project.

To the extent that the definition of a 'crisis' as a critical juncture in the life of a project or entity like the EU – rather than an isolated emergency – comes closer to our own use and understanding of the term, the crucial question to be asked is: a critical juncture in the evolution of what?

The perhaps easy answer is that the Eurocrisis itself is evidence of cracks in the foundational premises of the EU and the institutional structure that was built upon them. It signifies a critical moment in the evolution of the European project, a certain limit, or crossroads, that has been reached in respect of some of its fundamental objectives and the mechanisms constructed to support them. As we mentioned, this appears to be the direction the wind is blowing in more recent developments at the European level. In that context, however, the 'cracks' in the foundational premises of the EU continue to be linked primarily to the Eurozone and the critical moment rooted in an interpretation of the Eurocrisis as an isolated financial event. A more systemic and critical understanding of the 'critical junction' thesis, by contrast, would allow for a broader set of institutional and functional deficiencies to be explored that are not limited to the EMU. It would also make clear that it is the wider European project, rather than only the Eurozone, that has reached a limit or crossroads, on the basis that the current framework, with its normative hierarchy impliedly but firmly skewed in favour of free market principles and objectives, has failed to produce the equitable improvement of living standards and the protection of liberal principles it had evangelised. What it resulted in, instead, has been the embedding and locking in of a perpetual process of 'dys-integration'. Despite appearances that suggest the Member States are bound together and committed to the pursuit of a common fate, the principles, structures and mechanisms the EU embraces and utilises do not in reality ensure harmonious improvement for all. Rather, in a process of dys-integration, they reinforce and recycle stereotypical roles for Member States within the internal market (producer states–consumer states; industrialised North–service-providing South, etc.) and inherently push for a constant race to the bottom as regards social rights and social standards, as well as Keynesian assumptions and promises. What is eventually 'harmonised' is the embedment of market liberal and, increasingly, neoliberal assumptions.

Another answer is that we have not only reached a critical juncture in the evolution of the EU, but a tipping point in something more significant, in which the Eurocrisis is but a manifestation of more fundamental cracks not just in the EU's institutional architecture and constitutive (legal) foundation, but also in the economic and social model the Union is designed to promote and which, to a certain extent, it has helped bring about. Under that reading, the object under examination ought not to be limited to the EU itself but should encompass the wider liberal market ethos that permeates it and the transnational capitalist market system and structures it has produced. In this sense, what is really in crisis is market liberalism and contemporary capitalism as such, which in turn directly affects the variety of market liberalism upon which the Union has been based since its inception.

In that sense, the Eurocrisis would be inherently connected to a wider set of events, which cannot be considered as 'exceptional' but mark a critical point in the evolution of a certain form of capitalism and the political agendas attached to it. Indicative characteristics and effects of that broader crisis have manifested themselves across the developed western economies: growing inequality; reduction of the traditional social and labour protection networks of the post-Second World War social consensus; prioritisation of economic freedoms and, ultimately, of economic interests, and the apotheosis of the market as a regulatory factor; and disconnect between the demos and political actors, naturally resulting in the disillusion of the citizenry. All these symptoms connect the Eurocrisis with a nexus of global developments unfolding in sequence at an astonishing pace and that share not only the same wider context, but also similar characteristics and, to some extent, political consequences.

However, this is not to say the global financial crisis of 2008 was not felt particularly strongly in the EU. But the fact that it was should not be attributed to the severity of the circumstances and events of 2008 as much as to the inherent nature of the Union. It is not a coincidence that financial crises, grievous consequences though they may have, are rarely regarded as threatening the life of a nation state. The economic, financial and monetary spheres constitute only one of the elements comprising the realm of a state; statehood and national identity, however, are hardly premised exclusively upon these, which may explain why the nation state has been generally more effective both in defusing capitalist crises and creating the conditions for the renewal and reproduction of economic and social relations. These spheres, by contrast, lie at the heart of the EU's existence and its integration narrative. The illusion of post-state citizenship aside, especially since its EU variant is a peculiar market-based, market-compatible citizenship that is devised from above to correspond to the one-dimensional ideal of 'integration-by-free-market', the EU lacks an 'ideology of "belonging" [that] could be mobilised during periods of instability or crisis'.[24] It lacks not only a constitutional moment of popular consent and the constitutive myth of a democratically expressed transnational social and political

---

[24] Philip Marfleet, cited in C Cantat, 'Narratives and Counter-Narratives of Europe: Constructing and Contesting Europeanity' (2015) 3 Cahiers: Mémoire et Politique 5, 12.

contract, but even the fundamental objectives and features (such a primacy of civic, political and social principles over the economic) that could potentially draw allegiance and legitimacy. It is therefore hardly surprising that a potential danger to the particular form of free market capitalism the EU has been set up to promote – its 'market liberalism with a human face', to paraphrase Samuel Brittan[25] – and the aspirational narrative constructed around it – the ideal of liberal Europeanism – comes to be construed by its proponents as a potential threat to the very existence of the European project.

In other words, the fact that the EU was created upon, and continues to serve, predominantly economic premises and objectives does not just mean that it is more susceptible to the inherent cyclical nature of capitalist crises. More than that, the primarily economic ethos of the EU results in the EU effectively incorporating and internalising the cyclical crises of the system that forms its underlying basis. In that sense, the EU is not merely *affected* by transnational crises of capitalism such as the global financial crisis of 2008. The Union, with its ordoliberal structural DNA, its market liberal normative priorities and the neoliberal characteristics of some of its contemporary policy and governance, is intrinsically *connected to* these crises and internalises them, since the broader economic system that produces and experiences them – contemporary global free market capitalism – is not merely an inherent element of the EU, but the foundation stone of its existence. This inherent symbiotic link can explain the existential character ascribed to the Eurocrisis, even if it cannot detract from its real nature and deeper cause.

In sum, our hypothesis, and argument, is that, contrary to the emergency narrative, the Eurocrisis is indicative of deeper flaws and contradictions that are inherent to the European project but were revealed, magnified and aggravated by the global financial crisis of 2008 because of the EU's symbiotic fate with the broader global capitalist system. From that perspective, the Eurocrisis cannot be approached as an event isolated from the broader systemic crisis of global capitalism, but it also cannot be examined without having regard to the EU's specific institutional and normative set-up, as a crucial factor in understanding the specific way this broader crisis of capitalism manifested itself in the Union. As a result, our analysis does not disregard a micro examination of the EU's institutional and legal architecture. What we propose, however, is to conduct such examination on the basis of the overarching assumption that the crisis the EU faces is inherent to its nature as a sui generis project that nevertheless internalises the character and flaws of contemporary capitalism. It is thus ultimately the very (dual) nature of the EU that, almost inevitably, foreshadowed and fostered the Eurocrisis in all of its multifaceted nature – legal, political, economic and social. And it is therefore in the nature of the EU as a project that the heart of the 'crisis behind the crisis' ultimately lies.

---

[25] S Brittan, *Capitalism with a Human Face* (Edward Elgar 1995).

III METHODOLOGY: UNCOVERING THE 'CRISIS BEHIND THE CRISIS'

Methodologically, our attempt to reconstruct the character of this 'hidden' crisis builds on three pillars. First, the volume explores, and is organised around, different dimensions of the Eurocrisis. Looking at the Eurocrisis as a manifestation of a deeper crisis necessarily requires, in the first instance, to go beyond a conceptualisation of the Eurocrisis as a purely economic phenomenon and situate it instead in a broader narrative about the character of the EU itself. As we go on to outline in the next section, we identify four such dimensions of the Eurocrisis, although this grid does not claim to be comprehensive, or indeed exhaustive.

To that effect, second, we investigate not only the characteristics of, and solutions to, these various dimensions of the crisis, but also their underlying systemic causes, going back to the very roots of the European project, including its history, purpose, identity, as well as institutional and normative setup. Only by uncovering the commonalities between these different dimensions will it be possible to begin reconstructing an explanation of the crisis that sees its various dimensions and manifestations as part of a single set of operative events, as well as normative and ideological assumptions.

Finally, dialogue on these questions is sought between scholars from different disciplines and diverse backgrounds. From our perspective as lawyers, this is partly with a view to 'reconnecting' the relevant legal analyses with the themes that have been the focus of other fields across the social sciences. Although the reluctance to challenge traditional conceptualisations of, and narratives about, the EU arguably permeates much of the broader field of European studies, it has been particularly pervasive in EU law, notwithstanding what some have identified as a supposed 'critical turn'.[26] But interdisciplinary dialogue is more fundamentally required, we believe, by the task at hand. With varied disciplines comes an equal variety in theoretical frameworks and analytical starting points that inevitably may lead to different set of observations and conclusions. But it also opens possibilities for the emergence of common themes and explanations that are again crucial to the reconstruction of a more holistic narrative of the crisis.

IV STRUCTURE: THE MULTIPLE DIMENSIONS OF THE CRISIS

Before engaging with the various dimensions of the Eurocrisis as an example that concretises the inherent flaws of the current European framework, the volume aims to give the reader some general context about the conceptual aspects of what we identify as a systemic crisis of the EU. The volume thus opens with a chapter from Benjamin Farrand and Marco Rizzi, which reflects on the history and discourse of 'crisis' in the European project and further develops some of the points we touched

---

[26] Editorial comments, 'The Critical Turn in EU Legal Studies' (2015) 52 CML Rev 881.

upon in this introduction. They argue, in particular, that the 'crisis' narrative was not reflective of an actual emergency but was essentially used to codify a particular ideology into EU law and delegitimise alternative economic doctrines. In doing so, they go beyond recent critiques that merely challenge the integrationist and distinctively progressive account of crises[27] – the idea of crisis as 'opportunity'[28] – in the process of European integration and instead prompt us to think more seriously about the role these crises played and continue to play in the construction of the European project.

The four parts that follow explore various dimensions of the Eurocrisis. These different dimensions of the prism are presented here as those aspects of the crisis that relate to the identity of the EU (Part I), its political and democratic legitimacy (Part II), the specific economic model it follows and the architecture of the EMU (Part III) and what is left of its social character (Part IV).

As will become clear over the course of our analysis, we view these dimensions as integral elements of the systemic deficiencies in the conception and construction of the European project and hence as inherently intertwined. It is a combination of these different aspects of the same fundamental flaws that created the conditions for the crisis as a singular critical juncture to materialise. Once all the inherent flaws approached critical mass, mirroring a similar tipping point in the broader political and economic context of the EU, the crisis manifested in full. Each of these aspects of the Union is a *sine qua non* piece of its existence and function. They are supposed to form a coherent structural whole, served by principled consistency, devoid of prejudice or imbalanced priorities, working for the common good of the European people, who the more passionate proponents of the EU envisage as its future singular demos. And yet, no harmony or symmetry was to be found in how the EU approached the first major turmoil threatening the supposed heart of the integration project, especially when that turmoil was ultimately very much a problem of the Union's own making, as we will see moving through the different dimensions of the crisis.

This topology is not, however, to suggest that there are no other dimensions to the crisis, neither to essentialise the particular categories and themes around which we have chosen to organise this work. Notions like the 'justice deficit'[29] – to mirror the long-standing debates around the democratic deficit – or the 'rule of law crisis' could all potentially have provided fertile ground to think through the causes and nature of the crisis, even though many of the concerns that they tend to convey are covered under different labels in our analysis. Likewise, building on our conceptual grid, new terminologies and analytical lenses may yet be deployed. More fundamentally, however, approaching the Eurocrisis as a manifestation of an underlying hidden and systemic crisis implies that its full ramifications may yet to have fully unfolded, even

---

[27] eg D Dinan, 'Crises in EU History' in Dinan and others (n 6).

[28] ibid 28.

[29] D Kochenov, G de Búrca and A Williams (eds), *Europe's Justice Deficit?* (Hart 2015).

as the Eurocrisis has seemingly taken a backstage. Conversely, it also implies that the crisis's constitutive dimensions are not exhausted by any one particular moment like the Eurocrisis, however seminal it may have been for the process of European integration.

A *Deconstructing the Crisis*

1 The Crisis of Identity

The first dimension is conceptualised in Part I as a crisis of the EU's identity. The term 'identity' is used to refer to the nature of the EU, as it emerges from its historical and normative foundations and evolution. In that context, the EU's identity is examined not only as it is concretised in EU primary law, but also as it emerges from the EU's political ethos and the objectives prioritised by its institutional actors, whether they act within or outside of the strict confines of EU law. By the same token, the focus is not on how the Union portrays itself or the identity it might aspire to, be it that of a coherent constitutional legal order, a human rights-based organisation, a liberal and democratic transnational entity based on the rule of law or a quasi-federal project. Rather, the contributions in Part I move beyond the EU's legal framework and set of discursive practices, to offer a more contextual analysis of its roots, purpose and evolution, which ultimately challenge the professed aspirations and objectives of the EU's legal, political and economic framework and of European elites.

To that effect, in Chapter 2, Charalampos Kouroundis first retreads the historical development of the EU. He traces its roots in the hidden interplay of geopolitical and economic interests and rivalries and explores how they played and continue to play an important role in determining the contradictory nature and course of the European project. In Chapter 3, Hent Kalmo revisits the dominant assumption that arose out of the attempt to find common ground between the foundational interplay of interests, namely that building an economic and monetary union to achieve market integration would in itself ultimately lead to political integration through factual solidarity among the people of Europe. He argues that the Eurocrisis revealed not only the fallacy, but also the true nature and dangers of that assumption, as engineering closer economic ties may have the consequence of actually increasing resistance to closer political integration. Magnus Ryner then takes the argument forward, digging deeper into the nature of the European project. If Kalmo reveals the 'integration through common market' to be little more than a convenient myth, Ryner's chapter more fundamentally questions the nature of the EU as anything but an organisation created and developed to serve very specific economic and political aspirations, notwithstanding the EU's self-projection as a beacon of democracy, social protection and fundamental rights. In Ryner's account in Chapter 4, the 'crisis' appears indeed as nothing but the concretisation of authoritarian neoliberalism as an extension of disciplinary neoliberalism, itself the culmination of the free market centred ethos of the Union since its conception.

The common thread that connects the contributions of Part I is the argument that several characteristics of the 'crisis', that magnified its effects and fostered disillusionment with the European project, were in fact simply a consequence of inherent flaws in the EU's normative soul and structure. It was not a coincidence nor a result of contemporary politics that during the course of the crisis the Union swiftly painted itself in a corner from which 'there is no alternative'. It is not coincidental, in other words, that a singular vision of integration, based on a misconstrued monetary union and very specific conception of free market economy, became the established, but rigid, dogma. It was the unavoidable culmination of five decades of attempting to build a supposed constitutional legal order upon a skewed foundation that put very specific normative versions of economic freedom above all. Of course, that outcome was perhaps unavoidable. Any suggestion to carry on with the integration project at a more careful pace, through democratic debate and the reflection that would be prudent for the transition from an organisation of economic and trade cooperation to a potential future transnational polity, was arguably doomed from the start, stopped on its tracks by the ordoliberal DNA of the EU's fundamental objectives. There was no debate to be had as regards the heart of the EU project: economic integration was the sole indisputable means to achieve political integration.

2 The Crisis of Democratic and Political Legitimacy

The endogenous crisis of political and democratic legitimacy that this precipitated constitutes the theme of Part II. In Chapter 5 Michael Wilkinson picks up the baton from Ryner to trace the longer-term advent of authoritarian liberalism and de-democratisation of the economy. His analysis suggests that the essence of authoritarian liberalism, as a form of government ultimately designed to protect the material order of economic liberalism, is not only reflected in the EU's reaction to the perceived 'crisis' but that the resulting assaults on democracy appears to be a continuation of, rather than divergence from, the normal path of integration. In Chapter 6, Eva Nanopoulos and Fotis Vergis pursue a similar line of thinking, examining this time more specifically the EU's own democratic credentials, including the relationship between the present democratic meltdown and longer-term debates about the so-called 'democratic deficit'. Similarly, that chapter concludes that the EU's democratic predicament is hardly coincidental, since the undemocratic ethos has been engrained in the EU's psyche and telos since its conception and is not therefore a structural glitch in the form of a symptomatic 'deficit' that can be remedied through institutional change. In Chapter 7 Maria Tzanakopoulou then turns to examine how that undemocratic ethos, now fully revealed and almost reaching the authoritarian heights alluded to by Wilkinson, actively encroached upon the national constitutional structures of Member States, but also, and perhaps

more importantly, was used to shape popular perceptions that would foster resigna-
tion to the TINA dogma. And, as Elia Alexiou recounts in Chapter 8, whenever
popular reaction managed to supersede the narratives and attempt to voice dissonance through institutional means, most notably through referendums, their voice
was quickly muffled, either by the EU pushing towards a second referendum that
would deliver the 'right answer' or towards humiliating capitulation to the demands
electorates had voted against, as in the case of the Greek referendum of 2015. In
Chapter 9, Ozlem Ulgen more generally challenges the extent to which such
referendums, alongside other forms of civic participation, can in fact retrospectively
legitimise the EU, in a wider context where much of the EU's allegedly common
system of rules and values were neither collectively agreed, nor are equally applied.

The legitimacy issue, therefore, is far from new. Nor is its aggrandisement just
a by-product of the Eurocrisis.[30] Democratic deficiency has been a crack in the
foundations of the EU's structures since they were first laid, and depoliticisation
inherent in the economic theory and ideology that underpin it.[31] Part II seeks to
establish this thesis, by going back to the authoritarian and ordoliberal underpinnings of the European construct and the gradual constitutionalisation of neoliberalism, and by exploring the consequences these have had not only on the EU's
relationship to the European people, but also on the relationship between citizens
and the nation state. What emerges from these inquiries, is that the Eurocrisis
merely acted as a catalyst, exposing these deficiencies, and bringing the gradual
popular and political delegitimation that they produced to a critical stage.
Disillusionment was fostered and precipitated precisely by the crisis narrative and
the accompanying emergency shock treatment, often outside normal procedures
and rules, that was portrayed as an economic necessity.

3 The Crisis of the Economic Model

This brings us to that economic dogma and the nature of the framework devised to
serve it, which is the focus of Part III. Part III combines doctrinal analyses of the
EMU and the responses to the Eurocrisis with a normative assessment of the
underlying structure of the EU's economic constitution, as well as the economic
model and ideology that underpins it. The foundational framework of the Union has
always been tilted towards the promotion of a very specific version of the free market
economy envisaged as the centre of social and political development and the
impetus for European integration. The specific theoretical conceptions about the
role and value of the free market in a polity that underpin the European project
never sat well with ideas of strong democratic scrutiny, regulatory flexibility or

[30] cf F Scharpf, 'Monetary Union, Fiscal Crisis and the Preemption of Democracy' (2011) MPIfG
Discussion Paper 11/11 www.mpifg.de/pu/mpifg_dp/dp11-11.pdf accessed April 2018.
[31] See also H Macartney, *The Debt Crisis and European Democratic Legitimacy* (Palgrave Macmillan
2013).

wealth redistribution. Pisani-Ferry has dubbed the creation of the Euro as 'the last utopia of the 20th century',[32] a true *'ex abruption* creation',[33] to highlight the grandeur of the vision and the revolutionary aspirations of its creators. But the idea of promoting the EMU as a means to precipitate political union was arguably putting the carriage of monetary union before the horses of democratic debate, popular and social consensus and, ultimately, democratic legitimacy.

Vanessa Bilancetti opens Part III by engaging with one specific part of the institutional and normative architecture of the contemporary EMU: the Treaty on Stability Coordination and Governance (TSCG), as an emblematic example of the Union's 'New Economic Governance' (NEG). She describes the rigidity of its conditions and discusses the underlying theoretical premise of the fiscal discipline dogma, which prevents any flexibility that would allow for a policy that requires budget deficits, and hence removes a crucial financial tool that could be used to reinvigorate economies in crisis and ensure social protection for those affected. However, what distinguishes her chapter from other similar examinations is that she bases her analysis on a combination of two critical perspectives, namely governmentality studies and a historical–materialist approach inspired by Gramsci and neo-Gramscian scholars. Thus, she conceptualises the Fiscal Compact as a *fiscal governance machine*, in the Gramscian and Foucauldian sense, that serves the financialisation of the economy and perpetuates the uneven construction of the monetary union. As such, Bilancetti argues that the TSCG, and the NEG it is part of, are not only unable to rectify the economic, political and social divides plaguing Europe, but also exacerbate and perpetuate them.

In Chapter 11 Gunnar Beck turns to examine whether these new instruments of EU 'economic governance' and particularly the way the Court of Justice of the EU has approached them are compatible with the Union's own primary law. The result is a principled, robust critique of the Court's *Pringle* and *OMT* judgments, in which the Court upheld the contested legality of both the ESM and the ECB's bond-buying programmes. As Beck notes, the Court reached its conclusion by adopting a teleological approach that essentially ignored the wording of the EU Treaties. The judgments, Beck suggests, are difficult to reconcile with either the specific Treaty provisions that the Court was supposed to interpret and apply, unless one takes the view that every provision of the EU Treaties has to be read subject to a pro-integrationist proviso, or the Union's own supposedly fundamental principles and objectives of democracy and social market economy. By adopting this unhinged teleological method, the Court was essentially able to read purposes into the text, something that would allow it to justify almost any judgment. The CJEU judges, as a result, effectively fully embraced the narrative of the 'economic emergency', and exempted the ECB and the ESM from judicial oversight. In doing so, they followed

---

[32] J Pisany-Ferry, *The Euro Crisis and Its Aftermath* (OUP 2011) 19.
[33] ibid.

the Members States and other EU institutions in essentially bypassing the Treaties, retroactively providing a mantle of legitimacy to the actions taken in response to the crisis.

Lastly, Christakis Georgiou takes a step back and attempts to decipher the meaning of the conjuncture initiated by the crisis of the EMU and what it might tell us about the future trajectory of the EU. For Georgiou, the Eurocrisis is likely to lead to deeper integration and fewer and weaker Eurosceptic obstacles within it. However, his analysis is not based on some kind of neo-functionalist reading of integration. Instead, he traces the introduction of the Euro and the present conjuncture to the 'corporate reconstruction' of European capitalism. Under this view, the Eurocrisis, like other crises before it, would have brought the internal contradictions of integration to the fore and spurred the ruling elites to overcome them.

4 The Crisis of the Social Character

Part IV closes the exploration the EU's multifaceted crisis by asking if, after the Eurocrisis and the institutional change it precipitated, there is anything left from the coveted 'European Social Model'[34] that supposedly reconciles free market principles with fundamental liberal and socio-democratic values. In Chapter 13, Alan Bogg and Keith Ewing provide the overarching context that connects us back to the normative foundations of the EU, tracing the fate of the European social model from the Charter of the Fundamental Social Rights of Workers to the European Social Pillar. In the twists and turns from a clearer socio-democratic paradigm in the 1980s to the complete embrace of market liberalism today, they discern a clear deregulatory turn, reflected in the contracting influence of social rights and the declining collective empowerment of worker-citizens. Their chapter, however, sees a silver lining in the Social Pillar, as contrasted with the current political situation in the UK, including the British stance regarding collective labour institutions and, ultimately, the fate of the working class and its capacity for democratic participation. For Bogg and Ewing, the UK case provides a salutary lesson in the political dangers of social and economic deregulation. Its brutal social policies of austerity have exposed the dark linkages between social and economic precariousness and authoritarian state policies, that imply a grim repudiation of basic liberal commitments. However, the writers note that the mere declaration of the Social Pillar is not

---

[34] Indicatively, see J Kvist, 'The Post-Crisis European Social Model: Developing or Dismantling Social Investments?' (2013) 29 Journal of International and Comparative Social Policy 91; D Schiek (ed) *The EU Economic and Social Model in the Global Crisis* (Routledge 2013); MA Moreau and I Ulasiuk, *Before and After the Economic Crisis: What Implications for the 'European Social Model'?* (Edward Elgar 2011). For context, see also D Vaughan-Whitehead, *The European Social Model in Crisis: Is Europe Losing Its Soul?* (Edward Elgar 2015); D Schiek, U Liebert and H Schneider, *European and Social Constitutionalism after the Treaty of Lisbon* (CUP 2011); M Jepsen and AS Pascual, 'The European Social Model: an Exercise in Deconstruction' (2005) 15 Journal of European Social Policy 231; F Scharpf, 'The European Social Model' (2002) 40 Journal of Common Market Studies 645.

enough, if not followed by clear initiatives to guarantee social protection. Bogg and Ewing warn that the UK paradigm should stand as a lesson to European policy-makers on the likely political and democratic consequences of economic deregulation across Europe.

Roland Erne is not as optimistic about the prospects and intentions of European institutions, yet sees a possible exit route in empowering and redefining collective action. His analysis in Chapter 14 builds a bridge to Part III by engaging with the EU's NEG and assessing the margin of manoeuvre it leaves to social actors, predominantly collective labour institutions, to influence its effects or react to it. Erne observes that the NEG clearly aims to prevent transnational collective action by introducing league tables and country-specific interventions that nationalise social conflict. However, these methods resemble less those of a political, state or state-like entity, and more those of the corporate governance structures of multi-national companies that use coercive comparisons based on centrally chosen key performance indicators to control their notionally autonomous subsidiaries. In that, the new architecture, whose advent was fuelled by the Eurocrisis as the proper response to the supposed emergency, goes far beyond the principled constraint of collective action on the basis of the free market related 'fundamental freedoms' of the Treaties. It essentially attempts to seclude collective action and conflict to national boundaries, and to the narrowest possible level. As a means to counter these effects, Erne suggests taking a page out of the supranational playbook of the NEG: he proposes to set aside the established classical 'nation-by-nation' designs that are still dominating comparative industrial relations, political economy, and legal research. The depoliticisation of economic governance, according to Erne, can only be countered by the transnationalisation of social and political conflict and, hence, the political space, along transnational class or national cross-class lines.

Chapter 15 by Dimitris Dalakoglou, concluding Part IV, provides a radically different angle to the impact of the Eurocrisis on social cohesion than lawyers and political scientists are accustomed to. Dalakoglou goes beyond norms and institutions and examines the effects of the collapse of Europe's main sociopolitical balance after the end of the Cold War. This balance had been premised upon the traditional fundamental assumptions of the market-based European dream and its relevant constants. Its collapse, which followed the disintegration of that dream, led to overemphasising the boundaries of the privileged territorial condition of being part of the bordered European space as the dominant basis for identifying European identity against a new paradigm of 'the Other'. Dalakoglou suggests that the collapse of the 'micro-capitalist' dream of owning a private home or a private investment, that had already begun before the Eurocrisis, with the outburst of the property bubbles in the advent of the global financial crisis of 2008, and was only further advanced by it, left the EU stripped of the sociopolitical narrative that served to substantiate and delimit the privilege of its subjects vis-à-vis outsiders. The result of the collapse has been that the only privilege left for the EU to 'sell' to its citizens is the mere supposed privilege of a secure, bordered common space (almost in the sense of the old German Lebensraum). As the European economy slows and the construction and real estate sectors are further deregulated, Dalakoglou notes, the promises that the post-Cold War period brought wither alongside. The inevitable result is what we observe in the context of the current refugee crisis as the manifestation of Europe's ugly and discriminatory spatiality: the preservation at all costs of its border security.

B *Reconstructing the Crisis*

Part V, finally, brings some of the threads of the analysis together, and back to where we started. In this last part of the book, the Eurocrisis is anchored more firmly within the context of the real, broader systemic crisis the EU is faced with. The Eurocrisis, as merely the financial manifestation of the deeper EU crisis, is also partly reconnected with one of the symptoms that followed it, namely the Brexit vote, as an illustration of the systemic interconnections between the EU's manifest crises. The aim is to open a door towards the exploration of the connections between the various dimensions of the crisis and begin to construct a narrative that enables not only an assessment of the future of the Union but also, importantly, the formulation of alternative visions that could bring together the people of Europe, building transnational solidarity and a sense of commonality based on their needs.

To that end, Michelle Everson's chapter joins the dots and traces the origin of the EU's crisis to a wider crisis of economic liberalism and other institutions that have been characteristic of modernity. In her narrative, the multiple aspects of the EU crisis (financial and sovereign debt related; Brexit; migration and reintroduction of borders) share (in part) a common root. Indeed, as a feature of globalisation, Europeanisation creates an unbearable tension between the internationalised economy and still-local complexes of identity, welfare and security. It is this tension, she argues, that lies at the root of the multiple manifestations of the European crisis. And it is therefore impossible to understand this critical conjuncture, in all its various aspects, lacking a coherent rethinking of modern economic liberalism.

The two final chapters reflect on the way forward, drawing both from concrete experiences, notably the events and debates around Brexit and Grexit, and theoretical perspectives about the nature of the European project.

Costas Lapavitsas carries on from Everson, but moves beyond theory. His chapter grounds the concluding part of the book in the harsh reality of economics, critically examining an economic and monetary policy that is far from consistent in following normative theoretical principles. He draws upon the lessons of the Greek crisis, its roots, evolution and alleged resolution, both from an economic and political perspective, and from his own hands-on academic and political experience of the Greek paradigm. Making use of these lessons, theoretical and practical, he goes back to the EMU to critically analyse the inherent flaws in its primary assumptions, conception, structure, organisation and policies. But he also goes one step further to critically contemplate alternatives to the current Eurozone and EU constructs and develop much needed concrete suggestions for a different evolution of Europeanisation.

Lastly, Alex Callinicos closes this volume by casting doubt on the very idea of Europeanisation through institutional integration 'from above' on the basis of the current EU framework, thus reinforcing the idea of an inherently dysfunctional and, therefore, perhaps popularly doomed, conception of the EU. This thesis is tested against the Brexit referendum, with its result being, partly at least, a reaction to the present formulation of the Union. The constitution of the EU in its present form is argued to be dual from its very genesis. Approached from the perspective of the Marxist critique of political economy, which understands capitalist imperialism as the intersection of economic and geopolitical competition, the EU's dual constitution arises from (1) the consistent promotion of European integration by the US as a means of ensuring its hegemony in the 'Euro-Atlantic' space that now reaches deep into Eurasia; (2) the use of the EU by the major European imperialist powers as a platform for more effectively pursuing their interests globally. This dual constitution has persisted through all the different phases of European integration and is essential to explaining the Union's inherent dysfunctionality. Britain's more problematic positioning in this nexus has now exploded with Brexit. The chapter concludes by considering this new and dramatic phase in the EU's dysfunctional functioning, laying down the ground for a more comprehensive future discussion once the Brexit events have fully unfolded.

The last part of the book closes with an overall conclusion to the volume, which attempts to link the different points and analyses together and think about the questions they open up not only as regards the character of the Eurocrisis, but also its relationship to other manifestations of the EU's systemic crisis, the implications for the likely future trajectory of the project, as well as its longer historical legacies.

v SHEDDING LIGHT IN A DARK ROOM: UNDERSTANDING THE TRUE NATURE OF THE CRISIS

To tame a beast, it is imperative that you first come to know it and understand its true nature. To do that, you need to share your perspectives and cooperate both with others that seek to know it, and with those that simply need to find a practical way to domesticate it, and make it serve their needs. And in doing so, it might be that new ideas and approaches emerge, illuminating hidden aspects or opening avenues that were difficult to conceive by using old methods and tools and by being constrained to traditional ideological or epistemological boundaries.

Following the Brexit result, it is all the more evident that traditional analyses, based upon now shattered assumptions of the irreversibility of integration and upon particular institutional and economic preconceptions, are proving inadequate to assess the immediate circumstances surrounding the EU's multiples crises. Political and economic analysis will now require thinking outside the traditional box of EU studies. It will necessitate taking pause and rethinking the fundamental assumptions that have characterised the European project, and its consequent contemporary political and economic landscape. Regardless of the interests or prejudices of the various actors, novel approaches that challenge the established narrative could prove invaluable as a basis and springboard for further debate and for more imaginative responses to the multiple conundrums raised by the current EU crisis.

The combination of bringing together perspectives arising from multiple disciplines, with a deeper, critical analysis of the economic, financial and social features of not just the EU but its systemic context can provide for a far richer approach of the Eurocrisis and one that is essential to understand the true inherent crisis plaguing the EU and the economic system it embraces, embodies and promotes. It is that systemic crisis that is the elephant in the room. And it is that underlying systemic crisis that this collection ultimately aims to shed a light on. Only by recognising its true characteristics and complexity we can be brought in a position to understand and, ultimately, begin to tame it.

1

There Is No (Legal) Alternative

Codifying Economic Ideology into Law

Benjamin Farrand and Marco Rizzi

I INTRODUCTION

The purpose of this chapter is to further explore the nature of 'crisis', and how the incorporation of an economic ideology as 'solution' to that crisis in the form of legally binding obligations restricts the ability to pursue alternative courses of action, creating tensions within society. Focusing upon economic doctrine as reflecting ideological positions, the authors consider the way in which the framing of events as 'crises', and thereby establishing them as threats to the current political and economic system, enables political actors to facilitate changes that may not otherwise be politically feasible. In particular, by responding to a crisis through the creation of laws that codify an ideologically guided economic doctrine, a temporary state of crisis creates a permanent legal set of obligations. By doing so, prevailing (if not altogether hegemonic) political actors are able to delegitimise alternatives to that economic doctrine as falling outside of the rule of law: there is no legal alternative but to follow that legal obligation.

This chapter begins by explaining the theoretical framework guiding the work. It draws from a social constructivist perspective, highlighting the importance of ideas as a means of interpreting events. It combines analysis of structural economic changes with the role of actors in creating and framing narratives surrounding such changes and the ensuing struggles. The proposed thesis holds that while structural changes are analytically observable, there is no single true narrative of social reality, but instead competing and contestable truth claims about the social or political origins of events, what those events mean, and whether they constitute a challenge, an opportunity, or a problem. It also expands upon how economic ideologies, such as those represented in neoclassical economics, reflect ideologically oriented perceptions of the truth of our social and economic world. In so doing, instead of rigidly applying analytical tools and precepts of social constructivism or Marxism to the events described, the chapter adopts a more flexible framework. It builds the theory drawing from tools and precepts of both approaches, thereby creating a theoretical hybrid, which is more convincing in accounting for the complex variety of factors contributing to the understanding of how events can be framed so as to make specific policy choices legally binding – while there may be alternative policy options, there is no *legal* alternative.

The subsequent section further explores how a 'crisis' narrative served to structure arguments concerning the nature of the 2008 collapse of key financial institutions and the resulting economic fallout, and the appropriate responses to that perceived 'crisis'. In this respect, the existence of crisis is not an objective, immutable truth, but instead dependent upon our frames of reference, experiences and understandings of material events. The section also considers the process by which the existence of a crisis is framed, communicated and acted upon. The rest of the chapter analyses the development of the EU's economic model. The third section traces this development as a response to the perception of systemic economic 'crisis' that resulted from the identification of serious structural problems with the international financial system during the 1970s and the collapse of Bretton Woods. The section then discusses the reframing of this crisis as a legitimacy one, resulting from the alleged state capture by actors such as trade unions; and through to the rise of monetarism and 'balanced budgets' as the basis for legal obligations under the Stability and Growth Pact, granted further impetus by the Maastricht Treaty. The final section considers the economic crash of the mid 2000s, indicating that although this was the result of a myriad of different factors, what was arguably a 'crisis' of private sector lending practices became framed as a crisis of public sector profligacy, with economic ideas concerning 'expansionary austerity' serving as a frame for the reform of the public sector. By the codification of this emergency response to a perceived crisis resulting from imbalanced budgets and high levels of public debt, a permanent state of austerity becomes codified as law, restricting the possibility of attempting alternative economic policies as a means of managing structural problems. The chapter concludes by considering the implication of this – namely the creation of a new legitimacy crisis, in which the top-down, rule-making governance style of government becomes discredited. By creating no alternative in law, unhappy electorates seek alternatives outside of that legal framework, leading to a rise in populist parties, pursuance of referenda as a means of direct democracy, and in the extreme case of the UK's 'Brexit' from the European Union (EU), a desire to leave that legal regime altogether.[1]

---

[1]   In this context, we refer to the EU's legal order and membership of it, rather than that of the Eurozone, of which the UK is not a member. However, as will be discussed later, perceptions of the impact of the Eurozone crisis among UK voters are believed to have been one of the determinants of the decision to vote 'Leave' in the referendum.

II THE IDEAS THAT SHAPE OUR WORLD: A FRAMEWORK FOR ANALYSIS

The central thesis of this chapter is that 'ideas matter'.[2] Fundamental assumptions are important in understanding how certain concepts become codified in law and therefore restrict the policy options of governments. Understanding the contestation between competing ideas that seek to explain phenomena (and in so doing, give them meaning) is the first essential stage in framing social and political conflict. In this sense the approach of this chapter is inspired by a constructivist framework, according to which 'people do one thing and not another due to the presence of certain "social constructs": ideas, beliefs, norms, identities or some other interpretive filter through which people perceive the world'.[3] To put it another way, our interactions with the world, while based in direct engagement with material and objective facts, are filtered through social, cultural and political processes that serve to shape our understanding of the world around us.[4] 'Truth' in social and political matters, 'is not a property of the "world out there" but, with the exception of purely analytical statements, is always relative to a semantic system'.[5] What this means, for the purpose of this chapter, is that while structural changes and struggles normally (though not necessarily) linger behind a narrative of crisis, the 'truth' of it is partial in nature. Different perceptions of the causes and solutions to those structural conflicts (including solutions created by legal reform) give rise to contestations over what constitutes a crisis, and how best to address it.

This brings us to the importance of ideas. As Beland and Cox state, we can consider ideas to be 'interpretive frameworks that make us see some facts as important and others as less so'.[6] They are the beliefs held by individuals or adopted by institutions that influence their attitudes and actions.[7] Saurugger states that ideas influence policymaking in three specific ways: 'First, they help to construct the problems and issues that enter the policy agenda; second, they frame the basic assumptions that influence the content of reform proposals; finally, ideas can act as discursive tools that shape reform imperatives.'[8] Of particular relevance to this chapter is the notion that ideas can shape macro-level understandings of the world

---

[2] A Wendt, *Social Theory of International Politics* (CUP 1999).

[3] C Parsons, 'Constructivism and Interpretive Theory' in D Marsh and G Stoker (eds), *Theory and Methods in Political Science* (3rd edn, Palgrave Macmillan 2010) 80.

[4] EG Guba and Yvonna S Lincoln, 'Competing Paradigms in Qualitative Research' in NK Denzin and YS Lincoln (eds), *Handbook of Qualitative Research* (SAGE 1994) 110; T Christiansen, KE Jorgensen and A Wiener (eds), *The Social Construction of Europe* (SAGE 2001) 3.

[5] F Kratochwil, 'Constructivism: What It Is (Not) and How It Matters' in D Della Porta and M Keating (eds), *Approaches and Methodologies in the Social Sciences: A Pluralist Perspective* (CUP 2008) 82.

[6] D Beland and RH Cox, 'Introduction: Ideas and Politics' in Daniel Beland and Robert Henry Cox (eds), *Ideas and Politics in Social Science Research* (OUP 2010) 3.

[7] L Emmerij, R Jolly and TG Weiss, 'Economic and Social Thinking at the UN in Historical Perspective' (2005) 36 Development and Change 211, 214.

[8] S Saurugger, 'Constructivism and Public Policy Approaches in the EU: From Ideas to Power Games' (2013) 20 Journal of European Public Policy 888, 891.

and how it functions, which we can refer to as ideologies. Ideology is in essence an interpretive frame, which serves to act as a guide to action. In his discussion of *ideological state apparatuses* (hereafter ISA),[9] Althusser argues that ideology refers to the ideology of the ruling class, made manifest through private domain actors such as trade unions, churches, political parties, the media and the family.[10] The analysis conducted by Althusser is Marxist in nature, with the ruling class being synonymous with the capitalist class, and ideology constituting 'an imaginary assemblage, a pure dream, empty and vain',[11] an imaginary relationship of individuals to their real conditions of existence.[12] The notion of ISA, and the associated *repressive state apparatuses* (RSA) developed within this framework are useful beyond purely Marxist–structuralist analysis however, and will be expanded upon with regard to the ideological conditions of law. In doing so, we adopt a post-Marxist understanding of ideology as an ideational framework supported by a framing narrative that serves as the interpretive lens for decision-making.

In terms of ideas influencing economic policies, the resurgence of 'neoclassical' economic thought has been particularly important historically in framing under-standings of the relation between state and market throughout the world, and has served as the basis for market reform in numerous contexts, including the Pinochet dictatorship in Chile and the economic reforms undertaken in South East Asia during the 1980s. The ideas that served as the basis for the economic reforms that have shaped the EU, as well as the international trade system, can be traced back to the establishment of the Mont Pèlerin Society in 1947, which comprised notable economic thinkers such as Milton Friedman, Friedrich Hayek and Ludwig von Mises. For Mirowski and Plehwe, the Mont Pèlerin Society can be considered the birthplace of the 'Neoliberal Thought Collective', or NTC,[13] out of which devel-oped the distinct, yet cross-fertilising, Austrian legal theory school and the Chicago School of neoclassical economics. While German ordoliberalism, already on the rise since the 1930s with roots in authoritarian liberalism and in the legal and political discourse of Carl Schmitt,[14] is often considered to be a distinct form of economic thought, it nevertheless received from this cross-fertilisation a renewed impetus towards developing its core concept of a preordained social market economy.[15] What these schools have in common is a focus upon a small-state,

---

[9]   A useful concept, which shall be returned to in later sections of this work.
[10] L Althusser, *On Ideology* (Verso 2008) 17–18.
[11] ibid 34.
[12] ibid 36.
[13] P Mirowski and D Plehwe (eds), *The Road from Mont Pèlerin the Making of the Neoliberal Thought Collective* (Harvard UP 2009); P Mirowski, *Never Let a Serious Crisis Go to Waste: How Neoliberalism Survived the Financial Meltdown* (Verso 2014) 38.
[14] See for example L Vinx, 'Carl Schmitt and the Problem of Constitutional Guardianship' in M Arvidsson, L Brännström and P Minkkinen (eds), *The Contemporary Relevance of Carl Schmitt – Law, Politics, Theology* (Routledge 2016); R Cristi, *Carl Schmitt and Authoritarian Liberalism* (University of Wales Press 1998).
[15] Mirowski (n 13) 42.

market economy. In this schema, the state would not act as the libertarian 'night watchman', there to preserve private property rights and to protect from foreign invaders, but instead would act as a coercive entity, there to ensure the function of, and indeed removal of barriers to, market activity. The NTC, while not a formal institution, nevertheless constituted an epistemic community,[16] with similar learned experiences and understandings of how economies function. Through the establishment of these informal links, individuals with shared economic views increasingly became seen as the economic mainstream and were successful in gaining positions in academic institutions such as the University of Chicago, as well as in think tanks relied upon by leaders such as Prime Minister Thatcher and President Reagan, namely the Institute of Economic Affairs in the UK and the Heritage Foundation in the US. Both of these think tanks espoused conservative, classical economic 'solutions' to the range of crisis 'problems', from labour relations to trade between nations, creating the conditions for the existing ideological frame; namely, that it was not the role of the state to coordinate or plan markets, to be successfully contested, but to create the minimum conditions necessary for free markets to operate, with minimal state interference.[17] Friedman in particular served as adviser to both Thatcher and Reagan, and Hayek's *Road to Serfdom* was highly influential on Thatcher in particular. Thatcher stated that it was 'the most powerful critique of socialist planning and the socialist state which I read at this time [the late 1940s], and to which I have returned so often'.[18] In this respect, it is important to think of the new wave of economic liberalism, encompassing both neoliberalism and the variant of ordoliberalism, not as an ideology of state reduction, but of state *transformation*.

Within this framework, the role of the state is to support and regulate the margins of market activity. It is not to intervene in the running of markets, but instead to facilitate it. In neoliberalism, this is done through the 'maximisation of entrepreneurial freedoms within an institutional framework characterised by private property rights ... the role of the State is to create and preserve an institutional framework appropriate to such practices'.[19] However, some authors have argued that the rise of 'so-called' neoliberal thought has led to an increase in the number of regulatory agencies, and an increase in regulation reflective of a form of regulatory capitalism,[20] and that it is therefore wrong to describe this as neoliberalism. In comparison, Cahill

---

[16] On this point, see PM Haas, 'Introduction: Epistemic Communities and International Policy Coordination' (1992) 46 International Organization 1.

[17] V Tanzi, *Government versus Markets: The Changing Economic Role of the State* (CUP 2014) 134; K Birch and A Tickell, 'Making Neoliberal Order in the United States' in Kean Birch and Vlad Mykhnenko (eds), *The Rise and Fall of Neoliberalism: The Collapse of an Economic Order?* (Zed Books 2010) 4–5.

[18] R Bourne, 'Hayek and Thatcher' (Centre for Policy Studies, 11 September 2012) www.cps.org.uk/blog/ q/date/2012/09/11/hayek-and-thatcher accessed April 2018.

[19] D Harvey, 'Neoliberalism as Creative Destruction' (2007) 610 ANNALS of the American Academy of Political and Social Science 21, 22.

[20] See for example D Levi-Faur, 'The Rise of Regulatory Capitalism: The Global Diffusion of a New Order' (2005) 598 ANNALS of the American Academy of Political and Social Science 12;

argues that we can refer to 'actually existing neoliberalism', which separates a *laissez-faire* economic doctrine in theory from a top-down managerial form of capitalism in practice.[21] Mirowski disagrees, arguing that the NTC reflected by Friedman in particular never ascribed to laissez-faire, and instead saw a role for the state.[22] In this respect, neoliberalism closely mirrors its cousin ordoliberalism, insofar as they both consider the state to have an interventionist role to facilitate market practices based on principles of competition. A different stream of literature, focused on 'statecraft', reaches similar conclusions. It identifies the current evolution of the state as the 'market state', which replaces the previous 'nation state'. While the essential role of the latter was welfare provision to the nation, the emerging market state is strategically focused on maximising economic opportunities for market agents, guaranteeing the basic strategic market infrastructure without unduly interfering with economic competition.[23] The success of this new wave of liberal economic thinking has steadily developed in the last thirty years. Its hegemonic status is an expression of the accepted common sense of both state-level policymaking, as well as general public perception. As Monbiot has claimed, 'we're all neoliberals now'.[24]

III NEVER LET A GOOD CRISIS GO TO WASTE: CONCEPTUALISATION, RECOGNITION AND FACILITATION

Since 2008, many authors writing in the diverse fields of European Union studies have referred to the existence of a 'crisis'. Writing in a recent edited volume, legal scholars Chalmers, Jachtenfuchs and Joerges refer to the Eurocrisis as the 'most severe crisis in the history of the EU'.[25] Similarly, the prominent philosopher and sociologist Habermas has written that 'in the current crisis, it is often asked why we

J Braithwaite, *Regulatory Capitalism: How It Works, Ideas for Making It Work Better* (Edward Elgar 2008).

[21] D Cahill, *The End of Laissez-Faire?: On the Durability of Embedded Neoliberalism* (Edward Elgar 2015).

[22] Mirowski and Plehwe (n 13).

[23] P Bobbitt, *The Shield of Achilles – War, Peace and the Course of History* (Knopf 2002) 229: '[s]uch a State depends on the international capital markets and, to a lesser degree, on the modern multinational business network to create stability in the world economy, in preference to management by national or transnational political bodies … Whereas the nation-state justified itself as an instrument to serve the welfare of the people (the nation), the market-state exists to maximize the opportunities enjoyed by all members of society'; and, expanding on its defining characteristics, 'the market state is largely indifferent to the norms of justice, or for that matter to any particular set of moral values so long as law does not act as an impediment to economic competition' (p 230).

[24] G Monbiot, 'Neoliberalism – the Ideology at the Root of All Our Problems' *The Guardian* (15 April 2016) www.theguardian.com/books/2016/apr/15/neoliberalism-ideology-problem-george-monbiot accessed April 2018; see also D Harvey, *A Brief History of Neoliberalism* (OUP 2007) on neoliberal hegemony.

[25] D Chalmers, M Jachtenfuchs and C Joerges, 'The Retransformation of Europe' in Damian Chalmers, M Jachtenfuchs and C Joerges (eds), *The End of the Eurocrats' Dream: Adjusting to European Diversity* (CUP 2016) 1.

should continue to cling to the European Union at all'.[26] Political scientist Majone indeed titled a book *Rethinking the Union of Europe Post-Crisis*.[27] Such statements are not relegated to the academic sphere, however; one only needs to refer to policy documents published by the European Commission in the past eight years to see the term 'crisis' being used repeatedly, whether in light of a new policy agenda, known as Europe 2020, in which 'the crisis is a wake-up call, the moment where we recognise that "business as usual" would consign us to a gradual decline',[28] or in the context of reforming copyright laws in the digital environment, deemed essential to ensuring the EU's recovery from financial 'crisis'.[29] In discussions on the current direction, policies and challenges of the EU, the existence of 'crisis' is presupposed, constituting the material state in which the organisation finds itself.

Yet what is a 'crisis', and how are we cognisant of the 'fact' that one exists? Posing such a question may appear facetious – after all, is it not obvious that we are experiencing one? Whether we focus upon the negative humanitarian consequences of austerity-based politics in Greece,[30] Spain[31] and Portugal,[32] or the plight of Syrian refugees and their subsequent treatment in countries such as Hungary,[33] is the existence of crises not evident? 'Crisis', it is submitted, is not an impartial and objective assessment of an exogenous phenomenon, an observation of a material fact in the physical realm. While structural changes are analytically observable, they are not in themselves a crisis. A 'crisis' is not an objective fact. Rather, it is contextual and relational. It is contextual insofar as the circumstances in which the event occurs serve to give it meaning. It is also relational, insofar as our prior knowledge, experiences and understandings serve as an interpretive lens, making sense of the material event, and in turn causing us to identify it as a crisis. In order to better understand this, an example may prove useful. Let us take the example of narratives concerning crime. A person taking property that belongs to another is a physical, material act that can be observed. This is an act constituting theft, a crime. But a material fact, one person stealing from another, does not in itself constitute a crisis. Whether it constitutes a crisis is a contextual, relational assessment based on its

---

[26] J Habermas, *The Crisis of the European Union: A Response* (Polity 2013) 1.

[27] G Majone, *Rethinking the Union of Europe Post-Crisis: Has Integration Gone Too Far?* (CUP 2014).

[28] European Commission, 'Europe 2020: A Strategy for Smart, Sustainable and Inclusive Growth' (2010) COM(2010) 2020 final 2.

[28] European Commission, 'A Digital Agenda for Europe' (2010) COM(2010) 245 final/2 2.

[30] V Ioakimidis and DD Teloni, 'Greek Social Work and the Never-Ending Crisis of the Welfare State' (2013) 1 Critical and Radical Social Work 31.

[31] M Gili and others, 'The Mental Health Risks of Economic Crisis in Spain: Evidence from Primary Care Centres, 2006 and 2010' (2013) 23 European Journal of Public Health 103.

[32] D Cairns, K Growiec and N de Almeida Alves, 'Another "Missing Middle"? The Marginalised Majority of Tertiary-Educated Youth in Portugal during the Economic Crisis' (2014) 17 Journal of Youth Studies 1046.

[33] A Kallius, D Monterescu and P Kumar Rajaram, 'Immobilizing Mobility: Border Ethnography, Illiberal Democracy, and the Politics of the "Refugee Crisis" in Hungary' (2016) 43 American Ethnologist 25.

conceptual construction. Crime was historically not a political issue, but an observable part of life. This appeared to change in the 1970s in the US, when crime began to be discussed in terms of crisis, plague and terror.[34] An observed phenomenon, an apparent increase in crime rates, was conceptually constructed as a crisis, necessitating an urgent political response. While other countries also observed an increase in crime rates at a similar point in time, they did not frame the phenomenon in terms of 'crisis'.[35] Furthermore, even where a crisis is perceived to exist, the causes of, and indeed solutions to that crisis are ultimately interpreted and, then communicated, in terms of the underlying ideological position of the actors constructing the narrative. For example, in the dominant narratives in the US and UK, the causes of crime (and subsequently, crime-related crises) are ultimately related to individual moral failings, the breakdown of social relations and undesirable elements in society.[36] In comparison, in Scandinavia, crime at that point in time was considered to result from collective social failure, relating to socio-economic inequality or lack of opportunities.[37] Solutions also differed – whereas countries like the US and UK adopted penal policies based strongly upon performative punishment, often with zero tolerance policies and harsh prison sentences,[38] countries such as Norway and Sweden focused upon rehabilitative policies, with more lenient prison sentences (or, indeed, alternatives to imprisonment), and the reintegration of offenders into society. Ideology plays a part in this identification, both of crisis and the appropriate responses to it – in the late 1970s, both the US and UK were heavily influenced by more conservative political philosophies, within a liberal framework of personal responsibility and individualism, where individuals should be punished for their failings.[39] Scandinavian countries, in comparison, were largely dominated by centre-left parties based on socialist principles and social belonging, with policies instead focused on rehabilitation and reintegration.[40]

It is also important to consider how an event or phenomenon becomes understood as constituting a 'crisis'. A crisis is discursively constructed, or as Hay states, 'constituted in and through narrative'.[41] It is subjectively perceived[42] as 'a social event,

---

[34] See for example BI Page and RY Shapiro, *The Rational Public: Fifty Years of Trends in Americans' Policy Preferences* (University of Chicago Press 1992); S Iyengar, *Is Anyone Responsible?: How Television Frames Political Issues* (University of Chicago Press 1991); D Gardner, *Risk: The Science and Politics of Fear* (Virgin Books 2008).

[35] See for example L Zedner, 'In Pursuit of the Vernacular: Comparing Law and Order Discourse in Britain and Germany' (1995) 4 Social & Legal Studies 517.

[36] D Garland, 'The Culture of High Crime Societies' (2000) 40 British Journal of Criminology 347.

[37] F Estrada, 'The Transformation of the Politics of Crime in High Crime Societies' (2004) 1 European Journal of Criminology 419.

[38] K Beckett, *Making Crime Pay: Law and Order in Contemporary American Politics* (OUP 1999).

[39] Estrada (n 37); Garland (n 36).

[40] H Von Hofer, 'Crime and Reactions to Crime in Scandinavia' (2005) 5 Journal of Scandinavian Studies in Criminology and Crime Prevention 148; T Lappi-Seppälä, 'Penal Policy in Scandinavia' (2007) 36 Crime and Justice 217.

[41] C Hay, 'Narrating Crisis: The Discursive Construction of the "Winter of Discontent"' (1996) 30 Sociology 253, 254.

[42] ibid 255.

and therefore is always socially constructed and highly political'.[43] What is, and indeed, what is not a crisis is ultimately determined by the ability of well-placed actors, whether in politics or the media, to successfully identify and communicate the existence of a crisis to their target audience(s). The ability to do so is linked to the dominant ideologies and discourses – those arguments and framings that are coherent within the larger ideological framework dominant in society at that time may be more able to be effectively communicated and accepted by the target audience.[44] Referring to the previous example, where the dominant discourses concerning the way society functions are based in ideas of individualism, self-reliance and personal responsibility, discourses concerning crime tend to be based in ideas of individual fault and personal failing necessitating punishment. Alternatively, where society is understood as a collective endeavour with shared responsibility, rehabilitation may be favoured over harsh prison terms, and public discourse focuses on social causes of crime. In attempting to understand whether there is a crisis, and if so, what its root causes are, there may be competing ideas represented, with different narratives competing for public acceptance so as to discursively control understanding of that event. As Hay puts it, narratives of crisis 'compete in terms of their ability to find resonance with individual and collective direct, lived experiences, and not in terms of their "scientific" adequacy as explanations for the condition they diagnose'.[45] Hay provides the example of the construction of the 'Winter of Discontent', during which the tabloid media successfully framed the strikes of workers over pay and conditions in 1970s Britain using emotive terms of crisis, with the state being brought to a standstill by selfish actors holding the state to ransom, refusing to bury the dead, collect garbage, allow access to hospitals by patients, or unload food held in storage containers at ports in Liverpool.[46] Similarly, in the US in the 1980s, actors were able to frame job losses and recession combined with an ageing population as constituting a Social Security crisis in which excessive benefit payments and welfare provision to those not deemed to have 'paid in' to the system, rather than as 'a consequence of the failure of fiscal and monetary policies' enacted by successive governments.[47] Media discourses and the acts and statements of high-profile political actors can in turn shape understanding of events, constructing narratives within ideological frames with guideposts for knowledge, persuasion and action.[48]

---

[43] A Gamble, *The Spectre at the Feast: Capitalist Crisis and the Politics of Recession* (Palgrave Macmillan 2009) 38.

[44] J Mehta, 'The Varied Roles of Ideas in Politics' in Daniel Beland and Robert Henry Cox (eds), *Ideas and Politics in Social Science Research* (OUP 2010).

[45] Hay (n 41) 255.

[46] ibid 261.

[47] Carroll L Estes, 'Social Security: The Social Construction of a Crisis' 61 Milbank Memorial Fund Quarterly: Health and Society 445, 447–48.

[48] See generally DA Schön and M Rein, *Frame Reflection: Toward the Resolution of Intractable Policy Controversies: Toward the Resolution of Intractable Policy Controversies* (Basic Books 1995);

Yet just because one actor claims that something is a crisis does not make it one: the construction of a narrative of crisis is a process. In this respect, drawing from the literature on securitisation in international relations can be useful. The framing of an issue as being one which constitutes a security threat is a process, in which a subject, such as 'crime', or 'immigration' is discussed in terms of a security issue. This issue then necessitates a security response in the form of an immediate and exceptional act. However, this cannot be achieved without convincing a target audience, generally considered to be the general public, or policymakers with the ability to accept, legitimise or legislate for this exceptional response.[49] Through studying these processes of framing, communication and acceptance, we can then better understand how security can be used as a concept 'invoked to legitimise contentious legislation, policies or practices that would otherwise not have been deemed legitimate'.[50] Securitisation is the process by which something is constructed as a security threat necessitating a policy response.[51] As stated by Buzan et al., through this process, the issue being interpreted by observers 'becomes a security issue – not necessarily because a real existential threat exists but because the issue is presented as such a threat'.[52] The issue, be it an attack committed by a terrorist organisation, or even the mere existence of that group at all, is securitised through the use of security-framed language, 'as an existential threat, requiring emergency measures and justifying actions outside the normal bounds of political procedure'.[53] Key dimensions of securitisation are urgency and exceptionality; something poses an imminent security threat, thereby requiring an exceptional response to counter that security threat, something that must be accepted as 'true' by the target audience in order for it to be considered as having been securitised.[54] It is submitted that the process by which an event, issue or phenomenon is identified, communicated and accepted as constituting a crisis is analogous with that of securitisation. This process can be considered as one of conceptualisation, communication and facilitation. The first stage, *conceptualisation*, involves the identification of an event or phenomena as constituting a 'crisis' event. The ideological stance of the observer helps to frame that event, identifying what it is about it that creates a crisis, and why. Once the crisis has been conceptualised, the observer must then communicate the existence of a crisis necessitating an immediate and

    VA Schmidt, 'Speaking to the Markets or to the People? A Discursive Institutionalist Analysis of the EU's Sovereign Debt Crisis' (2014) 16 British Journal of Politics & International Relations 188.

[49] B Buzan, O Waever and J de Wilde, *Security: A New Framework for Analysis* (Lynne Rienner Publishers 1997) 41.

[50] AW Neal, 'Securitization and Risk at the EU Border: The Origins of FRONTEX' (2009) 47 Journal of Common Market Studies 333, 335.

[51] See for example J Eriksson, 'Observers or Advocates? On the Political Role of Security Analysts' (1999) 34 Cooperation and Conflict 311; J Huysmans, 'Defining Social Constructivism in Security Studies: The Normative Dilemma of Writing Security' (2002) 27 Alternatives: Global, Local, Political 41.

[52] Buzan, Waever and de Wilde (n 49) 24.

[53] ibid.

[54] See R Emmers, 'Securitization' in A Collins (ed), *Contemporary Security Studies* (4th edn, OUP 2015).

exceptional response in order to counter, combat or recover from that crisis event, with the acceptance of this narrative by the target audience. Another way of putting this is the idea that the crisis creates such uncertainty or instability that extreme measures must be taken; it may not be pleasant, but *there is no alternative*. This is akin to the securitising act in securitisation theory, by which, through discursive appeal, the event is communicated to an audience as a means to persuade them that action is necessary. The final stage is that of *facilitation*; once the event has been accepted as constituting a 'crisis' necessitating an urgent, exceptional response, that exceptional action can be legitimised, allowing for policies, decisions, or laws to be instigated that would not normally be considered acceptable or possible.

A practical example borrowed from global health governance can illustrate the transferability of this model. In the summer of 2009, the WHO officially declared a state of global pandemic[55] following the outbreak of a new strain of A-N1H1 virus, better known as 'swine flu'.[56] The outbreak started in Central America, in the state of Veracruz in Mexico, and spread globally, prompting a *conceptualisation* of a state of global health crisis by official governmental authorities. The ensuing increasing anxiety of the international community led to a generalised outcry advocating the adoption of extraordinary measures to avert a potential global health disaster – the *recognition* phase. As a result, massive quantities of A-N1H1 influenza vaccine, subject to 'fast-track' emergency approval procedures, were swiftly made available by regulatory agencies. In order to ensure the supply of the vaccine to soothe public opinion, states discharged companies from tort liability in case of damages,[57] and assumed full responsibility for the risks created by the widespread distribution of a not-thoroughly-tested vaccine in their communities – the *facilitation* phase. Yet, the following winter (2009–10), the pandemic gradually started to diminish, and by August 2010, the Director-General of the WHO, Dr Margaret Chan, declared the end of the A-N1H1 pandemic.[58] The pandemic could have been much worse, or arguably should have been much worse, in light of the level of alert and social anxiety triggered by the 'crisis' narrative. In the space of one year, the A-N1H1 virus had killed approximately 18,000 people globally.[59] That is about 4 per cent of the

---

[55] See statement to the press by the WHO Director-General, Dr Margaret Chan, www.who.int/media centre/news/statements/2009/h1n1_pandemic_phase6_20090611/en/index.html accessed April 2018.

[56] An interesting reconstruction questioning the constitutional implications of the case for EU health policy is A de Ruijter, 'The Constitutional Implications of European Public Health Policy', ACELG Working Paper Series, 2010/05.

[57] The contracts between producers and Member States in the EU for the sale and distribution of A-N1H1 vaccine are characterised, Europe-wide, by the explicit provision of liability exemption clauses. See for example the contract between Novartis and the Italian government www .altreconomia.it/allegati/contenuti/phpXkxWoS2095.pdf.

[58] See www.who.int/mediacentre/news/statements/2010/h1n1_vpc_20100810/en/index.html accessed April 2018.

[59] By late July 2010, the WHO was still considering the virus a pandemic, on the basis of the same statistics: see the relevant documents available at www.who.int/csr/disease/swineflu/en accessed April 2018.

250,000 to 500,000 annual deaths caused by 'regular' influenza.[60] Questions were thus raised about the necessity of states investing billions in the purchase of enormous quantities of a vaccine, the safety and efficacy of which was far from certain. Then, quietly and smoothly, this story slowed down and disappeared.

Within the dominant ideology of western liberal democracy and the system of capitalism fostered within it, we have a plethora of examples of the ways that crisis has been facilitative of actions or policies that might not ordinarily be accepted. From Klein's analysis of the 'shock doctrine', in which natural disasters such as Hurricane Katrina, wars as in Iraq and acts of terror serve to open up new 'markets' to significant economic reform along neoliberal lines,[61] to Lowenstein's work on 'disaster capitalism', where the provision of nominally state functions are privatised as a response to a perceived crisis, be it the existence of large numbers of refugees to be 'resettled' off the Australian coast or the housing of asylum seekers in the UK (and the 'cost to the taxpayer' that this would entail),[62] the successful construction of a crisis narrative allows for the enactment of policies it may otherwise be difficult to legitimise. Furthermore, by using this opportunity to make an idea legally binding, the question of solutions is changed from a political one to a legal one – what is legally permitted as a response to a crisis, and what is legally prohibited? Law can therefore be used to depoliticise a particular issue, taking it out of the venue of political debate and discourse, and moving it into the realm of technical rule-making and application. By using ideas 'as weapons',[63] contesting ideas, and in the context of this chapter, economic ideologies can therefore be depoliticised and, ultimately, delegitimised; through the use of the legal system, it can then be ensured that *there is no (legal) alternative*. Yet, this is not the end of political contestation, which can hardly ever come to a definitive halt. Instead, by normatively excluding the possibility of change from the constitutional order, one runs the risk of destabilising that order altogether, as the legal responses and constraints facilitated by these discourses serve to delegitimise those legal frameworks. If, as these arguments run, there is no legal alternative within the existing system of governance, opponents to that system will instead argue for the dissolution or disengagement from that system, as we shall further explore in considering the UK's decision to withdraw from the EU, as well as the rise of anti-EU rhetoric in political campaigning.

IV FROM BRETTON WOODS TO MAASTRICHT: MONETARISM AS IDEOLOGY, MONETARISM AS LAW

It is possible to reconceptualise the development of the EEC, and now the EU, in terms of integration as a response to perceived crisis, and crisis as a facilitator of

---

[60]   WHO fact sheet communication No 211, April 2009, ibid.
[61]   N Klein, *The Shock Doctrine: The Rise of Disaster Capitalism* (Penguin 2008).
[62]   A Loewenstein, *Disaster Capitalism: Making a Killing Out of Catastrophe* (Verso 2015).
[63]   M Blyth, *Great Transformations: Economic Ideas and Institutional Change in the Twentieth Century* (CUP 2002).

change. The 1970s was a period of significant political–economic upheaval. Since the end of the Second World War, many industrialised nations not part of the Soviet Union were party to the Bretton Woods Agreement, which was initially negotiated between the Allied powers in 1944, and which Germany gained membership of after the war was over. Bretton Woods formalised a monetary policy in which the US dollar was 'equated' with gold,[64] and national currencies pegged to the value of the US dollar as a means of ensuring international currency stability.[65] The key objective of the Bretton Woods Agreement, according to Ruggie, was to create an international economic order based on embedded liberalism,[66] in which a compromise was established, ensuring free-flowing trade between states while allowing nation states to intervene in their domestic economies to mitigate the impact of that trade. This domestic intervention was Keynesian in nature,[67] itself based on an internal compromise between the perceived interests of labour and capital; a corporatist model involving state planning, administrative bureaucratisation and corporate management on the basis of increasing productivity with social welfare provision and collective bargaining.[68] In this system, trade unions, in particular, played an important role, cooperating in the management of wages in response to economic fluctuations.[69] Within this framework, the state was the *dirigiste* state,[70] responsible for guiding, shaping and managing the economy.[71] During this period, beginning in the early 1950s and ending in the 1970s, impressive growth rates in the US, Europe and Japan led to this compromise being tolerated by corporate entities, if not welcomed with entirely open arms.

At this time, according to Mirowski, the Mont Pèlerin Society members were something of a downbeat and disenfranchised group, relegated to the sidelines of economic thinking as a result of their support for free market solutions to the Great Depression and the subsequent rise of Keynesian interventionist policies.[72] Those classical liberal economic ideas, which the Mont Pèlerin economists claimed to adhere to, were ones in which the international financial system was underwritten by a system based on an international gold standard. States could use the gold standard

---

[64] JG Ruggie, 'International Regimes, Transactions, and Change: Embedded Liberalism in the Postwar Economic Order' (1982) 36 International Organization 379, 406.

[65] E Helleiner, 'The Evolution of the International Monetary and Financial System' in John Ravenhill (ed), *Global Political Economy* (4th edn, OUP 2014) 178.

[66] Ruggie (n 64) 393.

[67] VA Schmidt and M Thatcher, 'Theorizing Ideational Continuity: The Resilience of Neo-Liberal Ideas in Europe' in VA Schmidt and M Thatcher (eds), *Resilient Liberalism in Europe's Political Economy* (CUP 2013) 10.

[68] See for example R Cox, 'Labour and Hegemony' (1977) 31 International Organization 385.

[69] A Hassel, 'Trade Unions and the Future of Democratic Capitalism' in P Beramendi and others (eds), *The Politics of Advanced Capitalism* (CUP 2015) 245.

[70] Or, in statecraft terms, the welfare providing nation state – see Bobbit (n 23).

[71] RB Du Boff, 'The Decline of Economic Planning in France' (1968) 21 Western Political Quarterly 98, 98.

[72] Mirowski (n 13) 6–7.

as a basis for the valuing of their currencies, but this also allowed for currency depreciation and 'beggar-thy-neighbour' economic strategies. Undermined by their apparent ineffectiveness during the early 1930s, the failing of these classical economic ideas resulted in a legitimacy crisis of the old order. Their ineffectiveness, which, as Judt argues, 'seemed to Americans especially to be the root source of the European (and world) crisis',[73] in particular allowed for the contestation of dominant economic ideologies, resulting in the shift from a classical economic model to a Keynesian one. In other words, the Bretton Woods Agreement, and the domestic economic policies that followed, were based in a post-war consensus, with 'the centre of gravity of political argument in the years after 1945 [lying] not between left and right but rather *within* the left: between communists and their sympathisers and the mainstream liberal–social–democratic consensus'.[74] The dominant discourse of political economy, the idea shaping economic conduct, was that of liberal interventionism. The role of states was to intervene in markets so as to ensure their continued functioning for the achievement of public policy goals such as social stability. Economics and politics were intertwined, and co-dependent.

By the 1970s, however, perceptions had shifted substantially. The war in Vietnam, combined with a rapidly growing US federal budget deficit, were seen as no less disastrous for the US economy due to an outflow of US dollars that exceeded the amount of gold possessed by the US.[75] Concerns over a possible recession in the US and international speculation against the dollar resulted in President Nixon unilaterally devaluing the currency, cutting its link to the value of gold, effectively breaking up the Bretton Woods system.[76] This collapse, both in Bretton Woods specifically, as well as in confidence in the system of international trade with a fixed currency exchange, resulted in the UK devaluing its currency in 1972, followed by France in 1973, and the establishment of a new floating-rate system; the cost of this, ultimately, was inflation.[77] The 'oil shock' of 1973, a consequence of an embargo imposed by the Organisation of Arab Petroleum Exporting Countries, resulted in the cost of oil quadrupling. The inaccessibility of these energy supplies resulted in drops in industrial output in affected countries, lowering gross domestic product (GDP). This combination of low-to-nil economic growth (stagnation) with the inflation caused by the collapse of Bretton Woods led to a phenomenon referred to as stagflation, defined by Blyth as a situation in which 'wages/prices (inflation) and unemployment rose together'.[78] The Keynesian consensus broke down. Economic

---

[73] T Judt, *Postwar: A History of Europe since 1945* (Vintage 2010) 107.

[74] T Judt, *Ill Fares the Land: A Treatise on Our Present Discontents* (Penguin 2011) 92.

[75] Judt (n 73) 454; J Shaoul, 'Defeating Neoliberalism: A Marxist Internationalist Perspective and Programme' in K Birch and V Mykhnenko (eds), *The Rise and Fall of Neoliberalism: The Collapse of an Economic Order?* (Zed Books 2010) 242.

[76] D Harvey, *The Enigma of Capital: And the Crises of Capitalism* (Profile Books 2011) 32.

[77] Judt (n 73) 454; Ö Orhangazi, 'Financialization and the Nonfinancial Corporate Sector' in U Mattei and JD Haskell (eds), *Research Handbook on Political Economy and Law* (Edward Elgar 2015) 140.

[78] M Blyth, *Austerity: The History of a Dangerous Idea* (OUP 2013) 40.

instability allowed for contesting voices to emerge, raising economic arguments considered fringe until then, claiming that the events being witnessed constituted a major structural and systemic crisis within Keynesian economics. The resolution of this crisis, these voices argued, must be found outside the Keynesian orthodoxy, which had rapidly become discredited.[79] This was, in part, because events 'seemed to show that unemployment and inflation could coexist, which was extremely unlikely in Keynesian theory'.[80] The ideas of the Mont Pèlerin Society, previously at the margins of policymaking, became newly influential as policymakers sought alternatives to the Keynesian model.

How did this progressive shift impact Europe? Originally, the Treaty of Rome establishing the European Economic Community and its relevant institutions such as the European Court of Justice, laid down the prohibition on tariffs, quantitative restrictions and national measures 'having equivalent effect' on trade, with a transitional period ending 1 January 1970.[81] Despite this general framework, however, economic policies were national in nature, based on the Keynesian compromise between the socialist state and capitalist production.[82] Within this framework, regulation was an issue of national, and indeed state public policy; for Laffont, regulation in this model was 'the public economics face of industrial organisation. It explored the various ways in which governments interfere with industrial activities for the good or for the bad'.[83] This is the golden age of what Ogus refers to as 'command-and-control' regulation, laid down and enforced exclusively by the state.[84] Distinct from the discourse of neoliberalism, in which the 'interference' of the state in market activities could always be considered bad, this was not a given under Keynesian policies. For the EEC states in particular, the US and Japan were perceived as having weathered the turbulence of the mid 1970s much more effectively.[85] This was considered to be the result of both the US and Japan representing unified state entities, whereas the EEC was characterised by national divergences in preferences and policies, resulting in the often-cited 'Eurosclerosis' typifying this period of European integration.[86]

The Trilateral Commission, a non-governmental think tank established in 1973 by David Rockefeller, issued a report in 1975 that was significantly influential in changing the understandings of the EEC Member States regarding economic policy. The title of the report is indicative of its findings, referring as it does to 'the

---

[79] See in particular RE Lucas, 'Econometric Policy Evaluation: A Critique' (1976) 1 Carnegie-Rochester Conference Series on Public Policy 19; Tanzi (n 17) 132–33.

[80] Blyth (n 78) 41.

[81] M Egan, *Constructing a European Market* (OUP 2001) 41

[82] S Strange, *States and Markets* (Bloomsbury Academic 2015) 128.

[83] JJ Laffont, 'The New Economics of Regulation Ten Years After' (1994) 62 Econometrica 507, 507.

[84] A Ogus, *Regulation: Legal Form and Economic Theory* (Hart 2004) 79.

[85] W Sandholtz and J Zysman, '1992: Recasting the European Bargain' (1989) 42 World Politics 95, 109–10.

[86] RO Keohane and S Hoffmann, *The New European Community: Decisionmaking and Institutional Change* (Westview Press 1991) 6–8.

crisis of democracy'.[87] Europe was considered increasingly ungovernable due to an 'overload' of participants with conflicting demands, and being overly bureaucratic[88] – the task was now to replace its corporatist models with 'more flexible models that could produce more social control with less coercive pressure'.[89] To do so, it would be necessary to relocate responsibilities away from states, and towards markets.[90] By framing the events of the 1970s as the result of a crisis of democracy, and indeed a legitimacy crisis in which the old model was discredited and a new model needed, these phenomena could be *conceptualised* as crisis-inducing, *recognised* by policymakers as a problem in need of a solution, *facilitating* significant ideational and policy change.

In Europe, this restructuring along market lines began with the actions of the European Court of Justice, through its case law implementing the free movement of goods and services, and the removal of state barriers to trade, and facilitation of both mutual recognition and inter-state competition.[91] It is for this reason that some commentators have argued that the Court has been a 'neoliberal' actor,[92] enshrining (or, as Weiler puts it, constitutionalising)[93] the logic of market-based solutions and economic reasoning into the EU legal order.[94] This approach was not restricted to the negative integration of the Court, however, but extended into the rationale of positive integration through market re-regulation taken by the European Commission and Council.[95] Furthermore the European Council, originally an informal meeting of the heads of state of EEC countries, was influential in the development of the European Monetary System (EMS) during its summits in 1978 in Copenhagen, Bremen and Brussels.[96] The Trilateral Commission's report identifying the roots of crisis in an overabundance of democracy facilitated a situation in

---

[87] MJ Crozier, SP Huntington and J Watanuki, 'The Crisis of Democracy: Report on the Governability of Democracies to the Trilateral Commission' (1975).

[88] ibid 12.

[89] ibid 55.

[90] CJ Bickerton, *European Integration: From Nation-States to Member States* (OUP 2012) 94.

[91] Majone (n 27) 99–100; M Thatcher, 'Supranational Neo-Liberalisation: The EU's Regulatory Model of Economic Markets' in VA Schmidt and M Thatcher (eds), *Resilient Liberalism in Europe's Political Economy* (CUP 2013) 186; SK Schmidt, 'The Shadow of Case Law: The Court of Justice of the European Union and the Policy Process' in J Richardson and S Mazey (eds), *European Union: Power and Policy-making* (4th edn, Routledge 2015).

[92] See for example W Sandholtz and J Zysman, '1992: Recasting the European Bargain' (1989) 42 World Politics 95; L Hooghe and G Marks, 'The Making of a Polity: The Struggle over European Integration' in Herbert Kitschelt (ed), *Continuity and Change in Contemporary Capitalism* (CUP 1999); M Thatcher, 'Supranational Neo-Liberalisation: The EU's Regulatory Model of Economic Markets' in VA Schmidt and M Thatcher (eds), *Resilient Liberalism in Europe's Political Economy* (CUP 2013); Cahill (n 21).

[93] J Weiler, 'The Transformation of Europe' (1991) 100 Yale Law Journal 2403.

[94] JP McCormick, *Weber, Habermas and Transformations of the European State: Constitutional, Social, and Supranational Democracy* (CUP 2007) 259.

[95] See generally F Scharpf, *Governing in Europe: Effective and Democratic?* (OUP 1999).

[96] E Mourlon-Druol, 'Steering Europe: Explaining the Rise of the European Council, 1975–1986' (2016) 25 Contemporary European History 409, 410.

which the states party to the EEC could make their voices more effectively heard. Ostensibly intended as a means of coordinating their international response to pressing issues,[97] this resulted in their inclusion as a formal institution within the European organisational structure, referenced in the Single European Act and included formally as an EU institution in the Treaty of Lisbon. Indeed, according to Mourlon-Druol, of the issues discussed by the European Council between 1975 and 1986, macroeconomic policy was the most common.[98] The election of Margaret Thatcher in 1979, and her 'there is no alternative' approach to economic reform, combined with the Mitterrand reforms in 1983, was considered to be the point at which the conditions for broader financial liberalisation in the European Community were set.[99]

The continuing codification of an economic ideology as legally binding obligations was given impetus by the 1985 European Council summit in Milan. According to the European Council conclusions, measures that should be pursued by the Community included the liberalisation of capital movements, the creation of a free market for financial services and the continuing removal of barriers to trade.[100] In the Commission's 'White Paper: Completing the Internal Market' published subsequently to the Milan summit, it was stated that actions should be taken to create 'a more favourable environment for stimulating enterprise, competition and trade'.[101] Demonstrating the impact on policymakers represented by the ideational shift from Keynesianism to neoclassical/neoliberal thought, the Commission concluded that 'a well developed free trade area offers significant advantages: it is something much better than that which existed before the Treaty of Rome'.[102] The resulting Single European Act, signed in Luxembourg in 1986, facilitated the liberalisation of financial services desired by the European Council members, 'altering the systemic relationships that govern monetary policy making',[103] empowering central banks by making them independent from governments. The goal was to ensure that 'irresponsible' governments could not abuse fiscal policy, reflected in increases in public debt: 'identified as the source of economic problems ... the remedies were identified in the realm of monetary policy'.[104] These actions served to separate the discursive links between politics and economics, with economic activity considered

[97] ibid 413.
[98] ibid 416.
[99] E Helleiner, 'A Bretton Woods Moment? The 2007–2008 Crisis and the Future of Global Finance' (2010) 86 International Affairs 619, 626–27.
[100] European Council, Conclusions of the European Council 28 and 29 June 1985 in Milan (1985) 9.
[101] European Commission, 'White Paper: Completing the Internal Market' (European Commission 1985) COM(85) 310 final, para 21.
[102] ibid 220.
[103] K Dyson, K Featherstone and G Michalopoulos, 'Strapped to the Mast: EC Central Bankers between Global Financial Markets and Regional integration' (1995) 2 Journal of European Public Policy 465, 446.
[104] ibid 482.

a largely technocratic or expert-led exercise, in which undue political influence could result in inefficiencies or distortions of that distinct sphere of activity.

The Economic and Monetary Union (EMU) was the next step in preventing the future likelihood of this 'problem' (regarded as being responsible for the crises of the 1970s), codifying economic ideology concerning monetary policies into legally binding obligations. The Delors Report, named after Commission President Jacques Delors, published in 1989, linked the idea of EMU as functionally linked to the internal market, and indeed necessary for its completion. Indeed, a report issued the following year, entitled 'One Market, One Money' made the case that 'if the move to EMU were not to take place . . . capital market liberalisation would not be achieved or maintained'.[105] The Delors Report regarded the economic shocks of the 1970s as damaging to the process of European integration.[106] EMU, characterised by the free movement of capital, locked exchange rates and a single currency, would help to prevent these shocks in the future, it was reasoned, as it would prevent market manipulation and currency wars between the Member States. However, as McNamara argues, the implementation of EMU through the Maastricht Treaty represented the realisation of a neoliberal consensus, namely that the goal of economic coordination was to achieve anti-inflationary monetary policies and the limitation of public spending deficits,[107] discouraging state intervention in market activity not only politically, but legally.

Mann refers to this process at the EU level as being the constitutionalisation of economic doctrine through rules-based approaches to monetary policy, strictly limiting governmental discretion, providing the example of the EU's 'aggressive' price stability requirements.[108] The economic shocks of the 1970s, perceived as a crisis caused by stagflation (i.e. lack of growth combined with inflation) resulted in a collapse of market confidence, and indeed, a collapse of confidence in Keynesian economics. A distrust of 'big government', related to Nixon's domestic spending, resulted in the 'solution' to the crisis: reining in public spending as a means of combating inflation. Indeed, in a Council Regulation known as the Stability and Growth Pact[109] (SGP), the very first recital states that the SGP is based on 'the objective of sound government finances as a means of strengthening the conditions for price stability and for strong sustainable growth conducive to employment creation'. This was then codified in the Lisbon Treaty, with the consolidated version of the Treaty on European Union stating in Article 3(3) that one of its core

---

[105] European Commission, 'One Market, One Money: An Evaluation of the Potential Benefits and Costs of Forming an Economic and Monetary Union' (1990) 44 17.

[106] Committee for the Study of Economic and Monetary Union, 'Report on Economic and Monetary Union in the European Community' (1989) 7.

[107] KR McNamara, *The Currency of Ideas: Monetary Politics in the European Union* (Cornell UP 1998).

[108] G Mann, 'Hobbes' Redoubt? Toward a Geography of Monetary Policy' (2010) 34 Progress in Human Geography 601, 611.

[109] Council Regulation (EC) 1466/97 of 7 July 1997 on the strengthening of the surveillance of positions and the surveillance and coordination of economic policies [1997] OJ L209.

objectives is the sustainable development of Europe through 'balanced economic growth and price stability', with the effect of 'locking-in political commitments to orthodox market–monetarist fiscal and monetary policies that are perceived to increase government credibility in the eyes of financial market players'.[110] In this system, referred to by Gill as 'disciplinary neoliberalism',[111] even should EU Member States wish to pursue alternate economic policies or goals, there is no legal alternative.

V A NEW CRISIS, A NEW CHALLENGE: WHEN THERE IS NO LEGAL ALTERNATIVE, BREXIT STAGE LEFT?

The global financial crisis of the mid 2000s is perceived to have begun with the collapse of the subprime mortgage market: economically vulnerable homeowners, who had been granted loans despite dubious creditworthiness, struggled to make their monthly repayments as a result of higher interest rates and falling property prices.[112] However, as Blyth astutely points out, numerous different academic explanations of what happened, and who is to blame, have been given.

> The crisis is both overexplained and overdetermined ... for example, three excellent books on the crisis stress, respectively, increasing income inequality ... the captured nature of financial regulation, and the political power of finance. Each book certainly captures an important aspect of the crisis. But are these factors absolutely necessary to adequately explain it?[113]

That the systemic spread of financial instability, resulting in the collapse of Lehman Brothers in the US and the revelations of significantly overleveraged European banking institutions loaded with 'junk' debt, was perceived as a 'crisis' internationally is both clear and indisputable. In addition to the statements of leading EU officials mentioned earlier in this chapter, figures such as the then US presidential candidate Barack Obama declared that 'the economic crisis we face is the worst since the Great Depression'.[114] Similarly, Ben Bernanke stated in 2009 that 'the current crisis has been one of the most difficult financial and economic episodes in modern history'.[115] What is clear, however, is that the crisis had its origins in the

[110] Cahill (n 21) 113.
[111] See generally S Gill, 'Constitutionalising Capital: EMU and Disciplinary Neo-Liberalism' in A Bieler and A David Morton (eds), *Social Forces in the Making of the New Europe* (Palgrave Macmillan 2001).
[112] D Hodson and L Quaglia, 'European Perspectives on the Global Financial Crisis: Introduction' (2009) 47 Journal of Common Market Studies 939, 940.
[113] Blyth (n 78) 22.
[114] B Obama, 'US Election: Full Text of Barack Obama's Speech on the Economy' The Guardian (13 October 2008) www.theguardian.com/world/2008/oct/13/uselections2008-barackobama accessed April 2018.
[115] B Bernanke, 'Four Questions about the Financial Crisis' Board of Governors of the Federal Reserve System (14 April 2009) www.federalreserve.gov/newsevents/speech/bernanke20090414a.htm.

practices of private sector institutions.[116] As Beck states with regard to the perception of the crisis in Europe however, the surface view of policymakers has been that it instead 'revolves around debts, budget deficits and problems of finance'.[117] For Angela Merkel in particular, the crisis was the result of 'cheap money' and profligate state spending, which therefore required that states tighten their belts.[118]

Indeed, as with previous crises, the crisis of the mid 2000s allowed for new ideas to influence policy responses to it. Unlike the paradigm shift represented by the change from Keynesian to neoliberal economic policies (including the ordoliberal off-shoot), here the ideas forming the cognitive filter served to reinforce existing preconceptions regarding the role of the state in economic policy. From the work of Reinhart and Rogoff that dominated policy circles in the US, in which it was argued that accumulation of public sector debt resulted in decline in growth,[119] to that of the 'Bocconi Boys' in Milan who argued for 'expansionary austerity' as a means to counter financial crisis,[120] prominent economically liberal thinkers were able to successfully argue that the *perceived* crisis was a crisis fuelled by public sector debts and deficits, a fact then *recognised* by policymakers, resulting in the *facilitation* of new legal changes.

According to Blyth, the Bocconi University of Milan public finance economics thinking began with the work of Luigi Einaudi in the early twentieth century, as a hybrid of the Ordoliberal school of economic liberalism and public choice economics.[121] The role of the state, according to this way of thinking, is to expand the boundaries of the market, facilitate competition and create 'the legal and political milieu in which men can organise, invent and produce'.[122] Blyth argues that it is a new generation of economics professors at Bocconi, such as Alberto Alesina and Francesco Silvia Ardagna, who have substantially influenced the EU's current policies, and subsequent law reforms, in light of the crisis.[123] Austerity, namely the cutting of public expenditure, would allow for economic expansion as the private sector moves to fill the gap, their line of thinking runs. Instead of raising

[116] As convincingly argued by S French, A Leyshon and N Thrift, 'A Very Geographical Crisis: The Making and Breaking of the 2007–2008 Financial Crisis' (2009) 2 Cambridge Journal of Regions, Economy and Society 287.

[117] U Beck, *German Europe* (Rodney Livingstone tr, Polity 2014) 20.

[118] Blyth (n 78) 52.

[119] CM Reinhart and KS Rogoff, 'Growth in a Time of Debt' (2010) 100 American Economic Review 573; CM Reinhart and KS Rogoff, 'The Aftermath of Financial Crises' (National Bureau of Economic Research 2009) Working Paper 14656 www.nber.org/papers/w14656 accessed April 2018; for criticism of their modelling, see J Cassidy, 'The Reinhart and Rogoff Controversy: A Summing Up' www.newyorker.com/online/blogs/johncassidy/2013/04/the-rogoff-and-reinhart-controversy-a-summing-up.html accessed April 2018.

[120] O Helgadóttir, 'The Bocconi Boys Go to Brussels: Italian Economic Ideas, Professional Networks and European Austerity' (2016) 23 Journal of European Public Policy 392.

[121] Blyth (n 78) 165–66.

[122] F Forte and R Marchionatti, 'Luigi Einaudi's Economics of Liberalism' (Centro di Studi sulla Storia e i Metodi dell'Econonmica Politica 2010) 02/2010 24.

[123] Blyth (n 78) 167.

taxes, or taking on more debt in order to facilitate public works programmes and ensure employment, as the Keynesian consensus argued in the mid-twentieth century, states should instead 'combine spending cuts in transfers, welfare programs and the governmental wage bill'.[124]

This can be seen most clearly in the case of Greece, as well as in Ireland, Italy, Spain and Portugal. Despite criticisms over the methodology and strength of their findings that led to state reforms based in cutting budgets,[125] and indeed the entire concept of 'expansionary austerity',[126] the work of Alesina and Ardagna was presented at a 2010 ECOFIN meeting in Madrid, and was highly influential on the European Central Bank, resulting in their support of state budgetary cuts.[127] In the media, as well as the corridors of power in Berlin and Brussels, the Greek case in particular was presented as one which consisted of a lazy and bloated public sector, incredible inefficiencies and an overly generous state pension system, all made possible as a result of successive Greek governments having easy access to capital because of membership of the Euro,[128] rather than as the result of significant macroeconomic imbalances and structural faults within the Euro monetary system itself. The European Commission, European Central Bank and International Monetary Fund, known as the Troika, implemented a system to 'bail out' Greece, as the financial markets were unwilling to do so. With a budget deficit of 13 per cent and debts of 120 per cent of GDP, within the monetarist system dominating economic thought since the Bretton Woods collapse, the Greek state was not considered credible or creditworthy. However, the bailouts given to Greece and the other 'debtor' states came with 'strict conditionality'. This conditionality was required with Germany as the 'indispensable nation',[129] with scholars agreeing that 'German power, interests and ideas would be crucial in determining whether EMU would fail, continue to muddle through or be put on a more sustainable path'.[130] Rather than focus on systemic reform, including the fabled 'Eurobonds', which would allow investors to grant money to the Eurobloc as a whole, which would then apportion it to individual states requiring financial aid, Germany instead focused on structural adjustments to individual countries, within a narrative frame in which the countries of Northern Europe were prudential saints, and Southern Europe,

---

[124] A Alesina and S Ardagna, 'Tales of Fiscal Adjustment' (1998) 13 Economic Policy 488, 490.

[125] Blyth (n 78) 175.

[126] See for example J Guajardo, D Leigh and A Pescatori, 'Expansionary Austerity: New International Evidence' (International Monetary Fund 2011) WP/11/58.

[127] Blyth (n 78) 175–76.

[128] Y Kitromilides, 'Stories, Fables, Parables, and Myths: Greece and the Euro Crisis, Toward a New Narrative' (2013) 47 Journal of Economic Issues 623, 628.

[129] R Sikorski, 'I Fear Germany's Power Less than Her Inactivity' *The Financial Times* (28 November 2011) www.ft.com/content/b753cb42-19b3-11e1-ba5d-00144feabdco accessed April 2018; see also Harold James, 'Cosmos, Chaos: Finance, Power and Conflict' (2014) 90 International Affairs 37.

[130] M Matthijs, 'Powerful Rules Governing the Euro: The Perverse Logic of German Ideas' (2016) 23 Journal of European Public Policy 375, 376.

profligate sinners.[131] According to Merkel, there was no alternative. 'The rules must not be oriented toward the weak, but toward the strong. That is a hard message. But it is an economic necessity.'[132] As with the creation of the price stability rules in the Growth and Stability Pact, however, it is one thing for something to be necessary; it is another to ensure that there is no *legal* alternative.

The first set of legal changes was the 'Six-Pack' of laws passed in 2011. The Six-Pack comprised three Regulations[133] and one Directive[134] intended to increase compliance with the Stability and Growth Pack Requirements, and two Regulations intended to ensure the prevention of macroeconomic imbalances and enforcement actions to 'correct' excessive macroeconomic imbalances in the Euro area.[135] In 2013, two further Regulations[136] were passed, which provided for closer budgetary scrutiny and coordination. According to Chalmers, this legislation serves to hem in states 'with a hedgerow of constraints and procedures'[137] based on the identification of the public goods of 'low debt, balanced budgets and balanced economic performance'.[138] In other words, economic policies based on an ideology of market liberalism and monetarism become codified as legally binding obligations, ensuring that, while competing economic visions may contest the use of these measures as a way of securing both the exit from 'crisis' as well as growth post-crisis, it is not possible to pursue such action. While there may be alternatives that could be pursued by national governments, there is no *legal* alternative.

These obligations, imposed during a time of perceived crisis, then facilitate a permanent legal change, in which the state of emergency becomes the 'normal'

---

[131] See M Matthijs and K McNamara, 'The Euro Crisis' Theory Effect: Northern Saints, Southern Sinners, and the Demise of the Eurobond' (2015) 37 Journal of European Integration 229.

[132] Chancellor Angela Merkel, as quoted in James (n 129) 530.

[133] Regulation (EU) No 1175/2011 of the European Parliament and of the Council of 16 November 2011 amending Council Regulation (EC) No 1466/97 on the strengthening of the surveillance of budgetary positions and the surveillance and coordination of economic policies [2011] OJ L306/12; Council Regulation (EU) No 1177/2011 of 8 November 2011 amending Regulation (EC) No 1467/97 on speeding up and clarifying the implementation of the excessive deficit procedure [2011] OJ L306/33; Regulation (EU) No 1173/2011 of the European Parliament and of the Council of 16 November 2011 on the effective enforcement of budgetary surveillance in the euro area [2011] OJ L306/1.

[134] Council Directive 2011/85/EU of 8 November 2011 on requirements for budgetary frameworks of the Member States [2011] OJ L306/41.

[135] Regulation (EU) No 1176/2011 of the European Parliament and of the Council of 16 November 2011 on the prevention and correction of macroeconomic imbalances [2011] OJ L306/25; Regulation (EU) No 1174/2011 of the European Parliament and of the Council of 16 November 2011 on enforcement measures to correct excessive macroeconomic imbalances in the euro area [2011] OJ L306/8.

[136] Regulation (EU) No 473/2013 of the European Parliament and of the Council of 21 May 2013 on common provisions for monitoring and assessing draft budgetary plans and ensuring the correction of excessive deficit of the Member States in the euro area [2013] OJ L140/11; Regulation (EU) No 472/2013 of the European Parliament and of the Council of 21 May 2013 on the strengthening of economic and budgetary surveillance of Member States in the euro area experiencing or threatened with serious difficulties with respect to their financial stability [2013] OJ L140/1.

[137] Chalmers, Jachtenfuchs and Joerges (n 25) 272.

[138] ibid.

of legal provisions, requiring that this budgetary surveillance and compliance remains post-crisis, resulting in a permanent reconfiguration of the state. Law acts therefore as both *ideological state apparatus* and *repressive state apparatus* in these circumstances – law is an ISA, as the rule-of-law narrative requires that 'good' states abide by their legal obligations, as do their citizens. Acting in direct contravention of those laws becomes socially unacceptable and politically infeasible. To do so would somehow delegitimise the actions taken – while they may have been *effective* they are nevertheless *illegal*, and therefore unthinkable in a constitutional system based upon the rule of law. As an RSA, the attachment of bailouts to strict conditionality gives law a coercive force; do this, or there will be penalties. Your legal requirement is to obey, and your punishment for you failing to do so is legally enforceable sanctions.

Let us return then to the notion of strict conditionality. The bailouts, and the attached conditionality, have been commented upon by Kilpatrick for their some-what unusual legal nature – carried out by EU institutions, and yet not based directly on EU law, instead relying upon Memoranda of Understanding to ensure cuts to specific sectors or budgetary fields.[139] These bailouts have required strict structural reform, including 'extensive cuts to, or limitations upon who can access, health and education provision; reduced access to and levels of pensions and other social benefits ... and reduced employment protection'.[140] In other words, this process of state transformation, based on the legal implementation of economic ideology, has resulted in the burden falling disproportionately on the poor, the vulnerable, the disabled, and the young.

And what of the consequences? As was discussed with regard to the events of the 1970s, what began as an economic crisis became increasingly perceived as a legitimacy crisis, caused by undue amounts of 'democracy' represented by the influence of actors such as trade unions in determining state economic policies. As a result, we saw a move to the regulatory market state, and more 'technocratic' modes of governance replacing government. We can consider that the events of the past few years have led to a repeat of the 1970s, with a twist; economic crisis begets legitimacy crisis, but in this instance, it is a crisis of the existing model based in technocratic governance. The philosopher Ulrich Beck wrote that there were risks to 'German Europe', reflected by the hegemony of German economic thinking and policy direction during the height of the crisis. This, according to Beck, creates division not just between Northern states and Southern states, but also between elected and electorate. In Beck's words, 'Governments vote for austerity measures, while people vote against them. What [this] reveals is the structural divide between a European project that has been devised and administered *from above*, by political and

---

[139] C Kilpatrick, 'Are the Bailouts Immune to EU Social Challenge Because They Are Not EU Law?' (2014) 10 European Constitutional Law Review 393.
[140] ibid 393–94.

economic elites, and the resistance that wells up *from below*."[141] The EU's move to halt the crisis through unpopular economic adjustments mandated by (and in turn justified by reference to) legislation reinforced a perception that the EU and its legal order was disconnected from the people of Europe, making life-changing decisions in a dispassionate, unrepresentative way. Gillingham argues that 'the gap between the elitist approaches of the ruling Eurocrats and the democratic consensus needed for political legitimacy is huge'.[142] In 2014 this resulted in a wave of nominations of 'anti-EU' and Eurosceptic parties to the European Parliament, as well as dramatic drops in support for the European project in Southern European states subject to the 'expansionary austerity' doctrine.[143]

Indeed, there is a growing body of literature that refers to the end of the EU as we know it; the crisis represents the end of the Eurocrats' dream,[144] the consideration that European integration has gone too far,[145] and indeed, that the EU deserves an obituary.[146] What is not considered, however, is that it is perhaps not the EU that needs an obituary, but the *way* in which integration has been pursued, namely through a technocratic 'rules and markets' approach. This is the basis for the legitimacy crisis. Whereas previously, democracy was perceived by expert groups as being detrimental to economic development, resulting in top-down restructuring of state relations through the imposition of neo/ordoliberal economic doctrine as binding legal obligations, this legitimacy crisis is *of* those binding legal obligations, and the manner in which they are imposed. According to Nicoli, based on a large-scale quantitative analysis of parliamentary elections throughout the EU Member States between 2008 and 2015, the economic crisis has led to a rise in the election of populist, anti-EU parties, 'particularly through the channel of negative growth, historically high levels of unemployment and governance arrangements'.[147] Interestingly, the results were found to pervade beyond both the Southern states directly subject to the externally imposed austerity measures, and even to countries outside of the EMU.[148] This goes beyond a simple left–right divide, as Innerarity argues, but instead results in a 'technocracy–populism' axis being added to the traditional political compass, which straddles both the left and right of the political spectrum.[149] This can be seen in the left-populist revolt against further proposed

---

[141] Beck (n 117) 6.

[142] JR Gillingham, *The European Union: An Obituary* (Verso 2016) 167.

[143] M Matthijs, 'Mediterranean Blues: The Crisis in Southern Europe' (2014) 25 Journal of Democracy 101.

[144] D Chalmers, M Jachtenfuchs and C Joerges (eds), *The End of the Eurocrats' Dream: Adjusting to European Diversity* (CUP 2016).

[145] Majone (n 27).

[146] Gillingham (n 142).

[147] F Nicoli, 'Hard-Line Euroscepticism and the Eurocrisis: Evidence from a Panel Study of 108 Elections Across Europe' (2016) Journal of Common Market Studies 1, 14.

[148] ibid 14–15.

[149] D Innerarity, 'What Kind of Deficit? Problems of Legitimacy in the European Union' (2014) 17 European Journal of Social Theory 307, 312.

austerity measures in the 2015 pyrrhic referendum in Greece, in which voters said 'Oxi' (no) to the Troika and further cuts to the public sector, which were nevertheless implemented by the defeated SYRIZA government. It can be seen as part of the large 'NO' vote that characterised the Italian constitutional referendum of December 2016, in which 60 per cent of the electorate refused a massive constitutional reform presented by mainstream politics as the natural 'European choice'.[150] It can also be seen in the (albeit fringe) 'Lexit' movement in the UK, which campaigned for leaving the EU on the grounds that the legal framework of EU law prevented progressive economic reforms.[151] More visibly, and arguably much more effectively, a populist right-wing rhetoric concerning the technocracy of the EU, its lack of legitimacy and its responsibility for worsening economic crises struck a chord with the British public. Michael Gove, a leading figure in the 'Brexit' movement, famously responded to an audience member at a Sky News debate on the merits of leaving the EU, 'people in this country have had enough of experts'.[152] According to Travers, the decision by British voters to leave the EU can be attributed to various factors, including immigration (i.e. the free movement of workers, particularly as a form of competition for low-skilled jobs perceived as facilitating a race to the bottom in terms of wages and conditions); a narrative of bureaucrats disconnected from the interests of the population imposing top-down regulation; a dislike of austerity; and a perception that the crisis in the Eurozone was having a negative impact on the British economy.[153] Several academic commentators, writing soon after the result was announced, have indicated concerns that this perception of an out-of-touch elite, coupled with a perceived failure of 'expansionary austerity' as public services have been cut, unemployment has risen and people have expressed publicly a desire to 'take back control', has led to a situation where populist ideas are serving to delegitimise the functions of the EU, and indeed the current regulatory framework.[154] Prime Minister Theresa May's comments and subsequent support for a 'hard' Brexit, on the grounds that 'no deal is better than a bad deal', further reinforces that where policy choices and ideologies are crystallised in the form of binding obligations, the perceived solution to their rigidity is to remove oneself from

[150] S Merler, 'Italy's Constitutional Referendum: A Roundup of the Political Commentary' http://blogs .lse.ac.uk/europpblog/2016/12/03/italys-constitutional-referendum-a-roundup-of-the-political-commentary accessed April 2018.

[151] See for example MA Wilkinson, 'The Brexit Referendum and the Crisis of "Extreme Centrism"' (2016) 17 German Law Journal 131.

[152] H Mance, 'Britain Has Had Enough of Experts, Says Gove' *Financial Times* (3 June 2016) www .ft.com/content/3be49734-29cb-11e6-83e4-abc22d5d108c.

[153] T Travers, 'Why Did People Vote for Brexit? Deep-Seated Grievances Lie behind This Vote' http:// blogs.lse.ac.uk/politicsandpolicy/why-did-people-vote-for-brexit accessed April 2018.

[154] R Ashcroft and M Bevir, 'Pluralism, National Identity and Citizenship: Britain after Brexit' (2016) 87 Political Quarterly 355; C Calhoun, 'Brexit Is a Mutiny against the Cosmopolitan Elite' (2016) 33 New Perspectives Quarterly 50; L Floridi, 'Technology and Democracy: Three Lessons from Brexit' (2016) 29 Philosophy & Technology 189; SB Hobolt, 'The Brexit Vote: A Divided Nation, a Divided Continent' (2016) 23 Journal of European Public Policy 1259.

that system of regulation altogether. It should be of concern to policymakers that when a framework is created in which There is No Legal Alternative, alternatives to that legal system begin to be sought.

VI CONCLUSION(S)

The central thesis of this chapter has been that ideas matter. We have argued that the way we look at structural challenges and the solutions we offer are ultimately based on our perception of material facts filtered through the shaping lenses of ideas and ideologies. We have discussed throughout the chapter how the Eurocrisis has been shaped and analysed largely as a debt and budget deficits crisis in which virtuous actors have had to bear the costs of sloppy partners, who in turn needed to pay their benefactors back. What has been largely missing from this mainstream narrative is an acknowledgement that different analyses and, indeed, alternative solutions exist. In this sense, the Eurocrisis is very much a perceived crisis and therefore, we have argued, ideologically biased in its perception. Our thesis is that this is essentially the net result of the integration process as carried out since the 1970s. In particular it is in the double move from Keynesian to liberal economics on the one hand, and from state politics to supranational technocracy on the other, that we find the inception of the move from 'there is no alternative', as a powerful economic and political discourse, to the definitive 'there is no *legal* alternative' by which, regardless of their existence, alternative analyses and solutions are not simply intellectually disregarded, but effectively made illegal. The Eurocrisis is in this sense the symptom of a much larger or (to borrow the words of this book's title) multi-systemic failure. Both actors and commentators have gone to a great deal of effort to shape the surrounding narrative as a failure delimited both theoretically (debt and deficit) and geographically (Greece and Southern Europe).

Yet what this narrative has failed to appreciate is the fact that ideas matter. Eventually a contestation between competing ideas is bound to emerge in a situation of structural conflict and uncertainty, such as the one pervading the EU as of the late 2000s. When this happens, if there is no legal alternative *within* the polity, competing narratives may very well identify solutions *outside* the polity. It is no surprise then that the controversial (Greece), unwisely packaged (Italy) or altogether shattering (UK) referendums held in the last few years have been essentially a net rejection of the dominant narrative and of its legal authority (albeit with very different connotations as discussed above).

In this sense, the codification of ideology into law constitutes a major grounding element of a multi-systemic failure of which the Eurocrisis is, in the end, but an epiphenomenon.

The Crisis as a Crisis of the EU's Identity

PART 1

The Crisis as a Crisis of the EU's Identity

2

The Roots of the European Crisis

A Historical Perspective

Charalampos Kouroundis

1 INTRODUCTION

This chapter focuses on the trajectory of the European Union in order to elucidate and discuss its current problems. My main argument unfolds on the historically proven premise that the uneven and combined development of different national economies produces a major contradiction between the trend for greater integration and the continued assertion of national interests, a contradiction which is not likely to be transcended in the near future. My analysis brings forward two points, through a historical exploration of the European integration process.

First, I suggest that what invites further research and guides the formation and the development of the European integration process is geopolitical antagonism. This antagonism has two dimensions. The first revolves around the EU Member States, as countries in competition with each other, and the second encapsulates the 'external' antagonism of these nations as parts of a single entity (Europe) vis-à-vis the big geopolitical powers outside Europe (the Soviet Union in a former period, the United States, Russia and China nowadays). This duality in the perception of the concept of antagonism contrasts the arguments put forward by many researchers who insist that the European project has been launched in order to provide peace and prosperity among the Member States and view the European integration process solely as a response to existing nationalisms. Instead, the prism of the antagonistic coexistence of countries with different levels of power is more accurate and productive and allows for an investigation of the different national views on the European project. This approach, therefore, zooms in on the nexus between France and West Germany which favoured the creation of the European Coal and Steel Community (ECSC) and places each enlargement of the European project in the broader cadre of its geopolitical implications at the time. At the same time, it takes into consideration the internationalisation of capital and its contradictory contribution to the European integration process. On the one hand, economic unity pushed towards the creation of a regional 'European state', while, on the other hand, economic crisis produced political obstacles to the process.

My second point suggests that throughout its history the European integration process functioned as a machine for the liberalisation of European economies. The example of the Economic and Monetary Union (EMU) is very indicative, as its particular structure permitted the management of the eurozone crisis to be dominated by Germany, who opposed any idea or alternate arrangement that would have included any form of subsidy of the poorer Member States by the richer ones. However, it is suggested that any analysis should take a step back and position the installation of a European regime of fiscal surveillance within the broader picture of the recent global crisis. To understand the European crisis, we need to examine and explain the relevant role of the economic crisis of 2007–08 on it. By elucidating the economic stakes, this chapter will also attempt to offer an insight into their impact on social policy at a European level.

This attempt, aiming to contribute to current discussions on the European crisis and the dilemmas faced by the EU, will unfold in two steps. First, my analysis reveals that the development of the European project was contradictory from its very beginning. It seeks to demonstrate that European integration involves competitive interests of different countries which cannot be transcended through the goodwill of national or European political leaders. Second, the chapter investigates the economic and social aspect of the European project in an approach which conceptualises the EU as structurally subordinated to the neoliberal logic, while being hostile to basic aspects of the welfare state or of social protectionism.

II THE BEGINNING OF THE STORY: FROM THE FORMATION OF THE ECSC TO THE EEC

European integration began after the end of the Second World War, which shattered the whole continent and ended with the partition of Europe into spheres of influence between the United States and the Soviet Union. The adoption of such a project was based upon both geopolitical considerations and economic motives.[1] The first move towards European economic integration came from outside the continent: it consisted of the European Recovery Programme, known as the Marshall Plan, which was announced in June 1947. It is no coincidence that the Marshall Plan, followed by the formation of NATO two years later, were both US initiatives. They were both born out of grave US concerns about the security of Western Europe against the 'communist threat' represented by the Eastern bloc. Moreover, both initiatives essentially promoted European integration in order to create a unified market for US enterprises which needed stability and safety to make investments.

---

[1]   A Callinicos, *Imperialism and Global Political Economy* (Polity 2009) 169–78.

Thus, the special form taken by the post-war reconstruction of the European states and the European integration process effectively comprised, from the very beginning, two processes not separated from each other, but actually concurrent and complementary. The 'Schuman Plan', announced by the French Foreign Minister Robert Schuman in 1950, and the Treaty of Paris, signed one year later, launching the European Coal and Steel Community, were a great move forward for the economic cooperation between France and the new Federal Republic of Germany, and created the institutional embryo of European integration. Even though six countries (West Germany, France, Italy, Belgium, the Netherlands and Luxemburg) signed the Treaty of Paris, the endeavour was predominantly, and firmly, under the influence of just two. The actual effect of the Treaty lay in the creation of a supranational cartel, aimed to integrate French and German steel production, placing the industrial zone of Ruhr under the shared control of these two countries.[2]

Six years later, in 1957, the six signatories of the Paris Treaty signed the Treaty of Rome, which launched the European Economic Community (EEC). The EEC basically provided the framework for a stronger alignment between France and West Germany. France backed the European project in order to strengthen its position after the loss of its standing in the global state system as a colonial power. General de Gaulle adopted this strategy in 1958, aiming the formation of a 'Europe of the nations' as a counterbalance to US power, through cooperation between sovereign countries and not through integration.[3] Insisting on this strategy, de Gaulle opposed the accession of the UK to the Community during the 1960s, as the British governments were preserving a close partnership with the US.[4] At first, Britain chose to stay away from the EEC, as it was still trying to maintain its old role as a colonial empire, and therefore retained its focus and orientation on imperial markets. The failure of this attempt to maintain a dominant position on the global map was marked by the UK's accession to the Community, alongside Denmark and Ireland, in 1973. West Germany's main preoccupation was to assert its economic interests, which were based on an expansion driven by rising productivity and exports, and advance its international role, without reviving the recent memories of German aggression. After two world wars the only way for Germany to participate in the global decision-making was to 'hide' itself inside a common European structure.[5] From the US point of view, the US reaffirmed their strategic commitment to European integration even by sometimes going against traditional stances and policies advocated by

[2] A Milward, *The European Rescue of the Nation-State* (Routledge 2000) 64.
[3] See General de Gaulle's letter to Paul Reynaud of 24 December 1958, quoted by E Jouve, *Le Général de Gaulle et la Construction Européenne (1940–1966)* (LGDJ 1967) 202; and more generally, C Morelle, 'Les Conceptions Européennes du Général de Gaulle' in Konstantinos Svolopoulos (ed), *De Gaulle et Caramanlis. La Nation, L'Etat, L'Europe* (Patakis 2002) 133–46.
[4] M Vaisse, *La Grandeur, Politique étrangère du Général de Gaulle* (Fayard 1998) 75.
[5] See Chancellor Helmut Schmidt's expression of this idea in TG Ash, *In Europe's Name: Germany and the Divided Continent* (Vintage 1994) 87.

its own political apparatus. As such, for example, the US government, during the EEC's formative period, displayed remarkable tolerance as to the high degree of protectionism involved in the EEC's Common Agricultural Policy, going as far as to overrule the objections of the Treasury, Department of Agriculture and Federal Reserve Board to the formation of a European common market that might cause harm to US economic interests.[6]

The first steps of the EEC were deeply determined by the virtuous economic circle between 1948 and 1973 and subsequently by the internationalisation of production and the growth of world trade. The internationalisation of capital had also occurred before the First World War but it was mostly related with colonialism, while the same trend after the Second World War affected the advanced industrial powers themselves. The integration of the economies of the advanced world took a special form, as the concentration of industry led to the emergence of huge firms, able to channel resources into innovation and productive investment on an unprecedented scale.[7] The multinational firms, which had already existed in the pre-war period, turned to an international mobilisation of resources, not only in terms of trade but also in terms of production. Thus, the EEC opened itself to the global system, and US enterprises took the opportunity to make investments that were based on recent technological innovations, but also benefitted from the post-war 'economic miracle'.[8] At the same time, West Germany's expansion provided a market for the manufacturing industries of the other Member States.[9] So, in a broad sense, the pioneer of the European integration process was the multinational capital in a way that lived up the general tendency of capital to encourage the growth of political structures under its own control.

The official constitutive documents of the Community reflect the economic considerations cited above. As illustrated by Article 9 of the Treaty, the EEC just aimed at the realisation of the common market: 'The basis of the Community shall be a customs union which extends to include the exchange of all goods'. This declaration, which supposed that the preoccupations of the Community as a whole were initially exclusively economic, reflected the stage-by-stage approach of the European integration process, adopted by Jean Monnet. Monnet believed that this gradually developed scheme might provide the trigger for a chain reaction resulting in a new European and global order.[10] The economic preoccupation of the EEC was also stressed by the fact that the Treaty of Rome conceived social

---

[6]   Callinicos (n 1) 173–74.

[7]   C Harman, 'The State and Capitalism Today' (1991) 51 International Socialism 27.

[8]   W Wallace, *The Transformation of Western Europe* (Pinter/Royal Institute of International Affairs 1990) 44–45.

[9]   For the pivotal role of West Germany in the economic advance of Western Europe's trade, see A Milward, *The European Rescue of the Nation-State* (Routledge 1994) 134–66.

[10] J Palmer, 'The EU Referendum: The Case for a Socialist Yes Vote' (2015) 148 International Socialism 78–79, 81–82.

objectives principally as a way of correcting distortions arising from the operation of the common market.[11]

The only 'social' (with a very broad sense of the term) provisions contained in the founding Treaty were those referring to the free movement of workers (Arts 48–50), the European Social Fund (Art 123) and the declaration of the Community's commitment on the improvement of life (Arts 117–122). Contrary to its traditional function at the national level, which is to bypass the market's monopoly of reward, European social policy was from the beginning not of the 'market-breaking' but of the 'market-making' variety.[12] The reason for this is that the economic liberalism of the founders of the EEC assumed that the unhindered function of the market would bring automatically the harmonisation of social policies. As is illustrated by Article 117 of the Treaty of Rome, the functioning of the common market was supposed to result spontaneously in the harmonisation of the national systems and the improvement of working conditions. For all these reasons, social policy has been correctly characterised as the 'stepchild' of European integration.[13] Moreover, during the same period, the European Court of Justice (ECJ) favoured the interests of European integration over everything else, and, therefore, it was not consistent in its protection of social rights.[14] It is illustrative that the ECJ in 1967 practically abandoned the goal of harmonisation of national social policies, stipulating that the aim of the Treaty of Rome is not the equalisation of the social security provisions across Europe.[15] So, in this period, the EEC is characterised by measures of *negative* integration, i.e. removing obstacles to the free competition and the unification process, while proposals for a more active social policy, such as the Social Action Programme of 1974, did not have any real institutional impact.[16]

Thus, the European project, on the basis of an intergovernmental agreement, resulted ultimately in creating a new political field, with its own institutions, but without direct legitimation or a common foreign and military affairs strategy. The aforementioned institutional framework and the ideology which supported it were also reflected in the jurisprudence of the ECJ. The ECJ declared the primacy of Community law over national law, justifying this primacy in part on the special nature and autonomy of the Community legal order and in part on the proper functioning of the common market and, consequently, of the Community.[17]

---

[11] E Moxon-Browne, 'Social Europe' in J Lodge (ed), *The European Community and the Challenge of the Future* (Pinter 1993) 152.

[12] G Katrougalos, *Constitution, Law and Rights in the Welfare State . . . and Beyond* (Ant N Sakkoulas 1998) 135.

[13] P Flora, 'The National Welfare States and European Integration' in L Moreno (ed), *Social Exchange and Welfare Development* (Consejo Superior de Investigaciones Científicas 1993) 11.

[14] J Coppel and A O' Neil, 'The European Court of Justice: Taking Rights Seriously?' (1992) 29 Common Market Law Review 669–92.

[15] Case 2/67 *de Moor v Caisse de Pension des Emploies Privés* [1967] ECR 265.

[16] Katrougalos (n 12) 140.

[17] J Wouters, 'National Constitutions and the European Union' (2000) 27 Legal Issues of Economic Integration 65.

III THE EUROPEAN PROJECT AFTER 1973: IN SEARCH OF
PROFITABILITY AND LEGITIMATION

The economic crisis of 1973 ended the post-war economic boom, whose levels of sustained growth remain without historical parallel ever since, and inaugurated an era of a long downturn.[18] Subsequently, the results of the crisis, which escalated in 1979, after the failure of successive governments to deal with it using Keynesian tools, created the need for amendments in state strategies seeking solutions to restore business profitability. From the late 1970s, Margaret Thatcher's Great Britain turned decisively to neoliberalism.[19] It was followed in 1983 by France, where the financial market pushed the Socialist–Communist coalition government to quit the policies of nationalisation and embrace free market policies.[20]

The crisis was of course visible at the Community level as well. During the first half of the 1980s there was a drop in investment throughout Europe,[21] while European private investments in the US were growing fast. The Commission responded by adopting a policy of further liberalisation of the Common Market, and neoliberalism became firmly embedded into the structure of the Community.[22] This orientation was ratified by the Single European Act (SEA), which was signed in 1986 and came into effect in 1987, providing treaty changes aimed at achieving a Single European Market by 1992. Its actual target was to boost EEC competitiveness, despite Jacques Delors's declarations, as the President of the Commission, that this process constituted a safe road to create the 'social dimension' or 'social space' of Europe.[23] The only move in this direction was the adoption of the Social Charter by the Community in 1989. The Social Charter faced hostility from Margaret Thatcher; she dubbed it a 'Socialist Charter', despite the fact that it was only a legally non-binding declaration on workers' rights.[24] In fact, the single European

---

[18] See the figures which identify the falling rate of profit in Germany as well as in USA and Japan in R Brenner, *The Economics of Global Turbulence* (Verso 2006) 7.

[19] See among many others D Harvey, *A Brief History of Neoliberalism* (OUP 2007) 39–63.

[20] As stressed in H James, *Making the European Monetary Union* (Harvard UP 2012) 197, 'the speculative attack on the French franc which began in March 1983' forced the government to take 'a stark and obvious choice between continuing in the ex-change rate mechanism (ERM) and imposing budgetary austerity, the course advocated by Finance Minister Jacques Delors and leaving the ERM to embark on a strategy of economic nationalism, as proposed above all by the minister of industry, Jean-Pierre Chevenement'.

[21] See the figures in United Nations, Internal Yearbook of Industrial Statistics (United Nations Industrial Development Organization 1998).

[22] S Gill, 'A Neo-Gramscian Approach to European Integration' in A Carfuny and M Ryner (eds), *A Ruined Fortress? Neoliberal Hegemony and Transformation in Europe* (Rowman & Littlefield 2003) 63.

[23] For these declarations see P Teague, *The European Community: The Social Dimension – Labour Market Policies for 1992* (Kogan Page 1989).

[24] This extract of her speech on 18 May 1989 is cited in B Greve, 'Development in the EC and Its Impact on the Welfare State in Europe – Trends Towards Convergence in the Last Ten Years' (1994) 19 History of European ideas 147.

market opened the road for the liberalisation of European capitalism, not for any improvement in social protection.[25]

Thus, there was a major difference in the results of that economic crisis compared to previous ones: instead of causing a fragmentation of Europe, like the one that took place after the First World War and the Great Recession of the 1930s, this crisis pushed the European integration process forward. The Tindemans Report, presented in 1975, underlined the Economic and Monetary Union as the EEC's primary goal and, for the first time, used the term 'European Union', setting it as a long-range goal for the following decade.[26] This goal proved to be very ambitious, but served to open the discussion about treaty changes. According to the detailed treaty changes proposed by the SEA, for example, a Member State's veto power was to be reduced, as the European Council could take decisions with a qualified majority. However, what is more important in terms of the power held by democratically accountable authorities is the subsequent relevant gradual creation of a complicated framework largely devoid of democratic checks. A significant number of competences were transferred to European institutions with no accountability, while a great part of negotiation processes began to take place outside the official mechanisms, through unofficial meetings and bodies.[27] Consequently, numerous networks (economic, political, institutional, ideological) emerged within the EU, related to each other and ruled by Community institutions, Member States, multinational companies, lobbying groups, etc. This amalgam is founded upon the relationship between private capital interests and the Member States which try to assure these interests' reproduction, using their power inside the European hierarchy, especially in the intergovernmental institutions.[28] Within this new complex power play arena, however, the determinant factor is no longer the 'direct' (geopolitical or economic) power of each individual Member State, but rather, each state's position within the function of the whole European structure.

The reality of EU institutions was therefore created on the basis of two major contradictions: the first is at the institutional level, where there is a coexistence of state and federalist elements, and the second is at the political level, with the existence, within the EU, of a plethora of states with uneven power and different goals. In this way, the European integration process has provided Member States with the ability to claim themselves not responsible for unpopular measures imposed to allegedly grow productivity, such as changes in labour legislation or cuts in the welfare state, and portray them as being adopted directly by the Commission.[29]

[25] W Streeck, *Buying Time: The Delayed Crisis of Democratic Capitalism* (Verso 2014) 105.
[26] B Olivi and A Giacone, *L'Europe Difficile, la Construction Européenne* (Gallimard 1998) 142.
[27] N Nugent, *The Government and Politics of the European Union* (Macmillan 1995) 130–33.
[28] B Rosamond, *Theories of European Integration* (Palgrave Macmillan 2000) 154.
[29] A Moravcsic, 'Preferences and Power in the European Community: A Liberal Intergovernmental Approach' (1993) 31 Journal of Common Market Studies 473.

Under this framework, the only possible source of popular legitimacy could be seen to be the European Parliament, which sought to participate in the configuration of the Community budget and the legislation process. The direct election of the European Parliament for the first time on 10 June 1979 seemed to be a move away from the intergovernmental national sovereignty status quo, towards a more federalist approach. Despite the fact that the competences given to the European Parliament were not enough to change the balance of forces inside the Community apparatus, which continued to be dominated by intergovernmental and unelected bodies, the importance of this change was that European integration became a major stake with important political implications. With the direct election of the European Parliament, the mainstream political parties, as agents which acted both at national and European levels, obtained a crucial role in the legitimation of the European integration process.[30] The divisions concerning the future of the EEC differed between each country, according to the role each one played in the integration process. Thus, the main German political powers, the Christian Democrats and the Social Democrats, were in favour of a more federalist approach, while the French political powers remained, at least at first, faithful to the Gaullist perspective of a 'Europe of the nations'.[31] Further, the Italians stressed the need to enforce European unity as a means of reducing the gap between the rich North and the poor South. These different points of view were expressed, in reflection, even within the big European Communist parties of the time. The French one (PCF) stressed explicitly its fear towards a 'German Europe', while the Italian one (PCI) argued in favour of an enforced European Parliament as a democratically legitimised counter-balance to the unelected Commission.[32]

Another source of legitimation for the Community in this difficult period came from the countries of the European South, as the fall of dictatorships in Greece, Portugal, and Spain during the 1970s and the subsequent adherence of these states to the EEC provided the latter with democratic credentials. In Spain, since the early 1960s, internal forces of General Franco's regime, such as the technocrats of 'Opus Dei', alongside the moderate opposition to it, used to connect the democratisation of the country with the European prospect.[33] The case in Portugal seemed rather similar, as the orientation to the EEC provided an alternative for a dictatorial regime unable to protect Portugal as a colonial power.[34] Greece was quite different, as it had already signed a link agreement with the EEC in 1961, in a period where the civil war institutional edifice was still in place in the country. That included a set of

[30] P Pierson, 'The Path to European integration: A Historical Institutionalist Perspective' (1996) 29 Comparative Political Studies 131.

[31] J Story, 'Monetary Union: Economic Competition and Political Negotiation' in D Webber (ed), *The Franco-German Relationship in the European Union* (Routledge 2005) 21–26.

[32] R Dunphy, *Contesting Capitalism? Left Parties and European Integration* (Manchester UP 2004) 57–58, 79.

[33] G Hermet, *L'Espagne au XXème siècle* (PUF 1992) 215–21.

[34] G Filoche, *Printemps Portugais* (Actéon 1984) 151–87.

emergency provisions, permitting measures prohibited by the 'normal' constitutional order, such as deportation orders, dismissal of civil servants and deprivation of nationality.[35] During the negotiation process regarding the link agreement, the EEC did not pose any questions about the violation of constitutional rights and freedoms of a large part of the population.[36] However, the fact that the link agreement was put on hold during the seven year period of the colonels' rule (1967–74), did help to connect, in public perception, the democratic with the European perspective.

IV THE ESCALATION OF THE CONTRADICTIONS AND THE UNEVEN DEVELOPMENT OF THE EMU

From the late 1990s, there has been increasing interest among scholars about 'Europeanisation', a notion which attempted to explain the impact of EU membership on the shape, structure or dynamics of Member States' domestic politics.[37] According to the Europeanisation formula, through membership of the EU, states' preferences and the way they shape their policies converge into a European agenda, and Member States adapt to a European way of conducting policy,[38] but also politics. By participating in the institutions and bargaining processes of the EU over a range of policy issues, individual policymakers and policymaking elites start to behave in similar ways and to espouse similar views. Similarly, states adapt to specific policy agendas to the extent that all Member States begin to act the same way. In fact, the concept of Europeanisation reflected the neoliberal consensus which was already dominating the European project. Moreover, the principal trend of the Maastricht era was precisely the ambitious goal of economic 'convergence'. The emphasis on the completion of the internal market rather than the social targets can be proved by the data which show that until 1992, whereas about 85 per cent of the economic proposals contained in the single market programme had been agreed, only 5–7 per cent of the social ones had concluded to positive results.[39] The spectre that seemed to haunt the European policies of those years was the fear of 'Eurosclerosis', a term used to identify the fact that Europe, unlike the USA and Japan, did not create new jobs and was left behind in global competition. Then, as now, it had come to be accepted almost axiomatically that the comparative

---

[35] K Mavrias, *Transition démocratique et changement constitutionnel en Europe du Sud. Espagne-Grèce-Portugal* (Ant N Sakkoulas 1997) 46–47.

[36] For a general account of Greece's link agreement with the EEC, see P Mioche, 'Les Six et l' Association de la Grèce à la CEE, 1959–1961: accueil généreux ou comptes d' épiciers?' in A Deighton and A Milward (eds), *Widening, Deepening and Acceleration: The European Economic Community 1957–1963* (Nomos and Bruylant 1999) 331–45.

[37] See among others T Börzel, 'Pace-setting, Foot-dragging and Fence-sitting: Member State Responses to Europeanization' (2002) 40 Journal of Common Market Studies 193–94.

[38] See T Börzel, 'Towards Convergence in Europe? Institutional Adaptation to Europeanization in Germany and Spain' (1999) 37 Journal of Common Market Studies 573–596.

[39] Katrougalos (n 12) 145.

advantage of the US is the flexibility of its market, if not its inherent greater social inequality.[40]

After the Maastricht Treaty, the EU attempted to overcome its lack of competitiveness by adopting the Anglo-Saxon model of 'squeezing' the labour force.[41] The tools that crystallised the initiative to improve its long-run competitiveness were presented in the 'White Papers', documents containing the Commission's proposals for EU action in specific areas. The 'White Paper' presented by the Commission in 1993 attested that the labour markets did not work efficiently because of a lack of flexibility, more particularly in terms of the organisation of working time, pay and mobility.[42] Moreover, it claimed that this rigidity was the root cause of what were relatively high labour costs, which had risen at a much greater rate in the Community than in its principal trading partners. According to this assumption, social protection schemes had had a negative impact on employment in that they had, in the main, tended to protect people already in work, making their situation more secure and consolidating certain advantages, and thus constituting an obstacle to the recruitment of jobseekers or of new entrants to the labour market. Although the 'White Paper' also made an appeal for the promotion of active labour policies, it embraced essentially a neoliberal strategy. That strategy was firmly oriented to the reform of the labour market through the introduction of greater flexibility in the organisation of work, the distribution of working time and the reduction of labour costs by cutting back employers' contributions to the social security systems, while the minimal standards of the European social legislation were to be considered just as 'a large framework of action'. The 1993 'White Paper' also suggested a greater convergence of social protection systems, fearing that the divergence of the national systems could constitute an advantage for the poor countries with lower standards of social protection.

The 'White Paper' of 1993 was followed by others in the following years, all of them moving in the same direction of creating a more flexible labour market. The implementation of this strategy caused a mismatch of capital and labour at the European level, generating a 'downward spiral' in social provision and eventually proceeding towards the 'lowest common denominator' of the welfare states.[43] Moreover, the criteria thresholds posed by Article 109 of the TEU to enter the EMU exerted a pressure towards the retrenchment of social expenses, especially

---

[40] G Esping-Andersen, *After the Golden Age: The Future of the Welfare State in the Global Order* (UNRISD 1994) 14.

[41] J Halevi and P Kriesler, 'Stagnation and Economic Conflict in Europe' (2004) 34 International Journal of Political Economy 19–45.

[42] Commission of the European Communities, Growth, Competitiveness, Employment: The *Challenges* and Ways Forward into the 21st Century (Office for Official Publications of the European Communities 1993).

[43] C Erickson and S Kuruvilla, 'Labor Costs and the Social Dumping Debate in the European Union' (1994) 48 Industrial and Labor Relations Review 28–47.

on the weaker economies.[44] In this context, Streeck and Schmitter proved to be right when they prophesised more than twenty-five years ago that the European Union would likely resemble a pre-New Deal liberal state, with, in Marshall's terms, a high level of civil rights, a low level of political rights, an even lower level of social rights and an almost complete absence of a European system of citizenship.[45]

The prospect of a common currency has also given another push to the European integration project, as the aforementioned economic 'convergence' was claimed to be necessary in order to conserve the cohesion of the Union in the process of EMU. At an early stage in the European project, monetary union was identified by the 'transforming leadership' of Jean Monnet as a decisive move towards a political union.[46] However, the road to the common currency has opened due to the particular needs of the German economy, not because of the federalist ambitions which some of the founders of ECSC and EEC used to have.[47] The exchange of complex manufactured goods produced by German companies to the European markets was based from the very beginning not only on the high productivity of their workers but also on the policy of a strong deutschmark, which kept import costs, and therefore inflation, low.[48] The stable exchange rates needed were disrupted not only by the fluctuations of the dollar, but also by the tendency of the weaker European economies to boost their competitiveness through devaluation. The European failure to maintain a Bretton Woods system led to the creation of the Economic and Monetary System (EMS) in 1978.[49] The EMS has pegged the European currencies against each other, making them more dependent on Bundesbank policies as devaluation became more difficult. The reaction of the other strong European economies, mainly France and Italy as Britain was forced out of the Exchange Rate Mechanism in 1992, was to press in the direction of creating a single currency, in order to transfer control over European monetary policy from the Bundesbank to a European central bank that took the particular institutional form of the European Central Bank (ECB).

The Maastricht Treaty, agreed on in December 1991, stipulated 1 January 1999 as the date European currencies participating in EMU would be irrevocably fixed against each other. In the three years following that date, national banknotes were to

---

[44] The peripheral countries were obliged to re-examine their social policy strategy in order to avoid an unbalanced growth that could enlarge the budget deficits. For the case of Greece, see the various contributions in P Kazakos (ed), *Greece and EC Membership Evaluated* (Pinter 1994).

[45] W Streeck and P Schmitter, 'From National Corporatism to Transnational Pluralism: Organized Interests in the Single European Market' (1991) 19 Politics and Society 152.

[46] F Duchêne, *Jean Monnet: The First Statesman of Interdependence* (Norton 1994) 390.

[47] A Callinicos, 'The Internationalist Case against the European Union' (2015) 148 International Socialism 109–16.

[48] According to G Carchedi, *For Another Europe: A Class Analysis of European Integration* (Verso 2001) 129–43, Germany has the highest analogy of technologically innovative companies which benefit from a strong currency.

[49] B Eichengreen, *The European Economy Since 1945: Coordinated Capitalism and Beyond* (Princeton UP 2007) 282–90.

be completely replaced with those issued by the ECB. The Treaty provided tough convergence criteria for the Member States to qualify, notably reducing the budget deficit to 3 per cent of national income and keeping government debt lower than 60 per cent of GDP. The new monetary union was also characterised by the reproduction of the main features of the German monetary regime, as the ECB was declared to be essentially unaccountable to elected politicians and was supposed to be responsible to maintain price stability.[50] As has been pointed out, Germany has been able to dominate trade and capital flows within the eurozone.[51] This happened because of the competitive advantage of German exporters, which, in turn was mainly the result of the high exchange rates at which peripheral countries have entered the eurozone. Moreover, the structure of the EMU deprived Member States of their ability to respond to recession by devaluating their currency in order to make exports cheaper and boost growth, while the Maastricht Treaty prohibited the EU or Member States themselves from assuming the liabilities of individual Member States. The differentiation inside the eurozone between countries with surpluses and countries with deficits made their coexistence difficult and unstable.[52]

All the while, the dominant parties of the European Parliament after the decline of the Communist left since 1989, the centre-right Popular Party and the centre-left Socialist Party, adopted an ethos and a line of action that would be more properly indicative of the oligarchic parties of Notables rather than of modern political parties. In the former case, democratic discourse was nothing more than a negotiation between fractions of a single class, namely aristocrats, ultimately sharing the same broad interests and, subsequently, between them (and the concluded sum of their interests) and the king. Similarly, parliamentary discourse within the EP in response to the crisis has been largely reduced to rather superficial negotiations between the two bigger parties. The character of their debates is determined by the fact that, although the European Popular Party and the European Socialist Party have different historical roots and social references, they both share the same beliefs with regard to the necessity of budgetary discipline, the inevitability of the EMU and the priority of economic rationales over any other considerations. At a second level, when a consensus is reached, negotiation tends to address the EU equivalents to the king, that is the Commission, the Council and the ECB. Nowhere did EP parties behave as modern mass parties of representative democracies are supposed to behave, turning to their base in times of paradigm shifting crises to consult with it, take its pulse, and realign their policy accordingly. From this point of view, the succession of referendums in which EU initiatives and institutions have been rejected by popular vote – Ireland (2001 and 2008), the Netherlands (2005), France (2005), Sweden (2003) and Denmark (1992) – can be

[50]   James (n 20) 267.
[51]   C Lapavitsas and others, *Crisis in the Eurozone* (Verso 2012) 28.
[52]   J Milios and D Sotiropoulos, 'Crisis of Greece or Crisis of Euro? A View from the European "Periphery"' (2010) 12 Journal of Balkan and near Eastern Studies 223–40.

explained more as a rejection of the EU's neoliberal policies than as an expression of xenophobic syndromes.

V THE GORDIAN KNOT OF THE CURRENT CRISIS

During the early 2000s, there was much talk about the successful European model which should be exported worldwide as it allegedly guaranteed economic stability, peaceful competition and respect for fundamental human rights.[53] The euphoria came to an end with the global economic crisis of 2007–08. Neoliberalism had responded to the previous crisis by opening up markets in spaces such as health or education, and had pushed for the deregulation and global integration of financial markets. This new economic policy regime has had the 'success' of creating financial 'bubbles' during the past two decades, but did not manage to restore profitability to the levels of the long boom. Its failure to overcome the contradictions that caused the collapse of the long boom and the protracted period of crisis that have followed, became obvious when the financial upheavals of 2007–08 led to a new global recession.[54] The 2007–08 crisis started with the burst of the real estate 'bubble' in the US, which led to the collapse of Lehman Brothers. The US state responded to the credit squeeze with massive rescues of the entire banking system. The Federal Bank of the US played a crucial role in this process as it intervened openly in the market, lending money to investment banks, among other measures.[55] The US ultimately managed to remain the country with the biggest profitability among the G-7 thanks to the power of the dollar, but also thanks to its military power and, therefore, its geopolitical influence.

In Europe, the response to the crisis was quite different, as it was mainly orchestrated by national governments who organised their own rescues of their respective banking systems, while the Commission looked on ineffectually. The fact that the monetary union did not lead to a political union had been evident even before the 2007–08 crisis, as the role of the Commission had weakened in favour of intergovernmental councils, such as the unofficial 'Eurogroup', comprising eurozone members' finance ministers. Similarly, the management of the eurozone crisis has been dominated by Germany's refusal to allow the currency area to become a 'transfer union', in which the richer Member States subsidise the poorer. The eurozone Member States, which have spent large amounts of money to rescue their banks, saw their public debt increasing, and the weakest European economies (Greece, Portugal and Spain) found themselves moving closer to defaulting, and

---

[53] See for example J Habermas, *The Divided West* (Polity 2006) 43; and more generally U Beck, *Cosmopolitan Vision* (Polity 2006).

[54] D Sotiropoulos, J Milios and S Lapatsioras, *A Political Economy of Contemporary Capitalism and Its Crisis: Demystifying Finance* (Routledge 2013).

[55] C Lapavitsas, *Profiting without Producing: How Finance Exploits Us All* (Verso, 2013) 279.

were forced to implement austerity policies.[56] However, ironically, the eurozone crisis has not only divided Europe into 'lenders' and 'owners', but it also led once more to further integration. As the crisis of the 1970s and early 1980s led to the creation of the Single European Market, and the crisis of the early 1990s formed the backdrop to EMU, the current crisis acted too, in the first instance, as an integration catalyst. Thus, in March 2012, twenty-five EU Member States signed the 'Fiscal Pact', the Treaty on Stability, Coordination and Governance in the EMU, according to which the signatories agreed to present balanced budgets and set up an independent fiscal coordination council to monitor compliance. This method of deepening integration by centralising even more the decision-making process in the EU shows that the response to the crisis was not moving towards a democratic political union, but rather pushing more decisively in the direction of unaccountable neoliberalism. The contradiction between integration and national interests has also been reflected in the ECB's position towards the current crisis. The ECB vacillated between the Bundesbank's policy of keeping inflation low (e.g. raising interest rates during the crisis, in July 2008 and again in the spring and summer of 2011) and following the example of the US Federal Reserve Board and playing a more active economic role (through, for example, buying indebted government bonds in 2011 and undertaking quantitative easing in March 2015).

The political and social results of not just the crisis, but also the specific methods adopted to deal with it, are illustrated by the Greek case. The Troika's bail-out programme enforced government measures that directly impacted living conditions, thereby violating human rights legally protected at the domestic, European and international levels.[57] Since 2010, the drastic measures imposed on Greek society have provoked a rapid deterioration of living standards. The dismantling of the welfare state had a particularly severe impact on the most vulnerable groups of people, such as the poor, pensioners, women, children, people with disabilities and immigrants, who tried to respond with grass-root social welfare projects.[58] The adoption of such measures undermined social cohesion and democracy and provoked a huge political crisis which damaged the traditional establishment parties.[59]

In geopolitical terms, the crisis underlined that there is a divided hegemony in Europe, with the US retaining politico-military primacy and Germany assuming economic leadership within the EU.[60] Moreover, Germany's economic position can be maintained only at the price of transforming – and destabilising – the configuration of power within the EU, even if this creates a degree of tension with France. On the other hand, the entire eurozone crisis underlined how EMU has increased

---

[56] For data about the Greek debt, see the figures presented in Truth Committee on Public Debt, Preliminary Report (Hellenic Parliament 2015) 11–32.

[57] ibid 38–41.

[58] T Rakopoulos, 'Resonance of Solidarity: Meanings of a Local Concept in Anti-austerity Greece' (2014) 32 Journal of Modern Greek Studies, 95–119.

[59] K Ovenden, *SYRIZA: Inside the Labyrinth* (Pluto 2015).

[60] Callinicos (n 47) 126.

national antagonisms, both between northern and southern Member States, and among three of the EEC's founding nations, the biggest economies in the eurozone – France, Germany and Italy. Fierce national antagonisms among Member States are also a marked feature of the current refugee crisis, engulfing eastern Member States, seeming relatively untouched by the Eurocrisis, but very much a part of its evolution.

Within this context, Britain's vote in the 23 June 2016 referendum to exit the European Union is an event of major geopolitical significance, despite the fact that Britain was always an 'awkward partner' of the Union.[61] The popular decision of the second biggest country and Europe's largest financial and military power to leave the EU is likely to destabilise the equilibrium inside the Union. The unexpected 'Brexit' reverses the perceived irrevocable tendency of the EU to enlarge, as, for the first time, a Member State has decided to quit the Union.[62] Other countries may find Britain's example more attractive than before, although a total disintegration of the EU is not likely to take place in the near future.

The recent discussion about the 'multi-speed Europe' shows exactly the impasse produced at a European level by the aforementioned multitude of contradictory pressures. In a previous period, the different 'speeds' used to give flexibility to the EU and was presented as proof of the Union's respect towards 'national identities'. Nowadays, multinational capital does not seem able to play a 'hegemonic' role in the way it did and many Member States of the EU prefer to defend national capitalist interests. In addition, economic crisis is accompanied by political crisis causing a vicious circle.

In this sense, the Gordian knot of the European integration process can be cut by three different Alexanders with very different swords: (a) from inside, that is from an institutional and political '(r)evolution' transforming the European Union into a federal state; (b) from above, that is with the initiative of some states which would find it easier to adopt protectionist policies for their national capitals rather than continue down the same path of disciplinary surveillance and fiscal stability; or (c) from below, that is from the European people, inspired not by narrow nationalist sentiment but by the internationally widespread hostility against the autocratic and neoliberal structures of the EU. However, even if the Union manages to restabilise itself after this serious injury, its Member States will continue to find themselves in the same trap that has confined them since the 1950s – too weak to stand up to the forces of global competition on their own, but with too strongly diverging interests to be willing to surrender their sovereignty definitively to a genuine economic and political union.[63]

[61] S George, *An Awkward Partner: Britain in the European Community* (OUP 1998).

[62] For the legal implications of withdrawal from the European Union, see C Hillion, 'Accession and Withdrawal in the Law of the European Union' in A Arnull and D Chalmers (eds), *The Oxford Handbook of European Union Law* (OUP 2015) 126–52.

[63] Callinicos (n 47) 127.

VI CONCLUSION

The EU integration process reflects the contradiction between the trend for the Europeanisation of capital and the continued assertion of the Member States. Thus, the EU functions as a historically new hybrid formation which involves cross-border cooperation and supranational institutions, but is very far from replacing the European state system and from transcending nationalism. The history of European integration has proved that the Member States are not living fossils, as some theorists of globalisation tended to believe,[64] but still powerful entities which try to serve their national capital interests through partially pooling sovereignty rather than operating on their own. Thus, national interests reign supreme in the EU and the supranational institutions function without any democratic account-ability or control. As a result, the EU's problems are intrinsic and systemic, allowing national antagonisms and class struggle to grow, threatening European integration with disintegration.

[64] See, among many others, M Hardt and A Negri, *Empire* (Harvard UP 2000).

3

The End of Self-fulfilling Europe

Hent Kalmo

I INTRODUCTION

Much of the criticism levelled against European policymakers since the eurocrisis has centred around the claim that the adoption of a common currency was an essentially political project which courted disaster by decoupling monetary from political integration. According to what has become a popular narrative, the European leadership chose political grandstanding and symbolism over pragmatism in recklessly pushing forward with a fatally deficient scheme of monetary union. Little wonder, then, that the hubris of political fiat found its nemesis in the hard facts of economics.

I shall argue that this narrative is in many ways incomplete as it leaves out entirely the intellectual background to the steps that have furthered the development of the EU. From the 1950s, the integration process has been underpinned, or at least accompanied and justified, by what might be called the theory of 'self-fulfilling Europe': the idea that economic integration, once set in motion, can remove political resistance to European unification by creating factual interdependence and a consciousness of solidarity. The euro strategy was similarly rooted in the idea of the primacy of economics. Many of the proponents of monetary unification recognised in the mid 1990s that the EU does not satisfy the conditions of an optimal currency area. But they expected these conditions to be realised performatively, as it were, i.e. by the very act of introducing the euro. Monetary integration was expected to bring economic convergence in its wake.

The theory of 'self-fulfilling Europe' posits a similarly providential relationship between economic integration and political unification. In speaking of 'self-fulfilling Europe', I don't mean to suggest some crude form of functionalism – as if the economy were able to bring about political union in Europe without the need for any active prodding by politicians.[1] What I have in mind, rather, is the widely

The research for this chapter has been funded by the European Union's Horizon 2020 research and innovation programme under the Marie Sklodowska-Curie grant agreement No 709386.

[1] Jean Monnet contested the idea (which he thought was implied by some proponents of neo-functionalism) that founders of the EEC could simply start the process and then step back and watch it unfold (G Grin, *Shaping Europe: The Path to European Integration according to Jean*

shared belief that economic integration favours a sense of community because it weaves together a great interconnected whole and thus produces a state of factual solidarity. The latter, in turn, can supposedly be counted on to slowly morph into voluntary solidarity embodied in joint political institutions. In other words, the crucial assumption is that interdependence, though at first a mere fact, sharpens the sense of belonging together among Europe's political leaders and the population at large. A version of this theory of market-bred solidarity remains popular among those promoting the European project. Not only are the net benefits of increased economic integration assumed to be positive (and more or less evenly distributed across Member States), these benefits are also 'recognized and appreciated by those affected'.[2] On this hypothesis, further economic integration – almost in whatever form – is invariably a step in the right direction, so that when the process of federation begins to stall, pro-European decision-makers can turn their attention to breaking down economic barriers. Such a 'strategy of the side street'[3] – as one negotiator of the Treaty of Rome called it – has been a fixture in the history of the Communities. Market building is assumed to be community building by other means.

The eurozone crisis has dispelled this optimistic notion. The effects of economic interdependence have turned out to be much more ambivalent than had been assumed. This fact has given cause for serious scepticism about the long-standing reflex of European policymakers to manoeuvre out of any constitutional deadlock by going back to what is perceived as the real, and largely non-political, business of functional integration. Sadly, we have discovered that those who believed in 'the indirect penetration of the political by way of the economic'[4] were only half right. Economic integration has indeed had momentous political consequences. But the economic side street did not lead to a perception of a more expansive European community. Supporters of European integration tend to argue that this has not *yet* happened – that the single market has not been given enough time to do its beneficial work.[5] If that were the case, carrying on with market building would

Monnet (Lausanne 2017) 27). Monnet espoused a much more pragmatic and sophisticated view according to which integration in one sector changed the political situation in a way that creative political operators (like himself) could exploit. Yet he, along with most other founders of the European Communities, also had great faith in the capacity of the economy to facilitate and speed up the process. They expected the economy to have the great pedagogic virtue of driving home to Europeans their state of factual solidarity.

2   Philippe C Schmitter and Zoe Lefkofridi have described this as one of the main assumptions of a neo-functionalist approach to European integration ('Neo-Functionalism as a Theory of Disintegration' (2016) 1 Chinese Political Science Review 3).

3   Interview with Jean-Charles Snoy et d'Oppuers in MG Melchionni and R Ducci (eds), *La Genèse des Traités de Rome, Entretiens Inédits avec 18 Acteurs et Témoins de la Négociation* (Economica 2007) 175.

4   EB Haas, 'Technocracy, Pluralism and the New Europe' in JS Nye (ed), *International Regionalism* (Little Brown 1968) 65.

5   As one report noted, 'the barriers may have been abolished, the countless regulatory obstacles still make it difficult to achieve an harmonious life inside this common space' (A Lamassoure, 'The Citizen and the

appear to be the obvious answer to Europe's troubles. However, the correct diagnosis is not that economic forces have proved unable to overcome deep-seated remnants of nationalism. The crisis has shown that engineering more economic integration may have the unanticipated consequence of actually increasing resistance to closer political integration. This presents us with a challenge quite different from market building. It forces us to rethink the intellectual foundations of the European project.

II THE VIRTUES OF INTERDEPENDENCE: A HISTORICAL EXCURSUS

If the promoters of European integration have a credo, it can be found in the memorable phrase of the Schuman declaration: 'Europe will not be made all at once, or according to a single plan. It will be built through concrete achievements which will create a de facto solidarity.'[6] By force of repetition, these words have come to appear so transparent that their original meaning has remained largely unexplored. Yet, in order to understand the intellectual foundations of the European project, it is important to appreciate that the expression 'de facto solidarity' carried a lot of historical baggage in 1950. The language of the Schuman declaration implied a rejection of the methods used in earlier attempts at political integration, such as the experiment of the League of Nations, but also suggested a programme for correcting the mistakes.[7] A disillusionment with the impotence of interwar politics wedded the founders of the European Communities, and Jean Monnet in particular, to the belief that ringing proclamations have no lasting impact unless underpinned by clever economic and institutional engineering. Monnet's memoirs convey a vivid sense of how he despised such post-war initiatives as the Congress of Europe of 1948, which, as he saw it, tried to simply conjure a unified Europe into existence.[8] In his view, there was no use trying to loosen the grip of nationalist myths by mere words. It was to the world of tangible things that one had to look instead. The correct method was an evolutionary one, aimed at exploiting and enhancing interdependence among European states. Monnet, 'the first statesman of interdependence',[9] considered the latter to have a double virtue as a lever for federalisation. Interdependence increased costs to a lack of cooperation. But it

Application of Community law: Report to the President of the Republic' (2008) www.tib.eu/en/search/download/?tx_tibsearch_search%5Bdocid%5D=TIBKAT%3A733250513 accessed April 2018). The unspoken assumption, of course, is that more openness, be it of economic or of another kind, is naturally conducive to an absence of conflict ('harmonious life').

[6] These ringing words are also set at the beginning of the Commission's recent White Paper on the Future of Europe. Reflections and scenarios for the EU27 by 2025 (1 March 2017) https://ec.europa.eu/commission/sites/beta-political/files/white_paper_on_the_future_of_europe_en.pdf accessed April 2018.

[7] For Monnet's critical assessment of the League experiment, see J Monnet, *Memoirs* (Doubleday 1978) 80–81.

[8] Monnet dismissed the 'enthusiastic resolutions' of the Hague Conference of 1948 as exemplifying an approach that 'would lead nowhere' (ibid 272–73).

[9] F Duchêne, *Jean Monnet: The First Statesman of Interdependence* (Norton 1994).

also created the will to cooperate by giving rise to professional, as opposed to national, identities: identity as producers, consumers, etc.[10]

The posture of abandoning declaratory politics in favour of concrete achievements had been common in interwar Europe, as impatience with political action in a traditional, discredited sense grew. In France, this attitude harked back to the obsession of the Saint-Simonians with 'real things'. As the journal *Producteur* declared after the end of the First World War: 'Don't ask our opinions on domestic or foreign politics. At least for the moment, we can only respond indirectly with words such as: coal, nitrogen, fertilizer, hydroelectric power, credit, organising bureaus, technical knowledge, general knowledge.'[11] This programmatic statement – which prefigured the sentiment of the founders of the European Communities – was enthusiastically taken up by Francis Delaisi, one of the most vocal proponents of European cooperation in the 1920s. Delaisi thought that the main obstacle to unification lay in the discrepancy between outdated notions of politics and the facts of modern economy. There already exists a high degree of interdependence in Europe, a de facto solidarity, but it is obscured by nationalist rhetoric, Delaisi argued in his book *Political Myths and Economic Realities* (1927).[12] The recipe for European integration, according to Delaisi, was to allow 'persons, goods and capital to circulate freely', so that the modern cross-border economy would be able to 'operate along normal lines'.[13] With the tightening of economic ties, professional interests would begin to dominate, creating 'a bond of solidarity which [acts] as a counterpoise to national egoism.'[14] In fact, from this demythologised point of view, it is the consumer who is the real representative of the national interest.[15]

Delaisi was hardly original in emphasising the transformative and community-building power of interdependence. The nineteenth-century wave of globalisation had been accompanied by an optimistic mythology of communication as a source of solidarity. Railways, tunnels, the telegraph and cheap newspapers were counted on to strengthen 'the ties of solidarity between people nationally and internationally by allowing them to communicate more rapidly, putting them in contact, causing them to vibrate instantly in unison and creating a community of shared interests and emotions'.[16] Writers who advertised themselves as offering an objective description of the social reality were keen to point out that, when they spoke of interdependence, what they had in mind was not a socialist slogan or a mere moral prescription. The factual solidarity brought about by economic links had the advantage of being directly observable and could therefore survive as an object of study in a hard-

---

[10]   Monnet (n 7) 114.
[11]   Cited in C Bouglé, *Socialismes Français: Du 'Socialisme Utopique' à la 'Democratie Industrielle'* (Armand Colin 1932) 107.
[12]   F Delaisi, *Political Myths and Economic Realities* (Viking 1927) 546.
[13]   ibid 392.
[14]   ibid 262.
[15]   ibid 391.
[16]   C Gide, *L'Idée de Solidarité en tant que Programme Economique* (Giard & Brière 1893) 4.

headed scientific age. For example, recent discoveries in medicine had supposedly revealed the undeniable fact that 'the microbes of poor neighbourhoods poison rich neighbourhoods'.[17] There was thus a form of solidarity, a community of fate, between the rich and the poor living in proximity of each other, independently of any sense of mutual obligation. Once the shared nature of the public health problem became known – so the reasoning went – no high morality was involved in inducing the rich to clean up poor city areas and to finance the building of social housing. It was a matter of enlightened self-interest. The same principles applied to relationships between nations. Charles Gide, a French economist and social philosopher, argued mid-way through the so-called long peace of 1871–1914 that international relations had been pacified by motives not unlike those of the microbe-wary rich.[18] Technological progress and the expansion of markets had already created a factual community between countries. What remained to be done was to induce the world to embrace its state of factual interdependence, elevating the latter into a true, consciously willed community.[19]

This was the programme we find echoed in the Schuman declaration: employing expert knowledge about factual links between groups in order to expand their sense of community. The emphasis was less on old-style international cooperation than on building novel institutions apt by their very nature to promote the general interest. Delaisi called for the creation of 'organs of interdependence', i.e. 'permanent institutions, specially devised to keep in tow the forces which are ever diverging from [interdependence]'.[20] He was putting a modern twist on Saint-Simon's century-old view that the general interest does not prevail merely by the force of its rationality, but needs to be enshrined in a standing organisation. On the eve of the Congress of Vienna, Saint-Simon had laid out a plan for achieving peace in Europe through a political union among its warring powers. He took exception to the view that commercial ties are enough to guarantee peace.[21] Lasting peace and industrial development could only be achieved by creating a body whose members would naturally consider everything from a wider European perspective. The new institution would develop an appreciation for functional relationships between things, irrespective of national boundaries. For example, it would undertake industrial projects serving the common interest of Europe, such as building channels to link up Danube and the Rhine, or the latter with the Baltic Sea.[22]

---

[17] ibid 7.
[18] ibid.
[19] L Bourgeois, *Pour la Société des Nations* (E Fasquelle 1910) 273.
[20] Delaisi, *Political Myths* (n 12) 392.
[21] M Le Comte de Saint-Simon, *De la Réorganisation de la Société Européenne, ou de la Nécessité et des Moyens de Rassembler les Peuples de l'Europe en un seul Corps Politique, en Conservant à chacun son Indépendance Nationale* (A Égron 1814) 14.
[22] Saint-Simon (n 21) 60.

The result of such focus on concrete things would be a sea change in political thinking, Saint-Simon prophesied.[23] In assessing the latter's work, Friedrich Engels spoke of 'the complete absorption of politics by economics', noting that, in Saint-Simon, we find already very plainly expressed 'the idea of the future conversion of political rule over men into an administration of things'.[24] It is certainly true that the objectivity associated with the methods of increasing industrial production would later often be contrasted favourably with political bickering. On the other hand, the post-First World War slogan of putting fertilizer and coal before ideological divides was not about abandoning politics in favour of economics. Rather, it was an oblique method of doing politics, involving a redefinition of its relationship to the economic world. Change was to be effected not by sermonising or rhetoric, not by simply putting pen to paper, but by engineering the material conditions for a transformation in the political consciousness of the age. The role of the politician, Delaisi wrote, is to apprehend the hidden movements of the economic structure, its 'basic principles', in order to keep making necessary adjustments in the social edifice it supports.[25] For too long, the modern industrial enterprise had to wedge itself into the narrow national frame. This had produced a 'violent clash between facts and ideas'.[26] The task of politicians was to clear up 'the confusion of mind' by doing the long-overdue unwedging.[27]

A very similar aspiration underlay the supranational style of the European Communities.[28] The latter combined, in a Saint-Simonian vein, a set of novel institutions with an idea of a new kind of political action. Walter Hallstein, the first president of the European Commission, sought to capture the essence of the Community method by describing it as 'a common administration of general interests'.[29] We should, of course, not read too much theory into the organisational set-up that emerged from the Rome Treaty. It seems excessive to assert that there lurked 'a deep Saint-Simonian meaning'[30] in what had to be a negotiated compromise between more than one rival views. But we should also avoid the opposite extreme of dismissing entirely the lofty ideas expressed by the Communities'

---

[23] See D Fisichella, *Il potere nella società industriale* (Laterza 1995) 86.

[24] F Engels, *Anti-Dühring: Herr Eugen Dühring's Revolution in Science* (International Publishers 1966) 61.

[25] Delaisi, *Political Myths* (n 12) 86–87.

[26] ibid 86.

[27] ibid 45.

[28] Paul-Henri Spaak had read Francis Delaisi's works and found inspiration in the idea that economic interdependence can be harnessed to dispel nationalism (G Duchenne, 'Francis Delaisi. Un Economiste au service de l'Europe et de la Belgique (1926–1946)' in É Bussiere, O Dard and G Duchenne (eds), *Francis Delaisi, du Dreyfusisme à 'l'Europe Nouvelle'* (Peter Lang 2015) 162).

[29] Cited in M Schönwald, '"The Same – Should I Say – antenna". Gemeinsamkeiten und Unterschiede im europapolitischen Denken von Jean Monnet und Walter Hallstein (1958–1963)' (1999) 50 Pariser Historische Studien 269.

[30] RJ Dupuy, 'L'Organisation Internationale et l'Expression de la Volonté Générale' (1957) 61 Revue Générale de Droit International Public 570.

founders about turning economic integration into an alchemy for European political unity. Ernest Renan famously argued that an affective bond is needed for the
emergence of a nation. Mere interests, he said, can only give rise to a customs
union.[31] The founders of the European Economic Community, by contrast,
believed that, although the transubstantiation takes time, interests are the stuff
emotions are ultimately made of. 'We mobilised interests when we saw that the
emotional forces were not strong enough to carry and propel our movement', wrote
Hallstein. 'Hence this historically unique reversal of steps, which appears so odd and
"illogical" to the outsider: first economic pooling, then direct elections and then
political union.'[32] Far from being a counterexample, the German *Zollverein* was an
inspiration for their idea that economic solidarity could progressively lead to political unity.[33] European integration was a continuation of the same process which
had earlier given rise to nations.[34]

There was an important practical implication associated with the belief that the
economy paves the way to a sense of solidarity (provided it is allowed to work freely in
the proper transnational frame). For if obstacles on the road to political union
originate in a mental inertia, in an inability of politicians and the population to
liberate themselves from antiquated ideas and appreciate the fact of interdependence, then the correct approach when faced with resistance is to turn away from
high politics and instead concentrate on the economic machine. Changing the facts
on the ground, the latter will slowly bring about a more favourable psychological
climate. Federal Europe will follow, self-fulfilling, as an entity corresponding to the
emerging economic unit, in the same way that nations emerged as psychological
correlates to a smaller industrial system. This piece of wisdom became a counsel of
despair when the project of a European Defence Community fell through in 1954,
bringing down the projected European Political Union in its wake. Statesmen
started to circulate less ambitious memoranda where the emphasis was squarely
on economic cooperation. As one negotiator of the Rome Treaty put it, the earlier
deductive approach was now replaced by an inductive one: 'There was only one
possibility, which was to start by factual necessities, without discussing theory or
politics anymore, but discussing concrete things: economy, transportation, nuclear
energy, etc.'[35]

---

[31] E Renan, *What Is a Nation? and Other Political Writings* (Columbia UP 2018) 31.

[32] W Hallstein, *Die Europäische Gemeinschaft* (Econ 1979) 49.

[33] See the interview with Jean-Charles Snoy and d'Oppuers in Melchionni and Ducci (n 3) 168.

[34] 'Have I said clearly enough that the Community we have created is not an end in itself? It is a process
of change continuing that same process of change which, in an earlier period of history, produced our
national forms of life. Like our provinces in the past, our nations today must learn to live together
under common rules and institutions freely arrived at. The sovereign nations of the past can no longer
solve the problems of the present. They cannot ensure their own progress or control their own future.
The Community itself is only a stage on the way to the organised world of tomorrow' (Monnet
(n 7) 524).

[35] Interview with Johannes Linthorst Homan in Melchionni and Ducci (n 3) 60.

Yet it is misleading to say that, in the negotiations leading to Treaty of Rome, 'all priorities were unambiguously economic'.[36] In the light of the intellectual background sketched above, it becomes clear that the dichotomy between economic and political priorities offers a truncated perspective of the motives which determined the relaunch of European integration after the sudden setback of 1954. Economic integration has a political nature, declared Walter Hallstein with an Aristotelian flourish, since it 'alters the social character of people as zooa politika [political animals]'.[37] Needless to say, we do not need to assume that such soaring notions loomed large in the mind of everyone negotiating the Treaty of Rome. They clearly didn't. Many statesmen likely found all musings concerning the community-building power of the economy vacuous. A consensus on 'concrete things' was, nonetheless, facilitated by the availability of a theory which fitted excellently with the political deadlock of the mid 1950s. The self-fulfilling mindset both predicted such difficulties (the continuing hold of nationalistic 'myths') and offered a realistic way out ('unwedging' the economy from its nationalist frame). The theory, vague as it was, also imposed a language to which even the most down-to-earth politicians had to pay lip service. For example, historians tend to ascribe to the Netherlands an especially narrow pragmatic focus on the advantages of the common market.[38] However, it is interesting to note that the Dutch advertised their plan for general economic integration as the best means to reinforce a sense of solidarity and unity in Europe.[39] Opposition to the plan was often expressed in similar terms. Even Ludwig Erhard, the hard-nosed West German Minister of the Economy, felt obliged to pay tribute to reigning ideals. He framed his criticism of an economic community limited to the original six by describing it as a wrong way to deepen 'European consciousness'.[40]

---

[36] A Milward, 'The Origins of the Treaty of Rome' in Björn Hettne (ed), *Development Options in Europe* (Gothenburg 1988) 10.

[37] W Hallstein, 'Wirtschaftliche Integration als Faktor politischer Einigung' in Franz Greiss and Fritz W Meyer (eds), *Wirtschaft, Gesellschaft und Kultur. Festgabe für Alfred Müller-Armack* (Duncker & Humblot 1961) 61.

[38] For an emphasis on Dutch economic interests, in contrast to the German and French's allegedly more politically minded strategy, see W Loth, 'Der Weg nach Rom – Entstehung und Bedeutung der römischen Vertrgäge' (2007) 30 Integration 42. By contrast, François Duchêne has argued that the Beyen plan for a common market 'was not a standard rationalisation of Dutch trading interests', for it created 'doubt verging on opposition at home' (n 9). The idea that the fusion of national economies could be an instrument of greater political convergence was also influential within the European Commission (H von der Groeben, *Combat pour l'Europe: La Construction de la Communauté Européenne de 1958 à 1966* (Communauté Européenne 1985) 157).

[39] Duchêne (n 9) 273; AG Harryvan, *In Pursuit of Influence: The Netherlands' European Policy during the Formative Years of the European Union, 1952–1973* (Peter Lang 2009) 89.

[40] 'Persönliches Schreiben von Ludwig Erhard an die Bundesminister' (October 1956) 1 www.cvce.eu /content/publication/2006/10/30/efied619-6e1f-4e86-b99e-456c29d32737/publishable_de.pdf accessed April 2018.

III A SELF-FULFILLING MONETARY UNION

There is, more generally, little sense in asking whether economic or political motives should be cast as the main engine of European integration in some period. In the words of Ernest B Haas, '[t]he supranational style stresses the indirect penetration of the political by way of the economic because the "purely" economic decisions always acquire political significance in the minds of the participants'.[41] Rather than separating the two according to our own notions, we should consider the assumptions those involved in promoting integration themselves made about the relationship between the political and the economic sphere. This caveat also applies to the discussion as to whether the creation of the monetary union was primarily an economic or a political project. It was both. Many supporters of the single currency thought that there was a strong economic case for the euro and, precisely for this reason, also a political one, i.e. that the beneficial economic consequences of monetary integration would have desirable knock-on effects politically.[42]

The link between monetary and political integration was explicitly spelled out in the Werner Report, the first blueprint for the European Monetary Union (EMU) drafted in 1970. The Report described economic and monetary union as 'a leaven for the development of political union, which in the long run it cannot do without.'[43] This kind of pairing, with its implication that monetary integration could serve as a circuitous path towards high political goals, was particularly attractive in the early 1970s. For it appeared to many at that time that the earlier movement towards federalism had run out of steam.[44] Instead of spillover, the Community risked experiencing spillback.[45] In the presence of stagnation, if not backsliding, a push for monetary union could jump-start the Community in the same way integration had been relaunched during the malaise following the failure of the European Defence Community. Yet there was no consensus on the details of what was to be achieved.[46] The Werner Report was cautious in wording and short on detail. It

---

[41] Haas (n 4) 65.
[42] As Amy Verdun and Thomas Christiansen have written, 'there was a widely held view that the economic effects of EMU would strengthen the integration process, and facilitate its further creation, even towards further political integration' (' Policies, Institutions, and the Euro: Dilemmas of Legitimacy' in C Crouch (ed), *After the Euro: Shaping Institutions for Governance in the Wake of European Monetary Union* (OUP 2000) 169). The adoption of the single currency was not justified with reference to an existing political community that requires such an instrument. On the contrary, EMU itself was to be 'the tool through which the architects [hoped] to achieve such a polity' (ibid 176).
[43] 'Report to the Council and the Commission on the realisation by stages of Economic and Monetary Union in the Community' (Werner Report) 12 http://aei.pitt.edu/1002/1/monetary_werner_final.pdf accessed April 2018.
[44] For a contemporary description of this sense of disillusionment, see DL Coombes, *Politics and Bureaucracy in the European Community* (Sage 1970) 294.
[45] R Price, 'Political Aspects of an Enlarged European Community' (1972) 27 International Journal 112.
[46] The Werner Committee's report also refrained from formulating 'detailed proposals as to the institutional forms to be given to the different Community organs' (Werner Report (n 43) 12).

nevertheless sketched out a series of steps in which the creation of a political union could follow. The Report noted that an effective EMU would need to be buttressed by a centre of decision for economic policy with wide powers over national budgets and 'other domains of economic and social policy which will have been transferred to the Community level'.[47] Moreover, the grant of economic powers would have to 'go hand-in-hand with the transfer of a corresponding Parliamentary responsibility from the national plane to that of the Community'.[48]

Here, then, was a sequence of functional and political necessity with something as technical as a wish to stabilise exchange rates at one end and a powerful European Parliament at the other. It was a perfect illustration of the point that starting with 'real things' was a more reliable path to political union than aiming for it directly with an appeal to European solidarity. Of course, 'political union' hardly had the same meaning for those who regarded European federalism as a self-standing goal and the more pragmatically minded supporters of EMU who were interested simply in pooling enough powers at the centre for ensuring an effective coordination of economic policies. While the former viewed economic integration in instrumental terms, the latter, on the contrary, considered supranationalism as a means in the service of economic realignment – as the only credible way to keep fiscally adventurous EC countries to their commitments regarding the management of the economy.

The debates on EMU are often depicted as a confrontation between 'economists' and 'monetarists.[49] 'Economists' embraced the view that monetary union presupposed, and could therefore only come after, the convergence of the economies of participating countries.[50] Hence their scepticism regarding any form of monetary integration not flanked by new powers at the European level in order to ensure that deeper fundamentals underlying exchange rates are also brought into line. Germans policymakers, in particular, thought that the French were in favour of monetary union because it would help them to solve their problems without going through the painful process of reforming their economy. The French indeed mostly fell into the camp of 'monetarists'. They argued that there was no need to wait for economic convergence before embarking on EMU since joint monetary policy would itself cause the synchronisation of national business cycles. This optimistic idea became known as the 'locomotive theory'.[51] Opponents were quick to point out that it fitted rather too well with the interests of the countries supporting it: to force the German

[47]   ibid 13.
[48]   ibid.
[49]   For an early account, see L Tsoukalis, *The Politics and Economics of European Monetary Integration* (Allen & Unwin 1977).
[50]   I Maes, 'On the Origins of the Franco-German EMU Controversies' (2004) 17 European Journal of Law and Economics 21.
[51]   See D Wolf, 'Neofunctionalism and Intergovernmentalism Amalgamated: The Case of EMU' in A Verdun (ed), *The Euro: European Integration Theory and Economic and Monetary Union* (Rowman & Littlefield 2002) 45.

Central Bank to automatically support them at times of financial turbulence without paying the price of reducing their budgetary sovereignty.[52] Yet, however justified such suspicious attitude may have been, the 'monetarists' had the functionalist legacy of the founding fathers on their side.[53] If monetary and economic integration were inseparable, as the 'economists' claimed, then wasn't this enough to prove that the adoption of one component of a fully sustainable EMU would quickly lead to the other?[54]

The 'locomotive theory' can also be described as a theory of self-fulfilling monetary union. At its centre was the claim that monetary integration brings about its own conditions of success. A similar line of argument was later developed against those who sought to show that a Community-wide monetary integration was incompatible with the theory of optimum currency area (OCA).[55] The theory of optimum currency area (OCA) claims that there are both costs and benefits associated with the adoption of a common currency in some area (or irrevocably fixing the exchange rates between existing currencies). The most important cost is the loss of the ability to absorb country-specific shocks by devaluation. Crucially, this cost can be attenuated by some forms of economic integration, such as a unified labour market, which offer alternative means to deal with country-specific downturns. From the perspective of the 'economists', these factors can thus be treated as a set of preconditions for moving forward with monetary union. In other words, as long as the unemployed cannot be expected to move in sufficient numbers from crisis-stricken countries to other parts of the Community, and as long as other adjustment mechanisms produced by economic integration are not yet present, the Community fails to satisfy the conditions of an optimum currency area (i.e. the cost of monetary inflexibility linked to a single currency would outweigh any benefits).[56]

The answer suggested by the self-fulfilling approach was that monetary integration would itself, locomotive-like, produce the kind of economic environment required by the OCA. For example, it would speed up the movement of labour inside the Community, with the consequence that there would be less need for future suffering countries to devalue themselves out of a crisis. In a working paper

[52] DC Kruse, *Monetary Integration in Western Europe: EMU, EMS, and Beyond* (Butterworths 1980) 69.

[53] Monnet himself lobbied in favour of creating a European Reserve Fund. The latter would force EC governments to jointly manage their reserves, which would, in turn, lead to an economic union (Duchêne (n 9) 335).

[54] As G Carli, the governor of the Italian Central Bank, put it: '[i]n accepting the fact that monetary unification precedes economic unification one must bear in mind that the former cannot last unless it is followed by the latter in a fairly short space of time. Monetary unification is thus instrumental' (cited in H James, *Making the European Monetary Union: The Role of the Committee of Central Bank Governors and the Origins of the European Central Bank* (Harvard UP 2012) 74).

[55] For the theory of optimal currency area as an argument against the single currency in Europe, see F Masini, 'European Integration: Contrasting Models and Perspectives' in R Fiorentini and G Montani (eds), *The European Union and Supranational Political Economy* (Routledge 2015) 53

[56] See eg B Eichengreen, 'Is Europe an Optimum Currency Area?' in S Borner and H Grubel (eds), *The European Community after 1992: Perspectives from the Outside* (Palgrave Macmillan 1992) 139.

defending the idea of a single currency, the European Commission noted that '[t]he costs of doing without exchange rate changes as an adjustment instrument will gradually diminish over time as economic integration becomes deeper'.[57] A similarly dynamic perspective was required to assess the benefits of the single currency, the Commission argued.[58] By locking in a credible policy deemed favourable to the business environment, the EMU would create 'optimistic expectations' which may 'become self-fulfilling'.[59] If this was wishful thinking on the Commission's part, it was not without endorsement from academics. Several studies were published in the 1990s arguing that EMU could obtain its justification, as it were, retroactively.[60]

But even if the debate among experts was tying itself in knots with such arguments, it is hardly likely that many 'economists' were convinced by the self-fulfilling story of the 'monetarists'. Why, then, did Germans agree to an asymmetrical monetary union? A pivotal factor was the acceptance of capital liberalisation by other prospective members, resulting in a flurry of measures devised by the Commission and directed at opening capital markets in Europe.[61] German experts calculated that free cross-border movements of capital would pave the way to economic convergence within the future currency area. Exposure of national governments to the daily supervision of financial markets was thought to introduce an equally, if not more, effective discipline than formal sanctions enshrined in legal rules.

For all their abhorrence of French dirigisme, German policymakers with ordo-liberal leanings revealed at this point an adherence to a set of ideas remarkably similar to the Saint-Simonian tradition. Their belief in the primacy of the economic order[62] was not very different from the obsession of this tradition with 'real things'. Neither took the Marxist line that politics was *inevitably* the expression of deeper economic forces. The idea they shared was rather that politics *must* be made permeable to economic fundamentals. Both decried the tendency of politics to veer off and become abstracted from functional necessities. There was an important role for political action, well beyond that of the night watchman state of extreme

---

[57] European Commission, 'One Market, One Money. An evaluation of the potential benefits and costs of forming an economic and monetary union' (1990) 24 European Economy 1 ec.europa.eu/econo my_finance/publications/pages/publication7454_en.pdf accessed April 2018.

[58] For an analogous emphasis on the dynamic gains from integration at the time when the Treaty of Rome was signed, see C Kaupa, *The Pluralist Character of the European Economic Constitution* (Hart 2016) 30.

[59] European Commission (n 57) 21–22.

[60] See eg J A Frankel and A K Rose, 'Is EMU More Justifiable en post than ex ante?' (1997) 41 European Economic Review 753; J A Frankel and A K Rose, 'The Endogeneity of the Optimum Currency Area Criteria' (1998) 108 Economic Journal 1009.

[61] K Dyson and K Featherstone, *The Road to Maastricht: Negotiating Economic and Monetary Union* (OUP 1999) 710

[62] For this idea in the run-up to the adoption of the single currency, see K Dyson, 'Hans Tietmeyer, Ethical Ordo-Liberalism and the Architecture of EMU. Getting the Fundamentals Right', in K Dyson and I Maes (eds), *Architects of the Euro: Intellectuals in the Making of European Monetary Union* (OUP 2016)

liberalism, but this role had more to do with framing and facilitation than with giving expression to a form of rationality independent of economics.

There is thus a sense in which the euro was a political project, but of a quite different kind than usually depicted: less an imposition of a predetermined political programme in wilful disregard of economic rationality than an attempt at harnessing the ordering power of economic laws to produce a new kind of enlightened politics. Michel Foucault has offered us a perceptive analysis of an earlier project of a similar nature. He described the ideological undercurrents of the liberalising agenda formulated and promoted in the aftermath of the Second World War by Ludwig Erhard in the Anglo-American occupation zone. Compared to other anti-interventionist experiments carried out in Europe at this time, the German programme of price deregulation had an important difference, argued Foucault: it was about more than specifically economic interventions in that it revolved around the legitimacy of the state.[63] A reference to a historical or legal legitimacy was equally unavailable to a nascent German central authority. Nor could a collective will properly manifest itself in a divided and occupied country. But what if price deregulation could itself generate a new state? If the existing administrative authority could create a space of economic freedoms, then the voluntary adherence by individuals to this framework might be considered as a form of consent to any decision aimed at securing the freedoms. The institution of economic freedoms would function 'as a syphon, as it were, as a point of attraction for the formation of a political sovereignty ... It was a matter of finding a juridical expedient in order to ask from an economic regime what could not be directly asked from constitutional law, or from international law, or even quite simply from the political partners.'[64]

Devising economic expedients for gaining what is not granted politically – this is exactly the kind of insidious strategy many have suspected to have been at work during the adoption of the single currency.[65] Yet the notion of a functionalist conspiracy flouting the will of the people fails to do justice to the main contention of the self-fulfilling theory, i.e. that the operation of the market is itself productive of a quasi-political community. The accusation of deception falls flat. The sociologist Robert K Merton described a self-fulfilling prophesy as 'a *false* definition of the situation evoking a new behavior which makes the original false conception come *true*'.[66] Such 'specious validity', he went on to say, 'perpetuates a reign of error', for

---

[63] M Foucault, *The Birth of Biopolitics: Lectures at the Collège de France, 1978–79* (Palgrave Macmillan 2008) 82.

[64] ibid 83.

[65] Ernst-Wolfgang Böckenförde, a highly prominent German voice, has claimed that a lack of frankness concerning the ultimate goal exemplifies the 'inauthenticity' of the whole European project since 1957. 'What is really wanted is a political integration, but officially one has chosen the indirect path via economic integration and is banking on an "inherent constraint" that this integration is supposed to give rise to' (EW Böckenförde, 'Which Path Is Europe Taking?' in EW Böckenförde *Constitutional and Political Theory: Selected Writings*, vol I (OUP, 2017) 356).

[66] RK Merton, 'The Self-fulfilling Prophecy' (1948) 8 Antioch Review 195.

'the prophet will cite the actual course of events as proof that he was right from the very beginning'.[67] While analogous in character, the act to launch a self-fulfilling monetary union does not merit the same reproach. No falsehood is involved. As we saw above, the politicians present at the foundation of the EEC also made no secret of their strategy of reversing the supposedly natural order of things. Theirs was less a subterfuge than a well-thought-out vision of politics.

For those who hold fast to a traditional constitutionalist outlook, the asymmetric EMU is deeply flawed because it disconnects money as a 'technical-functional construct' from the holistic sphere of politics, ignoring the fact that 'the monetary system of a people reflects what this people does, wants, endures, all its political and social happenings as well as mental realities.'[68] The conclusion is that the single currency can only come after all these more fundamental things have converged in the European space – as the coronation of a new political community (in the same way the 'economists' thought that monetary integration should be a coronation of prior economic convergence). Otherwise it is bound to have a free-floating and artificial character. Analogously to the theory of OCAs, this conception posits a set of cultural preferences (what the 'people does, wants, endures') as indicia for deciding whether an area is ripe for sharing a currency. However, as in the case of the OCA, the objection of those who had their sights on a euro polity would likely have been that these cultural conditions are endogenous, i.e. forged by the operation of the single market.[69] If indeed, as Walter Hallstein theorised, economic integration alters the character of Europeans as political animals, then the new currency, be it free-floating at first, will gradually bring about new 'mental realities'. In other words, it will create the political preconditions of its own success.

Here is where the comparison with the German post-war project of regeneration is especially illuminating. According to the ordoliberal reformers, the genesis of the state from the non-state space of economic freedom was not at all meant to happen by way of a top-down imposition. The idea was rather the opposite.

> This economic institution, the economic freedom that from the start it is the role of this institution to guarantee and maintain, produces something even more real, concrete, and immediate than a legal legitimization; it produces a permanent consensus of all those who may appear as agents within these economic processes, as investors, workers, employers, and trade unions. All these economic partners produce a consensus, which is a political consensus, inasmuch as they accept this economic game of freedom ... The free market, the economically free market, binds and manifests political bonds.[70]

---

[67] ibid.

[68] Böckenförde (n 65) 356.

[69] As one proponent of functionalism has put it, European integration brings about an 'endogenous common preference' (F Schimmelfennig, 'European Integration in the Euro Crisis: The Limits of Postfunctionalism' (2014) 36 Journal of European Integration 330).

[70] Foucault (n 63) 84–85.

This description provides a theoretically sophisticated counterpoint to the notion that a currency must be embedded in a pre-existing political community of which it is merely an expression. It is, admittedly, debatable whether the political thinking of German ordoliberal reformers was really as elaborate as Foucault suggests. Foucault himself concedes that he is teasing out what remains largely implicit in their writings.[71] Similarly, it would be quite incorrect to suggest that all, or even many, of those who were involved in the creation of the euro held carefully thought-out views about its political ramifications. But, in this case also, we can seek to synthesise as something approaching a theory the beliefs which made the euro's proponents curiously unreceptive to arguments concerning the possibly divisive effects of the new kind of economic reality that was being ushered in.[72] It appears that at least part of the explication why such pessimism had no traction among European policy-makers is that it was squarely at odds with the set of unspoken assumptions described here as the self-fulfilling mindset. The latter postulated an unambiguously positive relationship between economic integration and political convergence. From this point of view, the precise way the political would be indirectly penetrated by the economic did not matter. For the operation of the market was expected to bring Europe together and thus, almost by definition, create a sense of being together, in whatever shape or form, by reinforcing its incipient 'community of shared interests and emotions'.[73] To introduce the euro would be to carry on a successful decades-old project whose very essence was to bank on the providential character of economic integration.

IV THE EUROPEANISATION BACKLASH

Yet doubts soon emerged about how exactly to carry on. Only a few years after the launch of the monetary union, amid a general mood of celebration, the German Foreign Minister Joschka Fischer proclaimed the Monnet method to be in crisis. Apart from this note of caution, his famous Humboldt speech of May 2000 was a tribute to what had been achieved up to that point. The problem, in his view, was that functional integration had resulted in an overcomplicated institutional jumble incapable of giving rise to a European identity.[74] Fischer argued that, although the Monnet method had been successful in earlier stages of integration, it was not up to the task of endowing the European Union with a truly democratic character. Great

---

[71] ibid 82.

[72] For such arguments, see eg M Feldstein, 'The Political Economy of the European Economic and Monetary Union: Political Sources of an Economic Liability' (1997) 11 Journal of Economic Perspectives 41.

[73] For this expression, see Gide (n 16).

[74] J Fischer, 'Vom Staatenverbund zur Föderation – Gedanken über die Finalität der europäischen Integration' (12 May 2000) www.cvce.eu/de/obj/rede_von_joschka_fischer_uber_die_finalitat_der_europaischen_integration_berlin_12_mai_2000-de-4cd02fa7-d9d0-4cd2-91c9-2746a3297773.html accessed April 2018.

hopes were therefore placed in the convention method which was to experience its high tide in the ensuing period. It only took a few short years, however, before this method, too, was perceived to be in crisis. Its product, the Constitutional Treaty, was shot down by referendums in France and the Netherlands in 2005. At this juncture, the more historically minded protagonists of integration may have had a sense of déjà vu. There were clear analogies with the crisis of 1954. Back to real things, away from nominalism, the solutions advocated had a distinctly Saint-Simonian ring. The Monnet method was suddenly said to be staging a renaissance.[75] But when the eurocrisis struck, it was again claimed that we are witnessing the 'end of Monnet'.[76] One 'veteran Eurocrat' was quoted as saying that the European Union 'was not designed to deal with a crisis'.[77]

Is this really true? The contours of the 'Monnet method' have inevitably become blurred over time. But whatever meaning is given to this expression, it is difficult to deny that Jean Monnet himself was very much aware of the salutary effects of crises. It is at such times, he thought, that the existence of a de facto solidarity between the Member States is driven home to their leaders. The union of peoples is not a natural thing, Monnet remarked; 'they have to be pushed by necessity'.[78] Crises would build awareness of Europe as an interconnected economic unit.[79] The idea was that, first, a community of fact comes into existence and is then transformed into a true political community through jolts of consciousness provoked by moments of acute difficulties. As if to prove this point, the eurocrisis has made it possible to find agreement on things that would have otherwise been blocked by Member States. The latter had long resisted granting the EU supervisory powers in budgetary matters, but the arrival of a period of turbulence quickly eased the way to the adoption of a raft of measures empowering the Commission. The embryonic system of economic governance outlined in the Maastricht Treaty was now hastily finished up at the level of secondary EU legislation and intergovernmental agreements (the 'Six-Pack' of December 2011, the 'Two-Pack' of March 2013, the Fiscal Compact of March 2012).[80] A realisation that potentially ruinous links exist between private banks and sovereign borrowers has pushed towards a banking union. More grandly still, a fully fledged political union has come to be envisaged as a necessary add-on to any solution capable of terminally fixing the defects of the original EMU. These

---

[75]   W Wessels and A Faber, 'Vom Verfassungskonvent zurück zur "Methode Monnet"? Die Entstehung der "Road Map" zum EU-Reformvertrag unter deutscher Ratspräsidentschaft' (2007) 20 Integration 377.

[76]   'Charlemagne: the End of Monnet' *The Economist* (3 September 2011) www.economist.com/node/21528269/all-comments?page=4 accessed April 2018.

[77]   ibid.

[78]   'Dialogue avec Alan Watson, entretiens des 15–16 novembre et 2–3 décembre 1971' in H Rieben, C Camperio-Tixier and F Nicod, *A l'Ecoute de Jean Monnet* (Fondation Jean Monnet pour l'Europe, 2004) 340.

[79]   Monnet (n 7) 428.

[80]   F Schimmelfennig, 'European Integration in the Euro Crisis: The Limits of Postfunctionalism' (2014) 36 Journal of European Integration 330.

developments have proceeded quite in the way Monnet imagined. They seem to bear out perfectly the prediction of neo-functionalists that European economic integration is self-sustaining.[81] The free workings of the market produced a spillover from an incomplete EMU as gaps in its original architecture unleashed 'neofunctionalist forces' which led to a crisis.[82] Further integration then became feasible by virtue of 'endogenous preferences' (what was desired earlier changed what was desired now).[83] Seen through the lens of this story, the eurocrisis appears as a textbook case of the kind of sequential dynamic characteristic of European integration. Appropriately enough, it seems, commentators have spoken of the 'revenge of neo-functionalism'.[84]

The idea that the philosophy of the founding fathers has been entirely vindicated is not true, however. Most importantly, the belief that factual solidarity has a tendency to morph into political solidarity has endured a serious battering. With uncanny prescience, Milton Friedman warned in 1997 that, given the absence of an effective fiscal compensatory mechanism, the euro was likely to 'exacerbate political tensions by converting divergent shocks that could have been readily accommodated by exchange rate changes into divisive political issues'.[85] The point is not that the adoption of the euro has been revealed to have been a bad idea. One may persist in believing that the benefits of a single European currency outweigh the costs and yet perceive flaws in the argument that the deepening of economic unity through the breakdown of barriers always favours political union. The operation of the market may indeed give rise to complementary economic identities, such as producer and consumer. As we saw, the founders of the European Communities had a tendency to interpret this process as the supplanting – or at least tempering – of divisive nationalist passions by more rational social relationships. But the entrenchment of categories such as debtor and creditor nation does not necessarily have a pacifying effect. Formally speaking, of course, perfect complementarity reigns here, since, in virtue of the conventions of accounting, one cannot be a debtor without there being somewhere a creditor. The problem is also, in some sense, a shared one, just like the microbial problem between rich and poor neighbours described above. It is,

---

[81] See A Moravcsik 'Preferences and Power in the European Community: A Liberal Intergovernmentalist Approach' (1993) 31 Journal of Common Market Studies 474.

[82] E Jones, RD Kelemen and S Meunier 'Failing Forward? The Euro Crisis and the Incomplete Nature of European Integration' (2016) 49 Comparative Political Studies 1027.

[83] Schimmelfennig (n 80) 330.

[84] I Cooper 'The Euro Crisis and the Revenge of Neo-functionalism' EUObserver (21 September 2011) https://euobserver.com/opinion/113682 accessed April 2018; H Zimmermann 'The Euro Trilemma, or: How the Eurozone Fell into a Neofunctionalist Legitimacy Trap' (2016) Journal of European Integration 426.

[85] M Friedman, 'Whither the EMU?' Wall Street Journal (20 June 1997) 10. As noted by Jeffry Frieden and Stefanie Walter, '[r]ather than build cohesion among the members of the Economic and Monetary Union, the crisis has driven countries into warring camps, each side blaming the other for the crisis and for the extraordinarily slow recovery' ('Understanding the Political Economy of the Eurozone Crisis' (2017) 20 Annual Review of Political Science 381).

nevertheless, not the kind of complementarity that creates affective bonds among the European population. The sharing of a collective economic problem (i.e. the situation described as 'de factory solidarity' in the Schuman declaration) can, on the contrary, make differences more salient. When interdependence is felt as a burden, or as a shackle, its psychological effect may be to create a sense of losing control, kindling a desire to reassert national sovereignty.

In the nineteenth century, it was often taken for granted that division of labour fostered a sense of unity. The Ricardian trade theory offered a powerful conceptual framework for elevating this vision to the international plane.[86] Against this intellectual background, it is easy to understand the attitude of Paul-Henri Spaak who was content to rely on the general notion that factual solidarity had beneficial political consequences for the European project and left it to experts to determine how precisely to engineer such interdependence.[87] The authors of the Spaak Report duly obliged, sketching out a road to a unified Europe as a 'powerful unit of production' characterised by advanced division of labour.[88] Europe has indeed become one large factory from an economic point of view.[89] Especially after the great enlargement of 2004, Western production technology has been profitably combined with Eastern labour. As predicted by the Spaak Report, labour has flowed from one edge of Europe to another.[90] All this has undoubtedly engendered new forms of interdependence, but often of a rather painful kind. To mention just one typical example: in 2004, workers at two Siemens plants in Germany agreed to work five additional hours per week without extra pay in order to prevent their jobs from being relocated to Hungary.[91]

Workers in East and West were now subject to the same economic forces, sharing a 'community of fate', without there being a heightened sense of solidarity in the offing. When the British journalist James Meek followed a disassembled Cadbury chocolate factory to its destination in Skarbimierz, Poland, he asked the president of the local economic zone: what about solidarity with the British workers who lost their jobs when their factory got moved to Poland? The answer:

---

[86] Even those, like Thomas Malthus, who argued that free trade could be harmful to the interests of a particular country, admitted that it would serve the interests of Europe as a whole (see DA Irwin, *Against the Tide: An Intellectual History of Free Trade* (Princeton UP 1996) 97).

[87] Interview with Johannes Linthorst Homan in Melchionni and Ducci (n 3) 60.

[88] 'Rapport des chefs des délégations aux Ministres des Affaires Etrangères' (21 April 1956) 13 http://aei .pitt.edu/996/1/Spaak_report_french.pdf accessed April 2018.

[89] R Baldwin, *The Great Convergence: Information Technology and the New Globalization* (Belknap Press 2016) 133.

[90] On the large scale of the East–West migration after the 2004 EU enlargement, see eg T Baas, H Brücker and A Hauptmann 'Labor Mobility in the Enlarged EU: Who Wins, Who Loses?' in M Kahanec, K Zimmermann (eds), *EU Labor Markets After Post-Enlargement Migration* (Springer 2010) 50.

[91] B Eichengreen, *The European Economy Since 1945: Coordinated Capitalism and Beyond* (Princeton UP 2007) 411

These processes are going on all over the world, and the difference these days is that Western Europe society is noticing it more. These countries, until recently, were totally indifferent; they didn't pay attention to even more painful processes going on in Eastern Europe. The only advice they had for us back then was for us to work harder. We took it as good advice.[92]

Much to their chagrin, workers in one part of Europe were suddenly forced to pay attention to the industriousness of their colleagues elsewhere. The notion that the virtues of openness slowly work their way into the consciousness of people is at the centre of the philosophy of European integration. But, in this case, the interdependence resulting from openness took the form of a perceived conflict of interests.

This is indeed the crux of the matter: there is no European exceptionalism when it comes to the effects of economic openness. Of course, we do not have to see economic integration in Europe as a zero-sum game. It may very well be true that, in the long run, it is beneficial to the European population as a whole and that this fact will eventually be 'recognized and appreciated by those affected'.[93] Yet, quite apart from overall efficiency, at least in the short term international division of labour creates both winners and losers. This means that resistance to European integration cannot be laid at the door of something external to it, like the hold of nationalist 'myths'. It used to be thought, in the same vein, that the nineteenth-century wave of globalisation fell victim to outside pressures produced by militarism or political nationalism. Not so. Historians now emphasise that 'a political backlash developed in response to the actual or perceived distributional effects of globalization ... Far from being destroyed by unforeseen and exogenous political events, globalization, at least in part, destroyed itself.'[94] It is a fact worth pondering that, in the French referendum on the Constitutional Treaty in 2005, supporters tended to be those with higher skills, opponents those without.[95] Trade theory predicts that the first group mostly gains from economic openness in Europe, the latter group loses.

To say that the present Europeanisation backlash, like the globalisation backlash of the late nineteenth century (or the one we are witnessing today), is largely the product of its own internal dynamic does not amount to laying exclusive stress on economic factors. The distinction between economic and non-economic (cultural or identity-related) causes in the debate on populism is itself misconceived, for it often obscures the intimate interaction between the two. The phenomenon of secessionism in Europe is an excellent illustration. This phenomenon must be

---

[92]   J Meek 'Somerdale to Skarbimierz' *London Review of Books* (20 April 2017) www.lrb.co.uk/v39/no8/ james-meek/somerdale-to-skarbimierz accessed April 2018.
[93]   See Schmitter and Lefkofridi (n 2).
[94]   KH O'Rourke and JG Williamson, Globalization and History. *The Evolution of a Nineteenth-Century Atlantic Economy* (MIT Press 1999) 287.
[95]   R Findlay and KH O'Rourke, *Power and Plenty: Trade, War, and the World Economy in the Second Millennium* (Princeton UP 2009) 542.

truly baffling for someone who believes, like Jean Monet did, that economic integration goes hand in hand with the expansion of political communities. If the latter hypothesis holds, then creating a larger economic unit (like the 'powerful unit of production' mentioned in the Spaak Report) is bound to bring in its wake a more expansive political identity. Although this does not, as Monnet emphasised, obviate the need for the hard practical business of forging political unity, it makes it considerably easier. This belief in an unambiguously reinforcing relationship between economic and political unity (when applied to European integration) is precisely what I described above as the theory of self-fulfilling Europe. How, then, to explain the present puzzling conjunction between economic integration and political fragmentation? Are we witnessing another case of nationalist – or in this case regionalist – passions obstinately hampering adjustment with economic realities?

In fact, there is much more method in this madness. Underlying the secession movements is itself a form of rational adjustment. The creation of a continent-wide system of economic freedom protected by international legal rules has changed the cost–benefit calculus which favoured political integration in nineteenth-century Europe. The reason why numerous German statelets acceded to the *Zollverein* of 1834 was not only, nor even primarily, the resolution to sacrifice their provincial self-interest on the high altar of German unity. What weighed in the balance was rather the consideration that, in a territory rife with protectionist barriers, it is exceedingly cold outside an expanding customs union. Political independence carries a very high economic cost in such a setting for it means limited access to markets across the borders of other states. The benefits of guaranteed economic openness, along with those of collective defence, outweighed the cost of having to submit to the majority vote in a larger political pool.[96] The achievement of the EU (in addition to the rules of GATT/WTO) has been to produce a much more benign environment in this regard – an economic umbrella, complementing the security umbrella provided by NATO. If Catalonia is assured of access to the single market should it become independent, its population may reach the conclusion, in an entirely rational way, that the cost of being part of the Spanish state now looms larger (at least in their eyes) than the benefits (which have been revised downward as a result of the presence of the EU). To see that the old cost–benefit calculus is still at work, one only needs to observe the debate on Brexit. Is the cost of weathering the cold winds of globalisation superior to that of having to submit to the strictures of common European rules? Such are the eminently pragmatic terms in which Brexit is discussed in the UK. In other countries, a similar focus on material interests as opposed to sentiments would perhaps give offence. Yet the pull of the argument is the same, especially if there are no cold winds to be endured as a result of secession with continuing EU membership.

---

[96] For an analysis of the size of states along these lines, see A Alesina and E Spolaore, *The Size of Nations* (MIT Press 2005).

Secessionism is backlash only in the sense that it draws force from the successful establishment of the single market. It has not thrived on rhetoric aimed against the EU; quite the contrary. The effects of the divisive discourse which economic integration has fed, and sometimes generated, can be discerned elsewhere. The sinking in of this discourse in the public opinion of Member States has stacked the cards in favour of a less redistributional, or less solidaristic, form of centralisation at the European level. Before allowing ourselves to feel overly reassured by the onward march of European integration as a result of the eurocrisis, we should attend carefully to the nature of the organisation that is being forged. From the point of view of economics, there are several very different ways of completing the EMU: (1) to maintain fiscal policy decentralised and arrange for a supranational supervision/enforcement mechanism; or (2) to centralise budgetary decision-making in Brussels by setting up a true fiscal union.[97] Even if these solutions were functionally equivalent in terms of ensuring financial stability, they have radically different implications for the future of the EU. The creation of a common eurozone budget large enough to cover the smoothing of asymmetric shocks in Member States in need of help would, in all likelihood, spark a chain reaction towards political union. The logic for Germany would be that, 'if we are going to have a transfer union anyway, we need a political union to control things'.[98] The decentralising solution, by contrast, builds on what has been called 'the logic of discipline'.[99] It requires European institutions charged with budgetary surveillance and enforcement to be as neutral as possible. The European Commission, instead of being an active promoter of the common European interest à la Saint-Simon, would be drifting towards something like the German *Kartellamt* (the competition authority) writ large – or, alternatively, it would be yielding its crisis-management functions to an independent body modelled on the European Central Bank.[100] The European debate in Germany has been wavering between these two options. If, in Germany, recent years have witnessed an abiding fear of a slide into a transfer union, this is presumably in no small measure because of the experience of 'real solidarity', i.e. of sitting in the same boat with 'others', which accompanied the eurocrisis. It is yet another example of how, contrary to the self-fulfilling theory, de facto solidarity originating in economic integration can work against the emergence of a voluntary, actively willed solidarity.

[97] See MK Brunnermeier, H James and JP Landau, *The Euro and the Battle of Ideas* (Princeton UP 2016) 101.

[98] See Q Peel 'Germany and Europe: A Very Federal Formula' *Financial Times* (9 February 2012) www.ft.com/content/31519b4a-5307-11e1-950d-00144feabdc0 accessed April 2018.

[99] A Roberts, *The Logic of Discipline: Global Capitalism and the Architecture of Government* (OUP 2010).

[100] The German debate on the proposed European Monetary Fund has largely revolved around the question as to how independent the body should be. While the coalition agreement between CDU/CSU and SPD (signed in February 2018) envisages a European Monetary Fund 'anchored in EU law and controlled by parliament', Angela Merkel has spoken in favour of an independent body, like the ECB (G Chazan, 'Merkel pressed on transfer union fears' *Financial Times* (5 February 2018) www.ft.com/content/bd76b754-0a76-11e8-8eb7-42f857ea9f09 accessed April 2018).

What is the conclusion to be taken away from this? Clearly, it is not that the deepening of the single market is harmful and should be put on hold, if not reversed. One prominent supporter and well-wisher of the European project has, indeed, called for a pause in integration efforts in order to re-engage with the wider public lost along the way.[101] The problem with this view is the apparent assumption that setbacks like the foundering of the Constitutional Treaty and Brexit ('the latest symptom')[102] exemplify a common phenomenon: the psychology of nations[103] lagging behind the technocratic avant-garde. The sin which has supposedly been committed is to have ploughed ahead with integration without explaining its benefits. I am pleading for a less educational approach – or for one that is educational in another sense. Rather than seeking to ram the implications of interdependence into the consciousness of the European population, as the founding fathers were hoping to do, we – the scholars – should educate ourselves about the subtle ways in which the economic actually, as a matter of observed fact, penetrates the political. The theory of self-fulfilling Europe offers an overly simplified picture of this relationship and should be laid to rest. In addition to its conceptual flaws, the theory is contradicted by the empirical observation that partial steps towards European integration, far from furthering a pro-European sentiment among the population, have rather tended to create a political backlash.[104] Much is certainly to be salvaged from the idea that consciousness of interdependence facilitates the solution of collective action problems, sometimes to the point of engendering among those affected a willingness to be locked into the same political community. But we should also be on our guard against scenarios where the attempt to harness the providential power of the economy proves self-defeating.

---

[101]   H Védrine, *Sauver l'Europe* (Liana Lévi 2016) 50.
[102]   ibid 19.
[103]   This was Walter Hallstein's expression ((n 32) 49).
[104]   L Guiso, P Sapienza and L Zingales 'Monnet's Error?' (2015) 31 Economic Policy 247.

4

The Authoritarian Neoliberalism of the EU

Legal Form and International Politico-Economic Sources

Magnus Ryner

I INTRODUCTION

In its management of the eurozone crisis, the European Union (EU) reformed its economic policy regime and forged what has become known as the New Economic Governance (NEG). The NEG is constituted by an ensemble of directives, regulations and measures. It consists of the Six-Pack (five regulations[1] and one directive),[2] the Two-Pack (two regulations)[3] and the European Fiscal Compact (or the Treaty on Stability, Coordination and Governance in the Economic and Monetary Union (TSCG)). Together, they tighten up surveillance and procedures pertaining to the 1996 Growth and Stability Pact. As such, they form a quid pro quo for measures in the field of monetary policy, which attenuated the prohibition against the European Central Bank (ECB) lending to EU institutions and Member States, but which nevertheless became necessary to save Economic and Monetary Union (EMU) against collapse: the European Stability Mechanism (ESM), as well as the Long-Term Refinancing Operations (LTROs) but above all the Outright Monetary Transactions (OMT) of the ECB.

The NEG has been the object of several criticisms. Heterodox economists have critiqued it on substantive grounds for its damaging policy orientation, which is held to be based on a misdiagnosis of the crisis. Rather than addressing the fundamental problems arising out of deficient aggregate demand in a broadly self-contained continental economy and an asymmetric shock arising out of the bursting of a casino-capitalist speculative financial bubble, the crisis has been misdiagnosed

---

[1] See Regulation (EU) 1173/2011 [2011] OJ L306/1; Regulation (EU) 1174/2011 [2011] OJ L306/8; Regulation (EU) 1175/2011 [2011] OJ L306/12; Regulation (EU) 1176/2011 [2011] OJ L306/25; Regulation (EU) 1177/2011 [2011] OJ L306/33.
[2] Council Directive 2011/85/EU [2011] OJ L306/41.
[3] Regulation (EU) 472/2013 [2013] OJ L140/1; Regulation (EU) 473/2013 [2013] OJ L140/11.

as one of lack of competitiveness and fiscal discipline in the southern European Member States that faced bankruptcy and insolvency crisis. Hence, rather than implementing fiscal federalism, the NEG is implementing a highly one-sided adjustment on the deficit countries, which if it was seriously enforced would according to some estimates, *ceteris paribus*, generate the equivalent of two 1930s-style depressions.[4] Having observed that the bumblebee is still flying, other critical political economists have argued that the main objective is not macroeconomic rebalancing as such. Rather, the conditionalities entailed in the NEG has the aim, akin to Naomi Klein's 'shock doctrine', of deepening neoliberal privatisation and commodification in the EU in what Barroso himself called a 'silent revolution'.[5] In other words, a second set of literature has sought to identify the interests that are served by the NEG. Finally, others have focused on the increasingly authoritarian form through which neoliberal deepening is taking place giving rise to a research programme on 'authoritarian neoliberalism'.[6]

This chapter contributes to this research programme by extending the analysis of Europe's emergent authoritarian neoliberalism to include its politico-economic sources. Section II draws on Lukas Oberndorfer's analysis of the legal form of the NEG and finds direct parallels with Franz Neumann's conception of 'general clauses' as a symptom of increasing executive arbitrariness, corrosion of liberal democratic norms and creeping authoritarianism as observed in the unfolding crisis of the Weimar Republic. The conclusion is that the post-Second World War equation in Europe between capitalism and democracy is looking increasingly fraught. Section III draws on a line of argument developed in embryonic form by Nicos Poulantzas[7] and argues that this development towards an increasingly author-itarian neoliberalism is the culmination of a much longer erosion of the capacity of EU governance to mediate between capital accumulation and social legitimation imperatives, which in turn is due to the particular mode of post-Bretton Woods transatlantic economic integration, which is organic to the US social formation but not the European ones.

---

[4]   E Stockhammer and D Sotiropoulos, 'Rebalancing the Euro Area: The Costs of Internal Devaluation' (2014) 26 Review of Political Economy 210.

[5]   S Gill, 'Transnational Class Formation, European Crisis, and the Silent Revolution' (2017) 43 Critical Sociology 635; M Ryner, 'Europe's Ordoliberal Iron Cage: Critical Political Economy, the Euro Area Crisis and Its Management' (2015) 22 Journal of European Public Policy 275.

[6]   L Oberndorfer, 'From New Constitutionalism to Authoritarian Constitutionalism: New European Governance and the State of European Democracy' in J Jäger and E Springler (eds), *Asymmetric Crisis in Europe and Possible Futures* (Routledge 2015); I Bruff, 'The Rise of Authoritarian Neoliberalism' (2014) 26 Rethinking Marxism 113; S Sandbeck and E Schneider, 'From the Sovereign Debt Crisis to Authoritarian Statism: Contradictions of the European State Project' (2014) 19 New Political Economy 847.

[7]   N Poulantzas, 'Internationalisation of Capitalist Relations and the Nation State' (1974) 2 Economy and Society 145.

II THE EU'S NEW ECONOMIC GOVERNANCE AS AUTHORITARIAN NEOLIBERALISM

General clauses ... are not specific laws with true generality. They embody rather spurious generality. A legal system which derives its legal propositions primarily from [such] principles ... is nothing but a mask under which individual measures are hidden.[8]

There is nothing new per se in European governance protecting market relations from what could be construed as 'excessive' mass political pressure. Ever since the Treaty of Rome, competition policy, fortified by the direct effect and supremacy of EU law, has served in the common market and later the single market as a constraint on the extent to, and manner in, which democratically elected governments of Member States could intervene in economic affairs. The European Economic Community (EEC) was from the outset central in establishing the formal separation between the economic and the political in European post-Second World War capitalism.[9] However, in the first decades of the EEC, competition law was subject to many exemptions and opt-outs,[10] and the Bretton Woods arrangements allowed for capital controls.[11] In other words, the EC formed part of the 'embedded liberal' Fordist compromise which tempered economic openness with the cultivation of national state capacity to pursue discretionary economic policy as determined by the electoral mandates of governments.[12]

This changed in the mid 1980s with the Single European Act, and the 1983 realignment of the European Monetary System (EMS). The culmination of this transformation was the 1993 ratification of the Maastricht Treaty whereby the EMU was forged. Together these measures resulted in a neoliberal order, where the scope of intervention by mass politics into the market order was qualitatively curtailed to a different order. Increased capital mobility, and independence of competition authorities and central banks now exerted direct market discipline on political society. It has become commonplace to point to the parallels between the mode of EU governance that emerged and Friedrich Hayek's vision in the 1930s of a European 'inter-state federalism', which for him promised to constrain the development of the welfare state.

---

[8] F Neumann, 'The Change in the Function of Law in Modern Society' in F Neumann, *The Democratic and Authoritarian State* (first published in 1937, The Free Press 1957) 29.

[9] W Bonefeld, 'European Integration, the Market, the Political and Class' (2002) 26 Capital & Class 117; P Cocks, 'Towards a Marxist Theory of European Integration' (1980) 34 International Organization 1.

[10] H Buch-Hansen and A Wigger, *The Politics of European Competition Regulation: A Critical Political Economy Perspective* (Routledge 2011).

[11] E Helleiner, *States and the Re-emergence of Global Finance: From Bretton Woods to the 1990s* (Cornell UP 1996).

[12] A Milward, *The European Rescue of the Nation State* (Routledge 1992); JG Ruggie, 'International Regimes, Transaction, and Change: Embedded Liberalism in the Postwar Economic Order' (1982) 36 International Organization 379.

Although in the national state, the submission of the will of the majority will be facilitated by the myth of nationality, it must be clear that people will be reluctant to submit to any interference in their daily lives when the majority which directs the government is composed of people of different nationalities and different traditions ... The central government in a federation composed of many different peoples will have to be restricted in scope if it is to avoid meeting an increasing resistance on the part of the various groups it includes.[13]

Already at an early stage of development of the single market, Stephen Gill[14] perceptively captured the social purpose of this form of governance with his term 'new constitutionalism', understood as the

> political–juridical counterpart to disciplinary neoliberalism, where the latter refers primarily to the process of intensifying and deepening the scope of market disciplines associated with the increasing power of capital in organising social and world orders, and in doing so shaping the limits of the possible in people's everyday lives.[15]

But the NEG represents a rather significant radicalisation of new constitutionalism and disciplinary neoliberalism.[16] While new constitutionalism and disciplinary neoliberalism certainly restricted mass political intervention in the economic sphere, their remit and procedures were defined by the rule of law. That is to an ever-diminishing extent the case with the NEG and hence it is justified to talk about increased authoritarianism.

Franz Neumann's[17] analysis of the corrosion of democratic order in the Weimar Republic and the transition to the Nazi dictatorship in Germany in the 1930s is instructive in this regard. Neumann argues that with the corrosion of democracy comes a proliferation of what he calls 'general clauses' (*Generalklausulen*) in public law, through which political rule is increasingly practised through executive decree. General clauses are characterised by what he calls a 'spurious generality' which he contrasts with the 'determinate generality' of the rule of law. An example of 'spurious generality' that he invokes is the then Section 138 of the German Civil Code, which stated that 'contracts that violate public policy or are unreasonable or immoral are null and void'. The problem with such legal statements is that they are dependent on an arbitrary interpretation external to the law itself of what is unreasonable or immoral. By contrast, there is no such scope of interpretation in a legal statement

---

[13] F Hayek, 'The Economic Conditions of Inter-State Federalism' (1939) 5 New Commonwealth Quarterly 131 cited in P Anderson, *The New Old World* (Verso 2009) 30.

[14] S Gill, 'The Emerging World Order and European Change: the Political Economy of European Economic Union' in R Miliband and L Panitch (eds), *The Socialist Register 1992: New World Order?* (Merlin Press, 1992). See also S Gill and AC Cutler (eds), *New Constitutionalism and World Order* (CUP 2014); S Gill, 'European Governance and New Constitutionalism: EMU and Alternatives to Disciplinary Neoliberalism' (1998) 3 New Political Economy 5.

[15] Gill and Cutler (n 14) 6.

[16] Oberndorfer (n 6).

[17] Neumann (n 8).

of determinate generality such as 'the legal existence (rights and responsibilities) of a person begins with his birth' (Section 1 of the then German Civic Code).[18]

The EMS as well as the EMU prior to the NEG can be seen to have been characterised by determinate generality. The EMS was a purely intergovernmental fixed exchange rate system. The main determinate generality resided in the medium of money rather than law and was set by the fixed exchange rate bands that Member States had agreed to maintain. This was certainly highly constitutional and disciplinary neoliberal. Any divergence from the primary objective of maintaining price stability over fighting unemployment was likely to trigger capital outflows, requiring an increase of interest rates that would stem the outflow but also neutralise the initial macroeconomic stimulus. But Member States were free to shape their economic policy within these constraints and could in any case leave the fixed exchange rate system or be forced to leave by the other members. There were also precise criteria for when Member States would intervene in currency markets with very short-term financing to support members whose exchange rate came under pressure under the auspices of the European Monetary Cooperation Fund (EMCF).

The transition from the EMS to the EMU entailed a significant degree of juridification, but determinate generality was initially maintained. Juridification was necessary because, with the adoption of the common currency, the discipline of 'exit' – the discipline entailed by the threat of capital flight out of national currencies – disappeared. Hence, discipline had to be codified in treaties, directives and regulations. The most important of these were the treaty provisions that made the ECB essentially a Bundesbank writ large, with a high degree of independence (Article 130 of the Treaty on the Functioning of the European Union (TFEU)) the prohibition against direct lending to Union institutions and Member States (Article 123 TFEU), and the primary objective of price stability (Article 127 TFEU), and the Growth and Stability Pact that specified a set of fiscal policy norms that should not be violated. The most prominent of these were the 3 per cent deficit norm and the 60 per cent debt norm.

It would be wrong to suggest that the EMS or the EMU were devoid of executive arbitrariness. A memorandum from Bundesbank President Emminger to Chancellor Helmut Schmidt (the so-called 'Emminger Letter') issued the caveat that the Bundesbank reserved the right not to intervene through the EMCF should it see such intervention as being contrary to its mandate to maintain price stability of the German mark.[19] In November 2003, the Council of Ministers refused to activate excessive deficit procedures for France and Germany though it was clear that they had violated the 3 per cent deficit norm. Yet, with the NEG executive arbitrariness and spurious generalities have become central to the very regulations themselves.[20]

---

[18] ibid 29.

[19] B Eichengreen, *The European Economy since 1945* (Princeton UP 2007) 285.

[20] See C Joerges, 'Europas Wirtschaftsverfassung in der Krise' (2012) 51(3) Der Staat 357; AJ Menendez, 'Editorial: A European Union in Constitutional Mutation?' (2014) 20(2) ELJ 127.

First, the expanding scope of the Economic Partnership Programmes entails a major proliferation of spurious generality. Member States which are in an excessive deficit procedure and who seek assistance from the ESM need to implement agreed Economic Partnership Programmes that are encoded in European law. With the NEG, these are no longer merely concerned with macroeconomic stability. They now also include 'structural' policy intended to enhance economic competitiveness and address 'persistently large balance of payments deficits'. This entails spurious generality because what generates economic competitiveness is essentially contested and institutionally contingent.[21] Yet the Troika (the ECB, the International Monetary Fund and the European Commission) is engendered with executive authority to interpret what generates competitiveness and impose this in Economic Partnership Programmes and memorandums of understanding.

Second, with the Fiscal Compact the referent for excessive deficits changed from a maximum deficit of 3 per cent of GDP and 'striving to achieve a budgetary position close to balance or in surplus over a complete business cycle' to a maximum 0.5 deficit medium-term budgetary objectives (MTOs structural deficit). This entails a spurious generality because MTOs are notoriously difficult to calculate and are based on the concept of 'potential GDP', the future prediction of which is dependent on many assumptions. In this context, according to Regulation 1174/2011, DG ECFIN is the sole judge on what constitutes 'macroeconomic imbalance'.

These increased executive powers of interpretation of spurious generalities are further reinforced by the Six-Pack and the replacement of qualified majority voting (QMV) with reversed majority voting (RMV). Whereas it used to be the case that EDPs could only be activated by QMV in the Council of Ministers, they are now deemed to be in effect unless a qualified majority in the Council of Ministers votes to suspend an EDP. Together with the fact that European Parliament co-decision does not apply, this significantly curtails the authority of elected governments.

In short, the NEG leaves a considerable amount of substance open for arbitrary executive interpretation at the same time as the authority for unelected bodies to exercise such authority of interpretation has increased. In addition, Oberndorfer[22] argues that this enactment of authority took place on the basis of a questionable reading of what is substantively and procedurally permissible under the TFEU, effectively bypassing Article 48 TFEU on treaty revision. First Article 121 TFEU can only be used to adopt surveillance measures and recommendations and the changes clearly go beyond mere recommendations. Second, Article 121 TFEU grants the power to make such recommendations to the Council, making the introduction of

---

[21]   P Hall and D Soskice, *Varieties of Capitalism* (OUP 2001).

[22]   L Oberndorfer, 'A New Economic Governance through Secondary Legislation? Analysis and Constitutional Assessment: Crib New Constitutionalism, via Authoritarian Constitutionalism to Progressive Constitutionalism' in N Bruun, K Lörcher and I Schömann (eds), *The Economic and Financial Crisis and Collective Labour Law in Europe* (Hart 2014) particularly 40–42. See also Oberndorfer (n 6).

'Reverse Majority Voting', pursuant to which a decision of the Commission is deemed to have been adopted by the Council if the latter does not object to it, 'manifestly illegal'.[23]

III THE POLITICO-ECONOMIC SOURCES OF EUROPE'S AUTHORITARIAN NEOLIBERALISM

The NEG can be understood as a radicalisation of new constitutionalism and disciplinary neoliberalism,[24] which itself represented a significant curtailment of representative democracy in the economic sphere in Europe. Seen in this light, the compatibility of democracy and capitalism in the post-Second World War rested on a set of particular conditions that are increasingly fading, if they even still apply today. In particular, it depended on a US hegemon, leading a Cold War conflict against the Soviet Union, being willing to offer its allies in the common market sufficient policy space within a transatlantic sphere of increasing free trade. The 'double screen' of Bretton Woods, which *both* ensured economic openness by facilitating trade through monetary cooperation and national policy autonomy, e.g. by mutual support of capital controls, was crucial in that regard.[25]

However, Bretton Woods depended on the absolute supremacy of the US in the field of trade and the ability to maintain balance-of-trade surpluses. This supremacy was eroded already in the 1960s amid much talk about the end of US hegemony.[26] But developments confounded these predictions, and by the mid 1980s it was clear that the US had managed to reshape its hegemonic strategy so as to make it compatible with persistent government and balance of payments deficits. This was based on the US remaining the issuer of the world currency (the US dollar), the sponsoring of liberalised global financial markets that were institutionally complementary with corporate and retail finance in the US itself, and the global promotion of neoliberalism.[27] But this hegemonic strategy was based on a radical transformation of transatlantic relations. Rather than promoting policy autonomy for its European allies, it was based on maintaining US policy space at the expense of its

---

[23] Oberndorfer (n 22) 41.

[24] Oberndorfer (n 6).

[25] D Calleo, *Rethinking Europe's Future* (Princeton UP 2001); Ruggie (n 12).

[26] eg P Kennedy, *The Rise and Fall of Great Powers: Economic Change and Military Conflict from 1500 to 2000* (Penguin Random House 1988).

[27] M Ryner and A Cafruny, *The European Union and Global Capitalism: Origins, Development, Crisis* (Palgrave Macmillan 2017); L Panitch and S Gindin, *The Making of Global Capitalism* (Verso 2012); M Konings, *The Development of American Finance* (CUP 2011); Y Varoufakis, *The Global Minotaur: America, the True Origins of the Financial Crisis, and the Future of the World Economy* (Zed Books 2011); A Cafruny and M Ryner, *Europe at Bay: In the Shadow of US Hegemony* (Lynne Rienner 2007); L Seabrooke, *US Power in International Finance: The Victory of Dividends* (Palgrave Macmillan 2001); H Overbeek (ed), *Restructuring Hegemony in the Global Political Economy: The Rise of Transnational Neo-Liberalism in the 1980s* (Routledge 1993); S Gill, *American Hegemony beyond the Reagan Era* (St Martin's Press 1989).

European partners while forging consent for such arrangements.[28] Post-Bretton Woods US hegemony was based on the capacity to 'delay and deflect' adjustment costs onto other states in the world economy, including those of Europe.[29] Every major thrust towards European monetary integration has based on the turbulence generated by such major 'America first' policy initiatives and turning points, and the need of Europe to develop an appropriate coping strategy.[30] Vulnerabilities on the capital account has been based on pooled protection in the form of current account surpluses, for which Germany has been the ultimate sponsor. However, Germany is only willing to perform this function as long as it can shape the European monetary integration according to the interests of its export-oriented capitalist groupings and impose attendant conditionalities.[31]

The power that made it possible for the US to pursue such a hegemonic strategy was based on the dominance of US capitalist groupings in sectors that were fundamental in structurally shaping of the world economy, including most notably in the monetary and financial field. Though European capitalist groupings maintained autonomy in competition in capitalist markets, they were subordinate in these sectors that set the terms for competition in the emergent global capitalist economy. This determined a whole series of corporate 'practices, know-how, modes and rituals to do with the economic sphere' to which also European capitalist groupings had to submit.[32] Hence, a major component in the forging of the single market was strong and coordinated business pressure for the removal of capital controls. Subsequently, Wall Street investment banks (Goldman Sachs, Morgan Stanley, Citigroup and Merrill Lynch) played the leading role in European mergers and acquisitions following the single market. The emulation of US business models, including the principle of 'shareholder value' must be seen in this context.[33]

Post-Bretton Woods global capitalism has thus created, so-called finance-led regimes of capital accumulation. These differ significantly from the Fordist regimes of accumulation. In contrast to the latter, which were based on the integration of mass production and mass consumption underwritten by productivity growth, they are based on the extension of debt underwritten by the increase of asset values. Finance-led accumulation is organic to US social formation, because its underlying social accord has for a long time been underpinned by financialised retail finance in pensions and housing and deep capital markets in corporate finance, which made it

---

[28] A Cafruny, 'A Gramscian Concept of Declining Hegemony: Stages of US Power and the Evolution of International Economic Relations' in D Rapkin (ed), *World Leadership and Hegemony* (Lynne Rienner 1990).

[29] B Cohen, 'The Macrofoundation of Monetary Power' in D Andrews (ed), *International Monetary Power* (Cornell UP 2006).

[30] R Henning, 'Systemic Conflict and Regional Monetary Integration: The Case of Europe' (1998) 52 International Organization 537.

[31] Ryner (n 5).

[32] Poulantzas (n 7) 164.

[33] Panitch and Gindin (n 27) 199–203.

possible to maintain high growth rates based on debt-financed consumption despite a lower wage share with increasingly 'flexible' labour markets. Europe's more stringent macroeconomic regime and increasingly retrenched pay-as-you-go social insurance systems did not generate a similar pattern of internal growth.[34] Though European corporate governance has been financialised, it has been increasingly dependent on export outlets in the core.[35] Though the European periphery seemed to emulate debt-financed consumption based growth, the financial and eurozone crisis revealed the devastating effect of trying to do so while not possessing the central node of global finance as in the US dollar–Wall Street regime.[36] In short, anaemic long-term growth, decades of welfare state retrenchment culminating with the NEG has resulted in a cumulatively developing legitimation crisis in Europe to which the NEG is responding by increasingly authoritarian means.

IV CONCLUSIONS

This chapter has sought to elucidate connections between emergent legal forms in eurozone crisis management, based on what Neumann called 'general clauses', and their sources in power relations in the global political economy forming an increasingly authoritarian form of neoliberalism. Section II sought to specify what is meant by 'general clauses' and the problems they pose for the rule of law, and then sought to put their application in the NEG in a broader account of developments in European monetary cooperation. Section III found drivers for these developments in post-Bretton Woods international political economy, and Europe's dependence on a US-led finance form of capital accumulation. In this account, European monetary integration can be seen as a defensive coping strategy to a more predatory form of US hegemony based on German leadership. However, due to the structural subordination to the US and the German conditionalities, the difficulties in reconciling capital accumulation with societal legitimation are ever increasing. The increasingly fraught compatibility of capitalism and democracy in Europe as expressed by authoritarianism and general clauses are ultimately a manifestation of this.

---

[34] S Sturn and T van Treeck, 'The Role of Income Inequality as a Cause of the Great Recession and Global Imbalances' in M Lavoie and E Stockhammer (eds), *Wage-led Growth: An Equitable Strategy for Economic Recovery* (Palgrave Macmillan 2013).

[35] S Vitols, 'Negotiated Shareholder Value: The German Variant of an Anglo-American Practice' (2014) 8 Competition and Change 357; E Stockhammer, 'Some Stylized Facts on the Finance-Dominated Accumulation Regime' (2008) 12 Competition and Change 184.

[36] J Becker and J Jäger, 'Integration in Crisis: A Regulationist Perspective on the Interaction of Varieties of Capitalism' (2012) 16 Competition and Change 169.

PART II

The Crisis as a Crisis of the EU's Political and Democratic Legitimacy

5

Authoritarian Liberalism

The Conjuncture behind the Crisis

Michael Wilkinson

I INTRODUCTION

In the period spanning nearly a decade from the beginning of the financial crisis to the present, the constitutional state and state system in Europe has been affected by a series of challenges to its authority and legitimacy. With regard to the European Union, these challenges are fundamental in that they go to the very existence of the project and to the values it professes to be founded on. They seem increasingly interconnected *to* the EU and the trajectory of integration rather than merely external to it. For the moment, the EU remains relatively resilient; outside of the UK, appetite for ending the experiment mostly inhabits the political fringes, although even in core countries, anti-European pressures are mounting and Eurosceptic parties are on the ascendency. What is clear is that the challenges to the current system go as much to the legitimacy of domestic regimes and their political authority as to the EU itself, not least from the fragmentary pressures on the state from below in the context of subnational claims to autonomy. In short, the crisis of authority is not merely of the EU but of the regional state system and the governing order in Europe.

The material conditions for this decade of multiple crises were set in place in the era of the Treaty of Maastricht and the geopolitical reconfiguration of Europe that accompanied it. The Maastricht era established the constitutional structure of economic and monetary union (EMU), laid the groundwork for the Schengen regime, opened the door to differentiated integration and anticipated the enlargement of Europe to the East. It also marked a change in the material balance of power, reunification beginning the path to a 'German Europe', and the end of any 'really existing alternative' to liberal capitalism cementing a neoliberal ideological hegemony as not only centrists but erstwhile critical theorists called an end to emancipatory projects.[1]

---

[1] Most notably Jürgen Habermas, declaring that since 1989, 'it has become impossible to break out of the universe of capitalism; the only remaining option is to civilise and tame the capitalist dynamic from within' (*The Crisis of the European Union: A Response* (Polity 2012) 106). This is the same Habermas

This process of depoliticisation reached its apogee in domestic contexts of a 'third way politics' (made famous by Tony Blair's New Labour project, but imitated by social democratic politicians across Europe) that offered no alternative to the neoliberal paradigm, and in many cases deepened it.[2] European integration reinforced an edifice of 'extreme centrism', through its institutional procedures of consensual lawmaking, constitutionalisation of the Treaty, and basic commitments to market liberalism.[3] In the absence of any robust supranational democracy, this left Member States with politics but without policies, and the EU with policies but no politics.[4] Or, as Streeck more recently puts it in reflecting on the Eurocrisis phase, 'where there are still democratic institutions in Europe, there is no economic governance any more, lest the management of the economy is invaded by market-correcting non-capitalist interests. And where there *is* economic governance, democracy is elsewhere.'[5]

I have tried to capture the constitutional crisis of the current period as representing a reprise of 'authoritarian liberalism', revealing the politically authoritarian face of economic liberalism.[6] This phenomenon was identified by Hermann Heller as characteristic of the late Weimar regime before its collapse in 1933.[7] Karl Polanyi sketched authoritarianism as a more general feature of market liberalism in the period leading up to the interwar collapse of liberal democracy.[8] In this conjunction, then as now, norms of democratic constitutionalism (especially representative democracy and legality) are bypassed in order to maintain economically liberal commitments to currency and price stability, austerity and fiscal discipline, competitiveness and the avoidance of moral hazard. This inflection is not merely formal or impartial; it serves various class and – within the geopolitical context of European integration – national interests.

It is no surprise that authoritarian liberalism is accompanied by systemic and anti-systemic challenges to the prevailing order, as alternatives are sought out, political

---

who now declares Brexit the defeat of capitalism by populism (*Die Zeit,* 12 July 2016) www.zeit.de /kultur/2016-07/juergen-habermas-brexit-eu-crises-english accessed April 2018.

[2]   For analysis, see L Panitch and S Gindin, *The Making of Global Capitalism* (Verso 2012). The beginning of neoliberal dominance might be traced to Mitterrand's climbdown from a socialist programme in his first years as President of France under pressure of the financial markets.

[3]   The term 'the extreme centre' belongs to Tariq Ali. For discussion of Brexit as representing a crisis of 'extreme centrism', see MA Wilkinson, 'The Brexit Referendum and the Crisis of Extreme Centrism' (2016) 17 German Law Journal 131.

[4]   On Europe and depoliticisation, see P Mair, *Ruling the Void* (Verso 2013) 115.

[5]   W Streeck, 'Heller, Schmitt and the Euro' (2015) 21 European Law Journal 361.

[6]   MA Wilkinson, 'The Reconstitution of Postwar Europe: Liberal Excesses, Democratic Deficiencies' in M Dowdle and M Wilkinson (eds), *Constitutionalism beyond Liberalism* (CUP 2017); 'Authoritarian Liberalism in the European Constitutional Imagination: Second Time as Farce?' (2015) 21 European Law Journal 313; 'The Specter of Authoritarian Liberalism: Reflections on the Constitutional Crisis of the European Union' (2013) 14 German Law Journal 527.

[7]   H Heller, 'Autoritärer Liberalismus' (1933) 44 *Die Neue Rundschau* 289, H Heller (tr S Paulson) 'Authoritarian Liberalism?' (2015) 21 European Law Journal 295.

[8]   See K Polanyi, *The Great Transformation: The Political and Economic Origins of Our Time* (first published 1944, Beacon Press 2001).

populism returns, and authoritarian *illiberalism* beckons. This is most evident in Central and Eastern Europe, but is also represented in the growth in core Europe of Eurosceptic parties such as the Front Nationale, Alternative für Deutschland and Movimento 5 Stelle. These movements and counter-movements are uneven in Europe, splintered and fragmented across the region, and yet commonalities can be identified.

The purpose of this chapter is to analyse these common themes and explore the deeper roots of 'authoritarian liberalism', conceptually and historically. It will be argued that although heightened in critical moments, the phenomenon of authoritarian liberalism corresponds to a more basic tension in the constitutional state between the forces of capitalism and democracy. This material dynamic has recently been theorised by Wolfgang Streeck, but, as yet, is missing from constitutional enquiry.[9] Introducing it gives us a clearer perspective on the trajectory of European integration: from the very beginning of the post-war project through to the Eurocrisis phase, constitutional development hinges on this material dynamic, authoritarian liberalism protecting capitalism from democracy.

The argument will proceed as follows. I will first outline the features of the Eurocrisis regime that are both 'authoritarian and liberal', and suggest this represents a deepening of rather than divergence from the normal path of integration (section II). This confluence of authoritarianism and liberalism sounds curious because, taking liberalism for political liberalism, constitutional theory generally elides the material and conflictual dynamic between capitalism and democracy (section III). To explore this further requires a historical turn, taking first the interwar breakdown of liberal constitutionalism in Europe (section IV) and then the post-war and post-Maastricht reconstruction, forging an economic constitutionalism based on a profound misreckoning – a concern for the democratic threat to liberalism rather than the capitalist threat to democracy (section V). This reconstruction lays the ground for the present moment, a critical but as yet inconclusive phase when authoritarian liberalism assumes more active forms in an attempt to maintain the material order (section VI). Although in some ways reminiscent of the interwar breakdown of liberal democracy, the outcome remains uncertain: contestation has increased but without definitive rupture, with the possible exception of Brexit.

II AUTHORITARIAN LIBERALISM

The term 'authoritarian liberalism' captures two symptoms of the constitutional development of Europe. First, there is an authoritarian aspect to EU, and especially

---

[9] See W Streeck, *Buying Time: The Delayed Crisis of Democratic Capitalism* (Verso 2013); 'The Crises of Democratic Capitalism' (2011) 71 New Left Review 5. See also M Goldoni and MA Wilkinson, 'The Material Constitution' (2018) 81 Modern Law Review 567–597, for an attempt to integrate material factors into constitutional study.

eurozone, governance, represented by a twofold process of de-democratisation and de-legalisation.[10] This refers to the bypassing of parliamentary authority and parliamentary debate as well as the violating or circumventing of normal guarantees associated with the rule of law, including the protection of social rights. This dual development has been captured by terms such as 'executive managerialism' and 'emergency Europe'.[11]

But, second, and underemphasised in those accounts, which focus on mutations in the formal exercise of authority, is the material nature of this authoritarianism and its historical pedigree: its aim at the maintenance of a regime of economic liberalism represents a deepening of rather than diversion from the normal path of integration. It is, in that respect, a 'conservative revolution'.

The substantive conditions imposed through the euro-regime, by Member States of the Eurogroup as well as the 'Troika' of institutions (IMF, European Central Bank (ECB) and European Commission), are neoliberal 'austerity' measures (e.g. privatisation, liberalisation, labour market reforms, regressive tax increases). This demands extraordinary government intervention in society, dismantling social contracts and disrupting existing social relations. It has also been backed by class and country-specific injections of central bank liquidity, particularly through the OMT programme.[12] Conditionality (hypothetically in the case of the ECB's bond-buying under OMT) is justified on the basis of the need to return to or approximate 'market conditions' of competitive economic practices, in order to avoid the moral hazard of a rescue that might incentivise further government imprudence and avoid or defer neoliberal structural reform.[13]

Although these measures of conditionality impose very specific, intrusive and debilitating constraints on debtor countries, they are consistent with and *even a continuation of* the liberal economic bias of the European constitution. This has evolved unevenly over the last few decades but it affects the EU as a whole, not only the eurozone; and it affects creditor as well as debtor countries.[14] This is an important point because it puts the allegedly exceptional nature of the measures in fuller context. So, although care has to be taken to distinguish particular *institutional* mutations in the governance of EMU, especially the new powers and authority of the Eurogroup and the ECB, it is important to note that the neoliberal bias of

---

[10]   C Kilpatrick, 'On the Rule of Law and Economic Emergency: The Degradation of Basic Legal Values in Europe's Bailouts' (2015) 35 OJLS 325. Kilpatrick now offers the term 'liminal legality', which nicely captures the legal grey area of much of the eurozone conditionality, see 'The EU and Its Sovereign Debt Programmes: The Challenges of Liminal Legality' (2017) Current Legal Problems.

[11]   See C Joerges, 'A Crisis of Executive Managerialism in the EU: No Alternative?' in G de Búrca, C Kilpatrick and J Scott (eds), *Critical Legal Perspectives on Global Governance: Liber Amicorum David M Trubek* (Hart 2015); J White, 'Emergency Europe' (2015) 63 Political Studies 300.

[12]   See, especially, M Blyth, *Austerity: History of a Dangerous Idea* (OUP 2013

[13]   On the OMT programme, see MA Wilkinson, 'The Euro Is Irreversible, or Is It? On OMT, Austerity, and the Threat of "Grexit"' (2015) 16 German Law Journal 1049.

[14]   See F Scharpf, 'The Asymmetry of European Integration, or, Why the EU Cannot Be a Social Market Economy' (2010) 8 Socio-Economic Review 211.

the Eurocrisis response is symptomatic of broader trends in EU economic constitutionalism if not necessarily demanded with any precision in the letter of the Treaty.[15]

The hollowing out of social democracy through the Eurocrisis in favour of technocratic market-making and enforced market rationality is thus a feature of much longer trends. Concerns about the EU's democratic deficit long pre-date the financial crisis of 2008; perhaps the most well-known article on the democratic deficit was published in 2006, Hix and Follesdal depicting in painstaking detail the centrist free market bias of the ordinary legislative procedure, and without even any discussion of the constraints imposed as a result of EMU.[16] In response to the German Court's Maastricht ruling, Jürgen Habermas noted in 1995 that the democratic deficit was *already* 'expanding day by day because the economic and social dynamics even within the existing institutional framework perpetuate the erosion of national powers through European law'.[17] In reality, concerns among critical and Marxist scholars about the economically liberal bias of European integration and its impact on social democracy can be traced back to before the Single European Act and earlier (even during the so-called *Trente Glorieuses*).[18]

Although forces of authoritarian rule intensify once re-politicisation is threatened, the dynamic of de-democratisation is identifiable right from the start of post-war European reconstruction.[19] The difference through the Eurocrisis has been the increase in the degree of popular resistance as 'anti-austerity' social movements have been harnessed across the continent by political parties and in the case of Greece, obtained the reins of government. But if the era of permissive consensus is decisively over, there has not (as yet) been a definitive rupture of *re-democratisation* – either at the supranational or national level, with the possible exception of Brexit.[20]

If democracy was never the guiding thread of European integration, law, however, did play a central role, and right from the foundational stages.[21] The transition from

[15] For an argument that 'downturn austerity' is better understood as an ideological prescription rather than a legal obligation within the European constitutional framework, see C Kaupa, 'Has Downturn Austerity Really Been Constitutionalised in Europe? On the Ideological Dimension of Such a Claim' (2017) 44 Journal of Law and Society 32.

[16] See S Hix and A Follesdal, 'Why There Is a Democratic Deficit in the EU: A Response to Majone and Moravscik' (2006) 44 Journal of Common Market Studies 533.

[17] J Habermas, 'Remarks on Dieter Grimm's "Does Europe Need a Constitution?"' (1995) 1 European Law Journal 303.

[18] For an earlier discussion of the link between European integration and capitalist development, see P Cocks, 'Towards a Marxist Theory of European Integration' (1980) 34 International Organization 1.

[19] See Wilkinson (n 6).

[20] Representing, according to Habermas, the victory of populism (if not democracy) over capitalism (see n 1). Because of the UK's distinct relationship with Europe, leaving the EU does not represent the same likelihood of rupture as would a core country, such as France, Germany or Italy, leaving. See further, Wilkinson, 'The Brexit Referendum' (n 3).

[21] See eg A Cohen, 'Constitutionalism without Constitution: Transnational Elites between Mobilisation and Legal Expertise in the Making of a Constitution for Europe (1940s–1960s)' (2007) 32 Law and Social Enquiry 109 and A Vauchez, 'The Transnational Politics of Judicialisation: *Van Gend en Loos* and the Making of the EU Polity' (2010) 16 European Law Journal 1.

'integration through law' to 'integration through fear', as Weiler characterised crisis-era Europe, therefore appears significant.[22] The harnessing of fear can be captured in the new identification of a Schmittian enemy, not external and physical, but rather internal and *ideological*. According to Donald Tusk, the notion that there could be any alternative to austerity is a dangerous illusion.[23] Tusk associates resistance to austerity as somehow 'anti-German', and speaks approvingly of ordoli-beralism. The notional enemy is anyone who calls into question this new common sense, in particular those 'bad Europeans' who disregard the economic stability criteria.[24]

A domestic electorate may of course accept the idea that 'there is no alternative' to neoliberal structural reforms. But now that idea is imposed as a constitutional (even supra-constitutional) constraint, achieving ideological hegemony despite the fact that it still seems explicitly *partisan* in a political–economic and a geopolitical sense – the crisis has emerged with clear winners and losers, between nations as well as between classes within nations.[25]

But the novelty of the move away from legality can also be overstated. Thus the attempt to create a loose structure of public discipline within EMU, the 'Stability and Growth Pact' – setting deficit and debt levels that were violated almost immediately by France and Germany – was under-enforced before the crisis by the European Council and the European Court of Justice.[26] This fact was given relatively little attention at the time; in the era of the open method of coordination, soft law, new governance and other softer forms of de-legalisation were *celebrated* by many as sensible departure from a Community method of lawmaking that was too centralised and 'one-size fits all', unable to accommodate the constitutional diversity within the Union.[27]

It is important to grasp the way in which heightened authoritarianism is both transformative yet also conservative of the existing constitutional order. To be sure, the euro-regime can be said to have mutated from a nominally rule-based structure accompanied by market discipline to a discretionary order reinforced by bureaucratic power.[28] And this is not a temporary suspension of normality, in response to a situation with a clearly demarcated end point, or with the limits of a sunset clause. It is open-ended and future-oriented. But it has *a conservative aim*. The aim of this

---

[22] See JHH Weiler, 'Editorial: Integration Through Fear' (2012) 23 European Journal of International Law 1.

[23] See P Spiegel, 'Donald Tusk Interview: The Annotated Transcript' *Financial Times* (16 July 2015) https://www.ft.com/content/ff50e5a9-7b15-3998-a9f1-c11359dc01b8 accessed April 2018.

[24] See U di Fabio, 'Karlsruhe Makes a Referral' (2014) 15 German Law Journal 107.

[25] See Blyth (n 12).

[26] Case C-27/04 *Commission v Council* EU:C:2004:436.

[27] For discussion of the relation between new governance, legality and democracy, see MA Wilkinson, 'Three Conceptions of Law: Towards a Jurisprudence of Democratic Experimentalism' (2010) 2 Wisconsin Law Review 672.

[28] For a detailed exposition, see M Ionnanidis, 'Europe's New Transformations: How the EU Economic Constitution Changed During the Crisis' (2017) 53 Common Market Law Review 1237.

mutation, substantively, is not to change but *to maintain* the existing material constitution of Europe and its fundamental market-driven objectives.

This is not to say there is nothing new about neoliberalism, as a specific regime of accumulation, for example, so dependent as it is on financialisation of the economy for its resource accumulation and distribution.[29] The point is rather to pursue a more basic conceptual connection between authoritarianism and liberalism in the dynamic of constitutional change. The provenance of this conjunction in earlier phases in European history, specifically in the interwar period of late Weimar, suggests a longer and deeper linkage.

III POLITICAL AND ECONOMIC LIBERALISM OR DEMOCRACY AND CAPITALISM?

If the confluence of authoritarianism and liberalism appears incongruous, this may be because the constitutional imagination is captured by political rather than economic liberalism. During ideological battles of the Cold War period, liberalism was twinned with democracy (in western capitalism) and opposed to authoritarian socialism (in Soviet Communism).[30] This was buttressed by the 'end of history' thesis famously announced by Fukuyama, liberal democracy presented as the culmination of historical progress, a kind of Hegelian terminus *après la lettre*. In political theory, under the influence of Rawls and Habermas, liberalism is paired with democracy and even a certain progressive (in the sense of egalitarian) political–economic position.[31] Both theorists located their work within the context of a really existing liberal democracy and support broadly social democratic goals.

Neither Rawls nor Habermas, however, offers the prospect of any alternative to capitalism as a matter of political economy. Nor, more problematically, do they offer any robust analysis *of* capitalism, of the threat that capitalism poses to the democratic order.[32] Radical democrats and critical theorists have thus long criticised Habermasian and Rawlsian political liberalism (and not only Hayekian economic liberalism) for being insufficiently attuned to the question of power, whether it is the significance of cultural power in the struggles for ideological hegemony or the capacity for economic power to translate into or effect political domination.[33]

---

[29] For a useful recent account, see eg B Fine and A Saad-Filho, 'Thirteen Things You Need to Know about Neoliberalism' (2017) 43 Critical Sociology 685.

[30] For a discussion, see eg P Wagner, 'The Democratic Crisis of Capitalism: Reflections on Political and Economic Modernity in Europe' LEQS Paper No 41/2011.

[31] J Habermas, *Between Facts and Norms: Contributions to a Discourse Theory of Law and Democracy* (MIT Press 1995); J Rawls, *Political Liberalism* (Columbia UP 1993).

[32] The earlier Habermas was more attuned to problems of this sort, see eg J Habermas, 'What Does a Legitimation Crisis Mean Today? Legitimation Problems in Late Capitalism' (1973) 40 Social Research 643.

[33] See eg C Mouffe, 'Deliberative Democracy or Agonistic Pluralism' (1999) 66 Social Research 745; S Wolin, 'The Liberal/Democratic Divide: On Rawls' Political Liberalism' (1996) 24 Political Theory 97.

Ideology as well as capital can threaten the 'empty place of power' on which the autonomy of the political depends.[34] In this view, liberalism (as well as related traditions of neo-republicanism) neglects the danger of domination arising in, but not limiting itself to, the economic and social sphere.[35] It takes for granted the existence of a vibrant democratic culture, underestimates the fragility of democracy and the threats arising to it in a capitalist society – the extent to which individualism, marketisation, competition and the profit motive can and do lead to the erosion of the solidarity and community that democracy needs in order to thrive.[36]

Constitutional theorists also evade these questions, tending to devote their attention to the counter-majoritarian dilemma, typically evaluating the legitimacy of constitutional review of legislation to protect basic civil liberties.[37] There is less attention to the impact of market freedoms on equal liberties, or to justifications for the decision-making frameworks of political economy (the independence of the central bank, or the legitimacy of constitutionally restricting the micro- and macro-economic policy choices of the government) – even regarding their impact on 'liberal' commitments such as equality of opportunity. Celebration of the metaphorical 'marketplace of ideas' displaces concerns over the actual marketplace of goods, capital, services and persons, and more broadly over the effects of commodification and marketisation on social relations, short of exploring marginal instances of market immorality, things 'money can't buy'.[38] The dynamic of political–economic development is missed because dominant strands of constitutional theory adopt a normativist method of abstract analysis, depending, say, on a fictional state of nature in the social contract tradition, a momentary legal system in the tradition of legal positivism or a moralised commitment to the rule of law in the anti-positivist constitutionalist tradition.[39]

To be sure, economic liberalism has a more explicitly chequered history in its relationship with democracy. Hayek's distrust not only of social justice, but also of

[34] See further, MA Wilkinson, 'Public Law and the Autonomy of the Political: A Material Critique', in MA Wilkinson and MW Dowdle (eds), *Questioning the Foundations of Public Law* (Hart 2018).

[35] Rawls's own framework (unlike Hayek's version) may be thought to be compatible with social justice or even demand significant redistribution of wealth. But there remains insufficient attention given to the historical record of liberal societies in meeting its egalitarian claims and to the question of whether Rawls's solutions respect his own egalitarian intuitions. See G Cohen, *Rescuing Justice and Equality* (Harvard UP 2008).

[36] This threat would have been apparent from earlier work, not only in the European context (see Polanyi (n 8)), but in the US context, earlier pragmatists similarly critiquing the political impact of market liberalism, see eg J Dewey, *The Public and Its Problems* (Henry Holt 1927).

[37] See eg L Alexander (ed) *Constitutionalism: Philosophical Foundations* (CUP 1998).

[38] See M Sandel, *What Money Can't Buy: The Moral Limits of Markets* (Allen Lane 2012).

[39] Rawls's own later concern (when he moves from the general theory of justice to its more particular expression in *Political Liberalism*) is with the stability of the political conception of justice in the face of the challenge of multiculturalism and the pluralism of comprehensive doctrines rather than in the face of the challenges of capitalism, specifically its structural tendencies towards inequality, on which, see T Piketty, *Capital in the 21st Century* (Harvard UP 2013).

democracy and his flirting with political authoritarianism, is well documented.[40] Identification of the pairing of political authoritarianism and economic liberalism is thus not at all new or unique to the recent Eurocrisis. The notion has been used in the context of South East Asian capitalism and Latin America to refer to politically authoritarian and even autocratic and dictatorial measures to implement so called 'free market economics'.[41] This type of pairing is sometimes referred to as 'authoritarian neoliberalism', associated with a turn from a relatively consensual neoliberalism of the 'third way' to the more coercive type that resurfaces during financial crises.[42]

But there is a more general conceptual point to be made in order to capture the deep tension between political and economic spheres in a state which is both democratic and capitalist. As a democratic state, modern constitutional authority depends at root on some connection to 'we, the people'. 'The people' here represents the rhetorical and symbolic force of popular sovereignty. This expresses the relative autonomy of the political realm, not only from theological power, as in classic accounts of modern secularisation, but also from economic power. It is not merely a presupposition, or a worldview. It is a fragile and ongoing material process, attained, if at all, by social struggle against the fusion of political and economic power and class rule (which does not end with feudalism). Its narrative includes worker's movements, women's movements, anti-colonial movements, and other struggles for equality and recognition.[43] In a capitalist state, modern constitutional authority also demands the relative autonomy of the economic realm. This privatised domain is based on market logic – operating according to imperatives of depoliticisation (naturalisation) of inequality, commodification of social relations and competitive erosion of the bonds of solidarity. But this is not hermetically sealed off from the public realm. Its dysfunctionality affects the legitimacy *of the political domain of democracy* and of the relationship between rulers and ruled.

Liberal constitutional theory, and much constitutional theory more generally, evades this dynamic, taking as givens free market capitalism on the one side and democratic legitimacy on the other. It simply does not provide the tools to deal with the pathologies and contradictions of capitalism and democracy, the tension between public goods and private interests, and the structural inequalities of power embedded in the modern state and state system. These are not free-floating but constituted by and constitutive of legal and political features of the constitutional order.

---

[40] cf W Scheuerman, 'The Unholy Alliance of Carl Schmitt and Friedrich Hayek' (1997) 4 Constellations 172.

[41] See eg K Jayasuriya, 'Globalisation, Sovereignty and the Rule of Law: From Political to Economic Constitutionalism' (2001) 8 Constellations 442.

[42] On 'authoritarian neoliberalism', see I Bruff, 'The Rise of Authoritarian Neoliberalism' (2014) 26 Rethinking Marxism 113.

[43] These are struggle for what Cornelius Castoriadis calls 'effective autonomy', see C Castoriadis, *Philosophy, Politics, Autonomy: Essays in Political Philosophy* (D Ames tr, OUP 1991).

To get a better grip on this, we must turn to work that offers a conceptualisation of these dynamics, moving towards a more 'situational' approach, a mix of historical, comparative, critical, political–economic and geopolitical analysis.[44] The political and economic domains then look interrelated, reflecting a material tension between democracy and capitalism as real political and social forces. Wolfgang Streeck has popularised this tension and it is a useful heuristic for understanding the dynamic of constitutional change.[45]

In the post-war period, Streeck recounts how the democratic capitalist state is transformed from a 'tax state' during the *Trente Glorieuses*, to a 'debt state' in the neoliberal era beginning in the 1970s, to a 'consolidation state' in the last decade of austerity-driven political economics, under particular pressure of the single currency.[46] This transformational dynamic is configured by the tension between community and coercion, solidarity and individualism (represented by the figures of the *Statsvolk* and the *Marktvolk*, as Streeck puts it).[47]

In this more sociologically rich account, the state can be said to represent the unity in difference of the political and economic; it is no mere inert container, or abstract idea of reason, but reflects stages of democratic and capitalist development, associated, for example, with the extension of the franchise as well as the expansion of the market.[48] In critical periods, when capitalism and democracy come into explicit, direct conflict, both in terms of the interests and ideas they represent, the state is increasingly 'seen' as a representation of these tensions in political economy and in some cases as a partial actor in their resolution. The reason we can talk here about the state and not just about temporary elected government is that all the institutions of the state ('the ideological and repressive state apparatus' as Althusser calls it) reinforce and recalibrate the relationship between democracy and capital-ism – the military, police, judiciary, central banks, as well as cultural and media institutions.[49] For those states which are members of the eurozone, we can add to the governing apparatus the 'five unelected presidents', of the Commission, Council, ECB, Eurogroup and European Parliament. This repressive and ideological appa-ratus of the state system in Europe not only bypasses democratic accountability; it does not even have a strong democratic representative body as supplementary or corrective force.

Just as capitalism and inequality may threaten the democratic state, democratic material struggles for political and social equality may appear as a potential threat to the capitalist state. Democratic movements may threaten a basic structural re-differentiation of the political and the economic with political–democratic control

44   See further Goldoni and Wilkinson (n 9).
45   See Streeck, 'Crises of Democratic Capitalism' (n 9).
46   Streeck, *Buying Time* (n 9).
47   ibid.
48   For a material account of the state see, eg B Jessop, *The State: Past, Present, Future* (Polity 2016).
49   See L Althusser, *On the Reproduction of Capitalism: Ideology and Ideological State Apparatuses* (Verso 2014).

over the economy (in the case of democratic socialism). In such a context, in order to maintain the status quo, the ideological and repressive apparatus of the capitalist state and state system proffers a more active form of authoritarianism. To capture the development of these material constitutional dynamics in Europe, we can now present a brief diachronic overview.

IV INTERWAR EUROPE: A MISRECKONING?

In certain periods, the tension between the democratic state and the capitalist state is heightened, entailing deep-seated constitutional crisis. A particularly significant moment for grappling with the structure and dynamic of European integration is the interwar period, marking the end of the *jus publicum Europeaum* of the 'long nineteenth century' (from the French Revolution to the First World War). In late Weimar Germany, the democratic capitalist state reached breaking point, not only due to external factors, but because of the growing threat of a class-conscious and politically emancipated proletariat which threatened the liberal differentiation of the political and the economic established and protected by the Constitution itself.[50] The reaction of the governing elite to this threat was ultimately a combination of authoritarianism and economic liberalism, as identified by Social Democrat and constitutional theorist, Hermann Heller.[51]

The term 'authoritarian liberalism' was thus used by Heller to denigrate the attempts of the German state in alliance with big business to keep economic liberalism going at all costs, in the period between 1930 and 1933, maintaining the differentiation of the political and the economic by violating it, intervening in the economy in favour of capitalism.[52] Heller's target with the label was not only the centrist cabinets of Chancellor Brüning that governed Germany before the Nazi party took power, but also the constitutional theorist who had advised them, Carl Schmitt.[53] Schmitt had recommended a strong state in order to keep the free market economy going against the threat of democratic socialism and experiments of

---

[50]   The Weimar Constitution promised to protect economic liberalism as well as the social state, posing a dilemma well understood by its architect, Hugo Preuss, see H Preuss, 'The Significance of the Democratic Republic for the Idea of Social Justice' in A Jacobson and B Schlink (eds), *Weimar: A Jurisprudence of Crisis* (University of California Press 2000).

[51]   Heller (n 7).

[52]   ibid. This fear of social democracy wasn't restricted to the German authoritarian liberals. Austrian liberal von Mises noted that despite the dangers of Fascism and its makeshift nature, it will be forever acclaimed for saving the continent from socialism and the attendant dangers to private property, approving Engelbert Dolfuss's crushing of labour and social democracy in Austria in the 1930s. For further discussion, see A Somek, 'Austrian Constitutional Doctrine 1933 to 1938' in C Joerges and N Singh-Ghaleigh (eds), *Darker Legacies of Law in Europe* (Hart 2003). In 1935, the cabinet of Laval in France undertook authoritarian measures to save the franc under enabling laws that bypass ordinary parliamentary debate (K Loewenstein, 'Autocracy versus Democracy in Contemporary Europe' (1935) American Political Science Review 571).

[53]   See C Schmitt, 'Strong State, Sound Economy', reprinted in R Cristi, *Carl Schmitt and Authoritarian Liberalism: Strong State, Free Economy* (University of Wales Press 1998).

economic democracy, encapsulated in his address to the Langnamverein in 1932, 'strong state, free economy'.[54]

The Brüning cabinets bypassed parliamentary democracy, using presidential decrees under cover of emergency, in order to impose austerity and defend the social relations of capitalism and economic liberalism – competition, the profit motive, accumulation, private property and social inequality.[55] The aim of this formation was the frustration of any democratic solidarity, in order to maintain the capitalist form of the economy, in a critical period of deflation, high unemployment and political turbulence. For authoritarian liberals, the fear in these conditions was that democracy might turn towards socialism (a fear heightened by the earlier Bolshevik victory in the Soviet Union).[56]

This pattern of authoritarian liberal response and reaction to economic crisis was far from unique to late Weimar – right across the globe states tried to maintain the political–economic demands of the gold standard, fiercely resisting social demo-cratic programmes, until, eventually but unevenly, they abandoned gold, and market liberalism, leading, for example, to welfarism in Britain and the New Deal in the US.[57] According to Karl Polanyi, the more fiercely countries resisted social democracy through authoritarian government in the name of economic liberalism and sound finances, the stronger and fiercer the eventual backlash would be (the 'double movement'). Authoritarian government hollowed out democracy, ulti-mately weakening its ability to respond to the Fascist threat when it arrived. It was, in other words, authoritarian liberalism that prepared the ground for Fascism.[58]

Heller's own earlier considered view was that conditions of extreme socio-economic inequality were incompatible with the survival of a constitutional democ-racy, because democracy requires a certain degree of social homogeneity, or at least the prospect of such, to sustain political legitimacy.[59] He had warned, presciently, in 1928 that the relative tranquillity in the Federal Republic would be short-lasting because social homogeneity was 'lacking to an extent unmatched in previous eras'.[60] Capitalism, and the inequality it entailed, in other words, was a threat to the democratic constitutional order.

---

[54] ibid.

[55] For a full account, see E Kolb, *The Weimar Republic* (2nd edn, Routledge 2005) 116–35.

[56] cf Cristi (n 53).

[57] See Polanyi (n 8).

[58] It was reaction to the 'deadlock of the market system' that precipitated the 'conjoint disintegration' of the political and economic system across the globe. Although reactions were similar only in discard-ing laissez-faire principles, where liberals obstructed social and economic reforms that might involve planning, regulation or control, 'the victory of fascism was made practically unavoidable'. Rejecting purely local or historical explanations for the situation that gave birth to Fascism, 'in reality', Polanyi insists, the part it played was determined by one factor: 'the condition of the market system' (ibid, 250–65).

[59] H Heller 'Political Democracy and Social Homogeneity' in A Jacobson and B Schlink (eds), *Weimar: A Jurisprudence of Crisis* (University of California Press 2000).

[60] ibid 262.

Yet the message taken by mainstream constitutional theory in response to this extraordinary double movement and the interwar breakdown of liberal democracy it entailed in Germany (and elsewhere) would be quite different from the one Heller and Polanyi had conveyed. It was not the threat that economic liberalism (and capitalism) posed to democracy that resonated in the liberal constitutional imagination but the threat that democracy posed to liberalism. This came to prominence through the work of another constitutional theorist of the period, who had emigrated to the US, but became closely involved in post-war German reconstruction, Karl Loewenstein. Loewenstein, writing in 1935, thought that liberal democracy needed to be more 'militant' in the fight against Fascism (and, if to a lesser extent, also against Communism).[61] The structures of the Weimar Republic should have been more flexible in order for it to defend itself, by suspending constitutional rights, banning political parties, and preventing the rise of extremist groups and associations. Lowenstein, describing the opportunism of the Fascist opponents of the constitution, urged liberal democracy to pre-empt them, take the fight to its enemies, if necessary to 'fight fire with fire', echoing Carl Schmitt's own call for robust defence of the Weimar Constitution, by diktat and decree if necessary.[62]

In the aftermath of the Second World War, mainstream political and constitutional theory became preoccupied with liberal constitutional defence, neglecting the sociological examination of the power structures that could formally and informally undermine democracy in a capitalist state. The German example of entrenching strong constitutional guarantees became increasingly influential and widespread (however misleading the conventional narrative of the dignified reaction to Nazism).[63] Constitutional lawyers, and those tasked with designing legal and political institutions, were dedicated to the justification of various institutional arrangements – whether domestic, international or supranational – that would constrain majoritarianism, with the rationale (or pretext) of preventing democratic backsliding or avoiding democratic irrationality. Independent technocratic institutions such as constitutional courts, commissions and central banks, became the norm, and were gradually engrained in the liberal constitutional imagination. European integration was an intrinsic part of this post-war settlement, representing the construction of a militant democracy 'writ large'.

But as Jan-Werner Müller has recounted, 'restrained democracy' is a more accurate representation of this phenomenon than the inappositely named 'militant democracy'.[64] If anything, it was liberalism that was to be militantly protected, albeit

---

[61] See K Loewenstein, 'Militant Democracy and Fundamental Rights Part 1' (1937) 3 American Political Science Review 417 and ' Autocracy versus Democracy in Contemporary Europe Part 1' (1935) 29 American Political Science Review 571.

[62] ibid 432.

[63] See M Hailbronner, *Tradition and Transformations: The Rise of German Constitutionalism* (OUP 2015).

[64] See JW Müller, *Contesting Democracy: Political Ideas in 20th Century Europe* (Yale UP 2011).

in the name of democratic consolidation.[65] This militancy was driven more by concerns to keep the wheels of economic liberalism revolving than to defend political liberalism, still less to promote strong democracy.

   In constitutional enquiry, the focus undoubtedly was on the dangers of strong (unfettered) democracy, rather than, as Heller and Polanyi had warned, of unfettered capitalism and its tendency towards socio-economic inequality. If, in practice, the excesses of capitalism as much as democracy were tempered in the *Trente Glorieuses*, through the building of the welfare state and various forms of corporatism and social democracy, this did not capture the attention of constitutional scholars, lawyers and constitution builders. The seminal texts of liberal political and constitutional theory were preoccupied with resolving the counter-majoritarian dilemma through various devices of justification for constraints on the democratic will of the majority, both institutionally (through constitutional review) and ideologically (as in the Rawlsian idea of 'reasonableness').[66] The fragility of the constitution in the absence of constitutional review, and even legal positivism's relativising of the question of legitimacy, is blamed by constitutional theorists and legal philosophers for Weimar's collapse.[67] Capitalism passes under the radar.

   Mainstream constitutional theory thus leads away from any critical engagement with political economy. European integration itself – to the extent it is given any attention by constitutional scholars – is seen as an aspect of the broader project of restrained democracy, rather than a further stage in the reconstitution of the relation between politics and economics in the process of democratic capitalist development. The creation of an internal market is seen tamely and benignly as designed only to ensure peace and prosperity for all after half of century of war and destruction. Heller's and Polanyi's lessons and the democratic struggles for equality at their heart could then be forgotten, helped by the fact that post-war growth could mask the underlying issue of socio-economic inequality. Might this prove to be a misreckoning of calamitous proportions?

v ECONOMIC CONSTITUTIONALISM IN POST-WAR EUROPE

What is clear is that the post-war constitutional imagination in Europe was not characterised by any vision of a vibrant democratic state. It was encapsulated in the story of West German post-war constitutional development: 'we are (afraid of) the people'.[68] Reaction to this fear entailed a new vision not only of the governing

---

[65] ibid.

[66] See Rawls (n 31).

[67] See L Fuller, 'Positivism and Fidelity to Law – A Reply to Professor Hart' (1958) 71 Harvard Law Review 630 and Müller (n 64) 129. cf F Neumann, *Behemoth: The Structure and Practice of National Socialism 1933–1944* (first published in 1942, Ivan R Dee 2009).

[68] See C Möllers, 'We are (Afraid of) the People: Constituent Power in German Constitutional Thought', in M Loughlin and N Walker (eds), *The Paradox of Constitutionalism* (OUP 2008). The UK may be an exception to this, along with the sustained democracies of the Nordic countries.

function (in particular the technocratic functioning of government) but of the governing relationship, the relation between state and society, and specifically of the nature and limits of the right to rule over the economy. In other words, this is a vision of de-democratisation both of the constituent and of the constituted powers, of sovereignty and of government. It lays out a new vision of political society, of the individual as a market participant rather than a political citizen.

This vision was presaged in the work of the ordoliberals, whose founding meeting in Freiberg coincided with Schmitt's address to the Langnamsverein, 'strong state, sound economy'.[69] Sharing Schmitt's vehement anti-Communism, obsession with order, distrust of economic democracy and belief in a strong state, they nevertheless presented unfettered capitalism (and not only democracy) as a challenge to the competition-based market society.[70] Carl Joachim Friedrich identifies the ideological and constitutional significance of this 'new liberalism' as early as 1955. He notes how in Germany it signals a fundamental reordering of the basic ideas underpinning constitutional theory.[71] As Friedrich understood, and as Foucault would later explore in his lectures on neoliberal governmentality in 1979, the decisive theoretical turn triggered by German ordoliberalism had been to replace constituent power (or popular sovereignty) with individual economic freedom – a freedom to participate in the market – as the legitimating device for the whole constitutional order.[72] It is not only a question of delegating power to technocratic agencies to avoid temporary democratic impulses, but a basic elision or denial of political freedom. This reversed the original meaning of the economic constitution, which for Franz Neumann had meant democratic control of the economy.[73] Instead, the constitution itself becomes sovereign, emblematically in post-war Germany with the idea of an inviolable 'eternity clause' in the *Grundgesetz*.

For the ordoliberals, the new economic constitutionalism, based on formal equality, individual economic rights and competition, was intended to achieve the complete abolition of class as well as national conflicts from the political domain.[74] The class-conscious struggles of the interwar period would be repressed in order to

---

[69] On the link between Schmitt and the ordoliberals, and the significant of both for the euro, see W Bonefeld, 'Authoritarian Liberalism: From Schmitt via Ordoliberalism to the Euro' (2017) 43 *Critical Sociology* 747.

[70] Although it was already Franz Neumann who had identified the threat of organised capitalism to the rule of law in the 1920s. See F Neumann, 'On the Preconditions and the Legal Concept of an Economic Constitution' in O Kirchheimer and F Neumann (eds), *Social Democracy and the Rule of Law* (L Tanner and K Tribe tr, Allen & Unwin 1987). See further, W Scheuermann (ed) *The Rule of Law Under Siege* (University of California Press 1996).

[71] CJ Friedrich, 'The Political Thought of Neo-liberalism' (1955) 49 *American Political Science Review* 509.

[72] ibid; M Foucault, *The Birth of Biopolitics – Lectures at the College de France 1978–1979* (Palgrave MacMillan 2008.

[73] See Neumann (n 70).

[74] See EV Bonn, *Standard Texts on Social Market Economy: Two Centuries of Discussion* (ed Horst Friedrich Wunsche) tr Derek Rutter (Stuttgart, Gustav Fisher Verlag, 1982) ix.

secure political and economic *stability*, considered threatened by the democratic and capitalist forces that the interwar period had unleashed. The new civil religion for the post-war order would be fiscal prudence, efficiency and competition, the model of the German economic miracle. Democracy would be restrained not (only) for fear of its violating civil or political rights but out of concern for its impact on economic stability.[75] The strong state would protect the market economy, and disarm any democratic (or capitalist) threat to it.

Although it was far from straightforwardly applied (in practice softened by the social market economy and aspects of corporatism), this reconfiguration of the constitutional imagination would become ideologically ascendant, first in Germany and then elsewhere, not least through its influence on the process of European constitutionalisation.[76] The self-understanding of constitutionalism in Europe would be increasingly conditioned by ideologies and interests that correspond to economic rationality and the logic of market competition, effecting a new differentiation of the political and economic realms.[77] These trends become more acute in time and of course extend far beyond the EU.[78]

With the Treaty of Maastricht, the differentiation between politics and economics is taken to a new stage in the constitution of EMU. EMU is based on the twin pillars of the separation of supranational monetary policy and domestic fiscal authority and the avoidance of moral hazard. In this configuration, a Member State's ability to spend and repay its existing debts would be based on its own ability to raise resources, which – increasingly in the era of the 'debt state' (and not least due to tax arbitrage in a world where capital moves relatively freely) – was increasingly undertaken through financial borrowing.[79]

The new stage of EMU must thus be understood in the broader context of neoliberal globalisation of the 1980s, and the turn to financialisation of the economy.[80] This incorporated a loosening of capital controls, with the free movement of capital eventually becoming a fundamental right in the EU. But with its commitment to a depoliticised monetary policy based exclusively on price stability; and an independent but limited ECB with restricted monetary tools but without the guidance of any supranational economic policy capable of dealing with uneven development, socio-economic heterogeneity or exogenous fiscal shocks, the Maastricht Treaty

---

[75] See JW Müller, *Contesting Democracy: Political Ideas in Twentieth Century Thought* (Princeton UP 2012).

[76] cf A Wigger, 'Debunking the Myth of the Ordoliberal Influence on Postwar European Integration' in J Hien and C Joerges (eds), *Ordoliberalism, Law and the Rule of Economics* (Hart 2017).

[77] See eg EJ Mestmäcker, 'European Touchstones of Dominion and Law' (2007) Ordo Yearbook of Economic and Social Order 4.

[78] See Jayasuriya (n 41).

[79] See Streeck (n 9).

[80] See eg A Menendez, 'The Existential Crisis of the European Union' (2013) 14 German Law Journal 453.

attempted to supranationalise ordoliberal principles designed for domestic constitutional consumption.[81]

Maastricht would also signal a decisive end to the previous, functional logic that economic integration would prompt political integration, and that politicisation would then force elites to engage mass publics in European matters, precipitating a process of Euro-democratisation.[82] On the contrary, it removed an important lever of power from the political pillars of the Member States, but without reconstructing it at the supranational political level or establishing any plans to do so. And the new currency – a 'currency without a state' – was not only democratically unaccountable (which would hardly have differentiated it from national variants); it also lacked the social and political bonds of community to sustain it, offering a symbol of the new 'economic Messianism' of the era to follow.[83] To reprise Streeck's heuristic, it seemed a decisive victory for capitalism over democracy, just as commentators were proclaiming 'the end of history' with the collapse of the Soviet Union.

VI EUROCRISIS: AN INCONCLUSIVE CONJUNCTURE?

The post-war liberal constitutional imagination, though far from democratic, is more passively than actively authoritarian. It is technocratic, institutional and juridical in form. In substance it is economically liberal, dedicated to expanding markets, pursuing free trade and spreading economic rationality. Politically, it is moderate, extreme only in the centrism it espouses and the technocratic and managerial ethos it embodies. Democracy is restrained but not yet extinguished.

But this hollowing out of democracy presages the more active authoritarianism to come. Although democracy had never been a key component of the post-war construct, since Maastricht, it would be systematically overridden, and not only in parliaments but in popular referenda.[84] And when the Eurocrisis hits, liberal centrism struggles to hold, becoming subject to increasing political contestation, sometimes from social movements in the margins but sometimes from positions of governmental power. Having lost faith in normal institutional routes, the apparatus of the state (and European state system) increasingly resorts to cajoling and coercing, undermining even its own moderate checks and balances of constitutional accountability in an attempt to maintain order. Since the democratic support for liberal centrism was always thin, it can only compensate in other ways, presenting those

---

[81] See K Tuori and K Tuori, *The Eurocrisis: A Constitutional Analysis* (CUP 2012).

[82] See G Marks and L Hooghe, 'A Postfunctionalist Theory of European Integration: From Permissive Consensus to Constraining Dissensus' (2009) 39 British Journal of Political Science 1, 5.

[83] See MA Wilkinson, 'Economic Messianism and Constitutional Power in a German Europe: All Courts Are Equal But Some Courts Are More Equal Than Others' (2014) LSE, Law, Society and Economy Working Papers 26/2014 http://papers.ssrn.com/sol3/papers.cfm?abstract_id=2522919 accessed April 2018.

[84] The most conspicuous warning sign was surely the Dutch and French rejection of the EU Constitutional Treaty in 2005, which was followed by its repackaging in the Lisbon Treaty.

who contest it as irrational, unreasonable or un-European. Fear becomes its method in a more overt manner. If its 'success' was apparent in the Greek crisis, its limits may have been revealed through the recent Brexit referendum.

To be sure, the Eurocrisis, and the response to it, suggests that the material order of democratic capitalism in the European state-system is complex. The interests of capital are not always unified or aligned. They may diverge, marked by contests between *capitals* (between Paris, Berlin, Athens etc.) as much as between capitalism and democracy. Authoritarian liberalism thus now needs to capture not only de-democratisation and de-legalisation in combination with the aim of a substantively liberal economic order, but the hegemonic relations between capitals in a new 'German Europe', where every country is urged to be more like Germany despite the impossibility of such a demand.[85]

But this suggests that the constitutional crisis is not primarily about a conflict between emergency politics and the normal rules of the game. These have been relatively easily bent or circumvented when necessary. They are rather surface indicators of a deeper crisis of the material constitution. The 'rules' of the economic liberalism established by EMU (ordoliberal in content) – e.g. no central bank financing, no bail-out of countries in financial difficulty, the avoidance of moral hazard, emphasis on price stability – come into conflict with the imperative to maintain the symbol of economic integration, the single currency (e.g. the euro is 'irreversible', 'if the euro fails, Europe fails'). In turn, they both come into conflict with the democratic and social movements against austerity, and in the case of Greece this was pushed (nearly) to the limit with the election of an anti-austerity but pro-European government. Democracy and the rule of law, including the protection of social rights, are also nominally protected in the EU Treaties and its charter of fundamental rights, it must be recalled. There is, in other words, a clash of fundamental political objectives: ordoliberalism, European integration and democratic self-government.[86]

Democratically legitimate rescue would require a transnational solidarity that is proscribed by ordoliberalism and cannot simply emerge through a functional spillover effect. The institutional channels for it to be expressed do not exist. The result is rescue by the back door, in super-technocratic fashion, as the ECB and the powerful members of the Eurogroup take centre stage. The irresistible force of neo-functionalism then meets the immovable object of ordoliberalism and the German hegemony that it represents. This is not only an order of rules, but also an order of interests, predominantly those of a German political class for whom export-oriented policy is a *raison d'état*.[87]

---

[85] See H Thompson, 'Austerity as Ideology: The Bait and Switch of the Banking Crisis' (2013) 11 Comparative European Politics 729.

[86] See Wilkinson (n 13).

[87] See Thompson (n 85).

The circle is squared by permitting rescue, not as an act of democratic solidarity, but through a 'grey area' of Union law, and with strict conditionality attached.[88] In this way the narrative of moral hazard is switched from the risky behaviour of private creditors to the profligacy of public debtors – the greatest 'bait and switch' in history, as Mark Blyth calls it.[89] This permits a moralisation of the debt, and a (misleading) metaphor to take hold of the imagination, that of the frugal Swabian household, which saves before it spends. Fiscal indiscipline is avoided in substance, because states have to pursue the austerity programmes (the 'strict conditionality') that are said would be demanded were they still subject to the financial markets. States – and the banks they are indebted to – are rescued enough to avoid immediate default, but without the debt restructuring that would be necessary to escape future dependency.[90] The eurozone thus develops in a neocolonial manner, along the lines of a core–periphery relationship between 'creditor' and 'debtor' nations. Germany becomes the 'reluctant hegemon', and the Greek people are 'punished' for electing a left-wing government that dared to oppose the austerity agenda of the Troika and powerful members of the Eurogroup, only to capitulate to the 'TINA' narrative ('There Is No Alternative', to neoliberal structural reform).[91] The domestic clash between capitalism and democracy is displaced into a neocolonial regime of integration; but it is democracy that pays the price.

Neo-functional rescue and ordoliberal discipline can theoretically be maintained for the moment in a very tense and delicate balance. The long-term cost to the normative values of democracy, solidarity, social rights and legality, however, has yet to be fully calculated. Political equality has rarely looked so illusory, as relations between debtor and creditor countries came to resemble 'unconditional surrender'.[92]

VII CONCLUSION

Considered in the *longue durée* of the battle between economic liberalism and social democracy, Maastricht has been described as having put a decisive end to the European civil war between right and left that took place across the 'short twentieth century'. It signalled the triumph of economic liberalism. The victory of capitalism itself was even declared complete. As Etienne Balibar frames it, reflecting on the (re)

---

[88] See eg Menendez (n 80).

[89] Blyth (n 12).

[90] See further B Jessop, 'Finance-Dominated Accumulation and Enduring Austerity' in R Sturm, T Griebel and T Winkelmann (eds), *Austerity: A Journey to an Unknown Territory. Discourses, Economics and Politics* (Nomos 2017) 29–49.

[91] See P Altermann, 'Jürgen Habermas' Verdict on the EU/Greece Debt Deal – Full Transcript' (*The Guardian*, 16 July 2015) www.theguardian.com/commentisfree/2015/jul/16/jurgen-habermas-eu-greece-debt-deal accessed April 2018.

[92] See F Scharpf, 'After the Crash: A Perspective on Multi-Level European Democracy' (2015) 21 European Law Journal 393.

birth of the EU at the Treaty of Maastricht, what is extraordinary is the explicit and detailed setting of its liberal political–economic goals into rigid constitutional guarantees:

> The EU in its constitutive moment (Maastricht) was endowed with a quasi-constitution ... where, for the first time in this part of the world ... a principle of political economy deriving from a specific ideological discourse (namely neo-liberal deregulation and unrestricted competition, believed to produce 'optimal allocation of resources' and spontaneously 'just' redistribution) was presented as the sovereign rule which all member states ought to implement in their national policies under close surveillance of the federal (or quasi-federal) organs of the Union.[93]

If the argument of this chapter is accepted, however, this battle, or at least its preliminary stages, may have already long been lost. Once *politics* is reduced to a single political–economic logic, and the possibility of genuine renewal comes down to the possibility of exercising the constituent power, the autonomy of the political is reduced to a bare formality or the prospect of a revolutionary rupture. This resettlement occurs right at the beginning of the post-war reconstitution of the European state and the project of European integration. It is cemented at Maastricht, continued into a further stage, rather than overturned.

In theory and practice, post-war constituent power is (temporarily) absorbed into a new regime of constituted power, based on constitutional rights, protected by constitutional courts, and managed by other technocratic institutions. But this also signifies a cultural and material shift, captured in the fear of political freedom, so emblematic of the German case but also affecting countries with a limited experience of democratic self-government. Issues of appropriation, distribution and production are increasingly taken out of the public political sphere of contestation, and determined by market logic, or the technocratic bodies who are supposed to replicate it. De-democratisation is a more appropriate term for this process that depoliticisation, given that these were highly politicised changes. And to capture constitutional change is to capture not only formal channelling but also constitutional framing, the way political debate is to be organised, and what its limits are.[94] So the process of de-democratisation can effectively be constitutionalised not only through institutional means but also through political ideology, such as in the TINA refrain.

If the constitutional implications of neoliberal political economy are underscored by the reconstitution of Europe right from the beginning of the post-war period, the

---

[93]   E Balibar, 'The Rise and Fall of the European Union: Temporalities and Teleologies' (2014) Constellations 202.

[94]   As Gavin Anderson puts it, 'constitutional discourse is always more than the rules it generates or legitimates ... setting the parameters not just for how politics is contested, but what is deemed politically contestable' (G Anderson in S Gill, *New Constitutionalism and World Order* (CUP 2015) 283), quoting Emilios Christodoulidis.

current conjuncture has thrown this settlement into doubt, but not yet into oblivion. It has been strongly contested, but there has been no definitive rupture, with the possible exception of Brexit.[95] If the capitulation of Greece suggests authoritarian liberalism may survive, developments elsewhere, as right-wing Eurosceptic parties surge in popularity, suggests that the authoritarian liberal suppression of the democratic voice may, once again, tend not only to the victory of capitalism, but also to the resurgence of reactionary forms of authoritarian *illiberalism*.[96] Whether any reprisal of the interwar breakdown of liberal democracy will more closely resemble tragedy or farce remains to be seen.

[95] The UK is one of the few places in Europe to have avoided the 'Pasokification' (virtual annihilation) of the traditional centre-left party, the UK Labour party under Jeremy Corbyn performing extraordinarily well in comparison to its sister parties. It is therefore a possibility that the UK's departure from the status quo of EU membership might, ironically given its advanced neoliberal trajectory, lead not to a right-wing authoritarian illiberalism, but to a turn towards democratic socialism.

[96] The turn to 'authoritarian populism' in Eastern Europe has been described as an inflection of, rather than rupture from, neoliberalism (G Dale and A Fabry, 'Neoliberalism in Eastern Europe and the Former Soviet Union' in D Cahill, M Cooper, M Konings and D Pimrose (eds), *The Sage Handbook of Neoliberalism* (Sage 2018)).

6

The Inherently Undemocratic EU Democracy

Moving beyond the 'Democratic Deficit' Debate

Eva Nanopoulos and Fotis Vergis

I INTRODUCTION

Almost ten years since the eruption of the global and financial crisis of 2008 and its European manifestation as the 'Eurocrisis', there is growing consensus that the latter quickly escalated or mutated into (among other things) a more profound democratic crisis. A number of prominent public intellectuals put pen to paper to warn not only of a crisis of European democracy,[1] but of a crisis of the very 'political institution' of democracy,[2] and particularly its representative and liberal variants. Contemporary manifestations of the 'hollowing out' of democracy following the Eurocrisis have taken many forms and several contributions in this volume have dealt with various aspects of the phenomenon.

The focus of the present chapter is on one aspect of this crisis, namely the Eurocrisis as a crisis of the EU's own democratic credentials. Even as they insisted on its purely economic character, commentators were quick to criticise the undemocratic form that the emergency EMU-related responses to the Eurocrisis came to assume, particularly at the European level, where not only parliamentary processes, but also the Treaties' legal prescriptions, were systematically circumvented. The critique comes across particularly vividly in Majone's characterisation of the post-crisis condition as a 'democratic default',[3] echoing both the aggravation of the EU's so-called 'democratic deficit'[4] and the spectre of sovereign debt default that the broader crisis of capitalism produced on the European continent.

---

[1] A Sen, 'The Crisis of European Democracy' New York Times (22 May 2012) www.nytimes.com/2012/05/23/opinion/the-crisis-of-european-democracy.html accessed April 2018.

[2] E Balibar, 'Europe in Crisis: Which "New Foundation"?' (*Open Democracy*, 5 December 2017) www.opendemocracy.net/can-europe-make-it/etienne-balibar/europe-in-crisis-which-new-foundation accessed April 2018.

[3] G Majone, 'From Regulatory State to a Democratic Default' (2014) 52 Journal of Common Market Studies 1216. For a more elaborate version of the arguments, see G Majone, *Rethinking the Union of Europe Post-Crisis: Has Integration Gone Too Far?* (CUP 2014).

[4] Although Majone himself denied the existence of a deficit on the basis that the EU did not require democratic legitimacy. For a thorough engagement with his and similar arguments, see A Follesdal

One could hardly disagree with the diagnosis – any deficit, if sustained over too long a period of time, threatens eventually to result in a default. More important, and contested, however, are its causes. Particularly within legal circles, post-crisis criticisms of the EU's response suggested that the erosion of democratic processes was merely a symptom or consequence of the crisis, rather than the expression of a more fundamental malaise. Here the economic and democratic aspects of the Eurocrisis parted ways: the two may be linked, but their relationship was largely one of cause (economic crisis) and effect (democratic degradation), rather than of systemic inter-relation. It could thus largely be solved by some measure of institutional engineering. In other fields, some contributors dug deeper into the relationship between the EU's debt crisis and its crisis of democratic legitimacy,[5] challenging the artificial separation of the economic and political spheres, which is embodied in their disaggregation into two separate crises, and pointing out how, from the perspective of the ruling classes, democracy was on the contrary 'part of the set of problems that caused the crisis' and could not 'therefore simultaneously be part of the solution.'[6] Such approaches revealed the more fundamental tension between democracy and the EU's economic order, but they remained rather marginal and did not necessarily trace this tension to the roots of the European project, focusing instead primarily on the Eurocrisis.

In line with the broader tenor of this collection, this chapter argues that what is seen as a crisis of EU democracy is not merely a symptom of the Eurocrisis, but a manifestation of a more systemic displacement of democracy as an inherent feature of the European project, which, we argue, is inherently undemocratic. In section II, we begin by showing that the reluctance or failure to look at the root causes of the EU's democratic predicament is characteristic of a broader trend, which permeates much of the literature on the democratic deficit, and hence pre-dates and is not confined to the Eurocrisis. Indeed, just as inquiries into the EU's post-crisis democratic default have tended to shy away from exploring its systemic roots, so have earlier debates about its longer-term democratic deficit tended to eschew its connection to the nature of the EU.

In section III, we argue that the displacement of democratic processes is inherent in the deeper formational essence and fundamental character of the EU. To show this, we examine the ideological and normative influences that informed the EU's construction and cemented its institutional and constitutional DNA, as well as the forces and actors that have continued to provide a vehicle for those influences to take political and legal form. Brought together, these indicative elements suggest that the fundamentally undemocratic nature of the EU is necessary both for the survival and perpetuation of the EU's specific vision of a common (free) market, and thus for the

---

and S Hix, 'Why There Is a Democratic Deficit in the EU: A Response to Majone and Moravcsik' (2006) 44 Journal of Common Market Studies 533.

[5] eg H Macartney, *The Debt Crisis and European Democratic Legitimacy* (Palgrave Macmillan 2013).

[6] ibid 7.

survival and perpetuation of contemporary European capitalism, as well as for the existence, affirmation and continuity of the EU bureaucracy and the symbiotic world of socio-economic interests and actors it has sprung forth.

In section IV, we conclude with some brief remarks about the implications of our analysis. A conceptualisation of the EU's displacement of democratic processes as an inherent constitutive feature of the project not only implies that the deficit, or the democratic default, cannot be palliated through institutional reform. It also implies that, in order to preserve its economic and social order, the EU will increasingly engage in a dangerous process of building European identity and allegiance, based on a singular vision of a Europe in Union, and resulting in the gradual exclusion of those who do not share a commitment to the EU's market telos. This marginalisation of critiques to the EU variety of free market capitalism and its disciplinary shackles may itself explain why the Eurocrisis did not result in more widespread debate about the relationship between European capitalism and democracy, even though the Eurocrisis suggested the two were rather uncomfortable bedfellows.

II THE 'DEMOCRATIC DEFICIT': MISSING THE POINT?

1 *The Deficit as Epiphenomenon*

Explanations of the democratic deficit could be broadly speaking divided into two main camps, although the second remains relatively marginal. The first is what we call the 'democratic deficit as epiphenomenon' approach. Although much of the relevant scholarship has primarily focused on describing, rather than explaining the root causes of, the democratic deficit, such work, whether explicitly or implicitly, tends to view the democratic deficit as a by-product, rather than an innate, let alone necessary, feature of the European project. Under this approach, the democratic deficit would have grown somewhat incrementally as an unintentional or unintended result of an evolving and complex institutional framework, designed to preserve a balance of national interests and, legally, respect for the principle of conferral, all the while ensuring the effective functioning of a somewhat undefined and ever-developing supranational project.

The epiphenomenal approach is evidenced by various dimensions of the debate. Linguistically, the language of 'deficit' appeared to suggest that democracy was something the EU came to lack, rather than an institution it was meant to sideline, exclude or redefine by design. Historically, more widespread concern about the EU's democratic credentials coincided with the adoption of the Single European Act in 1986 and the Treaty of Maastricht in 1992,[7] both of which are seen as key moments, even paradigm shifts, in the process of European integration, away from

---

[7]   eg B Kohler-Koch and B Rittberger (eds), *Debating the Democratic Legitimacy of the European Union* (Rowman & Littlefield 2007) 1.

its original economic orientation. Many commentators indeed expressly associate the deficit with the increased complexity of the EU's decision-making structures,[8] the expansion of the EU's competences and the gap between power and accountability that these Treaties created.[9] Normatively, moreover, it resonates with the conceptualisation of European integration as some kind of experiment, with unforeseen, contingent, possibly even random consequences, and the EU as an organisation 'sui generis', whose essence and future development are impossible to capture or foresee.

More importantly, perhaps, this epistemological basis is reflected in the particular kinds of reactions that the democratic malaise triggered, both in terms of the methodology and substantive focus of academic inquiry and in terms of institutional and political responses. From an academic perspective, much of the (legal) literature on the democratic deficit has been characterised by a distinct prioritisation of descriptive over theoretical or normative analyses. Since Weiler's 'standard version' of the deficit critique was published in 1995,[10] numerous studies have attempted to identify, map and describe the constitutive features of the EU's democratic predicament, even as it came to be widely agreed that the deficit has 'no single meaning',[11] but multiple interconnected dimensions. Various aspects of the deficit were thus brought to light, although the below topology is by no means comprehensive and only aims to recall some of the key elements of the debate.

Some inquiries have focused on the limits to input legitimacy (i.e. to effective means for citizens to express their will) including most prominently the absence of a European demos or the weakness of the European Parliament. Other studies have emphasised the deficit in output legitimacy, including the 'unresponsive'[12] nature of the EU's decision-making processes and its failure to reflect the preferences of the citizenry. Others have ventured into the realm of accountability,[13] and the problems created by the multiplicity of, and complex interaction between, different levels of decision-making. Increased attention, moreover, has come to be paid to questions of transparency, fuelled by the EU's secretive practices and methods of deliberation, as well as the thickness of its bureaucratic structures. To the extent that theoretical inquiries entered the landscape, they were aimed primarily at providing the normative criteria or benchmarks against which the EU's democratic credentials ought to be tested and solutions articulated, rather than explanatory tools for a more elaborate

---

[8]   See D Curtin, 'The Constitutional Structure of the Union: A Europe of Bits and Pieces' (1993) 30 CMLR 17.

[9]   D Grimm, *The Constitution of European Democracy* (OUP 2017).

[10]   JHH Weiler, UR Haltern and F Mayer, 'European Democracy and Its Critique' (1995) 18 West European 4.

[11]   Follesdal and Hix (n 4) 534.

[12]   P Craig and G de Burca, *EU Law: Text, Cases, and Materials* (5th edn, OUP 2015) 152.

[13]   M Bovens, D Curtin and P Hart (eds), *The Real World of EU Accountability: What Deficit?* (OUP 2010); A Arnull and D Wincott (eds), *Accountability and Legitimacy in the European Union* (OUP 2003).

understanding of the root causes of the deficit. Of particular concern have been the issues of what notion of democracy should be used (or carry greater weight), whether existing models and theories were suited to the task and whether national democracies provided a useful metric of comparison. The concepts of demoi and demoicracy[14] are among the many new concepts and analytical categories that emerged out of attempts to think through the dilemmas of post-national democracy in the context of the EU.[15]

On one level, this intellectual terrain may reflect a natural positivist inclination of doctrinal lawyers, and long-standing divisions of labour within legal studies and political science between descriptive empirical inquiries and theoretical work, the former kind of work being seen as properly concerned with the study of legal and political institutions and the latter with abstract concepts like democracy.[16] But it may also be explained by, and hence seen as a direct product of, a particular epiphenomenal approach to the democratic crisis. If the starting point is that the deficit is an unintended product, rather than a systemic feature, of integration, it almost naturally follows that the path to understanding and overcoming the problem cannot lie in theoretical enquiry about the nature of the European project but needs instead to be rooted in careful empirical diagnoses of the phenomenon and its various institutional manifestations.

The result, ultimately, has been that solutions to the deficit have been sought primarily in institutional 'fixes' designed to ameliorate one or the other aspects of the perceived democratic deficiencies of the EU, even as, ironically, the process of Treaty revision itself has been oftentimes criticised as opaque and exclusionary.[17] Successive waves of treaty amendments thus increased the powers of the European Parliament, introduced mechanisms to enhance the participation of national parliaments and citizens, provided for greater transparency in the working of the EU institutions, and particularly the Council, or reinforced the EU's professed commitment to democratic values. Not all commentators were convinced that these developments went far enough or that institutional reform would ever be sufficient whether because of scepticism about the Union's ability to replicate even the 'imperfect habits of governmental control, parliamentary accountability, and administrative responsibility'[18] that are present at the national level or about the

---

[14]   eg K Nicolaïdis, 'European Demoicracy and Its Crisis' (2013) 51 Journal of Common Market Studies 351; K Nicolaïdis, 'The Idea of European Demoicracy' in J Dickson and P Eleftheriadis (eds), *Philosophical Foundations of European Union Law* (OUP 2012).

[15]   eg see EO Eriksen, *The Unfinished Democratization of Europe* (OUP 2009).

[16]   On divisions of labour within disciplines and disciplinary boundaries, see eg C List and L Valentini, 'The Methodology of Political Theory' in H Cappelen, T Szabó Gendler and J Hawthorne (eds), *The Oxford Handbook of Philosophical Methodology* (OUP 2016).

[17]   eg Curtin (n 8) 19.

[18]   JHH Weiler, 'The Political and Legal Culture of European Integration: An Exploratory Essay' (2011) 9 International Journal of Constitutional Law 678, 679.

possibility of a European demos.[19] Reformist strategies have nonetheless tended to prevail and testify to a particular conceptualisation of the deficit as a question of 'appropriate institutional engineering'.[20]

This approach continued to underpin much of the (early) analyses of the deepening of the democratic malaise that followed from responses to the Eurocrisis and explains why it was diagnosed as a mere symptom of the crisis. The further democratic drift was indeed readily associated with yet another wave of expatriation of power to the EU in the form of fiscal and budgetary supervision[21] – indeed often in blatant disregard of legal prescriptions.[22] Energies were thrown into mapping its constitutive elements, from the empowerment of executive bodies (e.g. the European Council) to the emergence of new executive actors (e.g. Eurogroup) and the sidelining of the European Parliament and national parliaments. As others in this volume have highlighted: 'new intergovernment-alism'; 'executive dominance';[23] 'executive federalism'; 'executive managerialism' or 'agentification' were among the many terms that appeared to describe the structures that emerged during the crisis period. To the extent that the intensity of the crisis forced a more serious engagement with the aggravation of the deficit and the EU's authoritarian turn, the initial analyses displayed a distinct tendency to externalise the problem, citing 'political sensitivity', 'necessity', 'urgency'[24] or the natural reinforcement of the executive arm of the state in times of emergency. Discussions moreover swiftly began about what mechanisms could enhance the democratic legitimacy of the EMU governance structures[25] within the existing legal framework, alongside further Treaty reform. Ultimately, any deeper theorising about the root causes of the crisis was not only eschewed in favour of descriptive analyses, in tune with previous approaches to the deficit such an inquiry was implicitly deemed to be essentially pointless. The real question, again, was whether and how the democratic default could be rectified.

2 The Democratic Deficit as a Systemic But Not Inherent Condition

Outside the community of legal scholars, a more critical strand of commentary has tended to take more seriously the root causes of the deficit[26] and to view it as a systemic, rather than unintended, feature of European integration. Although

---

[19]   Although see J Habermas, 'Remarks on Dieter Grimm's "Does Europe Need a Constitution?"' (1995) 1 European Law Journal 303.

[20]   M Tsakatika, 'Governance vs Politics: the European Union's Constitutive "Democratic Deficit"' (2007) 14 Journal of European Public Policy 867, 867.

[21]   eg F Nicoli, 'Democratic Legitimacy in the Era of Fiscal Integration' (2016) 39 Journal of European Integration 389.

[22]   See Chapter 5 in this volume.

[23]   A Hinarejos, *The Euro Area Crisis in Constitutional Perspective* (OUP 2015), especially ch 6.

[24]   ibid 92.

[25]   C Alcidi, A Giovannini and S Piedrafita, 'Enhancing the Legitimacy of EMU Governance', Study for the ECON Committee (2014) www.ceps.eu/publications/enhancing-legitimacy-emu-governance accessed April 2018.

[26]   eg Tsakatika (n 20).

they provide important insights, however, they ultimately tend to shy away from linking the causes of the deficit to the nature of the European project.

(1) The Deficit and Functionalism

One such approach draws on functionalist premises. Under this reading, the deficit did not arise accidentally over the course of the EU's development nor does it constitute a structural defect, but can be explained functionally, as a feature that was and remains necessary to achieve the economic objectives of the EU, namely the creation of an internal market. The idea is that such functions can be executed more 'efficiently' if they are insulated from democratic scrutiny and the meddle-some wishes of electorates and entrusted instead 'to competent, stable, impartial, and rational actors and institutions'.[27] In a recent book that attempts to construct a functionalist theory of (European) constitutionalism, for example, Isiksel argues that the *finalité économique* continues to dominate the EU and shows how, from their origins to their current form, the Treaties bear their 'framers' aversion to mass participation in politics'.[28] In her account, crucially, the democratic deficit is 'not a bug'[29] but a systemic feature of the EU and its aggravation during the crisis a continuation, rather than 'radical break with the EU's *modus operandi*'.[30] That this remains a defining feature of the EU can be illustrated by the case of *Pringle*, where the Court was arguably as much concerned with safeguarding the EMU, as it was with preserving the 'stability' that technocratic supranational governance can ensure by escaping scrutiny and unwanted revisions.

Such inquiries take the debate in productive directions. They bring to light the systemic character of the EU's democratic predicament. They contest the view that the EU has transcended its economic orientation (and functionalist logic), and hence that the deficit springs merely from integration in other fields, rather than the distinctively market-building purpose in which such further developments are embedded, and to which they are ultimately subordinated. They highlight the need for a proper theorisation of the deficit that links it to the nature of the European project, rather than an unintended consequence of its incremental development. And, finally, they point, albeit more hesitantly, to some of the pitfalls of framing debates about the EU, and its crisis, around the question of whether and how the EU could be more democratic, highlighting the fact that the problem is not so much the lack of citizens' participation, but the 'functionally differentiated forms of political agency' the EU has produced and which 'amplify the voices of citizens and groups who further market liberalization'.[31]

[27] T Isiksel, *Europe's Functional Constitution* (OUP 2016) 11.
[28] ibid 12.
[29] ibid 12.
[30] ibid 228.
[31] ibid 28.

Approaches that build on functionalist premises, however, also have a number of limitations. First, they tend not only to keep the economic functions of the EU separate from its political and social functions, however modest, but also to take the positive value of the former as a given. The assumption that the functions of international organisations are 'a-political' in the sense of a 'force for good'[32] has deep roots in functionalist thought. It was in fact on the basis of that functional legitimacy, premised on the assumption that the EU exercised only regulatory 'pareto-improving functions' that had no redistributive effect and merely improved the lives of European citizens, that some authors disagreed that the EU needed democratic legitimacy and/or suffered from a democratic deficit.[33] That basic premise does not disappear in Isiksel's more critical and constitutionalist account of functionalism, given that she accepts constitutionalism has been and can be legitimately concerned not only with realising democracy or protecting individual liberty, but also with delivering effective government.[34]

Second, as a result, the democratic problem becomes primarily a question of (im)balance between different functions, linked to the prioritisation of economic objectives and the 'colonisation' of other aspects of the public sphere, including democracy, by economic rationalities and subjectivities. As such, the democratic deficit is viewed primarily as 'the EU's failure to strike the right balance between alternate sources of constitutional authority, namely democratic rule on the one hand, and effective government on the other',[35] rather than any inherent displacement of democracy.

Third, ultimately the result is that the deficit is seen as systemic, but not a necessary feature of the European project. It is merely a means to an end, an expression of the functionalist logic that could be remedied by a more radical transformation of the telos of the European project. Even as she remains deeply sceptical of the possibilities offered by contemporary conditions, Isiksel thus points out that 'economic union does not exhaust the horizons of the European project'.[36] This approach, then, does not foreclose the possible democratisation of the EU. From that perspective, its main difference from the epiphenomenal approach is the character of the reforms that would be needed for conditions conducive to democratisation to be put into place.

More importantly, perhaps, approaches inspired by functionalist tenets, insightful as they may be in their attempts to dig deeper into the examination of the deficit, remain superficially ontological and narrowly pragmatic in essence, failing to connect the democratic crisis to the underlying nature of the European project. If

---

[32] J Klabber, 'The Emergence of Functionalism in International Institutional Law: Colonial Inspirations' (2014) 25 EJIL 645, 646.

[33] For an overview and critique of the 'no deficit' thesis, see Follesdal and Hix (n 4).

[34] Isiksel (n 27) 27.

[35] ibid 57.

[36] ibid 232.

'ontology' is defined, at a superficial level, as the examination of what (visibly) exists and what the units that comprise it are,[37] functionalist analyses tend to take the visible features of the EU (principles and objectives; institutional framework, competences and functions) at face value, as the basis for their critique. It is on that premise that they subsequently seek to assess this visible reality of the institutional framework and explain why specific decision-making processes or subsequent regulatory norms and policies were adopted. Like Isiksel, they might also tap onto the fundamental normative choices revealed within EU primary law, including that of a very specific (arguably skewed) balance of fundamental economic and social objectives. These normative choices, though, are also accepted as a 'given' in the functionalist problematique; as part of the *observable* elements of the Union as a political and institutional being.[38] Put otherwise, under Colin Hay's definition of political ontology,[39] functional approaches merely scrape the surface of the nature of the EU: its formal legal framework and its institutional edifice.

(2) The Deficit and State Transformation

Within the field of political science, an approach that seemingly seeks to transcend the pragmatic and somewhat ontologically superficial lens functionalism tends to adopt, has been put forward by Christopher Bickerton.[40] In his important examination of the transformational effect EU membership has had on the concept of statehood, Bickerton presents the EU as a cauldron in which national and supranational political structures are fused into a new arrangement, whereby there is no confrontational distinction between the two layers, but rather an amalgam of their features. To him, the EU is not a union of nation states (as the intergovernmentalists would suggest) nor yet a polity of people (as ardent integrationists might assert), but rather a union of member states, EU membership having become an inherent feature of statehood itself, defining national policy and interests. In this account, the democratic deficit likewise is not merely the result of an expansion of the competences of the EU. Rather, it is part of this deeper transformation of the state, from nation state to member state, as a special form of statehood with distinct characteristics, which include the exercise of power in forums outside public scrutiny and control and as part of a wider reshaping of state–society relations linked to the dismantling of the nation corporatist state in the 1980s and 1990s.

---

37   N Blaikie, *Approaches to Social Enquiry* (Polity 1993) 6.
38   This is clear in Isiksel's own account where she explains that she intends to 'examine the values that guide the EU's normative structure, rather than to isolate the causal factors that explain its existence' and that her work is therefore 'interpretative and critical, rather than explanatory and predictive' ((n 27) 7).
39   C Hay, 'Political Ontology' in RE Goodin (ed) *The Oxford Handbook of Political Science* (OUP 2011) 460, 463.
40   C Bickerton, *European Integration: From Nation-States to Member States* (OUP 2012).

Bickerton's analysis makes an important contribution to conceptualisations of the EU[41] and brings home the important point that the deficit cannot be seen as having been imposed from the top. Yet, while his analysis is seemingly more concerned with the nature and effects of the EU, it is not actually as remote from the methodology of functionalist inquiries. Their focus might be different, but Bickerton's theorisation of the EU is still rooted in a particular interpretation of the visible architecture of the EU and hence equally superficial ontologically: he primarily describes what the beast looks like (a union of member states) not what its inner essence is. It is telling that Isiksel too highlights the transformative effects the EU's functional constitution has had on domestic constitutional systems, even though she arrives at a different understanding of the phenomenon.

Some commentators have hinted at what an analysis that builds on these approaches but takes more seriously the nature of the EU might begin to look like. In a review of Isiksel's book, and reflecting on the implications of the EU's 'functional legacy', Möller[42] looks closer at the EU's core character and the forces that forged it. He highlights a tendency to overlook the fact that the 'founders' of the Treaties, the 'bureaucrats' or the 'legal engineers' 'were not simply technocrats investing their efforts in a type of functional normativity as an end unto itself' but that 'functional technocracy on the European level was deeply embedded in social and political conflict in the post-war era'.[43] The review itself describes some of the main political and ideological struggles of the period, without fully developing what the 'ends' of European integration might be. But in doing so, Möller brings home the important point that the democratic displacement may not only be a means to an end, but an end in itself, rooted in a deeper underlying project that is linked to, and sustained by, a specific web of interests and actors.

Similarly, authors like Jones[44] or Macartney[45] have further contextualised the notion of state transformation, showing how the insulation from democratic processes is not only a feature of the 'member state' but was specifically intended to enable the 'European elites to push through neoliberal policies that would have encountered tremendous – possibly fatal – resistance had this been attempted at the national',[46] rather than the European, scale. Under that view, and in tune with the insights of Gill's notion of 'new constitutionalism',[47] the democratic deficit would be part of a set of legal arrangements designed to 'lock in' the preferences of the elite,

---

[41] Although see also AS Milward, *The European Rescue of the Nation State* (Routledge 1992).

[42] K Möller, 'Book Review: Europe's Functional Constitution' (2017) 24 Constellations 652.

[43] ibid 654.

[44] eg L Jones, 'The EU Locked in Neoliberalism and Locked Out Its People. Brexit Is the Alternative' (*LSE Blog*, 10 June 2016) http://blogs.lse.ac.uk/brexit/2016/06/10/the-eu-locked-in-neoliberalism-and -locked-out-its-people-brexit-is-the-alternative accessed April 2018.

[45] Macartney (n 5).

[46] Jones (n 44).

[47] eg S Gill and AC Cutler, *New Constitutionalism and World Order* (CUP 2014).

and its aggravation during the Eurocrisis a means to 'channel the crisis hysteria'[48] into neoliberal reforms that had been previously opposed. While this would seemingly attribute an instrumental function to the democratic deficit, seeing it as a tool to cement neoliberalism, it also suggests that the insulation from democratic processes may be a more intrinsic characteristic of the neoliberal project that is today embedded at the EU level. In the section III, we build on some of these insights to show that, contrary to what is commonly assumed, the democratic deficit is not a symptom nor the by-product of fragmented evolution,[49] but a conscious inherent part of its nature. While it is beyond the scope and the narrow confines of this chapter to engage in the deep 'institutional psychoanalysis' that would be required to paint a complete image of the true ontology of the EU, we hope nonetheless to pave the way for a more complex understanding of its (un)democratic predicament.

III THE DEMOCRATIC DEFICIT: A REAPPRAISAL

1 *From Political Ontology to Metaphysics*

One of the problems with ontological approaches is that reality does not merely consist of the visible; it cannot be identified with mere appearances.[50] If the causes of the deficit are to be excavated, and its relationship to the legal and political ontology of the EU unravelled, the description and analysis cannot be carried out by reference only to the EU's visible characteristics and functions but requires a much more complex examination. That would entail exploring the historical, sociopolitical and even cultural context within which the EU emerged and continues to develop, the nature and the motives of the actors engaged in its functioning and evolution, and the dynamic of the various relationships and conflicting interests that have shaped it. It would also entail an understanding of the ideas and narratives that either played a constitutive role in the institutional DNA of the project or frame its current form. Going beyond appearances, therefore, and diving into the origins, ethos and, ultimately, psyche of the Union will reveal that the normative choices engrained in primary law and identified as the cause of particular functional trajectories are not just another superficial feature of the EU. Rather, these choices are engrained in the EU's core, inherent characteristics and are therefore inescapable and impossible to rectify.

Our approach thus moves from the superficially ontological to the substantive and the 'political metaphysical' level.[51] That is, it is concerned not only with a positivist oversight of the material, hence visible, aspects of the legal and institutional framework (e.g. treaty provisions and other legal norms; institutional functions) or the stated substantive principles and objectives of the EU, that, together comprise its

---

[48]   Macartney (n 5) 24.
[49]   D Dinan, *Europe Recast: A History of European Union* (Palgrave Macmillan 2004) 323.
[50]   Hay (n 39) 462–63.
[51]   I Adams, 'The Inevitability of Political Metaphysics' (1999) 4 Journal of Political Ideologies 269.

formal appearance. It is also interested in the more elusive underlying normative and ideological impetus[52] as well as the often underexposed power dynamics and conflicts of interests that together constitute the hidden justification[53] for the adoption of those particular formal and substantive elements.

That approach not only allows us to illuminate the root causes of the deficit. It also enables us to see how such a rigid framework based on preordained substantive choices can give rise to a narrative that has little in common with the real nature of the institutional structure it is called upon to serve and can in fact conceal it under a package of almost metaphysical allure that can ensure its survival and perpetuity. In particular, by including an abstract commitment to values like the protection of human rights or the promotion of democracy, this package takes on a positive connotation of almost moral character,[54] even though the real ethos, substance and function of the EU do little to prioritise them. It is then the narrative, rather than reality, that serves as the (ultimately false) premise upon which new identities are forged (construed against the 'other' that does not share the narrative, in a divide that can take an almost Manichaeistic form). And it is the narrative, rather than reality, upon which an equally false consensus is formed that is then used to allow the assumption that the democratic legitimacy of the real project (rather than its metaphysical transfiguration) could be achieved.

If we are to look into the 'political metaphysics' of the nature and effect of integration and locate the EU within the historical and sociopolitical evolution of Europe, in other words, we need to begin by attempting to understand the EU's real fundamental defining character and nature. In order to do so, we return to the ideological and normative influences that informed its construction and cemented its institutional and constitutional DNA, the actors that provided a vehicle for those influences to take political and legal form, but also those that continue to shape it today.

2 Normative Influences and Original Ideological Roots

The formal and conceptual ordoliberal[55] influences on the original institutional design of the EU in its EEC form, especially in the idea of eventually developing

---

[52]   cf ibid 272, 283–86, where Adams argues that ideology in itself is metaphysical in nature, inviting and provoking acts of faith that can have similar practical and, eventually, institutional results with any such acts driven by metaphysical (i.e. moral or religious) faith.

[53]   Adams (n 51); J Hampton 'Should Political Philosophy Be Done without Metaphysics?' (1989) 99 Ethics 791, 791–92, both drawing upon Rawlsian theory's striving to unearth hidden justifications of justice.

[54]   On the value and importance of infusing political philosophy (and, thus, we would argue, political discourse and the creation of narratives and constitutive myths) with an element of positive morality (that allows a Manichaeistic 'right vs wrong' divide) see Hampton (n 53) 807–14; Adams (n 51) 286.

[55]   There is no single definitive form of ordoliberalism nor a respectively ultimate ordoliberal concept of the market. The term, however, can be used to share the various strands of the relevant economic and political theory. See M Streit and M Wohlgemuth, 'The Market Economy and the State: Hayekian and Ordoliberal Conceptions' in P Koslowski (ed) *The Theory of Capitalism in the German Economic Tradition* (Springer 2000) 225, 226.

a particular economic constitution[56] for the Union, cannot be disputed. This is not to say that the EU, in its conception, was an explicitly ordoliberal project, or that it adheres fully to the original ordoliberal ideas, as they evolved in Germany through the 1920s[57] and the 1930s and emerged more prominently after the Second World War,[58] under the influence of the Freiburg School[59] and scholars such as Walter Eucken and Franz Böhm.[60] In fact, some of the founding architects of the EEC might dismiss a direct association between the EEC and ordoliberal tenets, even though others among them were prominent members of the ordoliberal school, like Alfred Müller-Armack.[61] However, those actors that participated in the drafting of the EEC's blueprint and its eventual emergence were certainly influenced in their understanding of economic governance and the relevant necessary institutional constructs by ordoliberal ideas and frameworks, especially those that had informed the German reconstruction project and its social market economy[62] model. Moreover, they shared the fundamental ordoliberal objective of ensuring economic stability,[63] with the transnational twist of applying it to intra-European trade.

In the original conception of the European project, the influence of ordoliberal principles was primarily reflected in its foundational core. The project was to be based upon the prioritisation of free market principles, embracing them as its central objectives and values. Similar to ordoliberal thought, which embraces a functional understanding of the market,[64] and contrary to an approach that would have reflected classical market liberalism,[65] in the EU, common market liberalisation was not to be an end in itself. Rather, it was seen as a means towards not only political

---

[56]   C Joerges, 'What Is Left of the European Economic Constitution? A Melancholic Eulogy' (2005) European Law Review 461, 465–67; S Razeen, *Classical Liberalism and the International Economic Order* (Routledge 1998) 106–11; W Sauter, 'The Economic Constitution of the European Union' (1998) 4 Columbia Journal of European Law 27, 46.

[57]   R Ptak, 'Neoliberalism in Germany: Revisiting the Ordoliberal Foundations of the Social Market Economy' in P Mirowski and D Plehwe (eds), *The Road from Mont Pèlerin: The Making of the Neoliberal Thought Collective* (Harvard UP 2009) 98, 108–12; W Bonefield, 'Freedom and the Strong State: On German Ordoliberalism' (2012) 17 New Political Economy 633, 633.

[58]   Sauter (n 56).

[59]   ibid.

[60]   F Böhm, W Eucken and H Grossmann-Dörth (eds), *Die Ordnung der Wirtschaft als geschichtliche Aufgabe und rechtsschöpferische Leistung* (Kohlhammer 1937).

[61]   C Watrin, 'Alfred Müller-Armack – Economic Policy Maker' in Koslowski (n 55) 192, 193–94; N Goldschmidt, 'Alfred Müller-Armack and Ludwig Erhard: Social Market Liberalism' (2004) Freiburg Discussion Papers on Constitutional Economics No 04/12 2, 16. See also A Müller-Armack, *Auf dem Weg nach Europa. Erinnerungen und Ausblicke* (R Wunderlich 1971).

[62]   A Müller-Armack, *Wirtschaftslenkung und Marktwirtschaft* (first published in 1947, Kastell 1990); A Müller-Armack, 'The Social Aspect of the Economic System' (1947) in Ludwig-Erhard-Stiftung (ed) *Standard Texts on the Social Market Economy: Two Centuries of Discussion* (tr D Rutter, ed G Fischer 1982) 9, 9–22.

[63]   Ptak (n 57) 109–10; W Bonefield, 'On the Strong Liberal State: Beyond Berghahn and Young' (2013) 18 New Political Economy 779, 780.

[64]   R Sally, *Classical Liberalism and the International Economic Order* (Routledge 1998) 106–11.

[65]   K Tribe, 'Ordoliberalism and the Social Market Economy' (2007) 49 History of Economic Thought 155, 158; M Streit and M Wohlgemuth, 'The Market Economy and the State: Hayekian and Ordoliberal Conceptions' in Koslowski (n 55) 225, 226.

cooperation but also sociopolitical integration. The market was approached as a means to an emancipatory end that would dispel old antagonisms. This functional angle as regards the market was complemented by the other main idea[66] of ordo-liberal thought: that its attainment requires the establishment, at primary level, of a specific legal framework,[67] that would impose a specific preordained 'order' on the market.[68] That order should primarily ensure that the market operates upon two bases that constitute the prerequisites of free market economy:[69] completely undis-torted free competition;[70] and the guarantee of individual economic rights and freedoms and of autonomous self-regulation (arbitration).[71] Consequently, the mar-ket does not enjoy self-determination.[72] Rather, it is restrained by an order that has been predetermined by the economic constitution as the manifestation of a specific constitutional *choice*.[73]

At first glance, this choice is not disembedded in principle from democratic processes, even though democratic input could only affect its construction at the constitutional level (its constitutional adoption or amendment), and not influence regular legislation or policy. However, it is clear that an ordoliberal institutional framework ultimately aims to achieve the depoliticalisation of the economy,[74] or, to put it more accurately, the de-democratisation[75] of economic policy. The institu-tional apparatus of the EU and its legal order that sits at the centre of this framework plays the role of the market-guardian watchman, ensuring the preservation and perpetuation of the preordained market order and its monetary arm, without itself directly participating in the market. That central 'order', though, is secured against political debate, democratic review and revision of its fundamental characteristics. Putting the EU fundamental economic order beyond democratic reach reflects the fundamental ordoliberal belief that by constraining the central institutional machin-ery (the ordoliberal state), and, therefore, political actors, within more or less rigid

---

[66] W Eucken, 'Die Wirtschaftsordnung als Zentralbegriff des Wirtschaftsrechts' (1936) Mitteilungen des Jenaer Instituts für Wirtschaftsrecht 31, 3–14.

[67] KW Nörr, 'Franz Böhm and the Theory of the Private Law Society' in Koslowski (n 55) 148, 156–60.

[68] Joerges, 'What Is Left of the European Economic Constitution?' (n 56) 465–67; W Devroe and P van Cleynenbreuge, 'Observations on Economic Governance and the Search for a European Economic Constitution' in D Schiek, U Liebert and H Schneider (eds), *European Economic and Social Constitutionalism after the Treaty of Lisbon* (CUP 2011) 95, 97; Sally (n 64) 111.

[69] F Böhm, 'Private Law Society and Market Economy' (1966) (tr) in Koslowski (n 55) 161–87. It is in this piece that Böhm pre-dates Margaret Thatcher in proclaiming 'there is no such thing as a society which, vis-a-vis the state, might be a body responsible for constitutionally protected rights and powers. Such rights are only assigned to individual members of society in so far as they are legal entities' ((n 69) 171).

[70] See F Böhm, *Wettbewerb und Monopolkampf* (Heymanns 1933).

[71] Streit and Wohlgemuth (n 65) 231.

[72] H Peukert, 'Walter Eucken (1891–1950) and the Historical School' in Koslowski (n 55) 93, 120.

[73] V Vanberg, 'The Freiburg School: Walter Eucken and Ordoliberalism' (2004) Walter Eucken Institut, Freiburg Discussion Papers on Constitutional Economics 04/11, 5.

[74] Sauter (n 56) 47–48; Bonefield (n 57) 641.

[75] Peukert (n 72) 101; Ptak (n 57) 111–12.

boundaries delimited by the predetermined 'order', populist changes, driven by specific interest groups,[76] and potentially violent shifts in regulation, that would also directly affect the functioning of the market, can be avoided.[77]

The present form of the EU continues to carry ordoliberal DNA, enhanced after the Treaty of Maastricht, in further cementing the centrality of a closely safeguarded pre-specified market 'order' founded upon specific principles and rights that are afforded primacy over all others. It has also gone a step further in embracing ordoliberal principles, though. The normative basis of the EU economic order is endowed today with a robust apparatus designed to insulate its contemporary heart, the EMU, complemented by semi-autonomous institutions, such as the ECB, that are now entirely beyond the reach of electorates or even the judiciary. These are entrusted with safeguarding the new fundamental incontestable dogmas of fiscal discipline and price stability against meddlesome electorates. The Union's pre-specified central 'order', in its specific normative and institutional form, is to be accepted without contestation, as the fundamental existential *conditio sine qua non*; it just *is*, and it ought to be preserved as such. Therefore, it is to be placed beyond the reach of 'normal' politics and hence, essentially, outside the reach of democratic scrutiny.

The inherently undemocratic tenets of ordoliberal structures as regards the economic order that sits at their centre, allow what could be superficially regarded as a peculiar kinship. In particular, they suggest that there is a thread that connects the underlying undemocratic rationale of ordoliberalism with classic (laissez-faire) market liberalism[78] and with Carl Schmitt's ideas as to the political[79] and economic[80] aspects of a constitutional polity.[81] All three schools indeed perceive dangers in leaving the regulation of the market or the polity to the political process.

The similarities of ordoliberal *'ordo'* and Schmitt's *'concrete order'*[82] and *'stable authority'*[83] as the basis of regulatory predetermination cannot be ignored. Schmitt argued in favour of central political processes that would be sanitised from the

---

[76] Peukert (n 72) 101.

[77] C Joerges and F Rödl, '"Social Market Economy" as Europe's Social Model?' in L Magnusson and B Stråth (eds), *A European Social Citizenship? Preconditions for Future Policies from a Historical Perspective* (Peter Lang 2004) 125, 130.

[78] F Block, 'Towards a New Understanding of Economic Modernity' in C Joerges, B Strath and P Wagner (eds), *The Economy as Polity: The Political Constitution of Contemporary Capitalism* (UCL 2005) 1, 13.

[79] See C Schmitt, *The Concept of the Political* (first published 1932; G Schwab tr, 2nd edn, University of Chicago Press 2007).

[80] On the similarity of Schmitt's economic ideas with those of some of the founders of ordoliberalism, see D Haselbach, 'Franz Oppenheimer's Theory of Capitalism and of a Third Path' in Koslowski (n 55) 54, 66; see also R Cristi, *Carl Schmitt and Authoritarian Liberalism: Strong State, Free Economy* (University of Wales Press 1998) 194 and the references therein.

[81] Cristi (n 80) 176.

[82] ibid 159–66.

[83] C Schmitt, *Legality and Legitimacy* ((first published 1932; J Seitzer tr, Duke UP 2004) 90).

democratic element[84] by establishing a strong centralised executive. Under Schmitt's theory democracy should not necessarily be abolished in theory[85] or as a symbolic source of power,[86] but it would become authoritarian in practice,[87] a pretext for a functionally authoritarian executive.[88] Democracy should be 'relativised'.[89] In turn, the central executive structure would have to operate within a *'concrete order'*, which, as Cristi has interpreted it,[90] would amount to the rigid, stable, predetermined core of the polity,[91] comprising the 'ultimate fundamental norms'[92] beyond the reach of contemporary politics, democratic processes and legal scrutiny. Furthermore, more related to the ideas of market regulation through economic governance, Schmitt suggested that the concept of the economy is part of a 'non-state but still public sphere',[93] within which autonomous economic administration[94] is the main regulatory tool.

The similarities with ordoliberal reasoning are striking and the implications chilling. In both cases, a specific order (constitutional or political) is predetermined, a constant to be taken for granted, which delimits the conduct of all actors participating in the polity or the market it defines. This central order is to be safeguarded by a strong central institutional apparatus, itself beyond democratic reproach.

This attachment to the idea of a central driving dogma and the respective aversion towards democratic processes, particularly in relation to the regulation of the market, is also shared not only between ordoliberalism and Schmittian theory, but also between those and neoclassical market liberalism and, especially, neoliberalism. It is interesting to note that the neoliberal market resembles the ordoliberal 'ordo' and the Schmittian 'concrete order' in that it needs to be constructed[95] through planning and careful rearrangement and use of political[96] and legislative[97] power. As such, contrary to the popular perception, it is not a strong

---

[84] Cristi (n 80) 21, 193; cf D Dyzenhaus, *Legality and Legitimacy: Carl Schmitt, Hans Kelsen and Hermann Heller in Weimar* (OUP 1997) 81.

[85] See Cristi (n 80); cf J Habermas, 'Sovereignty and the Führerdemokratie', *Times Literary Supplement* (26 September 1986) 1053, 1054.

[86] Cristi (n 80) 15–16.

[87] ibid 23.

[88] ibid 15.

[89] PE Gottfried, *Carl Schmitt: Politics and Theory* (Greenwood Press 1990) 4.

[90] Cristi (n 80) 159–66.

[91] ibid 159.

[92] ibid.

[93] C Schmitt, 'Strong State and Sound Economy: An Address to Business Leaders' (first published 1932; Renato Cristi tr) in Cristi (n 80) 225.

[94] ibid 225–26.

[95] P Mirowski, 'Postface: Defining Neoliberalism' in Mirowski and Plehwe (n 57) 417, 434–35.

[96] T Mitchell, 'How Neoliberalism Makes Its World: The Urban Property Rights Project in Peru' in Mirowski and Plehwe (n 57) 386, 386.

[97] Draft Statement of Aims of the Mont Pèlerin Society, 7 April 1947, Point 5: 'The preservation of an effective competitive order *depends upon a proper legal and institutional framework*. The existing framework *must be considerably modified* to make the operation of competition more efficient and beneficial' (emphasis added), reproduced in Mirowski and Plehwe (n 57) 23.

state (or central authority) as such that neoliberals are against.[98] State power and its apparatus are considered by them essential to create those norms and institutions that will bring about the desired preconditions[99] for the exercise of (market) free-dom. Moreover, they are crucial in preserving this arrangement and its conditions (which can be identified with what ordoliberalism would recognise as the central '*ordo*'), once in place, by guaranteeing the protection and prioritisation of the relevant principles and freedoms, addressing distortions to the market equilibrium caused by various externalities.[100]

What is important, however, is how these functional similarities between neoli-beralism, ordoliberalism and Schmittian constitutionalism are woven together with the idea of a central authority, be it a state or the transnational entity the EU became, which is democratically unconstrained.[101] Ironically, Hayek himself, despite having expressed aversion for Schmitt's political ideas, actually commends him for under-standing the 'weakness of the government of an omnipotent democracy'[102] and shares concerns with him as regards an 'ever growing domination over the economic process by politics'.[103] The conclusion he is also led to is that the regulatory process, insofar as it affects the market, ought to be depoliticised; that is, de-democratised. Rationality is an attribute that can only appear at an individual level, according to neoliberal reasoning; electorates are not rational and therefore should not be entrusted with regulatory power. But if the central regulatory and supervisory authority does have a role to play, who is to direct it to the 'proper' path of action to be taken? Not the electorate or democratically elected politicians, but qualified educated technocrats,[104] supposedly better equipped to digest market information, interpret the signs of the invisible market forces, and neutrally and objectively direct the necessary course corrections.

This is ultimately what differentiates ordoliberalism, market liberalism, especially in its neoliberal form, and Schmittian autocracy. All three share a fundamental distrust of political and democratic processes and, therefore, require that they are either pushed aside or narrowed down to a point that avoids interference with the fundamentals upon which economic and monetary policy rests. And under all three approaches, those central fundamentals, and the principles they embody, are placed above all other considerations, interests or rights, precluding any debate or scepti-cism. They only differ as to the actor that is entrusted with maintaining the order, and, therefore, essentially, with ruling. In all three cases that actor is not to be 'the

---

[98]   Mirowski (n 95) 436.
[99]   Bonefield (n 57) 634.
[100]   See (n 97).
[101]   F Hayek, *Law, Law, Legislation and Liberty: A New Statement of the Liberal Principles of Justice and Political Economy* (1st full edn 1983, vol 3, Routledge 1998) 137–39.
[102]   ibid 194, fn 11.
[103]   ibid 150.
[104]   Referring to the Chilean neoliberal project, see K Fischer, 'The Influence of Neoliberals in Chile Before, during and after Pinochet' in Mirowski and Plehwe (n 57) 305, 306–07.

people'. Ordoliberalism puts 'the state' at the centre, allowing some limited role for democracy in the construction of the central 'order', but entrusting its preservation to the executive. Carl Schmitt would not hesitate to give the guardian's role to a much more powerful executive, even if it involved a singular sovereign. Neoliberals, on the other hand, also support the existence of a state or state-like apparatus, but only insofar as it ensures that the primary guarantor of the neoliberal market order is the market itself, as expressed through the 'market forces' that follow the laws of free market economics. Coming closer yet to Carl Schmitt's position, the neoliberal central authority is not moreover necessarily required to come in the form of a democratically elected government. It can perfectly assume the form of enlightened technocrats and 'independent' market institutions.

The EU's 'order', safeguarded as it is by both a version of state bureaucracy (the EU institutions apparatus) and a neoliberal technocracy of experts (such as those that work to set up and inform the policies and measures that govern the EMU), seems perfectly fitted to cater for any variety of autocratic governance these three schools would espouse.

What emerges, from this discussion, therefore, is that the EU, since its conception, has adopted a foundational premise that has embedded an undemocratic character, especially as regards the economic and fiscal principles and objectives it holds as fundamental. The undemocratic DNA shared by free market liberalism and ordoliberalism had been transplanted in the original EU substructure, and, arguably, still dominates judicial and technocratic conceptions of the Union. Political consultation is limited, substantively, to a narrow margin for manoeuvring and, procedurally, to cabals of experts and officials. What this paradigm of political consultations that take place without the involvement of the public can only amount to is not any variety of democracy, but only, as Bettina Lösch remarks, to the 'privatisation of politics'.[105]

What is also revealed is that the foundational myth of the EU, that if the common market and economic integration are built, social cohesion, equity and, ultimately, substantive democratic legitimacy and even political integration[106] will follow, is shackled in ordoliberal reasoning: the inherent *conditio sine qua non* of European integration is a preordained market order (a customs-free internal, and subsequently common, market based on free movement and free competition), which is to be safeguarded, as a matter of priority, even at the expense of the social standards and the democratic integration its attainment is supposed to herald. Further, that order is what dictates the potential social and democratic models that can be born out of the EU project, as it can only accommodate those that conform to its fundamental principles and objectives.

[105] B Lösch, 'Die Neoliberale Hegemonie als Gefahr für die Demokratie' in C Butterwegge, B Lösch and R Ptak *Kritik des Neoliberalismus 2* (Verbesserte Auflage 2008) 279.

[106] D Urwin, *The Community of Europe: A History of European Integration Since 1945* (2nd edn, Routledge 1995) 76.

Where that leads us, inevitably, is the adoption of an inherently autocratic ethos that cannot provide the basis for a substantive and emancipatory democratic process. Since the fundamental 'order' is not to be questioned, even a change in formal procedures of participation would not allow for radical critique and review. The democratic deficit is not quantitative, in other words, but qualitative. 'EU democracy' is, therefore, fundamentally undemocratic. And this undemocratic ethos is deeply engrained within not only the EU's structure, but within the heart of the EU project since its formation.

3 *The Undemocratic Character of Formative Actors*

(1) Founding Processes and Founding Fathers

The EU's inherent scepticism towards democratic processes, reflective as it is of the specific economic reasoning it ultimately serves, can also be attributed to a much simpler factor: the actors that either forged its early shape and spearheaded its development or safeguard its present form today, working to insulate it from fundamental change that might be brought upon it by those forces seen as 'external' to its core structure.

Regardless of the proclamations of the EU as a 'closer union among the peoples of Europe' that supposedly rests upon the acquiescence of European populaces, binding themselves to an aspiration of a common future and the acceptance of a common good, the EU can hardly be considered a popular project created 'from below'. Even superficially examining its constitutive Treaties, its intergovernmental character is obvious. It is not 'We, the People' that have set up the Union. It is our respective governments, cooperating to create a new transnational organisation, carefully making sure, among words describing high ideals and good intentions, that the primacy of nation state powers and, hence, national governments, is retained; the 'ever closer union' is shackled in the bounds of conferral and subsidiarity, right there in the TEU Preamble. Mere appearances, however, are just indicative. What is important is to examine not so much the nature of Treaty signatories, but of those formative actors that designed the Union and held its hand to ensure it grew to its present form and nature.

The history that led to the emergence of the European Coal and Steel Community (ECSC), the EEC and, eventually, the European Community (EC), the precursors to the EU, is well documented,[107] while the power dynamics and geopolitical considerations hidden behind the early initiatives and the noble aspirations of early federalists like Spinelli are explored elsewhere in this collection.[108] As to this latter point, it is to be noted how even someone like John Gillingham, a once

---

[107] Indicatively, see Dinan (n 49); Urwin (n 106) 1–12.
[108] See Chapters 2 and 18.

ardent supporter of the European project[109] recently turned sceptic,[110] now argues that the primary drive behind European integration was always exogenous and certainly had nothing to do with any form of democratic impetus:[111] from the Bretton Woods collapse and Cold War US/USSR power conflicts and geopolitics,[112] through the oil crisis and the neo-mercantilism of the 1970s, and to the advent of globalisation and the dominance of market (neo)liberalism, the EU was never a project championed and driven by politics focusing on common European interests, much less by the popular will for such interests to be expressed through the particular transnational framework the current Union has come to be. Bernard Connolly has been even more cynical in his infamous suggestion[113] that the EU is the battlefield of a power clash between France and Germany,[114] with the EMU especially being constructed either to be used as a lever of power by the French over the Bundesbank or as a vehicle of German ambition, interested in making its institutions, functions and substantive core the mirror image of German monetary authorities and institutions.

In this context of perpetual antitheses, conflicts and politico-economic machinations, it is not hard to understand why the lowest common denominator on which some consensus could be found was free trade. Specifically, a form of economic cooperation that could be built without necessarily the meddlesome effect of electorates, since sensitive issues (such as social welfare, fundamental rights, healthcare, security and defence – much less citizenship) that appear as closer to the everyday lives of the citizenry than trade deals and tariffs or are popularly perceived as ingrained within the 'national psyche' and state sovereignty, were left out of the mix, at the hands of Member States, the 'masters of the treaties'. What could only be agreed upon is an arrangement whereby a new international organisation, formed of sovereign Member States, emerges, endowed with only limited and clearly confined powers that do not entail a considerable transfer of sovereignty.

Therefore, formally, as Mancini and Keeling have observed, 'shocking as it may seem, the Community was never intended to be a democratic organisation'.[115] They point out that not only the word 'democracy' does not even appear in the Treaty of Rome, but also that accession was originally open to all European states, irrespective

---

[109] Albeit because it fit with his Hayekian reasoning and his admiration for Thatcherite economic policies (J Gillingham, *European Integration: 1950–2003: Superstate or New Market Economy?* (CUP 2003)).

[110] J Gillingham, *The European Union: An Obituary* (Verso 2016).

[111] ibid.

[112] Urwin (n 106) 13–26.

[113] B Connolly (1st edn published 1996, Faber & Faber 2013).

[114] A point to which Gillingham concedes: see Gillingham *The European Union: An Obituary* (n 110). For a more nuanced account of Franco-German influence, see U Krotz and J Schild, *Shaping Europe: France, Germany, and Embedded Bilateralism from the Elysee Treaty to Twenty-First Century Politics* (OUP 2013).

[115] F Mancini and D Keeling, 'Democracy and the European Court of Justice' (1994) 57 MLR 175.

of their democratic character – making eligible even states that were dictatorships at the time (like Spain and Portugal).[116]

There is no doubt, however, that the founding fathers of the EU envisaged the project would ultimately encroach upon those issues more closely associated with sovereignty, social cohesion and identity. However, they did not clearly express *how* they felt that transition ought to happen and whether it should include the expression of the will of the peoples affected through transparent democratic processes. That can be perhaps attributed to the fact that some of the prominent figures of the Union's early days were not themselves major political actors, accustomed to democratic processes and scrutiny, if at all politically engaged. Jean Monnet, throughout the years when the European project was forged, was always the adviser backroom diplomat, never entering a political party, much less opening his grand plans to democratic dialogue.[117] In fact, he seemed to find little value in conveying his plans through official channels or even meeting with 'official' policymakers.[118] His much praised[119] network of confidants did not include political players or popular representatives.[120] And those that were political actors, like Paul-Henri Spaak, embraced a pragmatic approach to European integration that, even if carefully balanced with regard to the question of sovereignty and legitimacy, would keep the project and its economic character largely insulated from democratic processes that could possibly cast doubt on its fundamental features and objectives.[121] The Union's founding fathers, in other words, either because they were enthused with the possibilities their vision opened and feared the risk of its collapse under contemporary politics, or because, at the other end of the spectrum, they perfectly understood the limits of the political process and the red lines that precluded the transfer of power without the required legitimacy, did not endow their creation with a democratic ethos.

However, the creation of the EU was the result of much more complex institutional processes of geopolitical reshuffling and manoeuvring by economic and political elites.[122] These real origins of the project can probably provide us with a better explanation of why enthusiasm and pragmatism ought to have taken the specific form of conveniently leaving aside the participation of 'the peoples' the

---

[116] ibid.

[117] F Duchene and J Monnet, *The First Statesman of Interdependence* (Norton 1994) 64–97, 147–80; D Brinkley and C Hackett (eds), *Jean Monnet: The Path to European Unity* (St Martin's Press 1991); S Brown Wells, *Jean Monnet: Unconventional Statesman* (Lynne Rienner 2011).

[118] C Chira-Pascanut 'Discreet Players: Jean Monnet, Transatlantic Networks and Policy-Makers in International Co-operation' (2014) 52 Journal Common Market Studies 1242, 1246–47.

[119] ibid. cf. How such praise is rightly dismissed as simplistic 'worshipful hagiography' by Desmond Dinan (*Origins and Evolution of the European Union* (OUP 2006) 298).

[120] ibid 1249.

[121] Spaak Committee, 'The Spaak Report' (1956).

[122] A Milward, *The Reconstruction of Western Europe, 1945–51* (University of California Berkeley Press 1984); Y Karagiannis, 'The Origins of the Common Market: Political Economy vs Hagiography' (2016) 54 Journal Common Market Studies 233.

interests of which the project was supposed to promote in constructing it. The secrecy and personal-network diplomacy[123] that characterised the formation of the plan that led to the creation of the EEC,[124] perhaps had to do more with the fear that its specific characteristics, as envisaged by 'political entrepreneurs',[125] would not necessarily find sympathetic ears if opened to political actors and broad democratic debate. Perhaps it would have opened the plan to the valid critique that it was merely a project reflecting French and German concerns as to the control of German resources[126] and the new emerging antagonisms in the post-Second World War era of US hegemony that demanded[127] the French ensure that Western Germany be firmly incorporated into Western Europe's structures and relations. Or it might have been revealed to promote specific geopolitical and industrial interests[128] rather than the grand ideals it was dressed up in.[129] More importantly, even, there might have been backlash against a project presented as an agreement for cooperation and trade as regards coal and steel, but hiding a federal aspiration[130] for the creation of a polity not through political and democratic processes 'from below' but as a product of economic integration instigated by a supranational organisation 'from above'. Consequently, not only was there no open democratic debate to inform the construction of the plan that triggered the European project, but national parliaments were completely left in the dark, and working documents destroyed once the plan took its final form.[131] This was surely a great start for transparency and democratic participation as elements of the European project.

(2) The CJEU as a Formative Actor

Mancini and Keeling observe that, despite lacking democratic DNA, the EU was gradually 'infected' with the democratic ethos of the common traditions of its Member States.[132] The irony, however, was that this was achieved not through democratic processes but through the actions of an actor that was itself unaccountable and, therefore, of dubious democratic legitimacy: the Court of Justice of the EU (CJEU).

---

[123] Chira-Pascanut (n 118) 1250–52.
[124] ibid 1243.
[125] ibid 1242.
[126] Milward (n 122) 126–41.
[127] AW Lovett, 'The United States and the Schumann Plan. A Study in French Diplomacy 1950–1952' (1996) 39 Historical Journal 425. See also Lettre de D. Acheson à R. Schuman, 30 Octobre 1949, FJM, Archives Robert Schuman, dossiers 3: Correspondance, 3/1/4.
[128] Milward (n 122); Lovett (n 127) 425–31, 442–45.
[129] Chira-Pascanut (n 118) 1246.
[130] M Burgess, 'Entering the Path of Transformation in Europe: The Federal Legacy of the Schuman Declaration' (2011) 29 French Politics, Culture & Society 4.
[131] Discretion is the Order of the Day, Centre Virtuel de la Connaissance sur l'Europe (2016) www .cvce.eu/obj/en-058bff7e-e81e-4cb5-9491-40f124d36b2a accessed April 2018.
[132] Mancini and Keeling (n 115) 177.

Since the beginning of what had seemed to be merely a rather regular intergovernmental project, the Court would often take upon itself to circumvent political rigidity and take the lead in advancing the European project, in what has been suggested to be merely the fulfilment of its obligation as an EU institution.[133] Postwar enthusiasm for the European project was largely followed by political hesitation and stagnation. However, that could very well be attributed to Members States being content with the extent of the Union's reach under existing arrangements, or even, and perhaps more importantly, to the absence of popular, democratically expressed pressure for further integration. Regardless, it is characteristic of the void left by the inherent democratic deficit that the Court took upon itself to play the constitutive role usually reserved for the demos in its organised form of a constitutional assembly. Thus, it was the Court that devised the principles of direct effect and supremacy,[134] turned attention towards protecting fundamental rights[135] and used the language of constitutional courts, proclaiming the (then) EC an 'autonomous legal order' and primary law its 'constitutional' foundation. It was probably not audacity in the face of inaction by the political actors that prompted the judges to take the reins so much as the Court's more pragmatic need for self-preservation. The Court was conscious of the need to assert its authority and to convince national courts that the Community was not some shiny, empty, parochial political statement, but a source of actual, tangible and strongly enforced obligations. The Court thus tried from the very beginning to signal that Community law did not consist of obscure commonly agreed trade principles but actually had teeth and was to be respected and rendered effective. The toolbox of principles it quickly devised over the first couple of decades had precisely this purpose and was not directly intended to challenge national courts' authority.

As was to be expected, the Court's actions prompted a judicial discourse with national constitutional courts that only added to the progress of this bizarre new form of 'constitutionalisation' from above. The Court itself was conscious that the legitimacy, effectiveness and very cohesion of Community law depended on treading carefully so as not to ignite a judicial revolt by national judges that would outright deny its ultimate authority or indeed the fulfilment of Community law obligations. Thus, the development of judicial dialogue encompassing suggestion and acceptance, or at least toleration, of all the major principles of constitutional value crafted by the CJEU became a long and careful process.[136] That strand of judgments and the

---

[133]   ibid 186; cf T Hartley, 'The European Court, Judicial Objectivity and the Constitution of the European Union' (1996) 112 LQR 95, 107.

[134]   J Weiler, 'The Community System: The Dual Character of Supranationalism' (1981) 1 Yearbook of European Law 267.

[135]   Mancini and Keeling (n 115) 186–88; K Alter, *Establishing the Supremacy of European Law* (OUP 2001) 1–2.

[136]   ibid 64–123 (for German courts) and 124–81 (for French courts) for an excellent and thorough exposition and analysis of this process.

backlash they created earned the 'notoriety'[137] of the Court as an actor that led the transformation of an international organisation to a complex legal entity that challenges conventional constitutional theory. Moreover, it instigated a heated academic debate[138] that ultimately helped forge political perceptions and action. However, that political action through the national democratic processes would often simply entail acceding to principles and norms already crafted judicially; that is, outside of the democratic process itself.

It could thus be argued that the Court pioneered the judicialisation of constitutionalism within the EU legal system, forming the basic principles and subtext and managing to achieve acceptance and compliance by national courts, while also setting the agenda, influencing the strategies of Member States and the Commission and compelling them to act.[139] It has been suggested that this might be the inevitable but unintended by-product of the Court's inherent duty to interpret Union law so as to give effect to the original objective of a common market.[140] On the other hand, it could also have been a conscious and deliberate course of action by the CJEU judges. They were knowingly engaging in a 'didactic' exchange with national courts in order to devise carefully a legal order which national judges would accept and comply with,[141] while at the same time assert the Court's authority within it.[142] Isn't this latter conduct, however, elitist and self-serving by definition? Instead of a Court safeguarding (constitutional) principles, norms and rights delineated by the democratic representatives of its constituent subject, we have a Court that devises these principles, norms and rights itself, irrespective of a democratic process, and then endeavours to carefully train national constitutional courts to accept it as a legitimate discussant and a co-actor in the determination of the constitutional nature and substance of the Union. The CJEU had been careful in how to address national courts, so as to not appear as if encroaching upon their territory, to manage to convince them to

[137] M Everson and J Eisner, *The Making of a European Constitution: Judges and Law beyond Constitutive Power* (Routledge 2007) 4.

[138] Inter alia see Alter (n 135) 21.

[139] In what Alec Stone Sweet would deem, respectively, 'judicialisation of dispute resolutions' and 'judicialisation of politics' ('Judicialisation and the Construction of Governance' (1999) 32 Comparative Political Studies 147); K Alter, 'Tipping the Balance: International Courts and the Construction of International and Domestic Politics' (2011) 13 Cambridge Yearbook of European Legal Studies 1, 9.

[140] Everson and Eisner (n 137) 49; M Poiares Maduro, *We, the Court: the European Court of Justice and the European Economic Constitution: A Critical Reading of Article 30 of the EC Treaty* (Hart 1998) 8–10. See also the more thorough analysis of the CJEU as a 'trustee' in A Stone Sweet, *The Judicial Construction of Europe* (OUP 2004) 17, 27–30; cf A Cohen and A Vauchez, 'The Social Construction of Law: The European Court of Justice and its Legal Revolution Revisited' (2011) 7 Annual Review of Law and Social Science 417, 420, where the writers suggest a more complex sociological explanation.

[141] See (n 136).

[142] F Mancini, 'The Making of a Constitution for Europe' in F Mancini, *Democracy and Constitutionalism in the European Union: Collected Essays* (Oxford 2000) 1, 9.

accept the partnership. As a result, what Stone Sweet has called the Court's 'gambit'[143] succeeded in cementing its position.

It might be true that the CJEU had not been consciously self-servingly 'activist'.[144] It did not have an agenda, even impliedly. It simply tried to function as a constitutional court of the Union,[145] within the confines that role entails, and, therefore, any potential oversteps can be approached as a question of judicial reasoning.[146] Even if that approach is accurate, however, it does not dispel the fact that the Court's stance promoted an ethos of judicialisation, whereby there is no urgency to establish or enhance democratic participation as there are judges ready to act as the champions of democratic and liberal principles.

Moreover, it conveniently obscures a critical question. Whose court was the Court of Justice in the formative years of the Union? In other words, who had access to the court and made use of it so as to influence its conduct and, therefore, the trajectory of the Union? In the absence of a clear democratic mandate on its competences or at least of sufficient democratic acquiescence to its authority, upon which the Court could build, this question is crucial. Those with the interest and power to influence the court, would essentially assume the constitutive role of the demos as regards the extent of judicial powers. And, as it turns out, they were rather few, namely a professional and scholarly elite of jurists, whose role has remained largely under-examined.[147]

Whether one of these propositions or perhaps a combination of the two is true is now of only little importance. What is crucial is the product of that endeavour, the judicially constructed notion of a sui generis legal order that is the seed of the whole constitutionalisation discourse. And the ultimate indeed sui generis characteristic of that order is the marginalisation of the democratic process even as regards its own ascension to constitutionalisation.

(3) Bureaucratic Actors and Economic Elites

The 'infection' of the EU by democratic and social considerations, that Mancini and Keeling suggest, advanced further and became more tangible over the course of the 1980s and 1990s.[148] The centralising shift towards a more interventionist 'hands-on' approach by the EU institutions[149] infused with social goals could be attributed to not only a number of political and institutional factors of the period but also to the

---

[143] A Stone Sweet, *Governing With Judges: Constitutional Politics in Europe* (OUP 2000) 164.
[144] T Tridimas, The Court of Justice and Judicial Activism (1996) 21 European Law Review 199, 200–02.
[145] ibid 206–07.
[146] ibid 209–10.
[147] K Alter, 'Jurist Advocacy Movements in Europe: The Role of Euro-Law Associations in European Integration (1953–1975) (2009)' in K Alter, *The European Court's Political Power* (OUP 2009) 63.
[148] J Kenner, *EU Employment Law: From Rome to Amsterdam and Beyond* (Hart 2003) 23–215.
[149] M Streit and W Mussler, 'The Economic Constitution of the European Community: From Rome to Maastricht' (1994) 5 Constitutional Political Economy 319, 366.

interplay of various European elites.[150] As such, it provides a perfect example to examine how, beyond abstract ideas and ideological influences that coloured the Union's psyche, its nature was always influenced more by this interplay of bureaucratic and economic actors than it was by democratic processes.

In the 1980s, EU Member States were divided between a conservative bloc, members of which, such as the UK, were actively embracing post-Hayekian neoliberalism and consequent deregulation, and a social democratic one, pursuing social redistributive policies by publicly declaring their intention to insulate national economic, and thus social, policy from traditional EC interventions. However, it could be argued that, regardless of the national policies these various governments wanted to be perceived as pursuing against the rigidity of the EU project at that point, they were not against the EU's structures and their own potential therein. On the contrary, national governments and political elites could make use of the institutions and mechanisms to effectively internationalise domestic politics[151] and simultaneously overcome domestic opposition.[152] The conservative block saw the EU as a vehicle to expand the reach and scope of economic neoliberal rationales,[153] encompassing fields that had been beyond the reach of the market, while marginalising domestic protectionist opposition.[154] Conversely, social democrats,[155] beyond their national borders, still supported a common free market[156] that would assist their economic elites, promote trade and thus induce growth, without alienating their domestic electoral base or anti-market liberalisation institutional supporters, like trade unions.[157] Finally, new Member States in the South, such as Greece,[158] Portugal and Spain, all of which had recently come out of dictatorial regimes and thus largely authoritarian centrally

[150] W Sandholtz and J Zysman, '1992: Recasting the European Bargain' (1989) 42 World Politics 95, 100–01.

[151] See A Moravcsik, 'Why the European Community Strengthens the State: Domestic Politics and International Cooperation' (1994) 52 Harvard University, Center for European Studies Working Paper Series 2, 6; R Ladrech, 'Europeanization of Domestic Politics and Institutions: The Case of France' (1994) 32 Journal of Common Market Studies 69.

[152] G Marks, L Hooghe and K Blank, 'European Integration from the 1980s: State-Centric v Multi-Level Governance (1996) 34 Journal of Common Market Studies 341, 348–350.

[153] D Judge, 'Incomplete Sovereignty: The British House of Commons and the Completion of the Internal Market in the EC' (1988) 41 Parliamentary Affairs 441, 450; Sandholtz and Zysman (n 150) 99.

[154] For the example of the Thatcher government sidelining the opposition in the Commons, see Judge (n 153) 449–50.

[155] See K Featherstone, Socialist Parties and European Integration: A Comparative History (Manchester UP 1988).

[156] Sandholtz and Zysman (n 150) 99, 111–12.

[157] For an account of the French socialist government's position at the time, see A Moravcsik, 'Negotiating the Single European Act: National Interests and Conventional Statecraft in the European Community (1991) 45 International Organization 19, 29–31. A further example from the days of the very creation of the common market in the 1950s and how the French political elite used the European vehicle to circumvent domestic opposition can be found in Moravcsik, 'Why the European Community Strengthens the State (n 151) 30–36.

[158] See F Papageorgiou and S Verney, 'Regional Planning and the Integrated Mediterranean Programmes in Greece' (1992) Regional Politics and Policy 2, 139; Featherstone (n 155) 170ff.

controlled economies, had every interest in expanding the scope of the European project to include redistributive capacities and attract European reconstruction funds.[159] Regardless of the different political or ideological focus of national governments at the time, they all shared an interest in using EU structures as a tool for promoting their goals and extending their reach to areas beyond national competence,[160] overcoming various domestic political or institutional restraints.[161] No less, national governments were able, domestically, to point to the Union as the scapegoat for interventions that would be perceived as contrary to their domestic political proclamations,[162] though in reality sanctioned by the very same actors, wearing their EU Council member hats. Thus, the centralisation of power at the EU level and the expansion of Union competences and goals allowed national governments to reap the benefits while avoiding political costs. It was this convergence of transnational economic policy objectives and political interests[163] that accommodated the centralising shift.[164]

Furthermore, but closely connected to political necessity, the 1980s and 1990s change in paradigm has been explained as the result of the self-interest of the Commission[165] and EU bureaucracy to expand their own power and budget, by pushing for the further centralisation of intervening power and simultaneously advocating the expansion of the scope of their own competences.[166] Arguably this tendency had been accommodated by pressure groups within the European Parliament advocating further centralisation,[167] not to mention by lobbying in favour of transnational business elites. Some have in fact suggested that it was business lobbyists and the interests of transnational market actors, rather than political elites and governments, that not only instigated the centralising shift and set the relevant agenda,[168] but also effectively set its extensive market liberalisation terms.[169]

What this brief example reveals is, on the one hand, how national political actors have used the EU to advance national agendas. That implies, of course, the absence

---

[159] Sandholtz and Zysman (n 150) 101.
[160] Moravcsik, 'Why the European Community Strengthens the State' (n 151).
[161] ibid 4–6.
[162] ibid 23–24; 29.
[163] Moravcsik (n 157) 19, 21.
[164] See also Sandholtz and Zysman (n 150) 96–97.
[165] On the central role and influence of the Commission, see inter alia Marks and others (n 152) 365 and the further references therein.
[166] R Vaubel, 'The Political Economy of Centralization and the European Community (1994) 81 Public Choice 151; Sandholtz and Zysman (n 150) 107–08.
[167] Moravcsik, 'Negotiating the Single European Act (n 157) 19–20; GA Bermann George, 'The Single European Act: A New Constitution for the Community' (1988–89) 27 Columbia Journal of Transnational Law 529, 530–31; PC Schmitter, 'Examining the Present Euro-Polity with the Help of Past Theories' in G Marks, F Scarpf and W Streeck (eds), Governance in the European Union (Sage 1996) 1, 8.
[168] Sandholtz and Zysman (n 150) 95ff, 116–18.
[169] Moravcsik (n 157) 19–20.

of true allegiance to the EU as such and of genuine faith in its integration narrative. It can hardly be suggested that national political actors would be happy to see the project leading to a fully fledged and democratically legitimised political union, as that would mean, by definition, the transfer of power from their hands to the central level. Completion of the integration objective would mean the eclipse of national political elites. It is useful to recall a recent study which showed that, contrary to popular belief, political elites are less likely to wish further integration than their citizenry, for example on issues such as introducing a common tax or social security system.[170] On the other hand, the EU bureaucracy's self-preservation instinct compels it to make every effort to ensure the survival and perpetuation of the project, even if that means overseeing potentially unpopular or objectively socially devastating policies. Disintegration would mean the disappearance of the institutions and positions that EU officials, officers and employees serve. This perpetual exercise of centrifugal and centripetal forces, driven by the inherent interests of institutional players, is an inherent characteristic of the EU since its conception, only exasperated by its development and expansion. The current balance of an EU in limbo, an organisation not really in the path of full political integration, but also, albeit seen suspiciously by parts of the population, not in any real risk of disintegration either, is convenient for all institutional actors. It keeps the EU apparatus intact, to carry on business as usual, without the fear of possible popular revolt that might demand an institutional restructuring, or worse still, the dismantlement of the entire project as it currently stands. 'Integration only up to a point', that is just short of the introduction of those democratic processes that would have ensured legitimacy, but would also endanger the primacy of national political actors, also suits the interests of the national political establishments.

Moreover, this need for a delicate balance, also conveniences national political elites in the realm of national politics. The continued existence of the EU provides them with an easy scapegoat, someone to blame for all unpopular measures and to divert criticism towards. On the other hand, the EU is not to be granted further far-reaching powers, out of fear that electorates might react to relevant unpopular policies mandated by the Union by voting down national political elites.[171] Similarly, national economic actors, on which the respective political elites largely rest, simultaneously have an interest to retain access to the common market and the trade freedoms it entails, but would not necessarily welcome full competition from abroad.[172] The unifying proposition, seems to be, is not too little integration, but not too much either.[173]

---

[170]   M Wolfgang, J Marcello and E Alejandro, 'The Elites–Masses Gap in European Integration' in BH Best, L Gyorgy and V Luca, *The Europe of Elites: A Study into the Europeanness of Europe's Political and Economic Elites* (OUP 2012) 167, 182–85, 189–90.

[171]   Gyorgy and Luca (n 170) 6.

[172]   ibid.

[173]   See the relevant figures provided by Cotta and Russo (of a pre-Eurocrisis study) that indicated strong approval for development of the EU that has brought it to the current point of integration, but less so as regards a future that would bring more: M Cotta and F Russo, 'Europe à la Carte? European

This convenient balance of forces and interests requires a certain democratic deficit. Not too much, so as not to endanger the narrative of a democratic Union that respects fundamental rights and works towards full integration for the common good of the European people. But also not too little, as to either endanger the project's survival itself through revolt by referendums, or bring about a truly democratically legitimised federal structure that would reduce national elites to the relative unimportance of a local authority. Even if the Union lacked the ideological DNA that makes it inherently averse to fully embracing the democratic process, especially if that meant leaving its core economic and monetary objectives and policies at the mercy of electorates, the current balance would remove any impetus for the introduction of the necessary institutional change.

The undemocratic nature of European democracy, therefore, is not coincidental, but inherent and necessary both for the affirmation and perpetuation of the economic and monetary EU order and the specific variety of EU capitalism it serves, but also of the EU bureaucracy and the symbiotic world of interests and actors it has sprung.

IV BEYOND THE DEMOCRATIC DEFICIT

The democratic deficit therefore is not merely symptomatic; nor is it simply a question about the quantity or quality of the mechanisms and institutions in place at the European level, or the balance between the EU's mission of securing the internal market and other constitutional objectives. In that sense, the term 'democratic deficit' is itself misleading, as it alludes to something that is rectifiable by 'filling in' the holes through institutional change. What actually exists is an undemocratic variety of formal democratic structures. This, however, not only precludes democratic deliberation. By doing so it actively determines the tenor and reach of political debate, defines political subjectivities and rationalities, and more generally shapes the public sphere that the EU inhabits. What this suggests, as a result, is that the stakes reach much further than the question of whether the EU can be reformed.

The undemocratic affinities between ordoliberalism and free market liberalism we discussed and traced back to similar Schmittian musings, on the unimpeachable nature of a central dogma and the mechanisms designed to protect it, help bring to light another implication of the EU's undemocratic nature that can be related to a different element of Carl Schmitt's theory: the 'political', as the process that defines the entity that constitutes the subject of governance. The 'political' is defined by Schmitt as a process of constant existential conflict against an 'enemy' that threatens the existence of a given entity[174] whose political nature is revealed precisely in the

---

Citizenship and Its Dimensions from the Perspective of National Elites' in Best, Gyorgy and Luca (n 170) 14, 19–20.
[174] Schmitt (n 79) 27.

extreme situations of that existential threat. Moreover, every reaction against that enemy, no matter its intensity, is justifiable. This existence of an enemy, be it internal or external, is what crafts a community into a unified demos and allows it to be identified by drawing a clear red line between those that belong to it and those that do not.[175] The constitutive community and its members, thus, are defined and identified in constant opposition to whomever and whatever does not belong to it: the external; the 'enemy'.[176]

This divide that frames this fundamental existential conflict is not 'spontaneous', but can be influenced by institutional choices and preordained narratives. Over the years,[177] and surely by the time of 'On the Three Types of Juridical Thought,'[178] Carl Schmitt departs from his earlier suggestion that sovereignty, and therefore identity, emerge from 'nothingness' independently of an institutional framework, and comes to see the normative and the institutional as a symbiotic whole.[179] That implies that fundamental legal constructs, including any pre-prescribed foundational 'order' and its dogma, are not merely inherently connected to the political process[180] but they can in fact affect and frame it. Hence, they can eventually define the identity of the entity, depending upon how the friend–enemy divide is constructed, and delimit who ought to be recognised as its subject; as its citizen.

What that implies for an entity constructed upon an ordoliberal premise or market (neo)liberal dogma is that the pre-constituted formal normative centre of its existence, its fundamental 'order' with all of its basic principles, objectives and assumptions, is the criterion upon which the friend–enemy divide is constructed, fully embracing it, without question, as the Schmittian red line.

As with any ordoliberal 'order', therefore, the fundamental economic and fiscal premises of the current conception of the European project would have to be accepted as the undisputable constant that defines the EU. Consequently, dissent ought to be treated as radical Euroscepticism or opportunistic populism that endangers the European ideal and, therefore, would position those who espouse these critiques outside of it. They would be not only the enemies of progress, but the Schmittian enemy of the European project itself.

---

[175] On this topic: C Mouffe, 'Carl Schmitt and the Paradox of Liberal Democracy' (1997) 10 Canadian Journal of Law & Jurisprudence 21.

[176] T Strong, 'The Sovereign and the Exception: Carl Schmitt, Politics, Theology and Leadership' [Foreword] in C Schmitt, *Political Theology* (1st edn 1922, University of Chicago Press 2005) vii (xv–xvi).

[177] M Croce and A Salvatore, *The Legal Theory of Carl Schmitt* (Routledge 2013) 13–29. Terminologically, it ought to be noted that Schmitt doubts the accuracy of the term 'institutionalism', and its root concept of 'the institution'. Instead, he prefers to coin the terms 'concrete order' and 'formation thinking'. See C Schmitt, *On the Three Types of Juristic Thought* (1st edn 1934, J Bendersky tr, Praeger 2004) 89.

[178] Schmitt (n 177).

[179] C Schmitt, *Constitutional Theory* (1st edn 1928, J Sitzer tr, Duke UP 2008) 211.

[180] Croce and Salvatore (n 177) 34, 39–43.

This is certainly what appears to be emerging as regards how the contemporary political debate about the EU is framed along the Europhile–Eurosceptic divide and the meaning these categories have gradually come to acquire.

Let us return as an illustration to the EU's democratic deficit, which has not only been at the forefront of academic discussions but has come increasingly to dominate mainstream political debate around the EU and define support for or rejection for its institutions, turning the issue of whether the EU can be reformed into a more existential question. At the risk of oversimplification, in this particular context, Europhilia would be broadly associated with the belief in the possibility of democracy at the EU level, while Euroscepticism would be defined by a commitment to the nation state as the only possible level of political contestation.[181] Our approach would suggest that the reformist mindset, and hence that this particular framing of the divide, is misplaced, so it is worth exploring further the underlying terms of the debate.

On a closer look, debates around democracy and the EU have been increasingly cast as a question of political ontology or procedural democracy.[182] The primary question is where and how policy and law should be formed, and, hence, who should be the ultimate sovereign ruler.[183] Nowhere was this conceptualisation made clearer than in the infamous slogan of 'taking back control' that was so central to the right-wing Brexit leave campaign. But it also underpins the discourse of some sections of the social-democratic and liberal left, like DiEM 25, who call for a constitutional assembly and the creation of a 'full-fledged democracy with a sovereign Parliament' at the level of the EU. The democratic question, in other words, is portrayed primarily as a question of sovereignty, if not a matter of institutions and procedures – regardless of the quality and extent of democratic debate such enhanced structures of representation would actually allow.

This particular framing of the question has had at least two consequences for the way support for or rejection of the EU has come to be defined. First, it leaves much of the 'ensemble' which we have identified as lying at the heart of the displacement

---

[181] eg T Gallagher, *Europe's Path to Crisis: Disintegration via Monetary Union* (Manchester UP 2014). It should be noted that although Gallagher's analysis, that concludes in his support of a retreat to the nation state as the primary, and appropriate, hub of legitimacy and governance, rests on a strong critique of the premise and objective of the EMU, and its institutional architecture, he nevertheless shies away from making any connections to the broader normative economic underpinnings served by the EMU and its market context. cf J Mather, *Legitimating the European Union: Aspirations, Inputs and Performance* (Palgrave Macmillan 2006) 171–72, where Mather contests the thesis of the nation state as a homogeneous self-standing entity capable of bearing autonomous interests, albeit themselves a reflection of the 'common interest', which can be the ultimate collective institution capable of claiming democratic legitimacy.

[182] Under this approach, democracy is merely a mechanism for choosing and authorising government. See CB Macpherson, *The Life and Times of Liberal Democracy* (OUP 1977) 77–78 cited in AJ Ayers and A Saad-Filho, 'Democracy against Neoliberalism: Paradoxes, Limitations, Transcendence' (2015) 41 Critical Sociology 597, 598.

[183] Bickerton (n 40) 7.

of democratic processes out of the equation. Europhilia may continue to express strong support for the specific principles and form of market integration the EU espouses since its conception. But it has also come to include voices, like SYRIZA, who would have been traditionally opposed to free market liberalism. Euroscepticism, on the other hand, does not necessarily entail refuting the free market ideology that underpins the politico-economic ethos of the Union or contesting the idea that certain fields of policy need to be safeguarded against extensive democratic scrutiny or control by allowing their essence to be carved out by 'experts' and their implementation to rest on the executive, with little space for legislatures to have substantive influence. Taking again the Brexit example, it is telling that 'taking back control' is for many perfectly reconcilable with participation in the single market.

To use the terminology developed in political science, Euroscepticism as 'opposition to the regime',[184] namely to the 'political values, norms and structures of the EU' as serving the particular European variety of capitalist market economy and hence as opposition to European capitalism itself, is no longer a constitutive feature of the divide between Europhilia and Euroscepticism. As a result, it would seem that the fundamental economic and monetary premises of the project are to be accepted for anyone to even be allowed a place in the European public space, even as a 'Eurosceptic'. To continue with the Brexit analogy, rejection of the single market on the basis that it is inherently connected to free market capitalism would be branded as radical heresy.

Second, under this more procedural version of democracy devoid of more material considerations, decisions about the scale of democratic rule have become increasingly connected to questions of identity, i.e. framed as a choice between nationalism or Europeanism, as embodied by the EU. Rupture with the EU as a reassertion of sovereignty is seen as a retreat to national identity. Faith in the European project, by contrast, denotes a commitment to internationalism and the forging of common identities. In that context, Euroscepticism appears primarily in its nationalistic 'opposition to the community'[185] variant, i.e. as the expression of 'negative attitudes towards other citizens', whereas Europhilia almost becomes coterminous with more progressive and inclusive forms of politics.

The combination of these two trends is toxic. It is problematic already that a critique of the democratic deficit that raises its inherent character – and goes beyond a superficial, functional description of the problem that would lead to the conclusion that the issue is easily rectifiable within the EU system – would tend to be branded as 'Eurosceptic' in its 'community' variant, and thus left to share the negative connotation reserved for xenophobic, if not racist, nationalistic voices (indeed we would be disturbed if that were taken to be the message of our contribution). The more fundamental problem, however, is that any such critique and rejection of the EU on premises other than the fetishisation of the national unit

---

[184] F Serricchio, M Tsakatika and L Quaglia, 'Euroscepticism and the Global Financial Crisis' (2013) 51 Journal of Common Market Studies 51, 52.

[185] ibid.

or national sentiment is altogether excluded, that is to say it is placed outside the range of possible 'rational' alternatives to the EU, or indeed to nationalism. This creates the paradox that this supposedly inclusive and progressive EU formation somehow becomes more tolerable of Euroscepticism in its community variant, and hence to opposition to the EU's liberal values of equality and universal human rights, than it is to opposition to its market principles.[186] The real Schmittian enemy of the European project is thus not so much the nationalist, who may be depicted as reactionary and outdated but allowed to exist as an active political subject of the European sphere; rather the real enemy, in line with the EU's ordoliberal tenets, are those who oppose the EU's market dogmas.

That this form of enmity has been facilitated by the Eurocrisis is not, from that perspective, surprising. In the aftermath of the Eurocrisis, organised opposition to austerity in countries like Spain or Greece began to challenge the EU's economic order. In that context, the recalibration of the divide between Eurosceptic and Europhiles as one revolving around identity rather than support for or rejection of European capitalism, enabled a more powerful narrative to emerge, namely that there is no alternative to the EU other than reactionary nationalism, and hence that the EU's neoliberal 'iron cage' was not only an economic but also a political necessity. This ideology of Europeanism may explain much of the Greeks' fear to break away from the EU – there was just no progressive way of 'being' outside of the EU's structures. But it could also simultaneously explain why the leave campaign in the UK was almost entirely overtaken by the right: by silencing particular forms of opposition to the EU, Europeanism also helps the disenchantment and alienation of people suffering from the material realities of the neoliberal condition to be redirected in more nationalist and xenophobic directions.[187]

One ought to be clear about what the implications of this may be. Our conclusion that the displacement of democracy is inherent to the nature of the EU not only implies that institutional reforms in a more democratic direction would be ineffective, even if current mechanisms of participation were enhanced or new ones were created. Substantively, EU democracy would remain undemocratic, as the main features and premises of its market 'order' need to remain perpetually beyond the scope of contestation. Further, though, our conclusion also implies that, as the contradictions of the project intensify, as they did in the context of the Eurocrisis, the Union's continuing survival will increasingly hinge on the active suppression of opposition to its core normative and ideological tenets. In that context, the danger does not lie only in the institutional deficiencies of the formal democratic structures in place at the EU level and their complete marginalisation in times of crisis. The true risk comes from the marginalisation of substantive

---

[186]   Indicatively, one could compare the EU's reaction to illiberal regimes in Hungary and Poland and its reaction to opposition to neoliberal policies in Greece.

[187]   Empirical research also suggests national identity, rather than economic factors played a limited role in the rise of Euroscepticism after the financial crisis. See Serricchio and others (n 184).

democracy and the reconstitution of the public sphere along absolute exclusionary divides that fuel polarisation, heralding the redefinition of European identity into an illiberal variant based on shallow dichotomies.

This is not to say that the solution to the European crisis of democracy is necessarily a straightforward retreat to the national level as a sacred political unit. Our analysis on the contrary showed that the EU's undemocratic nature is sustained by a mixture of EU and national interests. Moving forward, any solution must begin with a revitalisation of the substantive debate around the conditions that are necessary for democratic processes to be put in place. We hope that our argument about the nature and causes of what has been traditionally described as a 'democratic deficit' and more recently a 'democratic default' (albeit with specific reference to the EMU-related measures) can contribute to that endeavour by illuminating the nature and causes of the EU's democratic predicament, and by recasting the debate as to democracy in the EU.

7

Europe and Constituent Powers

Ruptures with the Neoliberal Consensus?

Maria Tzanakopoulou

I INTRODUCTION

The European project has perhaps never been more thoroughly disputed across the whole range of the political spectrum, than it is today. From the far left to the far right, the ongoing crisis is precipitating robust reactions, sometimes caught up in extremist and xenophobic rhetoric and at other times motivated by progressive egalitarian demands. This analysis explores the constitutional relevance of the above developments with a special focus on the constitutional facets of the main outcome of the crisis, austerity, and the response given by European societies.

Constitutional discourse on the European crisis often tends to emphasise the constitutional mutations and institutional shifts of power equilibrium within both the Union and its individual Member States. Within Member States, the strengthening of the executive power has almost become a leitmotif as the safeguarding of austerity under the pretence of necessity and at the expense of democracy informs parliamentary routine. At the same time, externally imposed austerity measures render domestic constitutional principles of social justice virtually void of content. The judiciary, favouring as it does an economic-oriented reading of constitutional provisions and endorsing precarious interpretations of the 'national interest' in light of the need to shield the economy, aligns itself with dominant internal and external political imperatives. A parallel shift away from socio-economic welfare in Member States' political agendas can be read as both a trigger and a consequence of the institutional mutations. The above constitutional and institutional developments are frequently laid at the door of the European Union; an entity sometimes accused of being institutionally impotent to rebuild democracy and welfare and sometimes charged with structural neoliberal bias. According to both of the above views, but notably according to the latter, the European project is almost hopeless.

For all its importance, the above discourse, which largely emphasises the institutional dimensions of recent developments tells us only one part of the constitutional story of the European crisis. Of no less constitutional relevance is the actual embedment of austerity in societies: the perception of austerity as necessary or, worse even, as normal. The following analysis argues that this embedment safeguards the dominance of austerity to the same extent as does, for example, the EU-driven introduction of budgetary constraints in domestic constitutional documents. It is therefore important that constitutional discourse does not limit itself to a defence of pre-crisis, allegedly sovereign, constitutional business as usual but rather expands to a wholesale challenge of the logic and rationale behind the crisis, neoliberalism and austerity.

This entails the need to point the finger at those responsible for the present precarious situation. The following analysis argues that while the Union, represented by its political and economic elite, bears considerable responsibility, liability lies primarily with domestic political actors and economic elites. In this sense, it is argued that, whether structural or not, the problems facing the European Union need to be attacked at both domestic and regional levels. However, the poor constitutional quality of the Union renders the latter possibility practically unattainable.

In section II, the analysis reviews and reframes constitutional discourse by placing at the heart of constitutionalism, broadly understood, the effort to secure social consensus with a view to maintaining the status quo. This reading of constitutionalism also invites an understanding of constitutional arrangements as predominantly national arrangements. According to this reading, a broad national consensus around austerity suffices to render it constitutional. This is so, irrespective of whether austerity measures have been entrenched in the constitutional document, and regardless of potentially anti-democratic practices on the part of governors. As the violence of austerity policies deepens, notably in the southern parts of the European region, the hitherto strong consensus around austerity shows signs of disintegration. Drawing on these challenges against the logic of austerity, section III encourages an understanding of constituent power as a living emancipatory body that can counterbalance the constitutional transformations by building strong social structures and adding agonistic forms of democracy in to the constitutional equation. In the final analysis, it is concluded that, if the new consensus challenges the neoliberal logic of austerity, constitutionalism will have to embrace it. And while such constitutional challenge might fall on deaf ears in the quarters of the European Central Bank (ECB) and Commission, as it has done in the past, one can never be entirely confident that this will be the case indefinitely.

II THE CONSTITUTION, THE CRISIS AND AUSTERITY: REFRAMING THE DISCOURSE

At the outset, the relation between the European crisis and domestic constitutions appears to be anything but a dialectical one: the main by-products of the crisis, budgetary discipline and increased austerity, seem to threaten the integrity of national constitutional arrangements while domestic constitutions seems completely unfit to curtail the violent forces of austerity politics. There is much talk about the constitutional mutations brought about by – notably externally imposed – austerity measures on EU Member States. The discourse often takes the form of description of substantive changes in the constitutional rules of Member States, with a view to proving the mutating effect of the politics behind the crisis on the long-established welfarist constitutional consensus in the region.[1]

Within this context, constitutional rules are understood as the basic and relatively rigid set of checks and balances prescribing the main principles of organisation of a polity. In light of this reading, the argument is often that chaining the neoliberal economic model to the hard-and-fast rules of the constitution removes this model from the realm of politics and from democratic confrontation.[2] This is sometimes seen as a systemic failure of the Union;[3] a failure that was bound to result in disintegration once the strong-arm tactics of blocking democratic conflict were felt within European societies. At other times, it is viewed with less hostility, as simply marking a shift from the political to the legal constitution. In this latter case, the proposed remedy is to reintroduce the basics of democratic politics within budgetary decision-making through, for example, procedural constitutional changes within a broader context of deliberative constitutionalism.[4]

More specifically, much of the literature criticises the Union mechanisms for their failure to be effective and/or legitimate. According to this reading, the institutional machinery of the EU and EMU, as well as the constitutional framework of the Union, proved insufficient to withstand the pressures and institutional transformations brought about by the financial crisis.[5] The democratic deficit deepens, so the argument goes, because intergovernmentalism, enabled by the Lisbon Treaty, replaces the weak institutional apparatus of the Union, and fails to produce effective and legitimate results.[6] Proposed remedies range from the need to re-establish mutual trust between the EU and its citizens, to a call for abandonment of idealistic

---

[1] See eg M Adams, F Fabbrini and P Larouche (eds), *The Constitutionalization of European Budgetary Constraints* (Hart 2014) pt II, 151–296.

[2] See eg G Delledonne, 'A Legalization of Financial Constitutions in the EU? Reflections on the German, Spanish, Italian and French experiences' in Adams, Fabbrini and Larouche, *Constitutionalization of European Budgetary Constraints* (n 1) 181–204.

[3] See eg E Chiti and PG Teixeira, 'The Constitutional Implications of the European Responses to the Financial and Public Debt Crisis' (2013) 50 Common Market Law Review 683.

[4] For example, the argument sometimes is that '[procedural] constitutional change through scrutiny by fiscal councils may avoid' the problem of decision-making behind closed doors and through secret letters by, say, the ECB. 'The more discursive nature of such constitutional reform can create opportunities for correction of errors, and most importantly for debate and a plurality of sources of information' (T Prosser, 'Constitutionalising Austerity in Europe' (2016) Public Law 111, 129).

[5] Many attribute this failure to the construction of the European Economic Constitution on the example of the German ordoliberal model and the inflexibility of its rules. See, notably, C Joerges, 'The European Economic Constitution and Its Transformation Through the Financial Crisis' (2015) ZenTra Working Paper in Transnational Studies No 47/2015 http://ssrn.com/abstract=2560245 accessed April 2018.

[6] See eg S Fabrinni, 'Intergovernmentalism and Its Limits: Assessing the European Union's Answer to the Euro Crisis' (2013) 46 Comparative Political Studies 1003.

appeals to solidarity and for recourse to the constitutional responsibility of burden-sharing within the EMU.[7]

The discourse has taken a slightly different turn in light of the Brexit referendum results. As happens in times of major political change, polarisation fuelled more radical approaches. Constitutional critics have blogged, in a cry of despair, that the Union is not merely unable to withstand pressures. Instead, it is EU structures themselves that breed and perpetuate the crisis: 'EU Treaties not only contain procedural protections for capitalism ... they also entrench substantive policies which correspond to the basic tenets of neoliberalism'.[8] Thus, according to which stance one takes towards the structural matter, proposed solutions range from more or less marginal institutional amendments to getting rid altogether of an entity structurally doomed to fail.

Alongside the above attack against the Union's structural flaws or mere impotence to carry out either input or output legitimacy, the literature also focuses upon the constitutional significance of the relevant developments for national constitutions. Valuable comparative research has been conducted on the (in)ability of domestic constitutional structures to absorb and effectively contain the Fiscal Compact's distinctly German 'balance budget rule':[9] not every Member State is ready to speak the language of the German constitutional legislator.[10] The result is, inter alia, that the CJEU, which is now able to supervise the budgetary discipline of Member States, may have to dig deep into domestic constitutional systems that are unable to come up to the requirements for constitutional amendments tailored to the German constitutional model. It thus seems that even when the focus is on domestic arrangements, the blame bounces back to the EU and its structural fixation on a 'Germanness' often regarded as the main actor responsible for the crisis of the European project.[11]

In terms of purely internal constitutional arrangements, the relevance of the crisis reaches far beyond the need to incorporate fiscal constraints into hierarchically superior constitutional provisions. Of no less importance is the circumvention of

---

[7] On trust, see eg M Poiares Maduro, 'Foreword: Fiscal Capacity and Constitutional Reform in the EMU' in Adams and others (n 1) v–xiv; P Craig, 'Economic Governance and the Euro Crisis: Constitutional Architecture and Constitutional Implications' ibid 19–40; on burden-sharing, see P Lindseth, 'Power and Legitimacy in the Eurozone: Can Integration and Democracy be Reconciled?' ibid 379–98.

[8] D Nicol, 'Is Another Europe Possible?' (*UK Constitutional Law Blog*, 29 February 2016) https://ukconstitutionallaw.org accessed April 2018.

[9] Art 3(2) of the Treaty on Stability, Coordination and Governance in the Economic and Monetary Union (TSCG); for a review of the methods of constitutionalisation of EU countries see, Adams and others (n 1) pt II; Prosser (n 4).

[10] L Besselink and JH Reestman, 'The Fiscal Compact and the European Constitutions: 'Europe Speaking German' (2012) 8 European Constitutional Law Review 1.

[11] See M Everson, 'An Ideal, Not a Place: A Euro-Critic's Case for the UK Remaining in the EU' (*VerfBlog*, 11 June 2016) http://verfassungsblog.de/an-ideal-not-a-place-a-euro-critics-case-for-the-uk-remaining-in-the-eu accessed April 2018.

already existing constitutional checks and balances, notably in those countries that have implemented the most harsh austerity measures, mainly in response to conditionality demands imposed, inter alia, by the Union. The Portuguese and Greek stories that have developed in parallel are indicative of this. In Portugal, the government under Prime Minister Coelho, formed in 2011, defended the 2013 state budget, when the latter was challenged before the Constitutional Court, by making a plea to the country's state of emergency.[12] Worse still, in Greece 'acts of legislative content', supposed to be reserved for 'extraordinary circumstances of an urgent and unforeseeable need', have become a routine way of passing legislation implementing externally imposed austerity measures.[13] National Constitutional Courts tend, as they do in times of crises, to defer considerably to the domestic legislator, especially as regards the latter's initiatives related to compliance with EU or other international obligations.[14]

The constitutional discourse, as summarised above, tells a tale of two possible routes. One is to effectuate procedural change in the Union's institutional machinery. Such proposals may be essential, inasmuch as they highlight realistic amendments within the warp and weft of institutional arrangements in neoliberal political orders. The other route is to do away with the Union lock, stock and barrel. This could be an equally valuable proposal to the extent that the Union suffers from systemic failures at the constitutional level, which block any possibility for genuine radical change, a change much needed for increasing sections of the population that suffer most severely from austerity politics. Yet, as will be explained below, both approaches, while offering necessary insights, seem inadequate in getting to the root of the constitutional significance of the crisis.

In particular, constitutional discourse appears to be dominated by three tendencies, which offer a narrow perspective of the constitutional setting of both the Union and its Member States. First, procedural accounts seem to be driven by a bureaucratic-oriented or instrumentalist reasoning.[15] It is assumed that an adjustment of the constitutional and institutional machinery of the EU or of the Member

---

[12] 'Press Review: PM Invokes "National Emergency" to Defend State Budget in High Court' *Portugal Daily News* (8 January 2013) www.portugaldailyview.com/whats-new/press-review-prime-minister-calls-revision-of-state-budget-national-emergency accessed April 2018. The review notes: 'Prime Minister Passos Coelho is using the argument of "national emergency" to defend the coalition government's 2013 state budget after it was sent by the president and all opposition parties to be reviewed by the Constitutional Court'.

[13] See Art 44, para 1 of the Constitution of Greece, as revised by the parliamentary resolution of 27 May 2008 of the VIII Revisionary Parliament.

[14] In this context, many note the exception of the Portuguese Constitutional Court. See eg M Canotilho and others, 'Austerity Measures under Judicial Scrutiny: The Portuguese Constitutional Case-Law' (2015) 11 European Constitutional Law Review 155; for a comparative account of relevant case law, see C Fasone, 'Constitutional Courts Facing the Euro Crisis: Italy, Portugal and Spain in a Comparative Perspective' (2014) EUI Working Papers (MWP 2014/15) http://cadmus.eui.eu/bitstream/handle/1814/33859/MWP_WP_2014_25.pdf accessed April 2018.

[15] For a non-instrumentalist, sociolegal perspective, see K Nicolaides, 'European Democracy and Its Crisis' (2013) 51 Journal of Common Market Studies 351.

States will improve, or even suffice to rectify, both European and domestic constitutional missteps. Second, a sometimes explicit and sometimes implicit conclusion of the above discourse is that 'globalisation in its regional variety of Europeanisation marks the end not only of the political Westphalian paradigm but, in its wake, the economic Keynesian paradigm as well'.[16] The end of Keynesianism is at other times attributed to the untrustworthiness of the EU's institutional framework, which has forced Member States 'to push forward austerity measures as a precondition for financial support'.[17] Here, the focus shifts away from the nation state. Instead, the main responsibility for the constitutional mutations, evident in the shift away from welfarism and towards austerity, is rediscovered in either the systemic institutional failure of the EU or, more broadly, in the forces of globalisation. Third, there is an emphasis on the obligation of national courts to guard the constitution or, even, to become agents of political stability. This approach tends to disregard the fact that austerity policies usually go hand in hand with emergency situations in times of crises, namely with what has been termed 'mega-politics': 'core political controversies that define (and often divide) whole polities'.[18] In cases such as these, as Tushnet points out, albeit in a different context, 'the constitutional law of emergency powers is (primarily) political rather than legal'.[19]

For one, codified constitutions usually tend to express some inclination, whether explicit or de facto, towards a particular economic system. Nevertheless, as critics correctly point out, the Fiscal Compact's requirement for constitutionalisation of budgetary restrictions and fiscal constraints takes the neoliberal bias of European constitutions to unprecedented levels.[20] It is therefore both significant and necessary to explore the constitutional and institutional mechanics of implementation of austerity measures, as it is significant to examine the systemic depth of the problem. However, there is one element of constitutional significance that none of the above three tendencies touch upon – perhaps understandably so, given their different focus.

Next to the technical constitutional difficulties faced by the Union and its Member States, there is, domestically, a parallel construction of a discursive field that presents the choice for austerity policies as mirroring a state of exception. Within this context, domestic elites seek to legitimise austerity under the pretence

---

[16] L Besselink and JH Reestman, 'The Fiscal Compact and the European Constitutions: "Europe Speaking German"' (2012) 8 European Constitutional Law Review 6.

[17] See M Adams, F Fabbrini and P Larouche, 'Introduction: The Constitutionalization of European Budgetary Constraints: Effectiveness and Legitimacy in Comparative Perspective' in Adams and others (n 1) 4.

[18] R Hirschl, 'The New Constitutionalism and the Judicialization of Pure Politics Worldwide' (2006) 75 Fordham Law Review 721, 727.

[19] M Tushnet, 'The Political Constitution of Emergency Powers: Some Lessons from Hamdan' (2007) 91 Minnesota Law Review 1451, 1452.

[20] M Sah and T Daintith, 'Privatisation and the Economic Neutrality of the Constitution' [1993] Public Law 465.

that there is no alternative.[21] At this juncture, one has to pause and, first, re-evaluate the primacy (or not) of the nation state vis-à-vis the shift away from welfarism. Is austerity truly an externally imposed duty that Member States are coerced into implementing? Or is it, rather, a choice of Member States themselves? Second, in terms of the constitutional entrenchment and, therefore, depoliticisation of a particular economic model, one has to reflect upon what it is that differentiates the 'no alternative' narrative from the actual introduction of fiscal constraints or substantive neoliberal policies in constitutional documents. Once the 'no alternative' narrative is embedded in societies and treated as an irrefutable truth, the constitutional entrenchment of austerity offers no more and no less than a formal, if not merely symbolic, testimony of what has already occurred at a social level. Seen in this way, the constitutional significance of austerity is at least as much a matter of political discourse as it is of constitutional doctrine. Accordingly, even if one accepts the systemic nature of the crisis and the unavoidability of the changes precipitated by it, one must also accept that there is more to the constitutional story than simply the question of structure. What seems to be lacking in the constitutional discourse on austerity is an actual challenge to the underlying rationale of austerity *itself* and, concomitantly, an effort to infiltrate such a challenge into a constitutional narrative. Critically, this requires a shift away from thinking about the crisis in terms of European and domestic constitutional rules and a redirection of focus towards what is a broader concept, namely constitutionalism. The latter, as understood in this analysis, retains its relative autonomy from constitutional rules and is instead conceived as a project, which being permeated by the force of ideology, secures social consensus by acting out social conflict. Unlike analyses that focus on constitutional rules, the concept of constitutionalism offers the advantage of adding an extra element into the discourse, namely social relations. In the following sections, I explore the idea of constitutionalism and explain the importance of introducing the element of social relations within constitutional narratives of the crisis and of austerity.

1 Recasting Constitutionalism

Constitutionalism has been used so extensively and divergently that it has become associated with virtually everything, from the empowerment of citizens and democracy[22] to the depoliticisation of politics at national and transnational level,[23]

---

[21] See, for an analysis of the discursive framework, P Fonseca and MJ Ferreira, 'Through "Seas Never Before Sailed": Portuguese Government Discursive Legitimation Strategies in a Context of Financial Crisis' (2015) 26 Discourse & Society 682; on the use of the 'no alternative' rhetoric by MSs as an excuse to implement labour law reforms, see S Clauwaert and I Schömann, 'The Crisis and National Labour Reforms' (2012) 3 European Labour Law Journal 54.

[22] U Preuss, 'The Political Meaning of Constitutionalism' in R Bellamy (ed), *Constitutionalism, Democracy and Sovereignty* (Ashgate 1996), 12.

[23] J Gray, *Enlightenment's Wake* (Routledge 1975) 76.

and from the universal triumph of liberalism and the rule of law[24] to the alleged demise, or 'total crisis', of the nation state.[25] Constitutionalism has almost become a hackneyed concept; a concept the content of which appears to have been progressively frittered away. It is therefore not easy to give an account of constitutionalism without becoming caught up in the whirl of truisms and/or contradictions that accompany the concept. In fact, the following account does not claim to distance itself from any of the clichés of constitutional thinking. It merely seeks to frame constitutionalism in a way that is consistent with the latter's *raison d'être*.

In what would be a typical definition of constitutionalism, the latter would be presented, in the main, as prescribing the idea of specified political authority and of limited government.[26] Constitutionalism is about the marking off of the limits of public power and the removal from the latter's reach of 'certain favoured private activities'.[27] Constitutions reflect the will of people in their sovereign capacity and it is precisely for this reason that they can limit and control government.[28] According to this reading, constitutionalism marks the transition from the feudal society's irrational imposition of authority to adherence to the rule of law, checked, balanced and constrained state power, as well as to the guarantee of a minimum amount of personal autonomy for the people. It should follow that, when the constitution is no more capable of constraining state power because the latter no longer resides in the state, then constitutionalism ceases to fulfil its purpose and must perhaps be revamped at supranational level.

A slightly different reading would approach constitutionalism not merely as a response to the need for setting constrains to state power, but rather, primarily, in tandem with capitalism and the related demand to secure the peaceful coexistence of citizens and the smooth operation of national markets. Once constitutionalism is approached in this way, the weight of its purposes shifts from adherence to the rule of law to the need to create social consensus. Seen in this light, constitutionalism, seeking as it does to appease social conflict and to secure consensus, demarcates the legal framework within which this conflict materialises. Citizens are granted rights and freedoms in exchange for their harmonious coexistence in the face of social inequality. Constitutionalism can therefore be approached more as a political instrument that assists in the maintenance of the status quo and less as a legal tool that establishes the rule of law. It is in this sense that

---

[24] See eg L Diamond and M Plattner, 'Introduction' in L Diamond and M Plattner (eds), *The Global Divergence of Democracies* (John Hopkins UP 2001) xxi.

[25] L Ferrajoli, 'Beyond Sovereignty and Citizenship: A Global Constitutionalism' in Bellamy (ed), *Constitutionalism, Democracy and Sovereignty: American and European Perspectives* (Avebury 1996) 151.

[26] G Schochet, 'Introduction' in R Pennock and J Chapman (eds), *Nomos XX: Constitutionalism* (New York UP 1979) 10.

[27] R Kay, 'American Constitutionalism' in L Alexander (ed), *Constitutionalism* (CUP 1998) 22.

[28] See C Fritz, 'Alternative Visions of American Constitutionalism: Popular Sovereignty and the Early American Constitutional Debate' (1997) 24 Hastings Constitutional Law Quarterly 287.

constitutionalism retains a relative autonomy from the constitution. While the latter is a strong indicator of the quality and resilience of social consensus, it cannot always be relied upon as a measuring device of the status of social relations within a polity. This is so, not least because it is the very point of the constitution to be subject to divergent interpretations following, at best, the changing socio-economic and political climate but, at worst, the political project of any given political elite.

On the above account, it can be inferred that constitutionalism acknowledges the omnipresent existence of conflicting social interests, regardless of whether such conflict is conscious or not. This acknowledgement is, in and of itself, important. It is important, first, because it bespeaks an unbreakable link between constitutionalism and the nation state. The resolution of conflicting social interests cannot easily be attempted, let alone achieved, at extra-state level.[29] The German worker does not, and will not in the foreseeable future, be on the same wavelength or identify their interests, with the Romanian or Spanish one. This is only understandable. Different states, regardless of whether they belong to the EU/EMU or not, have different characteristics: insurance policies, taxation systems, employment relations, social rights and the institutions that protect them, prices and governmental budgets, wages and, in general, the factors that determine how profit is made, are not homogeneous in the different Member States of the Union. The structure and content of the above institutions reflect different national histories. Certainly, they also reflect different outcomes of the social struggles, and the balance of powers that emerged therefrom, within each national formation. Finally, they determine the scope and size of social conflict, the dimensions of which are therefore dissimilar within the Union's various Member States. This means that if constitutionalism is seen primarily as a tool that acts out social conflict, its purpose cannot easily be fulfilled unless constitutionalism is located in the nation state.

The acknowledgement on the part of constitutional arrangements of the ubiquitous existence of social conflict is important, second, because it indicates that, without a minimum legal recognition of conflicting social interests, social coexistence is non-viable. One might then wonder how constitutionalism achieves consensus so effectively, given the pervasive quality of social conflict. The answer is to be found in the notion of constitutionalism as ideology, in particular the ideology of the united and undivided nation, a nation with common interests and characteristics. The demarcation of the inside from the outside is vital for constitutionalism as it minimises the outward show of social antagonisms and the potential for eruption of violent conflict uncontainable by law.[30] The national interest is the idea upon which the state builds its unity and emerges as the representative of its people.

---

[29]   Even strands of the literature that support the internationalisation of the state and of collective social forces are hesitant to admit that anything akin to democratic conflict resolution is occurring at the global level: see eg A Demirovic, 'NGOs, the State, and Civil Society: The Transformation of Hegemony' (2003) 15 Rethinking Marxism 213; S Gill, 'New Constitutionalism, Democratisation and Global Political Economy (1998) 10 Pacifica Review: Peace, Security & Global Change 23.

[30]   See eg D Grimm, 'The Achievements of Constitutionalism and Its Prospects in a Changed World' in M Loughlin and P Dobner (eds), *The Twilight of Constitutionalism?* (OUP 2012) 12.

It is on the basis of the above understanding of constitutionalism that the present analysis sees the political offspring of the crisis, austerity, as a matter of constitutional importance. This is so, not so much because of the entrenchment of fiscal constraints in constitutional documents, but rather because of the attempt at legitimation of austerity in political discourse and practice through the rhetoric of austerity as national interest.[31] When austerity becomes legitimised and therefore unchallengeable in the social body; when, in other words, austerity becomes part of the social consensus, it has already become constitutionally anchored.

Before closing this section, two remarks need to be made. First, we need to accept that the effort to justify and endorse austerity could never succeed, were it to be undertaken by the Union alone. This endeavour has to be filtered through the national institutions. The maxim of austerity as national interest, if it is to be at all persuasive, must be expressed by state representatives acting in the name of this interest. It is therefore indispensable to re-evaluate the extent to which the political project of austerity challenges sovereign state powers. In particular, it is significant to reflect upon the question of primacy in this bundle of political developments. National authorities are no less busy trying to prove that austerity is unavoidable than are, for example, the ECB or the Commission. Without rejecting the major influence of external actors in national austerity tactics, the role of the nation state has to be reappraised. In fact, the role of the nation state has to be recognised as predominant, not least in terms of legitimation of austerity in the nation's collective unconscious.

At the same time, it is difficult – indeed, it would be inaccurate – to claim that the Union plays a minimal role in the breakthrough of austerity in EU Member States. Legitimating a political project in the eyes of the masses would be devoid of any tangible effects without this project's actual political and legal institutionalisation. Here the Union emerges as a catalyst for the surfacing of a debased form of European constitutionalism, which seeks to create pan-European consensus around the institutionalisation of austerity without acknowledging conflict. The result of this peculiar process of European constitutionalisation is the coming together of European elites and the knocking down of any possibility for pan-European struggles at the level of European societies. The latter increasingly tend to conceive conflict as a battle of nation versus nation. Enter Brexit.

The largely nationalistic and xenophobic discourse that has surrounded and driven the Brexit vote brings me to my second point. While the source of austerity, neoliberalism, is now deeply embedded at the social level of Member States and has

---

[31]   It is indicative, for example, that one of the countries most severely hit by austerity, Greece, has not proceeded to any constitutional amendment in order to include budgetary constraints within the constitutional document. Note that the relevant rhetoric reaches beyond the eurozone. For an account of austerity as national interest in the UK, see N Ritchie, 'Whose National Interest?' in T Edmunds and others (eds), *British Foreign Policy and the National Interest: Identity, Strategy and Security* (Palgrave Macmillan 2014) 91.

informed the ways in which we understand our role in the world and our relations with our fellow citizens, the recent violent outbreak of austerity is not equally well received in societies.[32] As already remarked, at pan-European level this challenge more often than not tends to take the form of fearmongering about the European 'other'. At Member State level, there is an apparent inefficacy of even the all-powerful idea of the national interest to fully absorb the enormous austerity-driven dissonance between different national social fractions. Crucially, this is the case regardless of whether budgetary and fiscal constraints have taken the form of constitutional provisions, and notwithstanding Constitutional Courts' proclamations that austerity and the national interest go hand in hand.[33] And, one might add, this will remain the case, whatever improvements, marginal or not, are made to the institutional framework of the EU and/or the Member States, as long as austerity remains the determinant factor of the organisation of societies. Herein lies an indication that the 'political' cannot always be contained by the 'legal'.

Most importantly, however, it becomes evident that, if constitutionalism is about the acting out of social conflict, then austerity has not been constitutionalised in a successful manner. In fact, far from securing social consensus and the maintenance of the status quo, austerity, despite the attempts at constitutionalising it, seems to have achieved precisely the opposite: an upswing in extreme right-wing ideology and activity on the one hand and a surge in public support for political powers that challenge the established order of things on the other. Coupled with the second tendency is an increase in social solidarity movements, notably in the states whose citizens are suffering the most. This situation brings Europe before an impasse that might always have existed, but which has come into view more strikingly than ever with the outbreak of the crisis, with both of the above tendencies undermining the foundations of the European project. The former, far-right ideology and nationalistic rhetoric, drives a coach and horses through the ever-closer Union of its people, the only truly emancipatory feature of the European endeavour. The latter tendency, social movements, debunks the basis of the neoliberal European economic and political project, as expressed and realised by the austerity agenda of national governments.

---

[32] On the dominance and embedment of (neoliberal) ideology, see L Althusser, *On the Reproduction of Capitalism: Ideology and Ideological State Apparatuses* (GM Goshgarian tr, Verso, 2014); M Foucault, *Power/Knowledge: Selected Interviews and Other Writings 1972–1977* (C Gordon ed, Harvester Wheatsheaf 1980) 119; A Gramsci, *Prison Notebooks* vol III (JA Buttigieg tr, Columbia UP 1975) 171. I say 'recent outbreak', because austerity is not a new phenomenon. However, it is only in its recent more intense form that it is being challenged to such an extent. On perceptions of austerity during the 1970s and the then powerful Italian Communist Party's Enrico Berlinguer's contentious reactions, see D Sassoon, *One Hundred Years of Socialism: The West European Left in the Twentieth Century* (Tauris 2010) 589–92.

[33] See eg Case 668/2012 (para 10) of the Council of State (Greece's Supreme Administrative Court) on the constitutionality of the first Memorandum of Understanding signed by the Greek government in 2010.

As the weak, one-sided European constitutionalism seems unfit or unwilling to curtail nationalistic tendencies and to enable a pan-European struggle that would allow European social fractions to come together and make possible the reimagining of a European idea, we are possibly left with one alternative: filtering political action and disobedience through national constitutionalism. Before I explore how constitutionalism can play an active and, this time, progressive role in the above state of affairs, it is important to explain austerity not merely in terms of budgetary constraints, limitations to sovereign decision-making, and technical details, but rather in terms of its effects on the social body.

2 A Note on Austerity-Knitting: Austerity and Constitutionalism

The endeavour to legitimise austerity is largely connected with the rhetoric of necessity. Austerity appears necessary because it will guarantee a state's economic survival; because it will ensure the smooth functioning of the economic system and hinder a bailout; because it will secure a state's participation in the EU and/or EMU; because it will save the common currency; because, finally, it is a condition for external economic assistance. This rhetoric, revolving as it does around necessity, is reminiscent of the state of exception. Such state, says Agamben, tends to become the dominant political paradigm in the largest part of the western world, for reasons ranging from the need to respond to financial crises to the need to return to conditions of political normality.[34] It is so much so, that the state of emergency tends to become normality in itself. Austerity thus emerges as a quasi-state of exception, which, instead of suspending the constitution, is aspiring to become a constitutional norm itself.

Be that as it may, once austerity is seen in broader terms than simple economic or legal technicalities, the disruption of social cohesion becomes almost self-evident. Austerity might bring with it the violent repression of any expression of opposition, but the story does not end there. As austerity deepens and jeopardises survival, its persuasive potential deteriorates. It is then possible that austerity becomes accompanied by recourse to threats, intimidation and moral dilemmas, which build up an impression of spread-out war and which reconstruct society as a force disseminated by precisely this sense: of spread-out war.[35]

Here, positive constitutional provisions play a diminished role, if any role at all. Instead, what seems to prevail is the penetration of authoritarian and militarist elements within the very structure of the state. If one now looks at the European history of the last century one will find out that such penetration in liberal regimes

---

[34]   G Agamben, *State of Exception* (K Attell tr, University of Chicago Press 2005) 1–31.
[35]   M Markantonatou, 'The State of Financial Crisis and the Rhetoric of Emergency, Economic War and Downfall of Sovereignty' (2012) 118 *Theseis* [in Greek] www.theseis.com/index.php?option=com_content&task=view&id=1172 accessed April 2018.

has constituted the necessary condition for the ultimate dominance of fascism.[36] This does not merely explain the upsurge of extreme-right and nationalist forces throughout Europe. It is also a reminder that the constitutional relevance of austerity is not limited to its constitutional entrenchment. We must, therefore, construct a constitutional narrative capable of absorbing the eminent dangers inherent in the modern politics of austerity. This narrative must pertain both to the Union, as the primary driver of austerity politics, and to its Member States, as the zealous enablers and facilitators of this political project. That said, the Union does not easily fit within a constitutional narrative that seeks to have an emancipatory dimension. This will be discussed in what follows.

III RECLAIMING CONSTITUENT POWER

It was argued above that constitutionalism is a legal and political instrument that facilitates the maintenance and longevity of established political arrangements, ergo of the status quo. To this end, constitutionalism seeks to achieve consensus. One therefore needs to explore the prerequisites for consensus and conditions of its maintenance. Aristotle, for example, a robust advocate of respect for the law and of political stability, taught that active disobedience was essential when it was driven by the need to preserve harmony.[37] For Machiavelli, enforced consensus would block out the antagonisms and dissent in society and, by preventing the creation of mobilised social forces able to further democracy, would result in bloodshed.[38] The same underlying idea appears to have been relied upon by many constitutional scholars who, in their study of the constitutional dimensions of austerity, have argued that constitutional entrenchment of budgetary constraints will prevent economic policies from being negotiated in the political arena.[39] This reading of post-crisis developments is largely correct. It does, however, seem to imply that constitutional crystallisation of a policy suffices to render that policy inalienable. Here, the constitution is equated with constitutionalism. However, the two need to be distinguished because the former is a document while the latter can be understood as a project comprising not solely the rules enshrined in the document but rather a whole range of social processes and dynamics capable of turning rules on their head.

What does it mean for a policy to be negotiated in the political arena? And, crucially, who negotiates it? Herein lies the need to conceive constituent power, not

---

[36] N Poulantzas, *Fascism and Dictatorship: The Third International and the Problem of Fascism* (Verso 1979) 65–66.

[37] J Frank, 'Aristotle on Constitutionalism and the Rule of Law' (2006) 8 Theoretical Inquiries in Law 37.

[38] N Machiavelli, *History of Florence and of the Affairs of Italy: From the Earliest Times to the Death of Lorenzo the Magnificent* (Pennsylvania State UP 2007) 121; F Ankersmit, *Aesthetic Politics: Political Philosophy beyond Fact and Value* (Stanford UP 1996) 171–72.

[39] See section III.

as a producer of constitutional norms who ceases to exist as soon as these norms are created, but rather as a living body that is ready to renegotiate constitutional certainties through democratic conflict. Surely, to reconcile such an understanding of constituent power with constitutionalism presents difficulties. Here is Antonio Negri:

> To acknowledge constituent power as a constitutional and juridical principle, we must see it not simply as producing constitutional norms and structuring consti-tuted powers but primarily as a subject that regulates democratic politics. Yet this is not a simple matter. In fact, constituent power resists being constitutionalized: 'Studying constituent power from the juridical perspective presents an exceptional difficulty given the hybrid nature of this power ... The strength hidden in consti-tuent power refuses to be fully integrated in a hierarchical system of norms and competencies. Constituent power always remains alien to the law.' The question becomes even more difficult because democracy, too, resists being constitutiona-lized: democracy is in fact a theory of absolute government, while constitutionalism is a theory of limited government and therefore a practice that limits democracy.[40]

Negri is right in claiming that 'the political' possesses a horizon not always able to be framed by what the constitutional order prescribes. He shows intellectual bravery in denying the constitutional, and therefore, according to his reading, also conser-vative quality of both the constituent power and of democracy: constituent power 'presents itself as the continual interruption of the constitutive rhythm and as revolutionary becoming with respect to political constructions and constituted being'.[41]

Can we make Negri's version of constituent power compatible with constitution-alism? I believe that we can. Constitutionalism, even in its version as an instrument directed towards protection of the status quo, leaves this possibility open. If we accept that the results of austerity policies reach further than mere economic and constitutional technicalities, into the very conditions of integrity of the social body; and if we further accept that constitutionalism is partly about preserving this integrity by allowing the acting out of conflict and the expression of dissent, then we have to detect within the constitutional arrangement a possibility for rupture in the established political order, when the latter is no longer viable. Such rupture will

---

[40] A Negri, *Insurgencies: Constituent Power and the Modern State* (M Boscagli tr, University of Minnesota Press 1999) 2–3. The quote inside the quote belongs to G Burdeau, *Traité de sciences politiques*, vol IV (Librairie generale de droit et de jurisprudence, 1983), 171, as cited in Negri.

[41] ibid 318. Negri eventually drifts into equating constituent power with an almost metaphysical idea of an undifferentiated multitude, a coming together of the people. This version of the constituent power is not accepted here. See, for a critique, L Corrias, *The Passivity of Law: Competence and Constitution in the European Court of Justice* (Springer 2011) 34–37 and D Dimoulis and S Lunardi, 'Constituent Power beyond Liberal Constitutionalism and the Impotency of the Multitude' (2012) 120 *Theseis* [in Greek] www.theseis.com/index.php?option=com_content&task=view&id=1192&Itemid=29 accessed April 2018.

often be able to take the form of an eclectic challenge against all dominant logics that co-occur with post-crisis developments. In particular, it may be able to challenge established constitutional understandings of principles whose meaning has been determined by a distinctly neoliberal rationale.

The logics of self-determination as self-help and of freedom as a natural universal certainty, rather than as a demand fought for and won at the political level, are a case in point. Although one could not by a long shot claim that collective projects of social solidarity are becoming a dominant practice, some of the European states that are most severely hit by austerity offer examples of collective movements that progressively challenge dominant understandings of principles, which conceptually back the idea and practices of austerity.[42] The Greek solidarity clinics test the neoliberal ideas of individualised risk, self-as-enterprise, and charitable activity by putting forward a philosophy of communal action and social solidarity in order to meet collective needs.[43] Similarly, the Spanish indebted homeowners movement questions, in practice, dominant conceptions of individual property and of economic freedom as the only available understanding of liberty.[44]

These are examples of how constituent power, understood, not as an undiversified multitude, but instead as collective social forces united under their common interests and needs, can produce cracks in the domestic constitutional order while remaining within its framework. Perhaps, we should be opting for a wholesale paradigm change. Perhaps, with Negri, we should demand that constituent power brings about the revolutionary conversion into what is beyond the vision of constituted being. But such conversion will occur neither instantly nor abruptly.

Constitutionalism does have a role to play in the meantime. This role should not be limited to an instrumentalist defence of pre-crisis adherence to the constitutional letter. The letter of the constitution is never too clear and never too firm to guarantee success of such a claim, however right it might be. This role should even less be linked to a fixation with institutional and procedural changes that will make austerity policies more transparent while leaving them, in principle, unchallenged. The constitutional dimension of the crisis lies more in the embedment of austerity and its paraphernalia in societies, in its appearance as a normality or necessity. Let us therefore renegotiate what is normal and necessary both in theory and in practice. The constitution will embrace the outcome of this renegotiation – it cannot do otherwise.

---

[42] There is much talk about such movements operating mainly in Spain and Greece, with the notable exception of Portugal. See C Príncipe, 'Hope for the Portuguese Left' (*Jacobin*, 10 August 2015) www .jacobinmag.com/2015/10/left-bloc-portugal-austerity-social-democracy accessed April 2018.

[43] For the relevant concepts, see eg N Rose and P Miller, 'Political Power beyond the State: Problematics of Government' (1992) 43 British Journal of Sociology 173.

[44] For more details on the activity of these movements, see M Zechner and BR Hansen, 'Building Power in a Crisis of Social Reproduction' *Roar Magazine* (2015) https://roarmag.org/magazine/building-power-crisis-social-reproduction accessed April 2018.

This process is difficult to replicate at European level. It is difficult, first, because the multi-tier system of states coexisting within the Union stands in the way of identification of common interests and of the building of pan-European movements from below. It is difficult, second, because the EU is immune from popular control. This is not so much a result of the (in)famous European democratic deficit and the lack of institutional transparency and accountability. It is rather a pragmatic conclusion emanating from the fact that the Union seems to be untouchable by domestic contestation.[45] Whether structurally flawed or simply politically unscrupulous, the Union is nowhere near enabling the formation of a European constituent power able to challenge its neoliberal rationalities, normalities and routines. Perhaps then the solution lies in spreading constructive opposition through the domestic route. Unlike the xenophobic and reactionary resistance that accompanied the largest part of the Brexit vote, such opposition can and has to be akin to a form of disobedience, defending rights and upholding the power of citizens to be involved in decisions that affect them. Another Europe might or might not be possible, but this is something that cannot be pre-empted. Lest we forget that structures, however difficult, are not impossible to shake.

IV CONCLUSION

The constitutional significance of austerity may well lie in the constitutional entrenchment of austerity rules in the constitutional document. Yet, the constitution can be seen in either technical terms, as the highest law of an entity or in broader terms, as the mode of organisation of social and political life. In the former case, the constitutionalisation of austerity refers to what the law prescribes. In the latter case, austerity insinuates itself in the social body emerging as the order of things, a routine or a normality. The preceding discussion argues that this latter form of constitutionalisation poses a far greater threat to societies. Interrupting embedded ideologies is always a process more tenuous than changing legal prescriptions. The threat has already materialised in Europe. Regardless of the degree to which different states have rendered austerity a constitutional command, austerity is constitutionalised. The European Union's neoliberal fundamentalism has been conducive to this process. Whether structurally designed as a neoliberal order or, simply, driven to pursue the goal of austerity by its political leadership and its Court's neoliberal agenda, the Union seems to always point to a predetermined winner in the battle between dominant and dominated social forces: the market. One response could be that, where winners are predetermined, there is no point in taking up arms. Another response could be to rethink of the European endeavour as one that could have

---

[45] See eg L Jones, 'The EU Locked in Neoliberalism and Locked Out Its People. Brexit Is the Alternative' (*LSE Blog*, 10 June 2016) http://blogs.lse.ac.uk/brexit/2016/06/10/the-eu-locked-in-neoliberalism-and-locked-out-its-people-brexit-is-the-alternative accessed April 2018.

never succeeded without the mediation of the state. The Union may be successful in imposing rules or conditionalities, but it is through the mechanisms of the state that these work their way into the level of dominant truths and hegemonic ideas. It may, therefore, be that Negri's continual interruption of the constitutive rhythm of austerity should commence at state level. Besides, until we are able to discern anything akin to a genuine constituent power at EU level, the state may be the only constitutional order able to be disrupted.

8

'Who's Afraid of the European *Demos*?'

The Uneasy Relationship between the European Union and Referendums

Elia Alexiou

I INTRODUCTION

In the midst of the multifaceted crisis the European Union (EU) is currently experiencing, almost every recent referendum held on European issues has been regarded as another crack in European unity. Not only have the questions addressed to the people – as well as the respective political campaigns – touched upon key areas of the European crisis such as finance and migration; the answers finally delivered were often also unexpected and sometimes even shocking from a European integration point of view.

The Greek 'no' to the bailout referendum in July 2015 and the Danish 'no' to an opt-out referendum six months later were followed in 2016 by a Dutch 'no' to the Ukraine–EU Association Agreement, by a Hungarian (invalid) 'no' to EU refugee-relocation quotas and, of course, by the famous Brexit referendum; the British 'no' to the EU itself. As diverse as they might be, all these recent referendums[1] form a rather dynamic series of 'no' votes across the continent, questioning and challenging the future of the European project itself. Henceforth, any new political pledge to hold a national referendum on EU issues might instantly be viewed as a threat to the Union's future. Yet, considering popular votes as threats appears rather paradoxical, if not contradictory and highly problematic, for a – supposedly – democratic organisation.

In fact, this recent round of EU referendums[2] forms part of a long-standing relationship between the Union and national popular ballots. Referendums held in both Member and candidate States have indeed shaped the Union over the years affecting its geographical borders, integration policies or even constitutional

---

[1] Instead of the plural 'referenda', we opt for the term 'referendums'. See JT Grant and Y Taoka, 'The Referendum Conundrum: Referenda or Referendums?' (2001) 44 Political Science and Politics 563.

[2] The 'EU referendum' is understood as a national referendum on EU-related issues and must be distinguished from the (hypothetical) 'pan-European referendum' meaning one eventually held on the EU level.

evolution. Since the first EU referendum held in France in 1972, Member States have turned to popular votes forty-six times in forty-six years, while more than half of these votes took place after 2000 (Table 8.1).[3] All major EU Treaty reforms have been subjected to at least one national popular vote in at least one Member State. And, as regards EU membership, it is noteworthy that, of the first fifteen Member States which respectively formed or joined the Communities, only two held referendums to ratify the accession decision (Ireland and Denmark), whereas, among the last thirteen accessions since 2000,[4] only two States did not hold a popular vote (Cyprus and Bulgaria). In this context, referendums are indeed emerging as an increasingly common and familiar feature of EU politics and, consequently, direct democracy seems to somehow expand beyond the traditional restricted national borders.

However, this recent proliferation of EU referendums must first be located within the broader context of a growing – regional,[5] but also global[6] – trend towards mechanisms of direct[7] and participatory democracy.[8] In recent decades, there has been a significant global increase[9] in the number of nationwide referendums[10] and a parallel adoption of new constitutional provisions on citizen-initiated votes[11] or legislative initiatives.[12] Over the last four years, several historic referendums have taken place worldwide, either on specific national issues (like the Colombian 'no' to the Peace Agreement Referendum in 2016), on international treaties (like the Swiss

---

[3] On the reasons behind this recent trend, see S Tierney, 'The People's Last Sigh? Referendums and European Integration' (2012) 18 European Public Law 683, 684; C Closa, 'Why Convene Referendums? Explaining Choices in EU Constitutional Politics' (2007) 14 Journal of European Public Policy 1311.

[4] The most recent accession is that of Croatia in 2013 after an EU-membership referendum held on 22 January 2012.

[5] ZT Pállinger and others (eds), *Direct Democracy in Europe: Developments and Prospects* (VS Verlag 2007); B Kaufmann and MD Waters, *Direct Democracy in Europe: A Comprehensive Reference Guide to the Initiative and Referendum Process in Europe* (Carolina Academic Press 2004).

[6] M Qvortrup (ed), *Referendums around the World: The Continued Growth of Direct Democracy* (2nd edn, Palgrave 2018); D Altman, *Direct Democracy Worldwide* (CUP 2011).

[7] For a definition of direct democracy, see Altman (n 6) 7–17. On new forms of democracy and a review of its history from antiquity to present, see T Kaplan, *Democracy: A World History* (OUP 2015); C Tilly, *Democracy* (CUP 2007).

[8] On the relationship between direct and participatory democracy, see T Schiller, 'Direct Democracy and Theories of Participatory Democracy – Some Observations' in Pállinger (n 5) 52–63.

[9] However, certain countries account for a disproportionately large share of referendums. Often described as a semi-direct democracy, Switzerland alone accounts for around 50 per cent of referendums worldwide. See M Qvortrup, 'The History of Referendums and Direct Democracy' in L Morel and M Qvortrup (eds), *The Routledge Handbook to Referendums and Direct Democracy* (Routledge 2018).

[10] See Qvortrup (n 6) 264 noticing that 'the zenith was reached in the 1990s with 63 nationwide referendums in democratic polities, or 6.3 per year. However, based on current trends, that total is likely to be surpassed in the second decade of the twenty-first century. So far there have been fifty votes or an annual average of 8.3 referendums. For additional statistical data, see the studies of the Centre for Research on Direct Democracy (C2D) of the University of Zurich, available at www.c2d.ch

[11] See Qvortrup (n 6) 268–70.

[12] M Setälä and T Schiller (eds), *Citizens' Initiatives in Europe: Procedures and Consequences of Agenda-Setting by Citizens* (Palgrave 2012).

TABLE 8.1 *Referendums on European integration*
R: Required **NR**: Non-required **B**: Binding **NB**: Non-binding **C**: Citizens' initiative

	Year	Date	Country	Object	Category	Type	Turnout (%)	Yes (%)	No (%)	Result
1.	1972	23 April	France	Enlargement of EEC (to admit UK, Denmark, and Ireland)	Single-issue	NR–NB	60.2	68.3	31.7	Yes
2.	1972	10 May	Ireland	EEC Membership	Membership	R–B	70.9	83.1	16.9	Yes
3.	1972	25 September	Norway*	EEC Membership	Membership	NR–NB	79.2	46.5	53.5	No
4.	1972	2 October	Denmark	EEC Membership	Membership	R–B	90.1	63.3	36.7	Yes
5.	1975	5 June	United Kingdom	EEC Membership (Staying in or leaving)	Membership	NR–NB	64.0	67.2	32.8	Yes
6.	1982	23 February	Greenland**	EEC Membership (Staying in or leaving)	Membership	NR–NB	75	47.0	53.0	No
7.	1986	26 February	Denmark	Single European Act	Treaty ratification	R–B	75.4	56.2	43.8	Yes
8.	1987	26 May	Ireland	Single European Act	Treaty ratification	R–B	44.1	69.9	30.1	Yes
9.	1989	18 June	Italy	Maastricht Treaty – Mandate for MEPs	Single-issue	NR–NB	80.7	88.0	12.0	Yes
10.	1992	2 June	Denmark	Maastricht Treaty (I)	Treaty ratification	R–B	83.0	49.3	50.7	No
11.	1992	18 June	Ireland	Maastricht Treaty	Treaty ratification	R–B	57.3	69.0	31.0	Yes
12.	1992	20 September	France	Maastricht Treaty	Treaty ratification	NR–B	69.7	51.0	49.0	Yes
13.	1992	6 December	Switzerland*	EEA accession	Membership	R–B	78.7	49.7	50.3	No
14.	1992	13 December	Liechtenstein*	EEA accession	Membership	NR–NB	87.0	55.8	44.2	Yes
15.	1993	18 May	Denmark	Maastricht Treaty (II)	Treaty ratification	NR–NB	86.5	56.8	43.2	Yes
16.	1994	12 June	Austria	EU membership	Membership	R–B	82.3	66.6	33.4	Yes
17.	1994	16 October	Finland	EU membership	Membership	NR–NB	70.8	56.9	43.1	Yes
18.	1994	13 November	Sweden	EU membership	Membership	NR–NB	83.3	52.7	47.3	Yes

(continued)

TABLE 8.1 (continued)

	Year	Date	Country	Object	Category	Type	Turnout (%)	Yes (%)	No (%)	Result
19.	1994	20 November	Åland Islands**	EU membership	Membership	NR–B	49.1	73.6	26.4	Yes
20.	1994	28 November	Norway*	EU membership	Membership	NR–NB	89.0	47.8	52.2	No
21.	1995	9 April	Liechtenstein*	EEA accession	Membership	NR–B	82	55.8	44.2	Yes
22.	1997	8 June	Switzerland*	EU membership	Membership	NR–B–C	35.4	25.9	74.1	No
23.	1998	22 May	Ireland	Amsterdam Treaty	Treaty ratification	R–B	56.3	61.7	38.3	Yes
24.	1998	28 May	Denmark	Amsterdam Treaty	Treaty ratification	R–B	76.2	55.1	44.9	Yes
25.	2000	28 September	Denmark	Single currency – euro	Single-Issue	NR–B	87.6	46.8	53.2	No
26.	2001	4 March	Switzerland*	EU membership	Membership	NR–B–C	55.8	23.1	76.9	No
27.	2001	7 June	Ireland	Nice Treaty (I)	Treaty ratification	R–B	34.8	46.1	53.9	No
28.	2002	19 October	Ireland	Nice Treaty (II)	Treaty ratification	R–B	49.5	62.9	37.1	Yes
29.	2003	8 March	Malta	EU membership	Membership	NR–NB	90.9	53.7	46.3	Yes
30.	2003	23 March	Slovenia	EU membership	Membership	R–B	60.4	89.6	10.4	Yes
31.	2003	12 April	Hungary	EU membership	Membership	R–B	45.6	83.8	16.2	Yes
32.	2003	11 May	Lithuania	EU membership	Membership	R–B	63.4	91.1	8.9	Yes
33.	2003	17 May	Slovakia	EU membership	Membership	R–B	52.1	93.7	6.3	Yes
34.	2003	8 June	Poland	EU membership	Membership	R–B	58.9	77.5	22.5	Yes
35.	2003	14 June	Czech Republic	EU membership	Membership	R–B	55.2	77.3	22.7	Yes
36.	2003	14 September	Estonia	EU membership	Membership	R–B	64.1	66.8	33.2	Yes
37.	2003	14 September	Sweden	Single currency – euro	Single-Issue	NR–NB	82.6	42.9	57.1	No
38.	2003	20 September	Latvia	EU membership	Membership	R–B	73.1	67.5	32.5	Yes
39.	2003	19 October	Romania	EU membership	Membership	R–B	55.7	91.1	8.9	Yes
40.	2005	20 February	Spain	Constitutional Treaty	Treaty ratification	NR–NB	41.8	81.8	18.2	Yes
41.	2005	29 May	France	Constitutional Treaty	Treaty ratification	NR–NB	69.4	45.3	54.7	No

42.	2005	1 June	The Netherlands	Constitutional Treaty	NR–NB	63.3	38.5	61.5	No
43.	2005	10 July	Luxembourg	Constitutional Treaty	NR–NB	90.4	56.5	43.5	Yes
44.	2008	12 June	Ireland	Lisbon Treaty (I)	R–B	53.1	46.6	53.4	No
45.	2009	2 October	Ireland	Lisbon Treaty (II)	R–B	59.0	67.1	32.9	Yes
46.	2012	22 January	Croatia	EU Membership	R–B	43.5	66.3	33.7	Yes
47.	2012	31 May	Ireland	European Fiscal Compact	R–B	50.6	60.3	39.7	Yes
48.	2013	20 October	San Marino*	EU Membership	NR–NB	43.4	50.3	49.7	Yes
							(invalid)		
49.	2014	25 May	Denmark	Unified Patent Court	R–B	55.9	62.5	37.5	Yes
50.	2015	5 July	Greece	Bailout	NR–NB	62.5	38.7	61.3	No
51.	2015	3 December	Denmark	Opt-out (Justice & Home affairs)	R–B	72.0	46.9	53.1	No
52.	2016	6 April	The Netherlands	EU–Ukraine Association Agreement	NR–NB–C	31.7	38.2	61.8	No
53.	2016	23 June	United Kingdom	EU Membership (staying in or leaving)	NR–NB	72.2	48.1	51.9	No
54.	2016	2 October	Hungary	Refugee-relocation quota	NR–NB	44.0	1.6	98.4	No
						(invalid)			

*Still non-EU Member States **Territories of Member States: Denmark (Greenland) and Finland (Åland Islands) 'yes' to the immigration-restriction referendum in 2014) or on major constitutional reforms (like those rejected in Italy in 2016 or those approved in Turkey in 2017; both with a significant impact on EU politics).

Considering also the numerous independence[13] and local referendums[14] held both in Europe and worldwide, one could arguably claim that we are witnessing a certain 'revival of direct democracy'.[15] Voters are increasingly given a direct say on major issues and, thus, somehow re-engaging with the political process,[16] while governments apparently seek to obtain a much-needed, renewed and uncontested popular mandate for important political decisions on sensitive issues requiring a broader consensus in society.

Nevertheless, this growing use of referendums is not necessarily an indication that the world has indeed become more democratic.[17] Certainly, the increasing frequency of direct citizen involvement in political decision-making carries in itself an inherent democratising potential.[18] But, beyond this apparent positive effect, the overall phenomenon cannot be viewed in isolation from the general context of modern democratic regimes. Referendums are, in reality, direct democratic devices which necessarily operate as decision-making processes within representative systems.[19] As such, they largely affect the 'interplay between voters and the institutions and actors of representative democracy, notably political parties'.[20] In this sense, the recent turn towards direct democracy can logically be associated with the numerous failures and deficiencies of the contemporary forms of representative democracy.[21] Referendums might, then, appear as constitutional safeguards,[22] alibis for governments' reluctance to act on sensitive areas,[23]

---

[13] Like those held in Scotland (2014), Catalonia (2014, 2017), Puerto Rico (2017) and the Kurdish referendum held in Iraq (2017). See: F Mendez and M Germann, 'Contested Sovereignty: Mapping Referendums on Sovereignty over Time and Space' (2018) 48(1) British Journal of Political Science 141; M Qvortrup (ed), *Nationalism, Referendums and Democracy: Voting on Ethnic Issues and Independence* (Routledge 2014).

[14] F Hendriks and others, *The Oxford Handbook of Local and Regional Democracy in Europe* (OUP 2011); T Schiller, 'Local Referendums: A Comparative Assessment of Forms and Practice' in Morel and Qvortrup (n 9) 60–80; T Schiller (ed), *Local Direct Democracy in Europe* (VS Verlag 2011).

[15] Tierney (n 3) 683.

[16] See Qvortrup (n 6) 136 arguing that '[t]he referendum as a legal, constitutional and political device allows citizens to make decisions that affect their lives, without the intervention of mediating representatives. It can give *a sense of proprietorship over the political process*' (emphasis added).

[17] On the 'stereotypes of portraying direct democracy as inherently *good* or *bad* for representative democracy' see Altman (n 6) 2 (emphasis in the original).

[18] M Qvortrup, *Direct Democracy: A Comparative Study of the Theory and Practice of Government by the People* (Manchester UP 2013) 12–25.

[19] See: S B Hobolt, *Europe in Question: Referendums on European Integration* (OUP 2009) 5, arguing that the distinction between direct and representative democracy is 'rather artificial since we know of no political regimes that use direct democracy as their main legislative system'.

[20] ibid.

[21] M Setälä and T Schiller, *Referendums and Representative Democracy: Responsiveness, Accountability and Deliberation* (Routledge 2009).

[22] Qvortrup (n 6) 266.

[23] ibid 265.

'second-order' elections,[24] instant legitimisation tools[25] or even 'institutionalised intermittent safety valves for political pressure'.[26]

Thus, despite its increasing popularity, the referendum device remains highly controversial. What may at first appear as an excellent instrument of pure Athenian democracy,[27] can easily be used as a powerful political tool to circumvent or outmanoeuvre well-established constitutional and democratic procedures. Interestingly, 'the list of non-democratic regimes that abuse plebiscites is pathetically high'.[28] Depending on the particular political conditions of their use or abuse, referendums may actually function as genuine Napoleonic plebiscites[29] – in both democratic and non-democratic regimes – by only demanding public approval for those in power in a rather authoritarian, manipulative way.[30] For instance, the timing of a referendum is carefully chosen and the specific question addressed to the people is strategically formulated in order to affect voting behaviour.[31] As for the – usually intense – 'yes' and 'no' political campaigns, they are often conceiving and framing the referendum issue in surprisingly distinct ways, in order to confuse and disorientate public opinion.[32] Besides, sometimes the very decision to hold a referendum is also a purely political one.[33] Hence, while undoubtedly serving their inherent democratic function, referendums are also being severely criticised in terms of their demagogic dimensions, especially when operating within highly sensitive political and historical contexts.

---

[24] On 'second-order' elections (eg local, regional or EU Parliament elections) as contrasted to the 'first-order' national parliamentary or presidential elections, see K Reif and H Schmitt, 'Nine Second-Order National Elections – A Conceptual Framework for the Analysis of European Election Results' (1982) 8(1) European Journal of Political Research 3, 8.

[25] Altman (n 6) 197.

[26] ibid 198.

[27] Without romanticising the ancient Athenian democracy or neglecting its strongly exclusionary character (eg towards women and slaves), citizens' assemblies in classical Greece remain rather unique cases of purely 'direct' democracy since 'issues were brought up, discussed, and decided directly without any institutional intermediation' (ibid 7).

[28] ibid 89.

[29] In the French literature, there is a common distinction between 'referendum' and 'plebiscite' with the latter denoting only the legitimisation of a person via a popular vote. See: M Guillaume-Hoffnung, *Le referendum* (PUF 1985) 14.

[30] MC Walker, *The Strategic Use of Referendums: Power, Legitimacy, and Democracy* (Palgrave 2003); M Qvortrup, 'Are Referendums Controlled and Pro-Hegemonic?' (2000) 48 Political Studies, 821.

[31] On the strategies of political elites in convening referendums, see F Mendez and others, *Referendums and the European Union: A Comparative Inquiry* (CUP 2014) 13, arguing that 'governments can gain tactical advantages in opting for a referendum and wield important agenda-setting powers when choosing its timing'.

[32] CH De Vreese, *The Dynamics of Referendums Campaigns: An International Perspective* (Palgrave 2007); *Political Campaigning in Referendums: Framing the Referendum Issue* (Routledge 2004).

[33] Paradoxically, this is true even for constitutionally mandatory referendums. For instance, the Danish Constitution (Art 20) requires a mandatory referendum whenever a transfer of national sovereignty to international authorities is not approved by five-sixths of the Parliament. Yet, even though the Danish government held a referendum on the Single European Act, the Nice and Lisbon Treaties were not considered to involve an analogous transfer of sovereignty.

Within the current European-crisis context, criticism against referendums appears even stronger – and sometimes truly provocative[34] – amounting to a veritable European 'plebiphobia'.[35] Indeed, the EU has a long and tempestuous history with referendums, and a rather problematic relationship with those which resulted in 'no' votes. Closely related to the compound EU processes of enlargement, integration, constitutionalisation and – progressively – democratisation, referendums have emerged as a significant, recurrent, and rather symbolic feature of EU politics, associated today with the multidimensional ongoing crisis and the risk of an eventual European 'dis-integration' following the Brexit vote. A comparative analysis of all those national 'no' votes – and the respective EU institutional reactions to each of them – can lead to the assumption of an apparent European neglect, if not outright contempt, towards the Member States' national *demoi*, combined with a widespread fear of new referendums ending in 'no' votes. Besides, the Union's relationship with its own emerging *demos* seems no less problematic, given the almost absolute absence of effective direct-democracy mechanisms at the EU level. Thus, studying this double-sided problematic relationship between the Union and direct democracy – first towards the different national European *demoi* and then towards its own emerging European *demos* – we will in fact review the story of European integration itself, through the prism of the current identity and democratic legitimacy crisis.

II NATIONAL REFERENDUMS ON EUROPEAN ISSUES

In the early decades of EU integration, direct democracy was strikingly absent. European governments made some crucial decisions affecting national sovereignty in unprecedented ways – and, therefore, some giant steps towards European uni-fication – without specifically consulting their *demoi*. Back in 1957, the founding members of the European Economic Community did not hold any referendum when establishing the organisation,[36] and, four decades later, the same policy was followed for the creation of the monetary union.[37] Yet, several referendums have

---

[34] In the aftermath of the recent 'no' votes, EU officials do not hesitate to openly despise referendums condemning them as 'instruments of distortion and massive disinformation' (Pierre Moscovici, 2016). See: P Wintour, 'Europe on Brink of US-Style Leap into Unknown, top EU Official Warns' *The Guardian* (14 November 2016) www.theguardian.com/world/2016/nov/14/europe-on-brink-of-us-style-leap-into-unknown-top-eu-official-warns accessed April 2018.

[35] P Wallace, 'Commentary: It's Time for Europe to Stop Holding Referendums' *Reuters* (20 September 2016) www.reuters.com/article/us-europe-referendum-commentary/commentary-its-time-for-europe-to-stop-holding-referendums-iduskcn11y22i accessed April 2018, arguing that '[t]he European lexicon, already stuffed with ugly words and phrases, needs to coin a new one: "plebiphobia". Unlike some anxieties, the fear of referendums is well-grounded.'

[36] On the reasons behind this absence of referendums, see F Mendez and M Mendez, 'The Promise and Perils of Direct Democracy for the European Union' (2017) 19 Cambridge Yearbook of European Legal Studies 48, 52.

[37] Only Denmark (2000) and Sweden (2003) held referendums on their Eurozone accession and they both resulted in 'no' votes.

been held at other critical moments of the EU enlargement and integration, progressively introducing a necessary element of public involvement in what was widely perceived as a rather 'elite-driven' project.[38] National popular votes on EU issues emerged like rare exceptional moments of public participation in a project almost exclusively discussed, designed and approved by national and EU political elites, with very weak lines of accountability between the citizenry and decision-makers,[39] and no apparent mass identification with or sense of attachment to Europe, as regards both its political and institutional dimensions.[40]

Since the first French referendum in 1972 paved the way for an EU-related direct democracy, Europe has seen sixty-two referendums on EU matters held in Member, candidate or third States,[41] and their territories.[42] Following a now common classification based on the subject matter submitted to the ballot,[43] these votes can be classified according to a threefold typology:[44] Twenty-eight referendums on membership issues[45] (including accession and withdrawal votes), sixteen on Treaty ratifications and eighteen on specific EU-policy issues[46] (including the eight Swiss referendums on the bilateral agreements between Switzerland and the Union). Among them, we can identify all possible types of referendums – mandatory or optional, binding or consultative/advisory, citizen-initiated or not[47] – depending on the respective national legal orders and constitutional provisions (Table 8.1).

Indeed, at first glance, the organisation of all these national-level votes depends exclusively on the internal constitutional order and political context of each Member or candidate State. Until now, popular votes have never been established or regulated by EU institutions. Referendums are only held by national governments

[38] M Haller, *European Integration as an Elite Process: The Failure of a Dream?* (Routledge 2008).

[39] N Nugent, *The Government and Politics of the European Union* (8th edn, Palgrave 2017) 120.

[40] R Hermann and others (eds), *Transnational Identities: Becoming European in the EU* (Rowman & Littlefield 2004) 260–62.

[41] EU referendums have been organised in third neighbouring countries with no official candidate status (Switzerland, Liechtenstein and San Marino).

[42] Greenland and the Åland Islands have voted on membership issues.

[43] On the typology and classification of the EU referendums based on the type of issues on the ballot, see Mendez (n 31) 22–29; Hobolt (n 19) 8–16.

[44] Although the labels may vary, most scholars adopt a similar working typology and identify at least these three basic types of EU referendums. Some scholars treat in a separate fourth category – regardless of their subject – all the 'Third-country referendums'. See F Mendez and M Mendez, 'Referendums on EU Matters: Study for the Committee on Constitutional Affairs' (European Parliament 2017) 26–27, www.europarl.europa.eu/supporting-analyses accessed April 2018.

[45] With eight of those held in non-EU Member States (Lichtenstein, Norway, San Marino and Switzerland).

[46] On this category of EU referendums, see DE Tosi, 'The Use of Referendums on European Topics in the Integration Process of the European Union' in X Contiades and A Fotiadou (eds), *Participatory Constitutional Change: The People as Amenders of the Constitution* (Routledge 2017) 178 noticing that '[t]hough very important aspects of the Union were affected by these referendums . . . the electorate did not get involved in deciding on a definitive resolution regarding continuing or not continuing to be part of the EU; nor was the ultimate destiny of the Union itself called into question. People were asked to decide only on the degree of their participation in the integration process.'

[47] On traditional classifications of referendums based on institutional criteria, see Hobolt (n 19) 10.

in accordance with their own domestic legal orders and involving only their own citizens. Thus, even when touching upon EU issues, the referendum device remains a purely national political and legal instrument. It is, therefore, 'the national framework that we have to look at in order to understand the different rationales for the use of this instrument and how it gives effect to the electorate's expression'.[48] In this sense, there can be various different reasons for holding, or not holding, a referendum on EU issues: it can be constitutionally mandatory or forbidden,[49] politically necessary or maybe extremely risky for a country, a government or a political party. Seen as purely national choices, certain EU referendums have, thus, been largely criticised by both EU officials and scholars on their 'legitimacy' or 'democratic-ness' regarding the specific question posed to the people or even the very decision to consult the electorate on a certain issue and at a certain political moment.[50]

In this context, a comparative analysis of all these national referendums seems rather difficult given their highly diverse national backgrounds. Apart from the wide variety of subject matter covering the whole spectrum of the EU integration process, one must also consider the different national thresholds for turnouts or results, the different legal effects of each vote and, above all, the different political and constitutional environments in which consultations have taken place. Most importantly, as illustrated in Table 8.1, the frequency of referendums conducted on EU matters differs significantly among the twenty-eight Member States. There are still five States which have never held a referendum on any aspect of the EU integration,[51] whereas Ireland and Denmark are leading the race with nine and eight referendums respectively. The Irish case remains, in fact, rather unique, being the only Member State to hold a referendum both on membership and on every major EU Treaty reform, in light of the famous Article 29.4 of the Irish Constitution.[52] Other remarkable cases include the French voting on EU enlargement (both the 1972 referendum and the modern relevant constitutional provisions)[53] and, of course, the two British votes on

---

[48]   ibid 174.

[49]   For instance, some national constitutions exclude referendums for taxes or public expenditure commitments.

[50]   For some recent critiques, see S Tierney, 'Was the Brexit Referendum Democratic?' (UK Constitutional Law Association, 25 July 2016) https://ukconstitutionallaw.org accessed April 2018; X Contiades and A Fotiadou, 'The Greek Referendum: Unconstitutional and Undemocratic' (European University Institute, 7 July 2015) http://eurocrisislaw.eui.eu/news accessed April 2018.

[51]   Belgium, Bulgaria, Cyprus, Germany and Portugal.

[52]   G Barrett, 'Why does Ireland Have All Those European Referendums? A Look at Art. 29.4 of the Irish Constitution' IIEA Economic Governance Paper n°4, Institute of International and European Affairs, Dublin (2013); 'Building a Swiss Chalet in Irish Legal Landscape?: Referendums on European Union Treaties in Ireland and the Impact of Supreme Court Jurisprudence' (2009) 5 European Constitutional Law Review 32; J O'Mahony, 'Ireland's EU Referendum Experience' (2009) 24 Irish Political Studies 429.

[53]   The French enlargement referendum in 1972 remains the only of this kind. France is also the only Member State with a constitutional provision (Art 88–5) regarding obligatory referendums on future EU enlargements. However, since 2008, this procedure can be avoided by a 3:5 Parliament majority.

EU membership in 1975 and 2016.[54] As for the referendums held in non-Member States, the case of Switzerland (Tables 8.1 and 8.2) remains certainly exceptional in light of the country's unique commitment to direct democracy.[55]

Nevertheless, beyond this inevitable focus on the national constitutional orders, we should constantly bear in mind that all these national referendums on EU issues have – by definition – an 'extraterritorial' nature which stems from their very use in a system of multilevel governance. Their *raison d'être* and impacts are far beyond national, affecting many States and – inevitably – the Union itself.[56] Each national 'yes' or 'no' vote on EU matters can have a significant direct extraterritorial impact on the rest of the Union. Even the 'yes' and 'no' political campaigns are not purely domestic, since they often include major external political influences and interventions, either from EU officials or from the other Member States' political elites.[57] This extraterritorial effect is rather evident in ballots on Treaty ratification or EU policies. Yet, even when the national *demoi* decide upon their own European future in membership referendums, they obviously affect and sometimes radically change the fate of the Union itself. For instance, the ten membership referendums held in 2003 led to the largest single European expansion which radically redrew the EU geographical boundaries to the East,[58] while a post-Brexit European Union will probably never be the same again.

When viewing these national popular votes from a broader European point of view, one can then easily perceive the signs of a problematic relationship between national direct democracy and the Union. Apart from seeing only the same few European *demoi* voting again and again on integration questions while others remain totally excluded from such procedures (which raises serious equality concerns among EU citizens),[59] a comparative synthetic study of past EU referendums

---

[54] C Gifford and B Wellings, 'Referendums and European Integration: The Case of the United Kingdom' in B Leruth and others (eds), *The Routledge Handbook of Euroscepticism* (Routledge 2018) 268–79; D Butler and U Kitzinger, *The 1975 Referendum* (2nd edn, Macmillan 1976).

[55] Via the prolific use of referendums and popular initiatives at all institutional territorial levels (federal, cantonal and local), direct democracy has emerged as an integral component of the Swiss political culture. See: A Auer, *Les origines de la démocratie directe en Suisse – Die Ursprünge der schweizerischen direkten Demokratie* (Helbing & Lichtenhahn 1996).

[56] See Thierney (n 3) 684 analysing 'the extent to which referendums on the future of Europe are, or indeed can be, *self-determination devices exclusive to the nation-State*' (emphasis added).

[57] See, for instance, the intervention of the EU Parliament's President Martin Schulz on the Greek referendum or the French President's Nicolas Sarkozy intervention after the first Irish vote on Lisbon: A Evans-Pritchard, 'EU Warns of Armageddon If Greek Voters Reject Terms' *The Telegraph* (London, 4 July 2015) www.telegraph.co.uk/finance/economics/11718296/eu-warns-of-armageddon-if-greek-voters-reject-terms.html accessed April 2018; M Hennessy and L Marlowe, 'Ireland Will Have to Vote Again on Lisbon, Says Sarkozy' *The Irish Times* (Dublin, 16 July 2008) www.irishtimes.com /news/ireland-will-have-to-vote-again-on-lisbon-says-sarkozy-1.945091 accessed April 2018.

[58] This fifth European enlargement in 2004 concerned the following ten countries: Cyprus, the Czech Republic, Estonia, Hungary, Latvia, Lithuania, Malta, Poland, Slovakia and Slovenia. Unable to join at the time, the accession of Bulgaria and Romania took place in 2007. With the exception of Cyprus and Bulgaria, all those countries held a membership referendum in 2003.

[59] R Rose and G Borz, 'What Determines Demand for European Union Referendums' (2013) 35 Journal of European Integration 619, 629.

can also reveal further aspects of this problematic relationship. Due to various non-legal factors (political, geopolitical, economic, social, etc.), the national EU referendums have had extremely different dynamics and impacts on the integration process. Producing largely different reactions, not all referendums enjoyed the same democratic credentials or polity-wide impacts and, finally, not all referendums were equally respected. Not surprisingly, the most problematic cases concern the referendums resulting in 'no' votes in which European *demoi* openly expressed themselves against the Union rejecting membership or further integration.

III THE 'NO' VOTES: EUROPEAN *DEMOI* AGAINST THE UNION

The most controversial EU referendums have always been those in which national *demoi* gave a seemingly 'wrong' – from an EU integration point of view – answer, which are basically the referendums resulting in 'no' votes. Since, in its binary logic, a referendum necessarily 'involves a change to the status quo, a pro-EU position usually takes the form of a 'yes' vote'.[60] However, 'yes' and 'no' apparently do not count equally within the EU context, while some 'nos' seem much more problematic than others. Since the first negative outcome delivered by Norway in 1972, the frequency of 'no' votes is progressively increasing, leading to the first ever series of five consecutive 'nos' from 2015 to date (Table 8.1). Starting at 20 per cent before the 2000s, the failure rate of EU referendums has almost doubled in the early 2000s to finally jump over 60 per cent since 2010.[61] As the EU crisis spreads and deepens, public support for the European project is indeed fading away. A fear of new 'no' votes is escalating across the continent and the very idea of involving citizens in the integration process starts losing support among EU circles. Apparently, the 'referendum euphoria' of the first decades is now succeeded by an era of 'referendum phobia'.[62] In this context, a brief overview of the history of EU integration seen through the national 'no' votes proves how difficult has been for the Union to take 'no' for an answer.

1 *The First 'No' Votes in Membership Referendums*

Even when they resulted in 'no' votes, the very first EU referendums did not really hinder the integration process. In 1972 several countries voted on membership issues in order to: approve (Ireland, Denmark) or reject (Norway) their own membership, consent to the European enlargement (France) or – some years later – decide upon their possible withdrawal from the Union (UK, Greenland). Between 1972 and 1992, we also see the first popular votes on Treaty ratification (Ireland and Denmark

---

[60] Mendez and Mendez (n 36) 49.
[61] ibid.
[62] S Seeger, 'From Referendum Euphoria to Referendum Phobia: Framing the Ratification Question' (2008) 10 European Journal of Law Reform 437–56.

adopting the Single European Act) and a rather prophetic Italian 'yes' to a future European constitution.[63] During these first two decades, the positive legitimising effect of direct democracy on the European project seems indisputable. With the exception of only two negative votes (concerning the not-so-surprising rejection of membership in Norway and Greenland's withdrawal),[64] whenever national *demoi* were asked, they offered relatively healthy majorities voting in favour of membership and further enlargement and integration.

2 The Danish 'No' to the Maastricht Treaty

The first referendum that dramatically reversed this general safe assumption of popular support for Europe took place in Denmark in 1992, resulting in the rejection of the Maastricht Treaty (even with the thin majority of 50.7 per cent). This Danish unexpected 'no' raised the first question-mark about future public reactions with the EU project and is generally viewed as the first 'warning shot' against 'the logic and trajectory of elite-driven treaty reforms'.[65] However, it also marked the starting point of a – now common – EU policy towards strategic 'no' votes on Treaty ratification; the so-called 'second-referendum' technique. A second referendum on the exact same subject was organised in Denmark the following year (1993),[66] after a number of legally binding 'opt-outs' were negotiated and finally achieved by the Danish government.[67] The initial 'no' was, then, overturned and the Treaty of Maastricht ratified,[68] though something had already deeply changed within the Union's relationship with direct democracy and – consequently – its own citizens. Paradoxically, the very same Treaty which endowed Member States' nationals with a formal EU citizenship became the starting point of the Union's turbulent relationship with popular votes.[69] Even though EU referendums have since proliferated and become a fundamental element of the overall politics of EU integration, this first popular 'no' to a European Treaty 'forced European elites to accept that public support for further

---

[63] This advisory Italian referendum held in 1989 (alongside the European elections) concerned the approval of a future constitutional-making mandate for the European Parliament.

[64] F Weiss, 'Greenland's Withdrawal from the European Communities' (1985) 10 European Law Review 173.

[65] J Shaw, *The Transformation of Citizenship in the European Union: Electoral Rights and the Restructuring of the Political Space* (CUP 2007) 161; M Franklin and others, 'Uncorking the Bottle: Popular Opposition to European Unification in the Wake of Maastricht' (1994) 32(4) Journal of Common Market Studies 455.

[66] H Krunke, 'From Maastricht to Edinburg: The Danish Solution' (2005) 1 European Constitutional Law Review 339, 345.

[67] Including assurances and clarifications in the areas of Security and Defence, EU citizenship, Economic and Monetary Union, Justice and Home affairs.

[68] After one more 'yes' vote in France in 1992 with a weak majority (51 per cent).

[69] C Schweiger, *Exploring the EU's Legitimacy Crisis: The Dark Heart of Europe* (Edward Elgar 2016) 13–82.

integration could not be taken for granted'.[70] The presumed 'permissive consensus'[71] that had characterised the EU integration in its first decades came to an end,[72] and fears for future negative votes increased among elites. What was carefully negotiated for years in diplomatic circles, what was widely supported by governments, political parties, EU officials, interest groups, and the media, might well be finally rejected overnight by a popular vote in a single EU Member State.

Nevertheless, in the following years, the enlargement and integration processes progressed with no big surprises regarding the 'no' votes. In May 1998, the Amsterdam Treaty was approved by both the Danish and Irish electorates, while negative outcomes occurred only in some membership referendums.[73] The only exception comes – again – from Denmark when, in 2000, the Danish electorate voted against joining the euro. However, this second Danish 'no' was much less problematic than that of 1992, since it only concerned an EU policy referendum on a specific issue – the single currency – and not an EU Treaty ratification.

3 The Irish 'No' to the Nice Treaty

The next 'no' to a treaty ratification referendum came in 2001 in Ireland. While the Maastricht and Amsterdam Treaties were rather comfortably approved in previous popular votes held in the country, the Irish electorate surprisingly voted against the Nice Treaty in 2001. Once again, the Union reacted using the 'second-referendum' technique. After a number of reassurances,[74] a second referendum was finally organised one year later (2002), resulting this time in a 'yes' vote and the final ratification of the Nice Treaty.

Then, between 2001 and 2003, the Union saw ten 'yes' votes in membership referendums[75] in light of the fifth and largest enlargement in Central and Eastern Europe and only one 'no' from Sweden in another EU-policy referendum on joining the Eurozone.

---

[70] W Wallace and J Smith, 'Democracy or Technocracy? European Integration and the Problem of Popular Consent' (1995) 18 West European Politics 137, 150–51.

[71] L Lindberg and S Scheingold, *Europe's Would-Be Polity: Patterns of Change in the European Community* (Prentice Hall 1970).

[72] L Hooghe and G Marks, 'A Postfunctionalist Theory of European Integration: From Permissive Consensus to Constraining Dissensus' (2009) 39 British Journal of Political Science 1; RC Eichenberg and RJ Dalton, 'Post-Maastricht Blues: The Transformation of Citizen Support for European Integration, 1973–2004' (2007) 42 Acta Politica 128.

[73] In the membership referendums between 1992 and 2001, there have been four 'yes' (Åland Islands, Austria, Finland, Sweden) and two 'nos' (Norway, Switzerland), as well as two 'nos' to the EEA Accession (Switzerland, Liechtenstein).

[74] Including explicit confirmations that Ireland's military neutrality would not be in any way threatened by the new Treaty and the common defence policy.

[75] A Szczerbiak and P Taggart (eds), *EU Enlargement and Referendums* (Routledge 2006).

4 The French and Dutch 'No' to the European Constitution

Maybe the most crucial moment in the relationship between direct democracy and the Union came in 2005, when – within only four days between 29 May and 1 June – French and Dutch voters rejected twice the Treaty establishing a Constitution for Europe, a major and, above all, symbolic Treaty reform which had been in the making for two years. Despite the instrument's fundamental character and the repeated calls for a certain uniformity in the ratification procedure,[76] Member States were finally left free to choose between parliamentary or popular approval according to their domestic national orders.[77] Thus, following the first successful parliamentary ratifications in sixteen Member States,[78] and two positive referendums (a previous 'yes' in Spain and a subsequent 'yes' in Luxembourg), the two negative popular votes in France and the Netherlands sent real shock-waves across the continent. The Constitution of Europe had obviously failed to win popular support and was practically rejected by its own citizens.[79] In response, instead of opting again for the 'second-referendum' technique, this time all other Member States were forced to postpone their own ratification processes and finally cancel their respective parliamentary votes or scheduled referendums.[80] The historic and symbolic feature of the Constitutional Treaty, combined with the fact that the 'no' vote came twice (from two founding Member States) and very early in the ratification process, apparently forced the EU elites to – at least temporarily – abandon the constitutional ambitions of the Union. Thus, for the first and only time in the history of EU integration, a Treaty was brought to an end by the people's verdict. Certainly, many tried to analyse and justify this huge 'no' as based on issues of national identity and social concerns over job losses using the famous Polish-plumber argument.[81] Yet, what remains is only this resounding 'no' to a historic European document, putting at stake the broader idea of European constitutionalisation. In an attempt to somehow reconnect the citizens with the Union, the European Council itself

---

[76] In a more brutal way, British Liberal Democrat Andrew Duff – a European Parliament Member at the time – questioned 'whether it was ever appropriate to submit the EU Constitution to a lottery of uncoordinated national plebiscites'. See B O'Neil, 'What Part of Ireland's "No" Does the EU Not Understand?' *The Guardian* (3 December 2008) www.theguardian.com/commentisfree/2008/dec/13/eu-ireland-lisbon-treaty accessed April 2018.

[77] A Dür and G Mateo, 'To Call or Not to Call: Political Parties and Referendums on the EU's Constitutional Treaty' (2011) 44 Comparative Political Studies 468.

[78] Austria, Belgium, Bulgaria, Cyprus, Estonia, Finland, Germany, Hungary, Greece, Italy, Latvia, Lithuania, Malta, Romania, Slovakia, Slovenia.

[79] A Peters, 'Referendums on the Constitutional Treaty 2004: A Citizens' Voice?' in D Curtin and others (eds), *The EU Constitution: The Best Way Forward?* (TMC Asser 2005) 39–57.

[80] Referendums on the European Constitution were scheduled but finally cancelled in the Czech Republic, Denmark, Ireland, Poland, Portugal and the UK.

[81] The 'Polish plumber' phrase was first used in a *Charlie Hebdo* cartoon by Philippe Val and was later popularised by Philippe de Villiers to become finally the symbol of a broader European debate over job threats for Western Europeans.

called, then, for a 'period of reflection';[82] a much-needed reflection since the whole constitutional project was precisely designed to overcome the democratic deficit of the Union and, instead, it further deepened – perhaps irreversibly – the EU legitimacy crisis.

However, even if the 'second-referendum' technique was wisely avoided, the Union apparently came up with a new way to overturn 'no' votes. Instead of coming back towards the same voters with a second referendum on the same Treaty, there is also the much safer way of coming up with a second – rather identical – Treaty and, this time, not submit it to a popular vote in the same electorates. And this is exactly what happened some years later with the Lisbon Treaty.

5 The Irish 'No' to the Lisbon Treaty

Four years after the rejection of the EU Constitution, ratification processes opened again in Europe for the Treaty of Lisbon. Specifically designed to rescue and replace the failed Constitutional Treaty, the new instrument could largely be seen (with the exception of some secondary aspects) as a carefully repackaged version of the Constitutional Treaty[83] only without the label of a 'constitution' or the references to EU symbols associated with a general federalist orientation and the emergence of a 'super-State'.[84] The new Treaty actually repeated the vast majority of the already rejected substantive reforms, only using less bold expressions in its preamble.[85] In fact, almost all institutional and policy reforms envisaged in the rejected Constitution were finally included in the new document by simply 'amending' the founding EU Treaties rather than replacing them with a single constitutional text. As for the French and Dutch voters, they were now denied a say on a Treaty reform they had practically already rejected in its near-identical 'constitutional' version. Similarly, with the exception of Ireland, all other Member States carefully avoided popular votes and ratified the Lisbon Treaty via parliamentary processes.[86] It is, thus, obvious that the gap which appeared in 2005 between the EU elites' integration plans and the European *demoi* had only further widened. Besides, the only referendum held in Ireland in 2008 delivered – again – a 'no' vote. Yet, this time, the

82 Declaration on the ratification of the Treaty establishing a Constitution for Europe, European Council, 16 and 17 June 2005, SN 117/05.
83 For a comparison of the two treaties in political and legal terms, see JC Piris, *The Lisbon Treaty: A Legal and Political Analysis* (CUP 2010) 326–31; S Griller, 'Is This a Constitution?' in S Griller and J Ziller (eds), *The Lisbon Treaty: EU Constitutionalism without a Constitutional Treaty?* (Springer 2009) 21–56.
84 These include references to the EU anthem and EU flag, as well as terms like 'minister for foreign affairs'.
85 For example, the Constitutional Treaty's reference to the intention of forging a 'common destiny' where the countries could 'transcend their former divisions' is carefully avoided in the Preamble of the Lisbon Treaty.
86 K Oppermann, 'The Politics of Avoiding EU Referendums on the Treaty of Lisbon' (2013) 35 Journal of European Integration 73.

other Member States continued normally with their ratification processes (all parliamentary) instead of stopping and negotiating a new Treaty like they did back in 2005 following the French and Dutch negative votes.[87] Rather than pausing for reflection, the 'second-referendum' technique was revived. After being promised certain legal guarantees in sensitive areas,[88] the Irish electorate was again 'convinced' and voted overwhelmingly in favour of the Lisbon Treaty in a second referendum held one year later (2009). After all, a second Irish 'no' to Lisbon and three overall Irish rejections on EU treaties in less than a decade would perhaps be impossible to handle. The Treaty of Lisbon was, then, ratified, finally bringing this first European constitutional adventure to an end.[89]

Nevertheless, only a few months after the Lisbon Treaty entered into force, the financial and Eurozone crisis begun and rapidly exposed the serious institutional deficiencies of EU economic governance. Although all three referendums held between 2009 and 2014 resulted in 'yes' votes (in Croatia on EU membership, in Ireland on the European Fiscal Compact, and in Denmark on the Unified Patent Court),[90] 2015 sees the beginning of the first-ever series of five consecutive 'no' votes. As the crisis deepens and spreads, the gap between EU elites and peoples apparently broadens. Starting from the Greek bailout referendum in 2015, the next 'no' votes successively emerged in Denmark, the Netherlands, the UK and Hungary.

6 The Greek 'No' to the Bailout Referendum

In the midst of the financial crisis, Europe witnesses unprecedented tensions between the Eurozone Member States. Tensions rise between EU officials and citizens, between creditors and debtors, between the North and the South. The legitimacy gap worsens as EU technocrats' estimations on the crisis and the common currency systematically prevail over national constitutions and EU constitutional principles.[91] Deeply rooted in the legal framework of the Economic and Monetary Union, this truly technocratic mode of governance leads to an increase in intergovernmental methods as well as to growing powers for the executive and the

---

[87] G de Búrca, 'The Lisbon Treaty No-Vote: An Irish Problem or a European Problem?' UCD Working Papers in Law, Criminology & Socio-Legal Studies, Research Paper No. 03/2009, University College Dublin (2009).

[88] Notably in taxation, neutrality, the right to life, education and family.

[89] A Arnull, 'Ireland and the Lisbon Treaty: All's Well That Ends Well?' in A Arnull and others (eds), *A Constitutional Order of States: Essays in EU Law in Honour of Alan Dashwood* (Hart 2011) 39–57.

[90] The Unified Patent Court is a proposed international court, open for participation only to EU Member States, which is to be constituted inter alia for litigation related to the EU patents.

[91] M Rodi, 'Power Shifts in the EU: Democracy and Legitimacy in the Context of the Financial Crisis' in PC Müller-Graff and others (eds), *European Law and National Constitutions* (BWV 2016) 97–114; B Crum, 'Saving the Euro at the Cost of Democracy' (2013) 51 Journal of Common Market Studies 614. For a general critique of the EU 'technocratic integration', see D Chalmers and others (eds), *The End of the Eurocrats' Dream: Adjusting to European Diversity* (CUP 2016).

European Central Bank (ECB).[92] In the dilemma 'market or democracy',[93] Europe seems to forget that the integration project had at some point sought to outgrow the purely market-driven model on which it was initially founded in order to progressively evolve towards a more political, democratic 'citizens' union'.[94] Thus, following several tough austerity-programmes, the disconnect between electorates and EU elites – between voters and unelected technocrats – became even more manifest. In this context, it is no surprise that the referendum held in Greece in July 2015 on the approval of further economic reforms proposed by the famous Troika (EU Commission/ECB/IMF) resulted to a resounding 'no' vote. In fact, the vote was rather exceptional for various reasons: (1) first, it concerned only working Eurogroup documents[95] and was organised within an extremely short timeframe (one week), since it was openly presented to the people by the Greek government as a negotiation tool, a means of putting pressure on EU partners; (2) second, it raised huge – and maybe exaggerated – legitimacy concerns mostly based on the argument that a decision involving the entire Eurozone could not be decided only by Greek voters,[96] obviously ignoring the inherent extraterritorial nature of every single EU referendum; and (3) it provoked major external interventions. Apart from the somehow common EU interferences during the campaign week,[97] there has also been a politically contested institutional reaction from the ECB. Almost immediately after the referendum announcement – and, thus, prior to the Greek 'no' vote – the ECB refused further support to the Greek banks leading to an immediate bank holiday and the inevitable imposition of strict capital controls across the country

[92]   On questions regarding the decision-making power shift to the executive level (including the problematic legitimacy of the Euro Summit and the Eurogroup) and the increase in competence of the ECB during the financial crisis, see Rodi (n 91) 100–08.

[93]   Ironically, in ancient Greece, democracy and market were connected by a single word, the term 'agora' meaning a central public space with multiple functions, both political and commercial.

[94]   N Copsey, *Rethinking the European Union* (Palgrave 2015) 72–98 at 94.

[95]   The wording of the referendum question was: 'Should the plan of agreement be accepted, which was submitted by the European Commission, the European Central Bank and the International Monetary Fund in the Eurogroup of 25.06.2015 and comprises of two parts, which constitute their unified proposal?' The first document is entitled 'Reforms for the Completion of the Current Program and Beyond' and the second 'Preliminary Debt Sustainability Analysis'.

[96]   For example, in the words of the EU Commission's President, Jean-Claude Juncker: 'In Europe, no single democracy is worth more than any other. And in the Eurozone there are 19 democracies, not one against 18, not 18 against one. Playing off one democracy against 18 others is not an attitude which is fitting for the great Greek nation' (President Jean-Claude Juncker's Press Conference on Greece, Brussels, 29 June 2015).

[97]   ibid ('You have to vote "yes", whatever the question because responsible, honourable Greek citizens, who are justly proud of themselves and their country, must say "yes" to Europe'). See also L Elliott, G Wearden et al., 'Europe's Big Guns Warn Greek Voters that a No Vote Means Euro Exit' *The Guardian* (30 January 2015) www.theguardian.com/business/2015/jun/29/greek-crisis-referendum-eurozone-vote-germany-france-italy accessed April 2018. However, voters in other Member States have experienced similar EU interferences, especially when the 'second-referendum' technique was applied.

during the campaign week.[98] These weekly and monthly limits in banking activities are still in force in Greece and, ironically, date from the day of the referendum announcement. As for the Union's reaction to the electorate's 'no' vote, this time it was faster and maybe much more brutal and undemocratic. There was neither a second referendum following negotiations for reassurances nor a second slightly amended document adopted without a new popular vote. Instead, only a week after the 61.2 per cent of Greeks rejected the bailout conditions – and despite the binding nature of the referendum according to the Greek constitution – the government agreed with the Eurogroup on a new bailout whose terms were almost identical to – and in many ways even worse than – those rejected in the referendum.[99]

7 The Danish 'No' to the Opt-Out Referendum

In December 2015, at the height of the refugee crisis and only three weeks after the Paris terror attacks, Denmark held its eighth EU referendum, this time on a policy-specific issue mostly related to the European Police Office (Europol). The referendum was held following a proposal by six parliamentary parties to abolish the country's long-standing full opt-outs on EU Justice and Home Affairs in favour of a case-by-case opt-in model, which would also allow the Danish continued membership of Europol.[100] By voting 'no', the Danish voters insisted on maintaining national control over specific policy domains and, thus, rejected the country's full Europol membership. However, even though Denmark was forced to officially exit the EU police agency on 1 May 2017 as a result of the referendum vote, a last-minute cooperation agreement between Europol and Denmark[101] secured the country's participation in the agency under a special – but rather problematic – status, since Denmark became the first ever EU Member State to be regarded as a third country with respect to Europol. The Danish prime minister's statements perfectly mirror the governmental – and European – reaction to the 2015 peoples' 'no' verdict: 'We had the keys to the main door to Europol, the ones we threw away when we voted no in

---

[98]   K Allen, 'Greece Crisis Timeline: The Weekend that Rocked the Eurozone' *The Guardian* (29 June 2015) www.theguardian.com/business/2015/jun/29/greece-crisis-timeline-the-weekend-that-rocked -the-eurozone accessed April 2018.

[99]   For a brief analysis on whether the referendum result was finally respected, see A Fotiadou, 'The Role of the People in Constitutional Amendment in Greece: Between Narratives and Practice' in Contiades and Fotiadou (n 46) 156, 165–66.

[100]   Since May 2017, Europol is governed by the new Regulation 2016/794 which grants extended powers to the agency in order to fight forms of cross-border crime, such as terrorism and cybercrime.

[101]   Agreement on Operational and Strategic Cooperation between the Kingdom of Denmark and the European Police Office, Brussels, 27 April 2017 www.europol.europa.eu/publications-documents accessed April 2018. According to this instrument, Denmark still enjoys access to Europol's databases as well as participation in joint investigation teams and in Europol's board meetings under an observer status with no voting rights.

December ... Ever since, we have worked hard to see if we could find a way in through the backdoor instead, and we can."[102]

8 The Dutch 'No' to the EU–Ukraine Association Agreement

In a rather unexpected citizen-initiated referendum held in April 2016, the Dutch electorate rejected the ratification of an Association Agreement between the EU and Ukraine.[103] Although the Dutch Parliament had already approved ratification[104] and the Treaty was even provisionally applied, a group of citizens used a new Dutch law allowing them to demand an advisory referendum on the issue.[105] The online citizen campaign had a clear Eurosceptic orientation[106] and gathered more than 450,000 signatures in favour of holding a referendum. Despite its non-binding character and the very low turnout (32.3 per cent with a legal threshold of 30 per cent), the referendum resulted in a valid 61 per cent 'no' vote, which was politically difficult to ignore. Therefore, the Treaty could not be ratified by the Netherlands in its current form. Along with the numerous political and geopolitical implications of this referendum outcome – ranging from increasing Dutch Euroscepticism to the Ukraine's progressive integration and the EU relations with Russia – there was also a major legal one: the emerging unprecedented situation in which a single Member State vetoed the conclusion of an EU 'mixed' international agreement.[107] The Union's Association Agreement with Ukraine could not enter into force because a single Member State denied ratification under a negative popular vote. Although most parts of the agreement were already provisionally applied, it seemed rather paradoxical to indefinitely provisionally apply a non-ratified document.[108] Thus, in

---

[102] L Kirk, 'EU Offers Denmark Backdoor to Europol' (*EU Observer*, 8 December 2016) https://euobserver.com/justice/136200 accessed April 2018 quoting the words of the Danish Prime Minister Lars Loekke Rasmussen.

[103] Association Agreement between the European Union and its Member States, of the one part, and Ukraine, of the other part, 29 May 2014 [2014] OJ L161/3.

[104] Including provisions that fall under the exclusive competences of both the EU and its Member States, this so-called 'mixed' agreement had to be ratified in both levels.

[105] According to the Dutch 'Advisory Referendum Act' which entered into force in July 2015, citizens can call for a national non-binding referendum on laws and treaties that both chambers of parliament have already approved, as long as they collect the right amount for signatures (ie 10,000 in the first and 300,000 in the second round). Nevertheless, after this first referendum on the EU–Ukraine Association Agreement and a second one scheduled for March 2018 on the controversial 'Information and Security Services Act', the Dutch government is already considering repealing this recent law which allowed for such citizen-initiated referendums on newly adopted legislative acts.

[106] The referendum was triggered by a right-wing Eurosceptic coalition. The left-wing anti-EU forces were absent in the campaign call for a referendum, but became actively involved in the no campaign once the referendum was announced.

[107] G Van der Loo, 'The Dutch Referendum on the EU–Ukraine Association Agreement: Legal Implications and Solutions' (2016) 47 Netherlands Yearbook of International Law 337.

[108] G Van der Loo, *The EU–Ukraine Association Agreement and Deep and Comprehensive Free Trade Area: A New Legal Instrument for EU Integration without Membership* (Brill/Nijhoff 2016).

May 2017, the Dutch Senate ended this political crisis and finally approved ratification. Ignoring one more popular 'no' vote, the agreement was finally fully ratified by the EU and all Member States in its initial form. The only response to the 2016 Dutch electorate's verdict was an added declaration noting inter alia that the Treaty does not guarantee EU membership or oblige the Netherlands to provide military assistance to Ukraine. Nevertheless, the Treaty itself was not amended and, thus, one more initial 'no' vote was finally overturned.

9 The British 'No' to the European Union

In the UK, the idea of questioning the country's EU membership is certainly not new. It has long been a topic of debate since the first referendum on continued membership of the European Communities was held in 1975, only three years after the UK's accession. Although this first popular vote resulted in a 67 per cent 'yes' to Europe, when the British electorate was asked again upon the same question in June 2016, the 'no' prevailed securing 51.9 per cent of the votes. Following the first referendum announcement during the 2015 British electoral campaign and an ensuing highly polarised referendum campaign between Brexit and Bremain, British voters finally decided to separate themselves from the Union by voting 'no' to Europe on 23 June 2016. Accordingly, in March 2017 and after necessary (following the famous *Miller* judgment)[109] parliamentary approval, the British government initiated the official EU withdrawal process which – according to Article 50 of the Treaty on the European Union – may include a negotiation period of up to two years. Although it is quite early to predict the final EU reaction to this British 'no' (since the exact withdrawal terms have not yet been negotiated at the time of writing), some first indicators might however be helpful. First, negative votes in membership referendums have, until now, always been respected, even in the unique case of Greenland's EU withdrawal. Yet, it is the first time that a Member State (and not just a territory) has voted to leave the Union, so various complications – both legal and political – may arise in the near future.[110] Second, the much-discussed non-binding character of the British referendum theoretically allows for future parliamentary votes against Brexit,[111] even if politically it is always difficult to ignore a popular vote. Finally, given that the British political landscape has radically changed after the snap general election in June 2017 and the

---

[109] R (Miller) v Secretary of State for Exiting the European Union [2017] UKSC 5, [2017] 2 WLR 583.
[110] R Wessel, 'You Can Check Out Any Time You Like, But Can You Really Leave? On "Brexit" and Leaving International Organizations' (2016) 13 International Organizations Law Review 197.
[111] On parliamentary and popular sovereignty in light of the *Miller* case, see M Elliott, 'The Supreme Court's Judgment in *Miller*: In Search of Constitutional Principle' (2017) 76 Cambridge Law Journal 257.

new hung parliament that emerged, voices in favour of an eventual second referendum – either on a reversal of Brexit or on the exact terms of the final Brexit agreement – are indeed getting louder.[112]

10 The Hungarian 'No' to EU Refugee Relocation Quotas

The most recent national 'no' on an EU issue came from Hungary in October 2016 in a referendum held about the EU refugee relocation quotas. According to the temporary emergency scheme established by the European Council in September 2015, Member States had committed to the relocation and resettlement of persons in need of international protection from Italy and Greece. While the number of asylum-seekers in Europe was constantly increasing, the Hungarian government initiated a referendum and openly campaigned for the 'no' side, in order to reject the imposition of mandatory EU quotas without the National Assembly's approval.[113] After a rather asymmetric campaign which progressively gained unprecedented racist and xenophobic dimensions,[114] an overwhelming majority voted for 'no' (98 per cent), but the low turnout rendered the vote invalid (44 per cent with a threshold of 50 per cent). Ironically, this invalid 'no' has been practically respected for over a year, since Hungary kept refusing to participate in the EU relocation programme. Despite the Commission's repeated calls for action, the country – together with Poland and the Czech Republic – still remains in breach of its legal obligations. Thus, in June 2017, the Commission launched infringement procedures against all three Member States and finally, in December 2017, decided to refer them to the Court of Justice of the EU for non-compliance with their legal obligations on refugee relocation.

11 The Swiss 'Yes' to EU Migration Quotas

Recently, this overall apparent EU reluctance to respect negative referendum outcomes has surprisingly been exported even to neighbouring Switzerland, despite the country's long and unique direct-democracy tradition. In a citizen-initiated referendum held in February 2014, the Swiss voters approved some restrictions on EU immigration, including the reintroduction of ceilings and annual quotas for foreigners, as proposed by the popular initiative 'Stop Mass Immigration' put forward by the right-wing Swiss People's Party. Nevertheless, being obviously inconsistent with the

---

[112] D Roberts, 'Brexit: Britons Favour Second Referendum by 16-point Margin – Poll' *The Guardian* (26 January 2018); www.theguardian.com/politics/2018/jan/26/britons-favour-second-referendum-brexit-icm-poll; A Rawnsley, 'How and Why Britain Might Be Asked to Vote Once More on Brexit' *The Guardian* (14 January 2018) www.theguardian.com/commentisfree/2018/jan/14/how-and-why-britain-might-be-asked-to-vote-again-on-brexit accessed April 2018.

[113] According to the EU plan to relocate 160,000 people across the bloc, Hungary should receive 1,294 asylum seekers.

[114] Especially during the broadly criticised 'Did you know' poster campaign.

EU–Swiss Agreement on the Free Movement of Persons, the proposed measures could have further serious implications for all other existing bilateral treaties between Switzerland and the Union. These treaties form a complex web of numerous economic and trade instruments, all linked by a so-called 'guillotine clause' whereby if one is violated, they might all collapse.[115] Thus, even with the weak majority of 50.3 per cent, this referendum outcome could indeed undermine the core of the EU relations with Switzerland. In fact, apart from the three Swiss negative votes on membership issues (regarding EEA accession in 1992 and EU candidacy in 1997 and 2001), all other eight Swiss referendums related to EU bilateral agreements have resulted in 'yes' votes (Table 8.2). However, this recent 'yes' to reducing free movement of persons is in reality a 'yes' in favour of Swiss sovereignty and a clear 'no' to Europe, obviously reversing the Swiss integration process so far. For the first time, even the formulation of the question was hostile to further integration, as the 'yes' vote corresponded to a rejection of the EU policies.[116] Finally, after a long period of negotiations in view of a compromise, the will of Swiss voters was not fully respected despite the referendum's constitutionally binding nature. In order to maintain the country's privileged access to the single market, the Swiss Parliament adopted in December 2016 a more balanced immigration law which simply prioritises national workers over EU citizens but avoids outright quotas on EU immigrants even though they were clearly approved by the referendum.[117] Thus, faced with this – unprecedented for the Swiss system of direct democracy – dilemma between the will of the people and the relations with the EU, the 2014 Initiative was finally not implemented to the letter. Instead, a 'lighter' and more EU-friendly interpretation was adopted proving that the uneasy relationship between referendums and the Union may also expand to popular votes in third countries.

IV CAN THE EU TAKE 'NO' FOR AN ANSWER?

A synthetic view of the various 'no' votes in EU referendums reveals how difficult it has been for the Union to accept negative answers. Undoubtedly, the juncture between EU integration policies and national referendum outcomes is a lot easier when national *demoi* approve their governments' commitments on EU issues through positive votes. In this case, direct democracy is seemingly 'legitimising' the EU-integration project by reducing – or at least masking – its overall elite-driven character. This is indeed the case for most popular votes held to date, since only eighteen out of the fifty-four referendums on EU integration resulted in 'no' votes

---

[115] Art 25(4) of the EU–Swiss Agreement on the Free Movement of Persons.
[116] The exact wording of the ballot question was: 'Do you accept the federal popular initiative 'against mass immigration?'.
[117] J Henley, 'Switzerland Makes U-turn over EU Worker Quotas to Keep Single Market Access' *The Guardian* (16 December 2016) www.theguardian.com/world/2016/dec/16/switzerland-u-turn-quotas-on-eu-workers-immigration accessed April 2018.

TABLE 8.2 *Swiss referendums on the bilateral agreements between EU and Switzerland*

	Year	Date	Subject	Category	Type	Turnout	Yes	No	Result
1.	1972	3 December	Free Trade Agreement with EEC	Treaty ratification	R–B	52.9	72.5	27.5	Yes
2.	2000	21 May	Bilateral Agreements I with the EU	Treaty ratification	NR–B	48.3	67.2	32.8	Yes
3.	2005	5 June	Schengen Agreement – Dublin Regulation	Single-issue	NR–B	56.6	54.6	45.4	Yes
4.	2005	25 September	Extension of the Free Movement of Persons Agreement to new EU Member States	Single-issue	NR–B	54.3	56.0	44.0	Yes
5.	2006	26 November	Eastern European Cooperation Act (Cohesion funds for the 10 new EU Member States)	Single-issue	NR–B	45	53.4	46.6	Yes
6.	2009	8 February	Extension of the Free Movement of Persons Agreement to new EU Member States	Single-issue	NR–B	51.4	59.6	40.4	Yes
7.	2009	17 May	Schengen Agreement – Introduction of biometric passports	Single-issue	NR–B	38	50.1	49.9	Yes
8.	2014	9 February	Reducing Free Movement of Persons (Immigration Referendum)	Single-issue	NR–B–C	56.6	50.3	49.7	Yes

Source: Centre for Research on Direct Democracy (University of Zurich, Faculty of Law). More information available at: www.c2d.ch

(Table 8.1). Yet, the recent series of five consecutive negative outcomes since 2015 – combined with the fact that eight out of the overall eighteen 'nos' have emerged since 2005 – indicates a clear recent trend towards negative answers and a growing difficulty to deliver pro-EU outcomes. Apparently, the European *demoi* – whenever consulted – are increasingly rejecting EU policies on further and deeper integration, while the Union keeps ignoring and reversing their negative votes in what might be regarded as a vicious circle in the context of a broader identity and legitimacy crisis.

The less problematic 'no' votes concern referendums in which the national *demoi* of member or candidate States decide first and mostly upon their own fate in the Union. These would certainly be the membership referendums, but also those single-issue votes concerning national participation in one specific aspect of the EU integration, like the monetary union. More specifically, these negative votes on *belonging* issues concern rejections of: EEC membership (Norway, Greenland), EEA accession (Switzerland), EU membership (Norway, Switzerland, UK) and Eurozone accession (Denmark, Sweden). Except, of course, for the ongoing Brexit negotiations, these negative referendum outcomes have in all cases been acknowledged and respected. On the other hand, the negative votes on issues about *deepening* the EU integration have practically never been fully respected. These referendums – which of course are held only in Member States – concern either the ratification of EU Treaties (Denmark, Ireland, France and the Netherlands) or some issue-specific integration policies covered by those treaties (France, Italy, Ireland, Denmark, Greece, the Netherlands and Hungary). It is, thus, about this second type of EU referendums that one may legitimately wonder if Europe can finally take 'no' for an answer.

In fact, the very process of EU Treaty amendment can explain – but certainly not justify – the general resentment against 'no' votes, as well as the overall hesitation about using referendums as a means to Treaty ratification. The requirement of unanimous consent via domestic ratification[118] (but without a parallel gradual harmonisation of the very diverse national ratification procedures) has led to extremely strict – and largely unequal as regards citizen participation – procedures of Treaty amendment. For every Treaty reform, the new text must be unanimously ratified by all Member States according to their domestic constitutional requirements, without any possibility of provisional application or partial entry into force of the amending Treaty.[119] Yet, several scholars argue that these strict EU procedures may have been appropriate for the smaller and much more homogeneous community of the past, but not for the modern diverse Union of twenty-eight Member States.[120] Since consensus is explicitly required, a rejection by a single State can

---

[118] Art 48(4) of the Treaty on the European Union.
[119] B De Witte, 'Treaty Revision in the European Union: Constitutional Change through International Law' (2004) 35 Netherlands Yearbook of International Law 51.
[120] G de Búrca, 'If at First You Don't Succeed: Vote, Vote Again: Analysing the Second Referendum Phenomenon in EU Treaty Change' (2011) 33 Fordham International Law Journal 1472, 1476.

eventually cancel years of intensive diplomatic work and halt the entire ratification process across the continent. This explains why referendums on Treaty ratifications are so rare and all 'no' votes are automatically and systematically viewed as 'unexpected'. Unless explicitly required by their constitutions, Member States usually choose to approve EU Treaty reforms through the much safer way of their national parliaments.[121] Thus, in the rare case of referendums on Treaty ratification, any negative answer significantly widens the gap between EU peoples and elites, since voters of a single Member State appear to reject a proposal openly supported by both EU officials and most national governments. Except for the Single European Act and the Amsterdam Treaty – which both gathered two 'yes' outcomes (Ireland, Denmark) – all other major Treaty reforms were at some point confronted by at least one popular 'no' vote. The Maastricht Treaty was rejected in Denmark, the Treaties of Nice and Lisbon suffered the same fate in Ireland, while the Constitutional Treaty was dismissed in France and the Netherlands and finally abandoned. As for the negative votes on single-issue referendums, they are sometimes equally hard to accept, since they often concern 'indivisible' EU issues for which even a single country's refusal to follow is seen as an impediment to further EU integration.

Indeed, the EU reactions to all these negative votes on issues about *deepening* the EU integration have been very similar. First of all, there has been a general tendency to hyper-analyse every 'no' vote – much more than the 'yes' – asking what people 'actually' voted 'no' to.[122] Apart from the obvious rejection of the explicit ballot proposal and – consequently – of further integration, other possible explanations include the dissatisfaction with the national government, the discontent about other policy areas, the choice of a random protest vote or the citizens' general attitude about Europe.[123] These arguments were largely invoked in the aftermath of the French and Dutch referendums, suggesting that the two 'no' votes did not really concern the idea of a European Constitution.[124] Similarly, for the Irish 'no' to the

---

[121]   On the politics of avoiding EU referendums, see K Oppermann, 'Derailing European Integration? Euroscepticism and the Politics of EU Referendums' in Leruth (n 54) 243–55; C Prosser, 'Calling European Union Treaty Referendums: Electoral and Institutional Politics' (2014) 64 Political Studies 182–199; G Tridimas, 'Ratification Through Referendum or Parliamentary Vote: When to Call a Non-Required Referendum?' (2007) 23 European Journal of Political Economy 674–92.

[122]   CH de Vreese and HG Boomgaarden, 'Immigration, Identity, Economy and the Government: Understanding Variation in Explanations for Outcomes of EU-related Referendums' in de Vreese (n 32) 185–205.

[123]   M Franklin and C Wlezien, 'Attitudes towards Europe and Referendum Votes: A Response to Siune and Svensson' (1994) 13 Electoral Studies 117.

[124]   A Glencross and A Trechsel, 'First or Second Order Referendums? Understanding the Votes on the EU Constitutional Treaty in Four EU Member States' (2011) 34 West European Politics 755, 769; P Svensson, 'Voting Behaviour in the European Constitution Process' in Pállinger (n 5) 163–73; K Aaarts and C Van Der Eijk, 'Understanding the Dutch "No": The Euro, the East, and the Elite' (2006) 39 Political Science and Politics 243; R Dehousse, 'The Unmaking of a Constitution: Lessons from the European Referenda' (2006) 13 Constellations 151; G Ivaldi, 'Beyond France's 2005 Referendum on the European Constitutional Treaty: Second-Order Model, Anti-Establishment Attitudes and the End of the Alternative European Utopia' (2006) 29 West European Politics 47.

Lisbon Treaty, the then Irish EU Commissioner argued that 'this is not a vote against the European Union. It is about a myriad of other issues'.[125] Indeed, several 'second-order' factors can have a significant impact on campaign dynamics and, thus, sometimes truly affect voting behaviour in EU referendums.[126] However, their impact cannot be limited only to the 'no' votes. They can similarly affect the 'yes' votes and the whole referendum process more broadly, or even the voting behaviour in the EU Parliament elections.[127]

After explaining the negative votes, a second-level EU reaction concerns the attempt to justify, and finally condemn them as 'wrong' answers. Interestingly, 'the approach adopted by Brussels, governments, and most other elite voices' is mostly articulated 'in *moral* terms, thus seeing little merit in discussing the outcome as an expression of a conscious *political* choice'.[128] 'No' voters are often depicted as nationalists, ignorant, irresponsible, uninformed, racist, intolerant, xenophobic or ungrateful.[129] The process of EU integration is, then, viewed as an ideal sacred path that needs to be followed unconditionally, while any deviation approved by national electorates has been presented like an unexpected, morally reprehensible and, above all, fatal mistake.

Then, at a third level, EU reactions to these 'no' votes become much more effective. In practice, all negative outcomes on *deepening* integration issues have been either exchanged for a 'yes' in a new vote or simply ignored. In the first case, EU elites use the 'second-referendum' technique, urging the people to 'think again' in order to finally 'vote correctly' in a second referendum held on the exact same issue (despite the first outcome being constitutionally binding). Thus, it took two

---

[125] J Smyth, 'McCreevy Pleads with EU States Not to Consider Irish Ungrateful' *The Irish Times* (13 June 2009) www.irishtimes.com/news/mccreevy-pleads-with-eu-states-not-to-consider-irish-ungrateful-1.1267003 accessed April 2018.

[126] J Garry, M Marsh and R Sinnott, 'Second-order Versus Issue-voting Effects in EU Referendums' (2005) 6 European Union Politics 201.

[127] Indeed, the European elections are widely perceived as a barometer of national governments' popularity. See: P Norris, 'Second-Order Elections Revisited' (1997) 31 European Journal of Political Research 109; G Irwin, 'Second-Order or Third-Rate: Issues in the Campaign for the Elections for the European Parliament 1994' (1995) 14 Electoral Studies 183.

[128] P Hansen and S B Hager, *The Politics of EU Citizenship* (Berghahn 2010) 7 (emphasis in the original). See also ibid 6, 'As borne out by practically all the post-referenda debates up until now, the reason for overturning a popular judgment is thus primarily motivated with a more or less implicit reference to a moral imperative. The popular verdict gets disqualified not because it is deemed political unfeasible, but because it is deemed morally reprehensible.'

[129] For some recent examples, see A Taylor, 'The Uncomfortable Question: Was the Brexit Vote Based on Racism?' *Washington Post* (25 June 2016) www.washingtonpost.com/news/worldviews/wp/2016/06/25/the-uncomfortable-question-was-the-brexit-vote-based-on-racism/?utm_term=.c52fdc8b75d2 accessed April 2018; N Nougayrède, 'Xenophobia and Nationalism Could Be the Greek Vote's Biggest Winners' *The Guardian* (6 July 2015) www.theguardian.com/commentisfree/2015/jul/06/greeks-no-austerity-yes-europe-collateral-damage accessed April 2018; on the critiques against the 'ungrateful Irish' following the first 'no' to Lisbon Treaty, see S Halimi 'European Style: Nobody Loves It' *Le Monde Diplomatique* (July 2008) https://mondediplo.com/2008/07/01european accessed April 2018.

referendums for Denmark to approve the Maastricht Treaty, and another two for
Ireland to approve the Nice Treaty and, later, the Lisbon Treaty.[130] In all three cases,
national governments negotiated concessions from the EU in the meantime and,
after being offered certain inducements, people indeed 'changed' their minds in
the second referendum and voted in favour of the Treaty reforms.[131] This opinion
change is perhaps unsurprising given the amount of pressure placed upon governments and voters while the ratification procedure continues with most or all other
Member States ratifying a new Treaty.[132] Yet, although quite effective until now, the
'second-referendum' practice has been severely criticised for its undemocratic
nature.[133] By promoting EU manipulation techniques in order to exchange EU
privileges for 'yes' votes, it clearly 'fails to respect the outcome of legitimate constitutional processes and undermines the democratically expressed will of the
people'.[134] As for the second case of simply ignoring negative outcomes, the so-
called 'denial of democracy' is even more apparent. Despite the people's verdict, the
initially rejected EU document is finally signed or ratified by national governments,
only in a slightly different form following some rather cosmetic changes: under
a new title (France and the Netherlands in 2005) or after adding or modifying some
rather secondary aspects (Switzerland in 2014, Greece and Denmark in 2015, the
Netherlands in 2016). However, the popular vote is manifestly ignored here, since
nothing can prove that these secondary modifications would even lead to a positive
vote in an eventual second referendum. Therefore, in both cases, refusing to respect
the will of the people – as legitimately expressed in the first referendum – clearly
undermines the democratic legitimacy of the Union and also raises serious constitutional concerns when the referendum result is constitutionally binding in the
national context.

Ultimately, this general EU problematic attitude towards 'no' votes is also leading
to a broader criticism of the very use of referendums as mechanisms for national
decision-making on EU matters. From the first Danish rejection of the Maastricht
Treaty to the recent Brexit decision, every single 'no' vote on integration issues has

---

[130]   J FitzGibbon, 'When "No" Means "Yes": A Comparative Study of Referendums in Denmark and
        Ireland' in Leruth (n 54) 280–90.
[131]   See L LeDuc, 'Opinion Formation and Change in Referendum' in De Vreese (n 32) 21, 42; T Worre,
        'First No, Then Yes: The Danish Referendums on the Maastricht Treaty 1992 and 1993' (1995) 33
        Journal of Common Market Studies 253; K Siune, P Svensson and O Tonsgaard, 'The European
        Union: The Danes Said "No" in 1992 But "Yes" in 1993 – How and Why?' (1994) 13 Electoral
        Studies 107.
[132]   De Búrca (n 120) 1472; E Edwards, 'Voters Being "Threatened" on Lisbon' *The Irish Times* (Dublin,
        18 August 2009); P Roberts-Thomson, 'EU Treaty Referendums and the European Union' (2001) 23
        European Integration 105, arguing that the EU referendums on Treaty ratification 'become asymme-
        trical devices as the status quo position 'moves' because of the ratifying actions of other members'.
[133]   ML McDonald and D Roche, 'Head to Head: Is the Second Referendum on Lisbon an Abuse of
        Democracy?', *Irish Times* (22 December 2008) 12; K Hayward, 'If at First You Don't Succeed ... :
        The Second Referendum on the Treaty of Nice, 2002' (2003) 18 Irish Political Studies 120.
[134]   De Búrca (n 120) 1475.

induced a broader political and academic scepticism about the very idea of EU referendums.[135] The arguments invoked vary significantly depending on the context of each specific 'no' vote. However, criticism has often targeted more broadly the very concept of modern direct democracy,[136] or even the very idea of introducing democratic mechanisms in a post-national context.[137] EU referendums have, thus, been widely criticised as being determined by 'second-order' factors unrelated to the ballot question, such as national governments' unpopularity,[138] but also as leading to excessive polarisation via the over-simplification of complex, multidimensional matters into a binary 'yes' or 'no' logic.[139] For instance, in the aftermath of the defeat of the EU constitution in France and the Netherlands, the then President of the EU Commission, José Manuel Barroso, condemned referendums as a 'populist trend' which threatens to 'undermine the Europe we are trying to build by simplifying important and complex subjects'.[140] Of course, the national strategies and tactics during the referendum campaign are often largely responsible for this disorientation and polarisation of voters. The information provided and the framing of a referendum issue by political actors and media during a campaign can be extremely influential to the referendum outcome.[141] For the opponents of EU referendums, when such 'complex issues are thrust into the maelstrom of a modern campaign, there can be little assurance that the result will always produce the most reliable reading of the popular will'.[142]

In the same logic, critiques have also focused on the voters' alleged 'lack of competence' to decide on technical and unfamiliar issues, which makes them

[135] For an overview of the critiques against direct democracy in the context of the EU referendums experience, see Mendez (n 31) 7–14.

[136] ibid 8, 'it is difficult to isolate current discussions about EU referendums ... from more general and normative attitudes towards direct democracy. The two are intimately connected such that many critical evaluations, i.e. arguments posed in favour of or against EU referendums, are simply rehearsing an age-old debate.'

[137] In fact, most of the arguments invoked against EU referendums could also concern the EU Parliament elections.

[138] The question on the ballot paper – as well as the overall citizens' attitudes towards Europe – are indeed intertwined with domestic concerns, national politics, ideological preferences or even one-off events and political personalities. See: M Qvortrup, 'Rebels without a Cause? The Irish Referendum on the Lisbon Treaty' (2009) 80 The Political Quarterly 59, 62, arguing that '[c]ampaining in a referendum is like solving an equation with many unknown variables and in which many singular events combine to create unforeseen circumstances'.

[139] Dehousse (n 124) 160 (criticising referendums as 'pseudo-simplifying mechanisms').

[140] Quoted in Hobolt (n 19) 23.

[141] In fact, voters' reactions to the discourse of a campaign 'can be as important to the voting decision as their opinions and beliefs on the issue itself'. See CH de Vreese, 'Context, Elites, Media and Public Opinion in Referendums: When Campaigns Really Matter' in de Vreese (n 32) 1–20. See also SB Hobolt, 'When Europe Matters: The Impact of Political Information on Voting Behaviour in EU Referendums' (2005) 15 Journal of Elections, Public Opinion and Parties 85; 'How Parties Affect Vote Choice in European Integration Referendums' (2006) 12 Party Politics 623; Hobolt (n 19) 4 arguing that the information provided to voters during a campaign influences 'whether feelings about the EU, partisan loyalties, or dissatisfaction with the government play a greater role in the ballot box'.

[142] LeDuc (n 131) 42.

victims of manipulation and demagogy.[143] This classic argument against direct democracy (suggesting that ordinary citizens are poorly informed and incapable to deal with the complexities of modern political decision-making)[144] acquires an even greater resonance in light of the EU decision-making intricacies. However, empirical research reveals that voters can be equally ignorant about party programmes and candidate positions in issues associated with EU or national elections.[145] After all, the competence argument can be seen as a rather 'misplaced critique against popular participation since, taken to its logical conclusion, a justification that is predicated on the faulty knowledge of citizens is an argument against democracy itself, including its representative variant'.[146] Yet, EU referendums (or, more likely, referendum threats when a 'no' vote seems highly possible) are further criticised for being strategically used either by national governments as a powerful negotiation tool to extract concessions from Brussels (Greece, Hungary) or by Eurosceptic parties in their electoral campaigns (France, Italy, Austria, etc.).[147]

Finally, another widespread critique against EU referendums highlights the alleged problematic veto power of a single *demos* in the Treaty ratification process.[148] Yet, the same argument might as well be used for an – eventual – parliamentary Treaty rejection by a single Member State. Whenever consensus is required,[149] any minority negative vote inevitably appears as more influential. Besides, the very idea of comparing the expression of the will of different *demoi* within the not-so-harmonised EU context raises numerous issues, both methodological and substantial: comparing parliamentary decisions and popular verdicts, comparing different types of referendums held in different dates and with varied

---

[143] Jean Monnet states in his memoirs: 'I thought it wrong to consult the people of Europe about the structure of a Community of which they had no practical experience' (J Monnet, *Memoirs* (Doubleday 1978) 367). See also: A Moravcsik, 'The European Constitutional Settlement' (2008) 31 World Economy 158, 178 arguing that referendums 'lead to unstable plebiscitary politics in which individuals have no incentive to reconcile their concrete interests with their political choices'; S B Hobolt, 'Taking Cues on Europe? Voter Competence and Party Endorsements in Referendums on European Integration' (2007) 46 European Journal of Political Affairs 151.

[144] More generally, on the alleged lack of knowledge and informed opinion of referendum voters, see A Lupia and JG Matsusaka, 'Direct Democracy: New Approaches to Old Questions' (2004) 7 Annual Review of Political Science 463; A Lupia and R Johnston, 'Are Voters to Blame? Voter Competence and Elite Manoeuvres in Referendums' in M Mendelsohn and A Parkin (eds), *Referendum Democracy, Citizens, Elites and Deliberation in Referendum Campaigns* (Palgrave 2001).

[145] J Grynaviski, 'Reflections of a Party Scholar on Direct Democracy and the Direct Democracy Literature' (2015) 38 Electoral Studies 238–40.

[146] Mendez and Mendez (n 36) 81.

[147] On the increasing referendum demands by Eurosceptic parties or party factions, see LK Topaloff, 'Euroscepticism and Political Parties: Theory and Practice' in Leruth (n 54) 63–74.

[148] Hobolt (n 19) 244.

[149] On the consensus model and the necessity of 'patiently negotiated compromises', see Dehousse (n 124) 161 arguing that EU referendums 'can imperil patiently negotiated compromises even when they are incapable of proposing an alternative'. See also Glencross and Trechsel (n 124) 769, arguing that the consensus model cannot act as a 'shield' protecting the integration project from direct democracy.

turnout and majority thresholds,[150] or even comparing different *demoi* with striking diverse constitutional and democratic traditions.

In any case, it becomes clear that, when it comes to national referendums on EU integration, the Union seems not only more and more unwilling to take 'no' for an answer, but also – maybe for fear of more 'no' outcomes – more and more critical of the very idea of using popular votes on integration issues, and more and more suspicious against direct democracy itself. This critique – coming from EU and national elites and a number of EU scholars – has of course a rather outcome-related character, given that we hardly ever witness the same rhetoric following a 'yes' vote. In addition, the recent series of five consecutive 'no' votes and the numerous implications of the Brexit vote have led to a renewed criticism of direct democracy mechanisms,[151] and an even greater referendum phobia in Europe, particularly regarding eventual new withdrawal votes.[152] In this context, this overall problematic relationship between Europe and direct democracy reveals and raises some serious legitimacy and identity concerns within the Union.

V DIRECT DEMOCRACY IN THE EU CONTEXT: LEGITIMACY AND IDENTITY ISSUES

The uneasy relationship between the EU and national referendums – especially those resulting in 'no' votes – is closely related to broader EU political and constitutional issues. The sudden eruption of EU referendums (or even of demands for such ballots), the proliferation of negative outcomes and the Union's reluctance to accept them, as well as the current referendum phobia and the increasing criticism against direct-democracy mechanisms following every recent 'no' vote, are certainly signs of a deeper political and constitutional crisis taking place within the Union, threatening its future and further integration.

In fact, the study of direct democracy in the EU context leads to an interesting paradox: the referendum device appears as an extremely powerful tool for both further integration and dis-integration of the Union. What was at first invoked to strengthen the common European identity and overcome the much-discussed legitimacy deficit is now slowly turning into a catalyst for an eventual EU dis-integration exposing some serious identity and legitimacy problems and even

---

[150] In 2016, the Hungarian 'no' vote was invalid due to a low turnout of 44 per cent, while the Dutch 32.3 per cent turnout led to a valid 'no' vote.

[151] The EU Commission President Jean-Claude Juncker stated: 'Regarding referenda on EU membership, I think it is not wise to organise this kind of debate ... because this will pile more controversy onto the huge number already present at the heart of the EU' (interview with Isabelle Kumar, *Euronews*, 26 November 2016).

[152] K Lyons, 'Frexit, Nexit or Oexit? Who Will Be Next to Leave the EU' *The Guardian* (27 June 2016) www.theguardian.com/politics/2016/jun/27/frexit-nexit-or-oexit-who-will-be-next-to-leave-the-eu accessed April 2018; J Henley, 'Would Brexit Trigger a Domino Effect in Europe?' *The Guardian* (10 June 2016) www.theguardian.com/world/2016/jun/10/brexit-domino-effect-europe-eu-referendum -uk accessed April 2018.

leading to Member States' withdrawals from the Union. In this sense, direct democracy can play a double role within the overall context of the current EU legitimacy and identity crisis. Depending on their type and outcome, EU referendums may well appear as both symptoms and remedies of the crisis. In other words, the Union seems now confronted to a real referendum dilemma: more referendums may be an answer to legitimacy and identity concerns, but they could also deepen the legitimacy deficit and further alienate (or, in the Brexit case, even exclude) citizens from the European project.

1 EU Referendums and Legitimacy Crisis

First of all, regarding the Union's democratic deficit which has preoccupied EU scholars for several decades now,[153] it mainly stems from the fact that the EU is losing contact with the basis of its legitimacy: the people.[154] As the EU integration deepens and progressively expands in policy-areas once at the core of Member States' national sovereignty (like the common security, defence, or monetary policy), the Union affects the lives of its citizens in unprecedented ways, evolving towards a truly supranational legal and political entity. Exercising state-like powers via the principle of conferral and endowed with a complex state-like institutional structure, the EU is indeed confirming its alleged *sui generis* nature, balancing between intergovernmental and federal models.[155] Thus, in order to maintain its legitimacy, the Union cannot continue to operate on the classic state-consent reasoning of international organisations[156] and certainly needs a more solid basis of legitimacy, more closely linked to the people. The indirect legitimation of EU decision-making via

---

[153] On the EU democratic deficit, see A Føllesdal and S Hix, 'Why There Is a Democratic Deficit in the EU: A Response to Majone and Moravcsik' (2006) 44 Journal of Common Market Studies 533; G Majone, 'Europe's "Democratic Deficit": The Question of Standards' (1998) 4 European Law Journal 5. For a recent approach in the crisis context, see L Papadopoulou, I Pernice and JHH Weiler (eds), *Legitimacy Issues of the European Union in the Face of Crisis – Dimitris Tsatsos in memoriam* (Nomos/Hart 2017).

[154] However, see A Moravcsik, 'In Defence of the "Democratic Deficit": Reassessing Legitimacy in the European Union' (2002) 40 Journal of Common Market Studies 603, 621, arguing that '[m]ost critics compare the EU to an ideal plebiscitary or parliamentary democracy, standing alone, rather than to the actual functioning of national democracies adjusted for its multi-level context'.

[155] SJ Bickerton and others, 'The New Intergovernmentalism: European Integration in the Post-Maastricht Era' (2015) 53 Journal of Common Market Studies 703; S Fabbrini, 'Intergovernmentalism and Its Limits Assessing the European Union's Answer to the Euro Crisis' (2013) 46 Comparative Political Studies 1003; AH Trechsel, 'How to Federalise the European Union ... And Why Bother' (2005) 12 Journal of European Public Policy 401; V Schmidt, 'The New EU Governance: New Intergovernmentalism, New Supranationalism, and New Parliamentarism' IAI Working Papers No 16/11, Rome: Instituto Affari Internazionali (2016) www.iai.it/sites/default/files/iaiwp1611.pdf accessed April 2018.

[156] Yet, similar arguments have also been invoked for classic international organisations exercising public authority. See: A Von Bogdandy and others (eds), *The Exercise of Public Authority by International Institutions: Advancing International Institutional Law* (Springer, 2010).

democratically elected national governments is no longer judged sufficient.[157] However, from its very conception in the post-war period, the EU integration has been a largely elite-driven project based on a strong bureaucracy with very limited popular involvement.[158] With the exception of the EU Parliament,[159] EU institutions are not directly elected by – or accountable to – EU citizens. Until now, and particularly during the current multifaceted crisis, the EU governance is clearly privileging technocratic efficiency over democratic principles.[160] This becomes obvious if one considers the pivotal role of the Commission's bureaucracy in legislation and decision-making,[161] the proliferation of non-majoritarian EU agencies[162] or the recent increased influence of the ECB's technocratic governance and the Eurogroup's 'informal' powers in the – largely criticised – Eurozone crisis management.[163]

In front of this continuous transfer of national sovereign powers to EU institutions – and, thus, mostly to unelected technocrats – calls for greater citizen involvement are indeed getting louder.[164] Although EU citizenship has certainly enhanced

[157] F Decker, 'Governance beyond the Nation-State: Reflections on the Democratic Deficit of the European Union' (2002) 9 Journal of European Public Policy 256.

[158] A Cohen, 'The Genesis of Europe: Competing Elites and the Emergence of a European Field of Power' in N Kauppi and MR Madsen (eds), *Transnational Power Elites: The New Professionals of Governance, Law and Security* (Routledge 2013) 103–20.

[159] Directly elected by EU citizens since 1979, the EU Parliament is the only international body whose members are directly elected by universal suffrage.

[160] On the dilemma between efficiency and legitimacy over the years of EU integration and in the current crisis, see C Schweiger, *Exploring the EU's Legitimacy Crisis* (Edward Elgar 2016); S Champeau and others (eds), *The Future of Europe: Democracy, Legitimacy and Justice after the Euro Crisis* (Rowman & Littlefield 2015); S Piattoni (ed), *The European Union: Democratic Principles and Institutional Architecture in Times of Crisis* (OUP 2015); FV Scharpf, *Governing in Europe: Effective and Democratic?* (OUP 1999); M Jachtenfuchs, 'Theoretical Perspectives on European Governance' (1995) 1 European Law Journal 115.

[161] A Ellinas and E Suleiman, *The European Commission and Bureaucratic Autonomy: Europe's Custodians* (CUP 2012).

[162] On the increasing delegation of powers to non-majoritarian EU agencies, see E Vos, 'EU Agencies and Independence' in D Ritleg (ed), *Independence and Legitimacy in the Institutional System of the European Union* (OUP 2016) 206–28.

[163] See P Craig, 'The Eurogroup, Power and Accountability' (2017) 23 European Law Journal 234–49; G Peroni, 'The European Central Bank and European Democracy: A Technocratic Institution to Rule All European States?' in L Daniele, P Simone and R Cisotta (eds), *Democracy in the EMU in the Aftermath of the Crisis* (Springer 2017) 249–66; N Scicluna, 'Integration through the Disintegration of Law? The ECB and EU Constitutionalism in the Crisis' (2017) Journal of European Public Policy https://doi.org/10.1080/13501763.2017.1362026 accessed April 2018; C Zilioli, 'The Independence of the European Central Bank and Its New Banking Supervisory Competences' in Ritleg (n 162) 125–79; FW Scharpf, 'Political Legitimacy in a Non-optimal Currency Area' in O Cramme and SB Hobolt (eds), *Democratic Politics in a European Union under Stress* (OUP 2015) 19–47; E Vaara, 'Struggle over Legitimacy in the Eurozone Crisis: Discursive Legitimation Strategies and their Ideological Underpinnings' (2014) 25 Discourse and Society 500.

[164] EO Eriksen and JE Fossum, *Democracy in the European Union: Integration through Deliberation?* (Routledge 2000).

the Union's legitimacy – via the EU Parliament elections[165] and the recent European Citizens' Initiative (ECI)[166] – it has not yet added new political rights 'significantly different to the ones Europeans already enjoyed in their respective countries'[167] nor opened new channels for civic involvement, analogous to the unprecedented supranational authority exercised on the EU level.[168] The EU Parliament may be directly elected by EU citizens, but the elections remain mostly nation-oriented, the turnouts are significantly low,[169] and the Parliament's powers – although reinforced after Lisbon – remain weak, especially when compared to the Commission's near monopoly on legislative initiative.[170] Besides, in the recent EU crisis management, this limited role of the EU Parliament became even more apparent.[171]

In this context, national referendums on EU issues may indeed appear as possible remedies to the Union's democratic deficit by introducing a significant element of popular involvement in the EU affairs.[172] After all, a popular vote seems capable to 'accord the highest degree of endorsement and legitimacy to a political decision'.[173] Yet, EU referendums have emerged as isolated sporadic moments of national direct democracy and, as such, they are certainly unable to offer an instant, automatic legitimisation of EU policies covering the Union's increasing democratic deficit in its entirety. In most cases, the use of referendums by national governments seems to be dictated by purely political reasons rather than from a deeper willingness to further involve the electorate in the integration process. Besides, the legitimisation effect of each popular vote largely depends on its specific type and outcome. For instance, the French and Dutch 'nos' to the EU Constitution had the exact opposite result, revealing the Union's legitimacy crisis and the increasing distance between

---

[165] The Lisbon Treaty highlighted the direct democratic mandate with which EU citizens vest the members of the European Parliament by replacing the wording of ex Art 189 EC ('representatives of the peoples of the States brought together in the Community') by the phrase 'representatives of the Union's citizens' (Art 14(2) TEU).

[166] See Section VI.

[167] PC Jiménez Lobeira, 'EU Citizenship and Political Identity: The Demos and Telos Problems' (2012) 18 European Law Journal 504, 506.

[168] Apart from the innovative ECI, Art 24 TFEU provides only for the EU citizens' rights to petition the EU Parliament, apply to the Ombudsman or address questions to the EU institutions and bodies.

[169] From the 61.99 per cent turnout of the first EU Parliament elections in 1979, we have passed to 42.61 per cent in the last elections in 2014 (source: European Parliament).

[170] Arts 17(2) TEU and 225 TFEU.

[171] On the role of the EU Parliament in the recent crisis, see B Crum, 'Parliamentary Accountability in Multilevel Governance: What Role for Parliaments in Post-Crisis EU Economic Governance?' (2018) 25 Journal of European Public Policy 268; F Neutel, 'Pushing the Union Forward? The Role of the European Parliament in the Union's Crisis' in KN Demetriou (ed), *The European Union in Crisis: Explorations in Representation and Democratic Legitimacy* (Springer 2015) 155–80; C Fasone, 'European Economic Governance and Parliamentary Representation: What Place for the European Parliament?' (2014) 20 European Law Journal 164.

[172] F Esposito, 'The European Referendum: A Tool to Legitimate the European Integration Process?' in SS Nagel (ed), *Policymaking and Democracy: A Multinational Anthology* (Lexington 2002) 15–38.

[173] Mendez and Mendez (n 36) 48.

the will of the people and the elite-driven integration plans. As for the most recent round of EU referendums, it is marked by the proliferation of negative outcomes and the sudden eruption of votes which are not constitutionally mandatory[174] and, therefore, more 'suspect in terms of democratic legitimacy'[175] and more likely to serve national political interests.[176] They have thus further delegitimised the EU policies and deepened the gap between the EU and national *demoi*. Even more, the Union's repeated disrespect towards 'no' votes further highlights its manifestly undemocratic attitude towards EU citizens expressing themselves in national referendums.

Hence, although asking voters to directly decide on EU matters seems to be one of the most democratic responses to legitimacy concerns, as long as these referendums remain purely national political devices and keep delivering negative answers, this legitimisation effort is clearly failing. Recent referendums have only revealed the broadened gap between elites and public opinion on EU matters.[177] In this sense, referendums seem like double-edged swords for the EU legitimacy, since opting for more direct democracy in Europe bears the risk of more and more resounding 'no' votes. Nevertheless, it remains undisputable that – regardless of their outcome – national referendums have at least provided a unique direct means of citizen participation in the otherwise mostly elite-driven EU integration process.

2 EU Referendums and Identity Crisis

Closely linked to the democratic legitimacy crisis, the so-called crisis of the EU's identity is similarly affected by the referendum device. EU citizenship – conceived as dependent on and 'additional' to national citizenship[178] – is generally associated not only with a palette of civil, political, economic and social rights, but also with the promotion of a collective European identity and civic engagement at the EU

---

[174] Among the five last EU referendums, which all delivered negative results, none was constitutionally mandatory.

[175] Mendez and Mendez (n 36) 84.

[176] In facultative government-initiated referendums, national governments control both the agenda and the timing of the vote, which provides them with opportunities for strategic manoeuvring pertaining to national or party interests. For an overview of the critiques against this discretionary deployment of the referendum device, see M Setälä, 'On the Problems of Responsibility and Accountability in Referendums' (2006) 45 European Journal of Political *Research* 699; L Morel, 'The Rise of Government-initiated Referendums in Consolidated Democracies' in M Mendelson and A Parkin (eds), *Referendum Democracy: Citizens, Elites and Deliberation Referendum Campaigns* (Palgrave 2001).

[177] L Hooghe, 'Europe Divided? Elites vs Public Opinion on European Integration' (2003) 4 European Union Politics 281.

[178] Art 9 TEU. The Lisbon Treaty replaced the term 'complementary' contained in the Amsterdam Treaty in order to 'reinforce the point that EU citizenship can only add rights, and cannot detract from national citizenship'. See: J Shaw, 'The Lisbon Treaty and Citizenship', European Policy Brief, Federal Trust, (2008) 2 www.fedtrust.co.uk.

level.[179] In the current legitimacy crisis context, the need to bring the EU institutions closer to the EU citizens is linked to a growing feeling at the national level that the Union constitutes a 'threat to their [national] identity'.[180] The unprecedented development of the EU supranational governance – particularly in the context of the recent financial and migrant crises – has led to an increasing public contestation of the Union. However, the collective EU identity is mainly understood as the citizens' identification with Europe, denoting their 'self-description as European and their attachment to Europe and other Europeans'.[181] As such, EU identity differs 'conceptually and empirically from EU support, which refers to positive or negative orientations towards the EU institutions and/or further steps in EU integration'.[182] In other words, we can perfectly imagine Europeans embracing their common identity but voting 'no' in referendums regarding their support to the current EU policies or next integration steps. In this sense, only the Brexit vote or any future withdrawal referendum could possibly challenge the EU identity.[183] Nevertheless, the two concepts are certainly inter-related. The continuously decreasing public support for Europe[184] inevitably casts doubts upon the very idea of a common EU identity. Although theoretical and empirical evidence shows that a collective EU identity has indeed somehow developed alongside the national ones,[185] the concept still remains

[179] IP Karolewski, 'The Citizenship–Identity Nexus in the EU Revisited' in V Kaina and others (eds), *European Identity Revisited: New Approaches and Recent Empirical Evidence* (Routledge 2016) 15–30; A Follesdal, 'A Common European Identity for European Citizenship?' (2014) 15 German Law Journal 765; R Bellamy, 'Evaluating Union Citizenship: Belonging, Rights and Participation within the EU' (2008) 12 Citizenship Studies 597; M Bruter, *Citizens of Europe? The Emergence of a Mass European Identity* (Palgrave 2005).

[180] Laeken Declaration on the Future of the European Union, Presidency Conclusions, European Council meeting in Laeken, 14–15 December 2001, 2. See also: LM McLaren, 'Opposition to European Integration and Fear of Loss of National Identity: Debunking a Basic Assumption Regarding Hostility to the Integration Project' (2004) 43 European Journal of Political Research 895; T Kuhn, *Experiencing European Integration: Individual Transnationalism and Public Orientations towards European Integration* (OUP 2015).

[181] S Bergbauer, *Explaining European Identity Formation: Citizens' Attachment from Maastricht to Crisis* (Springer 2018) 1.

[182] ibid. See also: D Fuchs and C Schneider, 'Support of the EU and European Identity: Some Descriptive Results' in D Fuchs and H D Klingemann (eds), *Cultural Diversity, European Identity and the Legitimacy of the EU* (Edward Elgar 2011) 61–85; LM McLaren, *Identity, Interests and Attitudes to European Integration* (Palgrave 2006); M Gabel, 'Public Support for European Integration' (1998) 60 Journal of Politics 333. For a further distinction between 'regime support' and 'policy support', see SB Hobolt and CE de Vries, 'Public Support for European Integration' (2016) 19 Annual Review of Political Science 415.

[183] L Scuira, 'Brexit beyond Borers: Beginning of the EU Collapse and Return to Nationalism' (2017) 70 Journal of International Affairs 109. However, see J Stone, 'More Europeans than Ever Say They Feel Like Citizens of the EU – The Continent Appears Undeterred by Brexit' *The Independent* (2 August 2017). www.independent.co.uk/news/uk/politics/eu-brexit-european-union-citizens-feel-like-euroba rometer-survey-results-a7872916.html accessed April 2018.

[184] K Armingeon and B Ceka, 'The Loss of Trust in the European Union during the Great Recession Since 2007: The Role of Heuristics from the National Political System' (2014) 15 European Union Politics 82; Hobolt (n 182) 413–32.

[185] Bergbauer (n 181) 101–31.

rather distant engendering confusion as to its exact meaning and potential.[186] In his 2016 State of the Union address, the EU Commission President Jean-Claude Juncker referred to an 'existential crisis' in Europe in which 'many [Europeans] seem to have forgotten what being European means'.[187] One year later and in the midst of the Brexit negotiations, he spoke of the Europeans' two choices: '[e]ither come together around a positive European agenda or each retreat into our own corners'.[188]

In a context of growing nationalism, Euroscepticism and Euro-pessimism across the continent[189] (especially following the EU management of the recent economic and migration crises),[190] opting for more EU referendums can have a double effect on EU identity. On the one hand, they can certainly enhance the crystallisation of an emerging EU public space by bringing direct public attention on EU issues and, therefore, encourage civic engagement beyond the Member States and strengthen a common 'we-feeling' among Europeans. Yet, on the other hand, as long as they keep serving national interests and resulting in 'no' votes, more referendums can also lead to a further growth of nationalism and a gradual European dis-integration.[191] Even though, in theory, more popular votes on EU issues could mean a closer connection among EU citizens and a growing sense of belonging to the Union, as long as these votes are organised in purely national contexts, they finally tend to

---

[186] P Bellucci, D Sanders and F Serricchio, 'Explaining European Identity' in D Sanders and others (eds), *The Europeanisation of National Polities? Citizenship and Support in a Post-Enlargement Union* (OUP 2012) 61–90; F Pichler, 'European Identities from Below: Meanings of Identification with Europe' (2008) 9(4) Perspectives on European Politics and Society 411.

[187] EU Commission, President Jean-Claude Juncker's State of the Union Address 2016, Strasbourg, 14 September 2016.

[188] EU Commission, President Jean-Claude Juncker's State of the Union Address 2017, Strasbourg, 13 September 2017.

[189] See R Wodak and S Boukala, 'European Identities and the Revival of Nationalism in the European Union: A Discourse Historical Approach' (2015) 14 Journal of Language and Politics 87; P de Wilde and HJ Trenz, 'Denouncing European Integration: Euroscepticism as Policy Contestation' (2012) 15 European Journal of Social Theory 537; HG Boomgaarden and others, 'Mapping EU Attitudes: Conceptual and Empirical Dimensions of Euroscepticism and EU Support' (2011) 12 European Union Politics 241; D Fuchs, R Magni-Berton and A Roger (eds), *Euroscepticism: Images of Europe among Mass Publics and Political Elites* (Barbara Budrich 2009). However, according to the latest Eurobarometer, there is a certain increase in optimism for the Union's future (European Commission, Standard Eurobarometer 88 – autumn 2017, 'Public Opinion in the European Union, First Results', available at: http://ec.europa.eu/commfrontoffice/publicopinion accessed April 2018).

[190] See HJ Trenz and A Triantafyllidou, 'Complex and Dynamic Integration Processes in Europe: Intra EU Mobility and International Migration in times of Recession' (2017) 43 Journal of Ethnic and Migration Studies 546; A Polyakova and N Fligstein, 'Is European Integration Causing Europe to Become More Nationalist? Evidence from the 2007–2009 Financial Crisis' (2016) 23 Journal of European Public Policy 60; EDH Olsen, 'Eurocrisis and EU Citizenship' in HJ Trenz and others (eds), *Europe's Prolonged Crisis: The Making or the Unmaking of a Political Union* (Palgrave 2015); R Wodak and S Boukala, 'European Identities and the Revival of Nationalism in the European Union: A Discourse Historical Approach' (2015) 14 Journal of Language and Politics 87.

[191] Interestingly, the very idea of EU citizenship was introduced in the Treaty of Maastricht, the first EU Treaty to be confronted at a 'no' vote in a national referendum (Denmark, 1992).

strengthen national identities rather than promoting the European one. A simple analysis of national campaigns' arguments and voting behaviour in EU referendums[192] leads to the assumption that voters generally tend to behave not as EU citizens, but rather as national citizens calculating costs and benefits from their relationship with the Union.[193] But still, despite the voters' overall limited identification with Europe when choosing between 'yes' and 'no' on the ballot paper, EU referendums remain the only medium whereby Europeans are put in such direct political contact with the EU project, feeling that their voices are – if not respected – at least clearly heard.

VI THE IDEA OF A PAN-EUROPEAN REFERENDUM AND THE QUEST FOR A EUROPEAN *DEMOS*

In view of such legitimacy and identity concerns, there have been several calls for an eventual cross-national coordination of EU referendums, mostly for those on EU Treaty reforms.[194] Organised on a more uniform and consistent basis following the example of the EU Parliament elections (maybe on the same day or week and in as many Member States as possible), these simultaneous national popular votes across Europe could eventually foster greater democratic legitimacy in the EU and a more genuine EU debate; a public debate focused more on EU rather than national questions. Interestingly, the first call for such coordinated referendums was launched back in 1949 when general de Gaulle declared: 'Europe will be born on the day on which the different peoples fundamentally decide to join. It will not suffice for members of parliaments to vote for ratification. It will require popular referendums, preferably held on the same day in all the countries concerned.'[195]

Such calls for simultaneous and coordinated national EU referendums inevitably lead to the idea of an eventual pan-European referendum; a popular vote organised on the EU level. Back in 1949, general de Gaulle had already imagined a referendum of 'all free Europeans'[196] while, in the early 1960s, the European federalist Altiero Spinelli suggested a popular vote on Europe as the ratification act

[192] For theoretical and statistical analysis of voting behaviour in EU referendums see Hobolt (n 19).
[193] L Hooghe and G Marks, 'Calculation, Community and Cues – Public Opinion on European Integration' (2005) 6 European Union Politics 419; L Hooghe and G Marks, 'Does Identity or Economic Rationality Drive Public Opinion on European Integration?' (2004) 37 PS: Political Science and Politics 415; L McLaren, 'Public Support for European Integration: Cost/Benefit Analysis or Perceived Cultural Threat' (2002) 64 Journal of Politics 551.
[194] There have also been calls for a certain coordination of membership referendums by requiring direct popular approval as a condition of a new EU accession (A Auer, 'National Referendums in the Process of European Integration: Time for Change' in A Albi and J Ziller (eds), *The European Constitution and National Constitutions: Ratifications and Beyond* (Kluwer 2007) 269–70).
[195] C de Gaulle, Press Conference in Palais d'Orsay, Paris, 14 November 1949.
[196] C de Gaulle, *Discours et messages, Vol 2: Dans l'attente. Février 1946–Avril 1958* (Plon 1970) 309, 'I think that the organisation of Europe has to proceed from Europe itself. I consider that the start shall be given by a referendum of all free Europeans.'

for a future European Constitution.[197] However, it was much later that the idea of a pan-European popular vote was translated into a concrete – yet unsuccessful – political proposal. In 1995, an EU Parliament resolution suggested 'a Union-wide referendum to ratify any Treaty provisions, on the grounds that a collective decision affecting the whole of Europe is at stake'.[198] The proposal was not given serious consideration but, ever since, calls for the establishment of an EU-wide referendum device have proliferated.[199]

Unsurprisingly, it was particularly during the preparation and ratification of the draft EU Constitution in 2005 that debates truly intensified, asking for a renewed form of legitimation for this fundamental text via the expression of citizens' direct consent.[200] At that time, a second concrete political proposal emerged. Representing a wide range of Member States and party groups, ninety-seven members of the European Convention[201] responsible for drafting the Constitutional Treaty came up with a new EU-wide referendum proposal for its ratification. Instead of following the standard system of uncoordinated national ratification procedures, they suggested an EU-wide referendum mechanism for ratifying the European Constitution[202] arguing that this was 'a real opportunity to democratise' the Union and 'empower the European citizens'.[203] Despite the evident legitimacy gains from such a 'popularly approved re-founding of the EU',[204] the proposal was widely judged as unrealistic and finally not acted upon by the Convention presidency. However, even in the aftermath of the French and Dutch popular rejections of the EU Constitution, proponents of EU-wide referendums were not discouraged. Instead, the idea of a pan-European referendum revived as a 'potential solution to the constitutional impasse'[205] or even as a possible remedy for the current crisis.[206] For

---

[197] A Spinelli, *Una strategia per gli stati uniti d'Europa* (Il Mulino 1989).
[198] Resolution on the functioning of the Treaty on European Union with a view to the 1996 Intergovernmental Conference – Implementation and Development of the Union, 19 June 1995, 56 (para 44). The text continues suggesting the alternative of simultaneous ratification: 'As an alternative, Member States could agree to hold any national referenda (or their respective parliamentary votes) at the same time or within a few days of each other'.
[199] Esposito (n 172); A Auer and JF Flauss (eds), *Le Referendum Européen* (Bruylant 1997); B Frey, 'A Directly Democratic and Federal Europe' (1996) 7(4) Constitutional Political Economy 267. For a critical overview of the EU-wide referendum proposals, see S Hug, *Voices of Europe: Citizens, Referendums and European Integration* (Rowman & Littlefield 2003) 101–15.
[200] J Habermas, 'Why Europe Needs a Constitution' in R Rogowski and C Turner (eds), *The Shape of the New Europe* (CUP 2006) 25, 35.
[201] The European Convention – established by the European Council in December 2001 and charged with drafting a European Constitution – finished its work in July 2003 with the Draft Treaty establishing a Constitution for Europe.
[202] European Convention, 'Referendum on the European Constitution: Adoption, Ratification and Entry into Force Procedure', Contribution Submitted by Several Members, Alternate Members and Observers, CONV 658/03, 31 March 2003, 2.
[203] ibid 4.
[204] Mendez and Mendez (n 36) 62.
[205] Mendez (n 31) 195.
[206] See J Habermas, 'The Crisis of the European Union in the Light of a Constitutionalisation of International Law' (2012) 23 European Journal of International Law 335.

instance, a recent EU-wide referendum proposal is contained in the – much discussed for its federal implications – 'Verhofstadt report' adopted by the EU Parliament in February 2017.[207]

Traditionally confronted with severe criticism for their unrealistic nature, the various proposals for EU-wide referendums have developed rather different theoretical conceptualisations of such a pan-European popular vote. It is, thus, important to study each of them in their own specific context and in light of the different EU integration stages. For instance, there have been calls for EU-wide referendums on the EU Constitution alone,[208] on Treaty ratification more generally,[209] on specific EU policy issues,[210] or even on a citizen-initiative basis.[211] Some proposals emerged quite early on, in the eras of the so-called 'permissive consensus' and 'referendum euphoria' before the recent EU enlargements, while others saw the light in the aftermath of resounding national 'no' votes, or in the midst of the Eurocrisis. A decisive criterion for the classification and evaluation of the various proposals is the role assigned to individual Member States in the overall procedure. The more modest proposals have mainly focused on a certain coordination and synchronisation of national EU ballots on the same date and issue and with the same turnout or majority thresholds.[212] In this case, the unanimity rule is applied and popular approval must be achieved at each Member State. However, several authors have insisted on the further Europeanisation of the procedure. The outcome could be, then, calculated either on a Member States' basis following the classic unanimity rule or even on a pure EU-population basis (maybe including some form of double majority of the EU electorate with additional quotas on a Member-State level).[213] Nevertheless, in light of the general EU preference for efficiency over legitimacy, both ideas have provoked a wide criticism on their practical feasibility: the former for converting the existing veto into a popular veto, which 'exacerbates the rigidity of the

---

[207]   European Parliament resolution of 16 February 2017 on possible evolutions of and adjustments to the current institutional set-up of the European Union (2014/2248(INI)), para 46.

[208]   Such proposals focused on a novel ratification mechanism exclusively designed for the Constitutional Treaty without suggesting a replacement of the existing treaty-revision procedure.

[209]   R Rose, *Representing Europeans: A Pragmatic Approach* (OUP 2013); F Cheneval, *The Government of the Peoples: On the Idea and Principles of Multilateral Democracy* (Palgrave 2011); M Efler and others, *Europe: Not without the People! The Dismal State of Democracy in the European Union and How to Mend It* (VSA Verlag 2009). Such proposals usually opt for a less extensive use of the EU-wide referendum only for larger-scale Treaty reforms.

[210]   eg on enlargement issues. See Efler (n 209) 132–46.

[211]   Hug (n 199) 101–15.

[212]   A Auer, 'Adoption, Ratification and Entry into Force: Article IV-8 Draft Convention' (2005) 1(1) European Constitutional Law Review 131; F Cheneval, '*Caminante, no hay camino, se hace camino al andar*: EU Citizenship, Direct Democracy and Treaty Ratification' (2007) 13 European Law Journal 647.

[213]   For instance, the members of the European Convention suggested: 'As Europe consists of citizens and member states, the fairest and most democratic means of consulting the people would be by a referendum based on a dual majority, i.e. a majority of citizens and a majority of states would be necessary to secure ratification' (n 202).

EU's rules of change',[214] and the latter for demanding a politically unrealistic federal step towards a truly political union through the requirement of a double majority of Member States and EU citizens.

This feasibility argument against EU-wide referendums is further reinforced with more general concerns regarding the Union's size and political diversity. Although e-voting could certainly facilitate the organisation of a continental-sized vote,[215] a pan-European referendum is still considered impractical or even 'particularly inappropriate' given the size of the Union.[216] In fact, opponents of referendums have always highlighted the difficulties of 'face-to-face debate and enlightened deliberation beyond a certain population threshold or geographic size',[217] to finally assume that direct democracy is mostly suited to the ancient city-state rather than the modern national state, let alone the EU's post-national context. Besides, the Union's political diversity is certainly not helping. Any EU-wide referendum scenario would also have to deal with the significant differences among Member States as regards the referendum device and their overall highly divergent constitutional structures and traditions of direct democracy. An eventual unification of referendum standards across the continent would need to take into consideration that some countries have a longstanding referendum culture (with largely different practices regarding initiatives, campaign regulations or turnout and majority thresholds), whereas in others there is a total absence of direct-democracy reflexes, since popular votes are not allowed by domestic constitutions.

Yet, the core critique against a pan-European referendum stems from the premise that Europe cannot be perceived as a unified political community, which leads back to the long-standing debates on the existence or emergence of a European *demos*.[218] Most scholars agree that there is no *demos* on the EU level, no shared sense of common past and future, common destiny, culture or a broad set of common values that could generate solidarity.[219] EU citizenship is not based on an EU-*demos* idea but rather on a conception of individuals as citizens of States which happen themselves to be members of a Union.[220] And, since individuals are not 'immediate

214   Mendez and Mendez (n 36) 63.
215   PC Schmitter, 'E-voting, E-democracy and EU-democracy: A Thought Experiment' in A Treschel and F Mendez (eds), *The European Union and E-voting: Addressing the European Parliament's Internet Voting Challenge* (Routledge 2005) 187–201.
216   J Weiler, 'To Be a European Citizen: Eros and Civilisation' (1997) 4 Journal of European Public Policy 495.
217   Mendez (n 31) 10.
218   J Weiler, 'Does Europe Need a Constitution? *Demos*, Telos and the German Maastricht Decision' (1995) 1(3) European Law Journal 219; LE Cederman, 'Nationalism and Bounded Integration: What It Would Take to Construct a European *Demos*' (2001) 7 European Journal of International Relations 139.
219   T Risse, 'No *Demos*? Identities and the Public Spheres in the Euro Crisis' (2014) 52 Journal of Common Market Studies 1207; V Pérez-Díaz, 'The Public Sphere and a European Civil Society' in JC Alexander (ed), *Real Civil Societies: Dilemmas of Institutionalisation* (Sage 1998) 211, 235.
220   However, see Case C-135/08, *Janko Rottmann v Freistaat Bayern* EU:C:2010:104, para 42.

bearers of EU citizenship',[221] it seems safer to conceive Europe as a 'demoi-cracy'; as a 'Union of peoples who govern together, but not as one'.[222] Thus, when trying to introduce an EU-wide referendum device and, consequently, a homogenous political debate and decision-making process across the continent, the size and heterogeneity of the EU electorate is a challenge in itself. In the absence of a clearly constituted EU demos, minorities would probably be rather unlikely to accept hostile majoritarian decisions coming from referendums, especially if the Member States' unanimity rule is abandoned and the referendum outcome is calculated on a pure EU-electorate basis.[223] In this sense, it seems rather illusory to imagine a pan-European referendum without a certain recognition of a European people.

However, instead of perpetually insisting on the lack of an EU demos, we could also focus on the lack of adequate mechanisms which would allow EU citizens – or even an existent or emerging EU demos – to manifest a collective will on EU matters. Depriving EU citizens of any chance of direct participation in EU affairs on the sole argument that an EU demos does not (yet) exist, may lead to a repeating vicious circle. On the contrary, more open and direct citizen involvement could lead to more active EU citizens, to sentiments of belonging and civic proximity and, ultimately, to the consolidation of an EU demos, meaning something more than the accumulation of the EU national demoi. Certainly, this demos will not be conceived on pure ethno-cultural terms,[224] but rather on a shared EU political conscience and set of values transcending national diversities. It would rather be a 'union among peoples' stemming from 'a political culture which learns new ways to deal with the other' by creating 'one people out of many'.[225] In this sense, the strong symbolic value of a pan-European referendum would certainly aid the formation of an EU demos.[226] Through such a political process, this emerging EU demos could be pushed forwards into realising its own existence and powers as a truly EU constituent power. Besides, the Swiss direct democracy system constitutes an

---

[221] PB Lehning, 'European Citizenship: Towards A European Identity?' 20 Law and Philosophy 239, 269.

[222] K Nicolaïdis, 'European Demoicracy and Its Crisis' (2013) 51 Journal of Common Market Studies 351; M Ronzoni, 'The European Union as a Demoicracy: Really a Third Way?' (2016) 16 European Journal of Political Theory 210; F Cheneval and F Schimmelfennig, 'The Case for Demoicracy in the European Union: Principles, Institutions, Policies' (2013) 51 Journal of Common Market Studies 334.

[223] On these 'dangers of majoritarianism', see Hobolt (n 19) 24.

[224] On the uncoupling of ethnos et demos in the EU context, see Lehning (n 221) 275 arguing that 'any comparison of people's sense of belonging to a nation-state with their sense of being citizens of the EU will be vitiated. To expect a strong sense of EU citizenship to arise only from people's subjection to a common set of political institutions would empirically expect more than any nation-state has probably ever achieved.'

[225] JHH Weiler, 'The Reformation of European Constitutionalism' (1997) 35 Journal of Common Market Studies 97, 117–18.

[226] However, see Hobolt (n 19) 247 concluding that 'the hopes of an EU-wide referendum bringing about a European demos should not be exaggerated, however. Elements of direct democracy might be helpful to the process of constituting a European public sphere, but are neither necessary not sufficient for a European demos to emerge.'

excellent example[227] of how referendums can progressively help develop a public sphere of diverse populations and a greater feeling of identity.

Therefore, in terms of the current legitimacy and identity crisis, an EU-wide referendum device could serve as an additional mechanism for strengthening both the Union's legitimacy and the common identity of its citizens. In terms of legitimacy, while national referendums concern only few national *demoi* and can only indirectly legitimise EU policies, the bold step of introducing an EU-wide popular vote could indeed foster greater democratic legitimacy by directly connecting EU citizens to EU institutions.[228] In this context, it would be easier to imagine 'a shift from the *demoi*-cracy to *demos*-cracy, a shift from accountability to the separate peoples of Europe . . . to accountability to the people of Europe as a whole'.[229] This could even affect the EU's problematic attitude towards 'no' votes, since an eventual EU-wide 'no' vote would be directly binding on the Union as a whole and not only on national governments. On the other hand, regarding identity issues, this deeper citizen involvement in EU affairs could foster the formation of a collective EU identity and the attainment of a certain sense of community. A pan-European referendum would promote transnational communication and help arousing genuine EU-wide political debates on concrete issues creating an integrated EU public sphere and an EU civil society.[230] Even though the risk of second-order voting will always be present, there is a crucial difference between the existing procedures of EU national referendums or EU elections and an eventual EU-wide popular vote. Whereas the former provide only a weak connection to actual EU policy outcomes, the vote choice in the latter would be clearly associated with a specific political outcome on the EU level.[231] Consequently, a truly European public space and a sense of belonging could then grow out of this collective will formation, which practically would mean EU-wide discussions and decisions upon a common European future. Besides, larger turnouts and deeper citizens' involvement could also be anticipated given that referendums enthusiasts have traditionally emphasised the educational and self-improving value of direct democracy in terms of citizens' political and voting behaviour.[232]

Although the Article 10 of the Treaty on the European Union only refers to EU representative democracy,[233] the same article also suggests that 'decisions shall be

---

[227] See the recent report of the BEUcitizen project titled 'Switzerland: A Future Model for the European Union? Similarities and Differences' (27 February 2017) http://beucitizen.eu/publications/switzer land-a-future-model-for-the-european-union-similarities-and-differences-d4-2 accessed April 2018.

[228] Rose (n 209) 84–97.

[229] P Van Parijs, 'Should the European Union Become More Democratic?' in A Føllesdal and P Koslowski (eds), *Democracy and the European Union* (Springer 1998) 298–99.

[230] C Closa, *The Politics of Ratification of EU Treaties* (Routledge 2013) 72–91.

[231] Hobolt (n 19) 245.

[232] On the idea that citizens' experience with direct democratic procedures enhances political efficacy inviting voters to discuss the issues at stake and seek out more information, see H Kriesi, *Direct Democratic Choice: The Swiss Experience* (Lexington 2005).

[233] Art 10(1) TEU.

taken as openly and as closely as possible to the citizens' who 'shall have the right to participate in the democratic life of the Union'.[234] In the current context of purely representative EU democracy, the EU Parliament elections remain the only actual EU-level vote empowering EU citizenship. It is, however, theoretically possible to enhance the Union's political life with some direct democratic EU mechanisms like a pan-European referendum. What is missing is certainly the political will to further involve EU citizens in the EU decision-making process in such a direct and effective way. The current EU crisis context and the increasing referendum phobia across the continent leave no doubt that – at least in the foreseeable future – these are indeed politically inauspicious times for ambitious proposals regarding EU-wide referendums.

Nevertheless, there has been a significant recent step towards European direct democracy with the establishment of the European Citizens' Initiative (ECI), the first and only direct democratic instrument institutionalised at the EU level. Introduced by Article 11(4) of the Lisbon Treaty, this EU participatory-democracy mechanism enables one million citizens (from at least seven Member States) to directly propose a legal act to the EU Commission.[235] Similar mechanisms have recently emerged in many national democracies allowing people to propose and vote on legislation and policies by gathering a certain number of signatures.[236] However, since the formal legislative initiative still belongs to the Commission alone, the ECI rather constitutes a pre-legislative instrument with an agenda-setting function. It is, thus, different from petition rights (since it lets people identify a problem and call for action), but also from referendums (since it can neither reject a legal act nor guarantee an actual impact on final legislation). Instead, it is only an invitation to the Commission to consider a legal change with no real effectiveness since it rarely leads to legislative action.[237] In September 2017 – and following a public consultation on ECIs – the Commission has finally proposed a long-awaited revision of the relevant ECI Regulation in order to render the mechanism more flexible and with more citizen-friendly formal requirements.[238] Despite its very limited success until now, this novel ECI mechanism could symbolically pave the way for a transnational participatory EU democracy with both horizontal citizen-to-citizen dialogues across the continent, and vertical citizens-to-institutions interactions initiated from 'below'.

---

[234]   Art 10(3) TEU.
[235]   Art 11(4) TEU; Art 24(1) TFEU; Regulation (EU) 211/2011 of the European Parliament and of the Council of 16 February 2011 on the Citizens' Initiative [2011] OJ L65/1.
[236]   H Krunke, 'Sovereignty, Constitutional Identity, Direct Democracy?' in Contiades (n 46) 200.
[237]   Since the mechanism entered into force in 2012, there have been only four successful ECIs which gained at least 1 million signatures ('Water and sanitation are a human right! Water is a public good, not a commodity!' 'One of Us', 'Stop Vivisection' and 'Ban glyphosate and protect people and the environment from toxic pesticides'). To date, the Commission has finally presented a legislative proposal regarding only the first one (February 2018). Yet, the promoters are not entirely satisfied with the text (www.right2water.eu).
[238]   Commission, 'Proposal for a Regulation of the European Parliament and of the Council on the European Citizens' Initiative' COM(2017) 482 final.

VII CONCLUSIONS

The EU seems to be confronted with an 'interesting' paradox regarding direct democracy. Although more referendums could mean more and better EU democracy, they could also halt, or even reverse, the integration project if they keep delivering negative outcomes. Following the term's Latin etymology, a referendum is supposed to 'refer' and bring questions back to the people. And this is indeed necessary in the EU context, where national sovereign powers are continuously transferred to EU institutions – and mostly to unelected EU officials – creating an obvious legitimacy gap. In this sense, referendums could easily legitimise the otherwise elite-driven integration process and enhance the common EU identity. Having more direct democratic mechanisms on EU issues or even at the EU level could progressively make European citizens feel both more 'European' and more like actual 'citizens', palliating the current identity and democratic-legitimacy crisis of the Union.

However, in EU circles, referendums are increasingly described as risky and dangerous, since well-designed EU policies might instantly be rejected by a single Member State's 'no' vote. Besides, following the recent series of consecutive 'no' outcomes, it seems that European electorates are increasingly voting against EU and national elites' advices, which might suggest deeper changes in the relationship between elected and electors; between governors and governed in this multilevel system of EU governance. The Union seems indeed afraid of national *demoi* every time they hold a referendum ballot paper. And, constantly ignoring calls for a pan-European referendum, the Union seems also afraid of its own emerging European *demos*. Apparently, the EU-integration project is so carefully designed in Brussels, to the slightest detail, that there is no need to bring it into ballot boxes across the continent asking for popular support, especially in the current times of crisis.

However, national EU referendums can ultimately be seen as the only rare moments of direct contact between EU citizens and the Union. Despite emerging in national contexts and concerning a very small number of EU citizens, this is for now the only available direct expression of EU citizens' will regarding Europe. And if Europe is indeed trying to become 'a more democratic union' taking 'a democratic leap forward' – as mentioned in last year's State of the Union[239] – a simple first step could be listening to its citizens and honouring their will, even when they vote 'no'. Instead of designing complex legitimation and democratisation strategies for clearly elite-driven current and future policies, there seems to be a simpler and much more basic first step in order to bring the Union closer to its citizens. And this includes a radical change of the EU's highly problematic attitude towards no-votes in national EU referendums.

---

[239] EU Commission, President Jean-Claude Juncker's State of the Union Address 2017, Strasbourg, 13 September 2017.

Listening to the EU citizens – even when they answer 'no' – can only enhance European democracy. Searching and addressing the causes of the recent first ever series of five consecutive no votes can only strengthen the Union. What Europe really needs is a more direct contact with its citizens within an overall truly democratic integration plan, not just some temporary legitimising clocks masking the deep democratic deficiencies of its institutions and decision-making mechanisms. The Union needs a real democracy, possibly even a more direct one, and not just some fake imaginary democratic clothes tailored by technocrats. Otherwise, there will soon be one more EU referendum, one more national *demos* through a new 'no' vote who – like the kid in Hans Christian Andersen's fairy tale – will shout again: 'the Emperor is naked'. It is just an Emperor. No fancy clothes of democratic legitimacy.

9

Can Public and Voluntary Acts of Consent Confer Legitimacy on the EU?

Ozlem Ulgen

I INTRODUCTION

Legitimacy is essential for any polity that seeks to exert law-making authority over its people. Although the EU is not a single state, it is a polity that has to obtain legitimacy for its power to make laws affecting some 500 million people across twenty-eight Member States (soon to be twenty-seven pending UK exit). And yet in the eyes of EU citizens the Eurozone crisis and Brexit vote call into question the EU's legitimacy as it cannot guarantee prosperity for all its peoples or shield against economic and political uncertainty. There is growing unease and disaffection, particularly among southern EU states' voters, and divisions between core–peripheral Member States, with emerging alternative popular representation structures (e.g. Podemos in Spain) and reappraisal of the EU, even among pro-EU politicians[1] (e.g. the British left-wing, albeit historically deep divisions have remained since the membership referendum of 1975 with vocal Labour Eurosceptics such as Tony Benn and Jeremy Corbyn).[2] In this context, 'core' Member States refers to the advanced economies and strong democracies including the original founding members (Belgium, France, Germany, Italy, Luxembourg and the Netherlands), and new members from the enlargement period between 1973 and 1995 (Denmark, Ireland, the UK, Greece, Portugal, Spain, Austria, Finland, Sweden). 'Peripheral' Member States denotes the southern, central, eastern European states that joined from 2004 onwards (Cyprus, Czech Republic, Estonia, Hungary, Latvia, Lithuania, Malta, Poland, Slovakia, Slovenia, Bulgaria, Romania, Croatia).[3] Added to this is a lack of

---

[1] K Demetriou (ed), *The European Union in Crisis: Explorations in Representation and Democratic Legitimacy* (Springer 2015); C Leconte, *Understanding Euroscepticism* (Palgrave 2010); N Fligstein, *Euroclash: The EU, European Identity, and the Future of Europe* (OUP 2008).

[2] KA Armstrong, *Brexit Time: Leaving the EU – Why, How and When?* (CUP 2017) 21–24; T Nairn, 'The Left against Europe?' (1972) I/75 New Left Review 1; T Benn, *Free At Last! Diaries 1991–2001* (Hutchinson 2002).

[3] On the core–peripheral and old–new Member State distinctions, see generally, JM Magone, 'Divided Europe? Euroscepticism in Central, Eastern and Southern Europe' in Demetriou (n 1); C Lequesne,

debate and public awareness of what the EU stands for and its practical benefits. It is, therefore, important to understand how legitimacy is (or is not) created and maintained in the EU.

A form of legitimacy may be conferred by EU citizens engaging in public and voluntary acts of consent. These are acts taken by individuals and groups which may confer legitimacy on the law-making authority of an entity (e.g. voting in European Parliamentary elections; national referendums on EU matters). Political theorists, such as Beetham,[4] have explored public and voluntary acts of consent in the context of understanding how state power is legitimised. Using Beetham's 'normative structure of legitimacy', especially the third component of 'expressed consent', this chapter considers whether public and voluntary acts of consent may confer legitimacy on the EU. Section II explores the relevance of Beetham's 'normative structure of legitimacy' under the criteria of rule-based validity, justifiability of power rules, and expressed consent. Section III evaluates expressed consent in three types of public and voluntary acts of consent: national referendums, with particular reference to the UK Brexit referendum of 23 June 2016, and the Greek bail-out referendum of 5 July 2015; the European Citizens' Initiative under Article 11(4) TEU; and civil society engagement under Article 11(2) TEU.

II BEETHAM'S 'NORMATIVE STRUCTURE OF LEGITIMACY' AND THE ROLE OF CONSENT

Legitimacy means different things to different people and Member States. It could mean perceived authority to make rules. It could mean perceived legitimacy of the rule-making process. It could also mean perceived authority to represent and act on behalf of people. Law-making authority, legitimacy of the law-making process and authority to represent EU citizens are all relevant to the question of the EU's legitimacy. Beetham and Lord argue that the EU needs direct legitimation through the people because it is a political entity that imposes goods and burdens on citizens.[5] This begs the question: can we say there is direct legitimation of the EU? Or is it legitimised through some other means? In *The Legitimation of Power* Beetham sets out three criteria for the 'normative structure of legitimacy': (1) rule-derived validity; (2) justifiability of power rules; and (3) expressed consent.[6] The last criterion is of most interest here but it is worth considering how all three are interconnected and relate to the EU.

'Old Versus New' in E Jones, A Menon and S Weatherill (eds), *The Oxford Handbook of the European Union* (OUP 2012).

[4] D Beetham, *The Legitimation of Power* (Palgrave 1991).
[5] D Beetham and C Lord, *Legitimacy and the EU* (Longman 1998).
[6] Beetham (n 4) ch 3.

1 *Rule-Derived Validity and the EU*

Legitimacy derived from rules means operating within a 'rule-governed social order' whereby the power to govern and the right to exercise such power are acquired through rules.[7] Beetham's reference to 'social order' and 'social rules' explains how basic rules emerge in social life to ensure predictability of behaviour, expectations and entitlements. This then translates into legal rules in a legal order, containing primary rules (e.g. rights and obligations) and secondary rules, which prescribe how primary rules are recognised, adjudicated and enforced.[8] Certain features of legal orders encourage respect for the law, serve as limitations on power, and make it difficult to challenge. In the EU legal order Member States are recognised as having rights and obligations; there are rules on free movement of persons, goods, capital and services that operate on the basis of their being regarded as basic freedoms and of a general prohibition of discrimination on grounds of nationality;[9] and, arguably, very restrictive rules on the standing of individuals to bring a judicial review claim against an EU institution.[10] But, as Beetham concludes, 'the law can never provide more than a primary, and therefore provisional, ground for legitimacy ... [because] ... rules cannot justify themselves simply by being rules, but require justification by reference to considerations which lie beyond them'.[11] So reference to EU law as evidence of the EU's legitimacy does not explain why those particular rules were chosen, nor does it account for reform.

A stark illustration of the limitations of legality as a source of legitimacy is seen in the Catalonian independence referendum of 1 October 2017. The Spanish Constitutional Court ruled that the referendum was unconstitutional, and that a law passed by the Catalan regional parliament authorising the referendum was against 'national sovereignty' and the 'indissoluble unity of the Spanish nation', protected under Sections 1(2) and 2 of the Spanish Constitution.[12] Section 1(2) refers to 'national sovereignty' that 'belongs to the Spanish people, from whom all state powers emanate'.[13] Section 2 states, 'the Constitution is based on the indissoluble unity of the Spanish Nation, the common and indivisible homeland of all Spaniards; it recognizes and guarantees the right to self-government of the nationalities and regions of which it is composed and

---

[7] ibid 65.

[8] HLA Hart, *The Concept Law* (OUP 1961) 77–96.

[9] Art 45 TFEU (free movement of workers); Arts 28–37 TFEU (free movement of goods); Art 63 TFEU (movement of capital); Art 56 TFEU (freedom to provide services); Art 18 TFEU (general principle of prohibition of discrimination on grounds of nationality).

[10] The Art 263 TFEU 'direct and individual concern' requirement for reviewing legislative acts, and 'direct concern' requirement for reviewing regulatory acts.

[11] Beetham (n 4) 68–69.

[12] 'Catalonia: Spain's Constitutional Court Declares Catalan Referendum Law Void' *The Independent* (17 October 2017) www.independent.co.uk/news/world/europe/catalonia-catalan-independence-referendum-spain-constitutional-court-void-a8004941.html accessed April 2018.

[13] 1978 Spanish Constitution, s 1(2).

the solidarity among them all'.[14] But Section 92 allows for advisory referendums to take place, subject to 'all citizens' being able to vote, and the King calling the referendum based on the president's proposal which should have prior authorisation from Congress.[15] In practice, a constitutional regional independence referendum would be virtually impossible if it requires the prior approval of Congress, the president, and the King. If all Spanish citizens are to vote in such referendum, then non-regional votes against independence will overwhelm regional votes supporting it. The 1978 Spanish Constitution therefore seems unable to cope with these conflicting interests and call for social change through democratic means of a referendum.

2 Shifting Belief Systems and Justifiability of EU Power Rules

Rules concerning the power to govern and the right to exercise power must be justifiable (i.e. open to justification) to the 'dominant', who invoke them to acquire power, as well as the 'subordinate', who are subject to these rules, within 'a common framework of belief'.[16] The 'common framework of belief' appears similar to Raz's formalistic notion that a constitution expresses a 'common ideology' governing public life.[17] A constitution may be one form in which shared beliefs are expressed. But Beetham is concerned about whether there are actual rather than assumed shared beliefs obtained through expressed consent. Such a belief system may derive from 'external' sources (e.g. religion; natural law doctrines; or the sciences) or 'internal' sources (e.g. traditions and customs, or the people). Any rule distinguishing dominant from subordinate must also be capable of justification under 'ideas of the common interest'.[18] If the dominant are simply reliant on rules that secure their own prosperity and well-being without any justification based on the common interest shared with the subordinate, then the system of rules is unsustainable. External belief systems are less prominent in the majority of states. With secularisation and multiplication of faiths, religious belief is incapable of providing a single coherent source of legitimacy. Natural law doctrines have played an important role in understanding human nature and trying to formulate rules based on morality and rationality. But they are not always egalitarian (e.g. Aristotle's justification of slavery and aristocracy; European Enlightenment rationality differentiating between men and women), and a single moral code is hard to formulate in a world of divergent beliefs and practices. Science appeals as an authoritative and independent source of legitimacy but it is incapable of producing normative principles on its own; not all issues of social organisation can be reduced to technical questions, and the idea of

[14]   ibid s 2.
[15]   ibid s 92.
[16]   Beetham (n 4) 69.
[17]   J Raz, 'On the Authority and Interpretation of Constitutions: Some Preliminaries' in L Alexander (ed), *Constitutionalism: Philosophical Foundations* (CUP 1998) 153–54.
[18]   Beetham (n 4) 77–90.

a depoliticised social and legal order is unattainable.[19] So it appears that internal belief systems, based on traditions and customs or the people, provide a stronger basis for the legitimacy of state-based power rules. What about EU power rules? Is there an internal belief system that legitimises them?

EU power rules can be seen in the overriding principle of EU law supremacy over national laws, areas of EU legislative competence, and EU institutional powers. Thus, to the extent that there is a conflict between national law and EU law, the latter prevails even over constitutional provisions and past or future national legislation.[20] However, there are 'two competing perspectives' (European and national) as to whether such a *grundnorm* represents formal constitutionalism, sitting at the apex of the EU legal order.[21] Many Member States have challenged the ECJ's non-nuanced approach to supremacy, especially where it potentially conflicts with national constitutional norms and fundamental rights.[22] Exclusive EU legislative competence exists in relation to the customs union, competition law, economic and monetary policy, conservation of marine biological resources, and the common commercial policy.[23] Shared EU–Member State legislative competence exists in the areas of the internal market, social policy, economic, social and territorial cohesion, agriculture and fisheries, environment, consumer protection, transport, trans-European networks; energy, area of freedom, security and justice,

---

[19] ibid 74.

[20] Case 6/64, *Costa v ENEL* [1964] ECR 585; Case 11/70, *Internationale Handelsgesellschaft* [1970] ECR 1126. Case 106/77, *Italian Finance Administration v Simmenthal* [1978] ECR 629.

[21] R Schütze, 'Constitutionalism and the European Union' in C Barnard and S Peers (eds), *European Union Law* (OUP 2014) 72–76.

[22] *Handelsgesellschaft v Einfuhr und Vorratsstelle für Getreide und Futtermittel (Solange I)*, BVerfGE 37, 271 [1974] 2 CMLR 540 where the German Constitutional Court refused to accept the unconditional supremacy of Community law, and held that, in the event of a conflict between Community law and guarantees of fundamental rights in the German Basic Law, the latter prevailed 'so long as' the EC had not removed the 'conflict of norms'; *Application of Wünsche Handelsgesellschaft (Solange II)*, BVerfGE 73, 339, [1987] 3 CMLR 225 where the German Constitutional Court qualified *Solange I* by stating that 'so long as' the EC and the ECJ ensured effective protection of fundamental rights, the German Constitutional Court would not exercise jurisdiction over fundamental rights; *Honeywell*, BVerfGE 126, 286 [2011] 1 CMLR 1067, paras 54–61 where the German Constitutional Court made it difficult to challenge EU law supremacy on the basis that the EU acted *ultra vires* by requiring prior ECJ determination of the issue and for the claimant to show any excess of power was 'manifestly in violation of competences' and 'highly significant'; *Czech Sugar Quotas*, Ústavní soud České republiky dne 8.3.2006 (ÚS) [Constitutional Court] [Decision of the Czech Constitutional Court of 8 March 2006], sp.zn Pl. ÚS 50/04, Part B para 4 where the Czech Constitutional Court asserted Czech sovereignty and conditional conferral of power to the EU; *Treaty of Lisbon*, Ústavní soud České republiky dne 26.11.2008 (ÚS) [Constitutional Court] [Decision of the Czech Constitutional Court of 26 November 2008], sp.zn Pl. ÚS 19/08, which approved ratification of the Lisbon Treaty on the basis of a conditional conferral of power; *Polish Membership of the European Union (Accession Treaty)*, Polish Constitutional Court, K18/04 Judgment of 11 May 2005, para 13 where the Polish Constitutional Court held that 'an irreconcilable inconsistency' between a constitutional norm and a Community norm cannot be resolved by assuming the latter's supremacy, and that it would be up to the state to amend the Constitution, seek modifications to Community provisions, or leave the EU.

[23] Arts 2(1) and 3 TFEU.

and common safety concerns in public health matters.[24] EU legislative competences that support and supplement Member States' legislative actions relate to protection and improvement of human health, industry, culture, tourism, education, vocational training, youth and sport, civil protection and administrative cooperation.[25] In terms of EU institutional legislative powers, the ordinary legislative procedure combines elected representatives in the European Parliament, with EU civil servants in the Commission, and ministers of each Member State in the Council of Ministers.[26]

Some consider these competences reflective of 'output legitimacy' whereby the EU is able to govern effectively for the people. Menon and Weatherill consider the EU's output legitimacy is based on its ability to undertake functions that individual Member States would not be able to (e.g. creation of the internal market; representation at international trade negotiations; and acting through the European Central Bank to coordinate responses to the Eurozone crisis).[27] Caporaso and Tarrow contend that output legitimacy derives from the 'social re-equilibration of economic liberalisation through the simultaneous movement/counter-movement of disembedding and re-embedding markets in society, with EU market-correcting alongside EU market-making, as in ECJ rulings in such areas as gender equality, regional equality, environmental protection, and laws promoting family solidarity in the case of labor mobility'.[28]

The power rules assume that the EU–Member State relationship is the most significant in terms of legitimising the EU, whereas the real question is whether EU citizens recognise an internal belief system that sustains legitimacy. To some extent, there is an internal belief system based on the Western liberal tradition of representative democracy and values of democracy, rule of law and respect for human rights.[29] These are clearly imported primarily from core EU Member States. For Central and Eastern European States (CEES), transitioning from totalitarian and authoritarian states to democratic EU Member States involved accepting pre-membership political conditions of 'stability of institutions guaranteeing democracy, the rule of law, human rights and respect for and protection of minorities'.[30] Within CEES, differences emerged regarding pace and extent of importation of

---

[24] ibid Arts 2(2) and 4.
[25] ibid Arts 2(5) and 6.
[26] ibid Arts 289(1) and 294; Arts 14(1), 16(1), 17(1) and (2) TEU.
[27] A Menon and S Weatherill, 'Transnational Legitimacy in a Globalising World: How the European Union Rescues Its States' (2008) 31 West European Politics 397.
[28] J Caporaso and S Tarrow, 'Polanyi in Brussels: European Institutions and the Embedding of Markets in Society' RECON Online Working Paper 2008/01 www.reconproject.eu/main.php /RECON_wp_0801.pdf?fileitem=50511945 accessed April 2018.
[29] Arts 2, 3, 10 TEU.
[30] *Bulletin of the European Communities* 6-1993, 13. Note, there were economic and legal criteria to fulfil as well (eg establishing a functioning market economy as well as the capacity to cope with competitive pressure and market forces within the Union; ability to take on the obligations of membership including adherence to the aims of political, economic and monetary union).

values depending on the level of democratic conditions already existing in the state. In the Czech Republic, Hungary, and Poland, as well as the two Baltic States of Estonia and Latvia, democratic consolidation existed prior to accession, whereas Romania and Bulgaria required domestic political reform before implementation of democracy and the rule of law.[31] Due to a 'quasi-mythical trust in Europe' as a result of mistrust of the Communist-era state, and a belief that anything emanating from the West is good, or at least better, the public in CEES were generally supportive of accession.[32]

But is this sufficient as, in Beetham's terms, 'a common framework of belief'? Arguably not, given divergent Member State views on the EU's purpose and objectives along with varying degrees of political and economic integration that undermine the notion of a singular basis for legitimacy. In CEES there was lack of national democratic deliberation about the harmonisation of laws, and lack of CEES participation in the creation of EU *acquis*.[33] The CEES' 'return to Europe' rhetoric camouflaged a 'profoundly asymmetric relationship' between, on the one hand, politically and economically integrated old Member States, with superior bargaining power to set and enforce value-based membership criteria; and on the other, emerging post-Communist democracies keen to gain entry.[34] By imposing values which had not been democratically deliberated within the new states, and which were not evident in the supranational governance structure of the EU, the enlargement process itself embedded problems of legitimacy. Priban likens this to the nineteenth-century 'administrative state', basing its legitimacy on efficiency and outcomes rather than values and democratic procedures.[35] Further distancing from 'a common framework of belief' occurred with the political condition of protection of minorities, which was not part of the EU legal system and not actually shared by all existing Member States themselves.[36]

For some states the national realities of integration may be politically costly.[37] In Greece, since 2008, and despite any long-term domestic reforms that may accrue from EU bail-out terms, successive governments trying to implement austerity measures have faced public opposition. There is political and economic instability

---

[31] F Schimmelfennig and U Sedelmaier, 'Governance by Conditionality: EU rule transfer to the candidate countries of Central and Eastern Europe' (2004) 11 Journal of European Public Policy 661, 669–71.

[32] W Sadurski, *Constitutionalism and the Enlargement of Europe* (OUP 2012) 145–47.

[33] Schimmelfennig and Sedelmaier (n 31) 661–79.

[34] J Priban, 'From "Which Rule of Law?" to "the Rule of Which Law?": Post-Communist Experiences of European Legal Integration' (2009) 1 Hague Journal on the Rule of Law 337; Sadurski (n 32) chs 2 and 4.

[35] Priban (n 34) 353; see Schmitt on features of the 'administrative state', C Schmitt, *Legality and Legitimacy* (Duke UP 2004) 5–6.

[36] Sadurski (n 32) 86–199.

[37] A Hinarejos, *The Euro Area Crisis in Constitutional Perspective* (OUP 2015), esp ch 7, argues that multi-speed or differentiated integration is on the rise due to different interests and immediate priorities of euro and non-euro countries.

(e.g. 20.7 per cent overall unemployment and 47.3 per cent youth unemployment; some 427,000 Greeks migrating overseas to find work; and the rise of the far-right Golden Dawn party).[38] Hungary, Poland, Slovakia, and the Czech Republic object to the quota system for refugee burden-sharing agreed by Member States in 2015, and there is rising anti-immigrant and xenophobic sentiments.[39]

It is also interesting to reflect on how the EU's traditions and values may have changed over time. Weiler identifies 'political messianism', the promise of a better land through European integration, as a form of legitimacy which the EU was originally successful at in terms of peace and stability.[40] But today's EU arguably has a weakened form of 'political messianism' legitimacy. Law and politics are conflated, as is evident in core–peripheral Member State citizens' calls for greater justice on many issues (e.g. migration burden-sharing; fiscal discipline; EU funding; or greater decentralisation and more autonomy for states and regions).[41]

Whatever the internal belief system of the EU supposedly entails, EU citizens may perceive and experience this (whether based on the common lineal Western liberal tradition, or the messianic mission towards further integration) as being paternalistically implemented by an EU elite disconnected from daily life. The autumn 2016 Eurobarometer indicates that only 36 per cent of EU citizens trust the EU and 35 per cent have a positive image of it.[42] Systematic paternalism and disconnection gradually erode any sense of a shared internal belief system, undermining the legitimacy of EU power rules. A perception of geographical under-representation of peripheral Member States in the EU's power structures and decision-making may also contribute to this delegitimisation process, although the majority in such states still tend to favour the EU and can be considered

[38] As at October 2017 http://ec.europa.eu/eurostat/statistics-explained/index.php/Unemploy ment_statistics#Youth_unemployment_trends accessed April 2018; S Karakasidis, 'Nearly Half a Million Greeks Have Left, Bank of Greece Report Finds' *Ekathimerini* (2 July 2016) www.ekathi merini.com/210072/article/ekathimerini/news/nearly-half-a-million-greeks-have-left-bank-of-greece-report-finds accessed April 2018; Magone (n 3), 33–56.

[39] J Rankin, 'Bitter Divisions over Migration Threaten Show of Unity at EU Summit' *The Guardian* (14 December 2017) www.theguardian.com/world/2017/dec/14/divisions-over-migration-spoil-show-of-unity-at-eu-summit-in-brussels accessed April 2018; A Byrne, 'Hungary's Anti-Migrant Campaign Takes Root as Villagers Vent Fury' *Financial Times* (6 October 2017) www.ft.com/content/4ae32ad0-a9cb-11e7-ab55-27219df83c97 accessed April 2018.

[40] J Weiler, 'In the Face of Crisis: Input Legitimacy, Output Legitimacy and the Political Messianism of European Integration' (2012) 34 Journal of European Integration 825.

[41] Migration and terrorism remain the main priorities for 45 per cent and 32 per cent respectively of EU citizens compared to 20 per cent concerns about the economic situation and 10 per cent about the EU's influence in the world, Eurobarometer Standard 86, autumn 2016, Public Opinion in the European Union http://ec.europa.eu/commfrontoffice/publicopinion/index.cfm/Survey/getSurveyDetail/yearFrom/1974/yearTo/2016/surveyKy/2137 accessed April 2018.

[42] ibid. The April 2017 Special Eurobarometer in response to the Commission's White Paper on the Future of Europe saw trust increase to 47 per cent. Yet this should be interpreted with some caution because the questionnaire sequence for this Special Eurobarometer was different from the one used for the biannual Standard Eurobarometer http://ec.europa.eu/commfrontoffice/publicopinion/index .cfm/Survey/getSurveyDetail/yearFrom/1974/yearTo/2017/surveyKy/2173 accessed April 2018.

'Eurocritical' rather than Eurosceptic.[43] The recent announcement of the relocation of the European Banking Authority and the European Medicines Agency to core Member States of France and the Netherlands respectively excludes peripheral Member States without any EU agency (Bulgaria, Romania, Croatia, Cyprus and Slovakia).[44] However, Beetham makes an interesting observation that profound social changes are marked by a shift in belief systems resulting in a disconnect between rules and beliefs, which creates a 'legitimacy gap or deficit'.[45] Arguably, this is what the EU is experiencing and exposure of the disconnect between rules and beliefs helps us understand how legitimacy may be weakened and restored.

3 Expressed Consent as a Legitimacy Criterion

Beetham's third criterion of legitimacy, expressed consent, refers to 'specific *actions* that publicly express and *confer* legitimacy on the powerful'.[46] Expressed consent makes a distinctive contribution towards legitimacy by approving of the power structures that limit freedoms. Beetham refers to the 'symbolic and normative force' of consent as making a distinct contribution to the legitimacy of power.[47] 'Symbolic' in public acknowledgement of power and 'normative' in creating obligations. For consent to have such dual effect it must emerge from 'positive actions taking place in public, since inaction or privacy can have no legitimating force'.[48] Locke, on the other hand, recognised the normative force of both express and tacit consent linking it to whether an individual was fully a subject of the state.[49] Express consent, he suggested, derived from men freely agreeing to be members of a society governed by rules, and 'entering into it by positive engagement and express promise and compact'. Such men, mainly property owners, were full subjects of the state and their express consent was needed before the state could tax them. Tacit consent to the state's authority, on the other hand, was given by all men enjoying the protections and privileges provided by the state. All men, including travellers, visitors and foreigners, could agree to abide by the rules governing continued enjoyment of protections and privileges but this did not make them full subjects of the state.

Locke's distinction is problematic for supporting an undemocratic elitist notion of consent privileging male property-owning classes with voting rights, and today universal suffrage has to some extent democratised the social contract between the

---

43 See Magone's survey of political parties in the European Parliament and southern, central, and eastern European state representation (n 3).

44 J Rankin, 'London Loses EU Agencies to Paris and Amsterdam in Brexit Relocation' *The Guardian* (20 November 2017) www.theguardian.com/politics/2017/nov/20/london-loses-european-medicines-agency-amsterdam-brexit-relocation accessed April 2018.

45 Beetham (n 4) 75.

46 ibid 91.

47 ibid 150.

48 ibid.

49 J Locke, *Two Treatises of Civil Government* (introduction by WS Carpenter, Dent & Sons 1962) 164–66, 177–79; J Locke, *Two Treatises of Government* (CUP 1967) 365–81.

state and people. But in the context of the EU where there is no single state or government, the tacit consent notion has some relevance in terms of peoples across the EU benefiting economically, socially and culturally from the Single Market; free movement of persons, goods, capital and services; and consumer and environmental protection laws. By continuing to enjoy such privileges and protections, are EU citizens providing tacit consent for the EU's authority and legitimacy? The passivity inherent in tacit consent is all too easy to legitimise any authority without requiring much proof or effort. There is a danger of silencing minority and different views, and assuming that participation in a political structure, no matter how directly or indirectly, leads to acceptance and consent. As Hume pointed out, tacit consent can lead to absurdities of the oppressed, vulnerable and weak accepting their lot, and the following criticism has particular relevance to the EU:

> Can we seriously say, that a poor peasant or artisan has a free choice to leave his country, when he knows no foreign language or manners, and lives from day to day, by the small wages which he acquires? We may as well assert, that a man, by remaining in a vessel, freely consents to the domination of the master; though he was carried on board while asleep, and must leap into the ocean, and perish, the moment he leaves her.[50]

Hume considers consent, especially tacit consent, irrelevant and the main reason for legitimation of state power is 'the general interests or necessities of society … because society could not otherwise exist'. Accepting that tacit consent is insufficient to confer legitimacy on the EU, positive actions are needed to demonstrate public support and create binding obligations.

III PUBLIC AND VOLUNTARY ACTS OF CONSENT IN THE EU

Public and voluntary acts of consent represent Beetham's third criterion for legitimacy of power, namely expressed consent. Beetham gives examples as swearing an oath of allegiance, participation in consultations and negotiations with the powerful (i.e. the 'dominant' who invoke power rules), public acclamation, and the electoral and mobilisation modes. Some or all of these may be relevant today to the EU.

1 Public Acts and EU Identity Formation

Swearing an oath of allegiance was traditionally used to legitimise monarchical power and colonial rule.[51] Modern versions are evident in certain professions, such as the army and police, where members swear an oath of loyalty to serve the commander in chief or the head of state in the exercise of their duties. An oath of

---

[50] D Hume, 'Of the Original Contract' in EF Miller (ed), *Essays Moral, Political and Literary* (Liberty Press Indianapolis 1985) 467–78, 480–81.

[51] Beetham (n 4) 92–93.

allegiance is a promise to obey pre-existing rules of governing power and the person or entity vested with that power. There is typically no choice in the person or entity to obey. This form of legitimation is non-existent in the EU. There is no unifying symbol, single authority or national anthem that could serve to galvanise EU citizens into a collective pledge of allegiance to the EU legal order. Entrenched national identities and the consequent lack of a common culture or European *demos* make it unlikely for a collective EU identity to emerge.[52] Some generational differences exist in terms of strength of feeling European or identifying as an EU citizen, which may also be connected to ideas of free movement and job prospects for the young.[53] Clearly, fostering some sense of collective belonging, identity or allegiance is necessary in order to connect the people to the EU and justify its existence. The 2017 European Identity Study for the European Parliament concedes that a 'proper' EU identity is unlikely but fostering a European 'sense of belonging' among citizens is possible and necessary if the EU is to exist with legitimacy and public support. It recommends that a 'sense of belonging' can be cultivated from a 'European culture of remembering' the past supported by 'policies that promote in parallel both a political and a cultural identity, and bring bottom-up initiatives centre stage'.[54] Such a fudged and forged identity lacks coherence or a focal point. It is both insular and chauvinistic in restricting identity formation to a historical perspective that is subject to differing interpretations by Member States and non-Member States.

2 Popular Consent, Elections and Public Mobilisation

Whereas historically consent was confined to politically and economically privileged sections in society (e.g. male property-owners), popular sovereignty changed this to widen the political community of those who could give consent to be governed and also decide on how they would be governed. Legitimacy today requires popular consent, which according to Beetham is expressed in 'the electoral mode', involving the act of voting directly or indirectly for governments, and 'the mobilisation mode', which involves mass participation in political activity at the grass-roots level.[55]

The electoral mode would support the EU 'input legitimacy' thesis, primarily concerned with structures and institutions of the EU that indicate the quality of EU representative bodies and electoral processes, and how these respond to EU citizens' demands.[56] It combines rule-making processes, representation and results. Thus, the

---

[52] Of Europeans, 53 per cent define themselves first by their nationality and then by their European citizenship (Eurobarometer Standard 86, autumn 2016, European Citizenship).

[53] More in the age groups 15–24, 25–39 and 40–54 identify as European than those in the age group 55+ (ibid).

[54] MJ Prutsch, *European Identity* (European Parliament, Policy Department for Structural and Cohesion Policies, Research for CULT Committee, Brussels 2017) 6–7.

[55] Beetham (n 4) 151.

[56] L Hooghe and Gary Marks, 'A Postfunctionalist Theory of European Integration: From Permissive Consensus to Constraining Dissensus' (2009) 39 British Journal of Political Science 1; H Kriesi and

European Parliament is an elected institution providing direct EU citizen representation, but low-level participation in European Parliamentary elections raises doubts about the strength of this representation and about public perception of its legitimacy.[57] Paradoxically, the lack of an elected central EU government (not particularly favoured or advocated by Member States or EU citizens) may diminish the EU's input legitimacy by not giving citizens the opportunity to vote in or out elected representatives who fail to deliver policies, as they would do national governments. Then there is the lack of a coherent EU strategy or policy to direct the direction of EU affairs for a period of term, as elected governments have to provide. Disparate issues, interests, and party political issues are cut across several Member States representing their own national interests before various institutions within the EU. There is an issue-based and representative-based loss of connectivity between citizens and the EU institutional apparatus. This has been referred to as resulting in EU 'policy without politics' and national 'politics without policy'.[58]

The 'public mobilisation mode' may provide legitimacy to those vested with power, and serve as an alternative to the electoral process for legitimising certain policies.[59] Unlike swearing an oath of allegiance, and participation in consultations and negotiations, public mobilisation carries no obligation. It is voluntary, needs to be continually demonstrated, and its legitimating effect depends on the quality of the action taken.[60] The latter is based on a belief system which the public can embrace and sustain through continuous engagement in political activity. Such a system may be re-legitimised through a shift from the mobilisation mode to the electoral mode. But the shifting from electoral to mobilisation mode is 'highly unlikely to prove effective, for the simple reason that the continuous mobilisation necessary to legitimation depends upon the vitality of a belief system or cause, and these are typically the product of popular movements of opposition, which cannot simply be called up to order from above'.[61] This raises a problem for the EU. Growing unease and disaffection among EU citizens, and claims of an EU democratic deficit are not resolved by electing members to the European Parliament and point to more fundamental normative issues such as the lack of a common European identity, and the lack of a belief system that can mobilise EU citizens to engage in political activity which would legitimise the EU's power.

---

others (eds), *West European Politics in the Age of Globalisation* (CUP 2008); S Hix, *What's Wrong with the Europe Union and How to Fix It* (Polity 2008).

[57] Overall turnout across the twenty-eight Member States at the 2014 European Parliamentary elections was 42.5 per cent with some very low and very high individual Member State turnouts (e.g. Czech Republic 18.2 per cent, Slovakia 13.1 per cent, Belgium 89.6 per cent, Luxembourg 85.6 per cent), see Eurostat, *Voter turnout in national and EU parliamentary elections* ec.europa.eu/eurostat/tgm/refreshTableAction.do?tab=table&plugin=1&pcode=tsdgo310&language=en accessed April 2018.

[58] VA Schmidt, *Democracy in Europe* (OUP 2006) 156.

[59] Beetham (n 4) 93–94.

[60] ibid 95.

[61] ibid 158.

This problem calls for a more grass-roots-based approach that can mobilise significant EU-wide public sentiment and commitment towards commonly held, perhaps even viscerally felt, values and expectations. Public deliberation, engagement and commitment needs to be at the forefront of creating and sustaining a belief system that can legitimise the EU's existence and purpose. Does this assume there is any ground for commonality? And is it a realistic prospect? We should perhaps understand commonality in terms of levels. At a functional level, core–peripheral, old–new Member States share commonality in being part of a polity that maintains peace and sustains trade. Short of conflict or trading wars impacting on all Member States, it is hard to see continuous public mobilisation around these issues. A belief system built on peace and prosperity is functional rather than viscerally felt as part of identity, and not unique to the EU. Many non-EU states, trading blocs, international organisations and military alliances fulfil the same purpose.

The idea of a viscerally felt belief system as part of identity is being taken to extremes by some EU Member State governments. Seizing on the belief-system gap, they are exploiting public sentiment towards the refugee, migrant, and/or Muslim 'other', and calling for the EU to be based on Christianity.[62] But, as noted previously, religion as a single source of legitimacy is unsustainable in today's world, especially in states with multi-ethnic groups, and secular and tolerant tendencies. There is a difference between religion as the source of rules, and religion as a factor to consider in the creation, interpretation, and application of rules. Contemporary resurgence in religious justification (e.g. debate on changing the abortion law in Poland; exclusion of migrants in Hungary) is an example of national power elites exerting their own interests and belief systems rather than providing a single source of legitimacy for the EU. With limited issue-based agendas, these elites occupy contested spaces of protest and opposition, and are unlikely to yield pan-European appeal. They may even cause public mobilisation in core Member States to reaffirm values of representative democracy, rule of law and respect for human rights.

Beyond the functional level, what are the common wants and aspirations of EU citizens that can translate into values? Although identifying 'basic human needs' (e.g. leading fulfilling lives in work; travelling for leisure and pleasure; interaction with different cultures; setting up business and community-based enterprises) seems unimaginative and unambitious, it offers a grass-roots-based approach that gets close to a viscerally felt belief system, with potential for continuous public mobilisation. Of course, 'basic human needs' is contestable and a more fundamental commonality may emerge whereby EU citizens consider 'the system broke' and in need of reform.

---

[62] J Brunsden, 'Orban: EU's "Christian Identity" under Threat from Muslim Migrants' *Financial Times* (30 March 2017) www.ft.com/content/7ecde2c2-af12-329a-9133-29a7bee08e31 accessed April 2018; I Traynor, 'Migration Crisis: Hungary PM Says Europe in Grip of Madness' *The Guardian* (3 September 2015) www.theguardian.com/world/2015/sep/03/migration-crisis-hungary-pm-victor-orban-europe-response-madness accessed April 2018.

3 National Referendums

National referendums may be considered the most advanced form of direct democracy with examples across the EU of Member States resorting to this mechanism. Ireland established the constitutional practice of referendums for EU Treaty reforms.[63] Section 20(2) of the Danish Constitution allows for transfer of powers to the EU by statute adopted by a five-sixths parliamentary majority or simple majority public vote. Ireland, Denmark and the UK are the only Member States constitutionally requiring a referendum. Referendums in France, the Netherlands, Spain and Luxembourg in 2005 on the Constitutional Treaty were not constitutionally required.[64] But extensive and ill-considered use of referendums represent a clumsy brake on EU decision-making and provide a hollow sense of empowerment for citizens.[65] Voting on technical areas may lead to voter apathy, low turnouts, greater disconnection from the EU, and an undermining of its legitimacy. Voting on more substantive issues, such as citizenship and free movement rights, connects more easily with daily lives and fosters an internal belief system that sustains legitimacy.

An example of the clumsy brake scenario is the UK's 2011 European Union Act requiring referendums in broad EU areas relating to the full range of EU institutions' competences, as well as broad policy areas. For example, an act of parliament and a referendum is required for: revisions to the TEU and TFEU; amendment of the TFEU under the simplified revision procedure; extension of existing EU exclusive, shared or supported competence, or conferral of a new one; social policy; common defence; participation in the European Public Prosecutor's Office; the environment; EU finance; enhanced cooperation; and border control.[66] This exceeds what some of the more active legislatures in Member States are required to do. In Germany, for example, where there is a developed understanding of democratic participation with a constitutionally protected right to vote from which state organs derive legitimacy, only prior legislative approval is necessary for participation in decisions under Article 48(7) TEU and Article 352 TFEU.[67] In contrast, the Czech Republic does not require prior parliamentary approval for use of Article 352 TFEU or Article 48(7) TEU.[68]

---

[63] Irish Supreme Court, Case 1986 No 12036P, *Crotty v An Taoiseach*, [1987] IR 713.

[64] See F Mendez and M Mendez, 'Referendums and European Integration: Beyond the Lisbon Vote' (2010) Public Law 223.

[65] O Ulgen, 'Strengthening European Union Democratic Accountability Through National and Treaty-Based Pre-legislative Controls' (2015) 16 German Law Journal 741–780.

[66] European Union Act 2011, c 12 (the EU Act). See in particular s 2(2) (Treaty revisions relating to the TEU or TFEU); 3(2) (amendment of the TFEU under the simplified revision procedure); 4(1) (extension of an existing EU competence or conferral of a new one); 4(1)(k)–(m) (changes to a voting procedure); 6(5) (social policy; common defence; participation in the European Public Prosecutor's Office; environment; EU finance; enhanced cooperation; and border control). For a fuller analysis of the Act, see Ulgen, ibid 751–56.

[67] *Treaty of Lisbon*, BVerfGE (German Constitutional Court), 2BvE 2/08, Judgment of 30 June 2009, para 409.

[68] *Treaty of Lisbon*, ÚS 19/08 (Czech Constitutional Court) (n 22) paras 150, 165.

The UK's Brexit referendum of 23 June 2016 is an example of an ill-considered popular vote mechanism on a crude question of whether to remain or leave the EU. The apparent empowerment of the British people was without full information or consideration of the political and economic conditions and consequences.[69] On such an important constitutional and EU-wide issue the referendum result (marginal majority of 51.9 per cent in favour of leaving and 48.1 per cent supporting remaining in the EU) cannot be considered authoritative and has created demographic and geographical divisions within the UK. Voting was likely to be different in England, Wales, Scotland, Northern Ireland, each voting on their own particular interests. In *Miller* v. *Secretary of State for Exiting the European Union* the Supreme Court considered that the devolved administrations had limited legislative and executive powers to affect the UK government's decision to trigger Article 50 TFEU to withdraw from the EU. A constitutional convention requiring prior consent of devolved administrations for constitutional decisions affecting them was deemed a 'political convention' without giving rise to a legally enforceable obligation.[70] Rather than 'facilitating harmonious relationships between the UK Parliament and the devolved legislatures'[71] such a pronouncement is likely to achieve the opposite.

The Greek bail-out referendum of 5 July 2015 can be seen as a symbolic gesture of real and imagined direct democracy.[72] After the EU imposed harsh austerity measures on debt-ridden Greece, the public expressed their discontent with the majority voting against the EU bail-out terms. Yet this was too little too late. Although the referendum restored a degree of national dignity it failed to achieve the desired effect of forcing the EU to recognise the expressed non-consent of EU citizens in Greece. The national government further cemented rejection of direct democracy as a means of (de)legitimising the EU by disregarding the vote and capitulating to the bail-out terms.

4 Article 11(4) TEU European Citizens' Initiative

One clear way in which citizens can engage in a participatory mechanism to try to influence EU policy-making is through use of the European Citizens' Initiative under Article 11(4) TEU and Regulation 211/2011. If one million citizens vote across at least seven EU Member States for change in EU law on a given matter, the

---

[69] PJJ Welfens, 'Cameron's Information Disaster in the Referendum of 2016: An Exit from Brexit?' (2016) 13 International Economic and Economic Policy 539 argues that key economic data was not presented to the public and this justifies holding a second referendum.

[70] *R (on the application of Miller and another) (Respondents) v Secretary of State for Exiting the European Union (Appellant)* [2017] UKSC 5.

[71] ibid para 151.

[72] For critical analysis of how hope and fear were used during the referendum, see S Boukala and D Dimitrakopoulou, 'The Politics of Fear vs the Politics of Hope: Analysing the 2015 Greek Election and Referendum Campaigns' (2017) 14 Critical Discourse Studies 39.

Commission is obliged to consider the petition. The Commission can reject an ECI for failure to meet admissibility requirements (e.g. manifestly beyond competence) or once it is considered by the relevant EU institution, it can still be rejected. The ECI process is a manifestation of evolved democratic principles based on public participation outside of the formal institutional structures of the EU. It combines elements of majoritarian voting, grass-roots organisation and influence by non-governmental organisations, and popular voting for new legislation.[73] It has the potential to create a 'public-opinion, mobilisation and contested space' where policies rather than the EU polity are contested, contributing to legitimacy.[74] It also has potential to act as a means of raising public awareness about EU matters, although perhaps not being a mechanism for direct citizen influence on policy formulation. There is a level of acceptance in the legitimacy of the process with participants believing it is a means to influence policy.

Strict voting requirements of at least one million citizens from at least one-quarter of Member States with minimum signatures from each of the latter (e.g. for the UK the minimum is 54,000),[75] sets a form of majority voting to attract sufficient public interest and justify Commission consideration. But the majoritarian analogy is not entirely relevant because ECIs do not compete against each other for popular votes. It is conceivable that several ECIs may satisfy the voting requirements and merit consideration, although they will compete for prioritisation by the European Parliament and Council. ECIs introduce a form of popular voting for new legislation by seeking and obtaining public support for a particular issue to be put before the Commission. Even though the Commission is not obliged to recommend legislative action, it must take account of the public will. To ensure ECIs are representative and similar conditions for supporting them apply in Member States,[76] certain minimum and procedural requirements must be satisfied before submission to the Commission. Signatories do not need to be registered to vote but they must be of voting age for the European Parliamentary elections, which is generally 18 years old except for Austria where it is 16. Apart from third country nationals being excluding, there are no residency restrictions. EU citizens living outside the EU can support an ECI, and the support from non-national EU citizens residing in another Member State can be counted in either state.[77]

But even if this form of popular voting could be considered a public, albeit voluntary, act of consent it is not pervasive to represent EU citizens' conferral of legitimacy on the EU. Problems exist in relation to the complexity of registration

---

[73]   See A Auer, 'European Citizens' Initiative' (2005) 1 European Constitutional Law Review 79, for discussion of ECI as 'a popular appeal to the Commission to initiate legislation' rather than a petition, popular motion or popular initiative.

[74]   ibid.

[75]   Regulation (EU) 211/2011 of the European Parliament and the Council on the citizens' initiative [2011] OJ L65/1 ('Citizen's Initiative Regulation'), art 7(2). See Annex I for minimum number of signatories.

[76]   ibid, recitals 5 and 6.

[77]   ibid, Art 3(4).

rules, the high rate of refusals to register proposed ECIs, the low rate of successful ECIs and their limited impact.[78] Although the Commission recently attempted to address these problems in proposing a new regulation (e.g. lowering the voting age to 16; partial registration of initiatives; simplification of signatories' data requirements; Commission helpdesk and online discussion forum),[79] these merely serve to illustrate the bureaucratic burden of such a process and do nothing to engender a sense of civic duty or empowerment of EU citizens. The autumn 2016 Eurobarometer indicates that 61 per cent of EU citizens are not likely to use ECIs.[80] Doubts have been raised as to whether it is used by more active civil society groups, and therefore can potentially have more impact, as opposed to lesser known ad hoc groups seeking to raise the profile of a particular issue.[81] Depending on how many ECIs are declared inadmissible, this could operate as a disincentive for groups who may consider the process removes the citizen further away from decision-making, therefore delegitimising it.

Neither Article 11(4) nor Regulation 211/2011 require citizens supporting the ECI to be from a cross-section of Member States (e.g. core–peripheral; northern–southern economies; old–new; eurozone–non-eurozone). Potentially, certain Member States' citizens may propose an issue for legislation that is not necessarily representative of citizens throughout the EU. Those in Member States with developed civil societies and non-governmental organisations, strong advocacy skills and high levels of engagement with domestic politics will have an advantage to promote their cause. Equally, there may be more of a realistic chance that a proposed ECI is successful with such resources and advocacy experience, and the ECI may benefit all citizens, including those from non-Member States. An example is the Right2Water ECI representing a global issue pursued by the European Public Services Unions.[82] Even if the proposed ECI secures the minimum number of signatories, the Commission is obliged to consult as widely as possible with relevant stakeholders before it proposes legislation, taking account of regional and local dimensions of the action and to ensure EU action is coherent and transparent.[83] Ultimately, the Commission decides whether to recommend legislative action to the European Parliament and the Council, and it is not obliged to do so. It must, however, give reasons for its legal and political conclusions on the ECI, and the action it intends to take.

---

[78] Commission, 'Proposal for a Regulation on the European Citizens' Initiative' COM (2017) 482 final.
[79] ibid.
[80] Eurobarometer Standard 86 (n 41).
[81] L Bo Garcia, 'How Could the New Article 11 TEU Contribute to Reduce the EU's Democratic Malaise?' in M Dougan, N Shuibhne and E Spaventa (eds), *Empowerment and Disempowerment of the European Citizen* (Hart 2012) ch 11.
[82] European Citizens' Initiative Official Register, 'Water and Sanitation Are a Human Right! Water Is a Public Good, Not a Commodity!' (10 May 2012) ECI(2012)000003 http://ec.europa.eu/citizens-initiative/public/initiatives/successful/details/2012/000003 accessed April 2018.
[83] Protocol (No 2) on the Application of the Principles of Subsidiarity and Proportionality, Arts 2 and 11(3) TEU.

The Right2Water ECI requested the Commission to propose legislation that: (1) obliged EU institutions and Member States to ensure that all inhabitants enjoy the right to water and sanitation; (2) water supply and management of water resources not be subject to 'internal market rules' and that water services be excluded from liberalisation; and (3) the EU increases its efforts to achieve universal access to water and sanitation. The Commission did not recommend introducing specific legisla- tion to recognise a right to water and sanitation per se, and referred to existing EU and international legislation. It noted its limited legislative competence in relation to national decisions governing the ownership regime for water undertakings, and referred to EU public procurement rules that require public authority outsourcing to be transparent and the most beneficial offer to users.[84] It was, however, prepared to take concrete measures in relation to universal access to water and sanitation, and in 2018 proposed revising the existing Drinking Water Directive.[85] Water is an issue affecting all EU citizens and the ECI managed to attract over 1.8 million signatures. Yet the power rules governing EU–Member State competences restricted the extent of any pan-European legislation. In the specific case of Greece, privatisation of drinking water services was incorporated in the bail-out agreement of August 2015 with ensuing conditionality reviews.[86]

5 Article 11(2) TEU Civil Society Engagement

Another means of voluntary participation in EU political activities is through civil society organisations engaging with EU institutions in policy formulation processes. Participation in consultations and negotiations is a promise to obey pre-existing rules of governing power and the person or entity vested with power.[87] An example is collective bargaining by trade unions with the employer over terms and conditions of employment. Under the Social Dialogue mechanism in Articles 154 and 155 TFEU, the Commission must consult management and labour at the Union level before making proposals in the social policy field. More generally, EU citizens can seek information and make representations to EU institutions in an attempt to influence policy. Article 11(2) TEU requires EU institutions to 'maintain an open, transparent and regular dialogue with representative associations and civil society', without defining who or what these 'representative associations' and 'civil society'

---

[84] Commission, 'Communication on the European Citizens' Initiative, 'Water and Sanitation Are a Human Right! Water Is a Public Good, Not a Commodity!' COM(2014) 177 final.

[85] Council Directive 98/83/EC of 3 November 1998 on the quality of water intended for human consumption [1998] OJ L 330/32; Commission, 'Proposal for a Directive on the Quality of Water Intended for Human Consumption' COM(2017) 753 final.

[86] European Commission (acting on behalf of the European Stability Mechanism), The Hellenic Republic and the Bank of Greece, 'Memorandum of Understanding' (19 August 2015), cl 4.4, and Annex 1 HRDAF Asset Development Plan (30 July 2015), which requires 11 per cent sale of shares in Athens Water Supply & Sewerage SA and 23 per cent in Thessaloniki Water Supply & Sewerage SA.

[87] Beetham (n 4) 93.

might be. This leaves room for well-established and ad hoc civil society groups to be involved. Its origins relate to established civil society groups wanting an institutionalised civil society dialogue.[88] This raises a question as to whether civil society engagement can be representative of EU citizens and EU-wide issues. It has been argued that whether a group is able to attract democratic and public debates could be used as a criterion of representativeness.[89] Ultimately, civil society groups may serve to inform policy but their status is consultative rather than formal, and there is no EU obligation of prior public consultation before passing certain policies or laws.

Civil society engagement comes closest to what Vivien Schmidt has dubbed 'throughput legitimacy'. 'Throughput legitimacy', which Schmidt describes as the 'black box' of EU governance,[90] is concerned with not only the efficacy of EU policy-making processes, but also their accountability, transparency, and openness to civil society. Unlike 'input' and 'output' legitimacy (derived from processes *by* the people, and *for* the people respectively),[91] more accountability or openness does not impact on public perception of legitimacy, or make up for problems with either input or output legitimacy.[92] In the Eurozone sovereign debt crisis, austerity-based output policies for Greece in need of a bail-out, and Ireland and Portugal protected under the European Financial Stability Facility, involved a trade-off with national input legitimacy, due to these governments having to surrender economic autonomy to the EU–IMF experts.[93] No matter how open, transparent, and accountable the Greek bail-out terms are, this does not compensate for the lack of national input. And after several years of austerity resulting in political and economic instability, the bail-out terms may prove to lack output legitimacy.

The 'throughput legitimacy' model considers processes through which EU citizens, not as voters but as interest groups, may influence policy-making.[94] There is some evidence of this already in the EU through consultative and representative status and involvement of interest groups, NGOs, consumer groups, think-tanks, environmental and social groups. Such EU citizen involvement may counter the voids left by the lack of a fully representative democracy within the EU. But there are a number of problems with this form of legitimacy acquisition. First, it atomises and localises certain issues and groups which may not translate or reflect national political concerns and citizens' interests. Second, lack of awareness and knowledge of these processes will prevent access, just as much as an unreachable and overly

---

[88] Garcia (n 81).

[89] ibid.

[90] VA Schmidt, 'Democracy and Legitimacy in the European Union' in Jones, Menon and Weatherill (eds) (n 3) 663.

[91] These terms were originally coined by FW Scharpf, *Demokratietheorie zwischen Utopie und Anpassung* (Konstanz, Universitätsverlag 1970). See also FW Scharpf, *Games Real Actors Play* (Westview 1997); FW Scharpf, *Governing in Europe* (OUP 1999).

[92] VA Schmidt, 'Democracy and Legitimacy in the European Union Revisited: Input, Output and "Throughput"' (2013) 61 Political Studies 2, 7–8 and 13–17.

[93] ibid 18.

[94] Schmidt (n 90) and (n 58).

bureaucratic accreditation and consultation process may dissuade many from participating. Finally, there are institutional policy-making rules which hinder accountability, transparency and openness. The unanimity rule, for example, means that any Member State may veto an agreement causing delays or no agreement. And Member States' resistance to differentiated or two-track integration may lead to less rather than more unity, solidarity, and integration. Interestingly, Schmidt regards 'throughput legitimacy' as supplementing rather than substituting 'output' or 'input' legitimacy.

IV CONCLUSION

Rule-based validity of the EU is insufficient to justify its existence and the rules. Reference to EU law as evidence of the EU's legitimacy does not explain why those particular rules were chosen, nor does it account for reform. EU power rules assume the most significant relationship is between the EU and Member States whereas the real question is whether EU citizens recognise an internal belief system that sustains legitimacy. The Western liberal tradition of representative democracy and values of democracy, rule of law, and respect for human rights exist as imports from core Member States. But as the enlargement process and Greek bail-out crisis show, these values are not necessarily sufficient to form 'a common framework of belief' legitimising the EU. The CEES enlargement process embedded problems of legitimacy by imposing values that were not democratically deliberated within the new states, and were not required of the older Member States or evident in the EU supranational governance structure. Even with the Greek referendum's symbolic gesture of real and imagined direct democracy, the same lack of national input occurred over the Greek bail-out. Terms were imposed, not negotiated. From these examples the EU can be likened to an 'administrative state'; more concerned about efficiency and outcomes than nurturing common values. This results in a disconnect between rules and beliefs creating a legitimacy gap.

Swearing an oath of allegiance is non-existent in the EU. There is no unifying symbol, single authority or national anthem to galvanise EU citizens into a collective pledge of allegiance to the EU legal order. Entrenched national identities, the lack of a common culture or European *demos* make it unlikely for a collective EU identity to emerge. But some sort of collective identity or allegiance is necessary to connect the people to the EU and justify its existence. A grass-roots-based approach is needed to mobilise EU-wide public sentiment and commitment towards commonly held, perhaps even viscerally felt, values and expectations. For example, a functional belief system may exist in relation to maintaining peace and sustaining trade. But short of conflict and trading wars, this is unlikely to inspire continuous public mobilisation. Beyond the functional, identifying 'basic human needs' may offer a grass-roots-based approach that gets close to a viscerally felt belief system, with potential for continuous public mobilisation.

As tempting as it is to regard national referendums a solution to the EU's legitimation problems, the UK and Greek examples show how they can be misused as clumsy brakes on decision-making, raising false expectations of citizens' empowerment. When used appropriately for voting on substantive issues, such as citizenship and free movement rights, referendums are more likely to connect with EU citizens' lives and foster an internal belief system that sustains legitimacy. The ECI process is not pervasive, does not engender a sense of civic duty or empowerment, and the majority of EU citizens would not use it. Civil society engagement on its own cannot serve as a means of legitimising the EU and supplements other more robust forms of legitimation, such as the justifiability of EU power rules within an internal belief system. On the sixtieth anniversary of the Treaty of Rome, what the EU is experiencing in terms of a disconnect between rules and beliefs represents a 'legitimacy gap or deficit'. But perhaps this is a necessary and transitory consequence in order to achieve social change and reform.

The Crisis as a Crisis of the EU's Economic Model

PART III

The Crisis as a Crisis of the EU's Economic Model

10

The Fiscal Compact

A *Paradoxical Fiscal Governance Machine*

Vanessa Bilancetti

I INTRODUCTION

This chapter analyses the Treaty on Stability Coordination and Governance (TSCG), as an emblematic example of the New Economic Governance. The New Economic Governance is the ensemble of economic and fiscal reforms that were introduced in the wake of the financial crisis. In this work, when we talk about New Economic Governance we refer specifically to: the European Semester;[1] the Six-Pack;[2] the Two-Pack;[3] and the TSCG, better known by the name of its Third

---

[1]   The European Semester was launched, first, as a code of conduct for the implementation of the Stability and Growth Pact (SGP), and was later codified in the Six-Pack. See Regulation 1175/2011 (EU) of the European Parliament and of the Council of 16 November 2011 on the strengthening of the surveillance of budgetary positions and the surveillance and coordination of economic policies [2011] OJ L306/12.

[2]   In the rest of this work when we use the term Six-Pack, we refer to the six normative measures that compose it: Regulation 1175/2011 (EU) of the European Parliament and of the Council of 16 November 2011 on the strengthening of the surveillance of budgetary positions and the surveillance and coordination of economic policies [2011] OJ L306/12; Council Regulation (EU) No 1177/2011 of 8 November 2011 amending Regulation (EC) No 1467/97 on speeding up and clarifying the imple-mentation of the excessive deficit procedure [2011] OJ L306/33; Regulation (EU) No 1173/2011 of the European Parliament and of the Council of 16 November 2011 on the effective enforcement of budgetary surveillance in the euro area [2011] OJ L306/1; Council Directive 2011/85/EU of 8 November 2011 on requirements for budgetary frameworks of the Member States [2011] OJ L306/41; and the so-called Macroeconomic Imbalance Procedure, namely Regulation 1176/2011 Regulation (EU) No 1176/2011 of the European Parliament and of the Council of 16 November 2011 on the prevention and correction of macroeconomic imbalances [2011] OJ 2011 L306/25 and Regulation (EU) No 1174/2011 of the European Parliament and of the Council of 16 November 2011 on enforcement measures to correct excessive macroeconomic imbalances in the Euro area [2011] OJ L306/8.

[3]   In the rest of this work when we use the term Two-Pack, we refer to the two instruments that compose it: Regulation (EU) No 473/2013 of the European Parliament and of the Council of 21 May 2013 on common provisions for monitoring and assessing draft budgetary plans and ensuring the correction of excessive deficit of the Member States in the euro area [2013] OJ L140/11; Regulation (EU) No 472/2013 of the European Parliament and of the Council of 21 May 2013 on the strengthening of economic and budgetary surveillance of Member States in the euro area experiencing or threatened with serious difficulties with respect to their financial stability [2013] OJ L140/1.

Title, 'Fiscal Compact'. All these measures have been adopted by European institutions to deal with the financial speculation on the euro and the financial crisis after 2008. Together with the Financial Aid Programmes[4] and the extraordinary measures of the European Central Bank (ECB), these financial and economic regulations form the institutional answer to the financial crisis in Europe. But if the Financial Aid Programmes and the ECB's extraordinary measures were thought of as temporary and exceptional, the New Economic Governance was conceived as the long-term legislative solution to the financial crisis.

While the measures that form part of the New Economic Governance each have their own specificities, they all share the same aim: to mitigate market pressures in the eurozone over the short term, and to resolve the financial crisis and ensure that it is not repeated over the long term. In doing this, they recognise and aim to tackle one main problem: the excessive deficits and debt of Member States. All the other problems faced by the European Union (EU) – the banking crisis, financial instability, unemployment, low or stagnant growth – have been considered effects of uncontrolled spending. For this reason, the New Economic Governance is a reaffirmation and reinforcement of the Stability and Growth Pact (SGP), and of the institutional architecture established by Maastricht. And since the TSCG was negotiated and voted to deal specifically with the excessive spending of Member States, we consider it is an emblematic example of, and thus able to explain, the overall logic of the New Economic Governance.

The incapacity to recognise any other structural problem beyond fiscal stability, we argue, reflects, above all, a broader problem about the way European integration has been traditionally conceptualised, that is to say a theoretical failure of European Studies itself. In that sense, this chapter seeks to contribute to the call for more dissenting voices in European Studies,[5] going beyond the debate between neo-functionalism and intergovernmentalism. It does so by drawing upon two critical

---

[4]   From 2008, different EU countries have received assistance under different programmes. The first programmes were signed in 2008/09 with non-euro countries. All aid programmes were agreed together with a set of structural reforms and a strict plan for the repayment of the loan. In October 2008, Hungary was the first country to ask and receive financial aid from the EU, followed by Latvia in December 2008 and Romania in May 2009 (renewed in 2011 and 2013). Greece was the first euro country to sign a financial assistance programme as a bilateral agreement – the Greek Loan Facility (GLF) – pooled by the European Commission along with IMF commitment in May 2010. In February 2015, a second programme for Greece was released by the European Financial Stability Facility (EFSF); in August 2015 followed by a third programme under the European Stability Mechanism (ESM) framework. Greece was followed by Ireland in December 2010 and Portugal in May 2011 while Spain agreed on a financial assistance for bank recapitalisation in July 2012. Finally, in May 2013, Cyprus signed a financial assistance programme with the ESM. All data bout the financial aid programmes can be found at https://ec.europa.eu/info/business-economy-euro/economic-and-fiscal-policy-coordination/eu-financial-assistance_en accessed April 2018.

[5]   I Manners and R Whitman, 'Another Theory Is Possible: Dissident Voices in Theorising Europe' (2016) 54 Journal of Common Market Studies 3.

approaches, namely governmentalities studies, and historical materialism, inspired by Gramsci and the neo-Gramscian in International Relations (IR).[6]

Section II of the chapter explains our conceptual framework. The chapter deploys governmentality to examine the legal text of the TSCG, its rationality and techniques. In particular, we use governmentality as a sort of 'radical institutionalism', to explore what we define as a *fiscal governance machine*. But this approach is unable to explain the broader socio-economic context. For this reason, it is necessary to intertwine it with a historical–materialist approach inspired by Gramsci. This will solve the apparent paradox that in the moment when the entire economy is based on debt, European Member States are asked to have their budget balanced or in surplus.

Section III introduces the negotiation process of the TSCG, which very clearly revealed the power relations, and the dominance of Germany, in the European space. However, this dominance did not manage to become fully hegemonic in Gramscian terms.[7] Eventually, and contrary to Germany's suggestions, the TSCG was approved outside the EU legal framework and the majority of Member States did not implement it at the constitutional level, but only through ordinary laws.

Section IV explores the TSCG in relation to what we refer to as a *fiscal governance machine*, comprising a set of technologies and an apparatus of knowledge and power set up by the SGP, and reinforced by the New Economic Governance. In particular we analyse Article 3 and its provisions, highlighting three important features of the overall New Economic Governance: a new discretionary power of the European Commission, the automatisation or semi-automatisation of rules, and the independence of the relevant national agency from state institutions.

Section V places the *fiscal governance machine* in the broader context of the financial-led regime of capital accumulation. The section sketches the pattern of indebtedness in the European space, and the transformation of the role of public debt, from a leverage for full employment to a mechanism of control of the financial

---

[6] Neo-Gramscian approaches have been labelled a 'school', a term that helps to identify a particular set of ideas and lines of research that today constitute among the most important alternatives to mainstream international relations and international political economy. Here we prefer to adopt the term 'approach' because it highlights the diversities between the different authors, while using the singular form to stress the similarities. See AD Morton, 'The Sociology of Theorising and Neo-Gramscian Perspectives: The Problems of "School" Formation in IPE' in A Bieler and AD Morton (eds), *Social Forces in the Making of the New Europe: The Restructuring of European Social Relations in the Global Political Economy* (Palgrave Macmillan 2001) 41. By contrast, governmentality studies are much less systematic and references to Foucault are employed in very different ways by different authors. In fact, Rose affirms that governmentality studies should not aim to become a general theory on power, but should offer a perspective for possible future studies. See N Rose, *Powers of Freedom: Reframing Political Thought* (CUP 1999) 21.

[7] For Gramsci, hegemony is the capacity to lead through consensus, protected by the armour of coercion (A Gramsci, *Prison Notebook* (Columbia UP 1996) Q 6, para 88).

market over states. In fact, in the European space, the process of financialisation has always been closely linked, rather than opposed, to the rules on fiscal discipline.

Section VI continues to contextualise the *fiscal governance machine* in relation to the uneven construction of the European Monetary Union (EMU). The EMU strategically privileges some actors and interests over others, increasing, rather than mitigating, disparities. In fact, given fiscal stability is simply unachievable for some Member States under the existing rules and economic conditions, such stability effectively becomes a way to control the political economy of Member States.

II CONCEPTUAL FRAMEWORK

When the crisis began in 2007, European Studies found themselves largely unable to come to grips with the socio-political and economic situation. As the crisis developed, it became even more evident that we lacked the instruments to fully comprehend it. One of the main problems is that European Studies are still centred on the debate between neo-functionalism and intergovernmentalism, between the centrality of supranational institutions or the centrality of Member States. From a neo-functionalist point of view, the Euro crisis can be read as the outcome of a 'functional dissonance' present in the EMU[8] and hence as a direct consequence of the incomplete architecture designed by Maastricht. As a result, the New Economic Governance should solve this functional dissonance, and eventually complete the process of integration. In this sense, the New Economic Governance is but a *spillover* effect of the integration process.[9]

During the crisis, new intergovernmental readings have flourished due to the new centrality assumed by Member States and by intergovernmental institutions, such as the Council or the Euro Summit. Schimmelfennig explains the New Economic Governance by looking into intergovernmental bargaining. These negotiations were based on convergent interests for maintaining the euro, but divergent interests on the distribution of adjustment costs. These different preferences, according to him, led to a 'chicken game' situation characterised by 'hard bargaining and brinkmanship'.[10]

The debate between neo-functionalism and intergovernmentalism initially prevented the diversification of theoretical inquiries of the crisis and marginalised dissenting voices in the discipline. In the last few years, however, many critical approaches arose in the analysis of European integration.[11] They have criticised

---

[8] A Niemann and D Ioannou, 'European Economic Integration in Times of Crisis: A Case of Neofunctionalism?' (2015) 22 Journal of European Public Policy 196, 198.

[9] The concept of spillover was first introduced by Haas and denotes the process through which sectors integrated initially spillover into neighbouring sectors (EB Haas, *The Uniting of Europe: Political, Social, and Economic Forces: 1950–1957* (Stanford UP 1968)).

[10] F Schimmelfennig, 'Liberal Intergovernmentalism and the Euro Area Crisis' (2015) 22 Journal of European Public Policy 177.

[11] For an idea of the different theories, see Manners and Whitman (n 5).

mainstream European integrationists mainly for: their rational understanding of actors;[12] a certain progressive idea of integration based on the assumption that more integration is positive per se;[13] and a problem-solving approach, rather than critical and holistic explanations.[14]

This chapter builds primarily on two main critical approaches: governmentality studies and a neo-Gramscian approach. There are many similarities and differences between Gramsci and Foucault. Here we focus on how governmentality studies have analysed power relations in the European space and how they have explained the diffusion of neoliberalism, before identifying their limits and trying to overcome them through a historical–materialist analysis inspired by Gramsci.

In the two lectures on governmentality,[15] Foucault connects his previous analysis on discursive formations[16] and disciplinary power[17] to a new set of problems: how power is exercised on a population and how this power rationalises itself. In these lectures, Foucault examines how a pluralisation of discourses is articulated in 'a rational art of government'.[18] First, he examines the emergence of the liberal art of government in the eighteen century,[19] and then, its reaffirmation with ordoliberalism and neoliberalism.[20]

International governmentality studies[21] have applied a governmentality approach to analyse the emergence and transformation of global governance. According to Walters and Haahr, governmentality as a form of political analysis explores mainly four issues: rationality, forms of power, subjectivity, and technologies.[22] First,

---

[12]   ibid.

[13]   MJ Ryner, 'Financial Crisis, Orthodoxy and Heterodoxy in the Production of Knowledge about the EU' (2012) 40 Millennium – Journal of International Studies 647.

[14]   For Cox, critical theory, differently from problem-solving theory, asks how orders have come about and how they might change. For this reason, Cox suggests that critical theory is more appropriate to analyse periods of crisis, when orders are under pressure (R Cox, 'Social Forces, States and World Orders: Beyond International Relations Theory' (1981) 10 Millennium Journal of International Studies 126–28).

[15]   M Foucault, *Security, Territory, Population* (Palgrave Macmillan 2009); M Foucault, *The Birth of Biopolitics* (Palgrave Macmillan 2008).

[16]   M Foucault, *The Archaeology of Knowledge and the Discourse on Language* (Pantheon Books 1972).

[17]   M Foucault, *Discipline and Punish: The Birth of the Prison* (Vintage 1995).

[18]   Foucault analyses how from the sixteen century the treaties regarding politics are no longer presented as advice to the prince, but as 'arts of government' (*Security, Territory, Population* (n 15) 88).

[19]   ibid.

[20]   Foucault, *Birth of Biopolitics* (n 15).

[21]   D Rosenow, 'Decentring Global Power: The Merits of a Foucauldian Approach to International Relations' (2009) 23 Global Society 497; T Fougner, 'The State, International Competitiveness and Neoliberal Globalisation: Is There a Future beyond "the Competition State"?' (2006) 32 Review of International Studies Foreign Affairs 165; M Merlingen, 'Foucault and World Politics: Promises and Challenges of Extending Governmentality Theory to the European and Beyond' (2006) 35 Millennium – Journal of International Studies 181; W Walters and W Larner, *Global Governmentality. Governing International Spaces* (Routledge 2004); W Walters, 'Some Critical Notes on "Governance"' (2004) 73 Studies in Political Economy 27.

[22]   W Walters and JH Haahr, *Governing Europe* (Routledge 2005) 6–20.

rationalities[23] can be disclosed looking at discursive formations, connecting discourse analysis to governmental practices, and ultimately revealing the materiality of discourses. A discursive formation according to Foucault is a set of ideas and practices within particular conditions of existence, which are more or less institutionalised, but which may be only partially understood by those that they encompass.[24] Second, governmentality is focused on the emergence of the liberal art of government, and on its re-elaboration by ordoliberalism and neoliberalism.[25] Third, governmentality reflects on the forms of subjectivities produced by the exercise of power, because power, for Foucault, is productive, and not only repressive.[26] Fourth, a governmentality approach looks at technologies of power, or, in other words, by what means and mechanisms power is constituted and rules accomplished.[27]

In the economic realm of the EU, the prevailing discursive formation is based on the interconnection between ordoliberal and neoliberal ideas.[28] This intersection is specific to the European space and it has shaped the formation of European institutions, fostering an idea of Europe as a competitive economic space, based on the fiscal responsibility of Member States, the construction of entrepreneurial societies, and individualised responsibility. Following this perspective, we could argue that the EU aims to 'conduct the conducts' of its Member States, shaping an ordo/neoliberal discourse that defines the language and objectives of its Member states.[29] This conduction takes the form of

---

[23] Walters and Haahr adopt the term mentality', but we think it is more appropriate to talk about 'rationality', because mentality bears a resonance to individual mentality, whereas rationality clearly refers to society. Merlingen defines rationality as 'a discursive formation, intimately linked to structures of power that produce effects of truth with regard to specific fields of governance' (M Merlingen, 'Governmentality. Towards a Foucauldian Framework for the Study of IGOs' (2003) 38 Cooperation and Conflict 369).

[24] M Foucault, 'Orders of Discourse' (1971) 10 Social Science Information 7, 21–30.

[25] Foucault, *The Birth of Biopolitics* (n 15).

[26] M Foucault, *The History of Sexuality: The Will to Knowledge Vol 1* (Penguin 1978) 49.

[27] M Dean, *Governmentality: Power and Rule in Modern Society* (Sage 1999) 33.

[28] In this chapter, we define ordoliberalism and neoliberalism through a Foucauldian lens. For Foucault, ordoliberalism is based on market as a foundational principle for the state; the active role of government to establish free competition; and a society ruled in the name of competition. For Foucault, the main difference with Hayekian and American neoliberalism is the role of government. For ordoliberals, government should play a role in the market, setting and safeguarding a particular 'order', whereas for neoliberals it should not (Foucault, *Birth of Biopolitics* (n 15) 79–100). Furthermore, for Foucault, neoliberals conceive all human behaviour in economic–rational terms, envisaging redefining society as a form of the economic domain (*Birth of Biopolitics* (n 15) 216–38). These two reformulations of the classical liberal art of government have both shaped the European institutions. In fact, the European Union has evolved differently from other free trade zones (eg NAFTA) merging neoliberal ideas of free market and abolition of tariffs with a rigid institutional architecture. Hence, the European Union has not only developed a single market but also a European Monetary Union (EMU) together with the Stability and Growth Pact (SGP).

[29] Merlingen talks about the conduction of states at the global level; we apply this concept to the specific context of the EU ((n 23) 368).

a government at a distance, through governmental,[30] disciplinary[31] and biopolitical techniques.[32]

Hence, this chapter analyses the legal text of the TSCG, examining which technologies have been envisioned in this Treaty to exercise this conduction at a distance. In our understanding, the TSCG reaffirms and reinforces the *fiscal governance machine* activated by the EMU and the SGP. With *fiscal governance machine*, we refer to a durable ensemble of technologies and regime of knowledge and power defined by an ordo/neoliberal rationality, intent on conducting national governments and sub-state actors in their decisions, controlling them *ex-ante* and *ex-post*.[33]

Although fiscal discipline has always been an aim of the EU, it has never been completely achieved. Since the approval of the SGP, except for Estonia and Sweden, all Member States have been under an excessive deficit procedure. The situation worsened during the crisis, and in 2011, 24 countries were under the procedure.[34] Yet the EU has been in a somewhat paradoxical situation: it has continuously reaffirmed the so-called 'austerity rules', whose objectives are repeatedly missed – at least by some of its Member States. Faced with this situation, however, the Union has systematically failed to apply fines or change the rules, which, as a result, have been misused, or applied with exceptions.[35]

In order to understand this paradox, it is necessary to go beyond international governmentality studies and engage with the broader socio-economic context, through a historical–materialist approach inspired by Gramsci. Therefore, although the chapter uses a governmentality approach to read the TSCG as a *fiscal governance*

---

[30] Governmental techniques are all those techniques that foster the responsibilisation of Member States, of their civil societies and their populations, such as the techniques envisioned in the Open Method of Coordination (OMC). JH Haahr, 'Open Co-ordination as Advanced Liberal Government' (2004) 11 Journal of European Public Policy 209–30.

[31] 'Disciplinary techniques' are all those that monitor, measure and control subjects over whom power is exercised. These include the techniques of visibility, such as European-harmonised statistics, benchmarks, European analyses of economic data, forecasts, annual growth surveys, economic reports and reviews. The TSCG envisages mainly this kind of techniques as we will see in the next section (W Walters, 'The Power of Inscription: Beyond Social Construction and Deconstruction in European Integration Studies' (2002) 31 Millennium – Journal of International Studies 83).

[32] 'Biopolitical techniques' are all those which aim to conduct the conduct of populations as a whole. In the European Union, these include all the techniques used to regulate migration, in what has been defined the 'border regime' (W Walters, 'Mapping Schengenland: Denaturalizing the Border' (2002) 20 Environment and Planning D: Society and Space 561).

[33] Deleuze and Guattari introduced the idea of machine in *Mille Plateaux* referring to the desiring machine (G Deleuze and F Guattari, *A Thousand Plateaus* (University of Minnesota Press 1987)).

[34] All the information about the Excessive Deficit Procedure can be find on the website of the European Commission: https://ec.europa.eu/info/business-economy-euro/economic-and-fiscal-policy-coordination_en accessed April 2018.

[35] For example, in 2016, the European Commission did not propose any fines for Spain and Portugal, which were not respecting the SGP criteria, even though after the approval of the New Economic Governance it has a much greater capacity to do it (D Gros, 'The Silent Death of Eurozone Governance' *CEPS Comment* (16 August 2016) www.ceps.eu/publications/silent-death-eurozone-governance accessed April 2018).

machine, it also goes beyond governmentality to explain the context in which this machine operates. In particular, we need to acknowledge the economic crisis, the transformation of the regime of capital accumulation through financialisation, and the uneven construction of EMU.

Through a neo-Gramscian approach, the EU can be seen as a space where different hegemonic projects compete.[36] These hegemonic projects are the expression of different ideas, discourses and rationalities supported by different social forces and Member States. For van Apeldoorn,[37] at the beginning of the 1980s, when the European project was relaunched, three main projects were competing: a neoliberal project, a neo-mercantilist project and a social-democratic project. The Maastricht Treaty represents a synthesis between the three projects, under the hegemony of the neoliberal project, what van Apeldoorn defines as 'embedded neoliberalism'.[38] In contrast to van Apeldoorn, we do not understand a hegemonic project as the direct expression of a transnational class, but we refer to it as a specific programme of actions and strategies,[39] able to foster specific discursive formations as expressions of specific rationalities. Second, in our understanding what van Apeldoorn's calls the neoliberal project, in the European space, is composed of two parts: a neoliberal project, for the single market, based on the elimination of tariffs and free competition, and an ordoliberal project, based on the idea of common institutions, fiscal stability and low inflation. For this reason, in this work, we refer to an ordo/neoliberal project to emphasize this duality.

Beginning in the 1980s, the ordo/neoliberal project struggled to become hegemonic, until it successfully became institutionalised in the 1990s with the Maastricht Treaty and later the SGP. This ordo/neoliberal project is related to a specific strategy of accumulation based on the financialisation of the economy and society in general, with financial capital at its centre. To understand the reinforced pressure for fiscal stability, we need to connect it with the new role of public debt in our economies, and this new regime of capital accumulation based on indebtedness.[40]

[36] For the concept of hegemonic project, see S Bulmer and J Joseph, 'European Integration in Crisis? Of Supranational Integration, Hegemonic Projects and Domestic Politics' (2015) 22 European Journal of International Relations 1; B van Apeldoorn, 'The European Capitalist Class and the Crisis of Its Hegemonic Project' (2014) 50 Socialist Register 189; B Van Apeldoorn, *Transnational Capitalism and the Struggle over European Integration* (Routledge 2002); B Jessop, 'Accumulation Strategies, State Forms and Hegemonic Projects' (1983) 10 Kapitalistate 89; B Jessop, *The Capitalist State* (Blackwell 1982).

[37] Van Apeldoorn (n 36).

[38] ibid 81.

[39] Focusing on strategies avoids deriving the actions of actors 'objectively' from their position in the social structure, therefore the same hegemonic project can be pursued by different actors (S Buckel and others, 'The European Border Regime in Crisis. Theory, Methods and Analyses in Critical European Studies' (2017) Rosa Luxembourg Stiftung Studien 8/2017, 17 www.rosalux.de/en/publica tion/id/38197/the-european-border-regime-in-crisis accessed April 2018.

[40] M Haiven, *Culture of Financialization. Fictitious Capital in Popular Culture and Everyday Life* (Palgrave Macmillan 2014); J Montgomerie, 'Bridging the Critical Divide: Global Finance, Financialisation and Contemporary Capitalism' (2008) 14 Contemporary Politics 233; GA Epstein,

On the institutional level, the concept of hegemonic project needs to be coupled with the neo-Poulantzian multilayered approach of Europe as a *multi-scalar European ensemble of state apparatuses.*[41] This ensemble is characterized by a cooperative–competitive interplay between different actors on different levels and scales. This 'unity in fragmentation' is not a lack of cohesion or programme, but the way through which the ordo/neoliberal project governs the European space, even though, this way of governing is unable to find a large legitimation in the different European civil societies.

To summarise, contrary to mainstream approaches, the chapter employs governmentality as a 'radical institutionalism' to look at the rationalities and technologies envisaged in the TSCG, as an emblematic example of the New Economic Governance. It will further combine this analysis with a historical–materialist approach inspired by Gramsci to frame the TSCG in the context of financialisation, economic crisis, and the uneven construction of EMU.

III THE NEGOTIATION PROCESS: A FAILED ATTACK ON NATIONAL CONSTITUTIONS

The European Council of 8 and 9 December 2011 endorsed the idea of a Fiscal Compact for the eurozone.[42] This concept was first sketched in an informal Franco-German meeting held earlier that December, just before the European Council. German Chancellor Merkel, and French President Sarkozy proposed to reinforce the economic governance of the eurozone through the approval of a 'debt brake', to be incorporated in national constitutions.[43] This proposal was opposed to the Eurobond project, which had been endorsed by the European Commission's Green Paper,[44] and, more generally, to any other kind of debt mutualisation.

The TSCG was negotiated within a few weeks, and the last version of the draft was ready by the end of January. Faced with the possibility of a new amendment to EU primary law,[45] the United Kingdom posed a veto, opposing any stricter budgetary

---

Financialization and the World Economy (Northampton 2005); G Krippner, *What Is Financialization?* (University of Los Angeles 2004).

[41] J Wissel and S Wolff, 'Political Regulation and the Strategic Production of Space: The European Union as a Post-Fordist State Spatial Project' (2017) 49 Antipode 231, 239.

[42] European Council, Conclusions of 9 December 2011 http://europa.eu/rapid/press-release_DOC-11-8_en.htm accessed April 2018.

[43] I Traynor and D Gow, 'Sarkozy and Merkel Unveil Two-Speed EU Plan to Shore Up Euro' *The Guardian* (7 December 2011) www.theguardian.com/world/2011/dec/07/sarkozy-merkel-two-speed-eu-plan accessed April 2018.

[44] European Commission, 'Green Paper on the feasibility of introducing Stability Bonds' COM (2011) 818 final.

[45] The first crisis-related Treaty amendment, that subsequently fuelled the UK's reservations, had been decided in March 2011 as regards Art 136 TFEU, so as to facilitate the establishment of the European Stability Mechanism.

discipline.[46] To bypass this problem the TSCG was signed outside the EU legal framework as an intergovernmental Treaty by twenty-five states[47] at the end of the European Council held on 2 March 2012.

In the drawing, negotiation and approval of the TSCG the German leadership was undeniable. The German government fully led the negotiation process, first through the joint letters with France, and then by deciding to go forward despite the British veto. In fact, after the second bailout with Greece and the creation of the ESM, the German government wanted to introduce a Treaty to ensure fiscal discipline in the eurozone. In that sense, the TSCG could be read as a direct expression of the German government's will to impose fiscal discipline as an aim per se. This is what led many scholars to claim a new centrality of Member States and of intergovernmental institutions, such as the Eurosummit or the Eurogroup, with Germany as the most powerful actor.[48]

At the same time, the TSCG empowered the European Commission – a supranational institution by definition – with a new role of surveillance and the capacity to impose sanctions.[49] In that sense, while the TSCG was concluded as an intergovernmental treaty outside the EU legal framework, it nevertheless reaffirmed the power of European institutions to control Member States, envisaging the possibility for certain Member States to control others (Art 8), with the fundamental aim to restore fiscal stability.

The SGP the Six-Pack, the Two-Pack and the European Semester are all commonly seen to have shifted some power from the national level to the European level either by completely transferring the decision-making level from the national to the supranational, or by imposing coordination between Member States. It could be argued this has also been the effect of the TSCG. However, in addition, the TSCG attempts to enforce fiscal discipline by demanding that the balanced budget rule be embedded in the national constitutions of Member States (Art 3). Despite its reforms, the SGP had repeatedly failed to ensure compliance with fiscal discipline.[50] The TSCG, while pursuing the same disciplinary objective, was intended to overcome such compliance issues by introducing specific obligations

---

[46]　In this British opposition, we could read a first step towards the process that will lead the Conservative government to call for a referendum.

[47]　The United Kingdom and Czech Republic did not sign the Treaty. Croatia, who joined the Union in July 2013, has not signed yet.

[48]　F Schimmelfennig, 'Liberal Intergovernmentalism and the Euro Area Crisis' (2015) 22 Journal of European Public Policy 177; U Puetter, 'The European Council and the Council: Perspectives on New Dynamics in EU Governance' (2012) 19 Journal of European Public Policy 161.

[49]　MW Bauer and S Becker, 'The Unexpected Winner of the Crisis: The European Commission's Strengthened Role in Economic Governance' (2014) 36 Journal of European Integration 213.

[50]　Council Regulation (EC) 1055/2005 of 27 June 2005 amending Regulation (EC) 1466/1997 of 7 July 1997 on the strengthening of the surveillance of budgetary positions and the surveillance and coordination of economic policies [2005] OJ L174/1; Council Regulation (EC) 1056/2005 of 27 June 2005 amending Regulation (EC) 1467/97 of 7 July 1997 on speeding up and clarifying the implementation of the excessive deficit procedure [2005] OJ L174/5.

of interventions at the national/state level. As the report of the Commission on the Fiscal Compact made clear, 'it was felt that the EU rules-based fiscal framework (the Stability and Growth Pact (SGP)) should be complemented by provisions at the national level in order to better achieve sound budgetary policies in all Member States'.[51] The TSCG therefore attempted to change not only the material but also the formal constitution[52] of Member States. The result is that sovereignty is not only being transferred at the supranational level but is being more fundamentally transformed, involving the active remaking of state apparatuses and of governmental practices.[53]

Furthermore, despite the UK's veto, the TSCG envisages its incorporation into the EU legal framework within five years (Art 16). In other words, opposition to its enactment was first bypassed through an intergovernmental Treaty, and will now be completely ignored through its absorption into the main corpus of EU law, probably without any changes. At any rate, in reality many provisions of the Fiscal Compact are already integrated in the EU law, as the requirement to have independent bodies monitoring national fiscal rules (Art 3(2)), the Economic Partnership Programmes for Member States under EDP (Art (5)), and the necessity to have an *ex ante* coordination on Member States' debt issuance plans (Art 6) are all provided for in the Two-Pack.

The TSCG, similarly to the German constitutional reform of 2009,[54] essentially demands that Member States constitutionalise a 'debt brake'. However, only Italy, Spain and Slovenia introduced the debt brake to their constitutions, all the other contracting parties having decided to implement the balanced budget rule as a special law or ordinary law.[55] Hence, while the Fiscal Compact can be seen as the highest moment of German domination in the EU, illustrating how Germany pushed for, and ultimately, to a certain extent, was able to impose the contents of its constitutional reform to the other Member States through an international treaty, it is also the lowest moment of German hegemony, since the Treaty needed to be

---

[51]　European Commission, 'Communication on the Fiscal Compact: Taking Stock' C(2017) 1200 final.

[52]　For the distinction between formal, material and normative constitution, see inter alia E Fossum and AJ Menendez, *The Constitution's Gift: A Constitutional Theory for a Democratic European Union* (Rowman & Littlefield 2011) 20–24.

[53]　S Gill, *Power and Resistance in the New World Order* (Palgrave Macmillan 2008); AJ Menéndez, 'The European Crises and the Undoing of the Social and Democratic Rechtsstaat' in JE Fossum and AJ Menéndez (eds), *The European Union in Crises or the European Union as Crises?* (ARENA Report 2/14 2014) www.sv.uio.no/arena/english/research/publications/arena-reports/2014/arena-report-2–14 .html accessed April 2018.

[54]　The new Art 109(3) of the *Grundgesetz* states that the budgets of the Federation and of the *Länder* shall in principle be balanced. This constitutional reform does not allow the federal government to run cyclically adjusted deficits in excess of 0.35 per cent of GDP, while the *Länder* cyclically adjusted budgets have to be balanced. For the federal government, the rule is fully operative since 2016; for the *Länder* it will be fully operative from 2019. But the Budget Rule does not include the municipalities and the social security system.

[55]　European Commission, 'Report Presented under Article 8 of the Treaty on Stability, Coordination and Governance in the Economic and Monetary Union' C(2017) 1201 final.

approved outside of the EU legal framework, and the majority of the contracting parties did not implement it through constitutional reforms. As such, while this authoritarian decision-making is the expression of a radicalisation of the ordo/neoliberal project, it also illustrates its incapacity to find a large consensus in the different European civil societies.[56]

IV A FISCAL GOVERNANCE MACHINE

Although only a handful of Member States incorporated the TSCG in their national constitutions, the latter was still implemented, and led to significant changes in the fiscal rules of twenty-five states, reinforcing what we have called the *fiscal governance machine* set up by the SGP. We use the term 'governance machine' in the Foucauldian sense, to refer to a set of technologies and practices that are put in place to shape the conduct of states, substate actors and their citizens, following an ordo/neoliberal rationality. Recourse to Foucauldian concepts serves in particular to highlight how pervasive a certain idea of fiscal discipline has become in European societies and how it is able to shape social relations. Furthermore, the idea of a 'machine' helps to show how different institutional devices, organised on different scales and levels, share the same apparatus of knowledge and power, with the aim of steering the political economy of Member States.

The TSCG is composed of four parts: the Fiscal Compact (Arts 1–8); the Economic Policy Coordination and Convergence (Arts 9–11); the Governance of the Euro Area (Arts 12–13); and the General and Final Provisions (Arts 14–16). Fundamentally, the essence of TCSG could be summarised by Article 3(1)(a), which establishes the balanced budget rule and according to which 'the budgetary position of the general government of a Contracting Party shall be balanced or in surplus'.

The balanced budget is the aim of the Treaty, however, the text never refers to this aim in relation to other objectives, such as reducing unemployment, avoiding deflation or enhancing growth. Instead balancing the budget is always referred to as an aim per se, and according to the rationale of the Treaty (Art 1), economic growth, competitiveness and social cohesion will simply follow from fiscal discipline. For a lack of space, in this chapter we will examine in depth only Article 3, with a particular focus on the Structural Deficit (Art 3(1)(b)), the automatic Correction Mechanism (Art 3(1)(e)), and the Fiscal Advisory Council (Art 3(2)). These techniques highlight three important features for the overall New

---

[56] On the authoritarian turn, see L Oberndorfer, 'A New Economic Governance through Secondary Legislation? Analysis and Constitutional Assessment: From New Constitutionalism, via Authoritarian Constitutionalism to Progressive Constitutionalism' in N Bruun, K Lörcher and I Schömann (eds), *The Economic and Financial Crisis and Collective Labour Law in Europe* (Hart 2014); I Bruff, 'The Rise of Authoritarian Neoliberalism' (2014) 26 Rethinking Marxism 113; AJ Menéndez, 'The Existential Crisis of the European Union' (2013) 14 German Law Journal Review 453.

Economic Governance: a new discretionary power of the European Commission, the automatisation or semi-automatisation of rules, and independence of the relevant national agency from state institutions.

1 The Structural Deficit

For the TSCG, the crucial indicator of pact compliance is the respect of the medium-term objective, with a lower limit of a structural deficit of 0.5 per cent (Art (3)(b)).[57] Since the revisions of the SGP,[58] the Medium Term Objective (MTO) is defined in structural terms, therefore taking into consideration business cycle swings and filtering out temporary measures. The structural deficit is presented by European institutions as a better way to calculate the deficit than nominal values, because it is more flexible and able to take into consideration the economic cycle.[59] This calculation is presented as a technical question of statistics, without any political implications.

But by whom and how to decide which measures are cyclical and which are temporary? In reality, the definition and calculation of the structural deficit is highly contested in the economic discipline. The structural deficit is the measurement of the gap between present and potential output, but its definition is difficult and subject to significant errors and revisions during the economic cycle.[60] In fact, in the last years, the calculation of the DG Finance has been questioned by different Member States,[61] and in 2015, the European Commission had to release a communication to clarify the issue.[62]

Decisions for structural reforms and austerity measures of each Member State are made on the basis of their compliance with the MTO. In other words, the calculation of the structural deficit influences the entire political economy of Member States. Here, it gives a new power of calculation assigned to the DG Finance, which

---

[57] Art 3.1d states that where the ratio of the general government debt to gross domestic product is significantly below 60 per cent the lower limit of the MTO can reach a structural deficit of 1.0 per cent.

[58] Council Regulation (EC) 1055/2005 of 27 June 2005 amending Regulation (EC) 1466/1997 of 7 July 1997 on the strengthening of the surveillance of budgetary positions and the surveillance and coordination of economic policies [2005] OJ L174/1; Council Regulation (EC) 1056/2005 of 27 June 2005 amending Regulation (EC) 1467/97 of 7 July 1997 on speeding up and clarifying the implementation of the excessive deficit procedure [2005] OJ L174/5.

[59] C Wyplosz, 'Europe's Quest for Fiscal Discipline' (2013) European Commission Economic Papers 498.

[60] L Eyraud and T Wu, 'Playing by the Rules : Reforming Fiscal Governance in Europe' (2015) IMF Working Papers 15/67, 19 www.imf.org/external/pubs/ft/wp/2015/wp1567.pdf accessed April 2018; H Radice, 'Enforcing Austerity in Europe: The Structural Deficit as a Policy Target' (2014) 22 Journal of Contemporary European Studies 318, 326.

[61] D Gros and C Alcidi, 'The Case of the Disappearing Fiscal Compact' (2014) CEPS Commentary www.ceps.eu/publications/case-disappearing-fiscal-compact accessed April 2018.

[62] European Commission, 'Communication on Making the Best Use of the Flexibility within the Existing Rules of the Stability and Growth Pact' COM (2015) 12 final.

is the European institution responsible for this and other measurements, as the expenditure benchmark[63] or the macroeconomic imbalances procedure.[64] An entire apparatus of knowledge and power has been elaborated around these measurements, based on the invoked objectivity of statistics and economy, providing the way through which the debate around economic issues is depoliticised. This depoliticisation of economic discourse, relegated to experts, is essentially the means by which the idea that there is no alternative is asserted.

2 *The Correction Mechanism*

The Fiscal Compact adds to the *fiscal governance machine* a new technique that goes beyond the simple surveillance of Member States from above. In fact, pursuant to Article (3)(e), in the event of significant deviations from the MTO or the adjustment path towards it, a prescribed correction mechanism has to be triggered automatically. The automatic mechanism is designed to set a path for the deviating Member State to return in line with the MTO within two years; a relevant independent body is granted responsibility for verifying the application of the mechanism for this period. This provision has been already integrated in the EU legal framework by the Two-Pack.[65]

The common principles of the correction mechanism are set in a communication of the European Commission.[66] Principle 5 states that the automatic mechanism shall correct the situation through the implementation of counter measures. These counter measures are supposedly designed to restore the structural balance at or above the MTO within a planned deadline, and they should give a prominent operational role to rules on public expenditure and discretionary tax measures.

Hence, Member States are required to adopt a corrective plan that has to be binding over the budgets covered by the correction period, with rules decided *ex ante* and not specific to the circumstances. Once this mechanism is adopted, it should be controlled not only by the national government, but by an independent agency, the Fiscal Advisory Council, which is discussed below. Furthermore, if a Member State believes that another Member State has not implemented the mechanism effectively, it can bring the matter before the Court of Justice (Art 8). This automatic correction mechanism can be read as a form of decentralised and peer surveillance, controlled by a national independent agency.

---

[63] Regulation (EU) 1173/2011 of the European Parliament and of the Council of 16 November 2011 on the effective enforcement of budgetary surveillance in the euro area [2011] OJ L306/1.

[64] Regulation (EU) 1176/2011 of 16 November 2011 on the prevention and correction of macroeconomic imbalances [2011] OJ L306/25.

[65] Art 5(2)(a) of the Regulation (EU) 473/2013 of the European Parliament and of the Council of 21 May 2013 on common provisions for monitoring and assessing draft budgetary plans and ensuring the correction of excessive deficit of the Member States in the euro area [2013] OJ L140/11.

[66] European Commission, 'Communication on Common Principles on National Fiscal Correction Mechanisms' COM (2012) 0342 final.

3 *The Fiscal Advisory Council*

As we have seen, all the provisions set out in Article 3 are to be monitored by an independent supervisory institution: the Fiscal Council (Art (3)(2)). The introduction of the Independent Fiscal Council at the national level was already mentioned in the Six-Pack, and later incorporated in the Two-Pack.

The creation of Fiscal Advisory Councils is part of an *agencification* process, that is to say the creation of independent bodies centred on the role of experts, that should regulate or control specific areas.[67] The IMF and OECD have promoted the formation of Independent Fiscal Councils for years, and already in 2006 the European Commission launched a survey about the institutionalisation of Fiscal Councils.[68] The crisis was the opportunity to enforce this kind of independent bodies in every Member State.

In line with the OECD and IMF, the Two-Pack envisages mainly two tasks for the Fiscal Council: first, monitoring compliance with fiscal rules, and second, producing or evaluating macro-economic forecasts.[69] Each national Fiscal Council is to be constituted as independent body structurally vis-à-vis any national budgetary authority (parliamentary commissions, ministries or any governmental department). Moreover, it is to be independent from a functional point of view, hence operating with its own budget and regulations.[70] Lastly, the Fiscal Council should be composed of economic experts rather than politicians, and it should have access to all economic data and information of the state.

The purpose of an independent authority controlling the application of fiscal rules is to depoliticise certain dimensions of fiscal policy, similar to what happened for monetary policy with the creation of an independent central bank, which was released from any formal relation with the Treasury.[71] Even more, Fiscal Councils are essentially designed to effectively control Member States 'from the inside', acting as a surrogate to European institutions. In other words, compliance with fiscal rules is not monitored and controlled by DG finance, or other European institutions, but rather directly by a national independent agency following European standards.

---

[67] J Jordana, D Levi-Faur and X Fernández i Marín, 'The Global Diffusion of Regulatory Agencies' (2011) 44 Comparative Political Studies 1343.

[68] All the three organizations have a dataset on national Fiscal Councils: the European Commission at https://ec.europa.eu/info/business-economy-euro/indicators-statistics/economic databases/fiscal-governance-eu-member-states/independent-fiscal-institutions_en accessed April 2018; the IFM at www.imf.org/external/np/fad/council accessed April 2018; the OECD at www.oecd.org/govern ance/budgeting/oecdnetworkofparliamentarybudgetofficialspbo.htm accessed April 2018.

[69] Art 5(2)(a) of the Regulation (EU) 473/2013 of the European Parliament and of the Council of 21 May 2013 on common provisions for monitoring and assessing draft budgetary plans and ensuring the correction of excessive deficit of the Member States in the euro area [2013] OJ L140/11.

[70] Art 2 of Regulation (EU) 473/2013.

[71] X Debrun and T Kinda, 'Strengthening Post-Crisis Fiscal Credibility: Fiscal Councils on the Rise – A New Dataset' (2014) IMF Working Paper 14/58, 4 www.imf.org/external/pubs/ft/wp/2014/wp1458.pdf accessed April 2018.

In this European process of *agencification*, two other developments are interesting: the establishment, in September 2015, of the European Network of Independent Fiscal Institutions (EU IFISI); and, the creation, in February 2016, of the European Fiscal Board (EFB), an independent advisory body with a consultative role towards the Commission.[72] Thus, at the centre of this decentralised network of fiscal advisory councils, at the national and European level, we find, again, the European Commission and its DG Finance.

From our perspective, the Fiscal Council is the agency that controls compliance with the ordo/neoliberal rationality. For this reason, it does not improve the democratic legitimation of the new Euro-national procedures.[73] On the contrary, it fosters a process of surveillance on the political economy of Member States, which now takes place not only in a top-down dimension, from the European level to the national level, but is instead organised directly at the national level.

To conclude, the discretionary power of the European Commission, the enhanced role of its DG Finance, the automatic mechanism to reimpose sound fiscal policies at the national level, independent agency to control national budget, the supposed objectivity of economic forecasts and economic calculation (such as the calculation around the structural deficit) and the diminution of national autonomy on budgetary decisions are all features of the *fiscal governance machine*. This is both a method of conducting and controlling Member States from the inside and outside, escaping democratic debate, and the expression of the shift from soft to authoritarian governance. In fact, this reaffirmation of the governance machine can even be said to change the functioning of European democracies, accelerating a reorganisation of Member States, which was already underway. European and national economic and executive institutions are gaining increased importance, accelerating the crisis of parliamentary democracy.

But, at this point we can ask: why are Member States so indebted, if this machine is so penetrating? Why are their deficits still growing? Why are they continuously asking for more flexibility? Governmentality studies are unable to answer these questions.

V FINANCIALISATION AND FISCAL STABILITY

To understand why some Member States are so indebted if the *fiscal governance machine* is so penetrating, we need to go beyond a governmentality approach and adopt a historical–materialist line of reasoning inspired by Gramsci. This can help us to link the *fiscal governance machine* with the financial-led regime of

---

[72] Commission Decision (EU) 2016/221 of 12 February 2016 amending Decision (EU) 2015/1937 establishing an independent advisory European Fiscal Board [2016] OJ L40/15.

[73] C Fasone and D Fromage, 'Fiscal Councils: Threat or Opportunity for Democracy in the Post-Crisis Economic and Monetary Union?' in L Daniele, P Simone and R Cisotta (eds), *Democracy in the EMU in the Aftermath of the Crisis* (Springer 2017).

accumulation, its crisis and its relation to the uneven construction of the EMU. If a governmentality approach can help us acknowledge the discursive dimension of the economic realm, and the relationship between knowledge and power in the construction of governing techniques, it needs to be situated in the broader context. Therefore, the neo-Foucauldian concern with rationality, technologies, form of powers and subjectivities needs to meet the neo-Gramscian focus on the economic, political and intellectual–moral bases of power, situating them in the broader context of the political economy of the crisis.[74]

The huge paradox of the Fiscal Compact, and of all the crisis measures related to it, is that they seek to impose the realisation of balanced or surplus budgets in Member States at a moment when the modern economic paradigm in its entirety appears to stand upon public and private debt. But, in reality, the request for fiscal discipline is intrinsically related with the financialisation of the economy, not opposed to it. There is indeed a large consensus in critical political economy that the financial crisis needs to be analysed in relation to the transformation of the accumulation strategy that occurred at the end of the 1970s, and took the form of the transnationalisation and financialisation of the economy.[75]

Following Streeck,[76] we can recognise three periods in the process of financialisation in Europe. First, in the 1980s, the level of public debt increased, while a first set of liberalisation of the credit system was organised, and some Member States were already transforming their central banks system.[77] This enabled banks to multiply credit faster, tying public finance to the expansion of financial services.[78]

Subsequently, in the 1990s, a first period of austerity measures stabilised the level of public debt. In the European space, this is the period when the ordo/neoliberal project was institutionalised through the creation of the EMU, and the adoption of the SGP. In fact, the Maastricht convergence criteria were coupled with a further set of liberalisation in the financial services sector, through the establishment of the full freedom of circulation for capital in the EU (now Art 63 TFEU). The stabilisation of

---

[74] B Jessop and N Sum, 'Towards a Cultural International Political Economy: Poststructuralism and the Italian School' in M de Goede (ed) *International Political Economy and Post-Structural Politics* (Palgrave 2011), 167.

[75] In a very general way, we can define financialisation as the increasing importance of financial markets, financial motives, financial institutions and a financial elite in the operation of the economy and its governing institutions (GA Epstein, *Financialization and the World Economy* (Edward Elgar 2005) 81). For the concept of financialisation, see, inter alia N van der Zwan, 'Making Sense of Financialization' (2014) 12 Socio-Economic Review 99; C Marazzi, *The Violence of Financial Capitalism* (Edizioni Casagrande 2011); C Lapavitsas, 'Financialised Capitalism: Crisis and Financial Expropriation' (2009) 17 Historical Materialism 114.

[76] W Streeck, *Buying Time: The Delayed Crisis of Democratic Capitalism* (Verso 2014).

[77] In 1973, the French government passed a law to separate the Treasury from the Bank of France (Law 73/7 of 3 January 1973 on the Bank of France). Similarly, in 1981, a letter between the Italian Treasury Ministry and the President of the Bank of Italy ratified the same separation.

[78] GR Krippner, *Capitalizing on Crisis: The Political Origin of the Rise of Finance* (Harvard UP 2011).

public debt was coupled with an increase of private debt, functioning in the form of a privatised Keynesianism,[79] or debtfarism.[80]

Yet the first round of austerity measures in the middle of the 1990s, and the turn to private indebtedness, did not stop public debt growing once more, increasing the intersection between public and private forms of debt. During the crisis, public debt levels – especially of Euro-Periphery Member States – skyrocketed. In 2016, more than half of eurozone Member States had a debt level greater than 100 per cent as a proportion of GDP.[81] This means than not only Euro-Periphery Member States, but also Member States such as France, Belgium and Austria are highly indebted.

It is important to acknowledge that the increase of public debt is not simply related to the misconduct of Member States or the mismanagement of the banking crisis of 2007/08. On the contrary, public and private indebtedness are intrinsic to the accumulation strategy of a financialised economy. This is why not only Euro-Periphery Member States are highly indebted, but many countries in the rest of the world, among which the Unites States and Japan. In fact, we can trace the first pattern of state indebtedness to the 1980s, together with the first round of liberalisation, and not simply to the 2008 crisis.

Debt is not a technical or neutral relation. It is a class relation that is both constituted through and reproduced by states. In this relation, creditors extract value from debtors, through the payment of interest. This is the reason why creditors need to have more and more performing loans in their portfolio. In other words, creditors do not aspire to have all their debts paid off, because they profit from the existence of the debt relation, in terms of money and power.[82]

The increasing centrality of the debt relation in our economy has transformed the role of public debt. It has turned it from being the leverage for full employment policies and welfare services, into a mechanism of control over the state in the hands of financial capital. This became possible because control over public debt is not in the hands of governments anymore, but public debt has effectively become an 'asset' to be directly sold and traded in the financial market. In the European space this is a process directly related to the institutionalisation of EMU that has created an independent central bank (Art 127 TFEU), and prohibited any type of credit facility with the any Central Bank (Arts 123, 124 and 125 TFEU).

Within the EU, therefore, the process of financialisation has assumed a specific form, inseparable from the institutionalization of the *fiscal governance machine*. In

---

[79] C Crouch, 'Privatised Keynesianism: An Unacknowledged Policy Regime' (2009) 11 British Journal of Politics and International Relations 382.

[80] S Soederberg, 'Student Loans, Debtfare and the Commodification of Debt: The Politics of Securitization and the Displacement of Risk' (2014) 40 Critical Sociology 689.

[81] Eurostat data http://ec.europa.eu/eurostat/web/government-finance-statistics/data/main-tables accessed April 2018.

[82] M Lazzarato, *Governing by Debt* (Semiotext(e) 2015); M Bersani, *Dacci Oggi Il Nostro Debito Quotidiano* (Derive Approdi 2017).

fact, the single market, the EMU, the SGP and their reaffirmation in the New Economic Governance have all been an essential part of this process.

VI THE UNEVEN CONSTRUCTION OF EMU

The process of financialisation, and the institutionalisation of the European and Monetary Union did not affect all Member States in the same way, and these differences and hierarchies that are shaping the European space must be acknowledged. In that sense, the *fiscal governance machine* does not work in the same way everywhere, but strategically privileges some institutional space/actors/interests over others.[83]

The EU has intensified, rather than mitigated, the lines of geographical division created by global capital in the European space. On the one hand, the single market, based on the free circulation of goods, services, capitals and people, has increased disparities between West and East, without fostering a homogenisation of working conditions, as well as labour and social rights. Consequently, it has exacerbated the competition between different national regulations and welfare systems in the attempt to attract more investment and capital. On the other hand, the EMU has increased the competition between North and South, inscribing in the construction of the euro the impossibility of devaluation or any kind of state aid, both thus blocking strategies used by the most fragile economies of the South/Periphery of the eurozone to remain competitive.[84]

The EMU has 'locked in' the power of capital, not in the abstract, but in the form of the capital based in the North–West/Core of the EU, itself centred around German capital. German capital took advantage of the constitution of a strong currency, and the ECB's restrictive monetary policy (until August 2007), reaffirming its growth model based on exports and low wages. Meanwhile the Peripheral countries had based their growth on a debt-based model. For years the cash inflows from the North–West to the South–East fed a growth model based on short-term investments and easy profit opportunities, much of which was very convenient for Peripheral countries for a while.[85]

During the crisis these economic differences increased, and in the eurozone Ireland, Spain, Portugal, Cyprus and Greece found themselves in need of asking for economic aid. The programmes of financial aid were the first step towards reinforcing and reaffirming the *fiscal governance machine*. This *fiscal governance machine* is thus the device through which a particular system of domination and

---

[83] B Jessop, *State Power* (Polity 2008), 47–52.
[84] C Lapavitsas and H Flassbeck, *Against the Troika* (Verso 2015).
[85] B Jessop, 'Variegated Capitalism, Das Modell Deutschland, and the Eurozone Crisis' (2014) 22 Journal of Contemporary European Studies 248; K van der Pijl, O Holman and O Raviv, 'The Resurgence of German Capital in Europe: EU Integration and the Restructuring of Atlantic Networks of Interlocking Directorates after 1991' (2010) 18 Review of International Political Economy 384.

control was able to affirm and reaffirm itself as 'neutral', supposedly objective and free of ideological influences. But, in reality, this system was based on the finance–industrial capital of the North–West of Europe, which constructed the EMU and the single market on the basis of its own needs of production and reproduction.[86] As such, the apparent neutrality of the *fiscal governance machine* was also the means through which the institutional construction of the EU is presented as if separated from any particular strategy of accumulation, and the crisis can be narrated as a problem of excessive spending at national levels, rather than relating this excessive spending to the centrality of debt to accumulation in our global economy.

Hence, on the one hand, Member States are increasingly involved in an economy based on private and public indebtedness, and on the other hand, become more and more limited by the *fiscal governance machine*. The rules on fiscal stability, and on excessive deficits, that apply to all EU Member States, were supposed to stabilise the intrinsic instability of the financial market. Instead, these rules have ensured the integration of Periphery States and helped foster an accumulation strategy based on indebtedness, while simultaneously trying to stabilise credit expansion. The *fiscal governance machine* is thus ensuring that states – especially Periphery States – can be constructed as performing debtors. And, as we have seen, a performing debtor pays its interest, but without extinguishing its debts, thus expanding the lending game.

Now we can return to answer our question: why are some Member States still so heavily indebted if the *fiscal governance machine* is so penetrating? The single market and the common currency exacerbated economic differences, instead of mitigating them, supporting a growth model based on short-term investments and easy profit opportunities, with cash inflows from the North and West to the South and East. The *fiscal governance machine* is the tool to control, stabilise and maintain these differences. In this way, some Member States can maintain their positions as creditors, while the others will remain debtors. This means that for some Member States, fiscal stability in the context of existing rules and economic differences is simply unachievable. Hence, it becomes a way to control the political economy of Member States, and to reaffirm the centrality of a financialised strategy of accumulation.

VII CONCLUSION

This chapter has analysed the TSCG as an emblematic example of the New Economic Governance, the institutional answer to the financial crisis of European institutions. We have conducted this analysis through the intertwining

---

[86] B Kogut and G Walker, 'The Small World of Germany and the Durability of National Networks' (2001) 66 American Sociological Review 317; EM Heemskerk, 'The Social Field of the European Corporate Elite: A Network Analysis of Interlocking Directorates among Europe's Largest Corporate Boards' (2011) 11 Global Networks 440; WK Carroll, *The Making of a Transnational Capitalist Class: Corporate Power in the Twenty-First Century* (Zed Books 2010).

of two critical approaches, governmentality studies and a historical–materialist approach inspired by Gramsci. First, through governmentality, we examined the techniques envisioned in the TSCG, defining this Treaty as a reaffirmation and reinforcement of the *fiscal governance machine* set up by the SGP. This Treaty gives new discretionary power to the DG Finance of the European Commission, and depoliticises the economic debate through the creation of an automatic mechanism and independent agencies, fostering an ordo/neoliberal rationality in the European space. This is a shift towards a more authoritarian governance and a radicalisation of the ordo/neoliberal project that demonstrates its incapacity to be legitimised in the different European civil societies. In that sense, the chapter has applied governmentality as a 'radical institutionalism', to analyse the legal text looking at techniques and rationalities.

Second, this analysis of the *fiscal governance machine* was placed in the broader economic context, enabling its functioning to be more fully grasped. This was done through a historical–materialist approach inspired by Gramsci, first looking at the regime of accumulation based on public and private debt, and then at the uneven construction of the EMU. We examined how the *fiscal governance machine*, and its set of rules on fiscal discipline, were not really intended to erase public debt, but to produce performing debtor states. Hence, the *fiscal governance machine*, we argued, is a way to control the political economy of Member States, and to reaffirm the centrality of a financialised strategy of accumulation, led by the North–West Member States of the EU. Overall, the intertwining between approaches inspired by Gramsci and Foucault can be inspiring for critical European Studies, and can help us shed new light on our understanding of the New Economic Governance, and of the crisis measures more in general.

11

The Rise of Unaccountable Governance in the Eurozone

Gunnar Beck

I INTRODUCTION

Since 2010 the EU has been in an 'emergency' situation due to the eurocrisis, where the crisis management by the EU institutions, notably the European Central Bank (ECB), and national governments has been increasingly out of step with the EU Treaties which define the scope of the mandate of the ECB and the EU's economic policy powers as well as the conditions and limits subject to which Member States have transferred policy and lawmaking powers to the EU in accordance with their national constitutions. The ECB is independent of parliamentary control, which means that it is not accountable to national parliaments and merely has a reporting duty to the European Parliament. Exempt from democratic control the ECB is subject only to judicial review at both EU and national level. At EU level, the competent court is the Court of Justice of the EU (CJEU) which claims the right to be the sole arbiter over the interpretation of EU law. At national law, constitutional courts have long claimed the right to review EU legislation and the acts of the EU institutions for compliance with the principle of conferral or the requirements of national constitutions. If the CJEU alone were competent to interpret EU law, it would be free to define the limits of the EU's powers in accordance with its own expansive interpretation of the Treaties. For this reason, many national constitutional courts including the German Federal Constitutional Court (FCC) have long claimed a jurisdiction of the last resort over EU legal acts and the acts of the EU institutions as a counterweight to the CJEU and to ensure that the EU does not extend its own powers through the judicial back door. This jurisdiction of the last resort includes the right to review any act of the EU institutions, including the acts of the ECB.

The first part of this chapter summarises aspects of my earlier work: G Beck, 'The Legal Reasoning of the Court of Justice and the Euro Crisis – The Flexibility of the Court's Cumulative Approach and the Pringle Case' (2013) 20 Maastricht Journal of European and Comparative Law 635.

There is no generally shared definition of the term 'governance' but it is clearly wider than 'government'. It includes the judiciary, certainly in situations where the courts, rather than the legislature or the executive, have the last say over the adoption of certain policies. The eurocrisis is such a situation because practically all measures adopted to stabilise the currency have given rise to litigation under the EU Treaties and/or national constitutional law. The ECB is explicitly exempted from political accountability at EU or national level. Judicial review is thus the only manner in which the central bank can be held to account. The courts also have the final say over the legality of acts of national parliaments where they may infringe national constitutions.

For this reason, this chapter focuses on the judicial response to the eurocrisis. It does so because to date the courts have been the main battleground where the principal issues of democracy and the limits of the EU's powers in the areas of monetary policy have been debated, not least because national parliaments throughout the eurozone did little more than rubberstamp executive decisions in defiance of treaty law. This is readily conceded by some EU politicians. The former French finance minister Christine Lagarde, openly admitted that 'to save the euro, we had to break the law'. In both legal and political terms, the EU's cavalier approach to the application of its own laws raises fundamental questions about a system where both the courts and national parliaments patently failed to discharge their function of safeguarding the rule of law against politically expedient action.

This chapter will demonstrate that the CJEU's general approach exhibits features which afford the Court extreme flexibility to take underhand account of extra-legal factors of judicial decision-making, notably political and ideological goals and institutional self-interest. In its *Pringle* and *Gauweiler* decisions the Court carries that approach to extremes, to a point where legal reasoning no longer imposes any meaningful constraints on judicial decision-making. It will be suggested, further, that the Court of Justice's integrationist, pro-Union response to the eurocrisis is mirrored by the politically compliant approach of the FCC which, in its judgments on the legality of the Greek financial aid measures, the eurozone's temporary and permanent rescue funds, and the ECB's so-called Outright Monetary Transactions (OMT) unlimited bonds buys programme, effectively abandons most central tenets of its long-established and well-considered case law on the principles governing the relationship between EU and national constitutional law, the principles of national sovereignty, the non-negotiable core identity of the German Constitution and the limits that imposes on the scope of the EU's supranational authority conferred by the EU Treaties. It is concluded that if the interpretative approaches adopted by the courts during the eurocrisis were universalised, they would free judicial decision-making from textual constraints and the power of relevant judicial precedent alike, and allow the courts to decide cases purely on putative teleological and subjective consequentialist considerations even in areas where judicial review is the only means of ensuring accountability. In effect, the courts adopted an approach that would leave them entirely free from methodological constraints. This is directly contrary to the axioms which purport to inform and legitimise both the EU Treaties and national constitutional law. Governance of the eurozone thus effectively became unconstrained.

II THE *ESM* JUDGMENTS

On 2 February 2012, the euro area Member States concluded the Treaty establishing the European Stability Mechanism (ESM) as an international treaty organisation with its own legal personality. The purpose of the ESM is to provide financial support subject to conditionality, to the benefit of ESM members which are experiencing refinancing problems on the financial markets. For that purpose, the ESM is authorised to raise funds by issuing debt instruments or via other arrangements with the eurozone governments, financial institutions or other third parties. The maximum lending and loans guarantee capacity is set initially at €500 billion but may be increased by the ESM members. The strict conditionality to which any support must be subject may take the form, notably, of a macro-economic or fiscal adjustment programme. Any bonds issued by the ESM on the capital markets are collectively and individually guaranteed by the eurozone governments, with Germany assuming liabilities of initially around €190 billion according to a set formula. Other Member States assume a lesser share broadly in line with the size of their economies. If one of the ESM members is unable to meet its financial commitments, its share of the guarantees shall be assumed by the remaining ESM members according to the same formula, with Germany again assuming the largest individual share of the burden.

Previous rescue packages for individual countries and the eurozone's temporary rescue fund, the EFSF,[1] were adopted outside the Treaty framework or, in the case of the EFSF, on the basis of Article 122(2) TFEU which provides for mutual financial assistance among EU Member States in exceptional cases, notably 'natural disasters'.[2] The eurocrisis has all the hallmarks of a disaster in slow motion. However, the disaster is hardly a natural one.

1 *The* Pringle *Judgment*

In April 2012 Thomas Pringle, a member of the Irish Parliament, brought proceedings against the Irish government on the grounds, first, that Council Decision 2011/

---

[1] European Financial Stability Facility

[2] To avoid renewed public controversy which had accompanied the use of the 'natural disasters' provision of the Treaties, the Member States chose to adopt Decision 2011/199 European Council Decision 2011/199/EU of 25 March 2011 amending Article 136 of the Treaty on the Functioning of the European Union with regard to a stability mechanism for Member States whose currency is the euro [2011] OJ L91/1 for the purposes of changing the EU Treaties to insert a new provision into the Functioning of the European Union Treaty (TFEU) authorising the eurozone governments to establish a permanent rescue mechanism.

199 entailed an alteration of the competences of the EU so that the simplified treaty revision provided by Article 48(6) Treaty on European Union (TEU)[3] should not have been used, and, second, that the proposed treaty amendment was inconsistent with the provisions of the Treaties concerning economic and monetary union and in particular the 'no bail out' principle under Article 125 Treaty on the Functioning of the EU (TFEU). The Irish Supreme Court referred the questions to the Court of Justice which applied the accelerated procedure. The case was heard by the Grand Chamber of then twenty-seven judges.[4] There were two principal grounds of the challenge against the ESM.

(1) The ESM: Economic or Monetary Policy?

First, Article 48(6) TEU states that the simplified revision procedure may only be used for amending provisions contained in Part III of the TFEU. The amendment of Article 136 TFEU envisaged by Council Decision 2011/199/EU authorises the eurozone members to do what otherwise appears prohibited by Article 125, namely to set up a mechanism for mutual financial assistance, and to do so outside the EU framework and by an international agreement which only binds the members of the eurozone. Mr Pringle submitted that, in the event that the Court should decide that Decision 2011/199 does not increase the powers of the Union and that the stability mechanism may be implemented by a multilateral agreement outside the framework of Union law, that agreement would still affect the scope of the Union's powers in so far as it directly encroaches on its exclusive competence in relation to monetary policy.

Mr Pringle's argument is convincing but was dismissed by the Court which emphasises that the TFEU 'contains no definition of monetary policy' and in addition refers 'in its provisions relating to that policy, to the objectives, rather than to the instruments, of monetary policy'.[5] The Court further stressed that the 'the primary objective of the Union's monetary policy is to maintain price stability' while the objective pursued by the ESM 'is to safeguard the stability of the euro area as a whole' which in the Court's view is 'clearly distinct from the objective of maintaining price stability, which is the primary objective of the Union's monetary policy'.[6] For this reason the Court concluded that the ESM 'clearly' falls within the Union's economic policy and not monetary policy notwithstanding the fact that 'the stability of the euro area may have repercussions on [sic] the stability of the currency used within that area', as 'an economic policy measure cannot be treated as

---

[3] Art 48(6) TEU introduces a simplified treaty revision which does not require Member States to convene a convention composed of representatives of the national Parliaments, of the Heads of State or Government of the Member States, of the European Parliament and of the Commission.

[4] Case C-370/12 *Thomas Pringle v Government of Ireland, Ireland, The Attorney General* EU:C:2012:756.

[5] ibid para 53.

[6] ibid para 56.

Gunnar Beck

equivalent to a monetary policy measure for the sole reason that it may have indirect effects on the stability of the euro'.[7]

Unsurprisingly, the Court's finding in this regard has received a favourable scholarly write-up. Adam and Parras have praised the 'legal pragmatism' of the Court's reasoning as the exclusive monetary policy prerogative of the Union would have precluded any intergovernmental mutual assistance.[8] The authors, it should be said, here rather casually, skirt over the narrow definition of the Union's complementary (and not shared) competence to coordinate the economic policies of the Member States.[9] Koutrakos commends the decision as 'fully reasoned' and 'tightly argued' in its argumentation which combines textual and purposive considerations in a manner that is 'convincing' and 'persuasive' in its conclusions.[10] And Hinarejos concludes her case note:

> The Economic and Monetary Union provisions in the Treaties were designed to prevent a crisis, but not to manage one; as such, they needed to be interpreted in a purposive and dynamic manner to ensure that the EU's legal framework does not become obsolete and that the eurozone is capable of dealing effectively with this crisis of confidence. This was the role of the court, and one that it discharged well.[11]

Paul Craig, like Koutrakos, recognises the multiplicity of interpretative criteria employed by the Court, but goes one stage further and commends the judgment as an almost ideal typical example of the synthetic use of teleological and text-based argumentation, i.e., of what he calls the 'conjunction of text, purpose, and teleology that informs legal reasoning'.[12] Craig, however, does not spell out what distinguishes the Court's putative exemplary fusion of these considerations from arbitrary judicial decision-making. And, finally, de Witte and Beukers add their voices to the generally uncritical reception of the *Pringle* decision when they conclude: 'All in all, the Court has given in Pringle a well-reasoned judgment expressing a good mixture of legal principle and political pragmatism'.[13] While the Court's 'pragmatic' deference to the eurozone governments no doubt appeased the financial markets, at least in the short term, its legal reasoning lays itself open to several objections.

---

[7] ibid.

[8] S Adam and FJM Parras, 'The European Stability Mechanism through the Legal Meanderings of the Union's Constitutionalism: Comment on Pringle' (2013) 38 European Law Review 848, 856.

[9] Thomas, for example, raises doubts as to whether the Union is competent to adopt the 'Six-Pack', ie the Fiscal Compact, adherence to which is a condition for aid under the ESM. See S Thomas, 'Commentaire de l'Arrêt "Pringle"' (2013) Revue du Droit de l'Union Européenne 198, 205.

[10] P Koutrakos, 'Political Choices and Europe's Judges' (2013) 38 European Law Review 291.

[11] A Hinarejos, 'The Court of Justice of the EU and the Legality of the European Stability Mechanism' (2013) 72 CLJ 237.

[12] P Craig, 'Pringle: Legal Reasoning, Text, Purpose and Teleology' (2013) 20 Maastricht Journal of European and Comparative Law 3.

[13] B de Witte and T Beukers, 'The Court of Justice Approves the Creation of the European Stability Mechanism: Pringle' (2013) 50 CMLR 805.

Although the Treaty does not define monetary policy it is misleading to suggest that the TFEU does not refer to specific instruments of monetary policy. Article 127(2) TFEU, for instance, mentions foreign exchange operations, the holding and managing of foreign reserves, and the operation of the payments system. Nor is it accurate to suggest that the ESM does not fall within the range of monetary policy instruments because it may merely 'have indirect effects on the stability of the euro' and the principal objective of monetary policy, the pursuit of price stability. The amended paragraph (3) of Article 136 inserted by Decision 2011/199 expressly states that the 'stability mechanism [may only] be activated if indispensable to safeguard the stability of the euro area as a whole'. That objective is central to the rescue fund. It is submitted that it is as implausible to suggest that a measure expressly designed to stabilise the currency, is nothing to do with monetary policy, as it is unconvincing to maintain that the ultimate objective of price stability is not also the stability of the euro and the currency union.[14]

The Court's strict separation between monetary and economic policy appears disingenuous in view of the various 'unconventional' measures by which the ECB has so far tried to prop up the euro. Its purchase of over €210bn of eurozone government debt in 2010 and 2011, especially of Greek government bonds, was occasioned by fears of a break-up of the eurozone, and so was the provision of emergency credit by the ECB to Cyprus and Greece as well the flooding of the money and capital markets with successive packages of up to €500 billion of near cost-free credit facilities, the so-called LTROs, to commercial banks to induce them to buy eurozone government debt. The ECB thereby locked governments and European taxpayers into a banking bailout as part of the general euro rescue operation, at a time when the indebtedness of many EU governments, namely, Ireland's or Spain's, had already been dramatically increased by a series of national banking bailouts and failing national property markets. The objective behind all the measures which manifestly exceed the mandate of the ECB, which is obliged by the Treaties to subordinate all goals to that of price stability, has been the bankrolling of individual governments and the easing of refinancing conditions for moribund banks. As such, the ECB's bonds buys have been justified as falling within the Bank's monetary policy and designed to stabilise the currency union. This likewise

---

[14] Art 119 TFEU further emphasises the close connection between the Union's monetary policy and its coordinating and supporting economic policy role, and it likewise draws attention to the link between stable prices, fiscal discipline and currency stability. The Court suggests that interstate financial assistance contributes to overall economic and economic stability, though it seems to deny that price stability does so too. On this questionable basis the Court is able to maintain that while price stability is the proper domain of the ECB's monetary policy mandate, mutual financial assistance and the easing of refinancing conditions for governments on the capital markets is a matter of economic policy which falls outside the Bank's mandate. This position would be tenable if the ECB had respected the limits of its Treaty mandate and not strayed into providing financial assistance to embattled euro governments, as the ECB has evidently exceeded its mandate with its subsequent OMT and QE programmes and progressive quantitative easing efforts and started buying bonds from embattled eurozone countries well before the ESM was set up. The Court scrupulously refrained from such criticism in *Pringle*.

applies to the ECB's assumption of extensive supervisory functions as part of the so-called banking union which lack any basis in the current EU Treaties, no less than ECB President Draghiavelli's so-called OMT and QE programmes announced in September 2012 and January 2015, which expressly link any future bond buys in support of indebted euro members to their compliance with the requirements of the ESM and the Fiscal Compact. The OMT programme therefore, while presented as falling within the Bank's monetary policy prerogative, is manifestly linked to fiscal and banking consolidation measures.[15]

Contrary to its general expansive *communautaire* reading of the Union's powers, the Court of Justice in *Pringle* for the first time interpreted the Union's competences narrowly in order to further the integrationist cause. If the Court had interpreted the scope of the EU's monetary policy more broadly – its usual expansive approach in interpreting the EU's powers – and had decided that the ESM fell wholly or partially into the area of monetary policy, the ESM would have encroached on the Union's exclusive monetary policy powers and would have been unlawfully adopted under the simplified treaty revision procedure. On the narrow monetary policy definition of the *Pringle* case the OMT and later PSPP bond-buying programmes would clearly fall outside the ECB's mandate.

(2) Compatibility with the EU Treaties, Especially Article 125 TFEU

Second, Pringle submitted that Decision 2011/199 and the establishment of the ESM irrespective of the legality of the Decision were inconsistent with the provisions of the EU Treaties concerning economic and monetary union, notably Articles 123 and 125 TFEU. Article 123 prohibits monetary financing of governments by the ECB, while Article 125 states that neither 'the Union institutions' nor 'a Member State' shall 'assume the commitments of central governments, regional, local or other public authorities, other bodies governed by public law, or public undertakings of another Member State'. The Court dismissed the applicant's argument in relation to both articles. Regarding Article 123 TFEU the Court found that the provision is addressed only to the ECB and so its wording does not preclude bond purchases via the ESM. This is correct but the Court's strict literal interpretation ignores the aid to construction of Article 123 TFEU which is provided by Council Regulation (EC) No. 3603/93.[16]

---

[15]   In reality, all these measures undertaken by the ECB are concerned with the stabilisation of the euro as much as, if not more than, with monetary policy traditionally conceived, just as the ESM authorises Member States to do more or less what the ECB is prohibited from doing by Art 123 TFEU but has nevertheless been doing since at least 2010, namely to purchase government bonds. It is therefore difficult to comprehend how measures adopted by the Member States, which share the same objective with the ECB's policies and broadly amount to the same category of measures best described as financial assistance to governments and the banking sector, should be construed as falling exclusively or predominantly within a different area of competence, namely economic policy, when the same measure must be regarded as part of monetary policy when resorted to by the ECB.

[16]   Council Regulation (EC) 3603/93 of 13 December 1993 specifying definitions for the application of the Prohibitions referred to in Arts 104 and 104b (1) of the Treaty [now Art 125 TFEU] [1993] OJ L332/1.

Council Regulation No. 3603/93 makes clear that Article 123 not only applies to primary market, i.e. direct, purchases but extends to secondary market bonds purchases where these might facilitate monetary state financing. As the ESM envisages bond purchases specifically for the purposes of easing refinancing conditions for national government (i.e. state financing), the only sensible conclusion must be that the ESM by intention and/or in effect operates to circumvent the prohibition on state financing in Article 123 TFEU. The ESM, therefore, although not in breach of the wording of Article 123 TFEU, clearly runs counter to its purpose.

The Court further upheld the compatibility of Decision 2011/199 with Article 125 TFEU based on a mixture of literal, teleological and practical arguments. The Court ruled:

> The granting of financial assistance by one or more Member States to a Member State ... [leaves that Member State] responsible for its commitments to its creditors provided that the conditions attached to such assistance are such as to prompt that Member State to implement a sound budgetary policy.[17]

It followed, the CJEU maintained, that 'the ESM will not act as guarantor of the debts of the recipient Member State [as] the latter will remain responsible to its creditors for its financial commitments'.[18] Furthermore, 'the granting of financial assistance to an ESM Member in the form of a credit line, in accordance with Article 14 of the ESM Treaty, or in the form of loans, in accordance with Articles 15 and 16 of the ESM Treaty, in no way implies that the ESM will assume the debts of the recipient Member State'.[19] The Court of Justice here resorts to a seemingly strict literal argument: mutual financial assistance between two or more eurozone countries and the assumption of existing debts of one such country by one or more other euro members, are two entirely different things because 'such assistance amounts to the creation of a new debt, owed to the ESM by that recipient Member State, which remains responsible for its commitments to its creditors in respect of its existing debts'.[20]

In essence the Court confines Article 125 TFEU to cases where the existing debt of one country is legally assigned to another Member State so that that state steps into the shoes of the original debtor and formally assumes legal liability for its pre-existing debt. Any other form of mutual financial assistance involving a transfer of the risk of default from the original debtor to the assisting state(s) but without a formal transfer of one and the same debt, the CJEU in effect maintains, is outside the scope of the 'no-bail out' clause. The Court's extreme only apparently literal construction effectively confines Article 125 TFEU to the narrowest of circumstances – the legal assignment of existing debts from one Member State to another. As the purpose of

---

[17] *Pringle* (n 4) para 137.
[18] ibid para 138.
[19] ibid para 139.
[20] ibid.

such an assignment – risk transfer – can easily be achieved by other means, be it the establishment of a rescue fund or other multi- or bilateral aid packages which leave the donor country formally responsible for the original debt, the Court's apparent literalism renders the prohibition in Article 125 TFEU effectively meaningless – all it does, on the Court's implausible reading, is to prohibit a particular legal construction, but neither the transfer of financial risk between eurozone governments nor the mutualisation of debt.

It is practically unprecedented for the CJEU to rely on an extreme literal interpretation which at the same time effectively reduces a central Treaty provision to absurdity. The Court's supposed literal interpretation even fails on its own terms. Under the ESM Treaty euro members guarantee loans and guarantees given by the ESM according to a contribution formula equivalent to their shares in the capital of the ECB. If one eurozone member is unable to honour its commitments, it falls to the remaining ESM members to assume the shortfall.[21] That would be precisely the 'assumption of liability' which, even on the CJEU's view, is prohibited by Article 125 TFEU. The supposedly literal interpretation of Article 125 TFEU patently conflicts with an equally literal interpretation of the ESM Treaty.

The Court further refers to 'the preparatory work relating to the Treaty of Maastricht' which discloses 'that the aim of Article 125 TFEU is to ensure that the Member States follow a sound budgetary policy'.[22] The ESM, the Court argues, takes account of this objective in that it links the award of financial assistance to 'strict conditionality . . . [designed to] ensure that the Member States pursue a sound budgetary policy'.[23] The ESM, the Court opines, therefore complies with Article 125 TFEU as it

> ensures that the Member States remain subject to the logic of the market when they enter into debt, since that ought to prompt them to maintain budgetary discipline. Compliance with such discipline contributes at Union level to the attainment of a higher objective, namely maintaining the financial stability of the monetary union.[24]

It is noteworthy that the Court here combines a supposedly strictly literal approach as its main argument, with a meta-teleological rationale for Article 125 TFEU nowhere spelled out in the Treaties, the ill-defined 'sound budgetary policy' objective which the Court chooses to read into the Treaties at a high level of generality in the absence of specific policy prescriptions.[25] The Court conveniently ignores that the Maastricht Treaty whose provisions have been retained in all subsequent

---

[21]   Art 25(2) ESM Treaty.
[22]   *Pringle* (n 4) para 135.
[23]   ibid para 143.
[24]   ibid para 135.
[25]   The Court maintains that 'strict conditionality' ensures Member States remain subject to the market. This confidence seems surprising indeed in view of the fact that a previous international agreement entered into by Member States, namely the Stability and Growth Pact signed in the 1990s, has been

revision treaties including the Lisbon Treaty currently in force, and made a clear choice, apparent from the wording of Articles 123, 125 and 127 TFEU, that budgetary discipline was to be achieved not through the mutualisation of debt but in accordance with the principle of individual national responsibility for public debts.

It is this teleological limb of the Court's argument which has found the most favour with academic commentators.[26] Contrary to the Court's appeal to the *travaux préparatoires*, however, the discussion surrounding the launching of EMU in the 1990s, confirms that Article 125 TFEU was intended to codify a policy choice by the prospective euro members that financial stability be best safeguarded by preventing any mutualisation of national public debt. That view is further supported by the words of Article 125 TFEU. Contrary to ECB President Draghi's announcement of 26 July 2012[27] the Treaties nowhere state either that the 'euro is irreversible' or even that membership of any one country in the currency union should or had to be irreversible. Article 125 TFEU on any ordinary language reading precludes mutual financial assistance, and there is nothing in the EU Treaties to suggest either euro members, or the EU institutions, should assume greater control over one another's fiscal policies or guarantee one's another debt.[28]

Adam and Parras,[29] in common with others,[30] praise the Court for its imaginative teleology. The more convincing construction of the rationale of Article 125 TFEU, it is submitted, would have been an ordinary language reading according to which 'the assumption of the commitments' of one Member State by another would have been taken to refer to, and strictly prohibit, any legal or any de facto transfer of the financial risk of public debt between Member States save where expressly provided for in the Treaties and strictly limited to the purposes of those exceptional provisions. This alternative interpretation is supported by the text of Article 125 TFEU which states that its provisions apply 'without prejudice to mutual financial guarantees for the joint execution of a specific project'.[31] That reference would in effect be otiose if

---

broken since its inception on a year-on-year basis by an average of two-thirds of the eurozone Member States. That pact, clear though its wording and annual as well as overall debt levels were, did nothing to ensure the observance of precisely that 'sound budgetary policy' which the Court now so confidently states it expects the ESM Agreement and the Fiscal Compact to promote.

[26] Adam and Parras (n 8) 859, for instance, are full of praise for 'this praetorian interpretation of Art. 125 TFEU [which] reproduces almost word for word the two conditions that form the guiding thread of the ESM Treaty itself, ie (1) the 'safeguarding the financial stability of the Euro Area' and (2) the granting of ESM aid only subject to 'strict conditionality'.

[27] M Draghi, 'Speech' (Global Investment Conference, London, 26 July 2012) www.ecb.europa.eu/ press/key/date/2012/html/sp120726.en.html accessed April 2018.

[28] Even in the long-established currency union of the United States individual states remain responsible for their liabilities – there is no mutual assistance between US states.

[29] Adam and Parras (n 8).

[30] See eg PA van Malleghem, 'Pringle: A Paradigm Shift in the European Union's Monetary Constitution' (2013) 14 German Law Journal 141, 162; Craig (n 12) 11; de Witte and Beukers (n 13) 805–48.

[31] At para 31 of the *Pringle* judgment the Court states:

Article 125 TFEU had been intended, as the Court conveniently decided, to be confined to situations involving the formal assignment of existing debt from one Member State to another.

It is difficult not to conclude that the CJEU's doctrinally and normatively unsystematic and ultimately unconvincing conjunction of literal, genetic and teleological arguments in support of its counter-intuitive and almost meaninglessly narrow interpretation of Article 125 TFEU is anything other than a very strained attempt to provide *ex post* judicial legitimation for a political decision, namely, the decision by the eurozone governments to try to save the single currency irrespective of the Treaties and in defiance of many of its specific provisions.

III THE BUNDESVERFASSUNGSGERICHT'S *ESM* JUDGMENT

The eurocrisis reached the German Bundesverfassungsgericht or FCC before it worked its way through the EU courts. The judicial response of the FCC, however, has been broadly similar and as methodologically and doctrinally unconvincing as the CJEU's: it provides in general a good example of the extreme reluctance of courts to assert constitutional restraints on executive action in areas of foreign and/or budgetary politics even where constitutional provisions or previous judicial decisions appear clear and sufficiently precise or to enforce national laws against major international financial institutions.[32] In short, where democratic accountability is suspended and replaced with judicial review as the principal or sole means of ensuring states or international bodies comply with treaties, the courts entrusted with the task of enforcing the treaty arrangements seem ill-equipped to discharge that function robustly and impartially and free from institutional or personal self-interest. For judges are rarely as independent as the Western mythology of the rule of law suggests but are part of the establishment of governance and are all too often appointed by bodies or groups to which they remain beholden.

Article 122(2) TFEU provides that the Union may grant ad hoc financial assistance to a Member State which is in difficulties or is seriously threatened with severe difficulties caused by natural disasters or exceptional occurrences beyond its control. If Article 125 TFEU prohibited any financial assistance whatever by the Union or the Member States to another Member State, Article 122 TFEU would have had to state that it derogated from Article 125 TFEU.

In view of the text of Art 125 TFEU it is difficult to construe this argument as anything other than disingenuous.

[32] It also illustrates that Germany's historical guilt complex, over seventy years after the end of the Second World War, appears to make it impossible for the country's political and judicial 'elite' to assert national self-interest and the rule of rule over the demands of European integration and appeals to Germany's special historical responsibility. This is all the more remarkable in that if anything the calamity of the Second World War imposes a special obligation on German government's to respect, and not to abandon, strict respect for the law.

1 Background

In its *Maastricht*[33] and *Lisbon*[34] judgments the FCC laid down a number of strict limits to further EU integration. These limits, the Court ruled, were an expression of the inalienable core of the Grundgesetz which could not be abandoned, at least for as long as Germany remains a sovereign state within the EU. However, as soon as the limits were put to the test by the German government giving consent to numerous euro rescue and mutual financial assistance measures, the FCC simply relaxed the conditions previously laid down and restated, modified and in the end all but abandoned its established constitutional position which it had carefully developed and fine-tuned over nearly forty years.

The FCC first considered the proposals for European Economic and Monetary Union (EMU) in 1992 when it had to consider the compatibility of the Maastricht Treaty with the German Constitution. In its so-called *Maastricht* judgment the Court concluded that the abolition of the Deutschmark and the effective subordination of the Bundesbank to the ECB were not in breach of the German Basic Law provided, and this is crucial, the treaty provisions for EMU do not, in the words of the German Constitutional Court, submit Germany to a self-propelling and uncontrollable automatism leading 'from monetary to full fiscal and political union'.[35] In the FCC's view the Maastricht Treaty met this condition 'because according to the [Maastricht] Treaty monetary union no more automatically entails a political union than an economic union'. Before any steps in this direction, the Court insisted, a fundamental treaty change was required, 'which cannot come about without a decision of the relevant national political institutions including that of the German parliament'.[36]

In the *Maastricht* judgment the FCC in particular considered whether the EU Treaties gave adequate protection to the objectives of price stability and national fiscal discipline and concluded that any fears to the contrary were 'far-fetched and unfounded' as 'the prohibition of monetary state financing by the ECB', i.e., against bond buying by the ECB, and the 'no bail out principle' provided adequate and reliable safeguards in this respect.[37]

To assess the judicial 'sense of judgment' it is instructive to compare the confident predictions of the FCC in the *Lisbon* and particularly the *Maastricht* judgment with the euro rescue scenario they were asked to assess in 2012. By the time of the *ESM* judgment in September 2012:

---

[33] BVerfGE 89, 155 decision of 12 October 1993, Az: 2 BvR 2134, 2159/92; *Brunner v European Union Treaty* CMLR [1994] 57.

[34] BVerfG, 2 BvE 2/08 decision of 30 June 2009, Absatz-Nr (1–421).

[35] BVerfGE 89, 155 (judgment of 12 October 1993), 2 BvR 2134, 2159/92, headnote 9.c) and paras 146–56.

[36] ibid para 151; see also para 155.

[37] ibid para 147.

- Germany had pledged well in excess of €100bn to assist other euro members, in addition to between €498 and €924bn so-called Target2 loans which the Bundesbank is owed by other euro system central banks.[38]
- The 'no bail clause', i.e., Article 125 TFEU, had been turned on its head, and Germany had pledged financial contributions of €190bn under the ESM alone, with additional funds available subject to simple parliamentary approval on top of funds already provided under different rescue and support mechanisms.
- The ECB had bought around €214bn of eurozone government bonds in 2010 and 2011 and in 2012 announced that in defiance of Article 123 TFEU it would be prepared to purchase unlimited amounts of euro government bonds if 'necessary'.
- Greece had two so-called haircuts, with further haircuts expected at regular intervals.
- The cost of the debt already written off and yet to be written off will be borne primarily by taxpayers not only in Germany but also other north European eurozone states.
- According to Article 127 TFEU the ECB is committed to price stability as its primary objective. Price stability literally means zero inflation, and, in practice, to keep inflation as low as possible. In numerous press conferences, speeches and written communications, however, ECB President Draghi nonetheless declared that he will interpret that commitment to refer to an annual inflation rate of 'below but close to two per cent'. He has brought the ECB's inflation target into line with those of the US Fed, the Bank of England, the Bank of Japan and other central banks notwithstanding the fact that the regulatory frameworks for all these central banks differs from that for the ECB and that the ECB's mandate is unique and unambiguous in confining monetary policy in the eurozone to the overriding objective of combating inflation.

In the opinion of Germany's top judges, the Maastricht Treaty provided adequate safeguards against each and all of these events: the Treaties were clear, the judges held, that there could be no bailouts, no joint liability, no money printing, no bond buys by the ECB, and the judges expressed confidence that there would be price stability in accordance with the Treaties. None of the things which subsequently happened, could have happened if we believe Germany's highest-ranking judges. So much for the judicial sense of judgement.

The FCC next evaluated the EU integration process in its *Lisbon* judgment of 2009.[39] In this case the Court identified a number of core areas of national

---

[38] Deutsche Bundesbank – Eurosystem website: www.bundesbank.de/navigation/de/aufgaben/unbar er_zahlungsverkehr/target2/target2_saldo/target2_saldo.html accessed April 2018.

[39] Like most other constitutional challenges to EU treaty reforms and the euro rescue measures this challenge was brought under Arts 20 and 38 of the German Basic Law, ie, on the basis of the constitutionally enshrined principle of democratic self-government and the right to elect popular representatives to the legislature. Judicial consideration in all these cases then revolves around the

policymaking including social security, the basic legal framework for the organisation of the people's economic and social living conditions, cultural policy including
linguistic policy and the status of religious communities, policies protecting national
identity and criminal justice, which, according to the FCC, collectively define the
minimum core of national sovereignty.[40]

The key to the exercise of sovereignty in these central areas of policymaking, the
Court went on, is the power to control taxation and expenditure. Only when the
Bundestag is able to determine the fundamental guidelines of taxation and expen-
diture, can Germany still be regarded as self-governing in accordance with the
principles of representative democracy as laid down in Articles 20 and 38 of the
German Basic Law (i.e. Grundgesetz, hereafter 'GG'):

> A transfer of the right of the Bundestag to adopt the budget and control its
> implementation by the government which would violate the principle of democ-
> racy and the right to elect the German Bundestag ... would occur if the determina-
> tion of the type and amount of the levies imposed on the citizen were supra-
> nationalised to a considerable extent. The German Bundestag must decide, in an
> accountable manner vis-à-vis the people, on the total amount of the burdens placed
> on citizens. The same applies correspondingly to essential state expenditure. In this
> area, the responsibility concerning social policy in particular is subject to the
> democratic decision-making process, which citizens want to influence through
> free and equal elections.[41]

This principle may be called the principle of national budgetary autonomy.
According to the FCC, it is a *sine qua non* of national sovereignty any meaningful
constitutional model of democratic self-government through representative
institutions.[42]

Representative democracy, according to the FCC, implies parliamentary budgetary autonomy. Or to put it differently, for as long as there still is a separate German
state, that state, the FCC declared, can only be described as democratic and
sovereign if its parliament retains budgetary autonomy. The German parliament
may not surrender that right until the German people have consented to the
submersion of their country within a larger European Union with its own constitution. That act would be tantamount to the self-extinction of Germany as a sovereign
state. The *Lisbon* judgment is crystal clear on this point.

The principle of parliamentary budgetary autonomy soon assumed centre stage in
the FCC's decision to uphold the various Greek aid packages and first temporary euro

---

issue of whether the proposed transfer of further powers to Brussels further undermines the ideal of
democratic accountability and progressively deprives the right to vote of any significance as fewer and
fewer decisions are taken at national level over which citizens have at least a measure of control in
national elections.

[40] See BVerfG, 2 BvE 2/08 of 30 June 2009, Leitsatz 4 and paras 249–51.
[41] BVerfG, 2 BvE 2/08, 30 June 2009, para 256.
[42] ibid paras 256–57.

rescue package, the so-called European Financial Stability Facility (EFSF) handed down in September 2011. Notwithstanding the clear guidelines in the *Lisbon* judgment the Second Senate of the FCC under its new president, Andreas Voßkuhle, concluded that the Bundestag's budgetary autonomy was not to any decisive extent diminished by Germany's assumption of total loans and guarantees for Greece and other eurozone countries of up to €170 billion, despite the fact that this was 60 per cent of the entire federal budget of €306 billion in 2011.[43] Bizarrely, the FCC at the same time affirmed its position articulated two years earlier that Articles 20 and 38 GG require the Bundestag to retain its budgetary autonomy and that, in consequence, the potential liabilities assumed by the German government must not be such that the possible interest and capital repayment on any potential losses sustained would effectively deprive the German legislator of its financial freedom.[44]

2 The FCC'S 'Reasoning' in Its ESM Judgment

It only took one further year for the FCC in all but name to abandon the principle of budgetary autonomy. On 12 September 2012, the Court in effect decided that the initial German contribution of €190bn to the permanent euro rescue fund, the European Stability Mechanism (ESM), and even unlimited German liability for the debts of other eurozone governments was compatible with Germany's parliamentary budgetary autonomy provided only that the Bundestag itself agrees to the assumption of further liabilities and itself authorises loans beyond the initial ESM ceiling, even if these increases were unlimited.[45] To Germany's agreed and possible future obligations under the ESM must be added the German government's pre-existing guarantees, loans and guarantees to Greece, Portugal and Ireland in so far as they are not absorbed into the ESM, as well as the pro rata cost of two haircuts for Greece and, importantly, the Bundesbank's total Target2 credit exposure to the eurozone periphery which over the last seven years has oscillated between €498bn and €879bn[46] no less than any losses Germany may possibly suffer qua guarantor for any losses sustained by the ECB from its unlimited government bond-buying programmes announced by ECB President Draghiavelli in September 2012 and January 2015. The apparent much noted limit set by the FCC on Germany's total exposure under the ESM – the €190bn which the Bundestag can extend by simple majority – thus is no limit at all. In the FCC's opinion, Germany's continuing budgetary autonomy is unaffected even by potentially unlimited liabilities amounting to several times the size of the annual federal budget of roughly €310–315bn

---

[43] BVerfG, 2 BvR 987/10 decision of 7 September 2011, Absatz-Nr (1–142), paras 133–36.
[44] ibid paras 122–29.
[45] BVerfG, 2 BvR 1390/12 decision of 12 September 2012, Absatz-Nr (1–319), paras 254–76 and esp para 279.
[46] As of 30 September 2017 – Deutsche Bundesbank-Eurosystem: www.bundesbank.de/Navigation/DE/ Aufgaben/Unbarer_Zahlungsverkehr/TARGET2/TARGET2_Saldo/target2_saldo.html accessed April 2018.

which in 2013 included a deficit of over €25bn and a supplementary mid-term budget of €8bn to account for unforeseen expenditure in connection with the eurocrisis.[47]

In 1993 the Bundesverfassungsgericht decided that the Maastricht Treaty, with its 'no bail-out' clause, strict limits on public borrowing, and an independent central bank committed by law to fighting inflation and prohibited by Treaty to engage in monetary state financing (Article 123 TFEU) adequately ensured that monetary union could not evolve into a fiscal and transfer union. In 2009, in its *Lisbon* judgment, the FCC affirmed its earlier strict 'no bail-out' stance by drawing a red line to protect core areas of national sovereignty beyond which EU integration must not constitutionally advance unless and until the German state is submerged within a newly constituted European nation. Central to national sovereignty, the Court decided in 2009, is the principle of parliamentary budgetary autonomy, the ability of the national parliaments to shape the living conditions of their populations through democratically accountable policies involving taxation and expenditure. Without budgetary autonomy in this sense, the Court appeared to leave no doubt in 2009, the constitutional principle of democratic self-government and the right to vote, enshrined respectively in Articles 20 and 38 of the German Basic Law, would lose all real significance.

With its euro rescue judgments of September 2011 and 2012 the FCC turned its previous 2009 interpretation of the German Basic Law on its head. Formally, of course, the Court maintains the fiction of judicial consistency and legal certainty, because not even in its ESM judgment of 12 September 2012 did the Court explicitly abandon the principle of budgetary sovereignty. In reality, however, the FCC reduced that principle to absurdity when it decided that with an annual budget of around €310–315bn in each year over the period 2011–13 the Bundestag could and would retain its budgetary autonomy even if it makes available unsecured loans and guarantees of hundreds of billions of euros to international organisations like the ESM or individual eurozone states, which would surpass the size of the annual budget several times over. It is difficult to conceive of a less principled and more inconsistent and politically expedient position than that developed by the FCC between 2009 and 2014.[48]

---

[47] Bundesministerium der Finanzen: www.bundesfinanzministerium.de/Content/DE/Standardartikel/ Themen/Oeffentliche_Finanzen/Bundeshaushalt/Bundeshaushalt_2013/2013_07_30_Nachtragsh aushalt-in-Kraft-getreten.html accessed April 2018.

[48] According to the Ifo-Institute, Germany's largest and most influential economic policy research institute, Germany's total exposure to the eurozone currently stood in excess of €583 billion as of 15 January 2014 including the volatile inter-central bank TARGET2-credits financed by the Bundesbank (www.cesifo-group.de/ifoHome/policy/Haftungspegel.html accessed April 2018). As a result of the gradual increase in the Bundesbank's Target2-loans to €879bn on 30 September 2017 and the ongoing ECB's QE programme launched in January 2015. Germany's exposure has since risen by at least another half a trillion euros and, conceivably, to well in excess of €1tn if account is taken of the fact that any country which may default on its debts, will not be able to assume responsibility of its share for any resultant ECB losses under the ECB share, profit and loss allocation

The FCC confirmed the 12 September 2012 ESM decision which, formally, was a preliminary decision on an interlocutory application, in its final *ESM* judgment of 18 March 2014.[49] In addition to affirming that, in principle, even unlimited liability was compatible with the principle of the Bundestag's budgetary autonomy, the FCC went so far as to declare that that principle would not be violated even if the guarantees and unsecured loans to other euro members in effect committed the Bundestag to one and only one 'specific budgetary and fiscal policy', because, as the post-2009 FCC argues according to the laws of its own private logic, the principles of budgetary autonomy and democratic accountability through national elections could still be safeguarded if the national parliament transferred far-reaching budgetary powers to 'the organs of a supra- or international organisation'. The decision 'whether and to what extent this is sensible', the FCC concluded, is a matter for the legislator.[50] The principles of national sovereignty and democratic self-government, the Court literally concluded, continue to be observed if the nation's representative organs decide to transfer the kernel of its sovereign powers, their budgetary control, to the EU. The judges of the German FCC have opened a new chapter in the theory of democratic government: democracy is safe where the demos is free to elect representatives who, in one single act of surrender, are free to extinguish their own powers and the prerogatives of their electors.

3 The Decision to Refer the OMT

Following a complaint by a record 37,000 German citizens against the ECB's so-called Outright Monetary Transactions (OMT) programme, the FCC in June 2013 held further hearings to consider whether the unlimited bond-buying programme announced in September 2012 exceeded the Bank's mandate which the Treaties confine to monetary policy. In particular the Court was asked to consider whether the OMT programme was compatible with Article 123 TFEU and Council Regulation (EC) No. 3603/93 of 13 December 1993 and especially Recital 7 thereof which provides that the prohibition of direct government bonds purchases by the ECB likewise applies to any attempt to circumvent Article 123 TFEU by other means including secondary market purchases. This includes purchases by the ECB of eurozone government bonds on the secondary market where these may facilitate the (re)financing of public debt.

---

distribution key. If one or more eurozone countries default, Germany's obligations under the ESM will likewise rise to make up for the shortfall (see Arts 21 and 25 ESM Treaty). If the European Commission's or French President Macron's proposals for further eurozone integration are adopted in anything approaching their current form, Germany's total exposure will rise further still.

[49]   BVerfG, Entscheidung decision of 18 March 2014, 2 BvR 1390/12, Absatz-Nr (1–245).
[50]   ibid 168.

On 7 February 2014 the FCC published its considered assessment[51] of the OMT programme which left little doubt that the ECB had manifestly exceeded its mandate. The court noted that:

> Art. 123 sec. 1 TFEU prohibits the European Central Bank from purchasing government bonds directly from the issuing Member States. It seems obvious that this prohibition may not be circumvented by functionally equivalent measures. [The] neutralisation of interest rate spreads, selectivity of purchases, and the parallelism with EFSF and ESM assistance programmes indicate that the OMT Decision aims at a prohibited circumvention of Art. 123 sec. 1 TFEU. The following aspects can be added: The willingness to participate in a debt cut with regard to the bonds to be purchased; the increased risk; the option to keep the purchased government bonds to maturity; the interference with the price formation on the market, and the encouragement, coming from the ECB's Governing Council, of market participants to purchase the bonds in question on the primary market.

On those grounds, the FCC concludes 'there are important reasons to assume that [the OMT programme] exceeds the ECB's monetary policy mandate and thus infringes the powers of the Member States, and that it violates the prohibition of monetary financing of the budget'. The FCC concludes that on the basis of its detailed analysis it 'is thus inclined to regard the OMT Decision as an ultra vires act'.

The FCC's analysis is comprehensive, clear and convincing in its conclusion that the OMT is incompatible with the EU Treaties and a manifest breach of the ECB's mandate as defined, inter alia, by Articles 123 and 127 TFEU. The FCC reached that conclusion on four distinct grounds: first, a literal analysis of the wording of Articles 123 and 127 TFEU in conjunction with Council Regulation 3603/03; second, a teleological argument based on the underlying purposes of those provisions; third, an economic analysis assessing the effects of the OMT programme and whether the OMT programme falls under the prohibition of monetary state financing; and, fourth, an assessment of the question of whether the relevant CJEU case law on whether the objectives of an EU act including ECB policy decisions had to be determined subjectively in terms of the stated aims or objectively in terms of their effects.

For over forty years[52] the FCC had insisted that the EU is not a sovereign state and thus cannot define its own treaty-based powers which have been conferred on it by the sovereign Member States subject to the requirements of their national constitutions. If the CJEU alone could define the EU's powers, the EU would effectively be

---

[51] BVerfG, Vorlageentscheidung decision of 7 February 2014, 2 BvR 1390/12.

[52] See the line of cases beginning with *Internationale Handelsgesellschaft von Einfuhr- und Vorratsstelle für Getreide und Futtermittel*, decision of 29 May 1974 (2 BVL 52/71 (also known as *Solange I*)), BVerfGE 37, 271 [1974] CMLR 540; *Maastricht-Urteil*, BVerfGE 89, 155 of 12 October 1993, 2 BvR 2134, 2159/92 (also known as and cited in English as *Brunner v European Union Treaty*) CMLR [1994] 57; *Lissabon-Urteil* BVerfG, 2 BvE 2/08 decision of 30 June 2009, Absatz-Nr (1–421); *Honeywell*, BVerfG, 2 BvR 2661/06 of 6 July 2010, Absatz-Nr (1–116).

sovereign. The FCC therefore always insisted that, within Germany, it retained a jurisdiction of final review in relation to the interpretation of any EU measure or policy that may exceed the EU's powers and to block, where necessary, the application of any ultra vires EU act within Germany. On the basis of the FCC's clear and, it seemed, settled interpretation of the relationship between EU law and German constitutional law, it would have been logical for the FCC to declare the OMT inapplicable within its own jurisdiction and to prohibit the Bundesbank from participating in any bond buys under the OMT programme. That the Court refused to do so and instead referred the issue to the CJEU for further consideration, is not in itself in purely formal terms an act of unconditional submission to the higher judicial authority of the Luxembourg court, but it represents a clear break with its own interpretation of the German Basic Law and of the scope of its own constitutional review up to and including the *Lisbon* judgment.

4 The CJEU's Preliminary Ruling and the FCC's Act of Submission

The CJEU handed down its requested preliminary ruling on 16 June 2015.[53] The CJEU openly dismissed the FCC's assessment, ignored the detailed literal, purposive and economic arguments put forward by the FCC and concluded that, first, 'safeguarding an appropriate monetary policy transmission and the singleness of the monetary policy' was a legitimate monetary policy objective and that, second, for this reason and contrary to the assessment of the FCC, bond buys were monetary policy and hence fell within the ECB's mandate. The CJEU's ruling is poorly reasoned, defies clear Treaty language (Art 127 TFEU) and relevant EU legislation (EU Regulation 3603/03, esp. Recital (7)), ignores the patently obvious underlying objectives of these provisions as well as the CJEU's own inconvenient case law on whether the objective of an EU measure must be determined subjectively or objectively, and contains absolutely no economic analysis at all.

Crucially, the CJEU affords the ECB such a wide margin of policy discretion, that it in effect exempts the central bank from any kind of judicial review and thus leaves it free to take over economic policy functions as and when it thinks fit – policy functions which the Treaties largely reserve for the Member States. Since the EU Treaties exempt the ECB from democratic including parliamentary control, the FCC had always emphasised the importance of strict judicial control over the observance of the central bank's mandate. The CJEU, without consideration of the well-reasoned objections raised by the FCC in its 2014 referral decision and in open defiance of the special responsibility the Treaties assigned to the judiciary in upholding the legal constraints limiting the ECB's powers in the absence of democratic accountability, has made the ECB into the least accountable political institution in post-war non-Communist Europe.

---

[53]   Case C-62/14 *Gauweiler and Others* EU:C:2015:400.

In its *Honeywell* decision[54] the FCC stated that before declaring an EU act ultra vires, it would afford the CJEU 'the opportunity to interpret the Treaties, as well as to rule on the validity and interpretation of the acts in question, in the context of preliminary ruling proceedings according to Article 267 TFEU, insofar as it has not yet clarified the questions which have arisen'.[55] However, the *Honeywell* judgment did not commit the FCC to accept and follow the CJEU's preliminary ruling in the *OMT* case. In its *OMT* ruling the CJEU had not in any detail addressed but simply either ignored or brushed aside the economically and legally persuasive arguments in the FCC's ultra vires 2014 assessment of the OMT. Nevertheless, in its final judgment which formally concluded the *OMT* litigation, the FCC submitted like a lamb, abandoning its earlier detailed objections as if they had been no more than the untrained opinions of a law school applicant.

For about forty-five years, beginning with its *Internationale Handelsgesellschaft* judgment,[56] and culminating in its *Maastricht*,[57] *Lisbon*[58] and *Honeywell*[59] judgments the FCC with some modifications but nevertheless uncompromisingly emphasised that the EU's powers were predicated on the principle of conferral, that the principle of the supremacy of EU law only applied subject to that of conferral, and that the question of the compatibility of an EU act with the EU Treaties in so far as its application in Germany was concerned, could not be decided in isolation from the democratic guarantees contained in the Basic Law. If the EU's powers are subject to the principle of conferral and the German legislature can transfer powers only subject to the provisions of the Basic Law as interpreted by the FCC, then it followed, the FCC had argued since the 1970s, that if the Bundestag seeks to transfer powers it is not constitutionally authorised to cede, or if the EU institutions subsequently exercise their powers in a manner incompatible with the Basic Law, it is the FCC and it alone which has the right conclusively to assess and to invalidate such a constitutional breach within Germany just as the CJEU alone has the authority to invalidate an act of the EU institutions for the EU as a whole.[60] As the CJEU has no jurisdiction to interpret the German jurisdiction and

---

54 *Honeywell*, BVerfG, 2 BvR 2661/06 of 6 July 2010, Absatz-Nr. (1–116).
55 The *Honeywell* principle only relates to the FCC's *ultra vires review* which the FCC decided it would no longer exercise without a prior opinion of the CJEU. It does not commit the FCC to follow the CJEU's guidance, nor concern the second limb of the FCC's last resort jurisdiction which was clarified in the *Lisbon* judgment, the FCC's identity review. Under its identity review the FCC reserves the right to examine any EU act for its compatibility with the non-negotiable core of the German Basic Law including the principle of budgetary autonomy. If it is not compatible, as the FCC suggested in its 2014 OMT Opinion, no reference to the CJEU should have been made and the FCC should have declared the programme unconstitutional within Germany.
56 *Internationale Handelsgesellschaft von Einfuhr- und Vorratsstelle für Getreide und Futtermittel,* Entscheidung vom (n 52).
57 *Maastricht-Urteil* (n 52).
58 *Lissabon-Urteil* BVerfG, 2 BvE 2/08 of 30 June 2009, Absatz-Nr (1–421).
59 *Honeywell*, BVerfG, 2 BvR 2661/06 of 6 July 2010, Absatz-Nr (1–116).
60 See also Art 5 Vienna Convention on the Law of Treaties 1968.

is empowered by the Treaties only to interpret EU law and not whether its interpretation also respects the fundamental guarantees and principles of the German Basic Law, it appears to follow that it can only express a preliminary opinion, and thus at best deliver a provisional answer, in relation to the question of whether an EU act is ultra or intra vires. The German constitutional judges were substantially correct in their 2014 assessment of the legal defects of the OMT programme, but ultimately failed to show the courage to follow their own reasoning when they decided to refer the matter to the CJEU.

The problem of Kompetenz-Kompetenz spawned some of the finest examples of subtle interdisciplinary and sociologically, historically and philosophically informed constitutional reasoning by any court. Yet, when its intellectually convincing reasoning was put to the test by a wily Goldman Sachs-trained central banker determined to offload the debt of reckless banks and feckless governments onto the taxpayers and savers of the eurozone's more prudent members and social groups, who was supported by an inherently integrationist federalist court, the German judges lacked the cardinal virtue of the Enlightenment and liberal republicanism identified by Immnanuel Kant: 'Sapere aude – to courage to follow one's one reason'.

IV THE ECB'S QE PROGRAMME: A RERUN OF THE OMT LITIGATION

Courts rarely admit that they change their mind, that they abandoned a previous position or ruled the way they did not because it was right but because it was expedient. The fact that they don't, is part of the noble lie of the rule of law. It comes therefore as no surprise that even after its humiliating climbdown in the OMT litigation, the FCC has not in a purely formal sense unequivocally abandoned its claim to exercise a jurisdiction of the last resort over the EU's Treaty-based competences. That claim has recently been affirmed by the FCC in yet another ECB-related ultra vires and identity set of constitutional complaints by, inter alia, leading German industrialists, legal academics and economics professors.[61] In essence, the complainants submit that the ECB's Quantitative Easing programme launched in January 2015, on a quantitatively and structurally more significant scale than the OMT programme, is in breach of Article 123 TFEU, represents an arrogation by the ECB of general economic policy powers which the Treaties reserve to the Member States, and that it undercuts the incentives to pursue a sound budgetary policy which the CJEU in its *Pringle* and *Gauweiler* judgments had accepted were a *sine qua non* of the EU Treaty provisions governing the monetary union. For this reason, the complainants submitted, the QE programme represented a manifest and

---

[61] BVerfG, Beschluss des Zweiten Senats of 18 July 2017 – 2 BvR 859/15 – Rn (1–137); Case C-493/17 *Weiss v Germany*.

structurally significant shift in the division of competences between the EU and its members.

After nearly two years of deliberation and, one may add, hesitation the FCC once more concluded that the multiple complaints were well founded and affirmed, as it had previously done in relation to the OMT, that 'there were doubts that the PSPP[62] was compatible with the prohibition of monetary state financing in Art. 127 TFEU'.[63] The FCC gives the following reasons for its assessment:

- Although Art. 123(1) TFEU only categorically prohibits the purchase of government bonds by the ECB and the central banks of the Member States directly from EU institutions or the Member States, purchases on the secondary market are likewise prohibited if they appear intended to circumvent the objective pursued by Art. 123 TFEU.
- Several factors indicate that the ECB's PSPP decision violates Art. 123 TFEU, namely the fact that details of the purchases are announced in a manner that could create de facto certainty on the markets that issued government bonds will indeed be purchased by the euro system; that it is not possible to verify compliance with certain minimum periods between the issuing of debt securities on the primary market and the purchase of the relevant securities on the secondary market; that to date all purchased bonds were – without exception – held until maturity; and furthermore that the purchases include bonds that carry a negative yield from the outset.
- To determine whether the PSPP falls within the ECB's monetary policy mandate, it is necessary to delineate matters of a monetary policy nature from economic policy, the latter being primarily the responsibility of the Member States. In this regard, decisive factors include the aim of a measure which is to be determined objectively, the means chosen with a view to achieving this aim as well as their connection to other provisions.
- Based on an overall assessment of the relevant criteria of delimitation, the PSPP decision must be deemed to constitute a measure that is primarily of an economic policy nature. The FCC notes that the PSPP officially pursues a monetary policy objective and that monetary policy instruments are used to achieve this objective; however, the economic policy effects flowing from the volume of the PSPP and the resulting foreseeability of purchases of government bonds are integral features of the programme which are already inherent in its design. As far as the underlying monetary policy objective is concerned, the PSPP could thus prove to be disproportionate. In addition, the decisions on which the programme is based lack comprehensible reasons that would

---

[62] Public Sector Purchases Programme, ie, the purchase of government bonds by the ECB and national central banks of the eurozone. The PSPP represents by far the largest part of the ECB's QE which, however, also extends to corporate bonds and so-called asset-backed securities and covered bonds, all of which represent high-risk debt instruments issued by banks or other financial institutions.

[63] BVerfG, Beschluss des Zweiten Senats of 18 July 2017 – 2 BvR 859/15 – Rn (1–137), para 76.

allow for an ongoing review, during the multi-year period envisaged for the implementation of these decisions, as to whether there remains a continued need for the programme.

- The ECB Governing Council may be able, as appears from its Statute and Rules of Procedure, to modify the rules on risk sharing within the euro system in a way that would result in risks for the profit and loss accounts of the national central banks and also threaten the overall budgetary responsibility of national parliaments. In that event, an unlimited risk sharing within the euro would amount to a violation of Germany's constitutional identity within the meaning of Art. 79(3) GG if it became necessary to recapitalise the Bundesbank through budgetary resources to such extent that approval by the German Bundestag would be required in accordance with the principles established by the FCC its previous case law regarding the principle of principle of budgetary autonomy.[64]

National references for a preliminary ruling by the CJEU are typically sketchy and confined to specific questions. The FCC's 2014 OMT judgment contained a full legal analysis and all the ingredients for a final judgment. The FCC nevertheless chose to refer the matter to the CJEU and in a humiliating volte face subsequently accepted the Luxembourg court's poorly reasoned and methodologically unconvincing pro-Union preliminary ruling.

In its assessment of the PSPP component of the QE programme, the FCC once more provided a comprehensive and conclusive legal analysis but stopped short of giving the ECB the thumbs down and again decided to refer further consideration of the matter to the CJEU. Predictably the CJEU, brushing aside the FCC's reservations, upheld the legality of the ECB's QE programme in December 1918.[65] The FCC will now take another year or more to conclude the litigation. Except perhaps for the politically naive who still believe in the fairy tale of the rule of law, no one[66] expects anything other than a rerun of OMT saga: self-assertion by the FCC in theory, and submission in practice.

v THE CJEU'S AND FCC'S APPROACH TO LEGAL REASONING IN CONTEXT

The primary materials of EU law, especially the EU Treaties, are characterised by a high degree of legal uncertainty.[67] The same applies to most provisions of national constitutions including the German Basic Law. The Court of Justice and national

---

[64] ibid paras 76–121.
[65] Case C-493/17 Weiss and Others.
[66] When the FCC officially released its assessment of the PSPP on 15 August 2015, the event was barely registered by the financial markets, and not a single commentator cited in the German and international financial press evinced any serious expectation that, in the end, either the CJEU or, eventually, the FCC could rule the programme unlawful.
[67] Legal uncertainty has its origin in a combination of linguistic vagueness, value pluralism, 'gaps in the law' and rule instability as a specific source of uncertainty which is associated with precedent. Legal

higher constitutional courts further rely on broadly the same kinds of established interpretative arguments and techniques of statutory and case law interpretation although subject to a few important differences. In general terms, the Court of Justice's interpretative reasoning, the author shows elsewhere, is best understood in terms of a cumulative and flexible approach whereby the Court justifies its decisions in terms of the cumulative weight of purposive, systemic and literal arguments.[68] That approach differs from that of other courts in that the Court gives added weight to purposive considerations and in particular meta-teleological consideration.

Its cumulative interpretative approach allows the Court to justify its decisions by reference to the variable respective weight of the literal, teleological and systemic criteria of legal argumentation, with no automatic primacy accorded to literal arguments and considerable discretion in determining the relative weight and ranking of the various interpretative criteria from one case to another.[69] This does not mean the Court will always depart from the wording and clear meaning of treaty or legislative provisions, yet ordinary meaning is typically less likely to be conclusive in Union law and more likely to be displaced by purposive considerations in the deliberations of the Court of Justice than it is in the decisions of most national courts.

The author has argued elsewhere[70] that case law analysis across most areas of EU law shows that the CJEU has used the interpretative discretion afforded by its

uncertainty in all its forms is a pervasive and inescapable feature of primary legal materials and judicial reasoning alike notwithstanding the fact that the process of judicial interpretative argumentation is designed to, or purports to, resolve primary legal uncertainty through the application of techniques and criteria of statutory and case law interpretation. The application of these techniques and criteria, however, cannot escape, and is itself governed by, uncertainty. That uncertainty is not merely contingent. See T Endicott, 'Law and Language' in J Coleman and S Shapiro (eds), *The Oxford Handbook of Jurisprudence & Philosophy of Law* (OUP 2002) 935–68; G Beck, *The Legal Reasoning of the Court of Justice of the EU* (Hart 2013) 52–75, 91–114. A key reason for the high degree of conceptual vagueness and value pluralism in EU law lies in the fact that the EU treaty framework and much of the secondary legislation made under successive treaties embody political compromises which manifest themselves in unresolved conceptual and norm uncertainties in the texts of EU law. The Member States, by failing to resolve underlying differences about the degree of integration desired, effectively left it to the CJEU to find what the Court regards as the best interpretation of European integration evolving over time. This is a general observation which may justify the CJEU's exercise of judicial discretion in relation to Treaty provisions which display genuine uncertainty. This does not apply to the provisions outlining the governance of the eurozone which contain clear prescriptions (Art 127 TFEU) and prohibitions (Arts 123, 125 TFEU).

68 'In interpreting a provision of Community law it is necessary to consider not only its wording but also the context in which it occurs and the objects of the rules of which it is part' (Case C-292/82 *Merck v Hauptzollamt Hamburg-Jonas* EU:C:1983:335, para 12); the Court therefore takes account of the 'spirit, general scheme and wording of [provisions of Community law] as well as the system and objectives of the Treaty' (Case C-6/72 *Europemballage Corporation and Continental Can Company Inc v Commission of the European Communities* EU:C:1975:50 para 10). For more detailed discussion, see KPE Lasok and T Millett, *Judicial Control in the EU: Procedures and Principles* (Richmond 2004) paras 656–85; A Arnull, *The European Union and Its Court of Justice* (2nd edn, OUP 2006) 601–21; G Conway, *The Limits of Legal Reasoning and the European Court of Justice* (CUP 2012) 201–71; Beck (n 66) 278–331, 437–44.

69 See Lasok and Millett (n 67), paras 656–85.

70 Beck (n 66) 332–443.

cumulative approach to resolve norm pluralism and vagueness in the Treaties broadly in favour of the 'meta-objective' of 'ever closer union' of the preambles of the EU on which it draws as and when desired to resolve uncertainties in an integrationist direction. This *communautaire* predisposition in the CJEU's justificatory argumentation, however, varies subject to (1) the degree of clarity and precision of the provisions under consideration, (2) the Court's political acumen, especially with regard to the political, constitutional and budgetary sensitivities of Member States, but, crucially, subject to (3) the extent to which any particular case engages the fundamental interests of the EU and the scope of its powers.

In summary, this means that in cases where two or more interpretative criteria pull into opposite directions the CJEU will not automatically, or even commonly, favour a literal over a purposive interpretation. However, the Court may give preference to the wording of a provision, typically where this would either favour a *communautaire* solution to the interpretative problem at hand, or allow the Court to defer in politically sensitive cases and do so in a way that does not fundamentally restrict the competences of the Union. In most cases where the issues involved are neither politically sensitive nor fundamentally affect the interests and competences of the Union, the Court tends to do what courts tend to do in all legal systems: it by and large follows, or at least does not openly flout, the wording and natural meaning of the rules under consideration, especially if other considerations favour the same solution. In extremis, however, the methodological pluralism and attendant flexibility of the Court's cumulative approach afford the CJEU the freedom to reach almost any conclusion.

Practically all commentators have defended the *Pringle* judgment not only as a politically desirable outcome for integration but as a model of the synthetic use of teleological and text-based argumentation or, as Craig puts it, of the 'conjunction of text, purpose, and teleology that informs legal reasoning'.[71] It is undoubtedly correct that the Court of Justice commonly relies on more than one interpretative criterion, and so do many national constitutional courts, and that the Court of Justice's fused or cumulative approach in turn allows the Court considerable interpretative freedom in choosing how much weight to attach to literal as opposed to purposive and consequentialist criteria and in deciding when to favour linguistic over teleological considerations or vice versa. However, judicial decisions differ, or should differ, from political decisions in that they are, or should be, constrained, by legal argumentation. Law is law not least precisely because anything does not go. Where constitutions and treaties, despite their often high level of generality and abstraction, lay down clear objectives and precise constraints on political action, as the EU Treaties evidently do in relation to the conduct of monetary and economic policy by the EU institutions and Member States, they constrain, or should constrain, the range of permissible political options. If, in these circumstances, judicial reasoning

---

[71] Craig (n 12).

is open-ended, ultra-flexible and indeterminate in constraining possible outcomes, then the distinction between law and politics is blurred and, ultimately, extinguished. Judicial decisions would be subject to political pressure and expediency as much as political action. In these circumstances, laws and treaties no longer constrain political action.

The *Pringle* and *Gauweiler* judgments provide ideal examples of the inherent dangers in the Court's cumulative approach – in these cases the Court of Justice carries the interpretative freedom inherent in its methodologically open-ended and almost unconstrained cumulative approach to extremes. It does so in several ways. First, in *Pringle* the Court oscillates unsystematically between literal, genetic and meta-teleological arguments in relation to the ESM's compatibility with Article 125 TFEU and the other specific interpretative issues in the case, opting for whichever argument favours the desired politically convenient conclusion to uphold the measures agreed by the euro members. At the same time the Court ignores those arguments where they point in the opposite direction, be it purposive considerations below the catch-all meta-objective of 'ever closer union' which clearly confine the ECB to the promotion of price stability as an overriding objective and define the eurozone as a currency and not a fiscal union, or the principle of national budgetary responsibility and the 'moral hazard' argument that Member States can only be deterred from incurring higher debts if they alone are responsible for them, or arguments based on the wording and *travaux préparatoires* and political context of the 1990s which likewise support the view that mutual financial assistance was always intended to be excluded as such assistance might act as a disincentive to budgetary discipline.

Second, on the main issue – the compatibility of the ESM with Article 125 TFEU – the Court does not only adopt an extreme literal interpretation, but does so in a way that renders the provision effectively meaningless.[72] Moreover, its purported literal interpretation conflicts with an equally literal interpretation of the ESM Treaty.

Third, the Court's reference to the alleged underlying objective of Article 125 illustrates that the Court, in its teleological argumentation does not only refer to specific purposes and objectives expressly stated in the Treaties but justifies its preferred solution by reference not to express but inferred purposive considerations nowhere to be found in the Treaties, such as the survival of the euro. By including putative rather than textual purposes, the range of argumentation options is broadened by the fact that there are not merely one single or a couple of purpose(s) to

---

[72] See *Pringle* (n 4), paras 137–47, in which the Court effectively restricts the meaning of Art 125 TFEU to situations where one Member State legally assigns its debts to another. The Court maintains that the provision does not prevent the transfer of risk associated with such debt between Member States. The *travaux préparatoires* and other contextual materials dating back to the early to mid 1990s, however, clearly indicate that the 'no bail-out' clause was intended to prevent precisely that transfer of risk from one euro member government to another.

a provision but a multiplicity of purposes and consequentialist considerations which the Court is free to bring to bear on legal provisions or judge-made rules and which can be stated at varying levels of generality and abstraction and which are contingent on different time frames. Put simply, while legal rules may sometimes have more than one literal meaning, they can generally be argued to have several purposes, depending on the time horizon and level of abstraction at which they are stated. This increases judicial freedom in the consideration of teleological considerations to extremes.

And, finally, while the Court typically uses the interpretative flexibility in its approach broadly to favour an expansive interpretation of the Union's competence, *Pringle* is unusual in that it indicates that the Court may do exactly the opposite and interpret the Union's powers narrowly – as it did in *Pringle* both with the non-application of the EU Charter to intergovernmental agreements as well as the scope of the Union's exclusive competence in monetary policy – when such a restrictive interpretation serves the interests of further EU integration, in this instance the preservation of the single currency.

In *Gauweiler* the CJEU's reasoning is much sketchier than in *Pringle*. The Court again employs only those arguments which suit its purpose and in particular altogether ignores relevant legislation, i.e. Council Regulation 3603/93 which clarifies that the prohibition of monetary financing in Article 123 TFEU extends to secondary market purchases of government bonds. Moreover, the CJEU ignores its own settled case law that the purposes of EU measures are to be determined not subjectively by the decision-maker, but objectively with regard to the effects of the EU legal act in question. In *Gauweiler*, the CJEU decided that the ECB is free to pursue objectives other than those enumerated in Article 127 TFEU and that those objectives become monetary policy simply because the ECB says they are, even when their effects patently encroach upon the Member States' prerogatives in the area of economic policy.

In relation to the FCC, German law, no more than EU law, too does not prescribe specific interpretative methods which courts must follow. The FCC, however, has made clear that in order to ascertain the intention of the legislator (in both its legislative and treaty-making capacity) it employs the following interpretative criteria: the wording of the provision, the legislative context, the teleological and the historical method.[73] Like EU law German law does not formally recognise judicial precedents as a source of law but they are widely followed in practice as authoritative interpretations of underlying written norms. As such, judges generally feel bound to follow previous decisions, subject to the proviso that precedents have no fixed authoritative wording.[74]

---

[73] BVerfGE 11, 126, 130. For detailed discussion, see S Vogenauer, *Die Auslegung von Gesetzen in England und auf dem Kontinent* (vol 1, Mohr Siebeck 2001) 29ff.

[74] Vogenauer (n 72) 226–27; Beck (n 66) 91–109.

The German Basic Law does not say much about Germany's participation in the EU integration process. Nor does it specify clear limits, but it contains so-called perpetuity clauses which enshrine the principles of representative democracy, national self-determination[75] and the right to vote[76] which must not be deprived of their essential function and cannot be surrendered. These provisions, the FCC has consistently argued, imply clear and precise limits in relation to the powers the Bundestag may, or may not, transfer to the EU institutions. The principle of the Bundestag's budgetary autonomy, the FCC held in 2009, should thus itself be construed as a perpetuity requirement of the German constitution.

The FCC did not in any detail consider the compatibility of the ESM with the EU Treaties. It essentially upheld the bailout fund on the grounds that it did not, in its highly debatable view, impose excessive demands on Germany's federal budget. In its *Lisbon* judgment the FCC had held in the clearest possible terms that, first, the principle of budgetary autonomy is an integral part of the principle of democracy as enshrined in Article 20(1) and (2) and Article 79(3) GG in combination with the right to vote under Article 38 GG which would be deprived of their essential significance if the Bundestag surrendered its overall budgetary responsibility and freedom of financial manoeuvre. In contrast to the Court of Justice which, in *Pringle*, upheld the ESM in defiance of the natural meaning of Article 125 TFEU by reducing that provision to an almost meaningless prohibition of direct assignments of public debt between eurozone member governments, and in disregard of the objectives of the Treaties which clearly indicate that the currency was to be based on the principle of national fiscal responsibility, the FCC could, and according to its settled case law, should have also considered the compatibility of the ESM with Articles 119, 125 and 127 TFEU but chose not to do so. It thus avoided, what the Court of Justice could not avoid, namely, the elaborate construction of a spurious argument why a clear Treaty provision does not mean what it says and why the no-bailout clause was apparently never intended to prevent the transfer of fiscal risks between eurozone members.

Yet, while the FCC could avoid making a travesty of a clear written constitutional provision of Article 125 TFEU, it did precisely that in relation to its established constitutional jurisprudence on the limits of EU integration: the constitutional judges stretched the principle of budgetary autonomy to the point of vacuity. In the absence of clear constitutional provisions and in the context of national constitutions which unlike the EU Treaties are not updated and revised at certain intervals, judicial precedents take the place of written provisions and are interpreted in the same reverential manner as written provisions subject in both cases to their level of clarity and precision. Otherwise constitutional jurisprudence

---

[75] Art 20 GG.
[76] Art 38 GG.

becomes meaningless. Through its case law since the *Solange I* case the FCC established that the German Constitution placed limits on Germany's transfer of sovereign rights to the EU. In 2009 it specified that under no conditions must those transfers encroach on certain key areas of national sovereignty and that Germany's fiscal and budgetary autonomy ruled out any crippling financial commitments on a scale where the Bundestag's future freedom of financial manoeuvre might be significantly impaired. Thus, although the Basic Law does not in any specific sense either authorise the sharing of sovereignty with the EU institutions nor place clear limits on the transfer of national powers to international bodies, the FCC had laid down clear and precise judge-made rules as to how far the integration process could go while Germany was still a nation state and the German Basic Law remained the supreme law of the land. It did so on the basis that the principle of democracy and national self-government implied that the right to control taxation and expenditure was the basis of national self-government.

Faced with the politically charged eurocrisis and a national government willing to save the common currency in defiance of clear Treaty rules and constitutional precepts, the FCC foundered with as little respect for its own clear judge-made rules as the Court of Justice failed to uphold the Treaty. As it did not have to deal with a concise written provision the FCC decided it did not have to engage in the embarrassing 'reasoning' process of justifying its decision based on the highly selective employment of the various literal, contextual and teleological argumentation forms which make up the traditional repertoire of judicial reasoning. Instead, the FCC avoided any discussion of the meaning of 'autonomy' or 'democratic accountability' and 'democratic control' and justified its decision with the implausible reference to the margin of appreciation the legislator should be accorded in all matters of taxation and public expenditure, with the absurd conclusion that additional liabilities of €190bn and even unlimited liability might be compatible with the future budgetary autonomy of Germany if the legislature so decided. The fact that the FCC went so far as to say that the Bundestag could extend its liabilities under the ESM by simple majority and that this was sufficient to ensure compliance with the principle of the democracy, suggests that the FCC in effect jettisoned the principle of constitutional representative democracy in the politically contentious area of EU integration. Subject to the proviso that in its *ESM* judgment the FCC chose to assess the legality of the ESM with reference solely to its own constitutional jurisprudence, its decision not to invalidate the ESM Treaty is as irreconcilable with own established constitutional position on the relationship between EU and national constitutional law as the Court of Justice's *Pringle* judgment patently makes a mockery of the wording of Article 125 TFFEU. What both courts have in common is the conviction that, in matters of EU integration, clear rules lose their meaning in emergency situations and that, where fundamental interests of the integration process are concerned, the rule of law is no more than a fair-weather phenomenon.

In the *OMT* case the FCC had outlined a fully reasoned and textually as well as teleologically convincing answer in its reference to the CJEU. When the CJEU dismissed that answer, the FCC willy-nilly abandoned its earlier view and accepted the CJEU's 'better' view, without in any way indicating where its earlier analysis had gone wrong. The FCC in effect abandoned legal reasoning for political and judicial expediency, which was motivated by the desire to avoid a judicial conflict which it had up to that point maintained since the early 1970s it would not avoid if the EU either exceeded its Treaty-based powers or encroached on the identity of the German Basic Law.

Little else remains to be said about the German FCC's response to the eurocrisis. By 2009 the FCC had developed a well-thought-out, clear and comprehensive judicial interpretation of the limits which the German Constitution places on future EU integration, and of its own constitutional right of last resort to review all EU acts and EU revision treaties without reference to the EU courts. In the face of the eurocrisis the FCC abandoned its established and clearly articulated constitutional provision in both respects. From the early 1970s to 2010 the judges of the FCC had worked out a controversial but doctrinally convincing answer to the question 'Who is master in the EU? The Court of Justice or the FCC, and hence the EU or its Member States?' With its *ESM* judgment and decision to refer the ECB's ultra vires OMT programme to Luxembourg, the FCC surrendered its established position without a whimper.

VI CONCLUSION

The EU is not a sovereign state with autochthonous legal powers but remains a treaty-based set of institutions whose powers are circumscribed by the principle of conferral: unless the Member States have conferred legislative or executive powers, these remain at national level. The powers of the EU are further constrained by national constitutions: when powers are conferred on the EU, this occurs subject to the proviso that the EU institutions will respect the Treaties as well as national constitutions which are interpreted by national constitutional courts. Unless Member States are willing to challenge the EU's authority by acts of non-compliance, the courts are therefore the ultimate arbiters over the limits of the EU's supranational authority as well as the actions of national governments in compliance or furtherance of that authority. Put differently, in matters involving the allocation of competences between the EU and its Member States, the courts are charged with enforcing the rule of law and the essential elements of national self-government. This position has been abundantly made clear by the FCC since the 1970s, and there is no national constitutional court in the EU which takes an antithetical position to that of the FCC. Paradoxically perhaps, the courts thereby became the ultimate executors of the democratic sovereign. In the eurocrisis the EU's and Germany's highest judges have defied Treaty language, judicial precedent and national constitutional law and jurisprudence in the interests of extending rather than scaling back the EU integration project. They were complicit in, as Christine Lagarde, the current head of the IMF put it, 'breaking the law, to save the euro'.

To allow the courts to pronounce and settle a political community's claim to sovereignty, carries with the risk that sovereignty may be asserted, arrogated or surrendered by judicial fiat rather than political decisions or a referendum. The governance of the eurozone, lawless as it has been since the beginning and patently so since 2010, illustrates that juristocracy (by transnational or constitutional courts) or technocracy (by central banks) are no substitute for democratic self-government.

12

Unification from Above, Its Contradictions and the Conjuncture Initiated by the Eurozone Crisis

Christakis Georgiou

I INTRODUCTION

At the time this chapter was being completed (December 2017), things had decidedly started looking up for the European Union (EU). A number of electoral hurdles had been cleared by pro-EU mainstream political forces, the economy was gaining momentum and the Brexit negotiations were shifting the mood both in the UK and the rest of Europe in a decidedly more pro-EU direction[1] as well as revealing the UK's direly weak hand and the extent of the EU's leverage. Emmanuel Macron's proposals for EU reform – laid out in his Sorbonne speech[2] – have crystallised a new optimistic mood, revolving around the issue of how to reshape Europe's federal order in order for the EU to take the next step in the process of integration. Although these developments are part of the ebb and flow of current affairs, they provide some added weight to the argument put forward in this chapter.

The recent developments should not lead one to forget how thick the clouds had been over the EU for the most part of the last decade, in particular during 2010–13 when the eurozone double dipped into recession and the prospect of its breakup was openly broached, in particular in English-speaking media outlets. The refugee crisis in 2015 and the result of the referendum on UK membership in June 2016 seemed to turn the eurozone crisis into a multidimensional crisis of the EU itself and the debate was wide open about what the future held for European integration.

But although the sense of crisis was palpable and the reality of the various crises was undeniable, there was – and still is – a debate about their deeper meaning. With

---

[1]   cf B Stokes, R Wike and D Manevich, 'Post-Brexit, Europeans More Favorable toward EU' Pew Research Center (15 June 2017) www.pewglobal.org/2017/06/15/post-brexit-europeans-more-favorable-toward-eu accessed April 2018; J Burn-Murdoch, 'Britons' Brexit Views Unchanged – But More Expect Bad Deal' *Financial Times* (6 December 2017) www.ft.com/content/70dca402-da7f-11e7-a039-c64b1c09b482 accessed April 2018; Flash Eurobarometer 458 on Euro Area December 2017.

[2]   E Macron, 'Initiative pour l'Europe' (26 September 2017) www.elysee.fr/declarations/article/initiative-pour-l-europe-discours-d-emmanuel-macron-pour-une-europe-souveraine-unie-democratique accessed April 2018.

the risk of oversimplifying, one could argue that there are broadly two opposing types of reading of the conjuncture initiated by the eurozone crisis.

The first sees the crisis as the inevitable result of the fateful and misguided decision to introduce the single currency ten years earlier without either introducing adequate supportive policies such as a sizeable federal budget and some harmonisation of fiscal policies or having sufficiently developed a sense of common belonging and shared identity among the EU's population (without building a European demos as this is sometimes summed up). These structural flaws were now coming back to haunt the EU and, crucially, could not be overcome under the weight of the crisis. The crisis was seen as reviving national antagonisms and Eurosceptic resistance to integration, thus unleashing powerful centrifugal trends leading either to a stationary state of semi-permanent crisis or even the disintegration of the eurozone if not the EU itself. In this view Brexit is a foretaste of things to come – the first instance of an open revolt by voters in a Member State leading to the unwinding of the EU itself. Moreover, in this view, the eurozone is still fragile and the economic recovery now underway is deceptive. The flaws haven't been repaired but only papered over and the medium-term prospect for the EU is far from bright. When the next crisis comes, the eurozone could still collapse and there is nothing irreversible about European integration.

The second reading of the eurozone crisis is in a way more traditional. It can be traced back to Jean Monnet himself, who wrote in his memoirs that 'Europe will be made through crises and will be the sum of the solutions provided to those crises'.[3] This could be dubbed the 'crisis as catalyst for further integration' reading of the last ten years. It is based on a broader understanding of how the EU is progressively built by a problem-solving approach involving compromises struck by the ruling circles in Member States and the supranational institutions. In this reading, the key event was the decision taken in 2011–12 to do 'whatever it takes' – to use the famous phrase by ECB president Mario Draghi – to preserve the eurozone. This decision accounts for the (quite substantial) innovations introduced to fight the speculative crisis on government bond markets in 2010–12 but it also inevitably entails further steps towards greater integration to provide firmer institutional foundations for the eurozone. In this view, how this process unfolds is a question of political opportunity and Macron's proposals are a natural outcome of the predicament in which the EU found itself due to the eurozone crisis. Moreover, there is little to suggest that public opinion has decidedly turned its back on integration.

The two readings also rest on two different assumptions about relations among European elites and their control of European societies overall. The first reading sees Europe's ruling elites as fundamentally divided along national lines. Their insurmountable contradictions loosen their grip on power and destabilise the EU's political order. In the second reading put forward in this chapter, national divisions

---

[3]   J Monnet, *Mémoires* (Fayard 1976) 615–16.

do exist among ruling elites, but every crisis while giving expression to such splits also contributes to overcoming them and forging ruling elite unity at the European level. This helps strengthen the elites' grip on power and eliminates splits as a destabilising political factor.

This chapter provides a particular version of this second reading that relies on what I term the 'corporate reconstruction of European capitalism' theory of European integration.[4] This is the basis for identifying the sources and pattern of the unification process such as it has been unfolding over the past seventy years or so (section II). Section III then uses this theoretical understanding to explain how the eurozone was created as an incomplete monetary union in the early 1990s, thus laying the ground for the eurozone crisis. Section IV looks at how Europe's ruling elites reacted to the crisis and how this has already initiated the next round of substantial integration in the EU. Section V provides an understanding of Brexit that flows from this analysis, arguing that it is a side effect of the renewed momentum towards integration rather than a foretaste of the EU's future. The conclusion offers some general predictions about how the EU will emerge from the conjuncture initiated by the eurozone crisis.

II THE SOURCE AND PATTERN OF EUROPEAN UNIFICATION FROM ABOVE

The ultimate source of the process that has given rise to the EU must be traced all the way back to the technological innovations that in the last quarter of the nineteenth century triggered what is usually referred to as the 'second industrial revolution'. The industries spawned by this wave of innovation – automobiles, rubber, steel, engineering, electricity, chemicals and pharmaceuticals, oil, agricultural machinery, agribusiness – have been the core sectors of twentieth-century advanced capitalism and have therefore determined the way economy, society but also polity have functioned in Europe. In a classic case of how advances in the forces of production have spurred historic shifts in social and political relations, the flourishing of these sectors – i.e. the transition from entrepreneurial to corporate capitalism – has entailed and triggered the economic and therefore political unification of Europe.

The transition to corporate capitalism has been synonymous with a substantially higher degree of concentration and centralisation of capital and with the oligopolistic transformation of market and industrial structures. This is down to the fact that the extensive capital investments required to exploit the new technologies could not be replicated by the myriad firms typical of entrepreneurial capitalism. Firms in the new sectors had to attain very high production volumes and thus significant market

---

[4]   This chapter is a highly condensed version of much of the research I have conducted over the past eight years. I refer readers interested in the full detail of the arguments to other publications referenced in the text.

share to make profits on these investments. This, crucially, also implied that their markets had to be enlarged to reach a continental scale.

This was not a major issue in the United States, although the advent of corporate capitalism did lead to the rise of federal regulation and the substantial strengthening of the powers of the federal administration to the detriment of the states.[5] But in Europe, the multiplicity of nation states pursuing their own trade, monetary and microeconomic policies was a huge obstacle to the transition to corporate capitalism. Europe, in other words, suffered from Balkanisation. Unification thus became a prerequisite for the transition to corporate capitalism.[6]

Unsurprisingly, then, Europeanism first emerged as a serious political ideology and a structured political current shortly after the turn of the century, when it became obvious that continued material, social and political progress in Europe entailed the economic unification of the continent and the establishment of a pan-European division of labour.[7]

What might seem more paradoxical is that Europeanism first emerged and became generalised on the left. Some of the first European political leaders to have publicly supported the prospect of a European federation – a United States of Europe – included Otto Bauer, Karl Kautsky and Leon Trotsky. The latter most consistently led the argument within the internationalist anti-war left that would form the basis for the Communist International and managed to convince his comrades to adopt the federalist perspective in 1923.[8] Social revolution and European unification were two sides of the same coin in his thinking. The Socialist International followed in 1926. The main theme on the left was that European federalism was the alternative to the militarism and commercial rivalry that had spawned the Great War, but Trotsky also argued openly that unification was a prerequisite for the further development of the forces of production and thus the realisation of socialism.

[5] L Panitch and S Gindin, *The Making of Global Capitalism: The Political Economy of American Empire* (Verso 2012) ch 2; MJ Sklar, *The Corporate Reconstruction of American Capitalism, 1890–1916: The Market, the Law and Politics* (CUP 1988); S Skowronek, *Building a New American State: The Expansion of National Administrative Capacities, 1877–1920* (CUP 1982).

[6] On the economic dynamic, see JC Defraigne, *De l'Intégration Nationale à l'Intégration Continentale: Analyse de la Dynamique d'Intégration Supranationale Européenne des Origines à nos Jours* (L'Harmattan 2004) in particular on the rise of the economic pressures towards unification, 53–70.

[7] On the birth and early growth of Europeanism, see JL Chabot, *Aux Origines Intellectuelles de l'Union Européenne: L'Idée d'Europe Unie de 1919 à 1939* (Presses Universitaires de Grenoble 2005); E du Réau *L'Idée d'Europe au XXe Siècle* (Complexe 1996) 62–96; CH Pegg, *Evolution of the European Idea, 1914–1932* (University of North Carolina Press 1983).

[8] L Trotsky, 'Is the Time Ripe for the Slogan "The United States of Europe?"' (June 1923) www .marxists.org/archive/trotsky/1923/06/europe.htm accessed April 2018. But the rise of Stalinism and its associated doctrine of socialism in one country soon discarded the slogan. The Kremlin soon reverted back to the typical policy of the Tsarist (and British) empire: opposing the formation of a unified power centre on the continent so as to preserve its capacity to play the European powers against each other. This is the ultimate source of West European communist Euroscepticism.

Bourgeois Europeanism also emerged soon after the end of the war and reached its pre-war apex in the second half of the 1920s. A number of transnational groups appeared and their efforts culminated in French foreign minister Aristide Briand's initiative for a federal EU in 1929–30.[9] Politically, bourgeois Europeanism was closely associated with the liberal internationalism that informed the attempts to build an organised international order through the League of Nations and its basic thrust was to find a compromise between France and Germany. Its main economic theme was the need to reverse the commercial rivalry among the European powers and ultimately create a customs union and a single market on a par with those of the United States so as to benefit from the same economies of scale and scope that big business was reaping there.

Finally, there was also a nationalist alternative to the two scenarios (socialist and liberal internationalist) referred to above that was based on the dynamics of power politics. This, of course, was the scenario that culminated into the First and Second World Wars, led by the dominant European power whose expansionism was based on the advance it had gained over its European rivals in exploiting the new technologies. German war aims during the two wars were based on various scenarios of economic unification with a customs union, industrial rationalisation and monetary unification and varying degrees of openness of the European economic bloc to the world market (as well as different political institutions to underpin this bloc).[10]

It was the failure of the first and third scenarios that opened the way for a return to the liberal internationalist method for unifying Europe after the Second World War. Indeed, in the 1950 Schuman declaration[11] that is usually cited as the speech that triggered the process of unification, the author refers to Briand's federalist schemes. This particular method of 'unification from above' (as opposed to the socialist version 'from below' that would have come through a deep transformation of social relations in Europe) is based on a Franco-German axis and a negotiated and step-by-step approach where France and Germany strike compromises on the most pressing issues of the day and then carry the rest of Europe's states with them. In this pattern, crises have an agenda-setting character: they reveal to the EU's ruling elites the issues that need to be dealt with through further integration and spur the process forward. They thus serve as catalysts for forging elite unity across Europe, which is then embodied in new supranational institutions and policies.

---

[9] 'Memorandum sur l'Organisation d'un Regime d'Union Federale Europeene' (1 May 1930) https://dl.wdl.org/11583/service/11583.pdf accessed April 2018.

[10] On the First World War, see GH Soutou, *L'or et le Sang: Les Buts de Guerre Economiques de la Première Guerre Mondiale* (Fayard 1989). On the Second World War, see A Barkai, *Nazi Economics: Ideology, Theory and Policy* (Yale UP 1990); A Tooze, *The Wages of Destruction: The Making and Breaking of the Nazi War Economy* (Allen Layne 2006).

[11] 'The Schuman Declaration' (9 May 1950) https://europa.eu/european-union/about-eu/symbols/europe-day/schuman-declaration_en accessed April 2018.

One can distinguish two major periods in this process of liberal internationalist unification from above prior to the eurozone crisis.[12] The first stretches from the early 1950s to the early 1970s. There follows a transition stage – usually known as 'Eurosclerosis' – interspersed by various crises before the second period really takes off in the early 1980s.

The first period is characterised by two developments running in parallel. The first is the realisation of the European customs union that substantially deepened the levels of commercial integration binding European states and their economies with each other and which transformed the EU[13] into a major international trading power[14] with a single external trade policy. The second is what has been referred to as the strategy of building national champion firms in each Member State through active microeconomic state intervention and preferential access to the domestic market for local firms. During these years, European governments – exemplified by the French – actively pursued the consolidation of capital within one or two national oligopolistic corporations in each industry with the purpose of preparing for the advent of a single European market.

During this first period, macroeconomic policies remained exclusively national. This was possible for three reasons. The first was the stability of the international monetary system set up at Bretton Woods in 1944 which ensured exchange rate stability and to some extent shielded individual states from the pressures of international capital markets. The second was the insufficient scale of these markets and the obstacles to international capital flows. Finally, because economic integration in Europe was still limited, financial systems remained nationally confined and therefore were put at the service of the policy of building national champion firms.[15] In France, for example, a system of bureaucratically administered finance was set up as a way of preferentially channelling funds to certain industries and firms within them and as a lever for forcing firms to merge into bigger corporations. French monetary policy proceeded from that basis and external imperatives were only secondary.

The first period came to an end in the early 1970s for three reasons. First, the customs union was completed in July 1968. Second, the Bretton Woods system collapsed and thereupon followed the rebirth of global finance, with international capital flows dramatically growing during the following decades. But the most important reason was that the policy of building national champion firms had reached its limits and these national champions were now expanding their investments across Europe and beginning to treat the customs union as their domestic

---

[12]   I follow Defraigne's periodisation here.
[13]   I use the abbreviation EU throughout the text for simplicity, despite its only having been introduced in the Maastricht Treaty.
[14]   See A Dür, *Protection for Exporters: Power and Discrimination in Transatlantic Trade Relations, 1930–2010* (Cornell UP 2010).
[15]   J Zysman, *Governments, Markets and Growth: Finance and the Politics of Industrial Change* (Cornell UP 1983).

market.[16] During the next two decades, these firms became truly pan-European corporations, operating regional value chains across the expanded European market.[17] In doing so, they further deepened commercial integration among EU Member States but also, crucially and much more importantly, productive and financial integration. Their production networks are entirely indifferent to Member State boundaries and form the cornerstone of what is now a European economy that operates as a single unit.

It is precisely this development that not only lies behind the 'relaunch' of European integration through the 1986 Single European Act,[18] but which also accounts for the creation of an imbalanced eurozone through the 1992 Maastricht Treaty.

III THE CREATION OF AN IMBALANCED EUROZONE AT MAASTRICHT

The official debate about an economic and monetary union began in earnest soon after the completion of the customs union and as the second stage described above was beginning to take off. A first report was drafted in 1970 by a group of central bankers and Commission officials under the responsibility of Luxembourg's Prime Minister, Pierre Werner.[19] The report envisaged both a federal central banking system and a 'centre of decision for economic policy' with real influence to set a fiscal policy stance for the whole of the community and influence 'the national budgets, especially as regards the level and the direction of the balances and the methods for financing the deficits or utilizing the surpluses'.[20] There followed the 1975 Marjolin report[21] which argued that at the final stage the EU's budget would have to fulfil all the functions of a typical state budget (stabilisation, redistribution,

[16] L Franko, *The European Multinationals: A Renewed Challenge for American and British Big Business* (Harper & Row 1976); Defraigne (n 6) 183–250.

[17] The European single market is in practice broader than the EU. Crucially, it also incorporates the European Economic Area (basically, Norway), Switzerland (through a web of bilateral EU–Switzerland sectoral treaties) and Turkey (but only for industrial goods, through the EU–Turkey customs union). These states practically apply all EU economic legislation without having a say in its formulation. The UK will soon find itself in this category if Brexit does indeed go ahead.

[18] The SEA's basic function was to remove the non-tariff barriers that stood in the way of the full Europeanisation of European corporations.

[19] Conseil-Commission des Communautés Européennes, 'Rapport au Conseil et à la Commission concernant la réalisation par étapes de L'Union Economique et Monétaire dans la communauté – Rapport Werner' (8 October 1970) http://aei.pitt.edu/1002/1/monetary_werner_final.pdf accessed April 2018.

[20] ibid 13. Note the radical difference with the Stability Pact, which is simply an anti-deficit surveillance mechanism with no ambition to define a community policy or any instruments for forcing Member States to spend more. The Commission has been calling on Germany and the Netherlands to raise public spending (and wages) for a few years now, but has no means to constrain them to do so.

[21] European Commission, 'Report of the Study Group "Economic and Monetary Union"' (8 March 1975) II/675/3/74 – E fin http://aei.pitt.edu/1009/1/monetary_study_group_1980.pdf accessed April 2018. The group was made up of various professors and representatives of industry and banking.

provision of public goods) but that this would happen over a very long period of time. Still, the report proposed to allow the Commission to issue its own debt, develop its regional policy and set up a European unemployment insurance scheme. Finally, the 1977 McDougall report[22] on the role of public finance in European integration proposed further counter-cyclical demand-management policy instruments and argued that beyond an immediate 'pre-federal integration' stage the EU would need to set up a minimum federal budget of around 5 per cent to 7 per cent of EU GDP.

I cite these reports so as to show that official thinking on macroeconomic integration in the EU was initially much more ambitious than what would later be set up at Maastricht; it can even be said to have anticipated the problems that would lead to the eurozone crisis. There was a clear understanding that monetary union would also require the development of at least strong coordination of fiscal and economic policy as well as the development of substantial federal fiscal powers to tax, borrow and spend. The 1970s reports all acknowledge the fact that the deepening of economic integration would create deeper macroeconomic imbalances within the EU and that those would require the development of federal policies to be dealt with. Indeed, as I argue below, the main driver of macroeconomic policy integration in the EU since the 1970s has been the financial and economic destabilisation generated by the growing accumulation of macroeconomic imbalances that were themselves the product of deepening productive and financial integration resulting from the Europeanisation of national champion firms. However, at Maastricht an imbalanced monetary union was created because neither banking nor fiscal policy were centralised.

The story of the eurozone is, then, largely the story of how the financial risk generated by these growing imbalances was dealt with in successive stages. Each time, the institutional structure of the EU gave rise to particular forms of financial risk (first currency, then sovereign and banking risk) and each time corporate elites responded by demanding of their political allies measures to reduce it.[23]

The onset of the second stage in integration described in section II went hand in hand with (and to a large extent even drove) the development of international capital flows, which gradually led to their full liberalisation by 1990. The context in which Member States defined and pursued their macroeconomic policies was thus radically altered during the 1970s and 1980s. National economies were now much more open and cross-border capital flows much more influential in defining the room for manoeuvre for national policies.

[22] European Commission, 'Report of the Study Group on the Role of Public Finance in European Integration' (April 1977) http://ec.europa.eu/archives/emu_history/documentation/chapter8/19770401en73macdougallrepvol1.pdf accessed April 2018. Again, the group was made up of professors and was chaired by the British CBI's chief economic adviser.

[23] I fully develop this line of argument in C Georgiou, 'The Eurozone Crisis and the European Corporate Elite: Bringing Corporate Actors into Focus' (2016) 45 Economy and Society 51.

At the same time, the growth of productive and financial integration also led to growing current account imbalances, with surpluses piling up in Germany and the Netherlands and deficits in the Latin Member States.[24] This point is quite important. In many discussions of the eurozone crisis, especially by authors who adhere to the pessimistic reading of the crisis, the macroeconomic imbalances (and the German surpluses) that lay behind the 2010–13 crisis were the product of the euro. As Harold James shows, this is incorrect. Imbalances and German surpluses have grown as a share of GDP since the early 1950s with every new round of integration 'mostly because international capital markets were deeper and thus allowed bigger imbalances to be financed for longer periods'. Imbalances are therefore an inevitable outcome of building a pan-European corporate economy in Europe. The issue for ruling elites is how to manage these imbalances through common institutions so that they become as least destabilising as possible.

Eventually, of course, imbalances tend to go into reverse, leading to capital flight (or 'sudden stops' as this is sometimes known). The macroeconomic history of European integration between 1971 and the launch of the euro is thus one of recurring sudden stops leading to instability in currency markets and wide fluctuations in exchange rates, with capital fleeing weak-currency Member States in the South of the EU and finding refuge in strong-currency Member States in the North. This happened more often than not in periods where inflation rates in Member States varied widely (as in 1973–83), but it also occurred later on (in the late 1980s and, in particular, the early 1990s)[25] despite the fact that deficit Member States had tightened policy and brought their inflation rates in line with the German rate and despite the fact that the EU had set up the European Monetary System of fixed but adjustable exchange rates in 1978. The only thing the EMS achieved was to politicise the issue because every time there was a speculative attack on Member State currencies, finance ministers would gather in Brussels and haggle late into the night over which currency should devalue and by how much.

Before the euro was introduced, then, imbalances within the EU gave rise to monetary instability and therefore to currency risk for European corporations. Moreover, the recurring devaluations threatened the principle of the single market (that was actively being pursued through the Single European Act and the 1988 directive[26] that fully liberalised capital flows) and pan-European corporate planning of productive operations as they regularly realigned relative costs and prices across Europe. But precisely because Europe's corporations had started becoming pan-European organisations with extensive investments outside of their national market, they grew decreasingly tolerant of currency risk. Corporations from weak-currency

---

[24] See H James, *Making the European Monetary Union* (Harvard UP 2012) 11.

[25] For the pre-Maastricht period, see D Andrews, 'Capital Mobility and Monetary Adjustment in Western Europe, 1973–1991' (1994) 27 Policy Sciences 425.

[26] Council Directive 88/361/EEC of 24 June 1988 for the implementation of Article 67 of the Treaty [1988] OJ L178/5.

Member States were even more exposed to such risk as a greater part of their investments was denominated in currencies that lost value when monetary crises occurred and so were more enthusiastic for a solution that would eliminate currency risk than their counterparts in, say, Germany or the Netherlands.[27] Nevertheless, the latter were also looking for such a solution and thus joined the campaign for a single currency that would simply do away with currency risk altogether.[28] As James concludes, 'the large cumulative imbalances were what convinced Europe's policy-makers that a monetary union was the only way of avoiding the risk of periodic crises with currency realignments whose trade policy consequences threatened the survival of an integrated internal European market'.[29] Far from imbalances and German surpluses being the consequence of monetary union, they were its cause.

But precisely because the problem that had to be dealt with was the persistence of currency risk arising from growing imbalances within Europe, the deal that was struck at Maastricht did not go beyond the creation of a single currency. In an interview I conducted with Stefan Collignon, director of research at the Association for the Monetary Union of Europe, I was told clearly that corporate executives were aware of the need to accompany monetary with fiscal union. But their main preoccupation was to succeed in getting the single currency introduced and they feared that it would be politically too much to also force onto the agenda the issue of a fiscal union.

> The main gist was that we wanted the euro to go through and we were aware that overcharging the project might sink it ... There was within AMUE a kind of neo-functional understanding of how monetary union would lead to fiscal and political union. We would have monetary union first, and at some point a crisis would force the move to fiscal union too.[30]

In fact, the most prominent voice in the early 1990s to argue for fiscal and political union to go along monetary union was the Bundesbank. But the Bundesbank was precisely the biggest obstacle on the way to a single currency because the new federal central banking system would dilute the monetary power it had accumulated since the early 1970s as the central bank issuing Europe's most important reserve currency. As a result, the Bundesbank's objections came to be seen by Europe's ruling elites in the same way that warnings by most Anglo-American economists were: as the quibbles of Eurosceptics who at heart were opposed to the whole project of

---

[27]   Accordingly, it was the state bureaucracies in France and Italy that led the political process that led to Maastricht. In terms of the distribution of bureaucratic power over Europe's money, the euro has clearly shifted power away from the Bundesbank in favour of French and Italian central bankers.

[28]   The empirical details can be found in Georgiou (n 23). On this issue, see also S Collignon and D Schwarzer, *Private Sector Involvement in the Euro: The Power of Ideas* (Routledge 2003) which tells the story of the Association for the Monetary Union of Europe, the corporate lobby set up in 1987 to campaign for the euro.

[29]   James (n 24) 12.

[30]   Interview, 28 February 2017.

integration.[31] Intellectually, policymakers also developed the idea that, in a monetary union, imbalances no longer mattered and that they could be indefinitely financed.[32]

As a result, all the political initiatives that took place after Maastricht and that aimed to move in the direction of a complete economic and monetary union failed. Debate in the early 1990s on the centralisation of banking supervision and regulation led nowhere. Without fiscal union, it was felt that potential bank bailouts could only be national. Moreover, European banks were still mostly national in scope and so were not interested in a European supervisor. Jacques Delors, the highly influential Commission president in 1984–94, had aimed for the EU's budget to rise to 3 per cent of EU GDP by the date when the euro would be introduced, more or less as the McDougall report had envisaged. German politicians regularly proposed ambitious projects of much greater federal integration – either through the famous Lammers-Schäuble 1994 paper on the CDU's European policy[33] or through Joschka Fischer's 2000 Humboldt speech 'From Confederacy to Federation'.[34] Finally, the commissioner for economic and monetary affairs in 1995–99 – the Frenchman Yves-Thibault de Silguy – proposed a European Treasury that would issue collectively underwritten debt and would then apportion the proceeds to the Member States – a much more fully developed version of the limited pooling of fiscal liability that has been introduced since 2010. The proposal was quickly buried because of opposition from French and German financial bureaucracies. Crucially, the corporate backers of the euro were also not interested.[35] Nobody had yet been tangibly confronted with how the problem of imbalances would re-emerge and generate financial risk in the form of sovereign risk. This was not yet a problem that needed to be solved.

IV THE EUROZONE CRISIS AND THE CRUCIAL DECISION TO MOVE TOWARDS GREATER INTEGRATION

German reunification's inflationary consequences inverted the traditional pattern of imbalances that had prevailed since the early 1950s. For the first time, Germany registered for a number of years in a row current account deficits whereas France joined the surplus club of Member States. Germany's expansionary course during

---

[31] On the economists, see L Jonung and E Drea, 'The Euro: It Can't Happen. It's a Bad Idea. It Won't Last. US Economists on the EMU, 1989–2002' (2009) European Economy Economic Papers 395 ec .europa.eu/economy_finance/publications/pages/publication16345_en.pdf.

[32] D Marsh, *The Euro: The Battle for the New Global Currency* (2nd edn, Yale UP 2011) 240–41.

[33] K Lammers and W Schäuble, 'Überlegungen Europäischen Politik' (1 September 1994) www .bundesfinanzministerium.de/Content/DE/Downloads/schaeuble-lamers-papier-1994.pdf? _blob=publicationFile&v=1 accessed April 2018.

[34] J Fischer, 'From Confederacy to Federation – Thoughts on the Finality of European Integration' (12 May 2001) http://ec.europa.eu/dorie/fileDownload.do?docId=192161&cardId=192161 accessed April 2018.

[35] Interview with Yves-Thibault de Silguy, 24 November 2017, Paris.

the 1990s both stabilised the system after the monetary storm of 1992–93 and eased the path to the introduction of the euro in 1999.

But this was ultimately only a parenthesis in post-war Europe's macroeconomic history. Reunification also had a substantial impact on the German labour market, as the supply of labour substantially increased overnight and downward pressure on wages in Western Germany quickly led to a fifteen-year-long wage moderation in German industry that lasted from the late 1990s to around 2013. As early as 1995, the president of the powerful IG Metall union, Klaus Zwickel, proposed a *Bündnis für Arbeit* (pact for work) where he explicitly proposed to trade off a real wage freeze for the preservation of existing jobs and the creation of new ones. When the red–green coalition government took over in 1998, it quickly moved to establish the *Bündnis für Arbeit, Ausbildung und Wettbewerbsfähigkeit* (pact for work, education and competitiveness) whereas as early as 1996 the unions had accepted the decentralisation of collective bargaining which further drove competitive dynamics into the process of German wage setting.[36]

The introduction of the euro also modified the composition of the imbalances. The Commission had envisaged that the single currency would facilitate capital flows to the traditionally deficit Member States that would have spurred a catch-up process through the funding of productive investments. But whereas capital flows to those Member States did increase, they did not fund productive investments but instead speculative bubbles in unproductive activities such as property markets (Spain is a case in point here) and consumption. In only a few cases (namely, Greece) did the flows lead to higher public debt. Crucially, these capital flows overwhelmingly took the form of interbank lending – banks in the traditionally surplus Member States lent capital to banks in the deficit states which used it to fund speculative investments in their home markets. To a lesser extent, the flows also took the form of direct investments in sovereign bonds – indeed, the proportion of public debt held by non-resident investors in eurozone Member States increased during the first ten years of the single currency.[37]

When the global financial crisis hit in 2008, it set off a worldwide process of financial retrenchment within home state borders and the scaling back of cross-border exposure. The eurozone crisis was a much more concentrated version of this global phenomenon. Imbalances began unravelling instantly and led as early as 2009 to a 'great bargain' between the national governments, the ECB and the

---

[36] See in particular P Bofinger, 'German Wage Moderation and the EZ Crisis' *CEPR's Policy Portal* (30 November 2015) https://voxeu.org/article/german-wage-moderation-and-ez-crisis accessed April 2018; C Dustmann and others, 'From Sick Man of Europe to Economic Superstar: Germany's Resurgent Economy' (2014) 28 Journal of Economic Perspectives 167.

[37] On cross-border capital flows in the eurozone crisis, see PR Lane, 'Capital Flows in the Euro Area' (2013) European Economy Economic Papers 497; A Hobza and S Zeugner, 'The "Imbalanced Balance" and Its Unravelling: Current Accounts and Bilateral Financial Flows in the Euro Area' (2014) European Economy Economic Papers 520.

banks,[38] whereby the ECB agreed to provide additional liquidity to the banks so that these could continue buying their home Member States' bonds and prevent what would be the defining feature of the crisis in 2010–12, namely a run on sovereign bond markets.

But neither the banks nor the ECB were happy with this bargain and they expected the governments to take other measures to ensure the liquidity of Member States. The banks resented what they saw as financial repression and the fact that they could no longer treat the EU as a single financial market, whereas the ECB resented having to take on too much risk by expanding its balance sheet for the purpose of ensuring Member State liquidity. Both the banks and the ECB were thus from the very beginning keen on measures that would in effect Europeanise, at least to some extent, banking policy and fiscal liability. The banks had indeed supported the 'euro-tarp' plan for bank recapitalisation mooted by the French government in October 2008, which came up against Berlin's resistance.

Indeed, the crisis would prove much harder to contain. In fact, it had two interlinked sources. The first was the run on sovereign bond markets, exacerbated by the Greek government's revelations in the autumn of 2009 about the extent of its budget deficit and, more importantly, by the fateful decision taken at the French seaside town of Deauville in October 2010 by Nicolas Sarkozy and Angela Merkel to introduce private sector involvement to all rescue operations for embattled Member States in the future. In other words, one key form that the financial risk generated by the unravelling of the imbalances took was that of sovereign risk. This was exacerbated by the fact that the regulatory treatment of such risk encouraged (and still does, despite the Bundesbank's vocal objections) banks to increase their exposure to it, as sovereign bonds were (and still are) treated as entirely risk-free for the purposes of calculating banks' capital ratios.

The second source was the interbank market. This instantly froze in the autumn of 2008. Banks in the deficit Member States were particularly hit. The solution that was found was for the balance sheet of the ECB to be substituted for it. Instead of borrowing from each other, banks would now borrow from the ECB, whose balance sheet would greatly increase as a result over the course of the eurozone crisis. In other words, the other form taken by financial risk was banking risk (this was also reflected in the collapse of the equity valuations of the banks and in the 'bank jog' on deposits in the deficit Member States).

The interplay between the two kinds of risk – or 'doom loop' as it came to be known – aggravated the speculative crisis of 2010–12. When a Member State was attacked by the financial markets, the deterioration of its sovereign creditworthiness devalued the balance sheets of the banks highly exposed to it. The same happened in the other direction. When substantial chunks of the domestic banking industry threatened to fail, implying the need for the local Member State to step in with

---

[38] C Bastasin, *Saving Europe: Anatomy of a Dream* (Brookings Institution Press 2015) 110–13.

a bailout, investors started questioning the capacity of the Member State to shoulder on its own the fiscal costs of such a bailout. They would thus ditch even more of the sovereign bonds of those Member States, aggravating in turn the run on sovereign bond markets.

It is important here to note that the link between banking and sovereign risk was to a large extent the product of the Europeanisation of big banks that took place in the two decades that preceded the eurozone crisis.[39] The European banking industry underwent extensive restructuring following the full liberalisation of capital movements in 1990. Consolidation first took place within national borders but by the early 2000s commercial banks[40] began merging on a cross-border basis. By the time the eurozone crisis hit, the bigger European banks had caught up with their industrial counterparts to become pan-European organisations. They had also become too big to bail out by their home Member States. Ireland, Spain and Cyprus are the basket cases here. The size of their banks' balance sheets was far too big a proportion of their GDPs and could hardly be back-stopped without sending their public debt to GDP ratios through the roof.

The issue, thus, became how to break the 'doom loop' between banking and sovereign risk and contain those two kinds of risk altogether. European corporations demanded measures to that effect (such as the pooling of fiscal liability to avoid debt restructuring, the pooling of fiscal resources for bank recapitalisation and the Europeanisation of banking policy to break the links between Member States and banks), although containing sovereign risk became the more controversial issue due to the insistence of the German government on private sector involvement. To a large extent, the speculative crisis of 2010–12 was the effect of Berlin's reluctance to clearly commit to the measures demanded by European corporations and the ECB. After Deauville, the banks broke their commitment to the 2009 grand bargain and began shedding the bonds of deficit Member States, thus piling up the pressure on politicians to act. The ECB followed them in the spring of 2011 (when it secretly stopped buying sovereign bonds on the secondary market),[41] and that is when the speculative crisis reached its feverish peak.

To ease the pressure, the European Council backtracked on private sector involvement in December 2011, established the European Stability Mechanism as

---

[39]   R Epstein, 'Choosing the Lesser of Two Evils: Explaining Multinational Banking Groups Push for Supranational Oversight in the EU' (2014) CERIUM Working Paper 2 http://cerium.umontreal.ca /en/research/cerium-working-papers/news/news/choosing-the-lesser-of-two-evils-explaining-mult -15626 accessed April 2018. Epstein draws a direct link between the Europeanisation of banks and their active support for banking union. The European Banking Federation had privately voiced strong support for the centralisation of banking policy as early as 2006 through its president, Michel Pébereau, chairman of France's biggest bank, BNP-Paribas. See F Autret 'Michel Pébereau, une Excellence à la Française: Portrait d'un Homme d'Influences' *Au fait n° 3* (September 2013).

[40]   Investment banking had Europeanised earlier, producing an agglomeration of investment banking activity for the EU market in the City of London. See D Mügge, *Widen the Market, Narrow the Competition: Banker Interests and the Making of a European Capital Market* (ECPR Press 2010).

[41]   Bastasin (n 28) 244–46 (banks) and 268 (ECB).

a way of pooling in an ad hoc manner Member State fiscal liability[42] and took the momentous decision in June 2012 to launch banking union, starting with the Europeanisation of banking supervision. This was the result of the decision to use ESM funds to recapitalise the Spanish banking sector, which was teetering on the brink after the collapse of Bankia in the spring of 2012.[43] By the time this chapter will have been published, the final push to complete banking union through the setting up of a European Deposit Insurance Scheme (EDIS) will have been made. The reforms also include the possibility for the ESM to directly recapitalise banks.[44] It is also important to note that banking union involves further fiscal liability pooling, through the pooling of resources to be used for bank resolution and for deposit insurance. Together with the ESM, these amount to decisive steps in the direction of a fiscal union.

Crucially, the rationale of these measures entails going down the path of a new leap in integration through banking and fiscal union. Indeed, the launching of banking union explicitly signalled that European political leaders had resolved to do so. Former European Council president, Hermann van Rompuy, has reported that the ECB president, Mario Draghi, told him during the crucial June 2012 European Council that banking union was the 'game-changer he needed' to fully commit the ECB balance sheet to calming down sovereign bond markets. Draghi himself later wrote that the decision to set up 'European banking supervision has been the greatest step towards deeper economic integration since the creation of Economic and Monetary Union'.[45] The decision was also accompanied by the launch of a process of official reports by the supranational institutions that explicitly mention the setting up of a eurozone Treasury with a eurozone budget and headed by a common finance minister as the ultimate aim of the process of reforming the eurozone. Macron's proposals are therefore not original. Rather, their significance lies in the fact that an explicitly pro-EU French president has fully endorsed them.[46]

---

[42] The ESM is an embryonic Eurozone Treasury, as it issues bonds to finance its operations. De Silguy told me that the ESM is similar to what he had proposed, although its scope is much less extensive. Interview, 24 November 2017, Paris.

[43] Around €100bn had fled the country in the first months of 2012 as a result. C Jones, P Jenkins and M Johnson, 'Spain Reveals 100bn Capital Flight' *Financial Times* (31 May 2012) www.ft.com /content/25c39204-ab01-11e1-b875-00144feabdc0 accessed April 2018.

[44] Through its Direct Bank Recapitalisation Instrument adopted in December 2014. See 'ESM Direct Bank Recapitalisation Instrument Adopted' ESM (8 December 2014) www.esm.europa.eu/press-releases/esm-direct-bank-recapitalisation-instrument-adopted accessed April 2018.

[45] Citations in N Véron, 'Europe's Radical Banking Union' (2015) Bruegel Essay and Lecture Series, 18–19 http://bruegel.org/2015/05/europes-radical-banking-union.

[46] The thinking behind Macron's proposals is laid out in a publication by the French Treasury (YE Bara and others, 'A Contribution to the Work on the Strengthening of the Euro Area' (2017) 190 Trésor-Economics www.tresor.economie.gouv.fr/Ressources/File/440712 accessed April 2018). The measures put forward include a eurozone budget to fund public investments, a eurozone unemployment scheme and a European corporation tax.

v THE ENTRENCHMENT OF UK EUROPHOBIA LEADING TO THE BREXIT REFERENDUM AS A SIDE EFFECT OF THE RENEWED INTEGRATIVE IMPETUS IN THE EUROZONE

How does Brexit fit into this picture? [47] The short answer is that the renewed integrative impetus generated by the eurozone crisis galvanised Europhobia on the right of the Conservative Party and that directly led to the calling of the Brexit referendum in 2016. But why is the UK different from France and Germany with respect to European unification? In other words, why is there in the UK such a depth of ruling elite suspicion and even antipathy towards the EU?

The UK has always entertained an ambivalent relation to the process of unification. This can to a large extent be explained by the economic strategy of UK capitalism. During an initial stage, running from the early 1930s to the early 1960s, the UK attempted to complete its transition to corporate capitalism via the setting up of a preferential trading bloc with the Commonwealth markets that would be an alternative to both the American economic bloc and the continental European one that would have to be formed around a Franco-German axis. The UK abandoned 'free trade' in favour of 'Empire free trade' when in 1932 it struck a deal with the dominions in Ottawa setting up a patchy system of imperial preference. The pound had come off the gold standard in 1931 and that allowed for setting up a sterling bloc. This was the basis for Churchill's famous 1946 Zurich speech,[48] in which he called for a United States of Europe to be formed on the continent and to partner the British Commonwealth and the United States in a Western liberal alliance. In fact, UK governments not only stood aside in the 1950s when the EU was being founded; they even attempted to dilute the project by proposing as an alternative to the customs union a European Free Trade Area. The miscalculation was that the coming about of a Franco-German axis could be prevented by luring the more free-trade-oriented Germany away from France.

When the EU was indeed instituted in 1958, the economic dynamism arising from the formation of the customs union brought about a reorientation of UK policy. UK firms were still weary of German competition, but the trade diversion and the additional economies of scale and scope arising from the customs union that were benefiting continental manufacturers were highly detrimental for UK corporations. The only way to take advantage of this process was to join it. Moreover, the Commonwealth fell far short of the initial hopes that UK elites had pinned on it. From this reorientation flowed the 1961 membership application. As membership negotiations progressed and stalled in the 1960s, UK industrial capital's interest in the EU grew into enthusiasm because of the potential for a pan-European industrial

---

[47]   This section summarises G Georgiou, 'British Capitalism and European Unification, from Ottawa to the Brexit Referendum' (2017) 25 Historical Materialism 90.

[48]   W Churchill (19 September 1946) www.churchill-in-zurich.ch/site/assets/files/1807/rede_winston_ch urchill_englisch.pdf accessed April 2018.

policy in high-tech sectors that alone could allow European corporations to compete with their American counterparts. The chief legacy of that 1960s–1970s push is, of course, the aerospace industry, with Airbus and the European Space Agency as the most significant achievements. Accordingly, the Conservative party was the pro-EU UK party of the day. Even Margaret Thatcher was counted as pro-European in the 1975 referendum campaign. The period stretching from the 1960s to the mid 1980s was the high point of UK Europeanism.

But with the Thatcher revolution things changed. The Tory governments of the 1980s carried out a deep restructuring of the UK economy that entailed a profound reorientation of UK economic strategy. First, they abandoned to foreign investors most of the manufacturing sectors that had been at the core of the national champions' period and that had formed the bulwark of Europeanism within UK ruling elites. The UK's industrial strategy became what can be called the 'gateway into Europe' strategy, namely one based on undercutting labour and social regulations and tax rates in the rest of the EU as a way of attracting extra-EU investment into the single market. Second, the Thatcher governments chose to specialise the UK economy in the international business services sector (financial, legal, accounting and other services) pivoting around the resurgent City of London. Again, the City's resurgence was based on its undercutting of international regulatory standards – indeed, it can be dated back to the early 1960s when it became the home of the Eurodollar market on the basis of the offshore treatment of dollar-denominated activity by the financial and monetary authorities in the UK. The City now became the pivotal section of capital in the UK.

These shifts boosted ruling elite Euroscepticism for two reasons. The first and overwhelming one was that UK economic strategy was now based on the preservation of regulatory and fiscal competition within the EU and it therefore created a vested UK interest in preserving political decentralisation within the Union. UK elites had always been intuitively suspicious of such centralisation because it represented the creation of a continental power centre draining power away from London, but now that suspicion acquired even stronger foundations in economic strategy. The second reason was that the renewed pre-eminence of the City within the UK strengthened the forces of globalism and Atlanticism that had traditionally coalesced around it since the days of British Imperial primacy.[49] These forces have always been suspicious of the protectionist aspects of the EU and their basic orientation is to provide services to the world's money capital holders. The City sees itself as the world's money dealer. City financiers therefore want to enjoy the greatest political freedom in pursuing this orientation and they correctly fear that they can influence Brussels much less than they can London.

As a result, the Thatcher revolution led to the entrenchment of Tory Euroscepticism. Even moderate and centrist Tories such as David Cameron and

---

[49]　K van der Pijl, *The Making of an Atlantic Ruling Class* (Verso 2012).

George Osborne and before them John Major are Eurosceptics in that they want the UK to stay detached from all the initiatives taken from Maastricht onwards and which aim to deepen the process of political unification, especially the single currency. These Tories are the real authors of the multi-speed EU which emerged in the aftermath of the Maastricht treaty.

But another wing of the party – which Thatcher herself came to embody in the late 1980s through her relentless and strident opposition to the prospect of a single currency – has rejected lock, stock and barrel all the integrationist initiatives. The split within the Tory party crystallised in the 1990s during the debate on the ratification of the Maastricht Treaty, which the moderate Eurosceptics accepted but the Europhobes fiercely opposed.

The Europhobes' failure to prevent the deepening of integration led them to radicalise and to turn openly secessionist by the time of the eurozone crisis. In fact, the turning point might be seen as the Europhobes' relentless opposition to the Lisbon Treaty. Crucially, the Lisbon Treaty included a provision for the extension of qualified majority voting and the co-decision procedure to financial services regulation. As soon as it came into force, the Commission used these new powers to introduce a raft of measures destined to produce a 'single rulebook' of financial regulation across the EU – i.e. to eliminate the regulatory competition that was widely seen as central to the City's success.[50] Moreover, after the 2009 de Larosière report, the EU began moving in the direction of the centralisation of microprudential supervision by setting up the European System of Financial Supervision.[51] Although the ESFS does not actually centralise supervision (it only creates a system of mandatory coordination), it amounts to a significant step in that direction and its ambitions are plain.

The renewed integrative momentum unleashed by the eurozone crisis added further to the Europhobic unrest within the Tory party. Initially, the Europhobes thought they could blackmail the EU into making significant concessions in exchange for them not blocking advances aimed at shoring up the eurozone. This thinking influenced Cameron's unsuccessful attempt to extract such concessions at the European Council meeting of December 2011, when he conditioned the UK's acceptance of the Fiscal Compact on the overturning of qualified majority voting on financial services.[52] But when it became obvious that the eurozone would push

---

[50]   Indeed, an April 2015 poll of City executives found that 75 per cent considered that the most important issue in the negotiations demanded by David Cameron for a new deal on UK–EU relations in advance of the referendum was the reform of the qualified majority voting system on financial services. Centre for the Study of Financial Innovation, 'The City and Brexit: A CSFI Survey of the Financial Services Sector's Views on Britain and the EU' http://static1.squarespace.com/static/54d620fce4b049bf4cd5be9b/t/5536a1e8e4b0eb6a74abafi6/1429643752526/CSFI+The+City+and+Brexit.pdf accessed April 2018.

[51]   Details on the ESFS can be found at https://ec.europa.eu/info/business-economy-euro/banking-and-finance/financial-supervision-and-risk-management/european-system-financial-supervision_en accessed April 2018.

[52]   A good account of the events surrounding the meeting can be found in A Barker and G Parker, 'False Assumptions Underpinned British Strategy' *Financial Times* (16 December 2011) www.ft.com/content/6c5e100e-27ee-11e1-a4c4-00144feabdc0 accessed April 2018.

ahead with deeper integration without the UK being in a position either to stop this from happening or to extract concessions, the Europhobes turned fully to the secessionist option.

Cameron had already pledged to hold a referendum on the ratification of the Lisbon Treaty when he was elected party leader in 2007. A party official would later claim that granting the Brexit referendum was the only way to prevent a split of the Tory party in advance of the 2015 general election.[53] But before holding the referendum, Cameron again attempted to extract concessions from the EU that could placate at least a section of Europhobic Tory opinion. His failure was an additional ingredient in the success of the Leave campaign.

VI CONCLUSION: THE COMING OVERHAUL OF THE EUROZONE AND THE EU

How will the trends I have described in this chapter develop over the coming years?

This chapter's analysis leads to the conclusion that we are now entering into a period of restructuring of the EU that should complete the overhaul initiated by the eurozone crisis. By the end of this process – at some point around 2025 – the EU will be significantly more integrated and the gap between its two concentric circles (the eurozone and non-eurozone Member States) will have substantially narrowed, although its outer periphery is likely to grow with the UK joining the ranks of EU satellite states.

The French and German general elections of 2017 have opened up a window of opportunity of about a year and a half in which major decisions can be taken. At the time this chapter was being finalised, the SPD and CDU had reached a pre-agreement on the formation of a new grand coalition in Germany that put front and centre EU policy and signalled a new German willingness to work with France on the basis of Macron's reform agenda.[54] The European Council has indeed prepared a precise schedule[55] that foresees substantial decisions on eurozone reform.[56] The December 2017 European Council decided to mandate the finance ministers to come to an agreement on completing banking union in the first half of 2018 (most importantly by agreeing on how to set up an EDIS), incorporating the ESM into EU law and transforming it into a European Monetary Fund with expanded powers. French President Macron and German Chancellor Angela Merkel also agreed to come up with a common proposal for setting up a eurozone

---

53   G Parker and A Barker, 'David Cameron's Adventures in Europe' *Financial Times* (22 January 2016) www.ft.com/content/26cbc524-bfb4-11e5-846f-79b0e3d20eaf.

54   See W Münchau, 'A German Coalition Deal to Radically Reshape Europe' *Financial Times* (14 January 2018) www.ft.com/content/a6e39acc-f796-11e7-88f7-5465a6ce1a00 accessed April 2018.

55   European Council, 'Leaders Agenda, Building our Future Together' (October 2017) www.consilium.europa.eu/media/21594/leaders-agenda.pdf accessed April 2018.

56   Significant decisions have already been taken on defence and military affairs too, but these fall outside the scope of this chapter.

budget and finance minister for the March 2018 European Council meeting[57] and the first substantial decisions on that front are scheduled to be taken in the June 2018 meeting.

It is important to see that Brexit is not only secondary on the EU's agenda, but that it has also added impetus to the process. Whatever the actual outcome of the ongoing negotiations regarding the terms of Brexit and the future UK–EU relationship, London's political standing within the EU has been profoundly damaged. As a result, one of the most important political obstacles to greater integration has been substantially weakened. This applies to eurozone reform too, as one of the issues involved in the ongoing discussions about a potential fiscal union is the harmonisation of corporation tax so that a European tax can be levied. The Commission has tabled a proposal for a Common Consolidated Corporate Tax Base, and Commission President Jean-Claude Juncker even floated the idea of moving to qualified majority voting on taxation (and foreign policy) in his 2017 State of the Union address to the European Parliament. Both of these initiatives become highly more likely without the UK exerting its leverage in Brussels.

There is another reason for which Brexit is adding to the integrationist momentum. When the UK ceases to be a Member State, the eurozone will overnight become a much greater part of the EU. The eurozone accounted for 72.4 per cent of EU GDP in 2017, but that will now go up to 86.2 per cent. The collective leverage of non-eurozone Member States will thus substantially decrease and consequently the strategic sense of being a non-eurozone EU Member State will too, especially as a number of Central and Eastern European Member States are waiting in the queue to join the eurozone. The Polish foreign minister, Witold Waszczykowski, echoed this assessment on the eve of the Brexit referendum when he expressed fears that the eurozone would 'dominate' and Poland would be sidelined after Brexit.[58] The UK's departure will also create more space for the Commission to insist that the Treaty creates a legal obligation to join the eurozone, as Juncker also explicitly pointed out in his State of the Union address. Moreover, if a redistributive eurozone budget is set up, that will further increase the incentives to join the single currency.[59]

The likely outcome of the 2010–12 eurozone crisis is therefore much deeper integration within the EU and fewer and weaker Eurosceptic obstacles within it.

---

[57] M Khan, 'Macron and Merkel Eye March Eurozone Agreement' *Financial Times* (15 December 2017) www.ft.com/content/db69cd93-4f1c-32fd-b1e8-9c92ae5c58e6 accessed April 2018.

[58] 'Brexit Could Sideline Poland in EU: Foreign Minister' *Radio Poland* (23 June 2016) www.thenews.pl/1/10/Artykul/258513,Brexit-could-sideline-Poland-in-EU-foreign-minister accessed April 2018.

[59] One fear is that such a budget could as a side effect reduce the redistributive effect of the EU budget itself, of which Poland and Hungary are important beneficiaries. A Spisak, 'Macron Sows Disunity over Euro in Eastern EU States' *Financial Times* (20 October 2017) www.ft.com/content/4b10af9e-962c-11e7-8c5c-c8d8fa6961bb accessed April 2018.

PART IV

The Crisis as a Crisis of the EU's Social Character

13

A Tale of Two Documents

The Eclipse of the Social Democratic Constitution

Alan Bogg and KD Ewing

I

Legal texts are the outcome of political processes. As such they provide an insight into the deep ideological changes that may be taking place within any legal system. In this chapter, we propose to contrast two important instruments of the EC/EU, the first being the Community Charter of the Fundamental Social Rights of Workers of 1989, and the other being the EU Social Pillar of 2017. The aim is not to engage in a literal compare and contrast of the two instruments, as one might compare and contrast apples and oranges; rather, it is to engage in a contextual compare and contrast of the two instruments, with a view to understanding what they tell us about the changing economic and political direction of the EU. In doing so we aim better to understand the evolution of social policy, the changing role of trade unions within the EU, and the inactivity in relation to employment rights despite the great changes in the global economy and working practices since the last employment law directive was produced in 2008.

In embarking on this project, we do so mindful of the objectives of this volume, one of which is to test the claim that there has been (1) a deep paradigm shift, caused by (2) the embrace of new theoretical models, leading to (3) an ideological distortion of institutional arrangements, and (4) the pursuit of policies which confound the purposes the EU had been established to serve, by (5) techniques that undermine the principles on which constitutional government should rest. That *paradigm shift* is reflected in the two documents identified for discussion, but also in other texts that form the dots to be joined between the Social Charter in 1989 and the Social Pillar in 1997. These include the Social Action Protocol concluded at Maastricht in 1992 and the EU Charter of Fundamental Rights concluded at Nice in 2000, achievements consolidated

The authors wish to thank Professor Tonia Novitz for her advice and encouragement in the preparation of this chapter.

and developed by the Lisbon Treaty in 2008. The great misfortune of the authors of the last is that it was signed just before the euro crisis, and the accompanying global financial crisis, which it was insufficiently robust to sustain.[1]

The good fortune of the European institutions in the wake of the crises is that they had great discretion under the constitution to respond as they saw fit. The EU constitution proved to be an enabling rather than a restraining constitution, particularly in relation to economic policy. This of course is unlikely to be a mistake, with ten years of neglect since 2008 suggesting that social policy was a thirty-year aberration in an institution that has *returned to the strict economic ambitions of its founders*, when labour rights were embraced only for economic reasons.[2] This was seen most obviously in the EEC Treaty, Article 119, designed to prevent unfair competition where some countries applied the principle of equal pay for men and women when others did not.[3] One of the arguments of this chapter is that we are experiencing a return to the liberal economism of that kind, with the institutional arrangements under the much-expanded constitutional structures facilitating such a retreat, notwithstanding a social agenda that had been promoted in waves since the 1970s.[4]

In terms of *ideological distortion*, the issue here has been the clash between the social democratic values that we believe were ultimately reflected in the European constitutional arrangements and their displacement by what some have argued are neoliberal values,[5] but which others may prefer to see as weak social liberal values.[6] We do not dispute that there has been a strong return to liberal economics since 2008, with the adoption of policies in the labour field that had much in common in tone and approach with the policies pioneered in the United Kingdom by the Labour governments of Blair and Brown. This approach may fairly to be said to be the intellectual source – intentionally or otherwise – of what is now being pursued in Brussels: (1) minimum standards in legislation; (2) representative rather than regulatory trade unionism; and (3) trade unions concerned as much with equipping members with adaptable skills as higher wages.[7] This is not the crude economics of Thatcherism or its contemporary heirs in the Brexit debate.

It is nevertheless an approach that is at *odds with the constitutional values* of the EU as it developed beyond the narrow constraints of the EEC Treaty. Weak social democratic values of the kind we believe to be reflected in the Treaty on European

---

[1]   The Lisbon Treaty was signed on 13 December 2007.
[2]   For an account, see C Barnard, *EU Employment Law* (4th edn, OUP 2012) 5–6; B Bercusson, *European Labour Law* (2nd edn, CUP 2009) 5–6.
[3]   Barnard (n 2) 253–54.
[4]   For an early account, see BA Hepple, 'The Crisis in EEC Labour Law' (1987) 16 Industrial Law Journal 77.
[5]   See C Crouch, 'Entrenching Neo-Liberalism: The Current Agenda of European Social Policy' in N Countouris and M Freedland (eds), *Resocialising Europe in a Time of Crisis* (CUP 2013).
[6]   See A Bogg, 'New Labour, Trade Unions and the Liberal State' (2009) 20 King's Law Journal 403.
[7]   For an account of the New Labour project relating to labour law, see P Smith and G Morton, 'Nine Years of New Labour: Neoliberalism and Workers' Rights' (2006) 44 British Journal Industrial Relations 401.

Union (TEU) are not consistent with economic liberalism of any variety, while the subordination of social policy to economic and employment policy which we outline seems difficult to reconcile with TEU constitutional values. That said, this is an era in which constitutional values have become greatly distorted, the most obvious example being the claim by the then EU President (Herman Van Rompuy) that the Commission's financial support for Greece during the euro crisis was an example of the constitutional principle of 'solidarity',[8] a scarcely credible claim given the conditions attached to the support which on some accounts led to the trampling on a national constitution, the destruction of a system of labour law, and according to many accounts the pauperisation of a generation.[9]

As already suggested, it is also an approach pursued by means that raise questions of *compatibility with constitutional principle*. In common with other instruments, the TEU expresses a commitment to the rule of law.[10] This is a principle the Commission takes seriously from time to time, usually in relation to the practices of Member States, notably Hungary and Poland (but shamefully not yet Spain). These interventions reveal a preoccupation with a conveniently narrow conception of the rule of law, relating principally to judicial independence.[11] But the rule of law is also about governing in accordance with the law, which means not using powers that have never been conferred on institutions, not using administrative powers of various kinds to take steps unavailable by using legislative powers, and not requiring or putting pressure on Member States to act in way inconsistent with if not contrary to the international legal obligations and national constitutional traditions of the Member State in question, the latter being most conspicuously the case in relation to Greece.[12]

If by these means there has been a deep paradigm shift, the question now is whether EU law is on a *journey to an even deeper and more authoritarian shift* of a kind which has been identified in the UK as a result of recent deregulatory measures going well beyond anything being demanded by the EU institutions.[13] The British experience is one in which (1) minimum standards have been eroded by

---

[8] 'EU President Herman Van Rompuy told a news conference after the summit that Europe was sending Greece a "clear message of solidarity", a line echoed by Germany and France'. See M Grajewski and J Toyer, 'EU Pledges to Support Greece But Offers No Details' *Reuters* (11 February 2011) www.reuters.com/article/us-eurozone/eu-pledges-to-support-greece-but-offers-no-details-idustre6181902010021 accessed April 2018.

[9] See I Katsaroumpas, 'De-Constitutionalising Collective Labour Rights: The Case of Greece' (2018) 47 Industrial Law Journal 465.

[10] Art 2 TEU.

[11] See European Commission Press Release, 'Rule of Law: European Commission Acts to Defend Judicial Independence in Poland', 20 December 2017; European Parliament Press Release, 'Rule of Law in Hungary Debated by MEPs with Government and Experts', 7 December 2017.

[12] This was most vividly expressed in International Labour Office, *Report on the High Level Mission to Greece: Athens, 19–23 September 2011* (Geneva 2011).

[13] A Bogg, 'Beyond Neo-Liberalism: The Trade Union Act 2016 and the Authoritarian State' (2016) 45 Industrial Law Journal 299.

changes to both substantive and procedural law; (2) the role of trade unions as industrial and political representative bodies has been eroded in line with neoliberal perceptions of the trade union function as service providers;[14] and (3) the legitimacy of trade unions as economic and political actors, whether on the demand or supply side, is now contested.[15] These developments in the UK since 2010 (picking up where Thatcher and Major had ended in 1997) both reflect the dangers of the deregulatory impulse now visible in Brussels, while also helping to contextualise the discipline and boundaries of that impulse.

As already indicated, in the pages that follow we trace these developments with a focus on two seminal texts, each produced at a different stage in the development of the Union. The first half of the chapter (sections II–IV) is concerned principally with the EU's social democratic past, beginning with the Community Charter of the Fundamental Social Rights of Workers, leading to the Social Action Protocol and the means better to implement the Charter, before examining first the EU Charter of Fundamental Rights, and then the TEU, which together provided a framework of objectives, methods for implementation, rights and values. The second half of the chapter (sections V–VII) in contrast is concerned principally with developments since 2008, the year coincidentally of both the Lisbon Treaty and the global and Euro economic crises. These developments reflect the contradictions sewn into the TEU, leading to the displacement of social policy by economic and employment policy, and in turn to the European Social Pillar as a pillar of economic and employment as opposed to social policy.

II

We begin with the Community Charter of the Fundamental Social Rights of Workers, an initiative associated with Jacques Delors, a French socialist politician who became President of the European Commission in 1985. Although influenced largely by the needs of the single market, the text was inspired also by ILO Conventions and the Council of Europe's Social Charter.[16] It was also a recognition of the need to take full account of the social dimension of what was then the European Community. As such, the rights proclaimed were organised under twelve headings in twenty-six paragraphs, as follows:

- freedom of movement;
- employment and remuneration;

---

[14] See FA Hayek, *The Constitution of Liberty* (University of Chicago Press 1960) 275–77.

[15] On the role of trade unions as valued 'supply side' agencies, see KD Ewing, 'The Function of Trade Unions' (2005) 34 Industrial Law Journal 1.

[16] The Preamble does not say which ILO Conventions, at a time when these conventions had not yet been formally segmented by the ILO Declaration on Fundamental Principles and Rights at Work (1998).

- improvement of living and working conditions;
- social protection;
- freedom of association and collective bargaining;
- vocational training;
- equal treatment for men and women;
- information, consultation and participation for workers;
- health protection and safety in the workplace;
- protection of children and adolescents;
- elderly persons;
- disabled persons.

It is hard to think that any of this was new, in the sense that comparable provisions would be found in the national constitutions of Member States,[17] the European Social Charter and its protocols, and ILO Conventions.[18]

What was new, however, was the embedding of these values directly within the Community (albeit initially excluding the UK), as well as the commitment to implement them. The Charter had no legal status and was not binding on Member States or enforceable in national courts, though it could be used as an interpretive aid. It was rather a manifesto for action and was accompanied by an Action Plan setting out how it would be implemented.[19] The problem with implementation, however, was that much of the programme was not within the competence of the EC as it then was, while most of what was within competence could be implemented only by the unanimous approval of all Member States in a union of expanding membership. Along with the Social Charter thus came new methods to implement it, finalised at Maastricht in 1992, the new Social Chapter of the Treaty increasing the competences of the EU while enabling much of the agenda to be implemented by qualified majority voting, a technical yet important constitutional reform.

The powers of implementation whether by qualified majority voting or unanimity were nevertheless incomplete in the sense that core matters were left beyond the competence of the EU, these being pay, freedom of association and the right to strike. In one sense these were crucial omissions because they strike at the very heart of a progressive labour law, which is about the redistribution of income through wages, and the industrial and political empowerment of workers through strong trade unions. But while it is tempting to see EU labour law as being concerned with secondary though not peripheral issues, one persuasive response is that EU labour does not stand in autonomous isolation, but operates symbiotically with national

---

[17] See KD Ewing, 'Economic Rights' in M Rosenfeld and A Sajo, *The Oxford Handbook of Comparative Constitutional Law* (OUP 2012) ch 50.

[18] Nevertheless, see B Bercusson, 'The European Community Charter of Fundamental Social Rights' (1990) 53 MLR 624; B Hepple, 'The Implementation of the Community Charter of Fundamental Social Rights' (1990) 53 MLR 643.

[19] European Commission, Social Action Plan, COM(89) 568.

law, and that European labour law is the synthesis or unity of the two.[20] In most members states at the time there were already comprehensive systems of collective bargaining dealing with pay (with high levels of coverage), as well as constitutional guarantees of freedom of association as well as the right to strike.

EU labour law was thus building upon a social democratic base established at national level in *most* Member States. Before talk of subsidiarity was fashionable, it was grounded in national law and was a bottom-up as a well as a top-down initiative. That sense that it was building on a social democratic base rooted in national constitutional traditions was reinforced by the other initiative taken at Maastricht, which was to strengthen the social dialogue procedures and to give to the social partners the power to create legal norms with an EU-wide application.[21] European law had previously permitted directives to be implemented at national level by collective agreements, provided the agreements in question were sufficiently comprehensive. The Social Dialogue procedures were different in the sense that they not only contemplated the social partners being consulted about legislative proposals and their content, but also enabled the social partners to take over the process and to create what was in effect legislation by negotiation between them.[22]

In this way, the Charter inspired (1) the introduction of new legislative powers, and (2) new legislative procedures. It also of course inspired (3) new legislative outcomes across a wide range of areas which it addressed. These included:

- transparency of the employment relationship;
- equal treatment for workers on non-standard employment contracts (such as part-time, fixed-term and agency workers);
- regulation of working time, including paid holidays;
- maternity protection and parental leave;
- strengthening of occupational health and safety;
- information and consultation procedures (on matters such as redundancy, the transfer of undertakings; and changes to contractual relations);
- the introduction of European Works Councils (EWCs).[23]

In the rich tapestry being woven at European level, what was emerging from this framework of legislative powers, legislative means and legislative outcomes was a framework of labour law that consolidated both the horizontal and vertical integration of trade unions. The former was reflected in Article 12 of the Charter which sought to guarantee the right to negotiate and conclude collective agreements, but which also provided that 'the dialogue between the two sides of industry

---

[20] Bercusson (n 2) 11–15, 403.

[21] For origins, see BA Hepple, *European Social Dialogue – Alibi or Opportunity?* (Institute of Employment Rights 1993).

[22] On the constitutional legitimacy of these arrangements, see Case T-135/96, *Union Européenne de l'Artisanat et des Petites et Moyennes Entreprises (UEAPME) v Council of the European Union* EU: T:1998:128.

[23] For a comprehensive account, see Barnard (n 2) 663–72.

at European level which must be developed, may, if the parties deem it desirable, result in contractual relations in particular at inter-occupational and sectoral level'. This was written into the social dialogue procedures, encouraging transnational sectoral bargaining which would build upon and be implemented by the comprehensive sectoral bargaining arrangements operating throughout the bulk of the EC as a result of developments at national level.

But the developing programme also made provision for the vertical integration of trade unions in the sense of corporate-level representation. Although the information and consultation procedures and the provisions for European Works Councils (EWCs) were silent as to the role of trade unions,[24] it seems clear that they created space which trade unions could occupy to provide representation for employees. This space could potentially have enabled trade unions to operate at all levels of the enterprise, though the agenda was seriously constrained by legal instruments that were too aspirational and not sufficiently prescriptive. It was constrained too by the failure to develop early ideas for a European company statute that would have led to trade union representation on company boards,[25] a feature of corporate structures in some Member States that remains a final step that has yet to be taken, there being no technical obstacle to its adoption at European level.

There are other failings of the vertical penetration measures, which have proved easiest to operate in countries where they are least needed. In the UK in contrast they have conspicuously failed to provide a stepping stone for trade union organisation. The agenda is nevertheless important for other reasons, not least because by the EWCs it provided an opportunity for the global reach of the European social model. The EWC Directive applied not only to EU-based companies but to all transnational companies operating in two or more Member States, provided they satisfied the minimum employment requirements in two or more Member States.[26] This included US multinationals now required to engage in conduct in the EU that they would never contemplate in the US. Indeed, there are now 151 corporations headquartered in the USA which have now established an EWC under the Directive.[27]

---

[24] On the expressly recognised role of trade unions in the British implementing legislation, see SI 2010 No 1088. See H Collins, KD Ewing and A McColgan, *Labour Law* (CUP 2012) 604–08, 638ff.

[25] For background, context and an assessment of the political complexities, see T Schulten and S Zagelmeyer, 'Board-Level Employee Representation in Europe' (*EurWORK*, 27 September 1998) www.eurofound.europa.eu/observatories/eurwork/comparative-information/board-level-employee-representation-in-europe accessed April 2018.

[26] Directive 2009/38/EC of the European Parliament and of the Council of 6 May 2009 on the establishment of a European Works Council or a procedure in Community-scale undertakings and Community-scale groups of undertakings for the purposes of informing and consulting employees (Recast) [2009] OJ L122/28 (European Works Council Directive (Recast)).

[27] See S de Spiegelaere and R Jagodzinski, *European Works Councils and SE Works Councils in 2015* (ETUI 2015).

III

It is easy to understand why British trade unionists should be won over to the European model by Delors. Here we see social democracy in embryo, a foothold for labour in the architecture of what was to become the European Union, reflecting the values embedded in the constitutional architecture of Member States. Here we also have a social action programme, social dialogue, and social integration of trade unions. None of it was perfect, but the social ambition and the social trajectory were clear enough, ambition and trajectory which underpinned these achievements by the language of fundamental rights. This is not to make inflated claims about the constitutional protection of rights – which history has shown to be easily vulnerable in times of crisis.[28] But equally we should not underestimate the importance of constitutionally protected rights, as a symbol of the values of the society to which they relate and in the case of the EU a consolidation of the legal and political achievements to date.[29]

The EU Charter of Fundamental Rights is striking for being a bottom-up initiative, reflecting the principles which it expressed (it was designed to be a 'showcase' of rights),[30] rather than a top-down initiative imposed or adopted by a new nation state (post-independence) or a recovering nation state (post-war). Although it differs from the Community Charter of the Fundamental Rights of Workers, in the sense that it was declaratory rather than programmatic, the EU Charter was equally important: while constitutional rights often guarantee citizens nothing when needed most, they tell us much about the political values of the country or community in which these citizens live and work. In that context, what is striking about the EU Charter is not only its comprehensive and wide-ranging embrace of civil and political rights on the one hand, and social and economic rights on the other, but crucially also its determination that these should have equal legal status and be enforced judicially in appropriate circumstances.

The EU Charter was of course not the first legal text to acknowledge the 'indivisible nature of all human rights, be they civil, political, economic, social or cultural', in the words of the Council of Europe's Revised Social Charter, from which the authors of the EU Charter drew inspiration. But it was the first international treaty formally to house these rights under the same roof and to embed them in the same way. This of course is not to say that there are other ways by which differences could

---

[28] This would be true of both civil and political rights on the hand, and social and economic rights on the other. See Katsaroumpas (n 9).

[29] See KD Ewing, 'Just Words and Social Justice' (1999) 15 Review of Constitutional Studies 53.

[30] See G Jones and Ambrose Evans-Pritchard, 'European Summit Charter on Rights "No More Binding than the *Beano*"' *The Telegraph* (14 October 2000) quoting Mr Keith Vaz, then Minister for Europe in the British government www.telegraph.co.uk/news/worldnews/europe/1370340/European-summit-Charter-on-rights-no-more-binding-than-the-Beano.html accessed April 2018.

be created and informal stratifications established within the text, as we find in the EU Charter's heavy qualification of social and economic rights in Chapter IV (Solidarity) in contrast to the more unequivocal tone of civil and political rights in Chapters I (Dignity), II (Freedoms) and III (Equality). Notably the right to collective bargaining and collective action in Article 28 was made conditional on 'Community law and national laws and practices', which is not much good if – as in the case of the right to strike – Community law has already trumped the right in question.[31]

It is also the case that the formal recognition of the equal status of rights does not prevent informal stratifications being established in the courts, which was not such an issue at the time the Charter was drafted (when it had no direct legal status), as it is since the Lisbon Treaty when it was given the same legal status as the Treaties.[32] This stratification can be achieved in various ways, for example in relation to Article 27 dealing with the right of workers to information and consultation by denying the provision in question any horizontal effect, so that it is binding only on the state and not on companies or other third parties. Thus, in *Association de médiation sociale*, it was held that the Charter right to information and consultation was not 'sufficient in itself to confer on individuals an individual right which they may invoke as such',[33] and could not be used to disapply French law from which some categories of atypical workers were excluded in determining whether statutory thresholds were met as a precondition of the employers' obligation to invoke information and consultation procedures.[34]

As pointed out, the Charter was given legal effect by the Lisbon Treaty in 2008. This was the apotheosis of Social Europe, for not only did the Treaty on European Union consolidate the foregoing achievements, it did so by wrapping them in constitutional language which is as good an expression of social democratic values as has been written since the end of the Cold War. Thus Article 2 TEU provides that the Union is 'founded on the values of respect for human dignity, freedom, democracy, equality, the rule of law and respect for human rights, including the rights of persons belonging to minorities'. Moreover, 'these values are common to the Member States in a society in which pluralism, non-discrimination, tolerance, justice, solidarity and equality between women and men prevail'. This is developed further in Article 3 TEU with the commitment to an internal market, 'based on balanced economic growth and price stability',

---

[31]   Case C-438/05, *International Transport Workers' Federation and Finnish Seamen's Union v Viking Line ABP* EU:C:2007:772; Case C-341/05, *Laval v Svenska Byggnadsarbetareforbundet* EU: C:2007:809.

[32]   Art 6(1) TEU.

[33]   C-176/12, *Association de Médiation Sociale v Union Locale des Syndicats CGT, Hichem Laboubi, Union Départementale CGT des Bouches-du-Rhône, Confédération générale du travail (CGT))* EU: C:2014:2.

[34]   For comment, see C Murphy, 'Using the EU Charter of Fundamental Rights against Private Parties after Association de Médiation Sociale' (2014) European Human Rights Law Review 170.

and 'a highly competitive social market economy', while 'aiming at full employment and social progress'.

This of course could all be cynical nonsense, recalling Kahn-Freund's famous dismissal of the Weimar Constitution as being meaningless platitudes binding on no one.[35] It is also the case that a social market is nevertheless a weak form of social democracy within a capitalist paradigm: it is a commitment to a social market economy not a socialised economy of the kind that might have been understood by earlier pioneers of social democracy. But equally it is a commitment to a social market economy, not a free market economy, which sets the TEU and the EU apart from the free market and liberal democratic constitutions to be found notably in the United States and Japan,[36] and the 'socialist constitution' under the 'people's democratic dictatorship' to be found in China.[37] What was in effect the European constitution (though it could not officially be referred to as such) thus offered a distinctive global voice, neither liberal nor socialist, nor equidistant between those of the other great economic powers. But different nonetheless.

These claims are reinforced by additional promises in Article 3 TEU, including specifically a commitment to 'combat social exclusion and discrimination', and to 'promote social justice and protection, equality between women and men, solidarity between generations and protection of the rights of the child'. Again of course this is as opaque (no doubt intentionally) as it is aspirational. What is 'social justice'? The answer depends to a large extent on who is being asked. Here, however, these legal values are set in a text defined in part by its Preamble, which refers to the inspiration drawn from the constitutional traditions of Member States as well as their international obligations. In this context, specific reference is made to the Council of Europe's Social Charters (original and revised), which provide a fuller crystallised framework of the principles of social justice than any other legal text, acknowledging that the Council of Europe 'agreed to secure to their populations the social rights specified therein in order to improve their standard of living and their social well-being'.[38]

Note the importance of 'social rights'. Social justice means social rights as a means to social justice; not social rights and free markets as the means to social injustice. This is not to say of course that rights create or guarantee social justice,[39] but it does suggest that they are a necessary precondition. Nor is it to say that the catalogue of social rights in the Social Charter underpinning the commitment to social justice in the TEU is adequate, sufficient or complete. This is a social democratic text first drafted in 1961;

---

[35] O Kahn-Freund, 'The Weimar Constitution' (1944) 15 Political Quarterly 235.
[36] In the United States this is most evident in the jurisprudence of the Supreme Court, which at various points has struck down regulatory legislation of various kinds on various grounds, most notably and significantly in *Schechter Poultry Corp v United States*, 295 US 495 (1935). Also of course *Lochner v New York*, 198 US 45 (1905).
[37] Art 1 Constitution of the People's Republic of China.
[38] European Social Charter (Revised) 1996, Preamble.
[39] Katsaroumpas (n 9).

the commitment is to social justice, not to equality. That said, unlike EU labour law the vision of social justice in the Council of Europe Social Charters represents the beating heart of a progressive labour law, which as we have said is through (1) high wages to equalise incomes; and (2) trade union freedom to strengthen the collective power of workers. To this end, the Social Charters not only seek to guarantee by social rights the right to a decent standard of living (Art. 4, where ensuring a decent standard of living is explicitly connected with the right to fair remuneration),[40] but the 1961 version was also the first international treaty to recognise the right to strike (Art. 6(4)).

IV

In consolidating developments in the twenty years since the Community Charter of the Fundamental Social Rights of Workers, the great achievement of the Lisbon Treaty is that it embedded a new framework of social values; provided a platform for legally enforceable fundamental social rights; and integrated the Maastricht social chapter with its legislative powers for making social legislation and its procedure for social dialogue in the making and implementation of such legislation. How has it all gone so awry so quickly? No one speaks of Social Europe any more, with a clear paradigm shift having taken place within the framework of the social democratic architecture that had been in the process of construction. It is convenient to blame the euro crisis and the global financial crisis.[41] That may be too easy: the seeds had already been sown in the *Viking* and *Laval* litigation some months earlier in which it was made clear that the social rights of workers were subordinate to the economic freedoms of employers.[42]

That subordination was carried forward into the Lisbon Treaty and the new legal status for the EU Charter. More generally, however, the Lisbon Treaty contained the seeds of its own destruction, with a Trojan horse in the TFEU, Title VIII capable of bringing down the entire social democratic structure. It is true that the provisions are not new and that they were carried over into the TFEU. But it does appear to be true that they are being used differently as economic policy has changed, with the soft law mechanisms of what are now Title VIII and to a lesser extent Title IX being used as one of the instruments of that change. Dealing specifically with economic policy, Title VIII states expressly that 'member States shall conduct their economic policies with a view to contributing to the achievement of the objectives of the Union, as defined in Article 3 of the TEU', but in a manner which seems directly contradictory, 'in accordance with the principle of an open market economy with free competition'.[43]

---

[40] Also notice ensuring a decent standard of living as one of the stated overarching objectives the signatories undertake in the Preamble and Part 1 of the ESC.

[41] For a critique, see Countouris and Freedland (n 5).

[42] Case C-438/05, *International Transport Workers' Federation and Finnish Seamen's Union v Viking Line ABP* (n 31) and Case C-341/05, *Laval v Svenska Byggnadsarbetareforbundet* (n 31).

[43] Art 120 TFEU.

It is unclear whether an 'open market economy' is compatible with a 'social market economy' or vice versa. If so why is the commitment not to an open social market economy? Contradiction apart, the other feature of Article 120 is that Member States shall conduct their economic policies in accordance with 'the broad guidelines referred to in Article 121(2)'. Article 121(2) in turn imposes a duty on the Commission to 'formulate a draft for the broad guidelines of the economic policies of the Member States and of the Union'. The draft is then submitted to the Council for approval in the form of a Recommendation. Thereafter, Article 121(3) provides that this soft law is to have a hard edge (Recommendations have no regulatory effect), with the requirement that a monitoring and surveillance procedure be established by the Council and the Commission to ensure that the economic policies of each Member State are consistent with the broad economic policy guidelines, now so well established that they are simply referred to as BEPL.

In addition to the process under Article 120 dealing with economic policy, Article 148 TFEU contains parallel provisions dealing with employment policy, also requiring the Council on a recommendation from the Commission to draft employment guidelines, which must be consistent with the economic guidelines. In contrast to the economic guidelines, which are not subject to any temporal limit, the employment guidelines must be reissued and if necessary revised annually. In addition, as the UK Parliament's European Scrutiny Committee spotted, these broad guidelines were adopted in two forms: the economic guidelines are included in a Council Recommendation, whereas the employment guidelines (subordinate to the economic guidelines) are to be presented in the form of a Decision (a powerful regulatory tool).[44] The employment guidelines are nevertheless subject to a similar process of annual monitoring and surveillance by the Commission, which may lead to recommendations for reform covering a wide range of issues.

Both sets of guidelines are in effect a charter for the reorientation of economic policy aggressively in the direction of an open market rather than a social market economy. Whether it is neoliberal is contestable; but it is certainly not social democratic, the six broad economic policy guidelines addressing a range of issues, beginning in the first guideline with public finances and a 'focus on expenditure restraint' along with an emphasis on 'growth enhancing expenditure'.[45] At the same time, 'tax and benefit systems should provide better incentives to make work pay', while measures to 'improve the sustainability of public finances' should include 'reform of age-related public expenditure, such as pensions and health spending, and policies contributing to raising employment and effective retirement ages to ensure that age-related public expenditure and social welfare systems are financially sustainable'. Related to this, the second guideline deals with macroeconomic imbalances, requiring Member States with large deficits 'rooted in a persistent

[44] HC 428-i (2010–11) para 9.16.
[45] Council Recommendation (EU) 2015/1184 of 14 July 2015 on broad guidelines for the economic policies of the Member States and of the European Union [2015] OJ L192/27.

lack of competitiveness' to take steps to 'address the underlying causes' by acting, for example, 'on wage developments' and 'labour markets'.

The second guideline also requires adherence to the four employment guidelines (numbered 5 to 8).[46] These provide an even more stronger flavour of market liberalism, with guidelines 5–8 dealing with boosting the demand for labour, enhancing labour supply, skills and competences, and most ominously enhancing the functioning of labour markets respectively. For example, so far as the first (guideline 5) is concerned, Member States should 'reduce the barriers business faces in hiring people, promote entrepreneurship and, in particular, support the creation and growth of small enterprises'. They should also 'encourage wage-setting mechanisms allowing for a responsiveness of wages to productivity developments', while ensuring that minimum wage levels have regard to their impact on 'in-work poverty, job creation and competitiveness'. And so far as the last (guideline 8) is concerned 'Employment protection rules, labour law and institutions should all provide a suitable environment for recruitment, while offering *adequate* levels of protection to all those in employment and those seeking employment' (emphasis added).

For public lawyers, the extent to which this coordination of economic policies is a benign or malign process depends to a large extent on how it is conducted, raising a number of questions about legality and accountability. As initially conceived, the process requires Member States to submit annual reports on economic developments: there is no requirement of engaging the social partners or national parliaments.[47] The reports are then considered by Commission experts – principally economists it seems – who produce assessments which deal not only with a wide range of economic questions, but also the impact of social institutions on economic performance and the need to reform the former in the interests of the latter.[48] These experts' reports unmediated by anything other than a detailed economic analysis are then the subject of a Commission recommendation to the Council, which invariably seems to be adopted in the form of a Recommendation addressed to the Member State individually, which the latter is expected to be followed.[49]

For labour lawyers, the extent to which this coordination of economic policies is a benign or malign process depends to a large extent on the substance of the guidelines, on the development of which the social partners appear to have had little influence. Thus, BEPL guideline 2 provides that

> Member States should encourage *the right framework conditions for wage bargaining systems* and labour cost developments consistent with price stability, productivity trends and the need to reduce external imbalances. Wage developments should

---

[46] Council Decision (EU) 2015/1848 of 5 October 2015 on guidelines for the employment policies of the Member States for 2015 [2015] OJ L268/28.

[47] Art 121 TFEU.

[48] These national reports, along with the Commission and then the Council Recommendations are already easily accessible on the Commission website.

[49] See section V for an account of this procedure operating in relation to France.

take into account differences in skills and local labour market conditions and respond to large divergences in economic performance across regions within a country. [emphasis added]

The words in italic are perhaps innocuous enough until it is understood what is contemplated, namely the reorientation of collective bargaining to make it 'effective', but not in the sense that effectiveness would be understood in social democratic terms as density and penetration, but effectiveness in open market terms to mean collective bargaining flexibility and decentralisation.

V

The guidelines and their application have significant implications for labour law. Whereas the Community Charter of 1989 offered the promise of improvements in living and working conditions, and drew inspiration from ILO Conventions, now the commitment is to adequate levels of protection for workers and the overt commodification and objectification of labour, the constitutional commitment to human dignity having been quickly forgotten. Gone too it seems is the constitutional commitment to the social market, social progress and social justice, unless it is thought that these are goals that open markets can provide. As already suggested, we have no desire to enter the debate about whether the economic policies of which the foregoing are merely a part can be characterised as neoliberal. Indeed, it could plausibly be argued that what is at work here is a weak form of social liberalism: there is still clear blue water between both the USA and the EU in terms of labour standards.

It is clear, however, that the EU economic programmes require high levels of deregulation and liberalisation in equal measure, and the introduction of initiatives that would be consistent with a neoliberal turn. But while the programme does not demand the elimination of regulation nor deny the role of social partners, it does have important things to say about collective bargaining. In this context, Crouch has written that

> The neo-liberal thesis contends that economic success depends on a willingness of policy-makers to expose labour to market forces. This requires dismantling industrial relations institutions such as collective bargaining and the role of trade unions. If bargaining has to be accepted, it should be as close to the market as possible and therefore at the level of the individual enterprise; co-ordinated and multi-employer bargaining should in particular be avoided.[50]

Behind the opaque language, this is precisely what guideline 2 requires, reinforced by an equally opaque passage that 'wage setting frameworks, including minimum wages, should allow for wage formation processes that take into account differences in skills and local labour market conditions and respond to large divergences in economic performance across regions, sectors and companies within a country'.

[50] Crouch (n 5) 44.

It is well known now of course that despite the commitment in the Community Charter of 1989 referring to the 'the right to negotiate and conclude collective agreements under the conditions laid down by national legislation and practice',[51] the policy of the Commission and the Council since 2008 has been to intervene at national level and to direct Member States to decentralise collective bargaining arrangements to the level of the enterprise.[52] This has been done in a number of ways, most famously in the case of Greece by using financial leverage during the economic crisis to make a number of profound changes to the multilayered collective bargaining system by decentralising to as low a level as possible. This has involved the charade of building structures of worker representation that clearly contradicted the terms of the ILO Conventions to which the Community Charter of the Fundamental Social Rights of Workers purported to draw inspiration.[53] Although the best known, Greece was of course not the only Member State to fall prey to this kind of leverage.[54]

But Commission policy has also been implemented by using the procedures set out above, which provide a more formal constitutionally based procedure for intervention, albeit one the use of which is not free of difficulty. At the time of writing, nevertheless, the country most famously the subject of this latter procedure is France, a country with high levels of social protection and collective bargaining density. Here it was noted by a Commission Working Document that

> The wage bargaining process in France is characterised by the interaction of industry-wide agreements and company-level negotiations, with a relatively stronger role played by the industry-wide agreements and few possibilities to derogate by firm-level agreements. As already underlined in the 2014 In-Depth Review, such agreements apply to unionised and non-unionised workers and extension mechanisms are widespread. Recent reforms have created only limited flexibility for employers to depart from industry-wide agreements. Since 2004, a company-level agreement can deviate from the provisions of a sectoral agreement unless such derogations are explicitly forbidden in the sector-level agreement. However, the favourability principle remains in force in terms of minimum wages, job classifications, supplementary social protection and multi-company and cross-sector vocational training funds. In practice, reductions in overall wage costs were mainly obtained by departing from sectoral-level agreements in terms of working time.[55]

The foregoing quote gives some indication of the economists' concerns, while also indicating that Commission surveillance of France on this issue has been on-going for a number of years.

---

[51] Community Charter of the Fundamental Social Rights of Workers 1989, Art 12.

[52] See KD Ewing, 'The Death of Social Europe' (2015) 26 King's Law Journal 76.

[53] ILO Committee of Experts, Observations 2011–2013, published 101st–103rd International Labour Conference (2012–14) (ILO Convention 98).

[54] See Ewing (n 52) for a fuller discussion.

[55] European Commission, 'Country Report France 2015 Including an In-Depth Review on the prevention and correction of macroeconomic imbalances' COM(2015) 85 final.

In 2014, a Council Recommendation proposed that France take steps to reduce labour costs, as well as 'further action to combat labour-market rigidity, in particular take measures to reform the conditions of the 'accords de maintien de l'emploi' to increase their take up by companies facing difficulties', in light of observations that 'very few companies have made use of the arrangements for company-level agreements created by the law to increase the flexibility of work conditions in the event of temporary economic difficulties'.[56] By 2015 the concerns were being expressed with greater urgency that France was not deregulating quickly enough:

> Recent reforms have created only limited scope for employers to depart from branch-level agreements through company-level agreements. This limits companies' ability to modulate the workforce according to their needs. Sectors and companies are given flexibility to determine case by case and after negotiations with social partners at which conditions working time should depart from 35 hours a week, but there are important cost implications. The law creating the *accords de maintien de l'emploi* has not brought the expected results. Very few companies have made use of the new arrangements for company-level agreements to increase the flexibility of working conditions. This scheme should be reviewed to give companies more scope to adapt wages and working time to their economic situation.[57]

This led to a Council Recommendation in 2015 that France should 'facilitate take up of derogations at company and branch level from general legal provisions, in particular as regards working time arrangements', and 'reform the law creating the *accords de maintien de l'emploi* by the end of 2015 in order to increase their take-up by companies'.[58]

The matter was revisited in the following year (2016) when the Commission expressed concern that

> Recent reforms have created only limited flexibility for employers to depart from branch-wide agreements. This concerns all aspects of employment conditions, including wages, working time, employment and working conditions and limits the possibilities for companies to adjust the workforce according to their needs. At present, branches may prevent companies from determining, on a case by case basis and after negotiations with social partners, the conditions under which working time could depart from branch-wide agreements. The take-up of derogations from branch agreements and general legal provisions on employment conditions, via firm-level agreements, could be facilitated, in consultation with social partners.[59]

---

[56] Council Recommendation of 8 July 2014 on the National Reform Programme 2014 of France and delivering a Council opinion on the Stability Programme of France [2014] OJ C247/42.

[57] Council Recommendation of 14 July 2015 on the 2015 National Reform Programme of France and delivering a Council opinion on the 2015 Stability Programme of France [2015] OJ C272/51.

[58] ibid.

[59] Council Recommendation of 12 July 2016 on the 2016 National Reform Programme of France and delivering a Council opinion on the 2016 Stability Programme of France [2016] OJ C299/114.

These concerns were duly echoed by the Council.[60] By early 2017, however, Commission staff were able to report progress that 'derogations through firm-level agreements from branch-wide and general legal provisions are becoming more systematic', reporting also that 'substantial progress' had been made in 'reforming the labour law',[61] referring specifically to the substance and procedure of the law relating to unfair dismissal.[62]

The same Staff Working Paper provided more detail of these changes, summarising them as follows:

> The Labour Act of 8 August 2016 addresses some of the rigidities of the labour market. This law paves the way for a reform of the Labour Code aiming at clearer differentiation between rules to be defined by regulation, branch-level and firm-level agreement, with the express intent to extend the perimeter of autonomous firm-level rules and to clarify individual economic dismissal rules. The law also contains measures to increase the effectiveness of collective bargaining, mainly by reducing the number of branches, introducing the majority principle for the adoption of collective agreements, reforming the rules underpinning the denunciation and revision of collective agreements, and introducing 'offensive agreements' that firms can use to adjust wages and working time arrangements, while maintaining or increasing the level of employment. In particular, firms will be able to adopt a collective agreement that will prevail over individual contracts, even in terms of working time and pay.[63]

The changes described above duly met with the approval of the Commission and the Council in 2017, the latter in its Recommendation noting with satisfaction that the effect of these changes – which are set out in great detail in the French government's national plan submitted as part of the process – is to increase 'the effectiveness of collective bargaining'.[64]

As suggested incidentally by the foregoing, the exposure of 'labour to market forces' in Crouch's terms is not simply about the decentralisation of collective bargaining: it is also about regulatory legislation, including specifically that relating to job security and unfair dismissal. Here Commission pressure was directed at France's tough laws on economic dismissals and then those relating to workers engaged on open-ended contracts. Rather than being celebrated as it would be by labour lawyers, France was condemned by the Commission's economists as ranking

---

[60] ibid.

[61] Commission, 'Country Report France 2017 Including an In-Depth Review on the prevention and correction of macroeconomic imbalances' (Staff Working Document) COM(2017) 90 final.

[62] ibid 55.

[63] ibid 33.

[64] The annual National Plans are to be found on the European Commission's European Semester webpage. See 'The European Semester in your country' for all the relevant documents going back many years. It is an extraordinarily rich resource and a compelling read for labour lawyers who still harbour uncritically benign views of the contemporary EU.

'among the countries with the strictest legislation of dismissal for open-ended and temporary contracts'.[65] As a result, the Commission staff noted with approval that

> Recent reforms have started to tackle the rigidities in the dismissal procedure for open-ended contracts and reduce their complexity and uncertainty. Strict, complex, and unpredictable employment protection legislation has negative implication for the capacity of the economy to reallocate resources and to respond smoothly to shocks. Early resolution of labour disputes reduces the cost of dismissal, leaving judges the possibility of focusing on the most difficult cases.[66]

These 'reforms' were encouraged by the Council's Recommendation in 2016 which expressed concern that the French 'legal framework governing labour contracts, in particular as regards the legislation on dismissal for open-ended contracts, may contribute to the high segmentation of the labour market'.[67] In 2017, Commission staff were able to identify a number of 'selected highlights' designed to 'promote flexicurity in France', with a view to 'improving the functioning of the labour market':

> Labour law has been reformed in order to increase hiring on permanent contract, by reducing legal uncertainties in the case of individual dismissal . . . and by setting indicative floors and ceilings for financial compensation in case of unfair individual dismissal. Furthermore, the functioning of individual work litigation courts (prud'-hommes) has been reviewed to reduce the procedural length.[68]

VI

It is at this stage that we turn finally to the European Social Pillar, a term that begs the question Pillar of what? A close examination of the background papers reveals quite quickly that this is not a framework of autonomous social policy in the way that the Community Charter was some twenty-seven years earlier, but paradoxically a consolidation of the economic and employment policy developments undertaken since. The most revealing text in terms of the ambitions of its authors is the first published draft in March 2016, which it is true declares in the explanatory note that its starting point is 'the social objectives and rights inscribed in the EU primary law', said to consist of the TEU, the TFEU and the EU Charter.[69] Although all three are referred to throughout the text to underpin or justify each of the twenty principles of what was then the proposed Social Pillar, there is no reference to the Community

---

[65] Commission, 'Country Report France 2016 including an In-Depth Review on the prevention and correction of macroeconomic imbalances' SWD(2016) 79 final, 28.
[66] ibid.
[67] Council Recommendation of 12 July 2016 on the 2016 National Reform Programme of France (n 59).
[68] Commission, 'Country Report France 2017 (n 61), Box 4.3.1, 38.
[69] Commission, 'First Preliminary Outline of a European Pillar of Social Rights' (Communication) COM(2016) 127 Final.

Charter of 1989. Admittedly not EU primary law, though this is a convenient basis for inclusion and exclusion, it is also the case that the latter is a monument to a period of EU history that has passed.

So, while the Social Pillar references the social policy instruments and social rights, it is nevertheless the case that the Social Pillar is located in TFEU, Titles VIII and IX. This is clear from the explanatory note to the first published draft where it is explained that the 'choice and formulation of the principles draw inter alia on existing guidance in the European Semester of economic policy coordination, on EU secondary legislation and on "soft" law guidance where it exists'.[70] That is to say that the Social Pillar is the progeny of economic and employment policy not of an autonomous social policy, and that it is both designed to facilitate while being subordinate to economic and employment policy. Social ends may help to inform economic and employment policy, but social justice (in the form of high wages) is not the end of economic and employment policy, nor is social democracy (in the form of strong trade unions, collective bargaining and social dialogue) the means of its delivery.

The first draft's twenty principles make clear the inspiration it draws from the economic and employment guidelines, while the latest version of the guidelines (2017) have been adapted to reflect even more fully the provisions of the Social Pillar.[71] This is not to deny that the initiatives are either important or worthy, which we believe to be self-evident. That said, however, the principles are a symptom of the collapse of the social model, the changing economic direction of the EU, and the role of EU labour law in supporting labour markets rather than advancing social policy. Thus, the first six principles of the Social Pillar deal with access to the 'labour market' (an economists' oxymoron). The issues covered by these principles include skills, education and lifelong learning (principle 1), flexible and secure labour contracts (principle 2), secure professional transitions (meaning support for workers who move from job to job) (principle 3), active support to employment (principle 4), and gender equality and work–life balance (principle 5).

Principle 5 is perhaps surprising but also very revealing. At first sight, it might be argued that a recommitment to gender equality is an indication that the presentation here of social rights as a complement to economic and employment policies is exaggerated and misplaced. Gender equality is not an economic issue but a human rights issue, which cannot be commodified in the manner suggested. Yet if we read the Social Pillar documentation carefully, we find no acknowledgement of human rights as a reason to address what is referred to as the underrepresentation of women in the workforce; rather the case for supporting female labour participation is that it is not only 'fundamental for ensuring quality of opportunities', but an 'economic imperative in a context of an ageing workforce'. The same case is made in relation to principle 6,

---

[70]   ibid.

[71]   Commission, 'Proposal for a Council Decision on Guidelines for the Employment Policies of Member States' COM(2017) 677 final.

which deals generally with equal opportunities, addressing in particular the continuing problems of discrimination against third country nationals and ethnic minorities, about whom there are also 'labour market' exclusion concerns.

To the extent that four principles deal with 'fair working conditions', this owes more to Hobhouse than Keynes, and more to Blair than to Delors, addressing respectively conditions of employment (principle 7), wages (principle 8), health and safety (principle 9) and social dialogue (principle 10). But while again much of this is welcome, the welcome cannot be unqualified, with raw liberal economism clearly visible. So, while on principle 7, there are good proposals for (1) more transparency about employment conditions, and (2) probation periods of reasonable duration, there are bad proposals on (3) security of employment. Thus, earlier proposals relating to principle 2 to address precarious employment and to encourage the move towards more open-ended contracts (to which we return in more detail in section VII) are to come at a very high price, with concern being expressed that 'complex, costly and uncertain regulation governing the termination of open ended contracts makes firms reluctant to hire and also [leads] to uneven enforcement of the rules in place'.[72]

The answer then is to make it easier for employers to fire, as the economic and employment guidelines scream loudly, the proposal attached to principle 7 being deregulatory for some (just as the Temporary Agency Workers Directive proved to be in some countries – most notably Norway, by liberalising as well as protecting).[73] What is now proposed in relation to dismissal (though by what regulatory means is unspecified) is that the dismissal of a worker is to be 'motivated' (by which presumably this means motivated by cause), 'preceded by a reasonable period of notice', with 'an adequate compensation attached to it as well as access to rapid and effective appeal to an impartial dispute resolution system'.[74] Purporting ironically to be based on the EU Charter of Fundamental Rights, Article 30, this represents a significant regression for workers in some countries, and would reduce EU standards to the minimum standards of ILO Convention 182.

The same liberal economism is to be seen in the proposals relating to wages. The right to wages that will guarantee a decent standard of living for workers and their families is now qualified by reference to wages of an 'adequate level', any notion that there should be a decency threshold (as in the case of the Council of Europe's Social Charter) being visible by its absence. Instead, minimum wages are to be used as a disciplinary tool in two respects – to (1) 'make work pay for the unemployed and inactive', and (2) 'evolve in line with productivity developments', the latter being

---

72 Commission, 'First Preliminary Outline of a European Pillar of Social Rights' (n 69), principle 7.
73 See AC Bergene and KD Ewing, 'Vikarbyradirektivet liberalisering eller likebehandling'? (2015) 32 Sokelys Pa Arbeidslivet Argang 137.
74 Commission, 'First Preliminary Outline of a European Pillar of Social Rights' COM(2016) (n 69), principle 7.

'crucial for competitiveness'.[75] Minimum wages are thus not to be a means of enhancing the 'human dignity' of the citizen or promoting equality between citizens,[76] but a way of enticing people into work and making them work harder once recruited. Decent wages are to follow higher productivity, rather than higher productivity following higher wages, and workers are to continue to be denied their share of the wealth already created.

It is in this process that the authors of the first draft of the Social Pillar rather optimistically proclaim that wages are to evolve in line with productivity developments, 'in consultation with the social partners and in accordance with national practices'.[77] If the latter proposal is serious, it would suggest a degree of co-optation of trade unions that even the most pessimistic had not anticipated, in addition to their marginalisation which appears to be reinforced by draft Social Pillar principle 10. As we have written elsewhere, this announces that 'well-functioning social dialogue requires autonomous and representative social partners with the capacities to reach collective agreements', but admonishes the social partners for 'the decreases in terms of organisational density and representativeness'.[78] Although the social partners 'need to further build their capacities to engage in a better functioning and effective social dialogue', no support is provided for this purpose, though they were to be further co-opted by '[consultation] in the design and implementation of employment and social policies'.[79] This is, if you like, 'collective laissez-faire' European style, within which are contained the seeds of organised labour's own destruction.[80]

VII

The draft of the Social Pillar has been heavily amended following consultations and the involvement of other social actors, that is to say when economics met politics.[81] This has produced a number of positive outcomes, though it is hard to escape the core concerns. The principles have been renumbered; *social dialogue has been restored* to a more prominent position; the employment guidelines have been

---

[75]   ibid, principle 8.
[76]   TEU, Art 2.
[77]   Commission, 'First Preliminary Outline of a European Pillar of Social Rights' (n 69), principle 8.
[78]   ibid, principle 10. See further A Bogg and KD Ewing, 'The Continuing Evolution of European Labor Law and the Changing Context for Trade Union Organizing' (2017) 38 Comparative Labor Law & Policy Journal 211, 221 (with reference to the relevant Social Pillar Proposals).
[79]   Commission, 'First Preliminary Outline of a European Pillar of Social Rights (n 69), principle 10.
[80]   On the significance of Social Dialogue, see AL Bogg and R Dukes, 'The European Social Dialogue: From Autonomy to Here' in Countouris and Freedland (n 5).
[81]   Commission, 'The European Pillar of Social Rights in 20 Principles' ('Proclaimed', 17 November 2017). See https://ec.europa.eu/commission/priorities/deeper-and-fairer-economic-and-monetary-union/eur opean-pillar-social-rights/european-pillar-social-rights-20-principles_en accessed April 2018.

modified to take on board the social pillar; and a new directive has been proposed. But the underlying rationale remains the same, the strengthening (?) of social dialogue is to give the social partners a louder voice on employment policy,[82] while the amendment to the employment policy guidelines paradoxically serves only to reinforce the point that this is about TFEU Titles VIII and IX, rather than Title X. Social policy continues to be subordinate to economic and employment policy rather than equal or superior thereto. Society serves economics (or a particular ideological version thereof), not vice versa, though it was ever thus.

The proposed Directive seems to be intended to reconcile the irreconcilable, its purpose as set out in Article 1(1) being about 'improving working conditions by promoting more secure and predictable employment while ensuring labour market adaptability'. As such it deals with the employer's obligation to provide information about the employment relationship (Part II), but also with 'minimum requirements relating to the employment relationship' (Part III). The former is a rewrite of the Directive of 1991 on Proof of Employment Terms, one of the most notable changes being the requirement that the information be provided no later than the first day of the employment relationship.[83] The latter is new, extending the boundaries of the 1991 Directive from matters of transparency to matters of substance, the draft Directive addressing matters never before the subject of EU law.[84] Notably, however, although the progeny of employment policy, the legal base for the draft Directive is said to be TFEU, Article 153.[85]

One area where the tension between 'secure and predictable employment while ensuring labour market adaptability' arises most acutely is in relation to zero hours contracts. It is here that the draft Directive makes its most important contribution, albeit one that serves only to highlight its ineffectiveness and its failure to begin to address the scale of the problem. Thus, so far as the duty to provide information is concerned, the written statement issued by employers to workers must include information about working time as follows:

> if the work schedule is entirely or mostly variable, the principle that the work schedule is variable, the amount of guaranteed paid hours, the remuneration of work performed in addition to the guaranteed hours and, if the work schedule is entirely or mostly determined, by the employer:
>
> > (i) the reference hours and days within which the worker may be required to work; [and]

---

[82] Under Social Pillar principle 8 as 'proclaimed', 'Support for increased capacity of social partners to promote social dialogue shall be encouraged'. See further, p. 342 below.

[83] Council Directive 91/533/EEC of 14 October 1991 on an employer's obligation to inform employees of the conditions applicable to the contract or employment relationship [1991] OJ L288/32.

[84] Commission, 'Proposal for a Directive of the European Parliament and of the Council on transparent and predictable working conditions in the European Union' COM(2017) 797 final.

[85] According to the Preamble, specifically Art 153(1)(b) and (2)(b).

(ii) the minimum advance notice the worker shall receive before the start of a work assignment.

It is further provided that a worker may be required to work only within the predetermined reference period, and only if reasonable notice is given of any shift.[86]

The foregoing proposals reflect either naivety or bad faith, failing realistically to encourage a transition to open-ended contracts. The suggestion that there should be guaranteed hours, the implication that there should be enhanced payments for working beyond those hours, the prohibition of any requirement that a worker could be required to work outside prescribed hours (guaranteed or not), and the duty to provide reasonable notice of a shift are all good. But as drafted there is no requirement that there should be any guaranteed hours, or that there should be a premium for non-guaranteed hours. Nor will the right of workers to work only in the reference period prevent them being asked to accept shifts outside the reference period, while the right to reasonable notice will not stop workers accepting shifts at short notice. The first two problems can be addressed only by creating financial incentives for employers to offer fixed and regular hours rather than flexible hours; and the latter two by addressing the question of pay from which working time cannot be divorced.

But apart from anything else, these proposals endorse and give legitimacy to the use of zero hours contracts, without beginning to tackle abuses. What about the rights of workers whose shifts have been cancelled at short notice and who incur loss as a result?[87] Not only is the problem not addressed, there is no duty to provide information about what it is to happen in such cases. So far as the transition to open-ended contracts is concerned, the only substantive provision is the proposal that workers should be entitled to request the transition to a more 'predictable' and 'secure' employment arrangement after six months' engagement with the same employer. But this applies only where 'predictable' and 'secure' employment is available, and does not require employers to change their business model or employment practices. Moreover, the draft Directive only requires the employer to 'reply' to the request within a month: it does not require the request to be considered seriously, or to be refused only if there are objectively justifiable reasons for doing so.[88]

All this falls far short of the approach taken in the new employment guidelines reflecting the language of the early Social Pillar documents, which held out the promise that 'misuse or abuse of precarious and non-permanent relationships shall be prevented', and that 'the transition towards open-ended contracts shall be

---

[86] Commission, 'Proposal for a Directive of the European Parliament and of the Council on transparent and predictable working conditions in the European Union' (n 84) Art 3.

[87] Compare Workers (Definition and Rights) Bill (2017–19), cl 2, proposing a new Employment Rights Act 1996, s 27D. This is a private member's bill introduced by Chris Stephens MP.

[88] This is a proposal with much in common with the insipid offerings of the Taylor Review, below. Compare the corresponding right in British law relating to the right to request flexible working: Employment Rights Act 1996, pt 8A. See *British Airways plc v Starmer* [2005] IRLR 862.

ensured'.[89] Amended in 2017 to take on board the Social Pillar initiative, the amended guidelines refer to the need to 'foster the transition towards open-ended forms of employment', and 'employment relationships that lead to precarious working conditions should be prevented, including by prohibiting the abuse of atypical contracts' (guideline 7).[90] These laudable aims are not, however, likely to be advanced by a legal instrument that (1) requires employers to provide information that taunts workers about their vulnerability, (2) offers no protection to workers against their treatment as disposable commodities, and (3) imposes no duty on employers to transition workers into secure and predictable employment.[91]

It is a hoax all the more deplorable for the fact that it is even less imaginative than the corresponding proposals of the heavily criticised Taylor Review in the UK.[92] There is, however, one bright spot in the proposed Directive. Thus, in the early Social Pillar documentation, concern is expressed about 'grey zones such as dependent and bogus self-employment leading to unclear legal situations and barriers to access social protection'.[93] This led in turn to the promise that 'equal treatment shall be ensured, regardless of employment contract, unless different treatment is justified on objective grounds'.[94] Needless to say, the promise is not delivered in the draft Directive, which does nevertheless adopt a wide and inclusive definition of a worker for the purposes of the proposed instrument: 'a natural person who for a certain period of time performs services for and under the direction of another person in return for remuneration'.[95] Although lifted from CJEU jurisprudence,[96] the challenge now is to extend this definition to other instruments (such as working time).[97]

---

[89] Commission, 'First Preliminary Outline of a European Pillar of Social Rights' (n 69), principle 2.

[90] ibid.

[91] It is no doubt not intended that the Directive should operate in this way and that the criticism advanced here is the jaundiced views of lawyers based in England familiar with the destructive behaviour of employers' lawyers which shows little commitment to the principles lawyers are expected to uphold.

[92] M Taylor, 'Good Work: The Taylor Review of Modern Working Practices (2017) www.gov.uk/govern ment/uploads/system/uploads/attachment_data/file/627671/good-work-taylor-review-modern-working -practices-rg.pdf accessed April 2018. For a critique, see K Bales, A Bogg and T Novitz, '"Voice" and "Choice" in Modern Working Practices: Problems with the Taylor Review' (2018) 47 Industrial Law Journal 46.

[93] Commission, 'First Preliminary Outline of a European Pillar of Social Rights' (n 69), principle 3.

[94] ibid.

[95] Commission, 'Proposal for a Directive of the European Parliament and of the Council on transparent and predictable working conditions in the European Union' (n 85) Art 2(1)(a).

[96] N Countouris, 'The Concept of "Worker" in European Labour Law: Fragmentation, Autonomy and Scope' (2018) 47 Industrial Law Journal 192.

[97] But the ambition to be inclusive and to revise definitions contrasts with the Taylor approach which has been to make more functional the existing dysfunctional definitions by greater transparency. The solution seems to have convinced no one, the author of the proposal conceding that it was unlikely to change the position of more than a small number of workers. See Taylor Review (n 92) 36. See generally, Bales, Bogg and Novitz (n 92).

With the social pillar already crumbling, the only consolation is that the existing social policy directives are not to be revoked, the Commission's deregulatory push at national level unmatched so far by any deregulation at EU level. This may tell us something about the limited nature of much of EU labour law and its peripheral concerns (no pay regulation or freedom of association instruments),[98] but may also reinforce the point that the project is social liberal rather than neoliberal in approach, though whether there is any virtue in dancing on the head of such pins is debatable. The fact is that while the development of EU social law has halted at the current time, EU initiatives at national level are eroding the social democratic base on which it would stand, a bleak regulatory/deregulatory impulse leavened only by the modest fruits of the social pillar. The latter is designed simply to ameliorate the worst symptoms of economic liberalism, in a manner that fails to satisfy the constitutional base on which the European Union purports to stand and the constitutional values it was established to advance.[99]

VIII

We have tracked the shift from the Community Charter of the Fundamental Social Rights of Workers to the European Social Pillar, a shift from what might be seen as a weak social democratic form to what is at best a weak social liberal form over a period of thirty years, and in the process the subordination of social rights to economic and employment policy. But for all, the British experience suggests that this is a journey which has some way to go. Recent legal and political developments in the UK reveal troubling and disturbing tendencies towards an even more authoritarian style of statecraft and governance that repudiates the liberal values that remain visible in the EU social liberal model. Taking this as our relevant contemporary political baseline, rather than the stronger traditions of social democratic constitutionalism in many European countries, the weak social liberalism of the European Pillar could operate as a progressive break on some of the worst excesses of populist authoritarianism. Whatever the problems in the EU, the position is much worse in the UK.[100]

There have been four main dimensions to this new authoritarian labour law in the British context: (1) a repressive approach to trade union regulation, reflected in an

[98] Both are addressed in the European Pillar of Social Rights, but only in aspirational terms.

[99] See also for a critical perspective on the Social Pillar, K Lörcher and I Schömann, *The European Pillar of Social Rights: Critical Legal Analysis and Proposals* (ETUI Report 139, 2016). We are grateful to Professor Novitz for bring this valuable report to our attention.

[100] We should also remember nevertheless that some social democratic movements in European countries are in disarray and in retreat (J Henley, 'From Spain to Germany and Italy, the Outflanked Centre-Left Cannot Hold' *The Guardian* (25 February 2018) www.theguardian.com /world/2018/feb/25/germany-spain-italy-elections-centre-left-cannot-hold accessed April 2018).

increasing reliance on direct criminal sanctions to promote 'social order' in industrial disputes and the coercive curtailment of the political voice of trade unions in
the democratic process; (2) the ratcheting criminalisation of 'irregular' migrant
workers and their employers, and the use of the criminal law to police the employment of migrants, in the Immigration Act 2016; (3) a reassertion of indigenous ethical
practices and 'British' human rights, rejecting the legitimacy of international and
European human rights law, and international courts such as the European Court of
Human Rights and the CJEU; and (4) attacks on the rule of law, including access to
courts, by imposing prohibitive fees on workers seeking to vindicate their statutory
employment rights. Taken together, these elements involve a strong reassertion of
the sovereign nation-state as the locus of civic allegiance.[101]

So, while we are dismayed by the gradual exclusion of trade unions within the
European legal order (both at EU and Member State level), the authoritarian
curtailment of intermediate associations such as trade unions in the UK is a yet
more profound development. Purporting to be taken in the interests of social unity
and public order, this is a move that has much wider implications as a way – along
with a number of other initiatives – of stifling pluralism and dissent in civil society.[102]
In this respect, the principles set out in the Social Pillar provide a progressive
counterpoint (which may be no more than a temporary respite) to the grim retreat
from liberalism witnessed in the UK, led by the hard Brexiteers of the Conservative
Government. That said, it took some political pressure to persuade the Commission
to include in the final version of the Social Pillar a provision to the effect that the
social partners are to be 'encouraged to negotiate and conclude collective agreements in matters relevant to them, while respecting their autonomy and the right of
collective action' (emphasis added). Although this provision was not in the original
draft referred to above, it can nevertheless be contrasted with the repressive measures
on strike action in the Trade Union Act 2016.

Particularly notable in relation to the Trade Union Act 2016 is the imposition of new
and stringent ballot thresholds in relation to 'important public services'. Thus, where 'the
majority of those who were entitled to vote in the ballot are at the relevant time normally
engaged in the provision of important public services', there is now a requirement that 'at
least 40 per cent of those who were entitled to vote in the ballot' supported the industrial
action.[103] Needless to say, the list of what counts as an important public service for these
purposes is determined not by objective legal standards but by considerations of electoral
expediency and the political needs of government. Coincidentally the final text of the

---

[101]   See Bogg (n 13).
[102]   Authoritarianism in the political sphere and in the workplace have always walked hand in hand. See
        Otto Kahn Freund's juxtaposition of democratic principles in the political and the workplace sphere
        in O Kahn-Freund, 'The Social Ideal of the Reich Labour Court – A Critical Examination of the
        Practice of the Reich Labour Court' (1931) in O Kahn-Freund, R Lewis and J Clark (eds), *Labour Law
        and Politics in the Weimar Republic* (Social Science Research Council 1981) ch 3.
[103]   See R Dukes and N Kountouris, 'Pre-strike Ballots, Picketing and Protest: Banning Industrial Action
        by the Back Door?' (2016) 45 Industrial Law Journal 337.

Social Pillar provides for a right of access to 'essential services', notable for the fact that the reference is to 'essential' rather than 'important' services, a concept with substantive content in international labour law. It is likewise significant that the 'right to collective action' is given specific recognition in the final text of the Social Pillar, enabling this to be taken into account in assessing the extent of the right to essential services.

The marginalisation of trade unions is for many reasons the most important symptom of the UK's slide into an authoritarian labour law, not least because of its implications for democratic structures and procedures generally. But as we suggest, this is not the only symptom. We consider the empowerment of employers in other ways also significant. Particularly important is the use of the criminal law to police the employment sphere, reinforcing the framing of a public discourse based on the preference for 'British workers'. The ideological underpinnings of these powers are perhaps best reflected in their irrationality, with Brexit exposing a hard reality that these 'British workers' may not exist, a reality that had already been exposed at the time of the fatuous and dangerous rhetoric of a former Labour prime minister who demanded 'British jobs for British workers'.[104] Where these British workers do exist, the workers in question may be unavailable for reasons of choice or incapacity, in a nation that has for various reasons effectively exported to other countries many of the labour supply needs of the domestic economy.[105]

Perhaps of greater practical significance has been the virtually complete disempowerment of workers by the removal of statutory protections at a time when trade unions were simultaneously under attack. Thus, the political attack on access to justice for workers through tribunal fees meant that rights were effectively unenforceable for most workers, reinforcing the disciplinary authority of the employer over an increasingly precarious workforce. In relation to dismissal protection, the Social Pillar provides for 'the right to access to effective and impartial dispute resolution', reflecting a strong rights-based commitment to access to justice in European law. This proved to be important in the vindication of the rule of law in respect of tribunal fees in *R (on the application of UNISON) v. Lord Chancellor* (*UNISON*).[106] While the principal basis of this judgment was the common law protection of access to a court, it should also be recognised that the UKSC concluded that the Fees Order breached the principle of effective judicial protection under EU law.

---

[104] C Barnard, '"British Jobs for British Workers": The Lindsey Oil Refinery Dispute and the Future of Local Labour Clauses in an Integrated EU Market' (2009) 38 Industrial Law Journal 245.

[105] See KD Ewing, 'Implications of Post-Brexit Architecture for Labour Law' (2017) 28 King's Law Journal 403.

[106] *R (UNISON) v Lord Chancellor* [2017] UKSC 51, [2017] 3 WLR 409. See M Elliott, 'UNISON in the Supreme Court: Tribunal Fees, Constitutional Rights and the Rule of Law' (*Public Law for Everyone*, 27 July 2017) https://publiclawforeveryone.com/2017/07/26/unison-in-the-supreme-court-employment-fees-constitutional-rights-and-the-rule-of-law accessed April 2018; M Ford QC, 'It's the Common Law Wot Won It' (Institute of Employment Rights, 31 July 2017) www.ier.org.uk/blog/its-common-law-wot-won-it accessed April 2018; M Ford QC, 'Employment Tribunals and the Rule of Law: *R (UNISON) v Lord Chancellor* in the Supreme Court' (2018) 47 Industrial Law Journal 1.

So, while the Social Pillar reflects a political direction of travel that is now unmistakable, and while the imperfections of the Social Pillar cannot be exaggerated, it nevertheless sits apart from the corresponding developments in the UK which pessimistically may yet be an indication of broader continental and global trends. For the moment, it stands, symbolically at least, as a rights-based normative alternative to the anti-liberal impulses of the Trade Union Act 2016 and the political attack on workers' access to justice,[107] albeit one that reflects a disturbing repointing of EU social, economic and political policies. The political commitment to non-regression of workers' rights after Brexit has already been exposed as a charade, with secret political plots to repeal the Working Time Directive stoutly and loudly but unconvincingly denied by the hard Brexiteers.[108] More remarkably, the recent and 'independent' Taylor Review of Modern Working Practices proposed to reintroduce 'rolled up' holiday pay,[109] an abusive practice that had been declared unlawful by the CJEU in *Robinson-Steele*.[110]

Whether the deregulatory features of the Social Pillar represent the protean germ of full-blown authoritarianism is an open question at the current time. Perhaps the 'free market' has always depended ultimately on a strongly coercive state that maintains the rules of the game, utilising penal methods to keep the growing legions of the poor and precarious in check. On this pessimistic view, the 'Social Pillar' is simply another deregulatory step in the journey away from liberal freedoms and social justice. From a European perspective, however, the UK experience should also give some pause to the political architects of the Social Pillar. The Brexit vote is a stark reminder that we may have all failed to appreciate the fragility of liberal institutions, and their vulnerability to the dark undertone of populist discontent in times of economic crisis and uncertainty. The protection of fundamental social rights of workers, such as those listed in the 'Solidarity' chapter of the EU Charter provide the constitutional basis for a social market economy. The social market economy and liberal freedoms depend upon social consent. In turn, social consent depends upon social and economic arrangements that are fair and equitable for all. Economic precariousness corrodes political citizenship, and it subverts democratic institutions.

---

[107] On anti-liberalism in certain strands of Conservative political thought, see D Dyzenhaus (ed), *Law as Politics: Carl Schmitt's Critique of Liberalism* (Duke UP 1998).

[108] J Moore, 'Burnout Britain Looms as Gove and Allies Plan to Axe Working Time Directive' *The Independent* (18 December 2017) www.independent.co.uk/news/business/comment/burnout-britain-looms-as-gove-and-allies-plan-to-axe-working-time-directive-a8116381.html accessed April 2018.

[109] See Taylor Review (n 92), and for a critique, see Bales, Bogg and Novitz (n 92).

[110] Case C-131/04 *Robinson-Steele v Retail Services* EU:C:2006:177. That the proposal constituted a serious departure from social rights jurisprudence of the CJEU didn't even warrant a footnote in the Review document.

As political events in Poland, Hungary, Spain, the US and the UK demonstrate, liberal toleration and civic respect cannot simply be taken as a given in a globalised world. In that respect, we recall the words in the Preamble to the ILO Constitution as the ILO celebrates its centenary, that 'Whereas universal and lasting peace can be established only if it is based upon social justice'. This must be something more than an elegiac epitaph for the social democratic constitution, if the European project is to have any kind of future, with or without the UK.

14

How to Analyse a Supranational Regime That Nationalises Social Conflict?

The European Crisis, Labour Politics and Methodological Nationalism

Roland Erne

I INTRODUCTION

After the adoption of the so-called Six-Pack of EU laws on economic governance in 2011, European Union (EU) interventions retrenched social welfare and collective labour rights in almost all EU Member States.[1] This chapter therefore aims to contribute to a better understanding of the EU's economic governance regime and the conceptual, methodological and political questions that it is raising.

Analytical concepts should always be 'elaborated in close connection with some set of substantive problems'.[2] The substantive problem that we address in our ongoing five-year-long research programme (www.erc-europeanunions.eu) is the following: what are the points of intervention or 'levers'[3] by which the EU's new economic governance (NEG) system may be changed by social actors?

In order to be able to answer this question, we use a conceptual framework that is able to distinguish between horizontal and vertical modes of European integration. We distinguish them based on *the different modes of constraints that are in operation*. We refer to horizontal integration if European labour movements are constrained by *transnational* (economic) market pressures. By contrast, we refer to vertical

I would like to thank Andreas Bieler, Colin Crouch, Bianca Föhrer, Darragh Golden, Jamie Jordan, Imre Szabó, Sabina Stan and Fotis Vergis for their comments on earlier drafts. I have also used sections of my ERC project application www.erc-europeanunions.eu: R Erne, 'Labour Politics and the EU's New Economic Governance Regime (European Unions): A New European Research Council Project' (2018) 24 Transfer: European Review of Labour and Research 237. This work was supported by the EU's Jean Monnet Chair programme [grant agreement 2016–2019] and the European Research Council grant 'Labour Politics and the EU's New Economic Governance Regime (European Unions)' [grant agreement 725240].
1   R Erne, 'A Supranational Regime That Nationalizes Social Conflict: Explaining European Trade Unions' Difficulties in Politicizing European Economic Governance' (2015) 56 Labor History 345; C de la Porte and D Natali, 'Altered Europeanisation of Pension Reform in the Context of the Great Recession' (2014) 37 West European Politics 732.
2   CB Mills, *The Sociological Imagination* (first published in 1959, OUP 2000) 125.
3   ibid 131.

European integration when they are constrained by interventions from a *supranational* political, legal and corporate authority. This distinction is pivotal because the two modes of European integration offer different crystallisation points for collective action. Horizontal integration is not questioning the formal autonomy of local or national unions and industrial relations systems, even if the Europeanisation of the economy is effectively constraining unions' choices. By contrast, vertical integration does question unions' and industrial relations systems' formal autonomy. Vertical constraints are thus more likely to trigger collective action than horizontal constraints; not only because they are more tangible and therefore easier to politicise but also because they are formally undermining social actors' and local and national institutions' autonomy.

We propose to operationalise 'modes of constraints' in relation to (1) the medium through which these constraints are communicated (market signals vs detailed prescriptions issued by a particular authority) and (2) the sanctioning mechanisms in case of non-compliance (the threat of a loss of market shares vs the threat of sanctions in case of non-compliance by a particular authority).

II HORIZONTAL INTEGRATION: CONSTRAINING BUT HARDLY TRIGGERING COLLECTIVE ACTION

Until recently, European unions have primarily been constrained by the horizontal integration triggered by the free movement of goods, capital, services and people. The subsequent increased competitive pressures effectively constrained union action. Since the 1990s, European workers have failed to get real wage increases that match productivity growth almost everywhere.[4] And yet, there had been surprisingly little change in formal institutional settings governing industrial relations systems.

Like the pre-crisis EU governance system, the EU industrial relations framework could not be 'defined in hierarchical terms with an EU layer added on top of national systems'.[5] Accordingly, Marginson and Sisson described the pre-crisis European industrial relations system as a multilevel governance regime that mixed cross-national (horizontal) influences with national (vertical) ones.[6]

Horizontal market integration did not lead to a collapse of multi-employer wage-bargaining or co-determination structures that are enforced vertically by legal enactment at the national level. However, European Economic and Monetary Union (EMU) did not lead to a transnational coordination of European unions' wage-bargaining policies either, despite the competitive pressures it triggered. Whereas the European Trade Union Confederation (ETUC) and sectoral

---

[4] R Erne, *European Unions: Labor's Quest for a Transnational Democracy* (Cornell UP 2008).
[5] P Marginson and K Sisson, *European Integration and Industrial Relations* (Palgrave Macmillan 2004) 25.
[6] ibid 289.

European trade union federations tried to stop the decline of wage shares as a proportion of GDP through joint wage coordination benchmarks, many of their affiliates got involved in arrangements that aimed at increasing national competitiveness to the detriment of their colleagues abroad. Increased transnational competition has led to transnational union action only in a small number of cases. As I have argued in *European Unions*:[7]

> Economic Europeanization and globalization do not explain transnational union cooperation. Markets create societies without facilitating association among workers. Or, as Karl Marx observed, the mutual 'relations of the producers, within which the social character of their labor affirms itself, take the form of a social relation between the products'.[8]

By contrast, the most successful cases of transnational collective action by European trade unions were triggered by decisions of supranational authorities, namely merger plans of multinational firms, the corresponding merger policy decisions of the Commission as well as Commissioner Bolkestein's draft Service Directive.[9]

III VERTICAL INTEGRATION: CONSTRAINING BUT ALSO TRIGGERING COLLECTIVE ACTION?

Since the adoption of the Six-Pack in 2011, the salience of vertical hierarchical integration has increased dramatically. Labour movements are increasingly constrained by EU interventions that put Member States' economic, fiscal, social and industrial relations policies under direct EU surveillance. The resulting EU's new economic governance (NEG) regime opens contradictory possibilities for labour politics in Europe.

On the one hand, NEG's reliance on vertical surveillance makes decisions taken in its name more tangible, thereby offering concrete targets for contentious collective action.[10] On the other hand, NEG mimics the governance structures of multinational firms.[11] By using performance indicators that put countries in competition with one another, it implicitly constitutes a deterrent to transnational collective action. Moreover, the interventionist strains associated with the NEG regime increase the threat of nationalist counter-movements. Whereas NEG has increased the salience of vertical integration, NEG's supranational governance regime also favours its politicisation along national rather than transnational class lines;[12] partly

---

7   Erne (n 4) 189.
8   ibid 189.
9   ibid 186–202.
10   ibid; T Kay, 'New Challenges, New Alliances: Union Politicization in a Post-NAFTA Era' (2015) 56 Labor History 246.
11   Erne (n 1).
12   ibid.

because pro-European neoliberals like to portray their critics as nationalists;[13] partly because visibility of the political NEG interventions may let people believe that renationalisation would solve unions' and workers' social and economic problems. In some cases, however, European unions did succeed in politicising NEG interventions across borders, namely in the case of the right2water campaign.[14]

IV TOWARDS A RESTRUCTURING OF THE EUROPEAN POLITICAL SPACE ALONG NATIONAL DIVIDES?

Leading scholars argue that the European political space is currently about to be restructured along a new divide, namely between a liberal–cosmopolitan and an illiberal–nationalist pole.[15] If this was true, the prospects for European democracy would be very bleak. A transnational democracy requires cross-cutting social cleavages that can unite national populations across borders (e.g. along transnational class lines). The prospects of a transnational European democracy are the weaker the more the critique of NEG is framed in nationalist institutionalist rather than transnational class-oriented terms.

Labour movements are integral to European politics and society. Labour mobilisations that followed the transnational Industrial Revolution homogenised political attitudes and behaviour within and across countries.[16] Furthermore, the mid-twentieth-century class compromises, on which Europe's social models were built, would not have been conceivable without the mobilisations of European workers and unions in workplaces and in national political arenas. A similar analogy can be made in a transnational context.[17] However, labour movements' capacity to (1) structure the (transnational) political space along class cleavages, (2) play a key role in public (and private) interest intermediation, and (3) enforce class compromises in industrial relations and social policy has been seriously challenged.

These three dimensions of labour politics are currently threatened by the new 'silent revolution'[18] in European economic governance. NEG's recommendations to commodify wage bargaining and public services are backing labour movements into a corner. We therefore aim to explore the tensions, challenges and possibilities that the interventionist turn in EU's NEG poses to labour politics in Europe. In the

[13] E Béthoux, R Erne and D Golden, 'A Primordial Attachment to the Nation? French and Irish Workers and Trade Unions in Past EU Referendum Debates' (2018) 56 British Journal of Industrial Relations 656.

[14] A Bieler, 'Fighting for Public Water' (2017) 9 Interface 300.

[15] T Börzel, 'From EU Governance of Crisis to Crisis of EU Governance' (2016) 54 Journal of Common Market Studies 8; H Kriesi and others, *West European Politics in the Age of Globalization* (CUP 2008).

[16] D Caramani, *The Europeanization of Politics* (CUP 2015); S Bartolini, *The Political Mobilization of The European Left* (CUP 2000).

[17] Erne (n 4).

[18] Barroso cited in ANSA, 'Barroso, Stiamo Facendo Rivoluzione Silenziosa' *Agenzia Nazionale Stampa Associata* (News Wire, Fiesole (Florence), 18 June 2010) www.controlacrisi.org/notizia/economia/2010/6/18/4925-barroso-ammette-il-colpo-di-stato-monetario-europeo;-stiamo accessed 23 March 2018.

context of increased social tensions arising from NEG,[19] our research programme aims to answer the following research questions: is NEG restructuring the European political space along national or class divisions? Are unions and new social movements politicising NEG along national cross-class or transnational class lines?

These are urgent questions in times when even proponents of neo-functionalist European integration theory envisage the following scenario: 'first, the collapse of the euro; then of the EU, and, finally, of democracy in its member states'.[20] However, posing such questions also calls for a broader analytical perspective, bringing interest politics and class conflict back into EU and social movement studies.[21]

Even before the Eurocrisis and the ensuing silent revolution in European governance, it has been argued that the formation of a new European political centre with strong regulatory and judicial capacities is potentially problematic.[22] This is because of the deficient 'system building' in the field of transnational social integration and democratic participation rights.[23] Yet, it is conceivable that transnational social integration and democratic participation will emerge after the creation of political authority at the EU level. Whether one is conceptualising *the political* in deliberative Habermasian terms or in power-struggle-oriented Weberian or Marxian terms, one has to acknowledge that political authority over a given population did not include democratic and social rights from the outset. In fact, the formation of political authority has usually been a product of 'coercion and capital'.[24] Democratic and social rights followed afterwards, as a result of social and political learning processes or struggles by 'countervailing powers'[25] in response to social tensions created by the making of integrated markets and political authority.[26]

The formation of much more robust EU governance institutions can paradoxically also favour the creation of a transnational democracy. Democracy requires not only a people (*demos*) but also an institutional manifestation of political power (*kratos*).[27] As democracy is dependent on political authority to enforce the results of democratic consultations, there is a dialectical relationship between popular mobilisations and the creation of political authority. Furthermore, democratisation usually occurred following struggles that politicised class conflict around tangible

---

[19]   VA Schmidt, *The Eurozone's Crisis of Democratic Legitimacy: Can the EU Rebuild Public Trust and Support for European Integration?* (Discussion Paper 15, Publications Office of the European Union 2015); W Streeck, 'Why the Euro Divides Europe' (2015) 95 New Left Review 5.

[20]   PC Schmitter, 'European Disintegration?' (2012) 23 Journal of Democracy 39.

[21]   D Della Porta, *Social Movements in Times of Austerity* (Polity 2015).

[22]   M Zürn and J Neyer, 'Conclusions' in M Zürn and C Joerges (eds), *Law and Governance in Postnational Europe* (CUP 2005).

[23]   S Bartolini, *Restructuring Europe* (OUP 2005).

[24]   C Tilly, *Coercion, Capital, and European States*, AD 900–1990 (Blackwell 2000).

[25]   JK Galbraith, *American Capitalism* (Transaction 1952).

[26]   TH Marshall, *Citizenship and Social Class* (first published in 1950, Pluto 1992); J Habermas, *Between Facts and Norms* (MIT Press 1996) 506; Erne (n 4).

[27]   Erne (n 4) 18.

social demands. Few of the participants were trying to create democratic institutions.[28] We will therefore explore whether established unions or new social movements, which have been triggered by NEG across Europe,[29] are capable of (a) politicising NEG, which means transforming technocratic NEG into a matter of political choice and (b) building transnational social integration and democratic participation rights through transnational collective action. After all, transnational democracy is not solely a result of innovative theorising, even if ideas play an important role in democratisation processes.[30]

Politicisation processes and the restructuring of the socio-economic and political space can be observed at three levels, namely individual (micro), organisational (meso) and systemic (macro). Most studies in the field have favoured analyses located at the micro or the macro levels.[31] It is quite easy to analyse data sets about changing voter attitudes at the micro level or to measure the salience of EU-related political issues in media debates at the macro level.[32] Yet, the emergence of new political and economic polarisations, as measured by the rise of new electoral cleavages or media discourses alone, cannot explain the restructuring of the European political space. The formation of new social cleavages also depends on the emergence of corresponding 'organisational networks';[33] hence, our focus on interest politics.

V BROADENING ANALYTICAL FRAMEWORKS

For 'several decades now the study of labour issues has been a specialist field, rather cut off from the rest' of sociology, politics and economics.[34] In the anglophone world, this discipline used to be called industrial relations. Given the relative decline of unions and industrial employment, many colleges have replaced it with human resource management. This has led to a narrowing of the field to 'a management perspective on how to get the most effective work out of employees'.[35] A similar tendency to economise labour policy can also be observed in the 'Law of the Labour Market',[36] as criticised inter alia by Ruth Dukes.[37]

---

[28] C Tilly, *Contention and Democracy in Europe, 1768–2004* (CUP 2004).

[29] A Bieler and others (eds), *Labour and Transnational Action in Times of Crisis* (Rowman & Littlefield International 2015); S Stan, I Helle and R Erne, 'European Collective Action in Times of Crisis' (2015) 21 Transfer: European Review of Labour and Research 131; M Vogiatzoglou, 'Workers' Transnational Networks in Times of Austerity in Italy and Greece' (2015) 21 Transfer: European Review of Labour and Research 5.

[30] Erne (n 4) 18.

[31] M Zürn, 'Opening up Europe: Next Steps in Politicisation Research' (2016) 39 West European Politics 164.

[32] ibid.

[33] Bartolini (n 16) 26.

[34] C Crouch, *Governing Social Risks in Post-Crisis Europe* (Edward Elgar 2015) 2.

[35] ibid 4.

[36] S Deakin and F Wilkinson, *The Law of the Labour Market: Industrialization, Employment, and Legal Evolution* (OUP 2005).

[37] R Dukes, *The Labour Constitution: The Enduring Idea of Labour Law* (OUP 2014).

In continental Europe, *la question sociale* was mainly a domain of social policy. When the incorporation of workers into welfare states apparently solved the social question, the discipline's big questions were increasingly replaced by technical issues, which required 'increased specialisation among academics, policy makers and practitioners'.[38] And yet, NEG may be bringing industrial relations and social policy together once more. These disciplines not only offer complementary vantage points but are also directly affected by these ongoing changes. The latter might bring them back to the big questions about capitalism, social equality and democracy that originally led to the creation of the social sciences at times of great political and social upheaval.

The more policymaking is depoliticised, the more sociology and political science are challenged by economics and management. Industrial relations and social policy are challenged even more directly by NEG. It is hardly a coincidence that the Commission's Industrial Relations Report 2014, which covered the period 2012–14, was the last of its kind.[39] And yet, the closer alignment of industrial relations to business studies also has paradoxical advantages. It enabled industrial relations scholars to capture the 'new' governance through 'coercive comparisons'[40] long before scholars in other disciplines theorised the EU's new 'governance by numbers'.[41] Industrial relations scholarship also suggests that the governance by coercive comparisons, as envisaged in the EU's NEG regime, will hardly lead to the end of social contestation. There are several examples where multinational firms have attempted to benefit from regime competition by involving workers and their representatives in 'whipsawing' games.[42] But workers in different production locations do not have to engage in the socially destructive games that management wants them to play. Instead, labour across countries can turn threats of social dumping into opportunities for transnational solidarity. In other words, workers can use the wedges that employers insert to divide them to build bridges and unite them. Competition can thus be seen as both a limiting and a triggering factor for cross-border action: 'competition can frustrate cooperation, but it also motivates it'.[43] Hence, cross-national collaboration can arise both despite and because of competition.

Before reviewing the literature on EU governance and transnational collective action, I will discuss the scholarly literature on the (re)structuring of the European political space and the politicisation of the EU integration process. Whereas the former is primarily a debate about the EU *level of governance*, the latter debate can

---

[38]   ibid 4.

[39]   Commission, *Industrial Relations in Europe 2014* (Publications Office of the European Union 2015).

[40]   A Ross, *Trade Union Wage Policy* (University of California Press 1948) cited in Marginson and Sisson (n 5) 11.

[41]   A Supiot, *La Gouvernance Par Les Nombres* (Fayard 2015).

[42]   I Greer and M Hauptmeier, 'Political Entrepreneurs and Co-managers' (2008) 46 British Journal of Industrial Relations 77.

[43]   M Anner and others, 'The Industrial Determinants of Transnational Solidarity' (2006) 12 European Journal of Industrial Relations 24.

be conceptualised as a debate about the democratic or technocratic *mode of governance*.[44] The following sections review the state of the literature in these fields separately. Subsequently, a concluding section will bring these two strands together once again, discussing the likely impact of NEG for democratic interest intermediation, social policy and (transnational) collective action.

VI RESTRUCTURING THE EUROPEAN POLITICAL SPACE

The labour movements triggered by the Industrial Revolution led to the formation of European party systems along class cleavages within and across countries.[45] But if one narrows the temporal focus of the analysis to the last two decades, then a new cleavage appears: namely, the cleavage between 'winners' and 'losers' of denationalisation.[46] This cleavage has also been discussed in terms of a conflict between cosmopolitan Europe-builders and illiberal nationalists.[47]

European labour parties and unions are indeed facing an increasingly Eurosceptic working class.[48] Compared to voters from higher classes, French and Dutch working-class voters rejected the EU Constitution in much higher proportions. The ETUC and almost all national union confederations endorsed it, but union leaders were arguably 'out of step' with their membership.[49] In turn, Hooghe and Marks explained the higher proportion of workers among the No-votes in Dutch and French EU referendums in terms of workers' alleged primordial attachment to 'pre-material values',[50] which is an explanation of labour Euroscepticism that has been challenged by our recent inductive content analysis of the French and Irish EU referendum debates.[51] It is worth noting that the framing of EU integration debates as a conflict between supposed enlightened elites and ethnocentric commoners may have been influenced by the cosmopolitan habitus of international journalists and scholars. The facility with which both cosmopolitans and nationalists frame contemporary cleavages as a conflict between globalising elites and 'more terrestrial ordinary nationals'[52] is striking for at least two reasons. First, the working class was the last social group to be nationalised,[53] which challenges explanations based on workers' primordial attachment to national values. Second, and more importantly, the reframing of socio-economic conflicts in nationalistic terms by elites has been an

---

[44] Erne (n 4).
[45] Caramani (n 16).
[46] Kriesi (n 15).
[47] Börzel (n 15).
[48] D Golden, 'Challenging the Pro-European Consensus' (PhD thesis, University College Dublin 2015); Béthoux (n 13).
[49] R Hyman, 'Trade Unions and Europe' (2010) 65 Relations Industrielles/Industrial Relations 3.
[50] L Hooghe and G Marks, 'Europe's Blues' (2006) 39 Political Science and Politics 247.
[51] Béthoux (n 13).
[52] J Friedman, 'Champagne Liberals and "Classes Dangereuses"' (2004) 96–97 Journal des Anthropologues 151.
[53] E Hobsbawm, *Nations and Nationalism Since 1870* (CUP 1992).

important feature of labour politics since its inception.[54] Consequently, any analysis of the restructuring of the European political space cannot rely simply on quantitative data on individual voter attitudes. Equally important are organisational mobilisations and the political structures of opportunities in which these mobilisations are taking place.[55] The processes that determine the lines along which debates are structured in the European political space are *social* processes, and this cannot be understood by an exclusive analytical focus on the individual.[56] The social habitus of a person is formed by experiences of collective agency and powerlessness.[57] Individual attitudes become a social force only if they are mobilised, and this very much depends on intermediary organisational networks located in the forecourt of party politics;[58] hence, our interest in European unions.

It is also important to note that the framing of socio-economic interests in national terms is hardly an exclusive property of anti-European populists, such as the Polish Law and Justice Party. If the politicisation of EU integration processes can no longer be avoided, neoliberal cosmopolitans also have an interest in politicising these along the nationalist vs cosmopolitan cleavage rather than along (transnational) class cleavages.[59]

Della Porta and Caiani avoid being captured by the politically charged conceptualisation of European protest movements along the nationalism–cosmopolitanism axis, by locating protests in broader (conflicting) networks.[60] By analysing the cognitive frames and discourses used by particular European protest movements, they were able to highlight the fundamental differences between 'critical Europeanists' – who were for example active in the campaign against the so-called Bolkestein directive – and 'populist Euro-scepticism on which research has focussed in the past'.[61] Although the neat distinction between progressive discourses of 'critical Europeanists' and regressive 'populist Euroscepticism' worked well in studies of social movements, the classification of protests based on discourses is problematic, as 'every union rhetorically supports a more social and democratic EU'.[62] I have therefore classified different European actor strategies leading to alternative EU-polity developments starting from actors' activities rather than from their discourses.[63] No European union is against a social and democratic Europe.

54   M van der Linden (ed), *Workers of the World* (Brill 2008), vol I.
55   S Tarrow, *Power in Movement* (CUP 1994).
56   Bartolini (n 23); S Saurugger, 'Sociological Approaches to the European Union in Times of Turmoil' (2016) 54 Journal of Common Market Studies 70.
57   B Föhrer, 'Collaboration Through Education? Transnational Competence and Trade Unions' Cross-border Commitment' (PhD thesis, University College Dublin 2015).
58   Bartolini (n 16) ch 6.
59   Béthoux (n 13).
60   D Della Porta and M Caiani, *Social Movements and Europeanization* (OUP 2009).
61   ibid 135.
62   Erne (n 4) 4.
63   ibid 21.

And yet, there is a long list of cases in which European labour movements mobilised along national cross-class lines rather than along transnational class lines.

Examples range from the truce of the German, French and British labour movements with their national bourgeoisies during the First World War; through labour's involvement in anti-colonialist national struggles in Ireland and elsewhere; to the national 'competitive corporatist' pacts of the 1990s and 2000s, through which unions aimed to increase their nation's competitive advantage in an increasingly Europeanised and globalised economy.[64] Finally, in cases in which political choices were apparently reduced to a choice between cosmopolitan neoliberals and nationalist anti-liberals, such as in Poland and Hungary, some unions sided with the latter. The union mobilisations along national cross-class rather than transnational class lines require detailed analysis of everyday practices across time.

The focus of the analysis on meso-level organisational dynamics, instead of on individual attitudes or macro-level observations, promises high gains. The same conclusions emerge from our review of the politicisation literature, which is discussed in the next section.

VII POLITICISING EUROPEAN INTEGRATION

Colin Hay appropriately conceptualised politicisation as a process that brings a subject from the 'realm of necessity' into the realm of the political, i.e. the 'realm of contingency and deliberation'.[65] Within European integration studies, politicisation is usually conceptualised as a process that can be empirically observed by studying (a) the growing salience of EU governance, involving (b) a polarisation of opinion and (c) an expansion of actors involved in EU governance at the macro level.[66]

If one compares the two conceptualisations, however, two problems become apparent.

1. *Pace* De Wilde,[67] the 'salience of EU issues' – for example in national media debates – is not necessarily a good indicator of European politicisation processes. If the political is the realm of contingency and deliberation, 'not every mention of the EU should count as politicization'.[68]
2. *Pace* Hay,[69] the location of the 'governmental sphere' in the political realm is problematic, as it assumes that all governmental action is automatically located in the political realm. Governmental action, however, has been increasingly delegated to 'apolitical' agencies, who claim to act in the 'non-political' realm of necessity.

---

[64] ibid.
[65] C Hay, *Why We Hate Politics* (Polity 2007) 79.
[66] P de Wilde, A Leupold and H Schmidtke, 'Introduction: The Differentiated Politicisation of European Governance' (2016) 39 West European Politics 4.
[67] ibid.
[68] Zürn (n 31) 167.
[69] Hay (n 65).

For this reason, Figure 14.1 maps the political realms in an alternative way. Although the claim of regulatory agencies being apolitical 'often masks ideological choices',[70] we locate their activities in the non-political realm of Figure 14.1.

(Democratic) governmental sphere	(Democratic) non-governmental sphere	(Technocratic) non-governmental sphere	(Technocratic) governmental sphere
Realm of contingency and deliberation ('political')		Realm of necessity ('non-political')	

FIGURE 14.1 Mapping the political revised
Source: author's adaptation based on Hay[71]

This conceptualisation maintains Hay's conceptualisation of the political as the realm of public choice.[72] In addition, however, it moves its focus from the public vs private sphere divide to the political vs non-political divide inside both governmental and non-governmental spheres of action. This allows us to distinguish between two types of governmental spheres at opposite ends of Figure 14.1, namely, a democratic and a technocratic one. Hence, I am not distinguishing technocracy from democracy based on technocrats' remoteness from citizens. Instead, my democracy–technocracy distinction relies on the articulation and acknowledgement of conflicting interests, respectively the lack thereof.[73] Accordingly, a policy issue remains 'non-political' as long as technocratic 'regulatory governance' is not challenged by social mobilisations for alternative public choices.[74] Hence, politicisation does not simply mean making technocratic governance subject to procedures of public scrutiny. Formal democratic procedures do not necessarily guarantee the availability of political choices. Alternative choices are only available if social actors mobilise people for them.

Our revised map of the political also captures 'collective governance' by non-governmental organisations – or 'private interest government',[75] in both the 'political' realm of contingency and the 'non-political' realm of necessity. This is particularly relevant in European industrial relations, where employers and unions – rather than the state – regulate wages and many other aspects of labour politics. Finally, the very same issue may be placed in the 'political' realm of contingency and deliberation at one level of governance (e.g. at national level), but in the 'non-political' realm of necessity at another level of governance (e.g. at EU level).

The first objective of the ongoing research programme on which this chapter draws, consists in the mapping of the different trajectories of shifting labour politics

---

[70] JHH Weiler, UR Haltern and FC Mayer, 'European Democracy and Its Critique' (1995) 18 West European Politics 33.

[71] Hay (n 65) 79.

[72] ibid 80.

[73] Erne (n 4) 23–26.

[74] ibid 15.

[75] W Streeck and PC Schmitter, 'Community, Market, State – and Associations? The Prospective Contribution of Interest Governance to Social Order' (1985) 1 European Sociological Review 119.

triggered by the EU's NEG regime. From an industrial relations perspective, this includes depoliticisation processes, such as shifts in wage setting:

- from a (national) 'democratic non-governmental' to a (European) 'technocratic governmental' sphere, as indicated by the shift from (national) collective bargaining to specific 'unit labour cost' benchmarks as included in the EU's new macroeconomic imbalance procedure scoreboard;[76] or
- from a (national) 'democratic non-governmental' to a (national) 'technocratic non-governmental' sphere, as indicated by the shift in (national) collective bargaining from redistribution to technocratic concession bargaining.[77]

In turn, however, the introduction of binding EU wage development benchmarks in NEG could also lead to an unintended promotion of wage policy benchmark-setting from a (European) 'technocratic governmental' to (European) 'democratic non-governmental' or 'democratic governmental' spheres; in other words, to a re-politicisation of wage policymaking at EU levels. Such multidimensional politicisation and depoliticisation processes, however, cannot be captured by the 'scale shifts' models of Euro-politicisation and transnational collective action that still dominate the field.[78]

Given the facility of access to media databases and the easy operationalisation of quantitative content analysis of media sources, it is not very surprising that most studies of EU politicisation processes are based on the salience of 'EU issues' in (national) media debates. Yet, if one conceptualises politicisation as a process that is promoting an issue into the realm of public choice, then 'even some seemingly political debates may remain in the realm of T[here] I[s] N[o] A[lternative] and thus stay apolitical'.[79]

If 'European political struggle [about competing political choices] is absent, there is no need to implement democracy as a mechanism of peaceful conflict resolution'.[80] As a result, NEG will lead to a politicisation of European governance only 'if the process of European integration becomes political in character'.[81] This, however, requires transnational social movements that challenge the power of depoliticised technocratic agencies, such as the ECB or the Economic Policy Committee, to define what are 'proper' and 'improper' economic policies.[82]

It follows that there is no alternative to a self-reflexive investigation of depoliticisation processes at the macro level and of counter-mobilisations at the meso level, as the categories by which individual attitudes are reported are themselves a product of corresponding politicisation and depoliticisation struggles. If, however, one focuses

[76] Erne (n 1) 347.
[77] Erne (n 4).
[78] S Tarrow, *The New Transnational Activism* (CUP 2005) 123.
[79] Zürn (n 31) 167.
[80] Erne (n 4) 23.
[81] ibid.
[82] Erne (n 1) 347.

the analysis on concrete activities of interest groups and social movements across time – instead of individual *attitudes* or media reports – it may be easier to control political classification struggles.

Hence, we need to pursue research strategies that go beyond the measuring of politicisation through an analysis of media debates. Instead, we are proposing an alternative research design, which investigates the politicisation of NEG through social mobilisations at the meso level. As shown by Bolkestein's intervention in the French EU referendum debate and its reverberations in both EU politics and the social sciences, analytical classifications always entail theory effects that consist of imposing a particular vision of social divisions.[83] Whether workers' Euroscepticism is best understood in (transnational) class or in (national) culturalist terms cannot be established by deductive, hypothesis-testing surveys of workers' attitudes at a particular point in time, however sophisticated they may be. Social classes are made by collective action, as shown by Thompson's study *The Making of the English Working Class*.[84] The same also applies to the making of a European working class.[85] Transnational collective action therefore seems to be a necessary condition for the structuring of the European space along transnational lines. The making of the English working class was not a result of growing inequalities, but a result of social struggles that often emerged below the radar of media attention.[86] Although socio-economic structures condition collective action, one should avoid static concepts of class.[87] People's attitudes are central to transformative action, especially perceptions of social injustice and power. Yet, attitudes lead to collective action only if activists involved in social mobilisations manage to convince a sufficient number of people to take action;[88] hence, our focus on established union and social movements. If NEG is a regime that is able to 'nationalise social conflicts',[89] however, then the prospects of a transnational democracy and a social Europe will be slim. Therefore, the following section reviews the opportunity structures for transnational collective action. This will then be used to outline an analytical framework for different actor strategies in relation to NEG to guide our ongoing empirical work.

VIII THE NEW EUROPEAN ECONOMIC GOVERNANCE REGIME: A SILENT REVOLUTION

The eurocrisis led to an unprecedented centralisation of power in the hands of EU institutions. This shift requires an explanation. Until 2007, the EU's business and

---

[83] P Bourdieu, 'Social Space and Symbolic Power' (1989) 7 Sociological Theory 14; Béthoux (n 13).

[84] EP Thompson, *The Making of the English Working Class* (first published in 1963, Penguin 1980).

[85] I Schmidt, 'Farewell to Europe's Working Classes' in Bieler and others (n 29).

[86] Thompson (n 84).

[87] Bieler and others (n 29).

[88] D McAdam, S Tarrow and C Tilly, *Dynamics of Contention* (CUP 2004); J Kelly, *Rethinking Industrial Relations* (Routledge 1998).

[89] Erne (n 1).

political leaders rejected the need for any coordination in the field of industrial relations and social policy at EU level.[90] After all, self-regulating market forces would, according to then dominant neoliberal beliefs, automatically lead to the desired adjustments in wages and social policies across Europe. But when it became clear that horizontal market integration did not lead to convergence but to major economic imbalances, the then president of the Commission announced a 'silent revolution' in EU governance.[91] The social–economic convergence that markets failed to achieve should now be realised through a more stringent vertical dimension of EU economic governance.

National governments and the European Parliament adopted six new EU laws in 2011 – the Six-Pack on European economic governance – with far-reaching consequences for labour politics.[92] In 2012, the Fiscal Treaty followed suit and the ECB used its power as lender of last resort within the euro system to impose its agenda also in Spain and Italy.[93] Finally, a Two-Pack of new EU laws that reinforced the supranational surveillance of national fiscal policies followed in 2013.[94] As a result, the Commission and Council are not only authorised to issue detailed country-specific recommendations (CSRs), but can – depending on the Commission's political will – also impose sanctions. Eurozone countries that fail to reduce 'excessive deficits' or cause 'excessive macroeconomic imbalances' risk substantial fines equal to 0.2 per cent or 0.1 per cent of GDP respectively. Although the Six-Pack introduces sanctions for non-compliant Member States, the new EU laws fail to define important key terms. What constitutes, for example, an 'economic imbalance'? Article 2 of the Regulation (EU) 1176/2011 on the prevention and correction of macroeconomic imbalances merely states that 'excessive imbalances' mean 'severe imbalances, including imbalances that jeopardise *or risk* jeopardising the *proper* functioning of economic and monetary union' (emphasis added).

As discussed elsewhere,[95] this definition of 'excessive imbalances' is so encompassing that no aspect of labour politics can a priori be excluded from its scope. The regulation also undermines the legal principle of *nulla poena sine lege*, as it does not specify what actions 'risk' jeopardising the 'proper' functioning of the EMU. Lawmakers delegated the definition of the regulation's key terms to EU executives, who are drafting and adopting CSRs and corrective action plans on an ad hoc basis. These executive orders, however, display neither the generality and democratic justification of a law that emerges out of the normal legislative process nor the

---

[90] E Leonard and others, *New Structures, Forms and Processes of Governance in European Industrial Relations* (Office for the Official Publications of the European Communities 2007).

[91] ANSA (n 18).

[92] Erne (n 1).

[93] S Blankenburg and others, 'Prospects for the Eurozone' (2013) 37 Cambridge Journal of Economics 463.

[94] MW Bauer and S Becker, 'The Unexpected Winner of the Crisis' (2014) 36 Journal of European Integration 213.

[95] Erne (n 1).

certainties of a rules-based ordoliberal policy regime.[96] National governments and parliaments cannot be sure in advance whether or not their reform programme will satisfy the EU executives. The ambiguous grounds for sanctions represent a risk that policymakers find difficult to assess.[97] The control of EU executives over national labour politics is also increasing because the Commission's fines apply automatically, unless a qualified majority of national finance ministers vetoes them within a period of ten days. This means that the decisive political decision in relation to the sanctioning (or not) of Member States is taken by the college of European Commissioners. Hence, the NEG laws substantially increase the political power of the Commission[98] to the detriment of national parliaments, the European Parliament and the social partners. The implications of NEG for unions are far-reaching.[99]

Keynesian policy advisers and labour leaders usually deplore the neoliberal bias of NEG.[100] However, the shifts caused by NEG also give rise to more profound conceptual questions. If economic policymaking is becoming an issue of technocratic implementation of 'proper' economic policies, then 'there is no longer any need for institutions of democratic interest intermediation between conflicting political preferences'.[101] Hence, NEG involves not only a *scale shift* in socio-economic policymaking, but also a *mode shift*, involving a de-democratisation of socio-economic policymaking. The problem is therefore not the neoliberal bias of NEG as such, but the contention that there are no alternatives to it.

Moreover, NEG governs the European economy not through universally applicable laws, but through key performance indicators and country-specific executive orders. In so doing, the 'EU's new governance regime does not follow the model of the classical federal state. It has much more in common with the corporate governance structures of multinational companies that control notionally autonomous subsidiaries through coercive comparisons based on centrally chosen key

---

[96] A Storey, 'The Myths of Ordoliberalism' (2017) Working Paper 17–02, ERC Project 'European Unions', University College Dublin www.erc-europeanunions.eu/working-papers accessed 23 March 2018; C Joerges, 'Integration Through Law and the Crisis of Law in Europe's Emergency' in D Chalmers, M Jachtenfuchs and C Joerges (eds), *The End of the Eurocrats' Dream* (CUP 2016) 314; C Joerges, 'Brother, Can You Paradigm?' (2014) 12 International Journal of Constitutional Law 769.

[97] C Degryse, M Jepsen and P Pochet, *The Euro Crisis and Its Impact on National and European Social Policies* (ETUI Working Paper, ETUI 2013) 29; C De la Porte and E Heins, 'Game Change in EU Social Policy' in E Xiarchogiannopoulou and PM Rodrigues (eds), *The Eurozone Crisis and the Transformation of Democracy* (Ashgate 2013).

[98] Bauer and Becker (n 94).

[99] P Marginson, 'Coordinated Bargaining in Europe' (2015) 21 European Journal of Industrial Relations 97; P Marginson and C Welz, 'European Wage-setting Mechanisms Under Pressure' (2015) 21 Transfer: European Review of Labour and Research 429; C De la Porte and P Pochet, 'Boundaries of Welfare between the EU and Member States During the "Great Recession"' (2014) 15 Perspectives on European Politics and Society 281; Erne (n 1).

[100] Erne (n 1) 350.

[101] ibid 347.

performance indicators."[102] Six-Pack Regulation (EU) 1176/2011 requires the Commission to design a Macroeconomic Imbalances Procedure (MIP) scoreboard of quantitative benchmarks to identify improper economic developments in Member States. Yet, a list of appropriate indicators and thresholds is not included in the regulation, despite its far-reaching implications. Instead, the list has been drafted by a Working Group of the Economic Policy Committee, which is one of the so-called 'comitology' committees of national and EU officials chaired by the Commission. The MIP scoreboard includes indicators relating to all economic policy areas, including those formally excluded from the competency of the EU, such as wages policy. Nominal unit labour costs (ULC), for example, that go beyond the benchmark set out in the MIP scoreboard may trigger the regulation's preventative and corrective mechanisms that range from CSRs, in-depth reviews, corrective action plans and surveillance visits, to the fines mentioned above. In contrast, *minimum* ULC thresholds are missing, despite the fact that macroeconomic imbalances can also be caused by beggar-thy-neighbour wage setting strategies.

The times when EU guidelines could be dismissed as 'soft law' have come to an end. In 2014, for instance, the Commission told the French government that its €50bn austerity plan and the €40bn reduction in employers' social security contributions and taxes, announced in early 2014, would still not go far enough 'in restoring private companies' profitability'.[103] Thus, France would require specific monitoring and decisive action, including further tax cuts for business, curbs on healthcare and pension spending, and a flexibilisation of its 'rigid' labour law and wage-setting system.[104] In 2015, the government adopted the Loi Macron to render French law more business-friendly. As elsewhere in Europe, however, the French government had to adopt the new law by executive order because the likely amendments adopted by a more labour-friendly parliament 'would have sent the wrong signal to the European Commission, a week before deciding whether to fine France for missing its deficit targets'.[105] As a result, the Commission refrained from sanctioning France. In order not to be penalised, however, the French government had to commit itself to a long list of additional reforms.[106] The list included a new labour law (now known as the Loi El Khomri), which the Socialist government adopted in 2016 by executive order, despite widespread opposition in its own parliamentary party, a strike wave culminating in a general strike and the popular *'nuit debout'* occupations.[107]

---

[102] ibid 353.
[103] Commission, *Macroeconomic Imbalances, France 2014* (European Economy Occasional Papers 178, March 2014, European Union 2014).
[104] Commission, 'Recommendation for a Council Recommendation on France's 2014 National Reform Programme and Delivering a Council Opinion on France's 2014 Stability Programme' COM(2014) 411 final.
[105] *Financial Times* (17 February 2015).
[106] Erne (n 1) 348.
[107] A Supiot, P Caïla and F Damour, 'Quand Les Nombres Nous Gouvernent' (2016)9 Études 53.

The Commission's reputation as advocate of social progress has been dwindling for a while. However, NEG represents a clear rupture with the social partnership approach of Jacques Delors. In 2012, the Commission's DG ECFIN even explicitly stated that the 'overall reduction in the wage-setting power of trade unions' would be one of its current policy objectives.[108] Although the new Commission President Juncker promised unionists at the ETUC congress in 2015 new 'social pillars' for the EU integration process, the realisation of this goal very much depends on unions and social movements mobilising for it, despite EU leaders' proclamation of its twenty key principles and rights at the Social Summit in Gothenburg in November 2017.

IX POLITICISING THE NEW EUROPEAN ECONOMIC GOVERNANCE REGIME?

Western democracies' retreat from their 'former heartland of basic economic strategy'[109] is undermining a vital power resource of organised labour, namely, *political* mobilisation and exchange power,[110] and one of labour's classical methods in the struggle for social progress, namely, *legal enactment*.[111] European unions' responses to the rise of centralised NEG structures, however, also represent a critical case for analytical reasons.

As mentioned above, unions have succeeded in triggering transnational collective action primarily in cases where they have been able to politicise the decisions of supranational corporate executives or public authorities in a transnational public sphere.[112] What remains to be explained, however, are the conditions behind successful transnational politicisation processes. The centralisation of decision-making processes within multinational firms and supranational organisations compels unions to act transnationally only if national options are deemed to be absent or exhausted.[113] Hence, the centralisation of policymaking at a supranational level seems to be a necessary, but not a sufficient, condition for their politicisation in a transnational public sphere. In many cases, European federations of civil society organisations fail to trigger debates about draft EU laws, however important they think the proposal may be.[114]

Furthermore, the construction of NEG makes it increasingly difficult to describe Euro-technocratisation and technocratic renationalisation as distinct

---

[108] Commission, *Labour Market Developments in Europe 2012* (European Economy 5, European Union 2012).

[109] C Crouch, 'Privatised Keynesianism' (2009) 11 British Journal of Politics & International Relations 398.

[110] Erne (n 4) ch 3.

[111] S Webb and B Webb, *Industrial Democracy* (Longmans 1897), vol II.

[112] R Erne and others, 'Introduction: Politicising the Transnational' (2015) 56 Labor History 237; G Harvey and P Turnbull, 'Can Labor Arrest the "Sky Pirates"?' (2015) 56 Labor History 308.

[113] Erne (n 4) 23.

[114] B Kohler-Koch and C Quittkat, *De-mystification of Participatory Democracy: EU Governance and Civil Society* (OUP 2013).

trajectories. The more national leaders follow EU recommendations, the more national and European technocratic strategies converge. As a result, the politicisation of technocratic governance at national level also requires a politicisation of NEG at EU level, and vice versa. Moreover, national and Euro-technocratic strategies share the same action repertoire, namely, the depoliticisation of economic governance. In contrast, Europeanist and nationalist politicisation strategies are still diverging, namely, in view of their different impact on the structuring of the European political space along transnational class or national cross-class cleavages. This is the case regardless of the economic or cultural foundations of nationalism. The difference between the two foundations may indeed not be as important as many post-functionalist EU integration scholars assume.[115] The two are converging, and not only in today's competition states.[116] Italian and Romanian pioneers of authoritarian corporatism also emphasised the importance of economic concerns when they justified fascism as a tool to 'harmonise' the 'antagonism between social classes' by force in order to succeed as a nation in the world economy.[117]

Given the disruptive nature of capitalist relations of production and exchange, capitalist societies require state structures in order to sustain their social reproduction. At times, this need for stable governance structures allowed organised labour to shift the conflict between workers and employers from the market place to the political arena.[118] As the working class is usually larger than the capitalist class, labour seems to retain an advantage in democracies. Accordingly, capitalists opposed universal suffrage for a long time, whereas labour fought for it.[119] Engels[120] even regarded democratisation as the strongest weapon for human emancipation. The social state would indeed not have been possible without labour's struggles for the democratisation of socio-economic policymaking.[121] It should be noted, however, that the neoliberal offensive against the social state was never meant to lead to the dissolution of the state as a law enforcement agency. Neoliberals only sought to block unwelcome popular interferences by delegating executive powers to technocratic agencies. In turn, democracy seems to be reverting to a democracy without choice, and not only in the periphery where 'predatory elites have learned to cite . . . external pressures as excuses for their own refusal to take responsibility for the welfare of ordinary citizens',[122] but also in developed capitalist states. The 'politics of constrained choice' is particularly challenging for left parties, as right-wing parties

---

[115] Hooghe and Marks (n 50).

[116] PG Cerny, 'Paradoxes of the Competition State' (1997) 32 Government and Opposition 251.

[117] M Manoïlesco, *Le Siècle du Corporatisme* (Felix Alcan 1936); F Pitigliani, *The Italian Corporative State* (King and Son 1933) ix.

[118] W Korpi, *The Democratic Class Struggle* (Routledge 1983).

[119] P Foot, *The Vote: How It Was Won and How It Was Undermined* (Viking 2005).

[120] F Engels, 'Introduction to Karl Marx: The Class Struggles in France, 1848–1850' www.marxists.org/archive/marx/works/download/pdf/Class_Struggles_in_France.pdf accessed 26 March 2018.

[121] A Wahl, *The Rise and Fall of the Welfare State* (Pluto 2011).

[122] I Krastev, 'The Balkans: Democracy without Choices' (2002) 13 Journal of Democracy 51.

usually support the business-friendly adjustments that are required from 'responsible governments'.[123] Centre-left parties have often paid a high electoral price for the implementation of austerity policies, even if they may seek new justifications as promoters of progressive causes in other areas, namely in the field of identity politics. In contrast, the legitimacy of unions depends on their capability to sway socio-economic policies in the interests of workers.

Despite the ongoing 'hollowing out of democracy'[124] in these 'post-democratic'[125] times, however, politicisation struggles of unions and new social movements are hardly becoming less significant. Drawing on nineteenth-century history, Wagner has argued that 'whenever capitalism exists without democracy it will be exposed to a critique of exploitation and injustice, likely to be expressed through calls for inclusive, egalitarian democracy'.[126] The shifts in socio-economic policymaking from the democratic social state to technocratic governance institutions are weakening the legitimacy of state structures that are essential for consolidating capitalism. Yet, the contradiction between our society's democratic values and the post-democratic state structures of transnational capitalism may also trigger social protest. At times, transnational union and social movement campaigns succeeded in politicising new technocratic governance regimes; as in the case of Commissioner Bolkestein's EU Services Directive or President GW Bush's Free Trade Area of the Americas.[127]

Conversely, however, NEG's particular governance model, which mimics the corporate governance model of multinational companies and therefore has the capacity to put Member States into competition with one another, may effectively deter transnational collective action. Certainly, the democratic legitimacy requirements of EU governance structures are higher than those of private multinational corporations. This suggests that the stronger vertical dimension of EU governance is increasing the likelihood of its politicisation. Given the ability of the 'new supranational EU regime to nationalize social conflicts',[128] however, it seems likely that this will occur in national rather than transnational arenas, unless social mobilisations succeed in politicising NEG along transnational class rather than national lines.

X NEG AND LABOUR POLITICS: A NEW RESEARCH PROGRAMME

Based on the discussion of the state of the art above, the following argument can be made: the more unions and social movements are politicising NEG in a transnational sphere as a conflict between labour and business interests, the more NEG will

[123]   P Mair, *Ruling the Void* (Verso 2013).
[124]   ibid.
[125]   C Crouch, *Post-Democracy* (Polity 2004).
[126]   P Wagner, 'The Democratic Crisis of Capitalism' (2011) LEQS Paper No 44, December www
        .lse.ac.uk/european-institute/Assets/Documents/LEQS-Discussion-Papers/LEQSPaper44.pdf
        accessed 23 March 2018, 14.
[127]   B Dobrusin, 'Transnational Labor Action in Latin America' (2015) 56 Labor History 270; Kay (n 10).
[128]   Erne (n 1) 345.

TABLE 14.1 *Actor strategies leading to different structures of the European political space*

Levels of action	Observable actor activities	Supporting a restructuring of the political space:	
		along transnational class divisions	along national divisions
Politicising NEG Transnational level	Transnational & contentious actions and action frameworks Euro-demonstrations Transnational strikes European Citizens' Initiatives	Yes	No
Depoliticising NEG Transnational & national level	Avoiding discussions about NEG Non-contentious actions and action frameworks Competitive adjustments of labour policies	No	Yes
Politicising NEG National level	Nationalist & contentious actions and action frameworks Nationalist counter-mobilisations	No	Yes

Source: adapted from Erne (n 1) 305 and (n 4) 25

lead to restructuring the European political space along transnational class lines. Conversely, the more they politicise NEG at national levels as a conflict between opposite national interests, the more NEG will lead to a restructuring of the European political space along national lines or even to its disintegration.

Table 14.1 outlines the framework for the analysis of different labour movement strategies and their operationalisation, outlining the observable activities through which unions and social movements can politicise (or depoliticise) NEG. Politicisation means the active promotion of an issue back into the realm of contingency and deliberation at the transnational or the national level, as outlined in Figure 14.1. We do not aim to place particular trade unions or social movements into a particular box of this typology, as this would inevitably entail the use of stylised evidence.[129] Our typology rather serves as a heuristic tool, which will enable us to assess varying strategic choices actors make across various cases.

XI GOING BEYOND METHODOLOGICAL NATIONALISM

So far, most studies on the responses of European trade unions and social movements to the Eurocrisis and the EU's NEG regime have relied on comparisons of different national cases. This is not surprising, given the dominance of

[129] Erne (n 4) 20.

methodological nationalism in comparative industrial relations and political economy that mirrors approaches in terms of varieties of capitalism,[130] unionism[131] and welfare regimes.[132]

The research design of Gumbrell-McCormick and Hyman's *Trade Unions in Western Europe* is representative of the field.[133] Its case selection includes unions from all West European Varieties of Capitalism (VoC), namely, from 'liberal market economies' of Britain and Ireland, the 'Nordic' countries, countries from the 'central group' around Germany and 'Southern Europe'. Consequently, they focus their analysis on national unions, even if this focus on national actors seems to be anachronistic given NEG's vertical dynamics. Sure, waning national autonomy does not disqualify national comparisons per se. However, the more features of national systems are shaped at EU level, the more national comparisons exhaust themselves in assessments of different ways of national adjustment while the processes that triggered the changes in the first place remain under the radar.

Yet, there are also practical reasons that explain the ongoing prevalence of methodological nationalism. Especially after the EU's enlargement to the East, the European political and social space may simply be too vast and the languages spoken in it too many for it to be captured through qualitative research. Consequently, researchers tend to limit their research field to countries and language areas they know well. This is the dominant strategy in industrial relations,[134] which is a discipline that values empirical findings also for their practical value. Theoretically more ambitious sociologists and political scientists, however, who tend to be less concerned about intricate idiosyncrasies in their empirical fields, often retreat from qualitative research altogether. Instead, they try to understand the workings of the European system on the basis of 'comparable' quantitative data.[135] However, as quantitative data are almost exclusively gathered at and for the national level, this methodological choice further reinforces institutionalist perspectives that treat nations as if they were independent from one another. The result is serious analytical distortion.

Research designs that are based on national variables are unable to capture the restructuring of the economy and society along transnational supply and value chains.[136] Likewise, the workings of NEG, and the mobilisations that are being triggered by it, cannot be adequately captured by national data sets either. Social

[130] PA Hall and D Soskice, *Varieties of Capitalism* (OUP 2001).
[131] C Frege and J Kelly, *Varieties of Unionism* (OUP 2004); C Crouch, *Industrial Relations and European State Traditions* (OUP 1993).
[132] G Esping-Andersen, *The Three Worlds of Welfare Capitalism* (Polity 1990).
[133] R Gumbrell-McCormick and R Hyman, *Trade Unions in Western Europe* (OUP 2013).
[134] ibid viii.
[135] Crouch (n 34); Caramani (n 16).
[136] A Simonazzi, A Ginzburg and G Nocella, 'Economic Relations between Germany and Southern Europe' (2013) 37 Cambridge Journal of Economics 653; P Dicken, *Global Shift* (Guilford Press 2011).

mobilisations that politicise European governance have to be studied (a) at the meso level of interest politics and (b) within and across national boundaries.

We should know more about politicisation below the macro level of public debates as presented in mass media. We also need to know more about the role of interest groups and civil society organisations in the process of politicisation. This should not only open avenues for 'thick descriptions'[137] of patterns of politicisation, but also help to elucidate the consequences of politicisation in terms of equality and democracy.[138]

Macro-institutionalist approaches are also often too abstract to appreciate the dynamics of socio-economic processes. Instead, I am making the case for disaggregation of both socio-economic and political process and of the units under study. This contextualised approach to the study of comparative labour politics will enable us to capture social dynamics that often fall under the radar of macro-level comparisons.[139] We are therefore arguing for comparative research designs that are no longer based on the comparison of seemingly autonomous national units. Accordingly, our new research programme involves two areas of labour politics (wage setting, provision of public services) and three sectors (public healthcare, transport and water services). This should enable us to contrast the NEG-related activities of unions and new social movements across sectors and subject areas.

XII CONCLUSION

The purpose of this chapter was first and foremost conceptual. Even so, it does not raise mere academic questions. The big questions we are addressing are relevant not only for the predominately institutionalist approaches in my field but also for the future of democracy and social justice. We believe that the growing vertical integration of Europe, and the counter-movements that these processes are triggering, are calling for a paradigm shift in industrial relations, social policy and other disciplines that are approaching comparative labour politics in terms of varieties of capitalism, unionism and welfare states. The more NEG is becoming a 'supranational regime that nationalizes social conflict',[140] however, the more difficult it will be to establish a new analytical paradigm that goes beyond methodological nationalism. Any yet, we also believe that our new research programme's focus on the mobilisation in three public sectors promises high gains. If transnational collective action occurs even in sectors that had been entrenched in domestic contexts – as implied by the transnational right2water campaigns of European unions and movements[141] – then

---

[137] C Geertz, *The Interpretation of Cultures* (Basic Books 1973).
[138] Zürn (n 31) 178.
[139] R Locke and K Thelen, 'Apples and Oranges revisited: Contextualized Comparisons and the Study of Comparative Labor Politics' (1995) 23 Politics and Society 337.
[140] Erne (n 1).
[141] Bieler (n 14).

we will be able to make inferences that are going far beyond the sectorial cases under study. This may help us to further develop analytical approaches that are better equipped to assess for the interplay between EU economic governance, labour politics, technocracy and democracy than most current approaches in my field, which are caught in methodological nationalism.

Co-funded by the
Erasmus+ Programme
of the European Union

15

Which Refugee Crisis?

On the Proxy of the Systemic Eurocrisis and Its Spatialities

Dimitris Dalakoglou

I DROWNING MIGRANTS*

Europe was shocked by the news that a boat full of migrants sunk into the Mediterranean Sea taking with it fifty-seven people. The episode occurred when the Italian Navy vessel *Sibilla*, in its effort to protect the common EU borders collided with the migrants' boat. Some serious debates took place then, raising questions as to whether it was an accident or part of a political effort to stop the flow of migrants or whether the Italian Navy could have intervened and rescued the migrants. The year was 1997 and the non-EU migrants were Albanians fleeing the 1997 civil war that followed the collapse of the 'pyramid' banking system in their home country. The transition of the country to market economy and the new ambitious financial innovations had been promoted by the World Bank (WB) and International Monetary Fund (IMF) but also the European Economic Community (EEC).

It is one of history's ironies that the name 'Sibilla' refers to the ancient oracles who foresaw the future. Almost twenty years later as the Albanian government together with most other European governments sealed off their borders to the Syrian refugees, sinking boats and dead migrants trying to enter the EU still are a common phenomenon in the Mediterranean. Obviously the then 'Others', who did not have the right to enter into Europe, were of a primarily different ethnic origin than the current 'Others'; yet, the persistent refusal of the right to mobility and, more generally, the border securitisation regime currently being witnessed was rehearsed and shaped in the early 1990s. Although the exact location of this border moves, qualitatively the border regime of 'Fortress Europe', as we know it today, remains the same over the last decades, protecting the core of Europe and its strategic peripheries.

However, I claim that today there is an additional reason why we focus so much on the security of the EU common borders and our governments ignore the right to life, and we thus accept the regular deaths on the sea in the name of the security of

---

*   A different version of this text was published in the journal City under the tile 'Europe's Last Frontier'.

'Fortress Europe'. This is because, spatially speaking, a symbolically privileged territorial belonging is the only benefit that the EU has to offer its citizens; the rest of the promises of united Europe are fading away.

It is well known that emergencies and the accompanying exceptional conditions often evolve into more permanent modes of governance.[1] The refugee crisis of 2015 is not different. It was an opportunity for European governments and the European elites to administrate the declining consent of European citizens for their policies. These are the elites that punished a great part of the EU's population (the majority of the impoverished PIIGS[2] residents) and implemented harsh neoliberal austerity to the rest of the people in Europe in the name of economic recovery. The EU's neoliberal economic project of several decades that promised certain spatial conditions for the everyday life of EU citizens (which can be summarised as territorial privilege and middle-class private property conditions and lifestyle for the masses) has been shaken since 2008. Within that context in 2015, increased disappointment among Europeans could be tackled instantly in the name of that vaguely defined urgent danger that comes from across our supposedly common borders. In this chapter, I wish to focus on the spatial dimensions of this process and explain how the collapse of a main spatial[3] pillar of post-Cold-War Europe (the novel private forms of real estate property, the renewal of the built environment and the related growth) led to the overemphasis on another spatial pillar, the boundaries of the privileged territorial condition.

II BUILDING EUROPE

Historically, the twentieth century witnessed two major pan-European construction projects that have taken place over the entire length and width of the continent, renewing its built environment. The first is the post-Second World War reconstruction and the second is the post-Cold War 'reconstruction'. Besides being a much larger-scale project, the post-Second World War project explicitly had a two-fold character. The two sides of the Cold War divide were each building their own urban and infrastructural materiality.[4] Via this material reconstruction, they aimed to engineer their respective social and political entity. Moreover, the construction project of the 1940s and 1950s was to (re)build a devastated continent. The ensuing physical construction project, from the 1990s to the 2000s, was tied to the metaphysical destruction of the Communist regimes' infrastructure and materiality – its very ethos. Thus, the building construction was part of the destruction both physical and symbolic of the defeated enemy.

---

[1]   G Agambien, *Lo stato di Eccezione* (Bollati Boringhieri 2003).
[2]   The term refers to Portugal, Ireland, Italy, Greece and Spain.
[3]   Spatial in the sense that is used in the anthropological and human geographic definition of space as a sociopolitical relationship (H Lefbvre, *The Production of Space* (Blackwell 1991).)
[4]   On materiality, see D Miller (ed.), *Materiality* (Duke UP 2005).

We have detailed ethnographies of the socio-material transformations that occurred in Eastern Europe at that time,[5] and these have also been recorded and recreated in art. For example, the celebrated film *Good Bye Lenin!*[6] describes on a fictional level this process of deconstruction of the enemy's material culture and its replacement by the capitalist version, which was novel to the former socialist countries. The movie's hero is desperately trying to reconstruct East Germany's material reality for his mother who wakes after a long coma – she must not get shocked to find the world has changed, lest she fall ill again. He tries to recreate the German Democratic Republic's material culture and with every passing moment this becomes more difficult as the material samples of the previous world are systematically erased.

Beyond fiction, the Cold War was a war, and at the end its outcome was one that most wars share: the winner occupied the territory of the defeated. Because this war was waged between two economic/political systems, this 'occupation of territories' meant the instant transfer of the vast majority of immobile resources and real estate of socialist countries from state, public or cooperative hands to private ones. The enormous influx of resources into the European capitalist economy resulted in its overnight expansion.

Another type of resource that was added in the early 1990s to the capitalist European economic system was the instantly impoverished masses of Eastern European populations who provided an inexpensive workforce either as migrants to the West or in their own countries – often for Western European interests and in the interest of the new local capitalist elites– while drawing on the private property of productive means as yet another source of power. Thus, it was only a matter of time until the construction sector evolved into the 'steam engine' of economic growth during the 1990s and 2000s, occupying an increasing percentage of GDP all over Europe. Certainly, the dilapidation and reconstruction of the socialist infra-structures, but also the big grids crossing what was once upon the time the Iron Curtain, aiming to physically connect the two Europes, were a great part of that activity. And yet, it was not only the East, as Western Europe witnessed some of the largest construction projects, both in terms of publicly funded works and in terms of private contracts. One sees here the radical metamorphosis of cities like Amsterdam or Dublin or even see the Spanish seaside or the transformations of London as typical examples. Within this context the whole phenomenon must also be linked with the emergence of the infrastructural mega-event of which the European continent saw at least four over a period of twenty years (Olympic Games of Barcelona, Athens, London or European football championships in

[5] M Salaru, 'Bloku: An Ethnography of a Rumanian Block of Flats' (DPhil University of Oxford 2017); D Dalakoglou, *The Road: An Ethnography of (Im)mobility, Space and Cross-Border Infrastructures in the Balkans* (Manchester UP 2017); V Buchli, *An Archaeology of Socialism* (Berg 1999).

[6] W Becker, *Good Bye Lenin!* (X-Filme Creative Pool 2003).

Lisbon, etc.) which fundamentally changed the entire built materiality of four of its metropolises.

This particular project of the built environment's reconstruction not only created profit but also contributed to the engineering of the new sociocultural capitalist subjectivities and relationships. For example, in the case of Eastern Europe, these subjects had to get used to the world of private automobility, the private housing market, the cosmology of supermarkets or malls, the new capitalist social hierarchies, etc. Similarly, the West was being re-engineered socially, first of all quantitatively, thanks to the intake of human and financial resources and accelerated growth, but also qualitatively. The post-Second World War housing policies, that were much more extended and inclusive in comparison to the current ones, have been replaced since the 1990s by an increasing expansion in private forms of property, financialisation of real estate and related price manipulation. This has changed most Western European metropolises and their demographics beyond recognition within three decades. As this chapter is written, in April of 2018, it was announced that a champion of affordable housing in the previous decade, Berlin, became the European city with the fastest increasing real estate prices. Certainly, as I will show below, this very same project of construction boom and economic growth is related with the bust that followed, but before going there, one should focus on the other spatial pillar of post-Cold-War Europe.

III BORDERS

Apart from this reconstruction of the built environment, the post-Cold War era also had another significant spatial dimension. Following 1990, an ongoing process of internal and external reconfiguration of the European borders ensued. Primarily, the new borders created a new privileged European space and identity, which was promising or even providing the dreams of wealth and growth alongside those of a supposed territorial and cultural exclusivity.

However, that process of symbolic and territorial integration between Western and Eastern Europeans to a new European identity was a gradual one. The sudden collapse of the main division between socialist and capitalist Europe made the previous internal Western division between core Western Europe (e.g. Germany, Benelux) and peripheral Western Europe (e.g. Ireland and Mediterranean countries) much less significant. In fact, given the common capitalist history, the western periphery and western core shared commonalities in comparison to the Easterners. Events such as the wars in Yugoslavia or the brief Albanian Civil War (1997) were attributed mostly to the primary 'sin' of communism and were used to confirm the former distinction, where the West had to intervene to 'civilise' the East of Europe. Despite the various infrastructural cross-border projects between EU and non-EU member countries on the continent that were promoted since the early 1990s, which attempted to materialise the new links, the new united Europe's identification processes became problematic.[7] The division had strong roots, as for over fifty years the archetypal enemy were the 'Other' Europeans and, as the Otranto tragedy shows, overcoming such old divisions is a long and hard process. So, this is a time bomb of symbolisms in the very project of (not so) united Europe.

The EU/non-EU borders became the favoured arena for testing, developing and shaping the policies of 'Fortress Europe'. Indeed, as more and more Eastern European countries enter the EU or gain potential member status, the geopolitical border is constantly redrawn. It is for example worth noting how, within just two decades, western governments' attitude towards the Easterners who crossed the borders of the old EU of the twelve member states has radically altered. When the first Eastern migrants started crossing the (former) Iron Curtain towards the West, western governments perceived this as a political success and as a positive develop-ment, which indisputably manifested the defeat of the enemy – the socialist regimes. However, within only a few months, the Eastern Europeans became an undesired flow for EU member countries. And yet, one after the other, the former infidels prove their fidelity to some of the most savage versions of the market economy and are welcomed into the EU. Despite this gradual inclusion of many Eastern European countries in the EU, the usual zones of the inexpensive sex or gambling industries along the old East–West European borders[8] – regardless of EU member-ship status for the Eastern neighbour – testify to the fact that the whole process of division and compartmentalisation between Eastern and Western Europeans is indeed ongoing.

So, during the refugee crisis of 2015–2016 we are witnessed the next stage of this ongoing identity crisis of the supposed common European identity. It was the turn of Eastern Europe to claim its right to Europeanness and westernness over the bodies of the new 'Others', precisely as the periphery of Western Europe did in the 1990s over the bodies of Eastern European migrants. Just as Greece or South Italy, Ireland or Spain saw in the 1990s and early 2000s their own 'economic miracles' after the collapse of socialism, largely thanks to the influx of economic and symbolic resources to the western capitalist economic system from Eastern Europe, the Eastern European elites confirm their upgrade into the hierarchies of Europe via the new 'Others' and especially based on the boundary. A good example is Albania. In the 1990s in Greece the phrase 'I became an Albanian' was commonly used to express the idea that some-one works hard for very little money and under generally conditions of exploitation. This was very much the case for most Albanian migrants in the 1990s when the Greek government took steps to ensure almost no Albanian would be able to acquire a green card (until 2001). Thus, a country of ten million people inherited over a million 'illegal' migrants as an inexpensive labour force, boosting the local and national economy. In February 2016, the Albanian Prime Minister of the Socialist Party, Edi Rama,

---

[7] Dalakoglou (n 5).
[8] eg the borders between Germany and the Czech Republic or Greece and Macedonia.

announced that he would seal off the borders of his country against Syrian refugees who use it as a passage on their way to Northern Europe via Greece.

At the same time, several Balkan countries came to an agreement with Austria to seal off their own borders, thus closing down the Balkan corridors to refugees. Meanwhile, the Hungarian governmental practices that refused to receive any refugee highlight a growing trend among the Eastern European states of the EU of openly racist and anti-refugee rhetoric and policy. In early 2016, the Dutch presidency of the EU silently accepted all these tactics and decisions. Greece's and Frontex security measures in combination with the EU–Turkey agreement led to the entrapment of millions of Syrians and other refugees in Turkey, providing again inexpensive labour for the struggling Turkish economy. Nevertheless, there is something important to note in this connection. The relative tolerance towards Hungary and other far-right and anti-refugee governments in Eastern Europe which break the EU agreement to host proportionally refugees, simply confirms that Western Europe sees such racism as a disturbing side effect of the proper inclusion of Eastern European states to the common European identity. This identification is the only attractive part of EU membership since the EU is in fact running out of financial resources to maintain the promises of the economic neoliberal dream of unlimited economic growth for everyone.

Taking the internal European divisions even further we see novel forms of old divides re-emerging. The emergence of PIIGS as the new infidels of the proper capitalism versus the careful Northern Europeans who do not 'spend their money on alcohol and women' as the then Dutch Minister of Finance, Jeroen Dijsselbloem claimed in 2017,[9] echoes precisely the divide between the core and periphery of old EU members that was predominant until the end of the Cold War . Even worse given all the new divides and alliances (e.g. see the agreements[10] between the states of the former Austro-Hungarian empire regarding the refugee flows), one can safely state that Europe faces an unrepresented crisis of its supposed collective identity since the end of the Cold War.

Europeans were forced to spend decades hating each other: socialist regimes disseminated fear and hate to their citizens in relation to westerners and vice versa; governments of core North-Western Europe disseminated fear of the western periphery and vice versa. These became the dominant schemes of creating collective national and regional identities orchestrated by ideological and violent state apparatuses for decades. So, in spite of the billions of euros spent on cross-border infrastructures, on trans-Europeans and inter-European corridors, highways, railways, natural gas pipelines, etc. it will take many generations before the symbolic

---

9   M Khan and P McClean, 'Dijsselbloem under Fire after Saying Eurozone Countries Wasted Money on "Alcohol and Women"' *Financial Times* (21 March 2017) www.ft.com/content/2498740e-b911-3dbf-942d-ecce511a351e accessed 7 January 2019.

10 'Europe/Migration: Five-Country Police Agreement Exacerbates Crisis and Puts Vulnerable Migrants at Risk' (reliefweb, 25 February 2016) https://reliefweb.int/report/austria/europemigration-five-country-police-agreement-exacerbates-crisis-and-puts-vulnerable accessed 7 January 2019.

and economic divides within Europe are bridged. Meanwhile, the crisis came, making the buying of consent unsustainable. If the EU and individual European governments had until recently the resources to finance all these major public works, bail out the banking sectors that generated too much money in the markets via credit economy, promising to the indebted Europeans state-sponsored middle-class lifestyles, the crisis brought an end to this utopia of unlimited growth and the related positive identifications. An emphasis on the undisputed common 'Other' (the non-European refugee) and on the boundaries that divide Europeans from these 'Others' can therefore potentially serve the purpose of holding together – for now – this divided population.

IV THE 'ACTUAL EXISTING' CRISIS

So, another reason that European governments emphasise so much the spatial column of Fortress Europe is precisely because the other spatial column of the post-Cold War European dream is collapsing with the 2008 crisis. This pillar in tangible everyday life terms was that of a private house for everyone, easterner or westerner. A private house/investment that would transform everyone into a micro-capitalist as house prices would rise *in perpetuum*. Nevertheless, despite the final boost that outlets such as Airbnb or the state-sponsored mortgages industry have offered to houseowners, in reality this dream seems to vanish. The mortgage industry that bails out the failed European banking sector leads to the occupation of real estate from the financial institutes leading to prices being manipulated artificially so much that the latest generation, the so-called 'millennials', are met with the peak of this financial bubble and are increasingly excluded from that much-vaunted asset: the private house. Today marks the first time since the Second World War, that we find as many young adults in Europe still living with their parents. Meanwhile, inflation in real estate prices is mirrored in products and services while real wages decrease as workloads increase in this form of European late capitalism. We therefore have a young European generation with very little in comparison to their parents' generation. Simultaneously, the soft infrastructural provisions of social democracy that were part of the parcel, are also vanishing under the triumphal neoliberal configuration of post-Cold War Europe: childcare, healthcare, care for the elders, social housing, etc. are no longer available as safety nets. After all, that was part of the excuse for 'Fortress Europe': 'Europe cannot take care of its own citizens; how can it care for so many refugees?' Simultaneously, the typical economic circle of capitalism has its risks. It eventually will turn once again, the real estate bubble will burst in certain cities and an enormous portion of the European population will potentially be trapped owning real estate in negative equity, condemned not just to repay huge mortgages, but also to bail out local and international banking sectors *ad infinitum*. The case of Spain, where riot police evict people who cannot afford to pay their mortgages, or of the Greek courthouses where house repossessions and compulsory distraints need to be approved in courtrooms occupied by riot police to keep the protesters out, the ghost suburbs of Ireland, built by developers during the boom who then went bust overnight, the empty holiday villages of Spain, the abandoned infrastructures of excess all around Europe, are all potential images of the collective European future. A future that scares European citizens. Britain has already opted to leave the EU as reaction, while the rest of the forces that support the dissolution of the EU were enhanced during the elections that took place over the last few years.

V RESCUING EUROPE?

After the outbreak of the European financial crisis in 2008, one of the main spatial pillars of post-Cold War Europe – the mass transformation of the built environment and real estate and the related economic growth – has either been deregulated or has slowed dramatically.[11] Meanwhile, the schisms within the hypothetically common European identity are deeper than ever since the foundation of the EU. In light of such events the only main spatial axis of reference of post-Cold War Europe that remains intact, and thus it is necessity for Europe to emphasise, is border securitisation. Thus, I suggest that the refugees in 2015 came like a *deus ex machina*, to rescue Europe from its deep political and economic crises.

The refugee flow was instantly declared by all European governments as a 'crisis'. The claim was that the richest continent in the world could not afford to rescue and carry out the welfare of two to three million people who crossed its common borders over a period of two years. Europe, which in recent decades was supposedly a champion of rights and democracy, pointing the finger at other regions for not applying them, sacrifices in the name of border security principles such as the respect for the right to life, protection of children, and the right to mobility, among others. It is telling that according to the Greek deputy immigration minister, his counterpart the Belgian interior minister allegedly proposed to him as a policy of preventing refugee flows that Greece 'should push them [migrants and refugees] back to the sea' and 'should let them drown'.[12] Refugee flows were reinvented as a pan-European emergency, which we are all facing and which became the means of governing the entire continent, as well of blackmailing social consent at a time when most European political elites are struggling to get some consent to their policies.

In early 2016 the whole humanitarian refugee tragedy that unfolded along the Syrian–Balkan corridor was of little importance – if any at all – compared to the question of the region's border policing. Europe's leaders have spent their time negotiating where exactly the European borders lie, to which countries Europe will

---

[11] See D Dalakoglou, 'Infrastructural Gap: Commons, State and Anthropology' (2017) 20 City 822.

[12] 'Belgian State Secretary Accused of Saying "Let Them Drown", Characterises Statements as "Grotesque"' *New Europe* (28 January 2016) www.neweurope.eu/article/let-them-drown accessed 7 January 2019.

externalise the refugee 'problem' and how it will guard its common borders in order to decrease the flow of refugees and filter people through. The life of a few million human beings became a secondary question to be debated by the European leadership – acceptable collateral damage for the protection of European spatial exclusivity. This is the only spatial privilege that can be provided by the common of the EU these days, which is phenomenally cost-free for EU citizens. On the one hand, this securitisation of the common EU border is one of the last things that might hold Europe together; on the other hand, this process exhibits more and more explicitly elements from what Marc Mazower[13] has called the history of our 'Dark Continent'. Europe is not only the continent that became, in the post-Second World War era, the champion of human rights, refugee rights, and bourgeois democracy, the rest of the liberal values it proclaimed to advance. It is also the continent that produced Nazism and Fascism, and previously had pioneered very effective versions of colonialism, imperialism and the genocide of various populations characterised as inferior and undesired 'Others'.

---

[13]   M Mazower, *Dark Continent: Europe's Twentieth Century* (Penguin 1999).

PART V

Joining the Dots and the Way Forward

16

The European Crisis of Economic Liberalism

Can the Law Help?

Michelle Everson

I INTRODUCTION

The European Union is caught in a trap; but is this a trap of the European Union's own making? Following Dani Rodrik's analysis, the problem might be argued to be akin to the 'trilemma' associated with economic globalisation.[1] For as long as the Union fails to overcome its founding functionalism and eschews its own (federal) 'statalisation', it will only ever be able to guarantee two out of three cherished notions of economic integration, national sovereignty and democracy. The parings might vary: sovereignty can always be combined with (national) democracy, just as trade liberalisation can be undertaken in a democratic manner (albeit of the Europeanised variety); yet, the simultaneous presence of all three concepts is an impossibility, a simple and inevitable consequence of the effort to move beyond the traditional structures of the nation state in pursuit of a single, integrated European market.

A distressing conclusion certainly, but perhaps also one which might be doubted, at least as regards the Union's culpability for various current crises: at the borders of Europe, within the discourse on democratic deficit and within a regime of crisis law that still struggles to contain the consequences of a sovereign debt crisis. History has, after all, played its part in forcing the pace of European integration, demanding, for example, a response to the geopolitical upheaval of Soviet collapse by way of the Economic and Monetary Union (Treaty for European Union (TEU)) and eastern enlargement (Nice Treaty to Lisbon Treaty)). Events have been a constant companion to integration, sometimes clearly outpacing the constitutive will of the political actors and peoples of Europe: the moving target of an 'ever closer Union' established by the 1992 TEU, tells its own story of reliance upon a *telos* of integration as substitute for impossible concord between Europeans.

---

[1] D Rodrik, *The Globalization Paradox: Democracy and the Future of the World Economy* (Norton 2011).

And yet, the story of European crisis might also be told in a more universal and universalising vocabulary; a vocabulary that establishes a link with projects of market-building per se, and one that simultaneously reveals and undermines the normative validity of a commitment to economic integration. The EU is now in the grip of a crisis of economic liberalism and, more importantly, has been in that state for most of its, and its predecessors' (EEC and EC) existence. Economic liberalism, it may be argued, has always struggled to reconcile the irreconcilable, to marry the founding economic autonomy of its individual citizens with their collective will, or governing spirit; a struggle which, in the European setting, has variously found a particular expression in the 'disembedding' of national markets,[2] the creation of 'a market without with a state' (or 'states without a market'),[3] the turn away from collective governing efforts to governance within functionalist bureaucracies and the 'regulatory (technocratic) state'[4] and, latterly, in the self-defeating reification of the economic constitution and the establishment of 'authoritarian liberalism', albeit without the usual partner mechanism of a 'strong state'.[5] Leaving the tricky concept of sovereignty aside, democracy and markets are *of themselves* uncomfortable bedfellows, and are even more so in a setting where the direction of European travel has always been buffeted by unforeseen happenings such as financial crises.

The latter point becomes particularly important for a critical legal discussion of the Union and its crisis of economic liberalism, which not only recalls, in its appeal to the trope of 'liberalism', the long and intimate role played by law in market-building, but also points to a specific problem of European law; namely the heightened challenge of legal adaptation to facticity, or, in Habermasian terms, the (failed) struggle to establish European legal validity, both in the absence of a constitutive act and in the midst of the historical crisis of European economic liberalism. The highpoint of the crisis of European economic liberalism might now be identified in the utilitarian 'scientism' into which current efforts to master sovereign debt crisis has descended (see section II). Yet, as noted, the problem is far older, dating at least to the first wave of European economic liberalisation in the 1980s. In detailing this history, and the failure of European law either to constitute a sustaining form of economic liberalism for the EC and the EU (sections III and IV), this contribution aims initially, in an instance of pure critique, to unveil the underlying crisis of economic liberalism that frames all other EU crises. Thereafter,

---

[2] The term is taken from K Polanyi, *The Great Transformation: The Political and Economic Origins of Our Time*, (first published in 1944, Beacon Press 2001).

[3] The couplet is taken from Christian Joerges, paradigmatically, C Joerges, 'The Market without the State: States without a Market?: Two Essays on the Law of the European Economy' (1996) EUI working paper LAW No 96/2 http://cadmus.eui.eu/handle/1814/125 accessed 17 April 2018.

[4] G Majone, *Regulating Europe* (Routledge 1996).

[5] The term is taken from H Heller, 'Authoritarian Liberalism?' (2014) 21 European Law Journal 295. Heller is commentating on Carl Schmitt, and his notions of the strong state: see for a good summary of Schmitt's position, R Cristi, *Carl Schmitt and Authoritarian Liberalism: Strong State, Free Economy* (University of Wales Press 1998), especially the chapter on Schmitt and Hayek.

however, in returning to analyse the traces of Carl Schmitt's 'authoritarian liberalism', as well as the remnants of 'ordoliberalism' within European (German) jurisprudence (section V), the chapter takes a brief constructivist turn, asking whether law can guide European economic liberalism through its current crisis.

II WHERE HAVE ALL THE LIBERALS GONE?

To conclude, the present euro regime amounts to an attempt to enforce the structural convergence of eurozone economies on the Northern model. In purely economic terms, this does not appear strictly impossible. If convergence should be achieved, it not only would stabilize the common currency but might also allow more attractive macroeconomic options to be realized in the eurozone. In contrast to some of their critics . . . I thus do not consider the promoters and defenders of the present euro regime to be either ignorant or dogmatically blindfolded. They should at least be given credit for constructing a gigantic, and indeed hubristic, gamble of technocratic social engineering whose visionary goal is the creation of an integrated European economy that is fit for competition in the ever more contested global markets.[6]

Writing about the treatment of debtor states within the European Stability Mechanism (ESM), and the concretisation of eurozone fiscal probity within the oversight regime established for national budgets within the Treaty on Stability, Coordination and Governance (TSCG) (which also builds upon the Stability and Growth Pact), Fritz Scharpf's analysis takes issue with, among others, Joseph Stiglitz: the regime is not a product of technical economic naivete, but rather a carefully planned process, which aims to pry the inward-looking economies of southern Europe out of their sheltered cocoons of domestic preference and retarded competition. They will instead be reshaped by a structural 'reform', consisting, for example, of the divesting of state assets (privatisation programmes), the reconfiguration of labour law and the sweeping aside of restrictive economic policy, in order to transform them into leanly competitive economies, mercilessly exposed to global competitive forces, just as are their outward-looking northern counterparts.

Faced with the ESM, the TSCG and the brutal economic conditionalities imposed upon debtor nations by 'misnamed' Memoranda of Understanding, the immediate temptation for modern critique must be to decry the European crisis regime as an instance of neoliberalism gone dictatorial within 'memoranda of indifference' to the suffering unleashed on the populations of southern Europe. Yet, should Scharpf be correct that planned economic convergence is the name of the European crisis regime game, the neoliberal appellation must surely be doubted, at least to the degree that 'liberalism', understood as the guarantee of secured (constitutionalised) economic autonomy, appears to have been misplaced

---

[6] FW Scharpf, 'De-constitutionalization and Majority Rule: A Democratic Vision for Europe' (2016) MPIfG Discussion Paper 16/14 www.mpi-fg-koeln.mpg.de/pu/mpifg_dp/dp16-14.pdf accessed 17 April 2018.

within the governing couplet of neoliberalism. Instead, this 'gigantic' and 'hubristic' exercise 'in social engineering' can only be understood in starkly utilitarian terms; either with regard to the functionalist project to salvage the euro, or, at a deeper level, as a reflection of the 'scienticism' or 'pseudo-rationalism',[7] which has assailed and overcome modern economic theory, replacing normative precepts of autonomy with a totalising faith in the steering capacities of a projected (objective) reality of economic and social processes.

For Scharpf, the utilitarian functionalism of an imposed convergence regime resides in its avowedly technocratic nature, or the stark refusal to countenance the democratisation of European Economic and Monetary Union. So, as Scharpf relates, the moral suasion that might thus be conceivably unleashed in favour of the immediate establishment of a transfer union would, in its opponents' view, most likely only result in a perpetuation of economic asymmetry and dependence, mirroring the continuing reliance of East German states upon their western counterparts, and replicating all of the political resentments that disfigure each and every dependency relationship, abusive or otherwise. In a European context, lasting economic and political asymmetry could only stand as an enduring barrier to a proper (politicised) union. In contrast, maintenance of the current regime and the veiled technocratic pursuit of European structural convergence certainly creates today's slaves, but might also, in a converged future, re-elevate debtor nations into equal contracting partners within a eurozone able to establish a full political union of redistribution.

Scharpf himself has little time for such prospective utilitarianism, correctly denouncing an absolutism of present economic suffering for future political gain, and suggests, instead, an immediate reform of EMU as an ERM mechanism (ERM II), designed to tackle also the often-overlooked problem exacerbating economic asymmetry in Europe: the lack of German profligacy.

But, for yet others, the utilitarianism of economic conditionality, or its common good of welfare maximisation, is not to be found in a posited future of redistributive political settlement, but rather, today as tomorrow, in an intrinsic commitment to efficient allocation, or to an objective reality of market-mediated steering capacities for maximised *universal* welfare.[8] The by-now famous crisis judgments of the Court of Justice of the European Union (CJEU) in *Pringle* and in *Gauweiler*,[9] giving

---

[7]   Scientism is a term belonging to Freidrich Hayek. The concept of pseudo-rationalism belongs to Otto Van Neurath. The two corresponded with one another around the terms, and although Hayek refused to recognise their complementary nature, each author was concerned with rebutting the assertion that economic process might ever be governed to certain ends. For details, see the work of John O'Neil, exemplary, J O'Neil, 'Knowledge, Planning and Markets: a Missing Chapter in the Socialist Calculation Debates' (2006) 22 Economics and Philosophy 55.

[8]   The point is perhaps best made by Ernst-Joachim Mestmäcker in his critique of Rischard Posner: economic rationality (neoliberalism) is 'socialism' (EJ Mestmäcker, *A Legal Theory without Law – Posner v. Hayek on Economic Analysis of Law* (Mohr-Siebeck 2007)).

[9]   Case C-62/14, *Peter Gauweiler and Others v Deutscher Bundestag* EU:C:2015:400; Case 370/12, *Pringle v Ireland* EUC:2012:756.

European legal approval, first, for the ERM and thereafter, for the European Central Bank's (ECB) secondary market transactions, are shocking, to the exact degree that they reproduce the predominant culture of reification of a science of objective reality. A culture within which markets supply a natural welfare, overseen, not by politics or the state, but by the mandated ability of technical expertise to guide and sustain *given* processes of economic and social organisation. Brute facts exist and supply welfare.

> This case is decided upon an economic theory which a large part of the country does not entertain. If it were a question whether I agreed with that theory, I should desire to study it further and long before making up my mind. But I do not conceive that to be my duty, because I strongly believe that my agreement or disagreement has nothing to do with the right of a majority to embody their opinions in law.[10]

For critical lawyers, natural fans of the dissenting opinion of Justice Holmes, the parallels between the majority opinion of the US Supreme Court in *Lochner* (1905) and the CJEU in *Pringle* are striking and enticing: embarrassed by the European Treaty's normative ban upon monetary inflation within the eurozone (Article 123 TFEU), the CJEU grasps at the notion of 'economic conditionality' in order to legitimise its condoning of ESM operation, thereby undermining the democratic processes of debtor Member States. Yet, the parallel is far from perfect, especially where the European Court's reliance in *Gauweiler* on the technocratic expertise of the ECB is considered contemporaneously. Unlike majority opinion within *Lochner*, the European Court cannot and does not draw on liberal notions of the freedom of contract to override democratic decision-making; neither is it drawing upon an economic theory that has established its own normative purchase in, say, the general commitment of the US Constitution to liberal autonomy. Instead, the European Court overrides both its own constitutional settlement[11] and democratic process in reliance upon an economic science that exists outside *all* structures of normative direction, and which is overseen by technocratic knowledge alone: 'a highly technical terrain in which it is necessary to have an expertise and experience which, according to the Treaties, devolves solely upon the ECB'.[12]

Here we might identify the apex of the crisis of economic liberalism within European crisis management, its self-unravelling subsuming of Hayek's bête noir of totalising scientism, first, in alienation of political and normative direction, or in adherence to the credo that market forces efficiently allocate resources in the material world of economic and social transactions. But, second, also in a reification of the technical expertise which, it is posited, can grasp and steer this

---

[10] *Lochner v People of State of* New York, US Supreme Court, 198 US 45 (1905), Justice Holmes dissenting.

[11] See G Beck, 'The Legal Reasoning of the Court of Justice and the Euro Crisis – The Flexibility of the Court's Cumulative Approach and the *Pringle* Case' (2013) 20 Maastricht Journal of European and Comparative Law 645.

[12] Case C-62/14 *Gauweiler* (n 9) EU:C:2015:7, Opinion of AG Cruz Villalón, para 111.

objective reality within its own scientific methodologies, intervening in order to guarantee maximised welfare, not as a normative project, but as a given part of objective reality, or as an observable outcome of natural human interaction. An anathema to Hayek, or to his commitment to the independent value of autonomy within human (economic) affairs,[13] scientism, or, in Otto van Neurath's 'complementary' left analysis, pseudo-rationalism,[14] is not only reproduced throughout the European crisis regime, but also dominates global schemes of risk regulation introduced to prevent a repeat of the 2008 financial crisis. The comparison is instructive: where a duty is placed upon global bankers, including the ECB, to expunge a technocratically construed notion of systemic risk from global financial systems, modern economic liberalism can only be grasped as an affront to Hayekian uncertainty, or to the normative primacy of unknown and unknowable outcomes within markets.[15] By the same token, however, it also reveals the underlying fallacy of a pseudo-rationalism that can never fully accept the outcomes of material reality and, needs to, indeed must, recolonise the 'objective' goal of welfare maximisation, ceding the political or constitutive component within its interventionism to central bankers who must now decide just how much uncertainty (lost-opportunity costs) or just how much risk (innovation) is required and when within the global economy.[16]

This all begs the question – where have all the liberals gone? Whether sacrificed to the utilitarianism of the functionalist integration impulse, dissolved within a scientific materialism of utilitarian welfare maximisation, compromised within the absence of constitutive effects, or wholly traduced within a pseudo-rationalism which inexorably concludes within the illiberally technocratic redistribution of resources, contemporary economic liberalism within the EU (and throughout the globe) has misplaced its liberal roots. It has lost its commitment to autonomy, or its aspiration to constitute individual and market autonomy, and has thereby also reneged upon its mission to regulate relations between autonomous and collective action (the market and politics).

III ECONOMIC INTEGRATION: DISEMBEDDING OR DISEMBEDDED LIBERALISM?

Indeed, by restricting the employer's ability to dismiss the workers collectively, the rule at issue merely gives the impression of being protective of workers. To begin with, that protection is only temporary until the employer becomes insolvent. Even more importantly, workers are

---

13   Continued even into his final writings, see, for an instructive example, with similar reference to the error of 'scientism', F Hayek, 'The Pretence of Knowledge' (1989) 79 American Economic Review 6.
14   See O'Neil (n 7).
15   For exhaustive explanation of the loss of 'uncertainty' in economic governing, J Pixley, 'Uncertainty: The Curate's Egg in Financial Economics' (2014) 65 British Journal of Sociology 200.
16   M Everson, 'Banking on Union: EU Governance between Risk and Uncertainty' in M Dawson, H Enderlein and C Joerges (eds), *The Governance of Europe's Economic, Political and Legal Transformation* (OUP 2015).

best protected by an economic environment which fosters stable employment. Historically speaking, the idea of artificially maintaining employment relationships, in spite of unsound general economic foundations, has been tested and has utterly failed in certain political systems of yesteryear. That provides confirmation that, in laying down an effective yet flexible protective procedure, Directive 98/59 affords genuine protection for workers, whereas a system of prior authorisation such as that at issue, which tellingly falls outside its scope, does not.[17]

Far less well known than *Pringle* or *Gauweiler*, the CJEU case of *Iraklis* dating from 2015, is nevertheless an exemplary child of the European crisis regime and of the anchoring of its economic utilitarianism within European law. The observations of the Advocate General are particularly revealing: faced with a Greek law requiring consultation with an independent Economic Council prior to mass redundancies in the concrete industry, the AG's argumentative language is one of economics and not of law. Shocking enough in its own right; nevertheless, critical outrage can only grow when confronted with the AG's economic fatalism. The Greek state is a naive child to be lectured about the economic facts of life. Markets are a given of observable human interaction and will supply workers with optimal welfare within their own objective realities and the technical frameworks of European regulation that are derived from observation of the market (Collective Redundancies Directive 98/59/EC). Voluntaristic human agency, or normative intervention within markets, is revealed in this AG's historical reading, to be a chimera akin to raging against the rising of the sun, and doomed only to end in counterproductive failure.

Naivety, however, is clearly the AG's alone, as he mislays vast swathes of successful industrial and economic policy from the New Deal to the present day. Yet, the mere fact that senior jurists so casually and confidently voice their childish reproductions of a dominantly utilitarian economic orthodoxy is disturbing indeed, hinting not simply at the totalising subjection of law to economic determinism, but also at increasing disjunction between law and liberalism, or law as mediator within a liberal market-making that takes seriously its mission to place markets in a normative context of governing. For many, the fault lies in the concept of economic liberalism itself, deemed to be a self-defeating project that falters on its own contradictions:[18] we shall return to this point (section VI). In the meantime, however, both taking a critical legal standpoint, and conceding the optimistic point that the European integration project continues to represent the most advanced and promising effort to tame a state of global economic nature, the analysis first asks how we got to where we are now. As it will be shown, the problem is twofold, relating both to the struggle of European law to establish its own validity, as well as the difficulties faced by European economic law and liberalism in adapting to 'happenings'. Though changing in its gestalt, this challenge has remained constant, as has the 'instructive' futility of all attempts to address it.

---

[17] Case C-201/15 AGET *Iraklis* EU:C:2016:429, Opinion of the Advocate General Wahl.
[18] H Brunkhorst, *Das Doppelte Gesicht Europas – Zwischen Kapitalismus und Demokratie* (Suhrkamp Verlag 2014).

1 'Integration through Law': Law of Its Own Making, Master of All It Surveys

Tucked away in the fairyland Duchy of Luxembourg and blessed, until recently, with benign neglect by the powers that be and the mass media, the Court of Justice of the European Communities has fashioned a constitutional framework for a federal-type Europe.[19]

The history of the European Court of Justice (ECJ) is one that has long fascinated since it seems to confirm the existence of a legal culture of argumentation that is accepted over and above national legal systems. The revolutionary ability of European law to assert its norms outside traditional structures of legal power lays the basis for its claim to be a law *sui generis*, but also leaves the observer with a tantalising question: can it really be that, like Baron von Münchhausen, European law extricated itself from the swamp by its own hair, achieving a status more powerful than that of international law and intergovernmental politics, to impose its validity on sovereign states?

The self-narratives of European lawyers leave little room for doubt. The interpretation of the European system as a supranational legal community was an ingenious ECJ invention. Its jurisprudence has found such widespread support, in the legal system and beyond, that it can be regarded as the dominant orthodoxy of Community law. The gradual construction of this legal architecture is a story that is often told, but perhaps nowhere better than in Weiler's foundational account, wherein 'direct effect', 'supremacy', 'pre-emption' and the transformation of economic freedoms into fundamental subjective rights as the 'law of the land', are born of the interpretative prerogative of the ECJ; a prerogative which has impressed itself upon generations of lawyers, and continues to do so within their reception of an integration though law orthodoxy.[20] By contrast, it took considerable effort on the part of critical legal and sociological study to remind us that the constitutionalisation of the EEC Treaty was an audacious, elite-driven exercise.[21]

The extraordinary success story of the integration through law orthodoxy continues to amaze. Joseph Weiler underlined early on in his writings that the supremacy of European law was anything other than self-sustaining; instead, acceptance for its operation was held in precarious equilibrium, and dependent upon continuous political processes of intergovernmentalism and continuing commitment to the defence of community spirit.[22] Yet, a later, much-cited, 1990 essay downplays the constitutional element within the saga, laying renewed emphasis upon the

[19]   E Stein, 'Lawyers, Judges and the Making of a Transnational Constitution' (1981) 75 AJIL 27.
[20]   A particularly noteworthy confirmation is the restatement of the orthodoxy by the London High Court: *R Miller and others v Secretary of State for Exiting the European Union* [2016] EWHC 2768 (Admin), [2017] 1 All ER 158.
[21]   See, for example, A Borger and M Rasmussen, 'Transforming European Law: The Establishment of the Constitutional Discourse from 1950 to 1993' (2014) 10 European Constitutional Law Review 119; highly critical, AS Sweet 'The Juridical Coup d'État and the Problem of Authority' (2007) 8 European Law Journal 915.
[22]   JHH Weiler, 'The Community System: The Dual Character of Supranationalism' (1981) 1 Yearbook of European Law 257.

integrationist impetus: law, we are told, could and should operate as 'the object and the agent of integration'.[23]

The flaws within this defining expression of the integration through law movement are many, but may, for our purposes, be summarised in three interrelated points. First, an integrationist trend suggests that legal diversity is bad per se and that legal uniformity is a defining feature of Europe's 'constitutional charter'; a command mode of law that must surely be questioned in its claim to outlaw the validity claims of constitutional democracies? Methodologically speaking, the integration through law movement equally assigns a mysterious strength to the 'law as such' and seems unhealthily fixated with the strictly legal operations of the judiciary and administrative bodies, avoiding any deeper investigation of the sources of legal legitimacy. But perhaps the most intriguing flaw within the integration through law movement is the camouflage which it has provided for an agenda that has at times been out of step with the post-war European welfare state consensus. The EEC was not designed to dismantle national social competences. Nevertheless, implicit within the law through integration movement was the destruction of the protective '"embeddedness" of post-war liberalism',[24] an agenda which had to be hidden.

2 Ordoliberalism: a Normative Outlier?

Law functions both as a mask and as a shield. It hides and protects the promotion of one particular set of objectives against contending objectives in the purely political sphere.[25]

Writing in 1993, Burley and Mattli's observation has been proved true many times over,[26] and particularly so, with regard to the close affinities between the dominant integrationist doctrines of European law and the radicalised political liberalism that dominated much western economic and social policy of the 1980s, just as the European project entered into its second stage of intensified market building. A body of law committed to integration and constrained only by its preoccupation with the coherence of its internal operations, became the perfect vehicle for totalising forces of market liberalisation. One close relation of the Thatcherism–Reaganism couplet, however, had already found some purchase within European institutions at the very founding of the EEC: German ordoliberalism.

Ordoliberalism has a unique place in any discussion of economic liberalism. Ordoliberalism distinguishes itself by virtue of its recognition of the interdependence

---

[23] R Dehousse and JHH Weiler, 'The Legal Dimension' in W Wallace (ed), *The Dynamics of European Integration* (Pinter 1990).

[24] On the concept, see famously JG Ruggie, 'International Regimes, Transactions and Change: Embedded Liberalism in the Postwar Economic Order' (1982) 36 International Organization 379.

[25] AM Burley and W Matti, 'Europe before the Court: A Political Theory of Legal Integration' (1993) 47 International Organization 41, 72.

[26] Exemplary, F Scharpf, 'Monetary Union, Fiscal Crisis and the Pre-emption of Democracy' (2011) 9 Zeitschrift für Staats- und Europawissenschaften 163.

of autonomous legal and economic orders in the establishment and protection of competitive processes (the market). An explicitly normative endeavour, given expression in the ordoliberal term 'economic constitution' (*Wirtschaftsverfassung*), to place market relations within a broader context of liberal governing, the operational history of ordoliberalism dates back to the Weimar Republic, where its founding fathers advocated a conflicts framework, designed to guarantee individual economic freedoms, but simultaneously to hold them in check through a system of law ensuring undistorted competition. At core, a theory of self-limiting liberal government designed to foster markets, 'ordoliberalism' become one of the founding elements of the young German federal republic, in particular, by virtue of compromises made with its opponents in its grudging recognition of the competing concept of the 'social market economy'.[27]

Various of its exponents, among them Walter Hallstein, Franz Böhm and Alfred Müller-Armack, engaged enthusiastically with the early processes of European integration: conceptually, ordoliberalism was particularly suited to the European realm, justifying, in its self-limiting liberal mode, the theorem of the primacy of European law and further detailing the precise, and similarly self-limiting 'constitutional' economic content of European integration: individual economic freedoms guaranteed by the founding Treaty, the opening up of national economies, non-discrimination principles and competition rules were all easily represented as a collective decision in favour of an economic constitution that mirrored and matched the ordoliberal framework conditions for establishment of a market economic system. More fundamentally, the simple fact that Europe began its life as an economic community, lent enduring plausibility to ordoliberal arguments: where Europe could be portrayed as a law-based order, committed to the guarantee of economic freedoms, it attained an 'apolitical' legitimacy of its own, independent of the institutions of the democratic constitutional state.[28] The constitution of the EEC as a 'market without a state' could go largely unremarked.

Today, German ordoliberalism has attained a striking prominence, albeit one with deeply irritating qualities. We will return to ordoliberalism below. In the meantime, however, it should be noted simply that the normative characteristics of ordoliberalism did not win widespread support in the formative European years, and barely registered outside Germany. Within Germany itself, and despite compromise, conflict still raged between the Ministry for Economic Affairs (pro) and the Federal Foreign Office (anti).[29] As Giandomenico Majone adds soberly and

---

[27] See, in particular, the contributions in J Hien and C Joerges (eds), *Ordoliberalism, Law and the Rule of Economics* (Hart 2017).

[28] A Müller-Armack, 'Die Wirtschaftsordnung des Gemeinsamen Marktes' in A Müller-Armack (ed), *Wirtschaftsordnung und Wirtschaftspolitik: Studien und Konzepte zur sozialen Marktwirtschaft und zur europäischen Integration* (Rombach 1966).

[29] W Abelshauser, 'Deutsche Wirtschaftspolitik zwischen Europäischer Integration und Weltmarktorientierung' in W Abelshauser (ed), *Das Bundeswirtschaftsministerium in der Ära der Sozialen Marktwirtschaft. Der Deutsche Weg der Wirtschaftspolitik* (de Gruyter 2016).

soberingly:[30] in the 1950s, *planification* and interventionist practices were common-place within the founding states. How could defeated Germany, of all states, have prevailed at the European level with a concept that had not even won full domestic approval?

3 'Self-limiting' Functionalism: a Road Not Taken

If one thing unites the integration through law movement and the ordoliberal vision of a transnational economic constitution, it is their failure to understand, let alone acknowledge the real character of the European machinery, the *factum brutum* that dominant practice was always functionalistic and technocratic. This phenomenon was instead captured as a conceptual legal orientation early on in the integration process by Hans Peter Ipsen in his characterisation of the (three) European Communities as 'purposive associations for functional integration'.[31] Experiencing a particular renaissance in the intense period of market integration beginning in the mid-eighties, the functionalist concept of the 'special-purpose association' allowed the development of Community law practices beyond the self-limiting strictures of ordoliberal economic constitutionalism, dispensing also with a liberal appellation, at least as regards its approbation for positive regulatory action. At the same time, however, it continued to obviate the demand for democratic legitimation of the Community in self-limiting terms: as a special-purpose association, Europe only *did* technical matters or administrative tasks that ought properly to be assigned to a supranational bureaucracy.[32] Ipsen rejected federal integration concepts and early interpretations of the Community as an international organisation. For him, Community law constituted a *tertium quid* between (federal) national law and international law, that was adequately legitimated through its 'specialized tasks'.[33]

Ipsen was highly influential in the Federal Republic but hardly noticed beyond its borders. A notable exception is the political scientist Giandomenico Majone, who acknowledged the affinities between Ipsen's conceptualisation of the integration project and his own renewal of the technocratic legacy in his reconceptualisation of the Community as a 'regulatory state'.[34] Was this the chance to contain totalising economic integration within Europe, albeit in functionalist rather than liberal terms? Like Ipsen, Majone insistently underlined that his functionalism was designed to restrict the reach of Community activities and to pay principled respect to the democratic legitimacy of the Member States. Also, like Ipsen, Majone identified the strength of the integration project within the problem-solving capacity of European institutions, or application of expert knowledge. The European level

---

[30] G Majone, *Rethinking the Union of Europe Post-Crisis. Has Integration Gone Too Far?* (CUP 2010).
[31] HP Ipsen, *Europäisches Gemeinschaftsrecht* (Mohr 1972).
[32] ibid.
[33] See Joerges (n 3).
[34] See Majone (n 4).

should be made up of 'non-majoritarian' institutions, including the Commission, and US-type independent agencies. The two authors nevertheless part company where Ipsen, writing in the 1970s, is functionalist *in se*, concerned simply to ensure the infiltration of the administration into society. Majone, by contrast, avails himself of modern theories of regulation and social choice to correct market failure, but also to maximise the economically defined welfare of consumers and citizens. The distinction is important: the institutionalisation of a 'fourth branch of government' to guard against 'regulatory failure' must also be legitimated and held accountable through indirect but effective control. At the same time, Majone considers the non-majoritarian institutions of European regulatory politics and the majoritarian institutions of the Member States to be complementary to one another, with European regulatory action confined to issues with no redistributive consequences.[35]

Separated from one another by two decades and different methodological backgrounds, Ipsen and Majone leave us with a single query: did their conceptualisations contain a legitimacy-generating potential? The answer is depressing: each conception found itself at odds with two competing forces, namely, the inexorable desire of European politics for more Europe on the one hand, and the totalising drive for more market on the other.

4 'Ever Closer Union': Facticity Unchained?

Looking back from a distance of almost thirty years, the enduring paradox of the closer Union announced in the Treaty of Union of 1992, is one that European reform following geopolitical upheaval was not presented to European publics within an explicitly (federalist) constitutive dialogue. However, still caught in the age-old trap between divergent national interests, Commission President Delors was careful to eschew constitutional discourse, establishing instead a modernisation package containing just enough social democratic and free market ingredients to ensure that the support of divergent Member States such as the UK and Germany was not alienated. In so doing, he continued the trend established in the 1980s of more (political) Europe and more market, without, however, solving and instead intensifying the evolving strains in the relationship between European economic liberalism and its wider environment of social and political interaction.

(1) Deregulation as Re-regulation

The legendary internal market initiative kick-started by the European Commission 1985 White Paper was one of the most successful planks in Jacques Delors's modernisation strategy, overcoming, at a stroke the majority voting barrier to the harmonisation of national economies, and ending, 'at the wave of its magical wand'

---

[35] See M Everson, 'Independent Agencies: Hierarchy Beaters' (1995) 1 European Law Journal 180.

economic stagnation.[36] Different explanations for this renewed impetus abound. Political scientists emphasise the neo-functionalist cunning of Delors and his ability to win the support of conflicting interests for the internal market.[37] Economists point to the economically rationalist shift in national opinion. Lawyers, by contrast, remain convinced that the negatively integrative approach of the ECJ to national economic regulation and its establishment of the principle of mutual recognition (*Cassis de Dijon* 1979)[38] was decisive, especially as mutual recognition became a founding feature of the Commission's White Paper. Whatever the background, however, the 1987 Single European Act confirmed this institutional innovation and introduced (qualified) majority voting for all internal market decision-making; a change of fundamental importance both for practical European policymaking and for the character of European law as an (economic) constitution.

Delors's internal market programme might have been rooted in the effort to promote economic rationality, but nevertheless also began the process of evolution of the multifaceted European polity which culminated in the TEU's commitment to a 'social Europe', its conferral of industrial policy competences upon the Union and its strengthening of social regulation. Market integration had inexorably given rise to its own re-embedding at European level.

A 'second generation' of ordoliberal scholars had attentively followed development of the integration project. Aware of the growing influence of a more aggressive form of Anglo-Saxon economic theorising, they were deeply concerned by the displacement of their commitment to 'free competition' by the principle of 'economic efficiency' within European competition policy,[39] but also by the broadening of Union competences in the Maastricht Treaty to include industrial policy.[40] They were nevertheless welcoming of *Cassis*, and the new emphasis laid on the principle of mutual recognition, which, the German economics ministry explained[41] would further regulatory competition, exposing national legislation to economic rationality tests.

Yet, expectations that further deregulation and privatisation would follow were thwarted. Instead, and far faster than either supporters or critics of the internal market programme had foreseen. New regulatory trends evolved. Regulatory interventions were intense, and most particularly so in relation to consumer and health interests. But even in the domains of private economic law, the 'completion' of the

---

[36] Joerges (n 3).

[37] A Moravcsik, 'Negotiating the Single European Act: National Interests and Conventional Statecraft in the European Community' (1991) 45 *International Organization* 19.

[38] Case 120/78 *Cassis de Dijon* EU:C:1979:42.

[39] See A Wigger, *The Politics of European Competition Regulation: A Critical Political Economy Perspective* (Routledge 2011).

[40] M Streit and W Müller, 'The Economic Constitution of the European Community: From "Rome" to "Maastricht"' (1995) 1 *European Law Journal* 5.

[41] Wissenschaftlicher Beirat beim Bundesministerium für Wirtschaft, *Stellungnahme zum Weißbuch der EG-Kommission über den Binnenmarkt* (Schriften-Reihe 51), Bonn 1986.

internal market was characterised by lacking faith in principles of mutual recognition between Member States and a concomitant growth and steady refinement of new, positive economic regulation and consumer protection policies, and the coordination of Community and national oversight competences, often within new administrative bodies located at European level.

(2) The Stability Community

All of this was incompatible with the ordoliberal vision of a European economic constitution. Intense regulatory activity documented mistrust in the self-regulatory potential of markets. This much is undisputed: as much as national and Member State interests may have coalesced around the internal market programme, the intense re-regulation that followed in its wake was not simply unloved but also raised both practical and normative demands for the legitimation and control of Europe's burgeoning administrative structures; demands to which refined regulatory theories still struggle to respond (see section V). At the same time, however, the internal market initiative was, in its outcome, an affront to ordoliberalism's commitment to the self-limitation of the state within the economic constitution, at least on the 'micro-economic' level.[42] It is all the more surprising therefore that ever closer Union was also noteworthy for the re-emergence of ordoliberal principles within the macroeconomic constitution of Europe.

Macroeconomic policies throughout post-war Europe were a Keynesian domain. Yet, Keynesianism faltered in the 1970s, undone by the pressure of simultaneously high unemployment and inflation. Monetarism and rational expectation economics became the new creed, with the Bundesbank adopting the new learning. European monetary policy was forced to follow, but, in EMU, evolved its own distinct features including: an exclusive European competence in the (undefined) field of monetary policy; the independence of the ECB and its primary commitment to price stability; the respect for national autonomy in fiscal and economic policy; and the addition to the new regime in 1997 of the Growth and Stability Pact, which was designed to coordinate national economic policy but which remained, in its soft law form, a *lex imperfecta*.

Today, debate on the EMU is dominated by a decade of financial crisis and doubts about the euro, including the extreme risks of deviating from it. It should not be forgotten, however, that the Maastricht Treaty was a catalyst for the politicisation of Europe and the creation of Eurosceptic publics in the years preceding its ratification. EMU was widely understood as a response to German reunification, as a counterweight to the potential dominance of the continent by the newly reunified Republic, its deutschmark and its Bundesbank: i.e., *preoccupation* with German dominance but no enthusiasm for an 'ever closer union'. Approved only by

---

[42]   K Tuori and K Tuori, *The Eurozone Crisis: A Constitutional Analysis* (CUP 2014) 13.

a slim majority in a French referendum, first rejected and then accepted by Danes, the Maastricht Treaty was also a subject of a constitutional complaint made before the German Constitutional Court. The complaint was rejected. Nevertheless, the Constitutional Court's judgment, delivered on 12 October 1993,[43] has gone down as a milestone in European legal history, as national constitutional judges rebelled against the self-enunciated constitutionalism principles of the ECJ, at the same time re-establishing the primacy within the process of European integration of German constitutional commitments, including a German constitutional commitment to price stability.

The Judgment is perhaps best known for the German Court's downgrading of the supranational character of the EU, their denoting of it as a mere 'association of states' (*Staatenverbund*), overseen by its Member States as the 'Masters of the Treaties', and by the German Court as a guarantor of the German Constitution; and, above all, as a guarantor for German national democratic process (paragraph 186). The judgment also caused significant disquiet within the European legal commentariat of the time,[44] appearing to herald a significant renationalisation of the European integration process. Its misguided reference to concepts developed by Herman Heller in particular, asserting that 'a certain degree of social homogeneity' was a prerequisite for democratic exchange, drew the ire of writers who noted that the Court's emphasis upon *ethnos* rather than the *demos* could only retard the pace of democratised European integration.[45]

In a final analysis, however, European legal response to communitarian German democratic recidivism has proved, with time, to be a mere distraction from the core problem created and left to European legal posterity by the Maastricht judgement, or its renewed reliance upon the underpinning constitutional norms of ordoliberalism, even though the facts of integration had moved Europe far beyond the self-limiting liberal government envisaged by the founding theory. The Maastricht Treaty was approved by the Court: in particular, EMU was held to be in full accord with the provisions of the German Constitution since, on the one hand, the German Parliament had the right, prior to completion of monetary union, to examine the fulfilment of the Treaty criteria on price stability and convergence (paragraph 202), and, on the other, since the German ratification law would no longer be valid should monetary union not follow the 'the agreed stability mandate' (paragraph 205). The core paradox in the Court's reasoning is readily apparent. First, it seeks to preserve the powers of the nation state. However, economic integration is perceived as an apolitical phenomenon occurring autonomously outside the states, and EMU as a project given functional legitimacy by its commitment to a politically neutral notion of price stability. Economic integration, in this reading, would never be

---

[43]   *Brunner v European Union Treaty* [1994] 1 CMLR 57.
[44]   JHH Weiler, 'Does Europe Need a Constitution? Reflections on Demos, Telos and the German Maastricht Decision' (1995) 1 European Law Journal 219.
[45]   See, in particular, Majone (n 4).

subject to ongoing constitutional review for its democratic qualities. Europe would become a 'market without a state' and the so-called 'Masters of the Treaties' would be left as 'states without markets'; a prescription that has come back to haunt Europe during financial and sovereign debt crises.

IV CONSTITUTION BY 'GOVERNANCE'

A familiar, if not widespread story of European integration is one that emphasises the disembedding of national economies within the economic rationalities of the new single market. The story is also well corroborated: long prior to hubristic techno-cratic efforts to enforce structural economic convergence within the eurozone, established and complex modes of cooperative or corporatist national regulation had fallen victim to rationalising European regulation, sometimes for an arguable good, but sometimes with unforeseen and highly prejudicial consequences.[46]

A natural corollary to this tale, however, is one that emphasises the role of economic liberalism, even in its more benign ordoliberal form, within this dissolution,[47] a conclusion that is hard to deny even where an 'ordoliberalisation' of Europe misrepresents the influence of an original German, economic constitu-tionalism: the Maastricht judgment of the German Constitutional court neverthe-less continues to a less than benign influence (section VI).

An overlooked component within this analysis, however, is the one of the con-temporaneous disembedding of traditional European economic liberalism, at the most obvious and simplest level, within the empty functionalism of a self-defining European law that appeared to concern itself with the 'constitutional' empowerment of individual autonomy when setting nation regulation aside, but which silently tolerated the re-materialisation of European law within a corollary impetus for social policy and regulation. In a more complex formulation: old-style, ordoliberal con-cern about the alienation of national social and economic policy competences and their reallocation to the European level, is not only an expression of a fear that the European market might be contaminated by illegitimate politics, lying far beyond the 'politics of order', or an *Ordnungspolitik* dedicated to preservation of undistorted supply and demand. It is also an expression of concern that the constitutive–regulative relationship established between the national market and the state would be shattered and no European equivalent established.[48]

In short, for as much as the EU's 'constitutional moment' of the early 2000s was a moment full of potential for progressive European forces of social or federal

---

[46] ibid.

[47] See Brunkhorst (n 18).

[48] See Wigger (n 39). Above all, the real time shift in European competition policy from an emphasis upon 'free and fair competition' to one of 'efficiency', was not a simple matter of concern about technical elaboration of competition law, but one about a fundamental shift away from a Hayekian dedication to supply and demand as guarantor for liberal autonomy within the market to a utilitarian preoccupation with markets as suppliers of optimal welfare.

renewal, it might also be argued to have been an instance pregnant with promise for economic liberalism; a moment in which a proper European Economic Constitution might be established and its relationship with other spheres of human endeavour be constituted. Both progressives and economic liberals were to be disappointed by the constitutional convention however; even though perspectives for reform at the day-to-day institutional level of market regulation and management was far greater.

> The question ultimately arises as to whether this simplification and reorganisation might not, in the long run, lead to the adoption of a constitutional text in the Union ... In order to pave the way for the next Intergovernmental Conference ... the European Council has decided to convene a Convention ... [I]t will be the task of this Convention to consider the key issues arising for the Union's future and try to identify the various possible responses. (Laeken Declaration 2001)

Given the cautiously vague language deployed by the European Council in launching the post-millennial European constitutionalisation programme, it is perhaps less than surprising that the sequence of constitutional reform begun by the Nice Treaty (2001) ended only in the disappointment of the 2009 Lisbon Treaty with all of its traditional EU elements of competence creep, paired with institutional compromise to paper over the cracks of incomplete federalisation. By contrast, the February 2000 speech delivered to the European Parliament by the President of the Commission, Romano Prodi, announced ambitious reforms to European governance. This was a message spoken in a new vocabulary with fresh reform agenda incorporating new political actors, as well as civil society. The promise was one of a package of innovation launched strategically into a legally non-defined space located somewhere between constitutional and administrative reform.

Nor was Prodi's speech mere rhetoric: in 2000, plagued by ongoing concern about the creeping competences of a re-regulated European market, faced with the organisational bombshell of eastward enlargement and confronted with the complaints of an increasingly Eurosceptic European public about 'the democratic malaise that Europe is suffering',[49] the demand for meaningful reform was unmistakeable and the programmatic subtitle of the Commission's Working Programme, 'Enhancing Democracy in the European Union', is particularly revealing in its millennial reform aspirations.

'Governance' has become such a commonplace term at all levels of private and public organisation that it is all too easy to forget its particular meaning and promise within systems such as the European Union. Long in vogue within international relations theory, governance was adopted by European political scientists to describe the decision-making processes formed within the EU system from the 1990s

---

[49] See Prodi's speech announcing the working programme on reforms (R Prodi, '2000–2005: Shaping the New Europe' Speech/00/41 (15 February 2000) 3 http://europa.eu/rapid/press-release_SPEECH-00–41_en.htm?locale=en accessed 17 April 2018.

onwards;[50] and, above all, to describe the proactive institutions of the single market designed to ensure its completion and to negate its social and political externalities. Accordingly, the term is analytically vague, dispensing with a normative charter to constitute institutions, and remaining open to the evolving modes of governing the expanding competences of the Union.[51]

This is not to reject the notion of governance however. As Philippe Schmitter convincingly argues,[52] the 'oversell and vagueness' of the concept notwithstanding, it is not simply an 'empty signifier'[53] but usefully designates 'a distinctive method/ mechanism for resolving conflicts and solving problems that reflects some profound characteristics of the exercise of authority that are emerging in almost all contemporary societies and economies'. It is a virtue of the concept that it captures actor configurations and problem-solving activities, which have emerged as responses to functional exigencies. Modern governance depends on, and similarly builds on, expert knowledge and the management capacities of enterprises and organisations. It cannot confine itself to law production and law application operating with the binary code of legal and illegal events and practices. It cannot be organised hierarchically. Seen in this light, the 'formalised' adoption of governance within European politics was an act full of promise and innovation. For years the Union had played host to extralegal developments and institutional innovations that had widened the discrepancies between the EU's activities and its formal legal structures. Where governance is a concept that also helps us to discover and to explain tensions between function and form, the Commission's Working Programme was a platform for constructive debate; or a debate that might achieve the impossible and reconstitute the relations between market and society, and do so within an evolving context of European integration.

Yet, debate disappointed, perhaps inevitably so: governance rather than 'government and administration' captures modern political action, its emphasis upon the social knowledge and the management capacities of enterprises and organisations, its eschewal of command and control policymaking and policy implementation, and its response to real social problems and to bottlenecks within the political system and its administrative machinery. This is the desired outcome, but it is also the problem, the point at which 'is' and 'ought' part company and the search for a sustaining governance *legitimation* is revealed as a simple chimera. In the final

---

[50] M Jachtenfuchs, 'The Governance Approach to European Integration' (2001) 39 Journal of Common Market Studies 245.

[51] On this concern, see C Joerges, 'Integration Through De-legalisation?' (2008) 33 European Law Review 289.

[52] P Schmitter, 'What Is There to Legitimize in the European Union ... and How Might This Be Accomplished?' in C Joerges, Mény, Weiler (eds), *Symposium: Mountain or Molehill? A Critical Appraisal of the Commission White Paper on Governance*, Jean Monnet Working Paper No 6/01, 79ff at 83 (the text is also available at www.iue.it/RSC/Governance and www.jeanmonnetprogram.org /papers/01/010601.html accessed 17 April 2018).

[53] C Offe, 'Governance: An 'Empty Signifier'?' (2009) 16 Constellations 550.

analysis, governance is a tool of political science and not of (constitutional) law; its value within the material context of political science is precisely one that it enables a necessary distinction between the efficiency of governance and its legitimacy. The European aspiration to marry governance to a programme of democratic legitimation could not but fail as the Commission's Governance Team responded to their brief within a metaphor of 'good governance', developing principles of openness, participation, accountability, effectiveness and coherence which,[54] while worthwhile individually, merely reproduced the technical mechanics of administrative legitimacy, and failed to address the underlying problems of autonomous versus collective action in and around market process. In its final version, the White Paper merely reproduced, alongside its delegalised commitment to coordination in the sphere of social policy (Open Method of Co-ordination), the unlimited functionalism of the original Community method; an unconvincing reproduction of Weber's bureaucratic rationality with regulatory competences for the market delegated from Council to Commission and then to the technocratic expertise of the EU's burgeoning 'fourth branch of government'.[55]

V BEYOND 'AUTHORITARIAN LIBERALISM'?

Through these references, a rough estimate of the substance of authoritarian liberalism appears to have been more or less adequately characterised: retreat of the 'authoritarian' state from social policy, liberalisation (Entstaatlichung) of the economy and dictatorial control by the state of politico-intellectual functions. According to Schmitt's quite credible reassurances, such a state has to be strong and 'authoritarian', for only a state of this type is able to sever the 'excessive' connections between the state and the economy. Of course, the German people would not tolerate for long this neoliberal state if it ruled in democratic forms.[56]

Hermann Heller's concluding excoriation of Carl Schmitt's assertion of the constitutional primacy liberal authoritarianism, unhappily recalls the arguments made by Fritz Scharpf: structural economic convergence is only possible within Europe in the *absence* of democratic process. At the same time, however, Heller's unpacking of Schmitt holds up a discomforting mirror, not simply to the immediate European (sovereign debt) crisis regime, but to the potential for the corruption of all economic liberalisms within economic integration.

Just as Prussian *Junckers* committed their original sin within a paradox of 'national liberalism',[57] or a forging of the 'free' market through aristocratic diktat, the category error of the European single market is to be identified in the negatively constitutive jurisprudence of the ECJ, in the *Cassis* Judgment, in the empty functionalism of the integration though law movement culminating in *Pringle*, as well as in the remedial attraction that ordoliberalism still holds for the contemporary German Constitutional

---

[54] Commission, 'European Governance: A White Paper' COM (2001) 428 final, 10.
[55] G Majone, 'The Rise of the Regulatory State in Europe' (1994) 17 *West European Politics* 77.
[56] Heller (n 5) 5.
[57] ibid 4.

Court (*TSCG/ESM*).[58] The direction of travel is inexorably one of *Entstaatlichung*, of divorce of the economy from Member States, from (European) democratic process, or from any source of the 'substantive liberal value', so derided by Schmitt as liberal nemesis:

> As the Bundestag can exercise the constitutionally required influence through its approval of stability support and can participate in the decision on the amount, terms and conditions and on the duration of stability support in favour of Members seeking help, the Bundestag itself lays the most important foundation of possible capital calls made in accordance with Article 2(9) TESM. (paragraph 274)

German constitutional approval for democratic process in the German Constitutional Court's parallel treatment of the European crisis regime (*ESM/TSCG*) is misleading. And not simply for the obvious reason that democratic voice for the German Bundestag is measured only in vassal status for debtor nations such as Greece. Rather, continuing the theme of its own Maastricht reasoning, the German Court is confident that parliamentarians will and can only exercise their democratic duty in service to the economic conditionalities of the German Constitution (price stability).

All liberal roads lead to the same authoritarian destination, and in Schmitt's analysis correctly so: economic liberalism can only survive within an authoritarian framework, which resists all materialisation efforts that would restrict the autonomy of markets; or within a 'strong state' that resits democratic process, and takes on the mantel of politics in nationalistic self-definition and in defence of authoritarian liberalism, or a notion that the market should be the sole realm of human freedom.[59]

> The detrimental impacts of such erroneous thinking are not only felt in the economic realm, but have also been manifest within the political and legal thinking of an entire epoch. The spirit of the era cannot but be disfigured where such an important sphere of common social life is given over to the wholesale worship of naked fact, in a manner which, in practice, cannot but end in annulment of the very idea of law. In a first instance, it was the proponents of the free economy who armed themselves with the power to pry the free economic system out of each and every social, political and legal hypothetical, and to batter the ordering concept to death with the aid of the notion of freedom. They were later joined by opponents of the free market economy who knew no better than to ensure that this now diluted and falsified market order be forever writ in stone.[60]

In a reversed mirror image, Schmitt's point is also famously made by Foucault. Writing in 1978, and sensing the post-Keynesian transformation of European politics,

---

[58] BVerfG Case No 2 BvR 1390/12 of 12 September 2012; an incomplete English translation is available at: www.bundesverfassungsgericht.de/entscheidungen/rs20120912_2bvr139012en.html accessed 17 April 2018.

[59] See Heller (n 5).

[60] F Böhm, 'Die Ordnung der Wirtschaft als geschichtliche Aufgabe und Rechtsschöpferische Leistung' in F Böhm, W Eucken and HaGroßmann-Doerth (eds), *Ordnung der Wirtschaft* (Kohlhammer 1937). The quotation is the author's own translation.

Foucault dismissed apparent (ordo)liberal rapprochement with the social market economy as a manifestation of the simple liberal fear of the rage of dispossessed social forces.[61] More tellingly still, he developed his own notion of 'anarcho-liberalism' in order to explain the modern absence of 'strong' (fascist) states within a newly globalising liberalism, which might be argued here to have found its new guardian in the functionalist, legal frameworks of regional and global trade, and its allocative inspiration in material scientism.

This final point is determinative for the analysis: certainly, the EU crisis regime displays authoritarian liberal characteristics. By the same token, German constitutional jurisprudence, has cemented authoritarianism through its misplaced reliance on ordoliberal constructions which have long been outpaced within the integration paradigm. However, this is not the whole of the story of European integration and crisis, nor yet a dominating characteristic of an extraordinarily complex and contradictory process of European integration. The evolving European polity is betimes functionalist, sometimes subject to political pressure for its socialisation (social Europe), occasionally punctuated by optimistic bursts of reforming intent (governance debate), and always subject to the conditionality of events. There is no single narrative of European crises. Nevertheless, within this multifaceted problem constellation, economic liberalism has mutated, has evolved a utilitarian outlook in posited welfare maximisation, which not only imposes itself on the European social and political realm, but also undermines the normative project of liberalism per se.

Writing in the midst of fascist dissolution, Franz Böhm recalls economic liberalism to its 'hypothetical' self. Economic liberalism is not a material project made up of the 'worship of naked fact'; nor may it tolerate any annulment 'of the very idea of law'. The founding fathers of the ordoliberal movement at least, were clear that economic liberalism remained a normative project, which must coexist with social and political hypotheticals. To this lawyerly ordoliberal mind, the enemies of ordoliberalism were also the enemies of political and social organisation and were to be found, first of all, within the 'free' market itself, and only then within efforts to correct the resultant parody of market freedom. Perhaps the same might now be said of the EU context, albeit that here, the market enemies of economic liberalism and democratic desire are not only the cartel kings of economic efficiency, but also the scientism that itself negates the freedom of autonomous economic action through its pre-emption of the political imperative in a distributive totality of welfare maximisation.

VI EPILOGUE

What might be the correct response to the current crisis of economic liberalism within the EU? Certainly, the historical precepts of ordoliberalism have proved themselves inadequate to the task of mastery the European markets, unable to

---

[61] M Foucault, *Birth of Biopolitics: Lectures at the College de France* (Routledge 2008).

establish a sustaining relationship with social and political organisation. Yet, in its early fundaments, and, above all, its grudging coexistence with the social market economy, this German variety of economic liberalism lays down its own self-limiting negatives – restriction of its own positive intervention to the ordering of autonomous markets, respect for political processes (of redistribution) and respect for the autonomous (autonomy securing) values of law.

In tandem with his eschewal of pseudo-rationalism, Otto van Neurath famously reminds us that all human projects of social, political and economic organisation are ships at sea: the European *telos* continues, we cannot park the Union in dry dock and start again with a comprehensive new design. Instead change must be discrete, performed when and where it can be. Seen in this limited light, perhaps one of the greatest services which law can perform for economic liberalism in crisis is its own act of self-limitation. Certainly, legal critique can play its own role in unveiling the dissolution of economic liberalism in utilitarian economic determinism. At the same time, however, European jurisprudence in its widest sense has demonstrated the utility of a legal refusal to decide.

Expanding upon the *Gauweiler* saga to include the judgment of the referring German Constitutional Court, we find an oddity in German constitutional history, the existence of two dissenting opinions.[62] The reasons given for her dissension by Judge Lübbe-Wolff are particularly illuminating. Courts should not judge upon the technical provisions of the OMT, because to do so would be to go 'beyond the limits of judicial competence under the principles of democracy and separation of powers' (paragraph 3). Taking a formalist legal position, Lübbe-Wolff nevertheless forcefully reminds us of the normative quality of law and the continuing significance of political hypotheticals. The law can refuse to judge. It can avoid its own transformation into a complacent instrument of a totalising economic outlook. Granted, such a legal stance will not solve the crisis of economic liberalism, but it may give pause for thought: the road we are travelling is not a 'natural' one; a mere facet of an observable human reality. We can constitute and we can engage in politics.

---

[62] BverfG, Case No 2 BvR 2728/13, of 14 January 2014.

17

With Time to Prepare

Planning an Exit from the EMU

Costas Lapavitsas

I A TRANSFORMED EU AND THE IRON CAGE OF THE EMU

Two dates help place the eurozone crisis in historical time, even though historical events are almost impossible to delineate with great precision. The sharp phase of the crisis began in May 2010 as the Greek government was shut out of the international markets, and was forced to accept the country's first bailout. By 2012 the sharp phase was over but the crisis continued for considerably longer, especially in the peripheral countries. In August 2018, a different Greek government, after fully submitting to the demands of the official lenders and completing the course of the bailout programmes, began to regain a form of regular access to the international markets. The eurozone crisis had been formally pacified.

The pacification of the eurozone crisis over the course of the last decade has involved a series of drastic measures imposed on the stricken countries by the 'Troika', i.e., the European Commission, the European Central Bank (ECB) and the International Monetary Fund (IMF). More broadly, the pacification of the crisis has taken place under terms dictated by Germany, the country which has emerged as the undisputed hegemon of the European Economic and Monetary Union (EMU), but also of the European Union (EU). In the course of the crisis, the EU has been firmly divided into core and peripheries, while neoliberalism has become embedded in its institutions and policies.

There can be little doubt regarding the institutional transformation of the EU in the course of the crisis. Despite extensive academic and political debate with respect to the 'architectural flaws' of the common currency, which presumably contributed to the long-drawn nature of the crisis, not a single reform was implemented in 2010 to 2017 that could potentially eliminate the notorious 'flaws'. That was not because of a shortage of proposals. The list put forth by academics and others included mutualising public debt by issuing Eurobonds, creating a system of fiscal transfers among EMU members, giving the right to the ECB to buy public debt in the primary markets and, needless to say, taking steps towards fiscal union.[1] All proposed reforms of this nature were consistently rejected, and the driving force behind their rejection was Germany.

Extensive institutional change has, however, taken place in the EMU and the EU since the outbreak of the crisis. Thus, the Stability and Growth Pact, which had failed to keep budget deficits within the 3 per cent limit of GDP in the 2000s, was considerably hardened. A battery of institutional reforms, including the Six-Pack, the Two-Pack, the Fiscal Compact, and the European Semester were introduced more effectively to police fiscal austerity. The key change in this respect was that Member States of the EU would no longer be penalised after registering an 'excessive' deficit, but would be policed by the EU prior to presenting a deficit. Thus, the institutions of the EU have acquired the power to impose fiscal austerity by directly interfering with the budget-setting processes of individual countries. Austerity has become institutionalised in the EU.[2]

Moreover, there was a sustained drive towards Banking Union, which has given the ECB supervisory rights over banking systems, as well as setting out terms for bank resolution that apply across national jurisdictions. Above all, the European Stability Mechanism (ESM), an unelected and unaccountable institution created in the course of the crisis, has been given substantial powers and considerable funds to prevent and confront turmoil similar to that which broke out in 2010. The ESM could potentially develop into a version of the IMF for the EU, though the political and institutional hurdles are formidable. In sum, all the institutional changes that have taken place have actually entrenched neoliberalism within the EU, and they have hardened the original practices of the EMU.

Furthermore, the pacification of the crisis occurred through a series of economic policies applied to stricken countries in the periphery of the EMU. These measures can broadly be found in programmes designed by the IMF to deal with several international crises since the 1980s, which were characterised by the sudden inability of countries to borrow in international markets, and thus to manage their existing stock of debt.[3] One key element of these programmes is to prevent the costs of crises

---

[1] For the public debate on mutualising debt, for instance, see J Delpla and J von Weizsäcker, 'Eurobonds: The Blue Bond Concept and Its Implications' (Bruegel Policy Contribution 2011/02, March 2011) http://bruegel.org/wp-content/uploads/imported/publications/110322_pc_blue_bonds.pdf accessed 1 April 2018; JD Juncker and G Tremonti, 'E-Bonds Would End the Crisis' *Financial Times* (London, 5 December 2010) www.ft.com/content/54253e90-038c-11e0-9636-00144feabdco accessed 1 April 2018; G Amato and G Verhofstadt, 'A Plan to Save the Euro and Curb Speculators' *Financial Times* (London, 3 July 2011) www.ftchinese.com/story/001039438/en accessed 1 April 2018. None of these recommendations came to pass.

[2] For an analysis of the neoliberal transformation of the EU and the ascendancy of Germany in the course of the eurozone crisis, see C Lapavitsas, *The Left Case against the EU* (Polity 2018).

[3] For the broader political consideration, the internal IMF politics and the compromises involved in the Greek programme, see International Monetary Fund, Independent Evaluation Office, 'The IMF and the Crises in Greece, Ireland and Portugal: An Evaluation by the Independent Evaluation Office' (July 2016) www.ieo-imf.org/ieo/files/completedevaluations/EAC__REPORT%20v5.PDF accessed 1 April 2018.

from falling on lenders, or at least to limit them as far as possible. A further important element is to provide urgently needed bailout funds to stricken countries, typically accompanied by severe conditionality which would seek to transform their economies and societies. In the case of the EMU, the bulk of the bailout funds needed by stricken peripheral countries were provided by the countries of the core. The costs and pressures of the subsequent adjustment of economies and societies fell almost entirely on the stricken countries in the periphery. Germany, in particular, has avoided major policy changes and has not borne any significant cost from confronting the crisis.

An exemplary instance of this process is the programme applied to Greece in several instalments since 2010.[4] To be more specific, the Greek programme – designed by the IMF – had two parts, both of which were imposed on the country through harsh conditionality attached to the bailout loans. First, stabilisation was to be achieved through the imposition of austerity, i.e., by cutting public expenditure and raising taxes, thus reducing aggregate demand. The effects of austerity were magnified through cutting wages and pensions, thus further reducing aggregate demand. Second, growth was to be achieved through 'reforms', i.e., by cutting wages in the first instance, but also by deregulating markets and privatising public property. The Greek programme exemplified the dominance of neoliberal ideology at the heart of the EU, which has become thoroughly entrenched and institutiona-lised in the course of the crisis. Greece functioned as testing ground for the institu-tions of the EMU and the EU allowing them to refine the approach of the IMF, giving it firmer foundations in the mechanisms of the Union, and applying it across broad swathes of Europe.[5] As for the social winners and losers from this process, and from the broader triumph of neoliberalism in the EU in the 2010s, there is no doubt at all: capital won heavily against labour.

The victory of capital over labour was also notable in Germany, the country that has emerged as the hegemon of the EU. During the years of the crisis, the domestic policy framework of Germany has remained fundamentally unchanged. To be specific, the ascendancy of the country in both the EMU and the EU has been predicated on the retreat of German labour in the face of German capital, a concomitant suppression of domestic demand and the extraordinary rise of German exports. Germany has engaged in a veritable 'neo-mercantilism' since the end of the 1990s, seeking wealth abroad, while keeping its domestic economy under permanent strain.[6]

---

[4] For a detailed analysis of the Greek programme, see C Lapavitsas, 'Political Economy of the Greek Crisis' (2018) Review of Radical Political Economy.

[5] See D Argyroulis, 'An Opportunity to Enhance the Cohesion of the Eurozone?' The Greek Sovereign Debt Crisis as a Negative Lesson' (UACES 47th Conference, Krakow, Poland, 4–6 September 2017) www.uaces.org/events/conferences/krakow/papers/abstract.php?paper_id=456#.Wjo7qN-gLIU accessed 1 April 2018.

[6] For the transformation in German policymaking and the implications for the eurozone, see F Scharpf 'Community and Autonomy: Institutions, Policies and Legitimacy in Multilevel Europe' (2010) 68

The success of German exporting capital has not been based on sustained productivity gains and rising investment in the economy; indeed, the performance of Germany in these respects has been quite poor. Rather, German industrial capital has emerged ascendant in Europe (and more broadly) by applying sustained downward pressure on wages since the late 1990s. The Hartz labour reforms implemented by the Schroeder government in the 2000s were vital in boosting the competitiveness of German exporters, particularly those referring to unemployment benefits (Hartz IV).[7] A guaranteed minimum living allowance was introduced, but the unemployed were also forced into seeking and taking work that hitherto might not have been considered. The social protection of German workers was profoundly weakened and downward wage pressures were worsened. Class differences were sharply exacerbated, inequality increased, and precarious employment swept across the labour force.[8]

Within the confines of the eurozone, which made it impossible for France, Italy and other countries to devalue their national currencies against Germany, the boost to German competitiveness through suppression of domestic wages proved a decisive factor, turning the eurozone effectively into a domestic market for German industrial capital. The institutionalisation of austerity and the application of neoliberal reforms in the 2010s helped embed this outcome in Europe. Germany has become the hegemon of Europe on the back of its own workers.

Publication Series of the Max Planck Institute for the Study of Societies www.mpifg.de/pu/mpifg_book/mpifg_bd_68.pdf accessed 1 April 2018; F Scharpf, 'Forced Structural Convergence in the Eurozone – Or a Differentiated European Monetary Community'(2016) MPIfG Discussion Paper 16/15 www.mpifg.de/pu/mpifg_dp/dp16-15.pdf accessed 1 April 2018. See also F Scharpf, 'Monetary Union, Fiscal Crisis and the Preemption of Democracy' (2011) MPIfG Discussion Paper 16/15 www.mpifg.de/pu/mpifg_dp/dp11-11.pdf accessed 1 April 2018.

7   The reforms were the result of recommendations put forward in October 2002 by the Committee for Modern Services in the Labour Market (Kommission für moderne Dienstleistungen am Arbeitsmarkt) chaired by Peter Hartz, a former human resources manager of Volkswagen AG and member of its board of directors. The reforms were in four parts enacted in two stages and are commonly referred to as Hartz I–IV. Hartz I and II were adopted in December 2002, while III and IV a year later. For the full text of the Committee's conclusions, see Hartz Commission, 'Moderne Dienstleistungen am Arbeitsmarkt: Bericht der Kommission für Moderne Dienstleistungen am Arbeitsmarkt' (October 2002) www.bmas.de/DE/Service/Medien/Publikationen/moderne-dienstleistungen-am-arbeitsmarkt.html accessed 1 April 2018.

8   For the rapid rise of precarious work and the decline of stable employment after the Hartz Reforms, see B Ruoff, 'Labour Market Developments in Germany: Tales of Decency and Stability' (2016) Working Paper No 39, International Labour Office, Global Labour University, Geneva www.global-labour-university.org/fileadmin/GLU_Working_Papers/GLU_WP_No.39.pdf accessed 1 April 2018; remarkably, Bispinck and Schulten drawing on the German Federal Employment Agency, report that 'as a rule of thumb' 40 per cent of the total labour force can be considered as having an 'atypical' employment relationship (R Bispinck and T Schulten, 'Trade Union Responses to Precarious Employment in Germany' (2011) WSI-Diskussionspapier Nr 178, Institute of Economic and Social Research (WSI), Hans Boeckler Foundation www.boeckler.de/pdf/p_wsi_disp_178.pdf accessed 1 April 2018).

The ascendancy of Germany has gone together with the entrenchment of a core–periphery division in the EMU and more broadly the EU.[9] The core comprises several countries in an uneasy coexistence with each other – France, Italy, the Netherlands, Austria, and so on. Coexistence is uneasy because neither France, nor Italy are able successfully to compete with Germany, and their relative standing has declined within the EMU and the EU. The true economic core of Europe is the industrial complex of Germany – automobiles, chemicals and machine tools.

German ascendancy has further defined at least two peripheries in the EU. First, the periphery of the South, i.e., Spain, Portugal and Greece, which belongs to the EMU. These are economies that have weak industry and large but uncompetitive service sectors, and have traditionally supported employment through their public sectors. Inevitably, the eurozone crisis and its aftermath has pushed unemployment to high levels, while encouraging large numbers of skilled labour to emigrate, including to Germany. Second, the periphery of Central Europe, i.e., Poland, the Czech Republic, Slovakia, Slovenia, and Hungary. Some of these economies belong to the EMU and some do not. Their distinguishing characteristic, however, is that they have joined value chains that are based on German industrial exporting capital, partly through substantial volumes of German foreign direct investment, which took advantage of low wages and high skills in those countries.[10] The Central European periphery comprises economies that have acquired significant industrial capacity in recent years, much of it dependent on the German industrial core. Unemployment has declined but, nonetheless, investment remains very low and income growth is weak.

Thus, in historical terms, the EMU has failed to bring convergence and mutual prosperity to its members and to the EU more generally. Indeed, it has exacerbated systemic divergences in Europe, helping to entrench peripheries and cause instability in the core. The euro has rebounded in the global interests of German exporting capital, while fostering deeply problematic domestic conditions for German labour. Far from easing the way towards greater European unity, the monetary union has emerged as the backbone of a thoroughly neoliberal EU, which has deleterious effects on economies and societies across Europe.

In view of these developments, it is clear that the political and social forces which have determined the path of the EMU and the EU are not going to adopt policies in the future that challenge neoliberal ideology and practice at the heart of European institutions. The adoption of quantitative easing by the ECB, for instance, as well as some budgetary compromises with France, Spain and other countries to reduce the

---

[9] For the emerging division of the European economy into core and periphery, see M Landesmann and S Leitner (in collaboration with R Stehrer) 'Competitiveness of the European Economy' (2015) Research Report 401, Vienna Institute for International Economic Studies; see also D Hanzl-Weiss and M Landesmann, 'Correcting External Imbalances in the European Economy' (2016) Research Report 410, Vienna Institute for International Economic Studies.

[10] See Lapavitsas (n 2) ch 3.

pressure of austerity in the second half of the 2010s, do not constitute fundamental structural change. Rather, they are acts undertaken with the aim of managing some of the worst tensions within the reshaped framework of the EMU. The monetary union and the EU as a whole are not amenable to the type of reforms that would mutualise costs and benefits in the name of partnership among the nations of Europe. The reforms which they actually admit (and plan) are in the direction of hardening the neoliberal outlook of institutions, defending the common currency as guarantor of neoliberalism in the EU, and taking steps to deal with the outbreak of new crises. This stance is perfectly consistent with the continuation of German hegemony.

In sum, the EMU has become an iron cage for the economies and the nations of Europe, which sustains the neoliberal transformation of the EU. Considering its trajectory, there is little doubt that the balance sheet of the monetary union has been negative for the people of Europe. The conditions that have emerged several years after the outbreak of the eurozone crisis are unstable, divisive and hierarchical. The only clear beneficiary of the common currency and the neoliberal hardening of the EU has been big business in Europe, while the costs have been borne heavily by labour.

Given the thoroughly unstable outlook of the EU in the aftermath of the eurozone crisis, it is a matter of time before another crisis materialises, possibly catalysed by political developments reflecting the frustration of broad layers of working people and even the middle class with the relentless pressures of neoliberalism in Europe. German hegemony is not based on conditions that are stable and long-lasting. It draws on persistent domestic austerity and wage suppression as well as the iron cage of the euro. A future crisis would be likely once again to threaten the existence of the monetary union and probably of the EU itself.

In this context, it is imperative to consider in broad outline the steps that would be required for individual countries to exit the monetary union thus acquiring scope for alternative economic policies that would remove neoliberal pall over Europe. This mental exercise is valuable not least because, for once, there is time to prepare. Moreover, the analysis could usefully draw on the experience of Greece in the 2010s, which is likely to remain the weakest link of the EMU in the future.

II GREEK EXIT FROM THE MONETARY UNION: A LONG-DELAYED ACT

Greece has suffered heavily from its membership of the EMU. The bailout policies since 2010 have inflicted significant damage to the economy primarily because the country has attempted to regain competitiveness by crushing wages and imposing extraordinary austerity. By 2018 Greece had attained a degree of stabilisation but at tremendous cost to its labour force, its productive structures, and its society in general.[11]

---

[11] For more on this issue, see Lapavitsas (n 4).

In this connection it is vital to note that during the last four decades the Greek economy has exhibited major weaknesses, including negative net saving and huge leakages abroad in the form of a strong propensity to import, especially by its industrial sector. The centre of gravity of the Greek economy has moved towards services at the expense of industry and agriculture, which has also meant favouring production of 'non-tradable' rather than 'tradable' goods. Greece has been able to grow reasonably rapidly in the 2000s only by borrowing from abroad. When that option disappeared in the 2010s, the country found itself at a developmental impasse to which the bailout strategy of liberalisation, privatisation and wage reductions has offered no fundamental answer. Indeed, one of the worst aspects of the bailout strategy is that it has not improved the structure of the economy practically at all. Stabilisation has come at great social cost, while leaving the Greek economy in a state of weakness and stagnation. The country is in need of a strategy that can deal with its exceptionally high unemployment and the deep contraction of GDP caused by the crisis.

To be more specific, for sustained growth and development Greece has to abandon austerity and boost aggregate demand. That is also the way to reduce unemployment rapidly. There are several areas of the economy, particularly in the service sector, that would be amenable to such a boost. Subsequently, the country would require a targeted industrial policy to limit its exposure to imports and to strengthen the growth of productivity. Such a strategy would simply be impossible to adopt within the EMU, thus making exit necessary.[12]

There is little doubt that the medium and long-term prospects of the Greek economy would be substantially better outside the iron cage of the eurozone. However, exit would not only be a difficult short-term task economically but also a political struggle, as was shown by the experience of the SYRIZA government in 2015.[13] The strategy of that government was to engage in 'hard negotiations' with the lenders and the EU to lift austerity and neoliberal policies as well as achieve substantial debt relief. It hoped to succeed in this endeavour because its efforts would draw legitimacy from the democratic mandate of the Greek people. The lenders would retreat in fear of the potential disruption to the world financial markets caused by Greek tenaciousness. SYRIZA would thus be able to keep Greece in the EMU, while reversing the stabilisation and adjustment policies of the EU, and continuing to receive liquidity from the ECB for Greek banks and funding for itself from the EU lenders.

Needless to say, this approach was based on a profound misunderstanding of the nature of the EMU, not to mention considerable make-belief among the SYRIZA

---

[12] For further analysis, see C Lapavitsas and others, 'Eurozone Failure, German Policies, and a New Path for Greece: Policy Analysis and Proposals' (2017) Rosa Luxemburg Stiftung Publikationen www .rosalux.de/fileadmin/rls_uploads/pdfs/Online-Publikation/3-17_Online-Publ_Eurozone Failure_Web.pdf accessed 1 April 2018.

[13] See Lapavitsas (n 2).

leadership. The result was an utter political defeat that was perfectly predictable and indeed was predicted.[14] The lesson from the debacle of SYRIZA is that negotiations are certainly necessary, but only to ensure a relatively smooth passage out of the iron cage of the eurozone. Determined use of national state power, plus social mobilisation, plus some international political support could help the government of even a small state achieve exit in ways that would lessen the difficulties of transition.[15] This option was proposed already in the early 2010s and contributed to forming a political current within SYRIZA during its first seven months in government, but it never prevailed and its exponents were forced out of SYRIZA when the third Greek bailout was signed in August 2015.

There is no formal method to exit the EMU but a legal basis for exit is available in the Treaties which does not, moreover, entail automatic exit from the EU.[16] Irrespective of legal treaties, a sovereign state retains both the right and the ability to act unilaterally to protect its people. Unilateral action does not mean hostility and refusing to negotiate with the EU, but rather setting a different framework within which negotiations would take place. There is no doubt, of course, that exiting the EMU and adopting a set of policies that would be in opposition to the neoliberal outlook of the Union would bring a direct confrontation with the EU. This should be understood as the beginning of a political and social process to change the balance between capital and labour domestically, as well as repositioning the country in the international domain. If the Greek people, or the people of any other Member State, also wish to leave the EU, that is their right, as the Brexit referendum of 2016 has already shown. The point of more immediate importance, however, would be to recapture key elements of sovereignty by leaving the EMU, for it is quite simply impossible to adopt alternative policies while remaining in the iron cage. To take this path, it would be necessary to have political legitimacy and active popular support. Such would be the basis on which the following steps of exit could be undertaken.

III THE STEPS OF EMU EXIT

Unilateral action to ensure EMU exit requires a series of steps, several of which have already been outlined in earlier work in relation to Greece.[17] The fundamental steps

---

[14] See H Flassbeck and C Lapavitsas, *Against the Troika: Crisis and Austerity in the Eurozone* (Verso 2015).

[15] See Flassbeck and Lapavitsas (n 14); see Lapavitsas and others (n 12).

[16] See P Miliarakis, 'Legal Issues of the Transition to a National Currency in the European Union' (Eurozone, Popular Sovereignty and National Currency, Athens University of Economics, 15–17 January 2016) www.maxome.gr/wp-content/uploads/2016/01/ΕΙΣΗΓΗΣΗ-ΠΕΤΡΟΣ-ΜΗΛΙΑΡΑΚΗΣ.pdf accessed 1 April 2018; P Miliarakis, 'The Legal Aspects of Greek Exit from the EMU' in Flassbeck and Lapavitsas (n 14).

[17] This section draws heavily on Lapavitsas and others (n 12).

are recapped below to help provide parameters for policy debate in Greece and Europe in the years to come. Thus:

1. By an Act of Parliament, the country would announce changing its standard of value on the basis of the *lex monetae*. Naturally, there should be no advance warning of the adoption of the new drachma, and the change of currency should take place over a weekend. The government should also immediately announce that:
   (a) All redemptions of principal and payments of interest on sovereign debt outside of the Greek payment system are suspended.
   (b) Greek participation in the EMU is suspended.
   (c) All bank operations and financial markets are closed until further notice.
   (d) The Greek Central Bank is placed under government control.
   (e) A Commissioner for Banking is appointed with full plenipotentiary powers over private and public banks.
   (f) A system of capital and bank controls is placed in operation for a period.
   (g) All accounts and all debts in the Greek payment system that are governed by national law are to be redenominated in the new currency at a rate of 1:1.
   (h) The government pledges to fulfil its obligations to all Greek agents.
2. All important decisions – from the choice of principles to be applied in the introduction of the national currency to the resolutions to be passed by Parliament – should be made immediately. Parliament should give the Government (particularly the prime minister and the minister of finance) the widest possible powers to implement the currency reform.
3. The Commissioner for Banking should take provisional control of Greek banks and the Central Bank to ensure:
   (a) Effective compliance with the system of capital and bank controls.
   (b) Re-denomination of bank assets and liabilities under Greek law.
   (c) The introduction of drachma banknotes into the vaults of banks to begin to use in the following weeks.
   (d) Possibly the 'voucherisation' of existing banknotes by using a special stamp to allow euro banknotes held by banks to be provisionally used as 'new drachma'.
   (e) In coordination with the Central Bank, the preparation of a list of Greek enterprises who have borrowed from non-Greek agents. The process should take no longer than a few days.
4. The decision to suspend external payments, thus allowing the national debt to go into arrears means in practice that Greece would be failing to redeem outstanding bonds held by the ECB, and failing to repay IMF loans. Greek debts to the EFSF, the ESM and other bilateral/multilateral debts arising from the bailout programmes have a significant grace period. After going into arrears, Greece should issue a call for an international conference to settle its debts,

including a substantial write off of the principal. Establishing an Audit Commission to consider the legitimacy of Greek public debt would be an important part if this process, not least to ensure democratic participation by the majority. It is probable that a 'growth clause' and a limit of debt repayments (interest and principal) relative to GDP, or to exports, would be set in all forms of debt settlement.

5. The conversion of all bank liabilities and assets that are governed by Greek law into the new drachma would take place at the rate of 1:1 to avoid the technical complexities of conversion at variable rates for different classes of asset and liability. Individual and enterprise bank deposits as well as individual and enterprise bank debts would be converted at 1:1. All employment contracts under Greek law would also be converted at 1:1. The government would immediately announce that it will no longer either accept or make payments in euro, giving effective monopoly of legal tender to the new drachma. The government should immediately issue a full guarantee of the new drachma-denominated deposits. During the initial weekend and for the first few days while the banks were closed, all charge and credit card transactions would be converted into the new currency.

6. Depending on the degree of preparedness, new banknotes could begin to enter circulation within a month and a half from the switch to a new currency. In the intervening period it would be possible to use stamped euro banknotes as drachma 'vouchers' in ATMs and at cashier's windows. It would also be possible to use government-issued scrip for official payments and for public salaries and wages for a short period of time. Incentives would be offered to attract the existing euro-denominated banknotes into the formal banking system following the change of currency.

7. The most complex issue with regard to payments would not be banknotes but reshaping the electronic systems of payment. The performance of banking IT systems should be immediately audited to ensure convertibility of euro into new drachma for the purposes of interbank and other electronic payments as well as limiting euro cash withdrawals shortly before and after the changeover. Compatibility with the IT systems of the banks of the eurozone should also be examined.

8. Ensuring the continued functioning of the payment system would be made easier by the full nationalisation of the four systemic Greek banks through conversion of the existing public holdings of equity into common stock with voting rights and through confiscation of the equity holdings of private funds without compensation. The government should simultaneously announce the continuation and strengthening of banking and capital controls that have been in operation since the summer of 2015, until such time as the economy would have recovered.

9. After nationalisation the banking system would be restructured, first, through establishing a 'bad bank' to relieve commercial banks from the bulk of the stock of non-performing debt and non-performing equity. The 'bad bank' would be capitalised primarily by newly issued public bonds in the national currency.

10. A public committee would be appointed to apply social and economic criteria to the allocation of problematic debts to the 'bad bank'. Two principles would be paramount to its functioning. First, to release households and SMEs from the enormous burden of non-performing debt, especially that which has accumulated in the 2010s. Second, to avoid saddling the public sector with the bad debts of dishonest private borrowers. The recovery of commercial credit, which has collapsed in Greece in the course of the crisis, would depend on rescuing the remaining vestiges of trustworthiness among private enterprises, and for that it is vital not to favour bad debtors.

11. The balance sheet of the National Central Bank would be redenominated and the Bank would be transformed fully into a public institution. The Greek Central Bank would remain a member of the European System of Central Banks, even after exiting the Eurosystem. However, a careful legal assessment would be necessary of the repayment of its liabilities to the Eurosystem as well as with regard to ELA.

12. The government would offer financial and legal assistance to companies and physical persons who hold contracts governed by foreign law, following the change of currency. More generally, there will be need for financial help to SMEs, households and large enterprises for weeks and months ahead. The aim would be to avoid bankruptcies and to deal with legal complications of making payments to and receiving payments from abroad.

13. Greece would rapidly regain monetary sovereignty and the new drachma would be re-established as the functioning money of the country as long as the state persevered with making and accepting payments in the new currency. However, it is likely that during the initial period there would be parallel circulation of several forms of money: new drachma banknotes, electronic new drachma units created by banks, regular euro banknotes, and perhaps newly issued scrip and stamped euro banknotes. Parallel circulation would create transactions costs as goods would be valued differently in different currencies, but they are likely to be limited and under no circumstances justify Greece remaining in EMU.

14. The new drachma would have an international exchange rate after the initial administrative conversion of assets, debts, wages and salaries at the rate of 1:1 with the euro. There is no doubt that global markets would immediately price the new drachma relative to the euro and to other currencies, and that the new drachma would depreciate. It is impossible accurately to predict the degree of depreciation – estimates of this kind are little more than guesses. It is worth

bearing in mind that Greece has reached a precarious balance on current account after six years of recession, and thus the depreciation pressures would be partially attenuated. Even so, it is likely that the exchange rate of the new drachma would follow a J-curve path, declining sharply in the initial period and rising gradually towards a new equilibrium. The initial period of sharp decline is unlikely to last longer than several weeks, while the adjustment to the new equilibrium would probably extend to several months. The ability to defend the exchange rate in the short run would depend on capital controls acting as a barrier to speculation. It would also be vital steadily to put together a stabilisation fund managed by the Central Bank. Further detail on the appropriate exchange rate policy is given below.

15. Provisioning of key markets – medicine, food and fuel – in the very short run would require administrative measures to ensure supply of key goods to industry and the most vulnerable social groups. There would be no need for rationing in the form of coupons, or ration cards for the population. Measures would be taken to prioritise access to medicine, food, and fuel of the most vulnerable and economically important groups. Note further that, at present, Greece has a huge underutilised capacity of both labour power and means of production that could be rapidly used to supply domestic markets. The country already has significant coverage of key food supplies from domestic sources. Moreover, it has good domestic coverage for energy to produce electricity, but it would certainly need an interstate agreement to boost the availability of car fuel for a short period. Greece, finally, has good domestic coverage of medicines, and it would be possible to immediately prioritise key imports of urgently needed drugs, including cheaply available generic drugs from a variety of suppliers across the world.

16. Depreciation would act as a vital lever for Greek enterprises to recapture the domestic market – since it would act as barrier to imports – and to expand exports. It can be expected to have beneficial effects on output and employment in Greece. It is also unlikely to lead to high inflation for reasons that are again discussed in the following section. The recovery of the Greek economy would probably begin between six and twelve months from the change of currency, if historical experience of similar monetary events is a guide. There is, of course, no doubt that the initial period of adjustment would affect output and produc-tion negatively. However, the combined effect of restoring liquidity, lifting austerity, and currency depreciation would deliver a strong boost to the econ-omy. Given the state of the Greek economy, the unused and wasted resources and the heavily repressed demand, it is reasonable to expect that the growth would be strong and sustained once the economy would have recovered from the currency change. Sustained growth in the medium term would, of course, depend on the implementation of a new development programme along the lines discussed in subsequent sections.

17. Following exit, Greece would follow a policy of managing a floating exchange rate in line with its small size in the world markets and its natural proximity to the markets of the EU. There is plenty of available guidance from other countries on how to manage a floating exchange rate to ensure stability, including from Sweden, which operates a floating currency within the EU. In this respect, minimum wages would be raised but, equally, collective bargaining must be put on a different footing to guarantee the new direction of the country. It would also be important to adopt measures to protect workers' incomes by abolishing high taxes on consumer goods (for instance, food, electricity, petrol), by providing increased social protection to the weaker strata of wage labour and the middle class, and by regulating key prices, including the rental cost of housing.

18. Finally, the huge stock of unpaid obligations by the public to the state (taxes, fines and so on) should be cleared by applying social criteria. The great bulk of the individual cases of unpaid obligations comprises small sums that have accumulated during the crisis. However, most of the debt in money terms (perhaps four fifths) is owed by a few thousand large debtors, mostly enterprises but also natural persons. In practice very little of the debt is actually collectible. Legislation should be passed to relieve the great bulk of small debtors, while encouraging large debtors also to pay. Once again, a vital issue would be to avoid favouring dishonest debtors.

IV SOME BROADER CONSIDERATIONS ON CONTROLLING CAPITAL FLOWS, STABILISING THE EXCHANGE RATE AND DEVISING A GROWTH STRATEGY

The steps outlined in section III could act as a broad guide for Greece and other peripheral countries, as and when the issue of exit arises politically. The precise policy of exit would, needless to say, depend on the political and social balance of forces in each member country. There is, however, one vital analytical point to make at the outset. A plan of exit is not – and could not be – a complete list of all possible eventualities and outcomes, with appropriate policy action attached, in case of exit. Such a thing would be impossible to devise for any economic policy, not merely one concerned with exiting the EMU.

The plan of exit is, above all, a series of coherent macroeconomic steps, such as those outlined in the previous section. Once the sequence has been identified, it would be incumbent upon policymakers to ascertain the modalities of each step, particularly with regard to stabilising banks, supplying key markets, and lessening the shock to the productive sector. This would not be an easy task but it would be entirely derivative of the fundamental problem, i.e., determining the series of steps for exit.

An important consideration in this respect would be dealing with the inevitable depreciation of the new currency. Depreciation would generally have a strongly beneficial effect on the international transactions of Greece, and probably of other Southern peripheral countries.[18] Nonetheless, it would be important to limit the extent of depreciation to help reduce the uncertainty generated by the exchange, thus creating a more stable environment for all economic activity. For a country of the size of Greece this would entail two problems.

First, it would restrict the independence of monetary policy, which is a fundamental element of the required mix of development policy. The underlying theoretical reason for this is that it is impossible to operate an independent national monetary policy when capital mobility is entirely free and attempts are simultaneously made to stabilise exchange rates.

Second – and related to the first – the Central Bank must have sufficient currency reserves to support the exchange rate, in conjunction with changing the level of the rate of interest. For an economy with a small footprint, such as Greece, the cost can be quite high.

In order to deal with these problems, it would be necessary to create a mechanism to restrict the cross-border mobility of capital. The mechanism should be particularly strict at the beginning and be gradually relaxed in line with the development trajectory of the economy. In essence, the mechanism should initially allow for only those currency transactions that, first, concern the current account of the balance of payments, second, relate to long-term (investment) inflows of money capital, and third, are conducted by the monetary authorities.

The mechanism must be retained even after the economy has entered the recovery phase, since there would then be a risk of heavy inflows of short-term ('speculative') capital that would create upward pressure on the exchange rate. More broadly, the inflow of short-term capital could create major problems in applying the recommended economic policy mix for growth during the recovery phase, as is shown by the examples of Mexico from 1991 to 1993 and Switzerland from 2009 to 2011.

Generally speaking, free capital mobility is a significant source of instability in the international economic system that raises the intensity and frequency of various crises (for instance, banking, foreign exchange, state debt). Furthermore, under conditions of stable exchange rates and free capital mobility the national authorities would be committing themselves to an endless process of competitive reductions in wages to stabilise or advance the position of the external sector of their economies. The simultaneous presence of these conditions is systematically inimical to the interests of wage earners.

---

[18]   See A Katsinos and T Mariolis, 'Switch to Devalued Drachma and Cost–Push Inflation: A Simple Input–Output Approach to the Greek Case' (2012) 3 Modern Economy 164.

It should be noted that foreign exchange crises, in which the currency reserves of the Central Bank tend to be depleted, typically rest on the expectation that the current exchange rate would prove unsustainable. Such expectations often arise when the foreign exchange markets detect contradictions in the mix of economic policies relative to the productive base of the economy. The adoption of a new development policy by Greece, combined with the imposition of restrictions on the cross-border movements of capital, would act as a deterrent for such expectations. In any case, given that a large proportion of Greece's trade is with countries outside the European Union, the exchange rate must be monitored with respect to an appropriately weighted 'basket' of foreign currencies (taking into account imports from and exports to the main trading partners). Forming a basket of currencies would allow for monitoring the country's competitiveness in relation to its trading partners, as well as facilitating greater precision in taking necessary adjustment measures.

Currency devaluation and expansionary fiscal policy financed by money creation would be prerequisites for a sustained rebound of the Greek economy, but they are not sufficient for long-term and rapid growth. The reason is that the growth potential of the Greek economy has been severely restricted due to its problematic structure, as was briefly argued above. Thus, it essential to induce changes in the structure of the Greek economy by encouraging growth of the primary and the industrial sector, while simultaneously strengthening the production of internationally tradable commodities.

Finally, the transformation of the structure of the economy would also have an effect on the productivity of the primary sector, which is particularly low. Generally speaking, a steady increase in productivity can be achieved in four interdependent ways: first, by restructuring the processes of producing and distributing goods; second, by providing material and moral incentives to workers and enterprises; third, by achieving technological progress; and fourth, by investing systematically in production, research, and education, which are the most decisive elements of the process of economic development.

It follows that raising productivity in the primary sector would require the creation of agricultural cooperatives whose crucial role would be to distribute the agricultural product. Agricultural productivity growth also requires the restructuring of the industrial sector along the lines developed above. A further prerequisite would be the creation of a specialised credit institution through the refounding of the Agricultural Bank on a healthy public basis. Rising productivity in the agricultural sector would, in turn, contribute to rising living standards and have a positive impact on the industrial sector by raising the quantity and quality of inflows from the primary sector. It would also create a basis for agricultural cooperatives in the sphere of agricultural production thus supporting the emergence of large agro-industrial enterprises.

Merely enumerating these steps is enough to show what a radical change of course the strategy of EMU exit would entail for Greece, or indeed for any other country. In effect it would be a wholesale rebalancing of both economy and society in the interests of wage labour, small–medium enterprises and farmers. On this basis a left government could address directly the existing structures of power in the country, potentially opening a path towards deeper social transformation. Movement in that direction could be accelerated by restoring labour rights, taking steps to redistribute income and wealth, revamping public administration to deal with corruption, and bringing deep reforms to justice and education.

EMU exit would be a vital step in restoring sovereignty and thus becoming able to challenge the neoliberal outlook of EU institutions. Sovereignty could potentially take a popular dimension by shifting the social balance against capital and in favour of labour. There would also be profound implications for political life, as popular participation could be encouraged and democratic practice strengthened. Exiting the EMU is far more than a mere technical question of changing the currency and adopting a different set of economic policies. It is potentially a major act in opposing and reversing the neoliberal advance that has gripped the EU. It remains to be seen whether the coming years will set in train political developments in Greece and elsewhere that could bring it to bear.

18

Brexit and the Imperial Constitution of Europe

Alex Callinicos

I INTRODUCTION

Brexit undoubtedly represents a crisis of the European Union, despite its leaders' attempts to deny this, or even to present Britain's departure as a moment of renewal and reinvigoration. But crises have the advantage of revealing the essential structures of a formation, and can offer X-ray vision of the antagonisms that constitute them. This is true in a fundamental sense of Brexit, since one of the main driving forces of the British vote to leave the EU – the potentially fatal tension between national sovereignty and the project of European integration – is inherent in that project.

It is important to emphasise that this tension is only potentially fatal. Indeed, as Alan Milward has shown in *The European Rescue of the Nation State* (a fundamental work largely ignored by the mediocrities of academic EU integration studies), the initial formation of the European Economic Community (EEC) allowed a reinvigoration of the West European nation states by providing a transnational framework of regulated trade that facilitated the realisation of a Keynesian welfare regime.[1] It is the further development of the European integration process, particularly since the Treaty of Maastricht (1992) and the resulting launch of Economic and Monetary Union (1999) that has turned the tension between this process and the persistence of national sovereignty from what Mao Zedong would have called a non-antagonistic into an antagonistic contradiction. But underlying it is the dual imperial constitution that has governed the European integration process since the 1950s – on the one hand, its promotion by the United States to secure a stable and prosperous junior partner at the western end of Eurasia, on the other, its function as a vehicle for the interests of the major European powers themselves. This constitution underlies the successive crises to have gripped the EU in recent years – over the eurozone, refugees and Brexit.

Thanks to Eva Nanopoulos and Fotis Vergis for organising the original conference from which this book developed, editing the book, and commenting on this chapter in draft.
[1]   AS Milward, *The European Rescue of the Nation State* (Routledge 1992).

11 THE ASYMMETRIES OF BREXIT

It is worth stressing that the tension between national sovereignty and European integration is in part merely a consequence of the success first of the EEC and then (since Maastricht) the EU in creating a powerful cartel of states. The sheer asymmetry of power between this cartel and most individual states, whether or not members, was on show during the eurozone-crisis, most notably in the relentless pressure exerted on Greece, for example, at the climactic summit in July 2015 where '[t]hey [notably Angela Merkel] crucified [Greek Prime Minister Alexis] Tsipras in there', according to a senior eurozone official, 'Crucified'.[2]

What is interesting is that we see a similar process taking place in the case of Brexit, as the British government has been forced to drop more and more of its initial stances after the referendum (no jurisdiction for the Court of Justice of the EU after Brexit, minimal exit payments to the EU, no participation in the single market or customs union, and so on) because of Brussels's refusal to budge. Greece is a small and (by European standards) poor country so it is interesting to see what remains a significant military power with one of the largest economies in the world suffer – not as rough treatment as Athens experienced – but a bracing education in the realities of power (or its lack).

Much of the more informed commentary on this process has been so filled with the *Schadenfreude* of journalists, academics and think tankers hostile to Brexit that it has obscured the underlying power logic. Interestingly, a similar logic was at work when Britain negotiated its entry to what was still the EEC back in the early 1970s. The *Financial Times* quotes the chief British negotiator, Sir Con O'Neill, reporting in retrospect: 'from the start, Europe's position amounted to making the UK "swallow the lot, and swallow it now". And this, he admitted, "by and large, we had to do".' The *Financial Times* continues:

[W]hat negotiators call Britain's 'accession in reverse' is drawing out similar EU reflexes and habits.

Both then and now, to London's great annoyance, Europe's approach has what one senior EU diplomat calls a 'mechanical' quality. Rather than a fluid exchange between equal parties, it approaches talks as more like a process where the weaker country eventually adapts. The main variable is the pace of change, the so-called transition.

Pascal Lamy, the former head of the World Trade Organization and two-time European commissioner, attempted to capture the asymmetry when describing Brexit not as a negotiation but 'an adjustment'. On hearing the quote, one senior EU figure involved in Brexit talks cried: 'Voila!'[3]

---

[2]   AS Chassany and others, 'Greece Talks: "Sorry, But There Is No Way You Are Leaving This Room"' *Financial Times* (London, 13 July 2015) www.ft.com/content/f908e534-2942-11e5-8db8-c033edba8a6e accessed 10 April 2018.

[3]   A Barker, 'Brexit: EU and UK Battle over "an Accession in Reverse"' Financial Times (London, 3 December 2017) www.ft.com/content/e4824a0a-d373-11e7-8c9a-d9c0a5c8d5c9.

The underlying structure of the situation is very similar in the case of both entry and exit. Reflecting the primarily (though not exclusively) economic focus of British policymakers, what they wanted in the entry negotiations was, more than anything else, access to what was then the common market at the heart of the original EEC. Now, after the Brexit referendum, they want to preserve as much as they can of the access Britain enjoyed to the single European market, constructed in the mid 1980s at the joint initiative of Margaret Thatcher and Jacques Delors, for the banks and insurance companies based in the City of London and the transnational corporations that have made Britain their European home for precisely this reason. Consequently, the original six in the early 1970s and the EU-27 now enjoy an enormous bargaining advantage: they control the access sought by London and so have been able more or less dictate their terms.

The Brexit negotiations have also drawn attention to the respect in which the EU has been most successful – something that is worth lingering over given how much stress there has been in the past few years on the Union's failings. Very quickly the EEC/EU developed into a formidable power in global trade – both as a negotiator of trade agreements and as an originator and exporter of market regulation. The latter function is particularly interesting. The very construction of the single market has required the formulation and imposition of regulations governing the production and circulation of commodities within the EU (in reality, a highly uneven and contested process). As Tobias Buck puts it:

> The EU's emergence as a global rule-maker has been driven by a number of factors, but none more important than the sheer size and regulatory sophistication of the Union's home market. The rapid expansion of the economic bloc to 27 nations [28 until Brexit takes effect] with a total of more than 480 m largely affluent consumers has turned the Union into the world's biggest and most lucrative import market. At the same time, the drive to create a borderless pan-European market for goods, services, capital and labour has triggered a hugely ambitious programme of regulatory and legislative convergence among national regimes.[4]

Consequently, other states have a powerful incentive to adopt these regulations as a means of gaining access. Moreover, trade negotiations between the EU and other states bring into play the bargaining asymmetry at the heart of Britain's Brexit dilemmas. Thus, access to the single market for those European states outside the Union requires them to accept the EU's 'four freedoms' – of goods, services, capital and people, even if this means, as it has in the case of Switzerland, overriding a referendum vote rejecting freedom of movement.[5]

In a way, this dynamic more than anything else vindicates the EU's self-image as a 'normative power'. The EU doesn't just export commodities and capital – it exports

---

[4] T Buck, 'How the European Union Exports Its Laws' *Financial Times* (London, 9 July 2007) www .ft.com/content/942b1ae2-2e32-11dc-821c-0000779fd2ac accessed 10 April 2018.

[5] C Barnard, *The Substantive Law of the EU: The Four Freedoms* (5th edn, OUP 2016).

norms as well. EU leaders wax lyrical about 'European values', but actually the norms in question are rather more hard-headed, since they have become about creating the optimal conditions for a certain kind of neoliberal capitalism – one that seeks to facilitate the global circulation of capital and commodities, but from a domestic base that respects the prevailing version of liberal democracy and offers some minimum of welfare provision. The adaptation required especially of neighbouring European states is not just to the minutiae of specific regulations, but to this broader set of norms (hence the embarrassment caused by the increasing authoritarian tenor of politics in Central and Eastern Europe).

The argument here is *not* that the European project was inherently neoliberal, despite the influence that some German ordoliberals may have had on the original Treaty of Rome. As Milward shows, the EEC in its initial phase permitted the consolidation of Keynesian welfare capitalism in Western Europe. It is more that the EU has become increasingly a mechanism for the promotion of neoliberalism, starting with the Exchange Rate Mechanism (1979), which tied participant currencies to the deutschmark and the hard-money policies of the Bundesbank, and followed by the Single European Act (1985) and the establishment of EMU. Apologists for the EU on the left sometimes object to this kind of claim by pointing to the survival of relatively generous welfare provision in north European Member States. But these are best understood as a case of path dependency, where the legacy of the Keynesian welfare capitalism that prevailed in the immediate post-war era manages (increasingly precariously) to hang on into the present. To see the direction of travel we must look at the neoliberal 'reforms' imposed on Greece and the institutionalisation of permanent austerity under the 2012 Fiscal Pact.[6]

III IMPERIALISM WITH EUROPEAN CHARACTERISTICS

The recurring theme of the discussion so far is the asymmetries of power in the relationship between a transnational, political formation and its constituent units and neighbours. One way of describing this would be to say that the EU has become an empire. Consider Michael Doyle's transhistorical definition of empire as 'effective control, whether formal or informal, of a subordinated society by an imperial society'.[7] The degree of control is clearly crucial here: Britain will probably emerge from the EU with much the same powers of initiative as it has now (which are already heavily circumscribed by prevailing economic and geopolitical relationships), maybe slightly more, but – to secure whatever access it retains to the single market – it will remain subject to EU regulations over whose making it will no longer have any influence: taking back control will turn out to involve a degree of persisting

---

[6] See the excellent treatment of the EU and neoliberalism in A Cafruny and M Ryner, *The European Union and Global Capitalism* (Palgrave 2017).

[7] MW Doyle, *Empires* (Cornell UP 1986) 30; for my own views on the subject, see A Callinicos, *Imperialism and Global Political Economy* (Polity 2009).

subordination. Nevertheless, Britain isn't powerless: there is an element almost of inter-imperialist competition in EU-27 discussions about seeking to reduce the size of the City of London and thereby its influence on the rest of Europe and planning sanctions to prevent British firms from undercutting their EU rivals after Brexit.[8] Greece, by contrast, remains inside the whale, a thoroughly 'subordinated society'.

Some EU apologists are happy to describe the EU as an empire that exports the norms of the European version of neoliberal capitalism to its barbarous near abroad, and now, they would probably add, defends them against 'populists' within and without.[9] This doesn't alter the nature of the relations of domination and subordination involved, even if the forms of coercion underpinning them are economic and not military. For students of empires there is the pleasure of comparative insights – for example, the enjoyment of their role on a larger stage taken by politicians from some of the smaller Member States (e.g. the Baltic) holding EU positions, which is reminiscent of the careers made in the service of the Ottoman Sultan by his Christian slaves or the ruthlessness with which Georgians transformed the Soviet Union into another Great Russian empire.

But the EU isn't just any old empire. It is a very distinctive kind of empire. In the first place, it has developed out of one of the key zones of advanced capitalism in an era when the United States exerted (and in my view continues to exert) hegemony over all these zones, including Europe. Second, empires vary in form but they have had a state at their centre (Michael Hardt's and Antonio Negri's conception of a centre-less empire is pure fantasy). But of course the EU is not a state, and no Member State, not even Germany, serves unproblematically as its centre. Minimally states are territorially based apparatuses of coercion and extraction, with a positive feedback loop between the two functions: coercive effectiveness facilitates extraction, while the greater the state's ability to tax and borrow the greater its ability to fund the means of coercion.[10] But what a Marxist would call Europe's repressive state apparatuses – army, police, security and intelligence – remain firmly under national control. The disruption of the Catalan independence referendum on 1 October 2017 by the Spanish Civil Guard is an interesting case in point: a post-Francoist government in Madrid drove the operation through, dismissing the doubts about its wisdom visible in Brussels and Berlin.

I return to this limitation below, but of more immediate political and economic importance is the EU's fiscal feebleness. While the budgets of EU Member States still average 49 per cent of GDP, representing expenditure primarily on social

---

[8] J Brusden, 'EU Rejects Brexit Trade Deal for UK Financial Services Sector' *Financial Times* (London, 31 January 2018) www.ft.com/content/7f7669a4-067f-11e8-9650-9c0ad2d7c5b5 accessed 10 April 2018; A Barker and J Brunsden, 'EU Seeks Powers to Stop Post-Brexit Bonfire of Regulation' *Financial Times* (London, 1 February 2018) www.ft.com/content/9052ed50-06d5-11e8 -9650-9c0ad2d7c5b5 accessed 10 April 2018.

[9] J Zielonka, *Europe as Empire* (OUP 2006); H Münkler, *Empires: The Logic of World Domination from Ancient Rome to the United States* (CUP 2007).

[10] C Tilly, *Coercion, Capital and European States: AD 990–1990* (Blackwell 1992).

provision, the Union budget remains stuck at around 1 per cent of EU national income.[11] Any attempt to allow the EU or eurozone to borrow by issuing its own bonds has been firmly blocked by Germany, fearful that this would turn Europe into a 'transfer union' in which rich Member States subsidise poor states. 'Transfer union' is really a metonym for 'state', at least of the modern kind. Minimally effective states even in the neoliberal era tax richer citizens and regions and transfer some of the revenues to poorer citizens and regions.

The fact that the EU is a fiscal midget helps to explain the eurozone-crisis. In an era of floating fiat currencies, a currency's strength depends in part on the size and condition of the economy supporting it and in part on the confidence of holders of the currency (and crucially of the bonds of the state issuing the currency) that the state is able to extract enough to service its debts. But the euro is issued by the European Central Bank, which has no state behind it and which is specifically forbidden to perform central banks' traditional function as lender of last resort in a financial crisis. It is this, more than individual incompetence or chronic internal divisions (though these played their part), than explains the ECB's sluggish and ineffective response to the 2008 crash, when EU institutions were initially bypassed by national governments.

The debt crises experienced by a number of weaker Member States (themselves made possible by the markets' mistaken expectation that Germany would rescue them if they got into trouble) were resolved by a series of 'memorandums' in which the affected states agreed to impose austerity on their societies in exchange for loans allowing them to repay their creditors (often north European banks) and by pro-tracted manoeuvres by Mario Draghi after he took over as ECB President in 2012 to reassure markets that vulnerable states would receive support and to prop up the banking system with large-scale bond purchases.

The only way of making sense of this business that I can see is the determination of the German economic and political establishment to block any rescue of the indebted Member States that might undermine the economic model painfully constructed under the Federal Republic after the Second World War of a high-export, low-inflation economy policed by the Bundesbank. This model has been invigorated in the past fifteen years by Germany's phenomenal export success, into which many of the new Member States in Central and East Europe have been drawn as providers of cheap skilled labour for the supply chains of German transnationals – a process that helps to explain Greece's isolation when, in the early months of Alexis Tsipras's government, it campaigned for debt relief. Meanwhile, France, which has traditionally advocated for a more politically regulated (and implicitly more growth-oriented) eurozone, has been marginalised by economic stagnation and a succession of dysfunctional presidencies.[12]

[11] European Commission Myths and Facts Sheet http://ec.europa.eu/budget/explained/myths/myths_en.cfm accessed 10 April 2018.

[12] This analysis is elaborated in A Callinicos, 'The Internationalist Case against the European Union' (2015) 148 International Socialism.

Another way of putting this is that the national interests of some Member States, above all Germany, prevailed. The EU undoubtedly has transnational institutions that function like state apparatuses (notably the Commission and the ECJ), and it has a much-vaunted Parliament, but at its core it remains a cartel of nation states. And, as in all cartels, some members are more powerful than others. The leading EU states – Germany, France, Italy, Spain, the Netherlands, Belgium, Poland and Sweden – bargaining among themselves and constructing differing coalitions of the other Member States depending on the issue, dominate the decision-making process.[13] In the past decade Germany has emerged as much more than *primus inter pares*. Does this make Germany Europe's hegemon? I don't think so. This is partly because of the negative and defensive way in which Berlin managed the eurozone-crisis. Gramsci argued that hegemony implied a willingness to make economic concessions, even sacrifices, to secure ethico-political leadership based on the claim to represent the universal interest.[14] While Germany did help fund the various debt settlements, the Tsipras government was publicly and humiliatingly disciplined in a brutal display of power designed as a lesson to anyone in any other European capital (notably Paris) not to step out of line.

It is important to emphasise that I am not making a moral judgement here (although, as a matter of fact I find the EU's treatment of Greece contemptible). Political leadership is often negative and defensive, and power is as frequently used brutally. The point is more about the kind of leadership that Germany under Angela Merkel has offered. After all, when Donald Trump was elected US president she was portrayed as the 'real leader of the free world'. But the only case when Merkel seriously stuck her neck out was when, in September 2015, she decided to let refugees in – a decision rapidly reversed and repented. Her leadership has been calibrated above all to staying in office, the management of crises geared to maintaining the ruling coalition, bending to Wolfgang Schäuble when as finance minister he vetoed debt relief to Greece, swaying towards the Social Democrats when, after the September 2017 election, they demanded support for greater EU integration as a condition of renewing a grand coalition government.

The problem, however, lies not simply in *how* the German political leadership has exercised its power, but in the limits of that power. Gramsci famously talked of 'hegemony protected by the armour of coercion'.[15] But, not only is coercive power

---

[13] I am developing here a suggestion from Fotis Vergis, whom I thank.

[14] The late André Tosel has provided an authoritative study of Gramsci's theory of hegemony: *Étudier Gramsci: Pour un Critique Continue de la Révolution Passive* (Éditions Kimé 2016). It is, of course, a matter of controversy how far Gramsci's theory of hegemony can be extended beyond the national plane for which it was originally formulated to the sphere of international politics: Lorenzo Fusaro makes a powerful case for the negative in his forthcoming book *Crises and Hegemonic Transitions* (Brill 2019). But the peculiarly hybrid character of the EU, with its combination of transnational institutions and intergovernmental policymaking makes it a comparatively easy stretch to use Gramsci to help anatomise its dysfunctions.

[15] A Gramsci, *Selections from the Prison Notebooks* (Lawrence & Wishart 1971) 263; *Quaderni del carcere* (V Gerratana ed, 4 vols, Einaudi 1975), II, 764; Q6 (VIII) para 88.

still exercised in Europe primarily at the national level, but Germany's military capabilities are also significantly less than those of Britain and France. This might not have mattered if the boosters of globalisation in the 1990s and early 2000s had been right to argue that greater transnational economic integration would have a pacifying effect on interstate relations. Evidently, they were quite wrong. This has important implications both within and without the EU. Claude Serfati, an early critic of the idea of an irenic globalisation, has argued compellingly that France has used its military clout, and its long tradition of intervention in its former colonies in the Maghreb and sub-Saharan Africa, to attempt to carve out a comparative advantage in EU decision-making that seeks to compensate for its poor economic performance compared to Germany.[16]

But even in the Mediterranean, France's ability to offer military protection to the rest of the EU is limited, particularly given that the threat is growing thanks the mutating forms of armed jihadism represented by Al-Qaeda and now ISIS. The heavy lifting is still done by the US, despite the battering it has suffered in Iraq and Afghanistan, by rivalrous regional powers – Saudi Arabia, Iran, Turkey, Egypt, Qatar – and by the new power broker in Syria, Russia. The ability of European states to manage the chaos in the Arab world is extremely limited, while their interventions across the Mediterranean have been mainly to contain the consequences of their past failures, and to regulate the flow of migrants and refugees (which is evidently related to these failures).[17]

Russia is of course active not just on the EU's southern flank, but to its east. The evolution of the Ukrainian crisis since its outbreak in 2013–14 is extremely instructive. The EU helped to precipitate the explosion by pressing the Yanukovych regime to accept a partnership agreement that Moscow interpreted as a step towards Ukraine joining NATO. But when Vladimir Putin reacted to Yanukovych's fall by seizing Crimea and supporting armed rebellion in south-eastern Ukraine it was the US that stepped in to orchestrate the western response, stiffening European backbones, redeploying military assets to Europe, and orchestrating NATO deployments to the Union's eastern borders with Russia.

Germany under Merkel took a tougher line with Moscow than it had at the time of the 2008 Russo-Georgian war (another intervention by Putin to keep NATO away from Russia's frontiers). But its main practical contribution lay in supporting and enforcing economic sanctions against Russia. It simply cannot begin to offer security guarantees to those eastern and central European states that fear a more assertive Russia. Even in the context of the collective security offered by NATO, Germany is a laggard that persistently fails to meet the shared target of spending at least 2 per cent of GDP on defence. Although Germany has participated in a number of overseas 'humanitarian' operations and is now committed to building up two new armoured

[16]   C Serfati, *Le Militaire: Une Histoire Française* (Éditions Amsterdam 2017).
[17]   L Pradella and S Taghdisi Rad, 'Libya and Europe: Imperialism, Crisis and Migration' (2017) 38 Third World Quarterly 2411.

divisions by 2032, the Bundeswehr suffers from chronic shortages of personnel and equipment. Christian Mölling, a defence expert at the DGAP German Council on Foreign Relations, says: 'Let's not make too fine a point about this: the situation of Germany's armed forces is dramatically bad. It will take a lot of time to turn this around.'[18]

The German domestic political constellation, with the right arguing that the fiscal surplus run up by the export boom and austerity should be used to fund tax cuts and the SPD advocating higher social expenditure, means that this situation is very unlikely to change any time soon. There is the alternative route of greater European military collaboration – given concrete shape in the decision of twenty-five EU Member States to sign up to permanent structured cooperation (PESCO) in military affairs. Brexit will remove an obstacle to the EU developing its own military capabilities (London always opposed anything that might duplicate or undermine NATO, and Washington has been quick to express reservations about PESCO for the same reason). But it is doubtful that this will offer much compensation for the departure of one of Europe's two genuine (though declining) military powers. The 'armour of coercion' that protects the EU externally thus remains American.

The implication is that, in the geopolitical domain at least, the US continues to play the hegemonic role in Europe. This is not simply an inheritance from the past or (as Trump would have it) a burden thrust on a weary American titan by free-riding Europeans. After the end of the Cold War successive US administrations intervened actively to reshape a continent thrown into flux to extend liberal capitalism eastwards under Washington's leadership. The expansion of the EU to incorporate ex-Communist states in Eastern and Central Europe was part of a package deal in which they also joined NATO (violating undertakings made to the last Soviet leader, Mikhail Gorbachev, when he agreed in 1990 to the reunification of Germany). The underlying logic was to expand the US-led Atlantic space eastwards. The response of the Obama administration to the Ukraine crisis indicates a commitment by Washington at the very least to maintaining that space (both that crisis and its Georgian predecessor also indicate a desire to continue to expand it).

The determination of the US security establishment to continue confronting Russia under a President whom it suspects of being Moscow's tool underlines the extent of that commitment. And Central and Eastern Europe is liable to become more problematic, thanks to the region's increasing economic penetration by Chinese investment and infrastructural projects that are threatening to make Beijing a rival centre of gravity to Brussels, thereby giving right-wing authoritarian governments greater room for manoeuvre. This development, reflected in the formation of the '16+1' grouping of China and sixteen East and Central European states, has already led to suspicions that some of the Member States involved have

---

[18] T Buck, 'German Military: Combat Ready?' *Financial Times* (London, 18 February 2018) www.ft.com /content/36e2cd40-0fdf-11e8-940e-08320fc2a277 accessed 10 April 2018.

been lobbying for weaker EU policies on the South China Sea and on the vetting of Chinese takeovers of European firms.[19] It is likely to increase the core EU states' dependence on the protective shield offered by the US and NATO.

So, if the EU is an empire, it is a peculiarly exocentric one, reliant for its security on an outside power, the United States, and offering a framework through which its most powerful Member States can pursue their interests. Indeed, I have argued elsewhere:

> From its inception, the process of European integration has involved a double imperialist constitution. In the first place, starting in the late 1940s, the US promoted integration in order to secure Western Europe as a stable and prosperous junior partner in managing global capitalism ... Secondly, the evolving forms of European integration (from the Iron and Steel Community through the Common Market to the EU) offered a platform through which the leading European states could pursue their imperial interests in a way that they were no longer able to individually.[20]

This constitution – by which I mean, not a legal structure, but the emergent properties of EU institutions – was there from the moment of genesis in 1950–51, but it persists into the present. It helps to explain the dysfunctions of the EU. The predominance of national interests – and therefore the failure, for example, to underpin EMU with a fiscal union – reflects the role that European integration has played in multiplying the power of the major Member States. This doesn't rule out further integration – Berlin is currently bending somewhat to the pressures for such emanating from Paris since Emmanuel Macron's election as French president – but it means that any changes will persist with the peculiar hybrid structure of intergovernmentalism and federalism that has characterised European integration since the Schuman Plan. The role of the US as military guarantor of European security explains the EU's restriction to the role of a 'normative power' – if this understood in the broader sense used above, as a generator and exporter of neoliberal economic regulation. The division of labour established between the US and Germany in the 1950s – a bifurcation of military and economic power – thus also persists, but in a more problematic form. For of course, Washington was always interested in European integration for economic and not just geopolitical reasons. The EEC offered US multinationals enhanced opportunities even if it restricted the access of American farmers to European markets. But the emergence of Germany as the EU's uncontested economic hub has limited American influence – as is indicated by the Obama administration's complete failure to persuade Merkel to offer greater support to indebted Member States during the eurozone-crisis.

[19] J Kynge and M Peel, 'Brussels Rattled as China Reaches Out to Eastern Europe' *Financial Times* (London, 27 November 2017) www.ft.com/content/16abbf2a-cf9b-11e7-9dbb-291a884dd8c6 accessed 10 April 2018.

[20] A Callinicos, 'Britain and Europe on the Geopolitical Roller Coaster' (2017) 21 Competition & Change 185, 187.

All this suggests that the EU's dysfunctionality is liable to grow in the post-Brexit era. This isn't a normative judgement based on comparing Europe with some ideal example of the nation state (after all, the US today is hardly a model of a well-ordered polity). But it is important to see that the EU's dysfunctions spring from its inner structure. Indeed, the dysfunctions drive the process of deepening integration, with new institutions being built to correct older problems, but creating problems of their own, sometimes (as in the case of EMU) worse that those they were intended to correct. The EU functions by dysfunction. In this sense it is comparable to the prison, as portrayed by Foucault:

> Prison 'reform' is virtually contemporary with the prison itself. It constitutes, as it were, its programme. From the outset, the prison was caught up in a series of accompanying mechanisms, whose purpose was apparently to correct it, but which seem to form part of its very functioning, so closely have they been bound up with its existence throughout its long history.[21]

The dysfunctionality of European integration was intended by its original architect, Jean Monnet, to drive it towards a federal state.[22] No such telos governs the actual development of the EU, which has been constrained by its double imperial constitution. The Union will continue on its tortuous path, amid a world that has yet to recover from the 2008 financial crash and which is driven by growing geopolitical rivalries. Europe today offers no refuge from this world.

---

[21] M Foucault, *Discipline and Punish: The Birth of the Prison* (Allen Lane 1977) 234.
[22] F Duchêne, *Jean Monnet: The First Statesman of Interdependence* (Norton 1994).

Conclusion

Eva Nanopoulos and Fotis Vergis

This volume brought together scholars from different disciplines to think through the systemic causes of the Eurocrisis across a number of its core dimensions and with a view to illuminating the 'nature of the beast', hidden in the large dark room, awaiting further apprehension. The analyses offered drew on a number of different disciplines, from law to political economy, as well as different theoretical perspectives, from Marxism to governmentality studies, to key figures of ordoliberal and neoliberal thought. It is inevitably difficult to synthesise such a wide pool of contributions, particularly since, informed by different theoretical starting points, assumptions and analytical tools, different analyses have inevitably at times produced different diagnoses, conclusions or prognoses. Nonetheless, section I attempts to distil the main ideas that emerge from the volume and that hold our basic thesis together. The common theme of a deeply rooted crisis and the need for a more principled critique indeed appears in all of the chapters, which proves both the necessity and value of dialogue and the sharing of perspectives. The remainder of this conclusion offers some thoughts about the implications of viewing the Eurocrisis as a mere symptom of a deeper systemic crisis and the further questions that this conceptualisation raises. Section II explores how our approach could inform inquiries about the relationship between the Eurocrisis and other similar events, including most notably Brexit and the so-called 'refugee crisis'. Section III ponders on the likely future trajectory of the EU. Section IV, finally, calls for a broader historical contextualisation of the EU as a way to shedding further light on the longer-term roots of its systemic crisis.

I THE NATURE OF THE CRISIS BEHIND THE EUROCRISIS

Regardless of the different approaches adopted by the various contributions, the common thread is clear: the Eurocrisis was not an isolated moment of imbalance, revelatory of merely structural deficiencies in the EMU architecture. Although the existence of flaws in the conception and particular institutional structure of the EMU are not disputed, the issue runs deeper. The crisis is revealed to be closely related to the nature of the EU and its inherent organic connection to particular geopolitical considerations, and, perhaps more importantly, to the particular economic rationale it was created to serve and primarily follows.

The Union was born out of the need to quickly settle the new antagonisms that would begin to emerge after the end of the Second World War, particularly between France and Germany, and the initiative to bind them into trade cooperation was heralded under the stark support – if not at the behest – of the US and its post-Second World War Euro-Atlantic policy. Regardless of its slow evolution into a transnational entity comprising supposedly equal partners, France and Germany remained the two fundamental pillars of influence, around which the European project was structured,[1] with the caveat of the distinct British angle that also exerted considerable effect on European policies and developments until 2016. This arrangement reflected a particular balance of economic and geopolitical power, as it was more or less set in place and stabilised in the post-Second World War period, operating within the broader context of the dualism of Cold War global antagonism. The end of the Cold War, however, propelled the EU into a more central position, as a new player in the global chess board, wishing to signify and project a unique political and economic paradigm that would distinguish it from its American counterpart. This was the premise upon which the old Eastern bloc 'enemies' were welcomed as equal partners, ushering in not merely a new era in the development of the EU, but, importantly, also an influx of new interests that would challenge the traditional established balance of power.

The main objective of promoting the creation of a common market by abolishing obstacles to trade was the appeasement of antagonisms; the promotion of cooperation among old rivals as a means to ensure that the plights of war would not reappear in the continent and European capitalism would be allowed to flourish. Peace among the EU Member States, though certainly not in the whole of Europe, has certainly been maintained for the last seventy years, even though it might be a stretch to attribute this achievement exclusively to the EU and not the post-war consensus, to which the Union was but a part. However, the fundamental flaw rested in the foundation upon which cooperation was to be built, with the supposed assumption that it would eventually lead to further deepened integration: the common market, and the entire nexus of ideological and normative assumptions and principles that come with it.

The transnational organisation that came to be the EU was never formed as anything more than a hub of trade cooperation, with a specific set of competences to serve the abolition of customs duties and the introduction of the fundamental economic freedoms, despite the declared aspirations of its founders. In fact, according to the plan of the Union's architects, those aspirations of further social and

---

[1] U Krotz and J Schild, *Shaping Europe: France, Germany and Embedded Bilateralism from the Elysée Treaty to Twenty-First Century Politics* (OUP 2013).

political integration explicitly were to be realised through, and as a result of, economic integration. However, the economic paradigm chosen was reflective of a particular vision of the market and, as such, inherently connected, since its inception, to a specific version of capitalism. Furthermore, the evolution of the new entity was to rely exclusively upon this vision and the institutional and normative choices inherent to it. The result was that the fragmented development which followed remained firmly founded upon the fundamental prioritisation of particular economic freedoms and objectives, with the common market 'ideal' at its core. Regardless of the changes in direction that gradually allowed for attempts to infuse more social considerations or a fundamental rights ethos to the project, the Razian 'common ideology' of this self-proclaimed new autonomous legal order was always defined predominantly by the absolute embrace and affirmation of the free market ethos that had been the Union's building block.

It is telling that the Union not only never came to shed its original ordoliberal characteristics (adherence to a particular normative and institutional market 'order' that is placed beyond questioning and needs to be safeguarded at any cost) but in many ways subsequently enhanced them, especially through the adoption of a very particular architecture for the EMU and the measures and institutions introduced in response to the Eurocrisis. What lies at the root of the political, institutional and structural imbalances that were revealed by the Eurocrisis, and the failure of the Union to react to the events of the 2008 global financial crisis with the flexibility and social reflexes that a traditional nation state would have at its disposal, was the invariable uniform economic nature of the core of its (constitutional) existence, impermeable by basic democratic and social principles. The real issue, therefore, is not the supposed deficits or flaws in the EU's architecture, but, rather, the character of the economic order the EU has been designed to promote, the neoliberal characteristics it has increasingly come to court, and the ordoliberal discipline with which it has sought to preserve this order and its constitutive dogma.

The most important consequence of this evolutionary path, a path that is certainly unique to any aspiring polity, is that the Union effectively irrevocably connected its existence, nature and fate to the economic system it was created to serve. Regardless of their recent constitutional dress-up, the EU and its structure remain existentially firmly attached in symbiotic embrace with transnational free market capitalism. As a result, it inherently internalises its crises, which then, understandably, take on an existential dimension as regards the current 'European project' as a whole. And as the EU fails to have any other reaction than the one demanded by its rigid preprescribed 'order' and its fundamental characteristics, since it is by nature inherently incapable of construing any solution that would question those foundational elements and their relevant assumptions, the embrace strengthens and the vicious circle perpetuates. Thus understood, the EU common market is nothing but a regional variety of the contemporary globalised free market. As such, the institutional features and life of the Union cannot but follow the features and life of contemporary capitalism. In other words, the Eurocrisis as such was not only a crisis of the Union and its framework, but rather part of a broader crisis of modern capitalism which seems to have reached a critical point.

What further exacerbates the potential effects of this process of imbalanced evolution and one-dimensional integration route is that neither the original conception of the EU nor its evolutionary path were crafted on the basis of popular democratic debate and acquiescence or any foundational social and political contract that might have granted it some legitimacy. The original draft, an exercise in geopolitics as it was, was forged and pushed forward outside of the popular spotlight and without direct democratic participation. Of course, this might only be natural for what was, at the time, simply an international treaty establishing yet another post-Second World War organisation. However, it is telling that, once the new entity, especially through the case law of the Court of Justice, started to claim for itself characteristics that would transcend its mere economic character (supremacy; direct effect; protection of 'fundamental rights'), and thus encroach upon more fundamental principles and structures that would resemble those of a liberal constitutional legal order, popular participation and consent in any form that would resemble acquiescence by a European demos were suspiciously absent. Moreover, a robust technocratic and bureaucratic apparatus attached to the EU slowly, and unsurprisingly, came to be, whose fate and ethos are intrinsically linked to the particular nature of the Union, and the specific vision of free market 'order' that rests at its heart.

The combination of (a) an ordoliberal DNA that embraces the requirement for that order to be closely safeguarded, (b) an institutional and bureaucratic construction set to serve that purpose but also feeding back into it and (c) the absence of either constitutive popular participatory structures or, at the very least, a common idea of belonging that goes beyond the shallow promise of political integration through market liberalism, provides for a dangerous mix, especially in times of turmoil. Perhaps that is exactly the reason why the mix also inherently demands sidelining, and narrowing the scope of, processes of democratic scrutiny. This marginal democracy ensures that, in moments of perceived crisis, the EU and its established order will not be at the mercy of immature electorates reacting in fear and panic. It might be, though, that it is not the electorates that are truly uneasy, but rather these actors, political and economic, whose interests primarily shaped the Union, and continue to define it today. And the source of their unease might be that, in moments when the cracks become apparent, and the underlining crisis gushes, the established narrative will collapse and the empty heart of the EU will be revealed.

II FROM THE EUROCRISIS TO THE REFUGEE AND BREXIT CRISES

How does this systemic crisis more specifically help us understand other events that followed the Eurocrisis, most notably Brexit, the refugee crisis or the election of far-right illiberal regimes in Hungary and Poland? Although these subsequent 'crises' featured in several contributions to this collection, the volume as a whole did not aim to draw concrete or systematic links between these different set of events. This is partly for want of space, as well as thematic coherence and focus: it would have been impossible to explore the systemic roots of the Eurocrisis and use them to illuminate other related events in a single volume. But it is also partly because these more recent 'crises' are still unfolding and the wider context in which they operate is constantly shifting. At the time this collection was completed, the UK's future relationship with the EU, and hence the exact challenge it poses to the process of European integration, remain largely unknown. At the diplomatic level, common ground between the UK Tory government and European elites remains thin, and shaky. The wider political establishment appears more generally in disarray. And many grass-roots social movements and organisations on the left still struggle to articulate a progressive vision of Brexit, which could form the basis for a test case of a successful reconstruction of social, political and economic life outside of the EU. Days before the collection was submitted, leaders of seemingly 'irreconcilable' clout and ideology – populists and defenders of the liberal order alike – found in their 'concern' about the humanity of the Syrian people and the 'defence of global rules and standards'[2] sufficient common ground to launch a series of attacks over Syrian territory. Whether those humanist instincts and concern for compliance with the rule of law will translate in greater openness to refugees and the de-securitisation of the EU's borders remains to be seen, but the unfolding of events thus far suggests humanitarianism is something Europe is only willing to practice at a distance and apparently, by force.

At the same time, our approach to the Eurocrisis and its conceptualisation as a deeper systemic crisis of the European project could not only offer a framework to begin thinking more seriously about their interconnections, but also a number of concrete hypotheses about the nature of these linkages. The European space is saturated with tangible signs of the links between these different sets of events: the overcrowded refugee camps in debt and austerity-ridden countries of the periphery, most notably Greece; the Nazi-inspired poster of Nigel Farage standing in front of refugees crossing the Croatia–Slovenia border in 2015 with the header: 'Breaking point: the EU has failed us all'[3] in the run-up to the Brexit vote; or the walls and fences now bordering the Union's territory in countries like Hungary. Empirically, there are thus many facts one could tap into to identify the links between these different events and indeed analyses that attempt to tease out these connections are proliferating. Indicatively, some commentators have looked at how the demands of

---

[2] M Weller, 'Syria Air Strikes: Were They Legal?' *BBC News* (14 April 2018) www.bbc.co.uk/news/world-middle-east-43766556 accessed 2 May 2018.

[3] H Stewart and R Mason, 'Nigel Farage's Anti-Migrant Poster Reported to Police' *The Guardian* (16 June 2016) www.theguardian.com/politics/2016/jun/16/nigel-farage-defends-ukip-breaking-point-poster-queue-of-migrants accessed 2 May 2018.

EU macroeconomic governance and the sovereign debt loan conditions imposed on Member States, and their dramatic effect on social rights and, hence, social cohesion, exacerbated processes that led to populist and nationalistic voices to emerge.[4] The 'rise of illiberalism' in Europe has also been connected to the Eurocrisis (alongside the EU's increasing 'inwardness' and its 'declining normative influence' and 'transformative capacity' towards not only its own Member States, but also third countries)[5] as a result of which the EU both ignored the political discontent that was brewing in populations ('illiberalism by omission') and facilitated the erosion of the social fabric, by, among other things, accentuating inequalities both between and within Member States ('illiberalism by commission').[6] The question, however, is not only how these interconnections should be interpreted, but how they should be contextualised and fit into a broader theoretical framework.

First, our approach implies that none of these crises are the products of unconnected or external factors[7] (even though in these contexts too, the EU has sought to deploy the language of emergency and exceptionalism) but that they must be routed instead in the same set of (geopolitical and socio-economic) interests and normative assumptions, as they are legally and institutionally reflected and operationalised in the EU, but also, to some extent, in the broader global capitalist order. Some contributions articulate this point more explicitly. Thus, for example, Alex Callinicos traced all three crises, and particularly Brexit, to the potentially fatal tension between sovereignty and European integration as an inherent feature, not of supranationalism as a mode of governance, but of Europe's dual imperial constitution as a vehicle for the interests of the US (external dimension) and major European powers (internal dimension). Similarly, for Michelle Everson, all three crises have in part a common root in the crisis of economic liberalism. But other contributions too, offer important evidence of the common grounding of the EU's multiple crises. Dimitris Dalakoglou thus situates the EU's reaction to the flow of refugees to longer-term processes of 'othering' that are crucial to the building of European identity and the maintenance of European unity.

Second, conversely, just like the Eurocrisis, Brexit and the refugee crisis would constitute but further symptoms of the EU's systemic crisis, which can be analysed against the latter's multiple dimensions. For example, in line with Dalakoglou's argument in this collection, several commentators have observed that the increase in number of people seeking asylum in Europe was only the trigger, rather than cause,

---

[4] C Kilpatrick, 'Constitutions, Social Rights and Sovereign Debt States in Europe: A Challenging New Area of Constitutional Inquiry' in T Beukers, B de Witte and C Kilpatrick (eds), *Constitutional Change through Euro-Crisis Law* (CUP 2017) 279.

[5] O Anastasakis, 'The Eurozone Crisis and the EU's "Sins of Illiberalism"' (*Hungarian Europe Society*, 4 June 2015) http://old.europatarsasag.hu/en/blog/met-blog/the-eurozone-crisis-and-the-eu-s-sins-of-illiberalism accessed 2 May 2018.

[6] ibid.

[7] For an analysis of the refugee crisis as 'systemic', see eg special issue, 'EU Refugee Policies and Politics in Times of Crisis' (2018) 56 Journal Common Market Studies 1.

of the so-called 'refugee crisis'. Whether the latter is attributed to 'persistent dys-functionalities and shortcomings of the Common European Asylum System',[8] to a more pervasive border crisis produced in large part by increased securitisation of the European border, or even to a more fundamental racial crisis produced by the postcolonial condition of Europe,[9] thus reframed, the refugee crisis could be understood, and analysed, as a product and reflection of the EU's crisis of identity. Similarly, under our conceptual grid, Brexit could be traced both to the EU's crisis of democratic and political legitimacy and to what we have termed a crisis of its economic model. Even before the Brexit vote, political scientists had noted the close symbiosis between the EU's economic and political crisis and British Euroscepticism,[10] looking at the ways Euroscepticism intensified as a result of the Eurocrisis but also how British sentiment towards the EU has been a persistent, and now growing, source of instability for the European project.

Ultimately, if these crises share common roots, and if their constitutive elements are but different manifestations of the same set of inherent dysfunctionalities, the interpretation of their visible interconnections in practice becomes arguably more complex. These tangible signs should not be seen as mere points of intersection in a European landscape inhabited by mutually aggravating but ultimately separate crises. Nor should they be interpreted merely in terms of cause and effects. Our approach to the EU's systemic crisis as inherent to the nature of the EU should prompt us on the contrary to see them as part of a single whole where the contradictions of the European project become both more visible and gradually intensify, and where the full ramifications of the EU's dysfunctional condition are being revealed.

To take but one example, the point is not only that the relationship between the refugee crisis and the Eurocrisis materialised in an increased number of attacks on refugee centres and homes – as it did even in countries like Germany – and that this can be explained by the fact political discontent and marginalisation have been channelled increasingly in nationalistic and xenophobic directions, which have facilitated the rise of far-right groups and illiberal regimes, in turn normalising racist and other attacks. The point, rather, is that these attacks are the culmination of processes that are inherent to the EU's condition. As Dalakoglou illustrates in this volume, the processes of 'othering' at play in these dramatic events and realised through spatial exclusivity and a sense of 'European belonging' premised on the differentiation between 'Europeans from non-Europeans',[11] are integral to the building of European identity and, after the Eurocrisis, to maintain European unity.

---

8   A Niemann and N Zaun, 'EU Refugee Policies and Politics in Times of Crisis: Theoretical and Empirical Perspectives' (2018) 56 Journal Common Market Studies 3, 4.

9   N de Genova, 'The "Migrant Crisis" as Racial Crisis: Do Black Lives Matter in Europe?' (2017) Ethnic and Racial Studies.

10   D Baker and P Schnapper, *Britain and the Crisis of the European Union* (Palgrave 2015).

11   C Cantat, 'Narratives and Counter-Narratives of Europe: Constructing and Contesting Europeanity' (2015) 3 Cahiers: Mémoire et Politique 5, 6.

Similarly, in our chapter, we suggested that nationalism was reinforced by the suppression of alternatives to neoliberalism, as a necessary means for the EU (and the Member States) to implement austerity policies. As such, these symptoms of the EU's crises are systematically interrelated and constitute inevitable manifestations of the EU's underlying systemic crisis. As the crisis deepens, these symptoms will worsen and evolve in sometimes violent or unpredictable directions. The Brexit vote, for example, may be partly a natural consequence of the disenfranchisement and intense reaction to incumbent elites by the electorates that can be observed across Europe since the advent of the Eurocrisis. But it also paradoxically took place at a time where the EU became 'closer to the traditional model of intergovernmental cooperation and market-led solutions encouraged by successive British governments'.[12]

III CRISES AS INTEGRATION, DISINTEGRATION OR 'DYS-INTEGRATION'?

What then is the likely impact of this systemic multifaced crisis whose various outgrowths have only began to emerge? Today, the cumulative effects of the Eurocrisis, the migration crisis, and a Brexit mandate that reverses a seemingly perpetual and irreversible forward movement, have for the first time seriously questioned the future of the 'further integration' dogma. If the narrative that the crisis of the EMU was 'exceptional' and could be contained found some purchase in the early days, there is far greater acknowledgement – and fear – that the EU's manifest 'crises' may not necessarily result in greater integration but may on the contrary have set the path for an outward disintegration of the EU. In that context, commentators have been particularly critical of the 'widespread belief that crises are not unusual occurrences in EU history and are perhaps essential to the success of European integration',[13] as well as the complacency about the self-sustaining capacity of the European machinery this served to produce.

Few contributions in this volume expressed a clear view on the likely future trajectory of the project. Among those that did, not all shared the prognosis of disintegration. Without falling into the trap of the somewhat mystical aura of the 'integration through crisis' approach and rooting the sources of unification in the evolution of European capitalism, Christakis Georgiou, for example, approached the present phase as one of corporate reconstruction and greater and deeper integration. On the whole, however, our approach to the Eurocrisis and European crises as systemic would tend to suggest that the integrationist–disintegrationist dichotomy somewhat misses the point. Empirical signs of its limits today abound. Even before Macron's more explicit promotion of the idea of 'multi-speed Europe', a prospect

---

[12] Baker and Schnapper (n 10).
[13] D Dinan, 'Crises in EU History' in D Dinan, N Nugent and W Paterson (eds), *The European Union in Crisis* (Palgrave 2017) 16–17.

that appeared unthinkable in traditional narratives of integration, the proliferation of à la carte arrangements and the gradual polarisation between Member States that characterised the immediate post-crisis period cast doubt over the narrative that integration was a uniform process with a clear and common telos. Within the academy, moreover, the acknowledgement that the EU machinery is facing an existential crisis has been met with increased calls, not necessarily for further or less integration – some commentators have indeed expressly argued for a move away from the 'sterile and counter-productive characterisation of every debate of the EU as one where all pro-Europeans must perforce desire political union, with those who want a more politically differentiated EU being dubbed anti-Europeans'[14] – but for the EU to rediscover or reinvent its very 'raison d' être'[15] and find novel ways to justify its existence to the people of Europe. This search for renewal confirms that the question is no longer about more or less integration, but about what kind of Europe.

Whether such performative transformation succeeds or not – and for whose benefit and at whose expenses is another question – our analysis suggests that the EU will remain deeply *dys*functional, ridden with asymmetries, contradictions and patterns of domination, hegemonic at times, but also authoritarian when the economic and social order comes under threat. As Callinicos puts it in his chapter: 'the EU functions by dysfunction'. The EU does not therefore oscillate between integration and disintegration in any linear manner; neither can its dynamics be productively – or accurately – captured by reference to either of these two trajectories. As such, the evolution of the EU can best be described as one of *dys*-integration, driven by an evolving but enduringly dysfunctional condition.

This is also in tune with our conceptualisation of crisis as a condition that lies within, not outside, the EU, as well as broader theorisations of crises as necessary for the reproduction and revitalisation of capitalism, be it in its global or European variant, the two being, in the final instance, closely interlinked. In that context, crisis is neither necessarily opportunity (integration), nor destruction (disintegration). It is a moment when the contradictions and limits of the system are revealed, when the historical process may accelerate and when the outcome – continuity or rupture – is both highly contingent, depending on the social forces on the ground, and over-determined by the existing machinery. Greece and SYRIZA are a case in point. The electoral victory of SYRIZA in 2015 was in many ways the product of mounting dissatisfaction with the austerity treatment imposed by the EU, and constituted the political organised form such resistance took at that particular historical moment. But its capitulation and subsequent alignment with European elites reflected both

[14] R Bellamy, 'The Democratic Deficit, Social Justice and the Eurozone Crisis' in R Bellamy and U Staigher (eds), *The Eurozone Crisis and the Democratic Deficit* (UCL European Institute 2014) 3 www.ucl.ac.uk/european-institute/ei-publications/working-paper-eurozone.pdf accessed 2 May 2018.
[15] G de Búrca, 'Europe's raison d'être' in D Kochenov and F Amtenbrink, *The European Union's Shaping of the International Legal Order* (CUP 2013).

the economic and ideological forces at play, whether imposed from the top, or from within the very changing base of SYRIZA's members and supporters.

IV FROM AN EU CRISIS TO A CRISIS OF CONTEMPORARY EUROPEANISM

What should be the way forward, thinking about the EU's multiple crises as systemic and emblematic of the deeply dysfunctional character of integration? If this systemic dysfunctional condition is rooted in the EU as a regional variety of the contemporary globalised free market, these dysfunctionalities should be traced not only to the workings of the capitalist system but also to the broader history of European capitalism. This means that the EU should be approached not on its own terms, but as the product and contemporary institutional manifestation of a set of dynamics with a much longer history. More importantly, it means that in tracing those lineages, one should avoid the trap that the EU marks a radical break from the continent's legacy of violence and imperial domination or that this legacy is somewhat of an uncomfortable parenthesis in Europe's history of enlightenment,[16] which the EU would today embody.

International lawyers have for some time understood the importance of historical contextualisation and critique. The 'turn to history'[17] produced invaluable work on the colonial origins of international law, the ways in which the colonial logic – what Anghie has coined 'the dynamic of difference'[18] – continues to permeate the structures and workings of the contemporary international order, as well as the relationship between international law and capitalism,[19] characterised by continuous inequality and exploitation, particularly of the Global South. Even doctrines like functionalism, which have been so central to the law of international organisations in general, and the law of the EU in particular, have been traced to ideas about colonial administration.[20]

The near absence of such inquiries within the EU legal community, and in European studies more generally, is not necessarily surprising.[21] EU law is largely seen to have emerged out of a voluntary alliance of states sharing a particular

---

[16] For an overview of these kinds of narratives, see in particular Cantat (n 11) 12–14.

[17] See for an overview of the literature, see T Skouteris, 'The Turn to History in International Law' Oxford Bibliographies (June 2017) www.oxfordbibliographies.com/view/document/obo-9780199796953/obo-9780199796953-0154.xml accessed 2 May 2018.

[18] A Anghi, *Imperialism, Sovereignty, and the Making of International Law* (CUP 2005).

[19] eg C Mieville, *Between Equal Rights: A Marxist Theory of International Law* (Pluto 2006); R Knox, 'Valuing Race? Stretched Marxism and the Logic of Imperialism' (2016) 4 London Review of International Law 81.

[20] J Klabbers, 'The Emergence of Functionalism in International Institutional Law: Colonial Inspirations' (2014) 25 EJIL 645.

[21] There are important exceptions, including the work of Nicholas De Genova, who frames the 'European question' as a problem of postcolonial whiteness. See N de Genova, 'The European Question: Migration, Race, and Postcoloniality in Europe' (2016) 34 Social Text 75.

heritage and eager to deepen their relationship inter se. Contrary to international law, it could not be accused of imposing western liberal values and norms upon other societies and cultures. The EU's disassociation from all matters imperial was also facilitated by the supposed autonomy of EU law and constitutionalisation of the EU legal order, suggesting a radical separation from the workings and logic of international law and the global capitalist order. Although progressive narratives of law and international cooperation abound,[22] the image of the EU as an enlightened, internationalist peace project has been particularly pervasive: it was in 2012, after all, as the humanitarian crisis was unfolding in Greece, that the EU was awarded its peace prize for the 'stabilising role [it] has played in transforming most of Europe from a continent of war to a continent of peace'.

The crisis made this dominant narrative and reading of the European project increasingly difficult to sustain. Our analysis of the Eurocrisis already revealed the weakness of the voluntarist and spatially uniform framework outlined above. Austerity was imposed through a range of disciplinary and coercive practices, implemented by legal instruments concluded outside the ordinary legal artillery of the Union and notwithstanding explicit rejection by the people. The crisis also blurred the lines between the inside and the outside of the EU, intensifying the divide between core and periphery and undermining the supposedly egalitarian European legal and political space. Several of our authors moreover remarked how the supposed common values of the EU, where neither commonly agreed, nor commonly applied: enlargement on the contrary involved a large process of social assimilation and state building.

The crisis also suggested that the roots of the asymmetries of power and the growing inequalities among European citizens are not only inherent in the EU project but have a much longer lineage. In this volume, this comes more explicitly across in Michael Wilkinson's reconstruction of the historical and intellectual roots of authoritarian liberalism. But it can also be seen in the stereotypical vocabularies and narratives that have emerged out of the crises, be it the distinction between 'virtuous' states and 'sinners', 'debtors' and 'creditors' or tropes like 'the lazy Greek' or 'PIGS' and that are reminiscent of 'old' classifications of societies (and humanity)[23] as 'civilised', 'semi-civilised', 'barbaric' or 'savage'.[24] These are among the few examples that draw attention to the urgent need to place the EU's systemic crisis in the context of the longer-term history of European capitalism, and indeed imperialism.

---

[22] eg T Altwicker and O Diggelmann, 'How Is Progress Constructed in International Legal Scholarship?' (2014) 25 European Journal of International Law 425.

[23] This also translates into a hierarchisation between subjects. See C Douzinas, 'Seven Theses on Human Rights: (1) The Idea of Humanity' (*Critical Legal Thinking*, 16 May 2013) http://criticallegalthinking .com/2013/05/16/seven-theses-on-human-rights-1-the-idea-of-humanity accessed 2 May 2018.

[24] eg L Obregón Tarazona, 'The Civilized and the Uncivilized' in B Fassbender and A Peters (eds), *Oxford Handbook of the History of International Law* (OUP 2012).

What is at stake is far more crucial than the survival of the EU. In his contribution, Christakis Georgiou introduced the various visions of Europeanism that dominated debates in the twentieth century: the socialist vision, a United States for Europe constructed from below; the bourgeois or liberal vision, a federal or quasi-federal union constructed from above; and the Nazi vision of a 'European New Order', to be achieved through the colonisation and 'authoritarian reconstruction of the continent'.[25] As Georgiou recounts, it was the 'failure of the first and third scenarios that opened the way for a return to the liberal internationalist method for unifying Europe' that is embedded in EU institutions. Today, that model of unification, alongside the wider international liberal order, are crumbling. If history supposedly ended with the victory of liberal (capitalist) democracy[26] over fascism and Soviet communism, then the historical process is on course to being 'relaunched'. The prospects ahead are neither daunting nor promising. Nationalist sentiment and far-right parties and regimes are on the rise. But there are also important pockets of progressive national and transnational resistance and solidarity. Luxemburg's famous warning – socialism or barbarism – should, however, give those unwilling to face the EU's systemic dysfunctional condition and/or, for that matter, the broader inhumanity of the capitalist system, at least pause for reflection. The Eurocrisis and its aftermath not only casts serious doubt about the narrative of European integration as a perpetual and irreversible forward movement. Most importantly, it casts doubt over its supposedly inherently progressive nature. The key question then is not whether the EU's systemic crisis will lead to more or less integration, or a different kind of EU but what kind of Europe will emerge when the crisis has run its full course and its effects have been revealed.

[25] M Mazower, 'Hitler's New Order, 1939–1945' (1996) 7 Diplomacy and Statecraft 29.
[26] F Fukuyama, *The End of History and the Last Man* (Free Press 1992).

Index

accords de maintien de l'emploi, 332
accumulation of debt strategy, 262
age-related public expenditure, 328
agentification, 127, 257, 258
Agricultural Bank, 417
agro-industrial enterprises, 417
Airbus, 311
Al-Qaeda, 426
Albanian Civil War (1997), 372
Albanian government, 369
Alesina, Alberto, 42
Amsterdam Treaty, 186
anarcho-liberalism, 401
anti-austerity social movements, 105, 118
anti-European populists, 354
anti-immigration rhetoric, 226
anti-inflationary monetary policies, 40
anti-interventionist experiments, 79
anti-refugee governments, 374
Ardagna, Francesco Silvia, 42
Association de médiation sociale, 325
Association for the Monetary Union of
        Europe, 304
asylum-seekers, 194
austerity politics
    bailouts and, 405
    constitutionalism and, 157–162, 165, 167–168
    domestic austerity, 408
    French government, 361
    German hegemony and, 408
    implementation of, 64
    institutionalisation of austerity, 165, 406
    introduction to, 29, 45
    missed objectives, 249
    neo-liberal 'austerity' measures, 104
    opposition to, 7
authoritarianism
    corporatism, 363

defined, 103–107
economic constitutionalism, 114–117
economic liberalisation and, 399–401
Eurocrisis and, 117–119, 382–383
inter-war Europe, 111–114
labour law, 341, 342
liberalism and, 15, 26, 101–103, 107–111, 121
neoliberalism, 89–90, 97
New Economic Governance as, 89, 90, 91–95
politico-economic sources of, 95–97
politico-economic sources of authoritarian
        neoliberalism, 95–97
Social Pillar, 344
summary of, 119–121
autonomous *vs.* collective action, 399
autonomy
    budgetary autonomy/discipline, 267–270,
        278–280
    in capitalist markets, 96
    collective action, 342
    economic administration, 137
    legal order, 144
    liberal autonomy, 385
    parliamentary budgetary autonomy, 277–278
    semi-autonomous institutions, 136

bailouts, 43, 45, 305, 403, 405, 409
balance budget rule, 159
balanced economic performance, 44
Balibar, Etienne, 119–120
bank jog, 307
Barroso, José Manuel, 201
basic human needs, 231, 238
Beck, Ulrich, 45
'beggar-thy-neighbour' economic strategies, 36
Bickerton, Christopher, 130–131
bilateral agreements, 195
Bocconi University of Milan, 42

Böhm, Franz, 390
borders and Eurocrisis, 372–375
Bretton Woods Agreement, 61, 95, 141, 300–301
Brexit
  asymmetries of, 420–422
  British 'no' to the European Union, 173, 193–194
  criminal law and employment, 343
  Euroskepticism by United Kingdom, 310–313
  foundering of, 88
  as ill-considered popular vote mechanism, 233
  impact of, 65, 295, 314
  introduction to, 3, 7, 21, 419
  post-Brexit European Union, 183
  reasons behind, 47–48, 159
  summary of, 433–437
  'taking back control' slogan, 152, 153
  Tory party split, 313
Brittan, Samuel, 11
Buck, Tobias, 421
budgetary autonomy/discipline, 267–270, 278–280
budgetary constraints, 168
Bundesbank, 304–305, 394, 424
Bundesverfassungsgerichtt. *See* German
  (Bundesverfassungsgericht) Federal
  Constitutional Court
Bündnis für Arbeit (pact for work), 306
Bush, George W., 364

Cameron, David, 311–312
capital liberalisation, 78, 101
capital/trade flow, 6
capitalism
  authoritarianism and, 97, 103, 107–111
  constitutionalism and, 163
  corporate capitalism, 297–298
  democracy and, 109, 364
  disruptive nature of, 363
  entrepreneurial capitalism, 297
  Eurocrisis and evolution of, 10
  European capitalism, 57, 371
  European Economic Community and, 91
  free market capitalism, 11, 109, 124, 153, 432
  global free market capitalism, 10, 11
  international law and, 439
  Keynesian welfare capitalism, 422
  liberal (capitalist) democracy, 441
  neoliberal capitalism, 422, 423
  new social hierarchies, 372
  transnational capitalism, 10, 364
  Varieties of Capitalism, 366
Cassis Judgment, 399
Catalonian independence referendum, 221–222
Central and Eastern European States (CEES), 224,
  225, 238

Chan, Margaret, 33
China, 326, 427–428
Christian Democrats, 58
Christianity, 231
citizen initiative, 212
citizen involvement in political
  decision-making, 178
civil liberties, 108
Civil Society Engagement, 236–238
Cold War, 19, 95, 141, 325, 371, 374, 427
collective action, 348–349, 358, 362, 367, 399
collective bargaining, 331, 415
collective governance, 356
collective labour rights, 346
Collignon, Stefan, 304
Colombian 'no' to the Peace Agreement
  Referendum, 174
'command-and-control' regulation, 37
Common Consolidated Corporate Tax Base
  (CCCTB), 314
Common European Asylum System, 436
common framework of belief, 222–223
communal action, 170
communautaire solution, 288
communication stage, 32–33
communist threat, 52
Community Charter of the Fundamental Social
  Rights of Workers (1989)
  amendments to, 337–341
  collective agreements and, 331
  European Social Pillar, 334–337, 339–345
  introduction to, 18–19, 317–320
  labor laws, 330–334
  overview, 320–323, 324
  paradigm shift, 327–330
  promises made by, 330
  social democracy overview, 324–327
Community Law *vs.* national law, 55
competitive corporatist pacts, 355
conceptualisation stage, 32
concrete order, 137
Connolly, Bernard, 141
constitution by governance, 396–399
constitutional accountability, 117
constitutional authority, 109
constitutional theory
  challenges to, 145
  counter-majoritarian dilemma, 108
  democracy and capitalism tension, 109
  democratic deficit and, 128, 129
  European integration and, 103
  political economy and, 114
Constitutional Treaty, 82, 85, 88
constitutional values of EU, 318

constitutionalism
  austerity politics, 157–162, 165, 167–168
  economic constitutionalism, 114–117, 135
  formal constitutionalism, 223
  introduction to, 156–157
  judicialisation of, 145
  ordoliberal economic constitutionalism, 391
  as political instrument, 168–171
  recasting of, 162–167
  reclaiming, 168–171
  referendums and, 187
  social democratic constitutionalism, 341
  summary of, 171–172
constructivist framework, 25
'core' member states, 219
corporate capitalism, 297–298
'corporate reconstruction of European capitalism'
    theory, 297
Council of Europe's Revised Social Charter, 324,
    326–327
counter-mobilisations, 357
country-specific recommendations (CSRs), 359
Court of Justice of the European Union (CJEU)
  Bundesverfassungsgerichtt judgment, 274–284
  Eurocrisis and, 37
  European integration and, 55
  European law and, 388
  as formative actor, 143–146
  legal reasoning in context, 286–293
  Pringle judgment, 266–274, 288, 384
  restructuring of, 38
  right as sole arbiter, 264
Craig, Paul, 268
crisis. *See also* Eurocrisis/Eurozone crisis; global
    financial crisis
  contemporary Europeanism crisis, 439–441
  of democracy, 37–38
  epiphenomenal approach to democratic crisis,
    124–127, 129
  European crisis management, 385
  European integration, 63–65
  hidden systemic crisis, 5
  of identity, 14–15, 19
  identity crisis, 14–15, 19, 81, 207–210, 373
  refugee crisis, 295, 375, 376–377, 433–437
  socioeconomic crisis, 4, 30
  sociopolitical crisis, 4
  sovereign debt crisis, 382
  Ukraine crisis, 427
critical junction thesis, 9
criticism against referendums, 180
cross-border capital flows, 302
cultural exclusivity, 372
cultural identity, 229

currency risk, 304
currency stabilisation measures, 265
Czech Republic, 232

Danish Constitution, 232
Danish 'no' to an opt-out referendum, 173, 191–192
Danish 'no' to the Maastricht Treaty, 185–186,
    199–201
de-democratisation, 15, 104, 118, 135
de Larosière report (2009), 312
de-legalisation, 104, 118
de-politicised monetary policy, 116
de Silguy, Yves-Thibault, 305
debt state, 110, 116
Delaisi, Francis, 70, 71, 72
Delors, Jacques, 40, 56, 305, 320, 324, 362, 392, 421
democracy. *See also* undemocratic EU democracy
  authoritarianism and, 97, 103, 107–111
  capitalism and, 109, 364
  constitutional power and, 169
  crisis of, 37–38
  denial of democracy, 200
  direct democracy, 174, 178, 185, 203–210
  liberal (capitalist) democracy, 441
  marginalisation of the democratic process, 146
  militant democracy, 113
  objectives of, 17
  participatory democracy, 174, 216
  peaceful conflict resolution and, 357
  post-communist democracies, 225
  representative democracy, 95, 215, 224, 238, 277
  restrained democracy, 113, 116
  technocracy vs., 356
  trade liberalisation, 381
  transnational democracy, 349, 350
  Treaty of Rome and, 141–142
  welfare state dismantling, 64
  Western liberal democracy, 34
democratic accountability, 274
democratic default, 122, 123, 124, 127, 155
democratic deficit
  bureaucratic actors and economic elites,
    146–150
  as epiphenomenon, 124–127, 129
  formative actors, 140–150
  founding processes/founding fathers, 140–143
  functionalism and, 128–130
  ideological roots of, 133–140
  influences and ideological roots, 133–140
  introduction to, 15, 16, 122–124
  meta-physics of, 132–133
  overview of, 124–132
  policies covering, 206
  political ontology and meta-physics, 132–133

popular control and, 171
problem with, 150–155
state transformation, 130–132
as systemic condition, 127–132
democratic legitimacy, 15–16, 127, 384
democratic non-governmental sphere, 357
democratic rights, 350
democratisation of socio-economic
    policymaking, 363
demoi-cracy, 214
demos-cracy, 215, 350
Denmark
    Danish Constitution, 232
    'no' to an opt-out referendum, 173, 191–192
    'no' to Maastrict Treaty, 185–186, 200–201
    referendums, 182
depoliticisation processes, 19, 357, 363
depreciation in Greek enterprises, 414, 416
deregulation, 319, 330, 392–394
dictatorships, 26, 58, 92, 109, 142, 147, 326
Directive of 1991 on Proof of Employment
    Terms, 338
Disaster Capitalism, 34
domestic austerity, 408. *See also* austerity politics
Doyle, Michael, 422
Draghi, Mario, 296, 309
Drinking Water Directive, 236
dual constitution of European Union, 21
Dukes, Ruth, 351
Dutch 'no' the Ukraine-EU Association
    Agreement, 173, 192–193
Dutch 'No' to the European Constitution, 187–188
Dutch working class voters, 353
dynamic of difference, 439
dysfunctional nature of Eurocrisis, 9, 437–439

e-voting, 213
Eastern Europeans, 372–375
Economic and Monetary Union (EMU)
    analyses of, 16, 20
    anti-inflationary monetary policies and, 40
    as conceptual and institutional mistake, 6, 9
    creation of, 61, 259, 309
    democratic legitimacy of, 127, 384
    economic liberalism, 118
    European integration and, 57
    features of, 394
    German interests and, 43
    Greek exit from, 408–418
    imposed constraints as result of, 105
    introduction to, 2, 4, 52, 403–408
    needed reform, 384
    nulla poena sine lege, 359–360
    optimistic expectations, 78

Soviet Union collapse, 381
    uneven development of, 59–63, 261–262
Economic Constitution *(Wirtschaftsverfassung)*,
    390, 394–396
economic elites, 46, 146–150, 157
economic freedom
    creation of, 86
    function of, 79, 80
    normative versions of, 15
    ordoliberalism and, 115, 390
    prioritisation of, 10, 432
    social rights of workers and, 327
    Spanish indebted homeowners movement, 170
    transformation into subjective rights, 388
    transnational organisation and, 431
economic governance, 17
economic ideology, 23–24, 25–28, 39
economic integration
    corruption potential, 399
    defacto solidarity, 87
    devaluation concerns, 77–78
    EU commitment to, 382
    European Union (EU) law and, 386–389
    impact of, 300, 426
    instigated by supranational organisations, 143
    introduction to, 52
    Maastricht treaty and, 117
    macroeconomic integration, 302
    as means to political integration, 15, 72–73, 74,
        80, 81, 139
    monetary integration and, 77
    potential benefits, 85–86, 87
    as self-sustaining, 83
    steps toward, 309
    summary of, 386–389, 395–396
    theory of 'self-fulfilling Europe,' 67–69
economic interdependence, 68, 69–74
economic liberalisation
    addressing problem of, 386–387
    authoritarian liberalism and, 399–401
    constitution by governance, 396–399
    deregulation as regulation, 392–394
    impact of, 383–386
    introduction to, 381–383
    ordoliberalism and, 389–391, 394–396, 401
    self-limiting functionalism, 391–392
    social re-equilibration of, 224
    summary of, 401–402
economic liberalism, 20, 102, 107–111, 118
economic Messianism, 117
Economic Partnership Programmes, 94, 253
Einaudi, Luigi, 26, 27, 42
electoral mode of popular consent, 229–231
'embedded liberal' Fordist compromise, 91

emergency Europe, 8, 104. *See also* executive managerialism
employment protection, 329
employment relationships, 338, 340
'end of history' thesis, 107
endogenous preferences, 83
Engels, Friedrich, 72
entrepreneurial capitalism, 297
entrepreneurial freedoms, 27
epiphenomenal approach to democratic crisis, 124–127, 129
Erhard, Ludwig, 79
ethico-political leadership, 425
EU Charter of Fundamental Rights, 343
EU Labour Law, 322
EU-Swiss Agreement on the Free Movement of Persons, 195
Euro-democratisation, 117
Euro-Periphery Member States, 260, 262
Euro-technocratisation, 362–363
Eurobond project, 251
Eurocrats, 46, 82
Eurocrisis/Eurozone crisis. *See also* constitutional discourse on European crisis; democratic deficit
  authoritarianism, 117–119, 382–383
  background, 1–5
  central thesis, 48
  coming overhaul, 313–314
  contemporary Europeanism and, 439–441
  crisis behind, 12
  crisis of identity, 14–15, 19
  decision to move towards European integration, 305–309
  deconstruction of, 14–20
  democratic and political legitimacy, 15–16
  dysfunctional nature of, 437–439
  economic model, 16–18
  as emergency narrative, 5–8
  ex abruption creation, 17
  as hidden systemic crisis, 5
  monetarism as ideology/law, 34–41
  multi-fold nature of, 437–439
  multiple dimensions of, 12–14
  nature of, 21–22, 430–433
  no legal alternative to, 41–48
  power shift from, 358–359
  as pre-supposed, 28–34
  real estate and, 375–376
  reconstruction of, 20–21
  refugee crisis, 295, 369–370, 375, 376–377, 433–437
  renewed integrative impetus, 310–313
  social character, 18–20

summary of, 430
  as systemic, 8–11
Eurocriticism, 227
Eurogroup, 63, 191
Europe 2020 policy agenda, 29
European Banking Authority, 227
European Central Bank (ECB)
  austerity politics, 165
  de-politicised monetary policy, 116
  Eurocrisis and, 64
  extra-legal judicial decision-making, 264–265, 269–270, 275, 281
  extra-ordinary measures, 244
  global financial crisis, 307
  intergovernmental methods, 190
  international trade negotiations, 224
  introduction to, 43
  lending prohibitions, 89
  prohibitive functions of, 424
  public debt purchases, 403–404
  Quantitative Easing (QE) programme, 284–286
  secondary market transactions, 385
European Citizens' Initiative (ECI), 206, 216, 233–236
European Coal and Steel Community (ECSC), 51, 53, 140
European Commission
  bureaucracy in legislation, 205
  market re-regulation, 38
  policy documents published by, 29
  role in Greek state bailout, 43
  White Papers, 60
European Community (EC), 140
European constitutionalism. *See* constitutionalism
European Council, 38, 39, 308–309
European Court of Human Rights (ECHR), 342
European crisis management, 385
European Defence Community, 73, 75
European *Demos*, 210–216, 229
European Deposit Insurance Scheme (EDIS), 309
European Economic Community (EEC)
  capitalism and, 91
  Common Agricultural Policy, 54
  establishment of, 53–55, 140, 419
  introduction to, 37–38
  referendums and, 180
  refugees and, 369
  transubstantiation, 73
European Enlightenment rationality, 222
European federalism, 76
European Financial Crisis (2008), 376
European Financial Stability Facility (EFSF), 237, 278
European Fiscal Board (EFB), 258

European Fiscal Compact, 89, 189
European Identity Study for the European
  Parliament (2017), 229
European integration
  beginning of, 52–55
  decision to move towards, 305–309
  elite-driven integration plans, 207
  EMU escalation and contradictions, 59–63
  Europeanisation backlash, 81–88
  global crisis (2008) impact, 63–65
  introduction to, 51–52
  monetary unification, 67, 75–81
  neofunctionalist European integration
    theory, 350
  politicalisation of, 352, 356f, 355–358
  pragmatic approach to, 142
  profitability and legitimation, 56–59
  public opinion on, 296
  referendum impact on, 184
  renewed integrative impetus, 310–313
  social welfare and collective labour rights, 346
  summary of, 66, 437–439
  support for, 68
European Medicines Agency, 227
European military collaboration, 427
European Monetary Cooperation Fund
  (EMCF), 93
European Monetary System (EMS), 38, 91, 303
European Monetary Union (EMU), 246, 275,
  347, 384
European Network of Independent Fiscal
  Institutions (EU IFISI), 258
European New Order, 441
European Parliament
  as elected institution, 229–230
  popular legitimacy of, 58
  responsibility of, 76, 205, 206
  Six-Pack on European economic governance,
    359, 361
  treaty amendments by, 126–127
  weakness of, 125
European Police Office (Europol), 191–192
European Political Union, 73
European Public Prosecutor's Office, 232
European Scrutiny Committee, 328
European Social Model, 18–20, 323
European Space Agency, 311
European Stability Mechanism (ESM)
  Bundesverfassungsgerichtt judgment, 274–284
  fiscal union and, 309
  legal reasoning in context, 286–293
  literal interpretation of treaty, 289
  private sector involvement, 308–309
  role of, 89, 94

transformation of, 313–314, 404
treatment of debtor states, 383
European System of Financial Supervision, 312
European Trade Union Confederation (ETUC),
  347, 353
European unification from above
  creation of imbalanced Eurozone, 301–305
  decision to move towards European integration,
    305–309
  Europhobia by United Kingdom, 310–313
  Eurozone overhaul, 313–314
  introduction to, 295–297
  source and pattern of, 297–301
European Union (EU)
  constitutional values of, 318
  decision-making process, 125–126
  dual constitution of, 21
  functional legacy of, 131
  fundamental legal framework, 6
  identity, defined, 14
  identity crisis, 14–15, 19, 81, 207–210, 373
  identity formation, 228–229
  monetary unification, 67, 75–81, 83, 296, 306
  as normative power, 421–422, 428
  ordoliberal form of, 136
  political authority of, 101
European Union (EU) law
  Community Law *vs.* national law, 55
  crisis ideology and, 13
  economic integration and, 386–389
  EU identity and, 14
  grey area of, 119
  human rights law, 342
  immigration law, 195
  labor laws, 330–334, 341
  monetarism as ideology/law, 34–41
  re-materialisation of, 396
  rule of law, 13, 92, 163, 284, 319
  social objectives, 334
  soft law, 361, 394
European Union (EU) Member States
  austerity measures, 157–158, 159, 165
  democratic ethos of, 143
  irresponsibility of, 3
  stereotypical roles of, 9
European Union (EU) referendums
  difficulties with, 195–203
  direct democracy and, 203–210
  identity crisis and, 207–210
  introduction to, 171, 174–180t
  legitimacy crisis and, 204–207
  national referendums, 180–184
  'no' votes on referendums, 173, 184, 196t
  Pan-European referendum, 210–216

European Union (EU) referendums (cont.)
  'second-referendum' technique, 188, 189, 199
  summary of, 217–218
  'yes' votes on referendums, 184
European Union Act (2011), 232
European Works Councils (EWCs), 322, 323
Europeanisation
  backlash from, 81–88, 347
  of big banks, 308
  formula, 59
  through institutional integration, 21
Europeanism, 298, 299
Europessimism, 209
Europhilia, 152, 153, 154
Europhobia by United Kingdom, 310–313
Euroscepticism, 153, 154, 192, 209, 227, 311, 353, 358
Eurosclerosis, 59, 300
Excessive Deficit Procedure, 94
excessive imbalances, 359–360
Exchange Rate Mechanism, 61, 422
exchange rates, 40, 61, 62, 76–78, 83, 93, 300, 303,
    413–418
executive dominance, 127
executive federalism, 127
executive managerialism, 104, 127. *See also*
    emergency Europe
'existential crisis' narrative, 6–7
existential threat, 32–33
expansionary austerity, 42, 43, 46
expressed consent, 220, 227–228
extra-legal judicial decision-making
  Bundesverfassungsgerichtt judgment, 274–284
  compatibility with EU treaties, 270–274
  decision to refer OMTs, 280–282
  economic or monetary policy, 267–270
  European Stability Mechanism, 266–274,
    278–280
  introduction to, 264–266
  legal reasoning in context, 286–293
  Pringle judgment, 266–274, 288
  Quantitative Easing (QE) programme, 284–286
  summary of, 293–294
extra-territorial nature of referendums, 183
extreme centrism, 102
extreme liberalism, 78–79

facilitation stage, 32, 33
fair working conditions, 336
fascism, 112, 113, 441
federalism, 188, 298
finalité économique, 128
Financial Aid Programmes, 244
Financial Times, 420
financialisation, 250, 258–261

Fiscal Advisory Council, 254, 256, 257–258
Fiscal Compact, 17, 159, 161, 253, 259, 312
fiscal governance machine, 243–246, 249–250,
    254–259, 261–263
fiscal indiscipline, 119
fiscal stability, 65, 244, 246, 250, 252, 258–261, 262
Fischer, Joschka, 81, 305
Foucault, Michel, 79, 81
France
  European project, 431
  Labour Act, 333
  monetary policy, 300
  'No' to the European Constitution, 187–188
  referendums, 181, 358
  voting on EU enlargement, 182
  wage bargaining process, 331, 361
  working class voters, 353
free capital, 416
free competition, 55, 135, 250, 327, 393
free economy, 112, 400
free market
  authoritarian liberalism and, 14–15
  creation of, 39, 392, 432
  European project and, 134
  European Social Model and, 18
  fundamental freedoms of treaties, 19
  Great Depression and, 35
  normative hierarchy and, 9
  role and value of, 16
  Socialist-Communist coalition and, 56
free market capitalism, 11, 109, 124, 153, 432
free market economics, 15, 16, 109, 111, 123–124, 135,
    139, 149, 326, 400
free market liberalism, 139, 150, 153
Freiburg School, 134
Friedman, Milton, 83
Friedrich, Carl Joachim, 115
functionalism
  conspiracy of, 79
  democratic deficit and, 128–130
  dissonance in, 246
  self-limiting functionalism, 391–392
  theory of 'self-fulfilling Europe,' 67
fundamental freedoms, 19

gender equality, 335
general clauses (*Generalklausulen*), 92
geopolitical antagonism, 51–52
German Central Bank, 76–77
German ordoliberalism. *See* ordoliberalism
Germany
  Basic Law, 275, 279, 283, 287, 291, 292
  Civil Code, 92
  constitution of, 292, 293, 395

constitutional court, 264, 274–284, 286–293, 395, 399–400, 402
crisis-management functions, 87
economic interests, 53
economic rise of, 73, 86, 407
European project, 431
foreign direct investment, 407
impact on Eurocrisis, 431
material culture, 371
Nazism in, 92–93, 441
onstitutional reforms
as *primus inter pares*, 425
response to Russo-Georgian war, 426
reunification's inflationary consequences, 305–306
Gide, Charles, 71
Gill, Stephen, 92
Gillingham, John, 140–141
global financial crisis (2008)
EU recovery from, 29
impact of, 10, 11, 41, 63–65, 306–307
introduction to, 1, 9
global free market capitalism, 10, 11
Global Health Governance, 33
globalisation, 70, 85, 86, 161, 348
Gobachev, Mikhail, 427
Gold Standard, 112
Gove, Michael, 47
governmentality studies, 247–248
grassroots-based mobilisation, 231
Great Depression, 35, 41
Greece
acts of legislative content, 160
bailout, 43, 403, 405
collective bargaining changes, 331
emergency provisions, 58–59
exit from EMU, 408–418
'no' to the bailout referendum, 173, 189–191, 233, 276
referendums, 16
solidarity clinics, 170
sovereignty of, 418
Greek Central Bank, 411
Growth and Stability Pact, 44

Haas, Ernest B., 75
Habermas, Jürgen, 28, 105, 107
Hallstein, Walter, 72, 73, 74, 80, 390
Hartz labour reforms, 406
Hay, Colin, 355, 356
Hayek, Friedrich, 91–92, 138
Heller, Hermann, 111, 112, 399
Heritage Foundation, 27
hidden systemic crisis, 5

historical legitimacy, 79
horizontal integration, 347–348
human resources management, 351
human rights, 133, 342
Hungarian 'no' to EU refugee relocation quotas, 194
Hungary, 374, 434

identity crisis, 14–15, 19, 81, 207–210, 373
identity formation, 228–229
ideological distortion, 318
Ideological State Apparatus (ISA), 26, 45
illiberalism, 103, 121, 353
ILO Conventions, 320–321, 331, 336, 345
Immigration Act (2016), 342
immigration law, 195
imperialism, 21, 310, 377, 422–429
Independent Fiscal Council, 257
individualism, 30, 31, 108, 110
industrial relations, 330, 351, 356, 366
Industrial Relations Report (2014), 352
industrial revolution, 353
input legitimacy, 237
Institute of Economic Affairs, 27
institutional integration. *See* Europeanisation through institutional integration
institutional legislative powers, 224
institutional psychoanalysis, 132
institutional transparency, 171
integrationist/dis-integrationist dichotomy, 437–439
inter-war Europe, 111–114
intergovernmentalism, 158, 246–247, 388
Internal Market programme, 393
international law and capitalism, 439
International Monetary Fund (IMF), 43, 64, 369
international organisations, 129, 145, 204
International Relations (IR), 245
international trade negotiations, 224
intra-European trade, 134
Ipsen, H.P., 391, 392
Iraklis case, 387
Ireland, 182
Irish 'No'
to the Lisbon Treaty, 188–189, 199–200
to the Nice Treaty, 186, 199–200
ISIS, 426

James, Harold, 303, 304
jihadism, 426
judicial decision-making. *See* extra-legal judicial decision-making
Juncker, Jean-Claude, 209, 314, 362, 399
junk debt, 41

justice deficit, 13
justifiability of power rules, 220, 222–227

Keynesian economic theory, 35–37
Keynesian welfare capitalism, 422
Klein, Naomi, 34, 90

Labour Act (2016, France), 333
labour laws
　authoritarianism, 341, 342
　collective labour rights, 346
　EU Labour Law, 322
　guidelines and application, 330–334
labour market, 60, 335–336
labour movements, 349
labour politics and New Economic Governance,
　364–365
Lagarde, Christine, 265
laissez-faire economics, 28, 136
Lamy, Pascal, 420
League of Nations, 299
legal enactment, 347, 362
legal legitimacy, 79, 80
legal orders, 181–182, 221
legal pragmatism, 268
legitimacy
　bailouts and, 45
　democratic legitimacy, 15–16, 127
　direct democracy in EU referendum process,
　　203–210
　EU referendums and, 204–207
　gap/deficit, 239
　input/output legitimacy, 237
　legal legitimacy, 79, 80
　limits on, 125
　normative structure of, 220–228
　output legitimacy, 224
　political legitimacy, 15–16, 46, 112, 410, 436
　'political messianism' legitimacy, 226
　referendums and, 182, 189
　throughput legitimacy, 237
legitimacy through acts of consent
　Civil Society Engagement, 236–238
　European Citizens' Initiative, 233–236
　expressed consent, 227–228
　introduction to, 219–220
　justifiability of power rules, 220, 222–227
　national referendums, 232–233
　popular consent, 229–231
　public acts of, 228–229
　rule-derived validity, 220, 221–222
　summary of, 238–239
The Legitimation of Power (Beetham), 220–228
legitimisation tools, 179

Lehman Brothers collapse, 41, 63
level of governance, 352–353
'Lexit' movement, 47
liberal autonomy, 385
liberal capitalism. *See* capital liberalisation
liberal democratic constitutions, 326
liberalisation, 330, 409
liberalism. *See also* authoritarian liberalism
　authoritarian liberalism, 15, 26
　capital liberalisation, 78, 101
　economic liberalism, 20, 102, 107–111, 118
　extreme liberalism, 78–79
　free market liberalism, 139, 150, 153
　market liberalism, 10, 11, 108, 138
　national liberalism, 399
　neoliberalism, 56, 59
　Ordoliberalism, 26, 27, 42, 46, 114–117, 119
　political liberalism, 103, 107–111, 114, 389
　universal triumph of, 163
　Western liberal democracy, 34
limited government, 169
locomotive theory, 76–77
Loewenstein, Karl, 113
Loi Macron, 361
Long Boom, 63
long peace (1871–1914) in international relations, 71
Long-Term Refinancing Operations (LTRO's), 89
Lösch, Bettina, 139
low debt balanced budgets, 44

Maastricht Treaty
　aftermath of, 60, 311–312
　birth of, 119–120
　Bundesverfassungsgerichtt judgment, 275–276
　competences in, 393
　court approval of, 395–396
　creation of imbalance Eurozone, 301–305
　Danish 'no' to the Maastricht Treaty, 185–186,
　　199–201
　democratic deficit and, 124–125
　geo-political reconfiguration of Europe, 101, 394
　introduction to, 40, 61–62
　neoliberal project and, 250
　ratification of, 91
macroeconomic imbalances
　failure to reduce, 359
　financial integration and, 303–305
　growing accumulation of, 302
　interpretation powers of, 94
　lack of competitiveness, 328–329
　unit labor cost, 357
Macroeconomic Imbalances Procedure (MIP),
　256, 361
macroeconomic integration, 302

macroeconomic policy, 39
Macron, Emmanuel, 8, 428, 437
Majone, Giandomenico, 390–391, 392
Major, John, 311–312
majority voting, 393
Making of the English Working Class (Thompson), 358
Mao Zedong, 419
marginalisation, 146, 343
Marjolin report (1975), 301
market immorality, 108
market liberalism, 10, 11, 108, 138, 329
market re-regulation, 38, 359
Marshall Plan, 52
Marx, Karl, 348
Marxism, 26, 423
material culture, 371
May, Theresa, 47
McDougall report (1977), 302
Medium Term Objective (MTO), 94, 255
Meek, James, 84–85
mega-politics, 161
Memoranda of Understanding, 94, 383
Memorandum from Bundesbank President Emminger to Chancellor Helmut Schmidt, 93
Merkel, Angela, 42, 44, 307, 313–314, 425, 426
Merton, Robert K., 79
methodological nationalism, 365–367
minimum living allowance, 406
minimum wages, 330, 331, 337, 415
mode of governance, 352–353
Mölling, Christian, 427
monetarism as ideology/law, 34–41
monetary integration, 67, 75, 76, 77, 80, 96, 97
monetary unification, 67, 75–81, 83, 296, 306, 403
Monnet, Jean, 6, 54, 61, 69, 81–82, 86, 142, 296, 429
Mont Pèlerin Society, 26, 35, 37
Müller-Armack, Alfred, 390
multi-ethnic groups, 231
multi-level governance regime, 347
multi-speed Europe, 8, 65, 312, 437
multilateral agreements, 267
mutual financial assistance between Eurozone countries, 271

National Central Bank, 413
National Constitutional Courts, 160
national referendums, 180–184, 232–233
nationalism, 7, 66, 165, 348
Nazism, 92–93, 441
Negri, Antonio, 169
neo-mercantilism, 141
neo-Poulantzian multi-layered approach, 251

neoclassical economics, 23
neofunctionalism, 83, 246–247, 350
Neoliberal Thought Collective (NTC), 26–27
neoliberalism
    austerity measures and, 104
    British turn towards, 56
    capitalism and, 422, 423
    common currency and, 408
    disciplinary neoliberalism, 41
    economic policy regime and, 63
    embedded neoliberalism, 6
    Europeanisation and, 59
    fundamentalism and, 171
    ordoliberalism and, 248, 249, 250, 258
    perceptions of trade union function, 320
    politico-economic sources of authoritarian neoliberalism, 95–97
    technocracy of experts, 139
Neumann, Franz, 92–93, 115
new constitutionalism, 131
new economic governance (NEG)
    analytical frameworks, 351–353
    horizontal integration, 347–348
    introduction to, 17, 19, 89, 90, 91–95, 346–347
    labour politics and, 364–365t
    methodological nationalism, 365–367
    political restructuring, 353–355
    politicalisation of European integration, 352, 356f, 355–358
    politicising of, 362–364, 367
    restructuring national divides, 349–351
    as silent revolution, 358–362
    summary of, 367–368
    vertical integration, 348–349
new intergovernmentalism, 127
Nice Treaty, 397
'no' votes on referendums, 173, 184–195, 196t
nominalism, 82
non-majoritarian institutions, 392
normative force of consent, 227
normative structure of legitimacy, 220–228
North American Trade Organization (NATO), 86
nulla poena sine lege, 359–360

Obama, Barack, 41, 427
O'Neill, Con, 420
online citizen campaign, 192
open-ended contracts, 334
Open Method of Co-Ordination, 106
open social market economy, 328
optimistic expectations, 78
optimum currency area (OCA), 77
Opus Dei, 58
Ordnungspolitik, 396

ordoliberalism
democratic deficit and, 133–140, 151–152
economic constitutionalism, 114–117, 391
economic liberalisation and, 389–391,
394–396, 401
impact of Treaty of Rome, 422
introduction to, 26, 27, 42, 46
neo-functionalism and, 119
neoliberalism and, 248, 249, 250, 258
Organisation for Economic Co-operation and
Development (OECD), 257
Organisation of Arab Petroleum Exporting
Countries, 36
organisational mobilisations, 354
organs of interdependence, 71
Osborne, George, 311–312
output legitimacy, 224, 237
Outright Monetary Transactions (OMTs), 89, 104,
265, 280–282, 284–286

pan-European movements, 171, 210–216
paradigm shift, 317–318
Paris Treaty, 53
parliamentary budgetary autonomy, 277–278
permanent structured cooperation (PESCO), 427
permissive consensus, 186
personal responsibility, 31
PIIGS nations, 374
pluralism, 288, 342
Polanyi, Karl, 102, 112
policy-making and ideas, 25
Political Myths and Economic Realities (Delaisi), 70
politics. *See also* austerity politics
authority of EU, 101
citizen involvement in decision-making, 178
conflicts, 19, 25, 131
constitutional theory and, 114
democratic deficit and, 150–151
disillusionment process, 7
diversity of, 213
economics and, 36
entrepreneurs and, 143
equality and, 110, 119
European integration, 352, 356f, 355–358
legitimacy and, 15–16, 46, 112, 410, 436
liberalism and, 103, 107–111, 114, 226, 389
mega-politics, 161
normality and, 167
ontology of democratic deficit, 132–133
Ordnungspolitik, 396
politicalisation processes, 351, 352, 362–364, 367
power of, 41, 58, 166, 350, 360
privatisation of, 139
stability and, 161, 168

popular consent, 10–11, 229–231
Popular Party, 62
populism, 85, 354
Portugal, 58, 147–148, 160
Post-Bretton Woods American hegemony, 96–97
post-Brexit European Union, 183
post-communist democracies, 225
post-state citizenship, 10
pre-federal integration stage, 302
pre-material values, 353
Pringle, Thomas (Pringle judgment), 266–274,
288, 384
private interest governance, 356
privatisation, 139, 409
Prodi, Romano, 397–398
protectionism, 7, 52, 54
protest movements, 354
pseudo-rationalism, 386, 402
public acts of consent, 228–229. *See* legitimacy
through acts of consent
public debt, 42, 260, 291, 306, 403–404
public involvement in referendums, 181
public mobilisation, 229–231
Public Sector Purchases Programme (PSPP)
decision, 285–286
Putin, Vladimir, 426

Qualified Majority Voting (QMV), 94,
312, 321–322
Quantitative Easing (QE) programme, 284–286,
407–408

racism, 194
radical institutionalism, 251
Rama, Edi, 373–374
Rawls, John, 107
reactionary resistance, 171
Reagan, Ronald, 27
recognition phase, 33
referendum phobia, 184
referendums. *See* European Union (EU)
referendums
refugee crisis, 295, 369–370, 375, 376–377, 433–437
religious belief, 222
renewed integrative impetus, 310–313
representative-based loss of connectivity, 230
representative democracy, 95, 215, 224, 238, 277
Repressive State Apparatus (RSA), 26, 45, 423
restrained democracy, 113, 116
Reversed Majority Voting (RMV), 94
revolutionary conversion, 170
rhetoric of necessity, 167
right2water campaign, 349
Road to Serfdom (Hayek), 27

Rockefeller, David, 37
rule-derived validity, 220, 221–222
rule of law, 13, 92, 163, 284, 319
Russia, 426
Russo-Georgian war (2008), 426

Sarkozy, Nicolas, 307
scale shift in socioeconomic policymaking, 360
Scharpf, Fritz, 383, 384
Schäuble, Wolfgang, 425
Schmitt, Carl, 26, 111–112, 113, 115, 136, 137, 151, 382–383
Schmitter, Philippe, 398
Schuman, Robert (Schuman Plan), 53, 69
Schuman declaration (1950), 299
secessionism, 85, 87
second industrial revolution, 297
'second-order' elections, 179
'second-referendum' technique, 188, 189, 199
securitarisation, 32–33
self-determination, 135, 170, 291
self-fulfilling Europe theory
    economic interdependence, 68, 69–74
    introduction to, 67–69
    monetary union, 75–81
self-limiting functionalism, 391–392
self-reliance, 31
semi-autonomous institutions, 136
shareholder value principle, 96
Shock Doctrine, 34, 90
short-term ('speculative') capital, 416
silent revolution, 90
Single European Act (SEA)
    changes proposed by, 57
    democratic deficit and, 124–125
    European integration and, 301
    introduction to, 39
    majority voting and, 393
    monetary instability and, 303
    signing of, 56
    social democracy and, 105
single European currency. *See* monetary unification
Single European Market, 421
Six-Pack on European economic governance, 359, 361
social
    character of Eurocrisis, 18–20
    conflict, 19, 164
    constructivist perspective, 23
    democratic constitutionalism, 341
    equality, 110, 352
    exclusion and discrimination, 326
    justice, 156, 330, 345

market economy, 17, 116, 330
movements, 166, 357
order and rules, 221
policies, 318
processes, 168, 354, 384, 410
rights, 327, 350
solidarity, 166, 170
welfare, 35, 64, 346
Social Action Program, 55
Social Action Protocol, 317–318, 320
Social Democrats, 58, 111, 147, 318–319, 335, 425
Social Dialogue procedures, 322
Social Europe, 327
Social Pillar, 334–337, 339–345
Social Security crisis, 31
Socialist-Communist coalition government, 56
Socialist International, 298
Socialist Party, 62
socialist principles, 30
socioeconomic policymaking, 360, 363
socioeconomic welfare, 116, 156, 164, 358
sociopolitical crisis, 4
sociopolitical integration, 135
soft law, 361, 394
solidarity, 68, 70
sovereign debt crisis, 382
Soviet Union collapse, 381
Spaak, Paul-Henri (Spaak Report), 84, 142
Spain, 58, 147–148
Spanish Civil Guard, 423
Spanish Constitution, 221–222
Spanish indebted homeowners movement, 170
spatial dimensions of Eurocrisis
    borders and, 372–375
    building Europe, 370–372
    real estate and, 375–376
    refugees and, 369–370, 375, 376–377
special-purpose association, 391
specious validity, 79
spill-over effect, 75, 118, 246
Spinelli, Altiero, 210–211
spread out war, 167
Stability and Growth Pact (SGP), 24, 40, 106, 244, 253, 259, 404
stable authority, 136
Staff Working Paper, 333
state-based power rules, 223
state transformation, 130–132
Stop Mass Immigration initiative, 194
Structural Deficit, 255–256
subprime mortgage market collapse, 41
supranationalism, 76, 116, 348
Swiss People's Party, 194
Swiss 'yes' to EU migration quotas, 194–195, 196t

symbolic force of consent, 227
Syrian refugees, 29
SYRIZA government, 409–410

tacit consent, 227–228
'taking back control' slogan, 152, 153
tax state, 110
Taylor Review of Modern Working Practices, 344
technical-functional construct, 80
technocracy, 46, 113, 356, 357
technocratic renationalisation, 362–363
Temporary Agency Workers Directive, 336
temporary contracts, 334
Thatcher, Margaret, 27, 39, 56, 311–312, 421
theory of 'self-fulfilling Europe,' 67–69
third way politics, 102
throughput legitimacy, 237
TINA, 16, 120
Tory party split, 313
trade liberalisation, 381
trade policy, 300, 304
Trade Union Act (2016), 342, 344
trade unions
    centralisation of decision-making, 362
    federalisations of, 348
    marginalisation of, 343
    mobilisations, 355
    NEG impact on, 360
    role of, 35, 323, 330
    vertical integration of, 322, 347
transnational
    capitalism, 10, 364
    collective action, 348–349, 358, 362, 367
    democracy, 349, 350
    economic market pressures, 346, 348
    organisations, 140, 431–432
    solidarity, 352
transnationalisation, 19, 259
transubstantiation, 73
Treaty of Lisbon
    Bundesverfassungsgerichtt judgment, 276–278
    EU participatory democracy, 216
    impact of, 317–318, 397
    intergovernmentalism, 158
    introduction to, 39, 40
    Irish 'No' to the Lisbon Treaty, 188–189
    legal status of, 325
    qualified majority voting, 312
Treaty of Maastricht. *See* Maastricht Treaty
Treaty of Rome
    democracy and, 141–142
    German ordoliberalism and, 422
    introduction to, 39, 53
    negotiations leading to, 74

social objectives, 54–55
theory of organisational set-up, 72
Treaty on European Union (TEU)
    Civil Society Engagement, 236–238
    European Citizens' Initiative, 206, 216, 233–236
    introduction to, 40
    Pringle judgment, 266–274, 288
    social democratic values, 318–319, 325
    Soviet Union collapse, 381
    summary of, 232
Treaty on Stability Coordination and Governance (TSCG)
    conceptual framework, 246–251
    correction mechanism, 256
    financialisation and fiscal stability, 258–261
    Fiscal Advisory Council, 254, 257–258
    Fiscal Compact, 17, 159, 161, 253, 259
    fiscal governance machine, 243–246, 249–250, 254–259, 261–263
    Growth and Stability Pact, 89
    introduction to, 17, 64, 243–246
    national budgets within, 383
    negotiation process, 251–254
    new economic governance, 243–246, 262–263
    Structural Deficit, 255–256
    summary of, 262–263
    uneven development of EMU, 59–63, 261–262
Treaty on the Functioning of the European Union (TFEU)
    decision to refer OMTs, 280–282
    extra-legal judicial decision-making, 266, 270–274
    NEG and, 94–95
    prohibition of monetary financing in, 290
    revisions to, 232
    Title VIII, 327
Trilateral Commission, 37, 38–39
Troika (EU Commission/ECB/IMF), 43, 47, 64, 94, 119, 190, 403
Trump, Donald, 7, 425
Tsipras, Alexis, 424, 425
Tusk, Donald, 106

Ukraine crisis, 427
unanimity rule, 212, 214, 238, 321
undemocratic ethos, 15
undemocratic EU democracy. *See* democratic deficit
unemployment reductions, 407, 409
unification from above. *See* European unification from above
unilateral action, 410
unit labour costs (ULC), 357, 361
United Kingdom (UK) Europhobia, 310–313

unity in fragmentation, 251
US Supreme Court, 385
utilitarian welfare maximisation, 386

van Neurath, Otto, 386, 402
Van Rompuy, Hermann, 309, 319
Varieties of Capitalism (VoC), 366
Verhofstadt report, 212
vertical integration, 322, 347, 348–349, 367
very short-term financing (VSTF), 93
veto powers in treaty ratification, 202, 212–213
violent conflict, 164
voluntary acts of consent. *See* legitimacy through
    acts of consent
voter involvement in referendums, 178, 232, 233

wages
    bargaining systems, 329–330, 331, 347
    minimum wages, 330, 331, 337, 415
    reductions in, 409
    sharing of, 97
    suppression of, 408
Wall Street investment banks, 96

Waszczykowski, Witold, 314
wealth distribution, 6
Weimar Constitution, 326
Weimar Republic, 113, 114, 390
welfare maximisation, 384, 386, 401
welfare state dismantling, 64
Werner, Pierre, 301
Werner Report, 75
Western liberal democracy, 34
White Paper (1993) EU Commission, 60
working class, 353, 358, 363
Working Group of the Economic Policy
    Committee, 361
Working Time Directive, 344
World Bank (WB), 369

xenophobia, 165, 171, 194, 226

'yes' votes on referendums, 184

zero hours contracts, 339
zero inflation target, 276
Zwickel, Klaus, 306